CENTRAL STATISTICAL OFFICE

Annual Abstract of Statistics

No. 121

1985 Edition

Editor: Ethel Lawrence

London: Her Majesty's Stationery Office

ISBN 0 11 620103 7*

BACKFILE VOLUMES

Complete volumes of *the Annual Abstract of
Statistics* from 1860 to date are now available on
microfilm from Microform Limited, Main Street,
East Ardsley, Wakefield, West Yorkshire WF3 2AT,
and volumes from 1970 to date are available on
microfiche from Congressional Information Service
Inc, 4520 East-West Highway, Bethesda,
Washington, DC, 20814, USA.

Her Majesty's Stationery Office

Standing order service

Placing a standing order with HMSO BOOKS enables a customer to receive
future editions of this title automatically as published.

This saves the time, trouble and expense of placing individual orders and
avoids the problem of knowing when to do so.

For details please write to HMSO BOOKS (PC 13A/1), Publications Centre,
PO Box 276, London SW8 5DT and quoting reference X02.02.27

The standing order service also enables customers to receive automatically as
published all material of their choice which additionally saves extensive
catalogue research. The scope and selectivity of the service has been extended
by new techniques, and there are more than 3,500 classifications to choose
from. A special leaflet describing the service in detail may be obtained on
request.

Introduction

The *Annual Abstract of Statistics* for the United Kingdom is prepared by the Central Statistical Office in collaboration with statistics divisions of other government departments. The name of the department or organisation providing the statistics is given under each table. Some of the statistics provided by government departments are actually collected by other organisations such as the national associations. The assistance provided by these organisations is gratefully acknowledged.

In addition, an Index of Sources is given on pages 328 to 334, which sets out the official publications or other sources from which the statistics are taken and to which reference can be made. The tables in this issue contain the latest statistics available, even though they may not yet have appeared in departmental publications.

Most of the tables in this *Abstract of Statistics* give annual figures, so far as they are available, for each of the years 1973 to 1983 and some include figures for the early months of 1984. Current data for many of the series appearing in the *Abstract* are contained in *Economic Trends*, the *Monthly Digest of Statistics* and in *Financial Statistics*, all prepared by the Central Statistical Office. Regional information, supplementary to the national figures in this *Abstract*, is published in *Regional Trends* also prepared by the Central Statistical Office. These publications are now available from Her Majesty's Stationery Office at the addresses given on the back cover.

Definitions

Area covered. Except where otherwise stated all statistics relate to the United Kingdom of Great Britain and Northern Ireland.

Time series. So far as possible annual totals are given throughout, but quarterly or monthly figures are given where these are more suitable to the type of series. Except where it is stated to the contrary all statistics are for calendar years ended 31 December.

For some series, weekly data are collected and not figures for calendar years. In such cases the figures appearing for particular years are cumulative totals for 52 or 53 weeks and attention to this is drawn by the footnotes to the tables. Since the series have not been adjusted to make them equivalent to a calendar year, care must be taken in making comparisons between annual figures for periods of different numbers of weeks.

Explanatory notes. Several sections of the *Abstract* are preceded by explanatory notes which should be read in conjunction with the tables. Definitions of many of the terms occurring in both the *Abstract* and the *Monthly Digest of Statistics* are given in the *Supplement of Definitions and Explanatory Notes* to the *Monthly Digest*, published annually. Detailed notes on items which appear in both the *Abstract* and *Financial Statistics* are given in a supplement to the latter entitled *Financial Statistics: Explanatory Handbook*, that is published annually. The original sources listed in the Index of Sources may also be consulted.

Consumption and stocks. Statistics of consumption and stocks should be used with care. The terms 'consumption', 'disposals' and 'stocks' are normally defined in detail in the *Supplement* to the *Monthly Digest of Statistics*. The stocks figures given may often relate to only part of the total stocks in the country.

Standard Industrial Classification

The Standard Industrial Classification has been prepared as a means of securing uniformity and comparability in the statistics published by government departments in the United Kingdom. It is a system of classification of establishments according to industry; it does not relate to commodities or occupations for which other systems of classification have been devised. It has been compiled to conform with the organisation and structure of industry as it exists within the United Kingdom.

A revised Classification, which replaces the 1968 Classification was published in 1979 and came into general use in 1983. One of the principal objectives of this revision is to eliminate such differences, as the structure of British industry allows, between the activity classification of the European Community, ('Nomenclature Générale des Activités Economiques dans les Communautés Européennes (NACE)') and the 1968 Classification. The 1980 Classification is a

different structure from its predecessor with 10 Divisions, 60 Classes, 222 Groups and 334 Activity Headings. Full details are available from *Standard Industrial Classification Revised 1980* (HMSO 1979, price £3.75 net) and *Indexes to the Standard Industrial Classification Revised 1980* (HMSO 1981, price £12.95 net). A detailed reconciliation between the 1980 and the 1968 Classifications has been prepared and is available only from Branch 7, Central Statistical Office, Great George St, London SW1P 3AQ, price £1.50.

Revisions and changes in content

Revisions. The scope of the *Abstract* is revised from time to time to include new statistical information as it becomes available. Some of the figures in this *Abstract* are regarded as provisional only and may be revised subsequently. In particular, this applies to the latest year.

New tables. The following new tables have been added:

4.12   Crimes and offences recorded by police—Scotland
4.13   Persons proceeded against—Scotland
4.14   Persons called to trial—Scotland
4.15, 4.16   Persons with charge proved—Scotland
7.8   Defence energy consumption
10.35   Seaport traffic of Great Britain
16.17   Water authority expenditure

Extended series and revisions. Other changes of contents in this compared with the previous issue, involve the addition of new series to existing tables and some substantial revisions. Some of the series which have hitherto been shown in the tables at 1975 prices or on base 1975 = 100 have now been rebased on 1980.

The following are the tables principally affected:

2.1   Population summary
2.3   Age distribution: census figures (N. Ireland revised)
2.4   Age distribution of Resident population: mid-year estimates
2.9   Geographical distribution of Home population: mid-year estimates
2.12   Acceptances for settlement on arrival
2.17   Live births by age of mother
3.7   Stock of dwellings
3.36   Fatal injuries at work
6.2   Distribution of total working population
6.4   Administrative, technical and clerical workers in manufacturing industries
6.14   Industrial stoppage
6.16   Size of manufacturing industries
6.19   Average earnings index
8.34   Volume index numbers of sales
9.2   Agricultural output and net product
9.4   Estimated quantity of crops
9.5   Cattle, sheep, pigs and poultry
10.3   Length of public roads
10.15   British Rail: assets and privately owned freight vehicles
10.18   London Transport railways: receipts, operations and assets
11.3   Retail trade: index numbers of value and volume of sales
12.2   Import penetration and export sales ratios
13.4, 13.5   UK public expenditure on overseas aid
17.5   Analysis of bank lending to UK residents
17.25   Acquisitions and mergers of companies
18.8   Index of purchase prices of means of agricultural production
18.9   Index of producer prices of agricultural products

Deletions. The tables listed below appeared for the last time in the *Annual Abstract* No 120, 1984 edition:

5.20   Educational building
6.17   Indices of basic wage rates of manual workers

Introduction (*continued*)

Symbols and conventions used

Change of basis. Where consecutive figures have been compiled on different bases and are not strictly comparable, a footnote is added indicating the nature of the difference.

Units of measurement. A table showing the various units of measurement used in this *Abstract* and, where appropriate, their metric equivalents, is given on the inside back cover.

Rounding of figures. In tables where figures have been rounded to the nearest final digit, there may be an apparent slight discrepancy between the sums of the constituent items and the total as shown.

Symbols. The following symbols have been used throughout the *Abstract:*

.. = not available

– = nil or negligible (less than half the final digit shown)

nei = not elsewhere included

nes = not elsewhere specified

Central Statistical Office,
Great George Street,
London SW1P 3AQ.

November 1984

CSO PUBLICATIONS

CSO Blue Book

UNITED KINGDOM
NATIONAL ACCOUNTS

Formerly titled *National Income and Expenditure* this is the essential data source for everyone concerned with macro-economic policies and studies.

Prepared by the CSO in collaboration with other government departments and the Bank of England, the *CSO Blue Book* contains estimates of the national product, income and expenditure for the United Kingdom. It covers industry, input and output, personal sector, companies, public corporations, central and local government, capital formation and financial accounts. Tables contain up to 22 years' data and there are definitions and detailed notes.

1984 Edition price £13.95 net

ISBN 0 11 620149 5

1985 Edition will be published in September 1985 ISBN 0 11 620155 X

CSO Pink Book

UNITED KINGDOM
BALANCE OF PAYMENTS

What are our total transactions with the rest of the European Community? What are the United Kingdom's overseas assets and liabilities? Can the North Sea oil and gas contribution to the balance of payments be identified? The answers are all in the *CSO Pink Book.*

The *CSO Pink Book* is the basic reference book for balance of payments statistics with data for the previous eleven years. It provides detailed information on visible trade, invisibles, investment and other capital transactions and official financing as well as sections on specific aspects of the balance of payments.

1984 Edition price £9.95 net

ISBN 0 11 620148 7

1985 Edition will be published in September 1985 ISBN 0 11 620154 1

CSO publications are available from Her Majesty's Stationery Office and through booksellers.

Contents

*New or revised in this issue of the *Annual Abstract*

Contents (*contd.*)　　　　　　　　　　　　　　　　　　　　　　　Page

*New or revised in this issue of the *Annual Abstract*

Contents (*contd.*)   Page

*New or revised in this issue of the *Annual Abstract*

Contents (*contd.*)   Page

*New or revised in this issue of the *Annual Abstract*

Contents (*contd.*)   Page

*New or revised in this issue of the *Annual Abstract*

Contents (*contd.*)   Page

*New or revised in this issue of the *Annual Abstract*

x

1 Area and Climate

1.1 Area of the United Kingdom
at 31 March 1981

	Total	Land	Inland water[1]	Total	Land	Inland water[1]
Metric measure	Thousand hectares			Square kilometres		
United Kingdom	24 410	24 088	322	244 100	240 882	3 218
Great Britain	22 998	22 740	258	229 979	227 399	2 580
England and Wales	15 121	15 032	89	151 207	150 319	888
England	13 044	12 968	76	130 439	129 681	758
Wales	2 077	2 064	13	20 768	20 638	130
Scotland	7 877	7 708	169	78 772	77 080	1 692
Northern Ireland[2]	1 412	1 348	64	14 121	13 483	638
Imperial measure	Thousand acres			Square miles		
United Kingdom	60 318	59 524	794	94 247	93 005	1 242
Great Britain	56 829	56 192	637	88 795	87 799	996
England and Wales	37 364	37 145	219	58 381	58 038	343
England	32 232	32 045	187	50 363	50 070	293
Wales	5 132	5 100	32	8 018	7 968	50
Scotland	19 465	19 047	418	30 414	29 761	653
Northern Ireland[2]	3 489	3 332	157	5 452	5 206	246

1. Excluding tidal water.
2. Excluding certain tidal waters that are parts of statutory areas in Northern Ireland.

Sources Ordnance Survey; Ordnance Survey of Northern Ireland

1.2 Mean daily air temperature at sea level

Degrees centigrade[1]

	Average 1941–70[2]	1974	1975	1976	1977	1978	1979	1980	1981	1982	1983	1984[3]
England and Wales												
Annual mean	10.0	10.0	10.4	10.5	10.0	9.8	9.3	9.9	9.7	10.4	10.4[3]	
January	4.0	6.5	7.2	6.2	3.5	3.9	0.9	3.1	5.2	3.6	7.0	4.3
February	4.2	6.1	5.2	5.0	5.7	3.1	1.9	6.3	3.7	5.5	2.6	4.2
March	6.2	6.2	5.3	5.4	7.5	7.2	5.3	5.4	8.3	6.6	7.0	5.3
April	8.8	8.3	8.6	8.3	7.7	6.8	8.1	9.0	8.2	8.9	7.3	8.4
May	11.6	11.3	10.1	12.2	10.8	11.5	10.3	11.3	11.6	11.9	10.6	10.1
June	14.7	14.1	14.8	17.1	12.8	14.0	14.3	14.3	13.8	15.7	14.6	14.7
July	16.3	15.5	17.5	18.5	16.2	15.1	16.5	15.0	16.0	16.8	19.2	16.8
August	16.1	15.7	18.7	17.6	15.7	15.4	15.4	16.3	16.6	16.4	17.6	17.8
September	14.3	12.6	13.9	13.8	13.7	14.5	13.9	15.2	15.1	14.8	14.2	
October	11.2	8.2	10.5	11.2	12.2	12.4	11.9	9.6	8.9	10.7	11.0	
November	7.2	7.2	6.7	6.8	7.0	9.0	7.3	7.0	8.1	8.5	8.1	
December	5.1	8.3	5.6	2.8	6.6	4.8	6.3	6.0	1.4	4.9	6.3[3]	
Scotland												
Annual mean	8.7	8.8	9.0	9.1	8.5	8.6	7.9	8.7	8.4	8.9	9.1[3]	
January	3.5	5.9	5.3	5.0	2.8	2.8	0.8	2.8	4.3	2.9	5.6	2.2
February	3.7	5.4	4.8	5.2	3.6	1.9	1.9	4.9	3.9	5.5	2.7	4.5
March	5.4	5.4	4.5	4.9	6.3	5.9	3.6	4.2	6.0	5.6	6.2	4.8
April	7.5	7.6	7.3	7.8	6.4	6.1	6.7	8.3	7.3	8.2	5.8	7.8
May	9.9	10.3	8.6	10.2	9.5	10.9	8.3	10.4	10.6	9.9	9.0	9.6
June	12.7	12.3	12.6	13.9	11.5	12.5	12.8	12.7	12.9	12.8	12.2	12.9
July	14.1	13.4	14.9	16.1	14.7	13.2	13.8	13.5	13.9	15.1	16.0	15.2
August	14.0	13.9	16.2	15.3	13.9	13.9	13.2	14.1	14.7	14.3	15.5	15.5
September	12.5	11.0	11.6	12.2	11.7	12.6	11.9	13.3	13.1	12.2	13.3	
October	9.9	7.7	10.2	9.8	11.2	11.0	10.6	8.1	6.7	9.6	9.4	
November	6.3	6.1	6.4	6.2	5.4	7.6	5.9	6.3	6.3	6.6	7.2	
December	4.6	6.5	6.1	2.2	5.8	4.2	4.7	5.5	0.8	3.9	6.1[3]	
Northern Ireland												
Annual mean	9.3	9.1	9.8	9.5	9.1	9.3	8.4	9.2	9.2	9.4	9.8[3]	
January	4.0	6.2	6.1	5.8	2.9	3.6	0.9	2.7	5.6	4.0	5.8	2.8
February	4.3	5.6	5.5	5.3	4.3	3.4	2.6	5.4	4.5	5.6	3.2	4.6
March	6.2	5.8	5.3	5.7	7.0	6.3	4.3	4.9	7.3	6.2	7.0	5.2
April	8.2	8.3	8.4	8.3	7.3	6.7	6.9	8.7	8.2	9.0	6.0	8.8
May	10.8	10.4	9.9	10.6	10.0	11.4	8.6	11.3	10.9	10.8	9.8	9.9
June	13.5	12.6	13.8	15.3	12.4	12.7	13.1	12.8	13.1	14.1	13.2	14.1
July	14.7	14.0	16.1	16.2	15.8	14.1	15.1	13.8	14.5	15.6	17.5	15.7
August	14.6	14.4	16.6	16.1	14.6	14.4	13.8	15.1	15.4	12.9	16.7	16.1
September	13.0	10.9	12.3	12.6	12.2	13.6	12.5	13.9	13.6	12.9	14.5	
October	10.4	7.9	10.7	9.2	11.6	11.9	10.9	9.9	7.2	10.3	10.1	
November	6.7	5.7	6.7	5.8	5.1	8.4	7.1	6.7	7.5	6.5	7.8	
December	5.0	7.4	6.0	2.4	6.2	4.5	4.8	5.7	2.2	4.4	6.8[3]	

1. To convert degrees centigrade into degrees fahrenheit: multiply by 9, divide by 5, and add 32.
2. The average for 1951–80 will be published in *Monthly Digest of Statistics* in 1985.
3. Provisional.

Source Meteorological Office

1.3 Rainfall

Millimetres[1]

	Average 1941–70[2]	1974	1975	1976	1977	1978	1979	1980	1981	1982	1983	1984
England and Wales												
Annual total	912	994	753	794	925	905	1 002	979	998	973	879	
January	86	117	117	60	101	111	86	78	58	72	92	144
February	65	98	31	40	138	86	66	93	52	44	42	57
March	59	47	81	43	73	78	125	104	153	101	67	59
April	58	14	71	21	51	52	68	18	64	23	108	11
May	67	40	47	64	52	47	124	32	91	46	117	59
June	61	66	21	17	85	70	42	128	49	129	37	43
July	73	77	66	32	24	89	33	74	55	39	40	26[3]
August	90	95	52	27	102	71	94	96	48	90	33	57[3]
September	83	144	106	160	36	54	38	67	141	78	101	
October	83	99	36	153	64	19	78	131	124	125	78	
November	97	125	73	83	104	54	87	87	69	126	53	
December	90	72	52	94	95	174	161	71	94	100	111	
Scotland												
Annual total	1 431	1 448	1 242	1 314	1 457	1 419	1 531	1 533	1 523	1 675	1 456	
January	137	228	245	185	127	158	120	120	157	154	220	223
February	104	118	48	87	137	104	38	95	91	107	59	111
March	92	73	58	130	129	166	178	113	152	153	149	103
April	90	18	100	60	116	52	96	20	33	46	74	60
May	91	78	48	118	74	40	102	18	87	92	115	24
June	92	71	67	65	78	69	75	150	103	72	86	66
July	112	102	112	64	63	90	105	125	92	57	43	54[3]
August	129	97	86	25	110	110	143	146	52	156	51	49[3]
September	137	141	184	141	146	177	112	172	235	200	172	
October	149	106	78	202	178	99	152	187	218	196	230	
November	142	190	128	127	207	198	204	181	216	229	49	
December	156	226	88	110	92	156	206	206	87	213	208	
Northern Ireland												
Annual total	1 095	1 074	825	1 008	1 027	1 077	1 142	1 159	1 209	1 165	952	
January	104	160	152	126	104	134	96	115	100	107	117	180
February	75	97	32	51	152	74	29	104	68	90	51	111
March	70	51	58	81	82	113	98	113	128	112	113	72
April	68	27	61	30	74	32	82	19	47	24	59	30
May	73	79	22	112	26	31	96	37	141	65	83	22
June	79	47	31	55	53	57	54	118	88	123	53	57
July	93	93	73	59	49	68	51	81	78	21	20	49[3]
August	103	79	54	16	98	80	137	84	43	92	35	76[3]
September	107	151	135	121	69	112	75	118	175	99	111	
October	107	67	91	191	105	54	138	148	154	126	132	
November	102	109	80	68	118	117	163	88	94	167	39	
December	114	114	36	98	97	205	123	134	93	139	139	

1. 1 millimetre = 0.0394 inches.
2. The average for 1951–80 will be published in *Monthly Digest of Statistics* in 1985.
3. Provisional.

Source Meteorological Office

1.4 Mean daily sunshine

Hours

	Average 1941-70[1]	1974	1975	1976	1977	1978	1979	1980	1981	1982	1983	1984[2]
England and Wales												
Annual mean	4.04	4.08	4.43	4.40	3.95	3.66	4.04	3.89	3.64	4.09	3.90[2]	
January	1.59	1.73	1.27	1.67	1.57	1.62	1.92	2.00	1.64	1.85	1.62	2.19
February	2.43	2.33	2.33	1.73	2.36	1.90	2.09	1.63	2.48	1.98	2.70	2.16
March	3.67	3.41	2.97	3.56	2.97	3.81	2.94	2.78	2.13	4.87	2.79	2.05
April	5.27	5.11	4.48	5.43	5.48	3.79	4.27	5.64	4.37	5.90	4.73	7.27
May	6.31	6.69	6.25	5.62	7.45	6.50	5.99	7.32	4.61	7.32	4.35	5.49
June	6.79	6.65	9.23	8.49	5.16	5.50	5.70	5.50	5.23	5.43	5.84	6.93
July	5.88	5.41	6.76	8.29	6.23	4.65	5.70	5.00	5.00	5.59	7.41	7.76
August	5.48	6.08	7.40	8.33	4.99	4.71	5.43	4.77	6.08	5.43	6.90	6.52
September	4.44	4.71	5.02	3.60	3.86	4.93	5.42	4.66	5.28	4.93	3.68	
October	3.25	2.89	3.54	2.18	3.48	2.96	3.41	3.58	3.71	2.31	3.64	
November	1.94	1.80	2.50	2.17	2.77	2.44	2.19	1.92	1.71	1.99	1.53	
December	1.47	1.51	1.47	1.85	1.31	1.12	1.68	1.75	1.48	1.46	1.64[2]	
Scotland												
Annual mean	3.53	3.57	3.88	3.53	3.81	3.20	3.37	3.17	3.49	3.53	3.14[2]	
January	1.40	1.13	1.18	1.12	1.74	1.47	1.53	1.26	1.19	1.19	1.02	1.28
February	2.53	1.80	3.04	1.72	2.61	2.50	3.04	1.52	2.53	2.16	2.40	1.62
March	3.36	3.26	3.83	3.02	2.55	3.16	3.42	2.69	3.19	3.74	2.18	2.25
April	4.99	6.04	3.94	4.24	4.99	3.84	3.94	5.54	6.18	4.84	4.42	5.89
May	5.74	5.45	7.23	4.48	6.72	6.37	5.28	7.40	5.45	6.89	3.67	6.71
June	5.79	6.37	7.47	4.86	6.48	5.44	5.62	4.57	4.92	5.27	5.50	4.92
July	4.81	4.71	4.95	6.40	5.72	4.28	3.56	3.70	4.14	6.01	5.87	5.62
August	4.48	4.52	5.38	7.35	5.82	3.32	4.03	3.36	4.79	4.39	5.02	4.71
September	3.71	3.97	3.75	3.01	3.45	3.08	4.56	2.93	3.52	3.34	2.89	
October	2.70	2.51	2.65	2.38	2.54	2.46	2.40	2.81	3.24	2.05	2.40	
November	1.73	1.73	1.87	2.28	1.95	1.66	1.85	1.45	1.56	1.45	1.52	
December	1.14	1.06	1.12	1.46	1.17	0.86	1.21	0.86	1.13	0.98	0.80[2]	
Northern Ireland												
Annual mean	3.54	3.61	3.97	3.50	3.75	3.11	3.28	3.08	3.04	3.56	3.04[2]	
January	1.51	1.18	1.53	1.21	1.66	1.84	1.66	1.46	1.15	1.53	1.30	1.43
February	2.45	2.08	2.72	1.74	1.67	2.50	2.52	1.81	1.94	2.19	2.35	1.59
March	3.29	3.29	4.54	2.53	2.73	3.22	3.49	2.96	2.66	4.73	1.90	2.37
April	5.01	6.91	4.86	5.46	4.96	3.91	4.21	4.91	5.51	5.16	5.30	5.76
May	6.15	4.55	8.12	4.00	7.63	5.47	5.10	7.26	4.43	5.78	4.12	7.56
June	5.71	5.88	7.48	5.88	6.05	4.28	4.80	3.31	4.28	4.51	4.05	4.74
July	4.36	4.01	4.75	4.14	5.58	4.05	3.18	3.62	3.31	5.75	5.80	5.71
August	4.52	5.06	4.97	8.05	6.15	2.89	4.38	3.20	4.02	4.02	4.38	3.69
September	3.58	3.69	3.69	3.19	3.33	3.08	3.76	3.01	3.72	3.65	2.61	
October	2.66	2.95	2.34	2.50	2.47	2.98	2.95	2.66	3.11	2.58	2.77	
November	1.95	2.52	1.95	2.36	2.32	1.74	2.05	1.83	1.52	1.54	1.17	
December	1.20	0.96	0.79	1.01	0.65	1.42	1.30	0.91	0.82	1.25	0.80[2]	

1. The average for 1951–80 will be published in *Monthly Digest of Statistics* in 1985.
2. Provisional.

Source Meteorological Office

2 Population and Vital Statistics

This section begins with a summary of population figures for the United Kingdom and constituent countries from 1851 to 2023 and for Great Britain from 1801 (Table 2.1). Table 2.2 analyses the elements of population change. Tables 2.3–2.4 give details of the national sex/age structure for years up to the present date. The marital condition of the population is given in Tables 2.5 and 2.6. Table 2.7 gives projections of the population by sex/age up to the year 2023. The distribution of population at local and regional level is summarised in Tables 2.8 and 2.9.

In the main, historical series relate to Census information while mid-year estimates are given for the recent past and the present.

Population (Tables 2.1–2.4).

Figures shown relate either to the population enumerated at successive censuses or to the annual mid-year estimates of population. Mid-year estimates are based on the latest Census with adjustments for births, deaths, migration into and out of the country and changes in the number of stationed armed forces. The series from 1981 includes residents who were temporarily outside the country at the time of the Census and excludes overseas visitors. Previously the overseas visitors were included and absent residents were excluded. This change in definition increased the population estimate for England and Wales by 278 000. In addition the 1981 figure is 52 000 higher than expected because of errors which have accumulated since 1971.

Home population: Persons actually present in an area.

Estimates prior to 1981 were given on two bases, Home and Total population. The series from 1981 will be for Home population only on the new definition.

Northern Ireland (Table 2.4)—the basis of the mid-year estimates from 1981 was not changed. The new series of estimates are still based on the 'population present' for the census. Only the Northern Ireland total has been revised for the inter-censal years.

Projected Home population of Great Britain and constituent countries (Table 2.7).

These projections are prepared by the Government Actuary, in consultation with the Registrars General, as a common framework for use in national planning in a number of different fields. A single principal projection for the next 40 years is made periodically on a set of assumptions which seems most appropriate on the basis of the statistical evidence available at the time. The projection is not, however, to be regarded as a 'forecast' in the normal sense of the word as population cannot be predicted over a 40 year period, and this is emphasized by the production every few years of supplementary projections made on assumptions differing from those of the principal projection.

The projections in Table 2.7 have been made on the following assumptions. Where appropriate, differing assumptions have been made for the constituent countries of Great Britain and the averages of the assumed rates are quoted here.

Base population: As estimated for mid-1983 by the Registrars General.

Mortality: Death rates at the outset are based on recent experience. Over a period of 40 years the rates are assumed to decline by ten per cent or more, although the improvement assumed at the different ages varies by up to 25 per cent.

Births: There were 720 000 in 1983. The estimates assume 694 000 in 1984, 708 000 in 1985 and 722 000 in 1986. Fertility rates then rise gradually until 2009 when they reach a level at which the population will approximately reproduce itself in successive generations, each woman on average producing 2.10 live-born children. After 1984, live-births fluctuate in line with the numbers of young women, reaching a peak of 797 000 in 1993, then falling to 701 000 in 2007 and rising again to 763 000 in 2023. A constant sex ratio of 106 boys to 100 girls has been assumed.

Migration: Allowance has been made for net outward migration of 22 000 persons a year for each year of the projected period.

Geographical distribution of the enumerated population: census figures (Table 2.8).

'The urban and rural districts and the conurbations shown in the table are based on local government administrative areas as they were prior to reorganisation in England and Wales in 1974 and in Scotland in 1975. Preliminary population counts from the 1981 Census were prepared for these areas in England and Wales, but it was not possible to continue the series to 1981 in Scotland or in Northern Ireland.

A new study of urban land and population based on the 1981 Census of Population has been made in Great Britain and the results published in 1981 Census, Key Statistics for Urban Areas, Great Britain. This gives the total population in Great Britain in urban areas in 1981 as 48 655 thousand and the population in remaining rural areas as 5 630 thousand, indicating that the division by administrative areas underestimated the urban population. However, it is not possible to give statistics of population in earlier years for the new urban areas, so the series based on administrative areas is given in table 2.8.'

Acceptances for settlement in the United Kingdom (Table 2.12).

This table now presents in geographic regions the statistics of individual nationalities, arranged alphabetically within each region as opposed to alphabetically within either Foreign or Commonwealth groupings as in previous years. It should be noted that information is not separately available for all nationalities and countries and therefore the group sub-totals shown are simply the totals of the countries listed.

Divorce (Table 2.14, 2.15).

Table 2.14 gives figures relating to dissolutions and annulment with duration of marriage and age of wife. Scottish figures relate only to marriages which took place in Scotland. Data in Table 2.15 relate to petitions filed and grounds for divorce and separation.

Births (Table 2.16).

For Scotland and Northern Ireland the number of births throughout are those registered. For England and Wales the figures up to and including 1930–32 are for those registered and later figures shown are for those occurring in each year.

Deaths (Tables 2.19–2.22).

The figures relate to the number of deaths registered during the calendar year, the normal time lag between occurrence and registration being a matter of days only.

Life tables (Table 2.23).

The interim life tables are constructed from the estimated Home population in 1981–83 and the total deaths registered in those years.

2.1 Population summary

Thousands

	United Kingdom			England and Wales			Wales	Scotland			Northern Ireland		
	Persons	Males	Females	Persons	Males	Females	Persons	Persons	Males	Females	Persons	Males	Females
Home population: census figures													
1801	..	..	..	8 893	4 255	4 638	587	1 608	739	869	..	..	..
1851	22 259	10 855	11 404	17 928	8 781	9 146	1 163	2 889	1 376	1 513	1 442	698	745
1901	38 237	18 492	19 745	32 528	15 729	16 799	2 013	4 472	2 174	2 298	1 237	590	647
1911	42 082	20 357	21 725	36 070	17 446	18 625	2 421	4 761	2 309	2 452	1 251	603	648
1921[1]	44 027	21 033	22 994	37 887	18 075	19 811	2 656	4 882	2 348	2 535	1 258	610	648
1931[1]	46 038	22 060	23 978	39 952	19 133	20 819	2 593	4 843	2 326	2 517	1 243	601	642
1951	50 225	24 118	26 107	43 758	21 016	22 742	2 599	5 096	2 434	2 662	1 371	668	703
1961	52 709	25 481	27 228	46 105	22 304	23 801	2 644	5 179	2 483	2 697	1 425	694	731
1966[2]	53 788	26 044	27 745	47 136	22 841	24 295	2 663	5 168	2 479	2 689	1 485	724	761
1971	55 515	26 952	28 562	48 750	23 683	25 067	2 731	5 229	2 515	2 714	1 536	755	781
Persons present													
1981	55 848	27 104	28 742	49 155	23 873	25 281	2 792	5 131	2 466	2 664	1 562[4]	765	797
Usually resident													
1981	55 113	26 815	28 298	48 522	23 625	24 897	2 750	5 035	2 428	2 607	1 556[4]	762	794
Home population: mid-year estimates[3]													
1956	51 184	24 644	26 540	44 667	21 517	23 150	2 608	5 120	2 446	2 674	1 397	681	716
1957	51 430	24 778	26 653	44 907	21 648	23 259	2 611	5 125	2 448	2 677	1 398	681	717
1958	51 652	24 887	26 765	45 109	21 744	23 365	2 615	5 141	2 459	2 682	1 402	684	719
1959	51 956	25 043	26 913	45 386	21 885	23 501	2 622	5 163	2 472	2 690	1 408	686	722
1960	52 372	25 271	27 102	45 775	22 097	23 678	2 629	5 178	2 482	2 696	1 420	692	728
1961	52 807	25 528	27 279	46 196	22 347	23 849	2 635	5 184	2 485	2 698	1 427	696	732
1962	53 292	25 826	27 465	46 657	22 631	24 026	2 652	5 198	2 495	2 703	1 437	700	737
1963	53 625	25 992	27 633	46 973	22 787	24 186	2 664	5 205	2 500	2 705	1 447	705	741
1964	53 991	26 191	27 800	47 324	22 978	24 346	2 677	5 208	2 501	2 707	1 458	711	747
1965	54 350	26 368	27 982	47 671	23 151	24 521	2 694	5 210	2 501	2 709	1 468	716	752
1966	54 643	26 511	28 132	47 966	23 296	24 671	2 702	5 201	2 496	2 704	1 476	719	757
1967	54 959	26 673	28 286	48 272	23 451	24 821	2 710	5 198	2 496	2 702	1 489	726	763
1968	55 214	26 784	28 429	48 511	23 554	24 957	2 715	5 200	2 498	2 702	1 503	733	770
1969	55 461	26 908	28 553	48 738	23 666	25 072	2 722	5 208	2 503	2 706	1 514	739	776
1970	55 632	26 992	28 641	48 891	23 738	25 153	2 729	5 214	2 507	2 707	1 527	747	781
1971	55 907	27 160	28 747	49 152	23 897	25 255	2 740	5 217	2 507	2 710	1 538	756	782
1972	56 079	27 253	28 826	49 327	23 989	25 338	2 755	5 210	2 503	2 707	1 542	761	781
1973	56 210	27 326	28 884	49 459	24 060	25 398	2 773	5 212	2 504	2 708	1 539	762	777
1974	56 224	27 345	28 879	49 468	24 074	25 393	2 785	5 217	2 508	2 709	1 540	762	777
1975	56 215	27 357	28 858	49 470	24 091	25 378	2 795	5 206	2 504	2 702	1 539	761	778
1976	56 206	27 356	28 850	49 459	24 089	25 370	2 799	5 205	2 504	2 702	1 541	763	778
1977	56 179	27 341	28 838	49 440	24 076	25 364	2 801	5 196	2 501	2 695	1 543	764	779
1978	56 167	27 327	28 840	49 442	24 067	25 375	2 804	5 179	2 494	2 685	1 546	765	780
1979	56 228	27 370	28 857	49 508	24 113	25 395	2 810	5 167	2 490	2 678	1 552	768	784
1980	56 314	27 405	28 910	49 603	24 156	25 448	2 816	5 153	2 480	2 673	1 558	769	789
1981	56 379	27 421	28 958	49 634	24 160	25 474	2 814	5 180	2 495	2 685	1 564	766	798
1982	56 335	27 399	28 936	49 601	24 143	25 459	2 807	5 167	2 489	2 677	1 567	767	800
1983	56 377	27 430	28 947	49 654	24 176	25 478	2 808	5 150	2 485	2 665	1 573	769	803
Home population: projections (mid-year)[5]													
1983 (base)	54 804	26 661	28 143	49 654	24 176	25 478	..	5 150	2 485	2 665	..	..	..
1993	55 382	27 018	28 364	50 335	24 575	25 760	..	5 047	2 443	2 604	..	..	..
2003	56 138	27 474	28 664	51 178	25 064	26 114	..	4 960	2 410	2 550	..	..	..
2013	56 383	27 627	28 756	51 582	25 291	26 291	..	4 801	2 336	2 465	..	..	..
2023	56 947	27 885	29 062	52 291	25 621	26 671	..	4 656	2 264	2 391	..	..	..

1. Figures for Northern Ireland are estimated. The population at the census of 1926 was 1 257 thousand (608 thousand males and 649 thousand females).
2. Except for Northern Ireland, where a full census was taken, figures are based on the 10 per cent sample census.
3. England and Wales revised series estimates 1961–80 and Northern Ireland revised series estimates 1971–80 are included in United Kingdom totals.
4. The figures include 74 000 non-enumerated persons.
5. 1983-based projections are for Great Britain.

Sources Office of Population Censuses and Surveys; General Register Office (Scotland); General Register Office (Northern Ireland); Government Actuary's Department

2.2 Population changes

Thousands

	Population at beginning of period[1]	Average annual change					
		Total increase or decrease(−)	Births	Deaths[2]	Excess of births over deaths	Net civilian migration	Other adjustments[3]
United Kingdom							
1901–1911	38 237	385	1 091	624	467	−82	
1911–1921	42 082	195	975	689	286	−92	
1921–1931	44 027	201	824	555	268	−67	
1931–1951	46 038	212	734	603	190	+22	
1951–1961	50 290	252	839	593	246	−7	+13
1961–1971	52 807	310	962	638	324	−32	+18
1971–1981	55 907	47	736	666	70	−41	+18
1981–1982	56 379	−44	722	669	53	−86	−11
1982–1983	56 335	42	722	660	62	−24	+4
1981–1991	56 252	66	788	679	109	−43	
1991–2001	56 912	106	832	691	141	−35	
2001–2011	57 968	44	760	681	79	−35	
2011–2021	58 403	90	806	681	125	−35	
England and Wales							
1901–1911	32 528	354	929	525	404	−50	
1911–1921	36 070	182	828	584	244	−62	
1921–1931	37 887	207	693	469	224	−17	
1931–1951	39 952	193	673	518	155	+38	
1951–1961	43 815	238	714	516	197	+30	+10
1961–1971	46 196	296	832	560	272	+7	+16
1971–1981	49 152	48	638	585	53	−18	+13
1981–1982	49 634	−33	628	587	41	−67	−7
1982–1983	49 601	53	629	580	49	−1	+5
1981–1991	49 593	72	686	597	89	−17	
1991–2001	50 314	110	730	611	119	−9	
2001–2011	51 416	60	671	602	69	−9	
2011–2021	52 011	103	715	603	112	−9	
Scotland							
1901–1911	4 472	29	131	76	54	−25	
1911–1921	4 761	12	118	82	36	−24	
1921–1931	4 882	−4	100	65	35	−39	
1931–1951	4 843	13	92	67	25	−11	−1
1951–1961	5 102	8	95	62	34	−28	+2
1961–1971	5 184	3	97	63	34	−32	+2
1971–1981	5 217	−7	70	64	6	−13	+1
1981–1982	5 180	−14	67	66	1	−15	
1982–1983	5 167	−16	66	64	2	−18	
1981–1991	5 150	−8	72	65	7	−15	
1991–2001	5 072	−5	74	64	10	−15	
2001–2011	5 018	−14	63	63	1	−15	
2011–2021	4 875	−12	65	62	3	−15	
Northern Ireland							
1901–1911	1 237	1	31	23	8	−6	
1911–1921	1 251	1	29	22	7	−6	
1921–1931	1 258	−2	30	21	9	−11	
1931–1951	1 243	6	28	18	10	−4	
1951–1961	1 373	5	30	15	15	−9	−
1961–1971	1 427	11	33	16	17	−7	+1
1971–1981	1 538	−3	28	17	11	−9	−5
1981–1982	1 564	3	27	16	11	−7	−1
1982–1983	1 567	5	27	16	11	−5	−1
1981–1991	1 509	2	29	16	13	−11	
1991–2001	1 526	1	28	16	12	−11	
2001–2011	1 534	−2	25	16	9	−11	
2011–2021	1 517	−1	26	16	10	−11	

1. Census enumerated population up to 1951; mid-year estimates of Home population from 1951 to 1981 and mid-1981 based projections of Home population thereafter.
2. Including deaths of non-civilians and merchant seamen who died outside the country. These numbered 577 000 in 1911–1921 and 240 000 in 1931–1951 for England and Wales; 74 000 in 1911–1921 and 34 000 in 1931–1951 for Scotland; and 10 000 in 1911–1926 for Northern Ireland.
3. For England and Wales, changes in Armed Forces, in visitor balance and other adjustments. For Scotland, this includes an adjustment to take account of 1981 census preliminary results.

Sources Office of Population Censuses and Surveys; General Register Office (Scotland); General Register Office (Northern Ireland); Government Actuary's Department

2.3 Age distribution of the enumerated population: census figures
United Kingdom

	1901	1911	1931[1]	1951	1961	1971	1981[2,3]
Persons: all ages	38 237	42 082	46 038	50 225	52 709	55 515	55 113
Under 5	4 381	4 516	3 531	4 326	4 213	4 505	3 349
Under 18	..	..	..	13 248	14 631	15 705	14 274
Under 21	..	..	..	15 162	16 667	17 993	16 936
5 – 14	8 040	8 452	7 643	6 999	8 123	8 882	8 106
15 – 29	10 808	11 180	11 853	10 328	10 258	11 678	12 417
30 – 44	7 493	8 923	9 717	11 125	10 526	9 759	10 767
45 – 64	5 706	6 764	9 877	11 980	13 400	13 384	12 306
65 – 74	1 278	1 624	2 461	3 689	3 971	4 713	5 050
75 and over	531	623	957	1 777	2 218	2 594	3 119
Under 1	938	915	712	773	893	891	712
1 and under 2	857	870	699	805	849	878	714
2 – 4	2 586	2 731	2 119	2 748	2 471	2 736	1 923
5 – 9	4 106	4 338	3 897	3 689	3 815	4 670	3 686
10 – 14	3 934	4 114	3 746	3 310	4 307	4 213	4 420
15 – 19	3 826	3 919	3 989	3 175	3 695	3 832	4 615
20 – 24	3 674	3 702	4 024	3 393	3 305	4 237	4 083
25 – 29	3 308	3 560	3 841	3 761	3 258	3 610	3 719
30 – 34	2 833	3 320	3 494	3 515	3 403	3 259	4 116
35 – 39	2 494	3 021	3 195	3 786	3 680	3 169	3 487
40 – 44	2 165	2 582	3 028	3 825	3 442	3 331	3 163
45 – 49	1 837	2 227	2 901	3 603	3 658	3 544	3 053
50 – 54	1 566	1 863	2 713	3 209	3 645	3 273	3 154
55 – 59	1 236	1 487	2 365	2 746	3 313	3 360	3 245
60 – 64	1 067	1 187	1 897	2 422	2 783	3 206	2 855
65 – 69	743	949	1 455	2 069	2 236	2 707	2 732
70 – 74	535	675	1 005	1 620	1 736	2 005	2 318
75 – 79	313	372	581	1 049	1 201	1 331	1 634
80 – 84	157	173	263	506	679	790	919
85 and over	61	78	113	224	338	473	565
Males: all ages	18 492	20 357	22 060	24 118	25 481	26 952	26 815
Under 5	2 190	2 269	1 784	2 215	2 162	2 312	1 717
Under 18	..	..	..	6 753	7 491	8 064	7 319
Under 21	..	..	..	7 658	8 507	9 223	8 675
5 – 14	4 024	4 228	3 859	3 566	4 159	4 561	4 159
15 – 29	5 191	5 382	5 804	5 073	5 159	5 915	6 298
30 – 44	3 597	4 290	4 495	5 461	5 225	4 909	5 404
45 – 64	2 705	3 225	4 647	5 554	6 397	6 452	6 008
65 – 74	565	716	1 099	1 561	1 602	1 976	2 211
75 and over	219	249	372	687	776	828	1 018
Under 1	471	462	361	397	459	457	365
1 and under 2	429	438	353	412	436	451	367
2 – 4	1 290	1 369	1 070	1 406	1 266	1 404	987
5 – 9	2 052	2 170	1 967	1 885	1 954	2 395	1 893
10 – 14	1 972	2 058	1 892	1 681	2 206	2 166	2 266
15 – 19	1 898	1 948	1 987	1 564	1 870	1 961	2 358
20 – 24	1 737	1 754	1 958	1 648	1 641	2 132	2 069
25 – 29	1 556	1 680	1 860	1 861	1 649	1 822	1 872
30 – 34	1 349	1 587	1 636	1 725	1 706	1 652	2 066
35 – 39	1 200	1 459	1 462	1 856	1 831	1 598	1 751
40 – 44	1 048	1 244	1 397	1 881	1 689	1 659	1 587
45 – 49	886	1 070	1 348	1 764	1 790	1 750	1 528
50 – 54	747	893	1 274	1 495	1 779	1 591	1 558
55 – 59	582	707	1 131	1 234	1 590	1 614	1 578
60 – 64	490	555	894	1 061	1 239	1 497	1 343
65 – 69	332	429	663	885	925	1 196	1 235
70 – 74	233	287	436	675	677	779	976
75 – 79	133	153	237	428	441	461	608
80 – 84	63	68	98	189	233	244	277
85 and over	23	28	36	70	102	124	133

1. Figures included for Northern Ireland are estimated.
2. 1981 data cover the 'usually resident' population and are not strictly comparable with other data.
3. Figures included for Northern Ireland are the revised Census population and include 74 000 non-enumerated persons.

Sources Office of Population Censuses and Surveys; General Register Office (Scotland); General Register Office (Northern Ireland)

2.3 Age distribution of the enumerated population: census figures
United Kingdom

(continued)

Thousands

	1901	1911	1931[1]	1951	1961	1971	1981[2,3]
Females: all ages	19 745	21 725	23 978	26 107	27 228	28 562	28 298
Under 5	2 190	2 247	1 747	2 111	2 051	2 194	1 632
Under 18	..	..	..	6 495	7 141	7 641	6 955
Under 21	..	..	..	7 504	8 160	8 769	8 260
5–14	4 016	4 225	3 784	3 433	3 964	4 321	3 947
15–29	5 618	5 798	6 049	5 255	5 100	5 764	6 119
30–44	3 895	4 634	5 222	5 663	5 300	4 850	5 363
45–64	3 001	3 539	5 229	6 425	7 003	6 931	6 296
65–74	713	908	1 361	2 128	2 369	2 737	2 839
75 and over	312	374	586	1 091	1 442	1 765	2 101
Under 1	466	453	351	376	434	434	348
1 and under 2	428	432	347	393	413	428	348
2–4	1 296	1 362	1 050	1 342	1 204	1 332	936
5–9	2 054	2 169	1 930	1 804	1 862	2 274	1 793
10–14	1 962	2 056	1 854	1 629	2 102	2 047	2 155
15–19	1 928	1 971	2 002	1 611	1 825	1 872	2 257
20–24	1 938	1 948	2 066	1 744	1 664	2 105	2 015
25–29	1 752	1 879	1 981	1 900	1 610	1 788	1 847
30–34	1 484	1 733	1 858	1 790	1 697	1 607	2 050
35–39	1 294	1 563	1 733	1 930	1 850	1 572	1 736
40–44	1 117	1 338	1 631	1 943	1 753	1 672	1 576
45–49	951	1 156	1 553	1 839	1 869	1 794	1 524
50–54	819	971	1 439	1 714	1 866	1 683	1 595
55–59	654	780	1 234	1 512	1 723	1 746	1 666
60–64	577	632	1 003	1 361	1 544	1 709	1 511
65–69	411	519	792	1 183	1 310	1 511	1 498
70–74	302	389	569	944	1 059	1 226	1 342
75–79	180	219	344	620	761	870	1 027
80–84	94	105	165	317	446	546	642
85 and over	38	50	77	154	235	349	432

	England and Wales				Scotland				Northern Ireland			
	1951	1961	1971	1981[2]	1951	1961	1971	1981[2]	1951	1961	1971	1981[2,3]
Persons: all ages	43 758	46 105	48 750	48 522	5 096.4	5 179.3	5 229.0	5 035.3	1 370.9	1 425.0	1 536.1	1 556.0
Under 5	3 718	3 597	3 905	2 910	470.8	469.2	444.3	308.4	137.8	146.5	156.2	130.6
Under 18	11 323	12 576	13 574	12 418	1 481.4	1 567.5	1 596.7	1 350.8	443.6	487.5	534.9	505.1
Under 21	12 965	14 335	15 563	14 737	1 688.3	1 780.6	1 822.3	1 609.0	508.6	551.1	606.8	589.5
5–14	5 974	6 987	7 671	7 053	784.5	869.9	910.5	769.6	240.9	265.6	300.8	282.9
15–29	8 912	8 925	10 236	10 859	1 107.3	1 034.1	1 099.2	1 183.1	308.9	299.2	343.2	375.2
30–44	9 767	9 263	8 593	9 541	1 083.8	1 000.3	912.7	947.2	274.4	262.5	253.4	278.3
45–64	10 563	11 836	11 849	10 884	1 143.0	1 256.9	1 217.9	1 116.3	273.9	307.3	316.5	305.2
65–74	3 257	3 520	4 178	4 488	343.6	358.4	426.5	444.3	87.9	92.3	108.2	117.7
75 and over	1 568	1 976	2 318	2 786	163.5	190.5	217.9	266.5	47.0	51.6	57.8	66.1
Under 1	659	764	774	619	87.6	97.8	86.0	66.1	26.7	30.8	31.1	26.9
1 and under 2	689	725	761	622	89.0	94.3	86.4	65.0	27.1	29.8	30.9	27.4
2–4	2 370	2 107	2 370	1 669	294.2	277.1	271.9	177.3	84.1	86.0	94.2	76.3
5–9	3 162	3 262	4 044	3 207	397.9	420.7	468.4	344.4	129.2	132.4	157.1	134.3
10–14	2 812	3 725	3 627	3 846	386.6	449.1	442.1	425.2	111.7	133.2	143.7	148.6
15–19	2 704	3 201	3 314	4 020	361.9	374.1	392.3	446.6	108.5	120.2	126.4	148.3
20–24	2 927	2 878	3 731	3 564	364.2	333.0	390.4	394.3	100.9	93.8	114.9	124.8
25–29	3 280	2 846	3 191	3 275	381.2	327.0	316.4	342.2	99.5	85.2	101.9	102.1
30–34	3 079	2 984	2 871	3 656	345.0	332.5	300.6	358.7	91.2	86.5	86.7	100.8
35–39	3 323	3 242	2 786	3 092	368.6	347.3	300.8	300.3	94.1	90.9	82.4	94.6
40–44	3 365	3 037	2 935	2 792	370.2	320.5	311.3	288.1	89.1	85.1	84.3	82.9
45–49	3 172	3 229	3 135	2 689	349.6	342.6	322.8	285.7	80.8	87.0	86.0	77.8
50–54	2 825	3 221	2 897	2 785	308.0	342.2	295.8	289.6	76.3	82.0	80.0	78.9
55–59	2 423	2 928	2 976	2 877	260.7	312.5	306.3	289.8	62.2	72.5	78.5	78.0
60–64	2 143	2 458	2 841	2 533	224.7	259.5	293.0	251.3	54.5	65.7	72.0	70.5
65–69	1 829	1 979	2 400	2 426	192.2	204.6	247.2	240.8	47.4	52.2	60.3	65.5
70–74	1 428	1 542	1 778	2 062	151.4	153.9	179.3	203.5	40.5	40.1	47.9	52.2
75–79	924	1 069	1 185	1 458	97.8	105.4	115.2	142.5	27.2	27.0	29.9	33.9
80–84	446	605	707	821	45.9	57.9	65.6	78.3	13.7	16.2	17.5	20.0
85 and over	198	302	425	507	19.8	27.2	37.2	45.6	6.1	8.4	10.4	12.2

1. Figures included for Northern Ireland are estimated.
2. 1981 data cover the 'usually resident' population and are not strictly comparable with earlier data.
3. Figures included for Northern Ireland are the revised census population and include 74 000 non-enumerated persons.

Sources   Office of Population Censuses and Surveys; General Register Office (Scotland); General Register Office (Northern Ireland)

2.3 Age distribution of the enumerated population: census figures

(*continued*)

Thousands

	England and Wales				Scotland				Northern Ireland			
	1951	1961	1971	1981[1]	1951	1961	1971	1981[1]	1951	1961	1971	1981[1,2]
Males: all ages	21 016	22 304	23 683	23 625	2 434.4	2 482.7	2 514.6	2 428.5	667.8	694.2	754.7	761.9
Under 5	1 904	1 846	2 003	1 492	241.0	240.1	228.5	158.3	70.6	75.4	80.3	66.7
Under 18	5 774	6 440	6 971	6 368	752.9	800.7	818.7	691.9	226.4	249.8	275.2	259.2
Under 21	6 554	7 320	7 978	7 549	844.4	905.6	932.4	823.5	259.6	281.2	312.6	302.9
5 – 14	3 045	3 578	3 940	3 619	398.2	445.2	466.7	394.5	123.0	136.2	154.9	145.3
15 – 29	4 388	4 502	5 184	5 506	532.8	507.8	554.4	599.7	152.0	148.8	176.0	192.7
30 – 44	4 804	4 612	4 337	4 794	523.7	486.5	446.9	471.2	133.2	127.1	124.9	138.7
45 – 64	4 902	5 663	5 728	5 331	523.7	588.6	573.5	531.9	128.3	145.5	151.2	145.1
65 – 74	1 372	1 419	1 755	1 971	148.9	143.7	174.5	188.9	39.9	40.0	45.9	50.8
75 and over	600	684	737	912	65.8	71.0	70.3	83.9	20.8	21.3	21.4	22.5
Under 1	338	393	397	317	45.0	49.9	44.2	33.8	13.8	15.9	15.9	13.7
1 and under 2	353	372	390	319	45.6	48.4	44.5	33.4	13.9	15.4	15.9	14.1
2 – 4	1 213	1 080	1 215	857	150.4	141.8	139.8	91.0	42.9	44.1	48.5	38.9
5 – 9	1 616	1 671	2 074	1 647	202.5	215.1	240.1	176.3	66.1	68.1	81.1	69.2
10 – 14	1 429	1 907	1 865	1 972	195.7	230.1	226.5	218.2	56.9	68.1	73.7	76.1
15 – 19	1 335	1 622	1 696	2 054	173.2	187.4	199.4	227.8	55.4	60.3	65.1	76.4
20 – 24	1 427	1 434	1 876	1 805	172.4	159.4	196.6	199.8	48.7	46.9	59.3	64.1
25 – 29	1 626	1 446	1 612	1 648	187.2	161.0	158.3	172.2	47.9	41.6	51.6	52.2
30 – 34	1 514	1 502	1 460	1 835	166.1	162.8	148.1	180.5	44.6	41.6	43.5	50.8
35 – 39	1 633	1 616	1 410	1 554	177.6	170.5	147.4	149.5	45.5	43.9	40.7	47.1
40 – 44	1 658	1 494	1 467	1 405	180.0	153.2	151.4	141.3	43.0	41.6	40.7	40.9
45 – 49	1 556	1 584	1 552	1 351	168.7	163.9	157.0	139.5	38.8	42.1	41.7	37.9
50 – 54	1 318	1 575	1 412	1 381	141.3	164.3	139.6	139.6	36.1	39.6	39.1	37.7
55 – 59	1 089	1 408	1 434	1 403	115.8	147.3	143.2	138.4	28.9	34.4	37.4	36.9
60 – 64	939	1 096	1 330	1 196	97.9	113.2	133.7	114.4	24.4	29.4	33.1	32.6
65 – 69	781	819	1 063	1 100	83.2	83.4	106.6	105.7	21.6	23.0	26.4	29.1
70 – 74	591	600	692	871	65.7	60.2	67.9	83.2	18.3	17.0	19.5	21.7
75 – 79	375	389	410	544	41.6	40.2	39.4	50.9	12.4	11.3	11.6	12.6
80 – 84	165	205	217	248	17.8	21.7	20.5	22.5	6.0	6.7	6.4	6.5
85 and over	61	90	110	119	6.4	9.0	10.4	10.5	2.4	3.2	3.5	3.4
Females: all ages	22 742	23 801	25 067	24 897	2 661.4	2 696.6	2 714.3	2 606.8	703.1	730.8	781.4	794.2
Under 5	1 814	1 751	1 902	1 418	229.8	229.1	215.8	150.1	67.2	71.2	75.9	63.9
Under 18	5 550	6 136	6 603	6 050	728.4	766.9	778.0	658.9	217.2	237.8	259.7	245.9
Under 21	6 411	7 015	7 585	7 188	844.0	875.0	889.9	785.5	249.0	269.9	294.3	286.6
5 – 14	2 929	3 410	3 732	3 434	386.1	424.8	443.8	375.1	117.9	129.4	145.9	137.5
15 – 29	4 523	4 423	5 052	5 353	574.4	526.4	544.8	583.4	156.9	150.4	167.2	182.5
30 – 44	4 963	4 651	4 256	4 747	559.7	513.8	465.7	475.9	141.2	135.4	128.5	139.6
45 – 64	5 660	6 172	6 122	5 554	619.2	668.3	644.4	584.4	145.6	161.9	165.3	160.1
65 – 74	1 885	2 102	2 423	2 517	194.5	214.8	252.0	255.4	48.0	52.3	62.2	66.9
75 and over	967	1 292	1 581	1 875	97.7	119.5	147.7	182.5	26.2	30.3	36.4	43.6
Under 1	321	371	377	303	42.6	47.9	41.8	32.3	12.9	14.9	15.1	13.1
1 and under 2	337	353	371	303	43.4	45.9	41.9	31.6	13.2	14.4	15.0	13.3
2 – 4	1 157	1 027	1 154	812	143.8	135.3	132.1	86.2	41.2	41.9	45.8	37.4
5 – 9	1 546	1 592	1 970	1 560	195.3	205.7	228.3	168.1	63.1	64.3	76.0	65.1
10 – 14	1 383	1 818	1 762	1 875	190.8	219.1	215.5	207.0	54.8	65.0	69.9	72.5
15 – 19	1 369	1 579	1 618	1 966	188.7	186.7	192.9	218.8	53.1	60.0	61.2	71.8
20 – 24	1 500	1 444	1 855	1 760	191.7	173.7	193.8	194.6	52.2	46.9	55.6	60.8
25 – 29	1 654	1 400	1 579	1 627	194.0	166.0	158.1	170.0	51.6	43.6	50.3	49.9
30 – 34	1 565	1 483	1 411	1 822	178.8	169.7	152.4	178.3	46.6	44.9	43.2	50.1
35 – 39	1 691	1 626	1 376	1 538	190.8	176.9	153.4	150.8	48.6	47.0	41.7	47.4
40 – 44	1 707	1 543	1 468	1 387	190.1	167.2	159.9	146.9	46.0	43.4	43.6	42.1
45 – 49	1 616	1 645	1 584	1 338	180.9	178.8	165.8	146.2	42.0	44.9	44.4	39.9
50 – 54	1 507	1 646	1 485	1 404	166.6	177.9	156.2	150.1	40.3	42.5	41.0	41.2
55 – 59	1 334	1 520	1 542	1 474	144.9	165.2	163.1	151.3	33.3	38.2	41.1	41.1
60 – 64	1 204	1 362	1 511	1 337	126.8	146.4	159.3	136.8	30.1	36.3	39.0	37.9
65 – 69	1 049	1 160	1 336	1 326	108.9	121.1	140.6	135.1	25.8	29.2	33.8	36.4
70 – 74	837	942	1 086	1 191	85.6	93.7	111.4	120.3	22.2	23.1	28.4	30.5
75 – 79	549	680	776	914	56.2	65.2	75.8	91.6	14.8	15.7	18.3	21.3
80 – 84	281	401	490	573	28.0	36.2	45.1	55.8	7.7	9.4	11.1	13.4
85 and over	137	212	315	388	13.5	18.2	26.8	35.1	3.7	5.2	6.9	8.8

1. 1981 data cover the 'usually resident' population and are not strictly
   comparable with earlier data.
2. Northern Ireland figures have been revised and include 74 000 non-
   emunerated persons.

Sources Office of Population Censuses and Surveys; General Register Office
(Scotland); General Register Office (Northern Ireland)

2.4 Age distribution of the Resident population: mid-year estimates[1]

Thousands

	1973	1974	1975	1976	1977	1978	1979	1980	1981	1982	1983
Persons: all ages	56 218	56 231	56 213	56 202	56 173	56 161	56 218	56 304	56 379	56 335	56 379
Under 5 years	4 301	4 114	3 937	3 718	3 519	3 391	3 374	3 405	3 455	3 520	3 582
Under 18 years	15 869	15 796	15 669	15 500	15 282	15 067	14 874	14 681	14 473	14 213	13 952
Under 21 years	18 188	18 125	18 027	17 929	17 771	17 619	17 500	17 386	17 251	17 057	16 852
5 – 14	9 149	9 201	9 192	9 168	9 077	8 922	8 684	8 416	8 147	7 846	7 588
15 – 29	12 055	12 125	12 226	12 375	12 332	12 386	12 527	12 698	12 854	12 987	13 121
30 – 44	9 808	9 867	9 915	9 989	10 284	10 516	10 710	10 856	10 961	11 028	11 118
45 – 64	13 251	13 144	13 050	12 963	12 868	12 742	12 616	12 518	12 486	12 483	12 551
65 – 74	4 938	5 022	5 075	5 109	5 142	5 176	5 205	5 221	5 197	5 113	4 970
75 and over	2 716	2 757	2 798	2 880	2 950	3 027	3 103	3 189	3 278	3 359	3 447
Under 1 year	793	734	706	677	645	655	710	734	730	713	715
1 and under 2	842	788	730	702	673	643	653	707	731	725	711
2 – 4	2 667	2 592	2 501	2 339	2 200	2 092	2 010	1 963	1 994	2 082	2 156
5 – 9	4 694	4 634	4 536	4 480	4 371	4 242	4 063	3 889	3 678	3 490	3 364
10 – 14	4 454	4 566	4 655	4 688	4 706	4 680	4 621	4 527	4 470	4 356	4 224
15 – 19	3 962	4 027	4 134	4 251	4 363	4 471	4 590	4 689	4 739	4 760	4 729
20 – 24	3 960	3 912	3 868	3 886	3 935	3 992	4 060	4 172	4 286	4 379	4 493
25 – 29	4 133	4 186	4 223	4 238	4 034	3 923	3 876	3 837	3 830	3 848	3 893
30 – 34	3 341	3 420	3 497	3 630	3 924	4 072	4 136	4 178	4 184	3 964	3 848
35 – 39	3 214	3 247	3 259	3 223	3 225	3 280	3 373	3 460	3 591	3 874	4 023
40 – 44	3 253	3 200	3 160	3 135	3 135	3 165	3 202	3 218	3 186	3 191	3 247
45 – 49	3 386	3 332	3 298	3 261	3 228	3 191	3 146	3 112	3 091	3 089	3 118
50 – 54	3 564	3 677	3 531	3 424	3 338	3 280	3 234	3 206	3 182	3 152	3 115
55 – 59	3 096	2 937	3 038	3 150	3 267	3 399	3 507	3 370	3 274	3 193	3 142
60 – 64	3 206	3 198	3 184	3 127	3 034	2 872	2 728	2 830	2 938	3 049	3 175
65 – 69	2 801	2 830	2 845	2 849	2 849	2 850	2 849	2 844	2 804	2 714	2 568
70 – 74	2 137	2 192	2 230	2 260	2 294	2 326	2 356	2 378	2 394	2 398	2 402
75 – 79	1 388	1 412	1 434	1 499	1 541	1 592	1 638	1 676	1 708	1 738	1 772
80 – 84	819	824	836	846	863	878	897	930	968	1 000	1 040
85 and over	508	520	528	536	546	558	568	583	602	620	636
Males: all ages	27 330	27 348	27 356	27 354	27 338	27 324	27 366	27 400	27 421	27 399	27 430
Under 5 years	2 209	2 114	2 024	1 911	1 809	1 741	1 732	1 748	1 772	1 805	1 837
Under 18 years	8 144	8 106	8 042	7 956	7 845	7 734	7 638	7 537	7 431	7 300	7 166
Under 21 years	9 326	9 294	9 246	9 198	9 115	9 033	8 974	8 914	8 844	8 750	8 648
5 – 14	4 693	4 720	4 717	4 708	4 664	4 584	4 463	4 322	4 184	4 028	3 897
15 – 29	6 123	6 162	6 217	6 295	6 269	6 296	6 374	6 458	6 530	6 598	6 669
30 – 44	4 949	4 985	5 016	5 052	5 199	5 312	5 409	5 476	5 516	5 542	5 586
45 – 64	6 405	6 358	6 320	6 283	6 243	6 188	6 138	6 100	6 092	6 100	6 142
65 – 74	2 098	2 145	2 178	2 201	2 221	2 240	2 257	2 270	2 265	2 230	2 168
75 and over	853	864	883	905	933	962	993	1 026	1 062	1 097	1 132
Under 1 year	408	378	362	348	332	336	365	377	374	366	367
1 and under 2	432	406	375	360	346	330	335	363	374	371	365
2 – 4	1 368	1 331	1 286	1 203	1 132	1 075	1 032	1 008	1 024	1 068	1 106
5 – 9	2 410	2 378	2 328	2 301	2 244	2 179	2 090	1 998	1 889	1 793	1 728
10 – 14	2 284	2 342	2 389	2 407	2 419	2 405	2 373	2 323	2 295	2 235	2 169
15 – 19	2 028	2 061	2 116	2 174	2 227	2 282	2 345	2 400	2 426	2 445	2 430
20 – 24	2 006	1 986	1 965	1 979	2 006	2 033	2 069	2 122	2 172	2 214	2 276
25 – 29	2 088	2 116	2 136	2 142	2 036	1 980	1 958	1 937	1 932	1 939	1 963
30 – 34	1 691	1 733	1 773	1 839	1 986	2 059	2 090	2 107	2 105	1 991	1 935
35 – 39	1 628	1 645	1 651	1 630	1 629	1 655	1 704	1 747	1 808	1 947	2 019
40 – 44	1 630	1 607	1 592	1 582	1 584	1 599	1 616	1 622	1 602	1 604	1 632
45 – 49	1 681	1 655	1 639	1 622	1 608	1 592	1 574	1 560	1 550	1 548	1 564
50 – 54	1 740	1 799	1 732	1 685	1 644	1 618	1 597	1 583	1 573	1 560	1 544
55 – 59	1 483	1 406	1 458	1 513	1 572	1 638	1 694	1 631	1 592	1 557	1 535
60 – 64	1 501	1 497	1 490	1 463	1 418	1 340	1 274	1 327	1 378	1 434	1 498
65 – 69	1 244	1 260	1 271	1 274	1 276	1 279	1 279	1 277	1 262	1 222	1 155
70 – 74	855	885	908	926	945	962	978	993	1 003	1 008	1 013
75 – 79	475	483	500	521	544	569	592	612	630	646	662
80 – 84	250	250	252	251	256	259	265	275	290	306	323
85 and over	128	130	131	132	133	134	136	139	141	145	148

1. The figures for 1973 to 1980 incorporate the revised intercensal estimates for
England and Wales, but old series estimates for Scotland and Northern
Ireland.

Sources Office of Population Censuses and Surveys; General Register Office
(Scotland); General Register Office (Northern Ireland)

2.4 Age distribution of the Resident population: mid-year estimates[1]
(continued)

Thousands

	1973	1974	1975	1976	1977	1978	1979	1980	1981	1982	1983
Females: all ages	28 888	28 883	28 857	28 848	28 835	28 837	28 853	28 904	28 958	28 936	28 947
Under 5 years	2 092	2 000	1 913	1 807	1 710	1 650	1 642	1 658	1 683	1 715	1 745
Under 18 years	7 725	7 690	7 627	7 544	7 437	7 334	7 236	7 144	7 043	6 913	6 787
Under 21 years	8 862	8 831	8 780	8 732	8 656	8 586	8 525	8 472	8 407	8 307	8 204
5 – 14	4 456	4 481	4 474	4 460	4 414	4 338	4 221	4 094	3 964	3 817	3 691
15 – 29	5 932	5 962	6 008	6 080	6 062	6 091	6 153	6 240	6 324	6 390	6 452
30 – 44	4 859	4 882	4 899	4 937	5 085	5 204	5 301	5 380	5 446	5 485	5 532
45 – 64	6 846	6 786	6 731	6 680	6 626	6 554	6 478	6 418	6 393	6 383	6 409
65 – 74	2 840	2 877	2 897	2 908	2 922	2 936	2 948	2 952	2 932	2 892	2 802
75 and over	1 862	1 894	1 936	1 976	2 018	2 065	2 110	2 163	2 216	2 262	2 315
Under 1 year	384	357	343	330	314	319	345	358	356	348	348
1 and under 2	409	382	355	342	327	313	319	344	356	354	347
2 – 4	1 299	1 261	1 215	1 136	1 069	1 018	978	956	970	1 014	1 050
5 – 9	2 285	2 258	2 208	2 179	2 126	2 063	1 973	1 891	1 789	1 697	1 636
10 – 14	2 171	2 223	2 266	2 281	2 287	2 275	2 248	2 203	2 175	2 121	2 055
15 – 19	1 934	1 966	2 019	2 078	2 136	2 189	2 244	2 290	2 313	2 316	2 299
20 – 24	1 954	1 926	1 903	1 907	1 929	1 958	1 991	2 050	2 113	2 165	2 224
25 – 29	2 045	2 070	2 087	2 095	1 998	1 943	1 918	1 900	1 898	1 910	1 930
30 – 34	1 650	1 687	1 724	1 791	1 937	2 013	2 046	2 071	2 079	1 973	1 913
35 – 39	1 586	1 602	1 608	1 593	1 596	1 625	1 670	1 714	1 783	1 926	2 005
40 – 44	1 623	1 593	1 567	1 553	1 552	1 566	1 586	1 595	1 584	1 586	1 614
45 – 49	1 706	1 677	1 659	1 639	1 620	1 599	1 572	1 552	1 542	1 540	1 554
50 – 54	1 823	1 878	1 799	1 739	1 694	1 662	1 638	1 624	1 609	1 592	1 571
55 – 59	1 613	1 531	1 580	1 637	1 695	1 761	1 814	1 739	1 682	1 637	1 607
60 – 64	1 704	1 700	1 694	1 664	1 616	1 532	1 454	1 503	1 560	1 615	1 678
65 – 69	1 558	1 570	1 574	1 575	1 572	1 571	1 570	1 567	1 542	1 493	1 413
70 – 74	1 282	1 306	1 322	1 333	1 349	1 365	1 378	1 385	1 390	1 399	1 389
75 – 79	913	929	954	978	997	1 023	1 045	1 064	1 078	1 092	1 109
80 – 84	569	574	584	594	607	619	633	655	677	694	717
85 and over	380	390	398	404	413	423	432	444	462	476	488

1983

	England and Wales			Scotland[2]			Northern Ireland[2]		
	Persons	Males	Females	Persons	Males	Females	Persons	Males	Females
All ages	49 653.7	24 175.9	25 477.8	5 150.4	2 485.0	2 665.4	1 572.7	769.3	803.4
Under 5	3 119.5	1 599.9	1 519.6	328.0	168.4	159.6	134.5	68.5	66.0
Under 18	12 147.7	6 240.5	5 907.2	1 311.2	672.3	638.9	493.0	252.7	240.3
Under 21	14 684.6	7 536.4	7 148.2	1 587.0	813.0	774.0	580.4	298.6	281.8
5 – 14	6 602.4	3 391.7	3 210.7	716.2	367.1	349.1	269.7	138.3	131.4
15 – 29	11 478.6	5 830.3	5 648.3	1 252.0	637.9	614.1	390.7	200.7	190.0
30 – 44	9 852.0	4 954.1	4 897.9	981.8	490.0	491.8	284.1	141.8	142.3
45 – 64	11 100.6	5 451.0	5 649.6	1 143.5	544.6	598.9	306.4	145.9	160.5
65 – 74	4 415.8	1 932.8	2 483.0	437.5	184.6	252.8	116.5	50.2	66.3
75 and over	3 084.8	1 016.1	2 068.7	291.6	92.4	199.2	70.8	23.9	46.9
Under 1	623.1	319.5	303.6	64.8	33.3	31.5	26.9	13.8	13.1
1 and under 2	618.7	317.4	301.3	65.8	33.6	32.2	26.7	13.5	13.2
2 – 4	1 877.7	963.0	914.7	197.3	101.5	95.9	80.8	41.1	39.7
5 – 9	2 922.5	1 501.7	1 420.8	314.4	161.3	153.1	127.4	65.2	62.2
10 – 14	3 679.9	1 890.0	1 789.9	401.8	205.8	196.0	142.3	73.1	69.2
15 – 19	4 129.6	2 122.6	2 007.0	452.0	231.2	220.8	147.4	76.6	70.8
20 – 24	3 934.2	1 986.1	1 948.1	431.1	220.1	211.0	134.0	69.5	64.5
25 – 29	3 414.8	1 721.6	1 693.2	368.9	186.6	182.3	109.3	54.6	54.7
30 – 34	3 403.9	1 711.4	1 692.5	344.5	173.3	171.2	99.1	50.0	49.1
35 – 39	3 582.1	1 798.0	1 784.1	342.6	171.6	171.0	98.7	49.1	49.6
40 – 44	2 866.0	1 444.7	1 421.3	294.6	145.1	149.5	86.3	42.7	43.6
45 – 49	2 750.2	1 384.1	1 366.1	289.0	141.2	147.8	79.0	38.7	40.3
50 – 54	2 748.0	1 367.7	1 380.3	290.2	139.7	150.5	77.0	36.9	40.1
55 – 59	2 779.0	1 362.9	1 417.0	286.3	136.5	149.8	76.0	36.0	40.0
60 – 64	2 822.5	1 336.3	1 486.2	278.0	127.2	150.8	74.4	34.3	40.1
65 – 69	2 279.0	1 029.1	1 249.9	227.1	98.5	128.5	61.6	27.3	34.3
70 – 74	2 136.8	903.7	1 233.1	210.4	86.1	124.3	54.9	22.9	32.0
75 – 79	1 581.5	593.4	988.1	153.1	55.2	97.9	37.0	13.7	23.3
80 – 84	931.0	290.0	641.0	87.6	25.9	61.7	21.0	6.7	14.3
85 and over	572.3	132.7	439.6	50.9	11.3	39.5	12.8	3.4	9.4

1. The figures for 1973 to 1980 incorporate the revised intercensal estimates for England and Wales, but old series estimates for Scotland and Northern Ireland.

2. Data has been rounded individually and may not sum exactly.

Sources Office of Population Censuses and Surveys; General Register Office (Scotland); General Register Office (Northern Ireland)

2.5 Marital condition: census figures

Thousands

	United Kingdom						England and Wales					
	Males			Females			Males			Females		
	1961	1971	1981[1]	1961	1971	1981[1]	1961	1971	1981[1]	1961	1971	1981[1]
All ages:												
Single	11 340	12 014	11 860	10 829	11 055	10 585	9 738	10 399	10 363	9 242	9 513	9 199
Married	13 279	13 976	13 563	13 355	14 050	13 630	11 813	12 433	12 042	11 860	12 488	12 093
Widowed	760	762	749	2 860	3 139	3 182	658	666	657	2 528	2 773	2 808
Divorced	102	200	606	185	318	863	94	185	563	170	293	797
Age groups												
0 – 14: Single	6 321	6 873	5 861	6 015	6 515	5 564	5 424	5 942	5 111	5 160	5 633	4 852
15 – 19: Single	1 850	1 921	2 328	1 709	1 713	2 152	1 605	1 661	2 031	1 475	1 477	1 878
Married	20	40	26	116	159	101	17	35	22	104	140	88
Widowed	–	–	–	–	–	–	–	–	–	–	–	–
Divorced	–	–	–	–	–	1	–	–	–	–	–	1
20 – 24: Single	1 139	1 350	1 536	719	848	1 080	990	1 186	1 350	607	737	945
Married	501	779	517	941	1 244	896	444	687	443	834	1 107	782
Widowed	–	–	1	2	2	2	–	–	1	1	2	2
Divorced	1	3	12	2	10	34	1	3	11	2	9	31
25 – 34: Single	799	703	973	461	374	534	688	617	866	382	320	471
Married	2 537	2 727	2 802	2 808	2 940	3 113	2 243	2 414	2 469	2 466	2 597	2 753
Widowed	4	4	5	15	14	15	4	3	4	13	12	13
Divorced	14	41	154	24	67	230	13	38	143	22	61	212
35 – 44: Single	439	363	346	371	247	195	374	315	304	308	206	167
Married	3 032	2 828	2 806	3 104	2 868	2 836	2 692	2 502	2 487	2 748	2 525	2 505
Widowed	19	15	13	74	57	48	17	13	11	63	48	41
Divorced	29	51	169	53	72	230	27	47	157	49	66	212
45 – 54: Single	346	325	288	447	298	200	291	278	251	375	248	167
Married	3 126	2 913	2 617	2 973	2 885	2 577	2 783	2 593	2 319	2 642	2 565	2 276
Widowed	63	53	44	258	218	176	54	46	38	221	187	149
Divorced	33	50	134	57	75	164	31	46	124	53	69	151
55 – 59: Single	145	140	148	251	177	127	120	118	128	210	148	105
Married	1 373	1 397	1 326	1 201	1 290	1 259	1 225	1 248	1 184	1 074	1 151	1 124
Widowed	60	56	53	251	246	214	52	48	46	217	213	186
Divorced	12	21	50	20	33	65	11	20	47	19	30	60
60 – 64: Single	106	125	115	234	207	125	87	105	98	196	173	104
Married	1 042	1 268	1 120	926	1 095	1 018	931	1 135	1 003	830	982	911
Widowed	84	87	72	370	380	316	72	75	62	323	330	274
Divorced	7	16	35	14	27	51	7	15	33	13	25	47
65 – 74: Single	130	158	183	381	392	305	106	130	154	322	328	254
Married	1 232	1 550	1 732	1 015	1 242	1 403	1 105	1 391	1 558	917	1 122	1 266
Widowed	235	253	252	961	1 075	1 062	203	220	220	852	948	934
Divorced	5	15	41	12	27	67	5	14	38	11	26	62
75 and over: Single	66	58	82	241	285	304	53	47	69	206	243	257
Married	415	474	616	269	326	426	373	428	558	246	298	389
Widowed	294	294	310	929	1 148	1 348	257	259	276	837	1 034	1 208
Divorced	1	3	10	2	7	22	1	2	9	2	6	20

1. 1981 data cover the 'usually resident' population and are not strictly comparable with earlier data.

Sources Office of Population Censuses and Surveys; General Register Office (Scotland); General Register Office (Northern Ireland)

2.5 Marital condition: census figures
(continued)

Thousands

| | | Scotland | | | | | | Northern Ireland[1] | | | | | |
| | | Males | | | Females | | | Males | | | Females | | |
		1961	1971	1981[1]	1961	1971	1981[1]	1961	1971	1981[1]	1961	1971	1981[1]
All ages:	Single	1 206.0	1 197.6	1 113.0	1 205.9	1 153.8	1 034.2	396.0	417.5	384.7	381.1	388.5	352.3
	Married	1 187.7	1 225.9	1 201.5	1 209.2	1 241.8	1 211.3	278.0	317.6	319.3	284.9	320.4	318.1
	Widowed	82.4	78.0	74.4	268.0	295.2	301.5	19.7	18.5	17.3	63.6	70.4	73.0
	Divorced	6.6	13.2	39.6	13.5	23.6	59.9	0.5	1.1	3.9	1.2	2.0	6.2
Age groups 0–14:	Single	685.3	695.1	552.8	653.8	659.7	525.1	211.6	235.2	197.2	200.6	221.8	187.1
15–19:	Single	185.2	194.8	224.2	175.9	177.6	207.8	59.9	64.3	72.3	58.0	58.2	66.1
	Married	2.2	4.6	3.6	10.8	15.2	10.9	0.4	0.9	0.8	2.0	3.0	2.7
	Widowed	–	–	–	–	–	–	–	–	–	–	–	–
	Divorced	–	–	–	–	–	–	–	–	–	–	–	–
20–24:	Single	112.2	121.2	140.2	83.6	81.5	101.7	37.0	42.3	45.9	28.7	29.7	33.1
	Married	47.1	75.0	58.3	89.6	111.2	89.8	9.8	17.0	15.5	18.1	25.9	24.8
	Widowed	–	–	–	0.2	0.2	0.3	–	–	–	–	–	–
	Divorced	–	0.4	1.2	0.2	1.0	2.7	–	–	0.1	–	–	0.2
25–34:	Single	80.4	60.7	80.7	56.0	37.0	47.4	30.6	25.0	26.4	22.9	16.2	15.7
	Married	242.1	242.6	261.1	276.1	266.8	282.8	52.4	69.8	71.4	65.1	76.5	76.6
	Widowed	0.5	0.4	0.6	1.8	1.6	1.7	0.1	0.1	0.1	0.4	0.4	0.6
	Divorced	0.9	2.8	10.4	1.8	5.2	16.5	0.1	0.2	1.0	0.1	0.4	1.6
35–44:	Single	46.4	34.9	30.9	46.1	29.6	20.0	18.7	13.5	10.9	16.5	11.3	7.7
	Married	273.2	259.0	247.4	284.9	271.3	256.1	66.1	67.2	71.9	71.4	71.8	73.1
	Widowed	2.3	1.6	1.6	8.9	6.8	5.6	0.5	0.4	0.5	2.2	1.7	1.9
	Divorced	1.8	3.3	11.0	4.3	5.6	16.0	0.2	0.3	1.1	0.4	0.5	1.7
45–54:	Single	40.2	33.7	27.7	55.1	37.3	24.5	15.0	13.6	10.0	17.2	13.2	8.9
	Married	278.3	253.8	237.2	268.1	254.4	239.6	64.8	65.4	60.4	62.9	65.3	60.6
	Widowed	7.5	5.9	5.2	29.7	24.6	20.5	1.7	1.4	1.2	7.0	6.2	5.7
	Divorced	2.2	3.2	8.8	3.8	5.7	11.6	0.2	0.3	0.9	0.3	0.6	1.2
55–59:	Single	17.9	15.7	14.8	31.8	22.0	16.3	6.2	6.2	5.4	8.7	7.2	5.7
	Married	121.4	119.9	114.6	104.5	111.9	108.1	26.5	29.6	28.8	23.3	27.1	26.3
	Widowed	7.2	6.4	5.9	27.6	27.1	22.4	1.5	1.5	1.4	6.1	6.5	6.2
	Divorced	0.8	1.3	3.2	1.4	2.2	4.5	0.1	0.1	0.3	0.1	0.2	0.5
60–64:	Single	13.5	14.7	11.7	29.7	26.0	15.7	5.3	5.6	4.9	8.6	7.9	5.8
	Married	89.6	108.2	92.9	77.5	91.6	84.7	21.8	25.3	24.3	18.5	21.4	20.8
	Widowed	9.6	9.7	7.7	38.3	39.9	33.2	2.3	2.1	1.9	9.1	9.4	8.6
	Divorced	0.5	1.0	2.0	1.0	1.8	3.3	–	0.1	0.2	0.1	0.2	0.4
65–74:	Single	16.4	19.5	20.6	46.3	49.8	38.2	7.7	8.2	7.9	12.7	14.4	12.3
	Married	101.3	127.6	140.2	79.2	97.4	109.9	26.3	31.7	34.7	19.0	23.4	25.8
	Widowed	25.6	26.4	25.7	88.4	103.2	103.4	6.0	6.0	5.9	20.6	24.2	24.8
	Divorced	0.4	1.0	2.3	0.9	1.7	3.9	–	0.1	0.3	0.1	0.2	0.4
75 and over:	Single	8.7	7.2	9.6	27.5	33.3	37.5	3.9	3.7	3.8	7.4	8.6	9.9
	Married	32.6	35.3	46.2	18.5	22.2	29.4	9.8	10.7	11.4	4.7	5.9	7.5
	Widowed	29.6	27.5	27.7	73.3	91.8	114.4	7.5	7.0	6.3	18.3	21.9	25.1
	Divorced	0.1	0.2	0.6	0.2	0.4	1.2	–	–	–	–	–	0.1

1. 1981 data for Scotland and Northern Ireland relates to the enumerated
'usually resident' population and are not strictly comparable with earlier data.

Sources General Register Office (Scotland); General Register Office (Northern Ireland)

2.6 Marital condition of the Home population[1]: mid-year estimates

Thousands

	England and Wales						Scotland					
	Males			Females			Males			Females		
	1980	1981[2]	1982[3]	1980	1981[2]	1982[3]	1981[2]	1982[2]	1983	1981[2]	1982[2]	1983
All ages												
Single	10 495.2	10 717.5	10 737.8	9 269.1	9 502.5	9 504.6	1 149.2	1 148.2	1 147.4	1 067.5	1 065.5	1 062.8
Married	12 322.8	12 189.2	12 098.8	12 356.4	12 252.9	12 173.9	1 226.3	1 216.8	1 206.2	1 239.1	1 227.2	1 211.4
Widowed	678.8	669.8	667.4	2 909.5	2 903.5	2 902.5	77.5	77.6	78.1	316.7	316.6	316.7
Divorced	538.3	583.6	641.4	726.0	815.3	880.4	41.8	46.8	53.2	62.1	67.8	74.6
Age groups:												
0 – 14:												
Single	5 284.6	5 180.6	5 076.4	5 005.0	4 909.9	4 812.2	563.5	548.9	535.5	534.9	522.1	508.7
15 – 19:												
Single	2 042.8	2 096.3	2 104.7	1 864.9	1 940.6	1 943.4	230.4	229.9	227.5	214.0	213.1	211.0
Married	21.9	17.8	16.5	100.5	74.3	70.9	3.7	4.0	3.7	11.1	10.7	9.7
Widowed	–	0.1	–	0.1	0.2	0.1	–	–	–	–	–	–
Divorced	–	0.2	–	0.1	0.3	0.1	–	–	–	0.1	0.1	0.1
20 – 24:												
Single	1 364.8	1 464.4	1 529.6	895.7	1 051.5	1 130.8	149.2	157.2	164.9	109.8	120.1	129.3
Married	483.4	421.3	402.3	848.1	765.6	732.4	59.9	56.6	53.3	92.0	85.0	77.9
Widowed	0.3	0.5	0.4	1.5	1.8	1.8	0.1	0.1	0.1	0.3	0.3	0.3
Divorced	8.4	10.2	10.5	20.8	28.4	28.2	1.3	1.6	1.8	2.7	3.0	3.5
25 – 34:												
Single	821.8	936.9	970.5	420.5	511.5	545.5	86.9	92.7	99.7	51.1	56.2	63.2
Married	2 576.2	2 481.6	2 341.1	2 856.0	2 777.7	2 649.1	266.1	254.2	244.8	289.5	278.3	268.3
Widowed	3.8	4.1	3.9	10.0	13.1	12.0	0.5	0.5	0.5	1.7	1.8	1.7
Divorced	143.0	146.5	157.4	182.0	214.9	226.3	10.9	12.5	15.0	17.0	18.5	20.4
35 – 44:												
Single	287.2	319.7	339.9	151.8	174.1	182.6	32.4	34.2	35.7	20.8	21.4	21.8
Married	2 516.7	2 528.2	2 612.5	2 510.0	2 540.3	2 639.6	252.5	260.2	264.4	261.7	269.1	273.0
Widowed	9.7	11.3	11.3	37.8	40.5	40.0	1.6	1.6	1.6	5.6	5.6	5.5
Divorced	158.0	164.7	188.0	196.6	217.2	244.4	11.7	13.4	15.1	16.5	18.4	20.3
45 – 54:												
Single	258.4	256.6	251.4	173.2	170.2	163.8	28.5	27.5	26.9	25.2	24.0	22.9
Married	2 358.8	2 341.2	2 320.4	2 316.3	2 295.6	2 274.5	240.6	238.5	237.3	243.5	242.1	240.7
Widowed	37.1	37.0	35.7	151.4	146.8	142.7	5.3	5.3	5.3	20.8	20.5	20.1
Divorced	118.1	129.0	142.0	143.0	155.3	169.2	9.3	10.2	11.4	12.1	13.3	14.6
55 – 59:												
Single	126.8	130.2	127.3	110.1	106.5	101.4	15.1	14.6	14.2	16.7	15.9	15.2
Married	1 232.9	1 190.6	1 158.6	1 174.4	1 134.2	1 102.8	116.2	113.5	112.5	109.9	108.0	106.9
Widowed	48.4	45.2	44.2	197.3	184.5	177.5	6.0	6.0	5.9	23.0	22.8	22.6
Divorced	44.1	48.5	51.9	60.0	61.6	63.8	3.4	3.6	3.9	4.7	4.8	5.1
60 – 64:												
Single	91.7	101.6	106.1	107.1	107.2	107.6	12.2	12.6	13.1	16.3	16.5	16.7
Married	990.6	1 028.5	1 067.6	890.3	941.9	978.5	95.7	99.2	102.4	87.6	90.7	93.3
Widowed	63.9	62.4	65.4	280.6	280.9	287.8	8.1	8.5	9.0	34.9	35.5	36.3
Divorced	29.4	34.3	38.3	44.9	49.9	55.2	2.2	2.4	2.7	3.5	3.9	4.5
65 – 74:												
Single	149.5	158.8	156.0	273.0	261.1	247.3	21.1	20.2	19.3	39.3	37.1	34.8
Married	1 598.4	1 597.5	1 571.9	1 286.0	1 309.5	1 292.6	143.9	141.1	136.5	113.1	111.6	108.3
Widowed	228.7	223.2	218.7	982.0	963.0	947.6	26.8	26.5	26.1	108.8	107.3	105.2
Divorced	32.2	40.3	42.1	63.0	65.7	68.9	2.4	2.6	2.7	4.2	4.4	4.5
75 and over												
Single	67.6	72.4	75.9	267.8	269.9	270.0	10.0	10.3	10.6	39.3	39.2	39.3
Married	543.9	582.5	607.9	374.8	413.8	433.5	47.8	49.4	51.4	30.6	31.7	33.3
Widowed	286.9	286.0	287.8	1 248.8	1 272.7	1 293.0	29.2	29.2	29.7	121.4	122.9	125.0
Divorced	5.1	9.9	11.2	15.6	22.0	24.3	0.6	0.6	0.7	1.3	1.4	1.6

1. See introductory note on page 5 on the 1981 census.
2. Revised.
3. Provisional.

Sources Office of Population Censuses and Surveys; General Register Office (Scotland)

2.7 Projected Home population at mid-year[1]
Great Britain

Thousands

	1983 Base	1984	1985	1986	1987	1988	1993	1998	2003	2013	2023
Persons all ages	54 804	54 820	54 839	54 868	54 909	54 961	55 382	55 852	56 138	56 383	56 947
0–4	3 448	3 457	3 448	3 458	3 493	3 542	3 854	3 906	3 699	3 508	3 761
5–9	3 237	3 221	3 255	3 311	3 382	3 446	3 541	3 853	3 905	3 505	3 644
10–14	4 082	3 908	3 740	3 536	3 356	3 235	3 444	3 538	3 851	3 696	3 506
15–19	4 582	4 500	4 389	4 313	4 203	4 076	3 230	3 439	3 533	3 896	3 499
20–24	4 365	4 487	4 586	4 624	4 621	4 567	4 062	3 219	3 428	3 833	3 679
25–29	3 784	3 847	3 946	4 059	4 181	4 300	4 501	3 998	3 157	3 459	3 822
30–34	3 749	3 690	3 646	3 648	3 684	3 728	4 243	4 443	3 942	3 313	3 716
35–39	3 925	3 990	4 032	4 040	3 833	3 717	3 698	4 210	4 410	3 078	3 378
40–44	3 161	3 245	3 327	3 456	3 742	3 891	3 686	3 667	4 176	3 879	3 259
45–49	3 039	3 072	3 087	3 055	3 061	3 115	3 837	3 633	3 616	4 315	3 012
50–54	3 038	2 994	2 960	2 939	2 937	2 964	3 039	3 746	3 547	4 026	3 741
55–59	3 066	3 025	3 000	2 972	2 946	2 911	2 843	2 917	3 599	3 397	4 059
60–64	3 101	3 198	3 071	2 980	2 908	2 861	2 720	2 661	2 735	3 206	3 657
65–69	2 506	2 380	2 478	2 577	2 678	2 788	2 579	2 460	2 415	3 092	2 940
70–74	2 347	2 349	2 344	2 307	2 237	2 116	2 375	2 205	2 115	2 165	2 575
75–79	1 735	1 762	1 779	1 790	1 797	1 802	1 635	1 858	1 735	1 672	2 204
80–84	1 019	1 053	1 079	1 102	1 124	1 147	1 200	1 104	1 280	1 180	1 262
85–89	442	456	478	499	518	540	620	664	616	703	723
90 and over	182	186	194	201	208	216	273	330	380	458	509
Males all ages	26 661	26 673	26 688	26 708	26 735	26 768	27 018	27 296	27 474	27 627	27 885
0–4	1 768	1 773	1 770	1 776	1 795	1 821	1 982	2 009	1 901	1 804	1 934
5–9	1 663	1 655	1 672	1 700	1 736	1 767	1 820	1 981	2 008	1 802	1 873
10–14	2 096	2 008	1 921	1 817	1 725	1 662	1 767	1 820	1 980	1 901	1 804
15–19	2 354	2 312	2 254	2 214	2 155	2 091	1 659	1 763	1 815	2 003	1 799
20–24	2 206	2 273	2 330	2 358	2 363	2 339	2 078	1 648	1 752	1 963	1 885
25–29	1 909	1 938	1 986	2 040	2 102	2 165	2 297	2 036	1 607	1 764	1 949
30–34	1 884	1 856	1 835	1 837	1 853	1 873	2 128	2 260	2 001	1 678	1 889
35–39	1 970	1 999	2 020	2 024	1 919	1 863	1 852	2 106	2 238	1 556	1 710
40–44	1 590	1 632	1 672	1 736	1 877	1 948	1 842	1 831	2 084	1 958	1 642
45–49	1 525	1 541	1 548	1 530	1 533	1 559	1 913	1 808	1 798	2 175	1 512
50–54	1 508	1 487	1 474	1 464	1 462	1 477	1 511	1 855	1 754	1 987	1 869
55–59	1 499	1 480	1 467	1 453	1 441	1 425	1 398	1 432	1 760	1 659	2 011
60–64	1 463	1 512	1 457	1 419	1 388	1 368	1 303	1 282	1 316	1 535	1 752
65–69	1 128	1 072	1 120	1 167	1 216	1 268	1 189	1 138	1 125	1 437	1 368
70–74	990	992	990	978	948	895	1 018	962	927	960	1 141
75–79	648	662	673	680	686	690	629	730	695	685	910
80–84	316	331	343	354	363	374	405	374	446	429	471
85–89	108	111	117	124	132	141	171	190	180	220	236
90 and over	37	37	38	39	40	42	56	72	86	112	131
Females all ages	28 143	28 147	28 150	28 160	28 174	28 194	28 364	28 556	28 664	28 756	29 062
0–4	1 680	1 683	1 679	1 682	1 698	1 721	1 873	1 898	1 797	1 704	1 828
5–9	1 574	1 566	1 583	1 611	1 648	1 679	1 721	1 872	1 898	1 703	1 770
10–14	1 986	1 900	1 818	1 719	1 631	1 573	1 677	1 718	1 871	1 795	1 702
15–19	2 228	2 189	2 136	2 101	2 048	1 984	1 571	1 676	1 718	1 895	1 701
20–24	2 159	2 214	2 256	2 267	2 257	2 227	1 985	1 571	1 676	1 870	1 795
25–29	1 875	1 909	1 960	2 019	2 079	2 135	2 203	1 961	1 549	1 696	1 872
30–34	1 864	1 833	1 811	1 811	1 831	1 855	2 115	2 183	1 941	1 635	1 827
35–39	1 955	1 990	2 014	2 017	1 914	1 854	1 846	2 105	2 172	1 523	1 668
40–44	1 571	1 613	1 654	1 720	1 865	1 943	1 844	1 835	2 092	1 921	1 618
45–49	1 514	1 532	1 539	1 525	1 528	1 555	1 924	1 825	1 817	2 139	1 500
50–54	1 530	1 506	1 487	1 475	1 474	1 487	1 528	1 891	1 793	2 038	1 872
55–59	1 567	1 546	1 533	1 519	1 504	1 485	1 444	1 485	1 839	1 739	2 049
60–64	1 637	1 685	1 613	1 561	1 521	1 493	1 417	1 380	1 420	1 671	1 906
65–69	1 379	1 308	1 358	1 410	1 462	1 520	1 389	1 321	1 290	1 655	1 574
70–74	1 357	1 356	1 352	1 331	1 290	1 221	1 356	1 243	1 187	1 206	1 434
75–79	1 086	1 100	1 106	1 109	1 111	1 112	1 005	1 128	1 039	988	1 293
80–84	703	722	737	749	760	773	801	730	833	752	791
85–89	334	345	360	374	386	399	448	473	437	483	487
90 and over	145	150	155	161	169	174	217	259	293	347	378

1. The assumptions on which these projections are made are described in the introductory note on page 5.

Source Government Actuary's Department in consultation with the Office of
Population Censuses and Surveys, the General Register Office
(Scotland) and the General Register Office (Northern Ireland).

2.7 Projected Home population at mid-year[1]

(continued)

Thousands

	1983 Base	1984	1985	1986	1987	1988	1993	1998	2003	2013	2023
England and Wales											
Persons all ages	49 654	49 685	49 719	49 762	49 815	49 878	50 335	50 838	51 178	51 582	52 291
0–4	3 120	3 130	3 124	3 136	3 170	3 215	3 498	3 551	3 369	3 215	3 455
5–9	2 923	2 911	2 945	2 998	3 063	3 122	3 218	3 501	3 554	3 207	3 348
10–14	3 680	3 526	3 376	3 191	3 031	2 923	3 123	3 218	3 501	3 373	3 219
15–19	4 130	4 054	3 953	3 883	3 785	3 674	2 918	3 118	3 213	3 548	3 203
20–24	3 934	4 049	4 142	4 180	4 178	4 127	3 672	2 919	3 118	3 495	3 368
25–29	3 415	3 472	3 564	3 670	3 783	3 895	4 087	3 634	2 883	3 176	3 511
30–34	3 404	3 349	3 307	3 307	3 337	3 377	3 856	4 047	3 596	3 046	3 421
35–39	3 582	3 640	3 676	3 680	3 490	3 382	3 356	3 832	4 023	2 829	3 121
40–44	2 866	2 947	3 028	3 152	3 417	3 555	3 357	3 331	3 805	3 548	3 006
45–49	2 750	2 783	2 798	2 769	2 775	2 827	3 508	3 312	3 288	3 943	2 774
50–54	2 748	2 707	2 677	2 658	2 658	2 685	2 761	3 428	3 236	3 674	3 427
55–59	2 780	2 742	2 718	2 693	2 668	2 636	2 578	2 653	3 297	3 095	3 716
60–64 Males	1 336	1 381	1 329	1 293	1 265	1 246	1 187	1 169	1 203	1 406	1 603
60–64 Females	1 486	1 531	1 465	1 416	1 378	1 352	1 280	1 248	1 289	1 526	1 742
65–69	2 279	2 164	2 255	2 347	2 440	2 543	2 346	2 235	2 197	2 840	2 686
70–74	2 137	2 139	2 135	2 103	2 040	1 929	2 171	2 010	1 925	1 979	2 362
75–79	1 582	1 607	1 623	1 633	1 640	1 645	1 494	1 702	1 585	1 528	2 032
80–84	931	962	987	1 008	1 028	1 050	1 105	1 012	1 176	1 080	1 159
85–89	405	419	439	458	476	496	570	611	567	647	665
90 and over	168	172	179	186	193	200	253	307	353	427	473
Scotland											
Persons all ages	5 150	5 135	5 120	5 106	5 094	5 083	5 047	5 014	4 960	4 801	4 656
0–4	328	327	324	322	323	327	356	355	330	293	306
5–9	314	310	310	313	319	324	323	352	351	298	296
10–14	402	382	364	345	325	312	321	320	350	323	287
15–19	452	446	436	430	418	402	312	321	320	348	296
20–24	431	438	444	444	443	440	390	300	310	338	311
25–29	369	375	382	389	398	405	414	364	274	283	311
30–34	345	341	339	341	347	351	387	396	346	267	295
35–39	343	350	356	360	343	335	342	378	387	249	257
40–44	295	298	299	304	325	336	329	336	371	331	253
45–49	289	289	289	286	286	288	329	321	328	372	238
50–54	290	287	283	281	279	279	278	318	311	352	314
55–59	286	283	282	279	278	275	265	264	302	302	343
60–64 Males	127	131	128	126	123	122	116	113	113	129	149
60–64 Females	151	154	148	145	143	141	137	131	131	145	164
65–69	227	216	223	230	238	245	233	225	218	252	254
70–74	210	210	209	204	197	187	204	195	190	186	213
75–79	153	155	156	157	157	157	141	156	150	144	172
80–84	88	91	92	94	96	97	101	92	104	100	103
85–89	37	37	39	41	42	44	50	53	49	56	58
90 and over	14	14	15	15	15	16	20	23	27	31	36
Northern Ireland											
Persons all ages											
0–4											
5–9											
10–14											
15–19											
20–24											
25–29											
30–34											
35–39											
40–44											
45–49											
50–54											
55–59											
60–64 Males											
60–64 Females											
65–69											
70–74											
75–79											
80–84											
85–89											
90 and over											

1. The assumptions on which these projections are made are described in the introductory note on page 5.

Source Government Actuary's Department in consultation with the Office of Population Censuses and Surveys, the General Register Office (Scotland) and the General Register Office (Northern Ireland).

2.8 Geographical distribution of the enumerated population: census figures[1]

Thousands

	Area in square kilometres[2]	1911	1931	1951	1961	1971	1981[4]
Urban and rural districts							
England and Wales:							
Urban areas	21 765	28 163	31 952	35 336	36 872	38 151	37 324
Rural districts	129 360	7 908	8 000	8 422	9 233	10 598	11 687
Scotland:							
Cities and burghs	1 300	3 140	3 362	3 563	3 646	3 705 }	5 131
Landward areas	75 879	1 620	1 481	1 534	1 533	1 524 }	
Northern Ireland:							
Urban areas	240	587	678[3]	728	770	846 }	1 562
Rural districts	13 330	664	602[3]	643	655	690 }	
Standard regions of England and Wales							
North	19 349	2 815	3 038	3 137	3 250	3 296	3 104
Yorkshire and Humberside	14 196	3 877	4 285	4 522	4 635	4 799	4 860
East Midlands	12 179	2 263	2 531	2 893	3 100	3 390	3 819
East Anglia	12 565	1 192	1 232	1 382	1 470	1 669	1 872
South East	27 408	11 744	13 539	15 127	16 271	17 230	16 796
South West	23 660	2 687	2 794	3 229	3 411	3 781	4 349
West Midlands	13 013	3 277	3 743	4 423	4 758	5 110	5 148
North West	7 993	5 796	6 197	6 447	6 567	6 743	6 414
Wales	20 763	2 421	2 593	2 599	2 644	2 731	2 792
Conurbations							
Greater London	1 580	7 160	8 110	8 197	7 992	7 452	6 696
West Midlands	678	1 651	1 951	2 260	2 378	2 372	2 244
West Yorkshire	1 255	1 590	1 655	1 693	1 704	1 728	1 682
South East Lancashire	983	2 328	2 427	2 423	2 428	2 393	2 245
Merseyside	394	1 157	1 347	1 386	1 384	1 267	1 127
Tyneside	235	761	827	836	856	805	738
Central Clydeside	778	..	1 690	1 759	1 802	1 728	1 718
Cities							
Birmingham	209	526	1 003	1 113	1 107	1 015	1 007
Liverpool	113	746	856	789	746	610	510
Manchester	110	714	766	703	662	544	449
Sheffield	184	455	512	513	494	520	538
Leeds	164	446	483	505	511	496	705
Bristol	110	357	397	443	437	427	391
Coventry	81	106	167	258	306	335	314
Nottingham	74	260	269	306	312	301	272
Bradford	103	288	298	292	296	294	457
Kingston-upon-Hull	71	278	314	299	303	286	270
Leicester	73	227	239	285	273	284	280
Cardiff	80	182	224	244	257	279	274
Wolverhampton	69	95	133	163	151	269	255
Stoke-on-Trent	93	235	277	275	265	265	253
Glasgow	157	784	1 088	1 090	1 055	897	766
Edinburgh	135	320	439	467	468	454	437
Dundee	50	165	176	177	183	182	180
Aberdeen	50	164	167	183	185	182	204
Belfast	73	387	438[3]	444	416	362	330

1. Populations of urban and rural districts and cities are for the administrative areas as constituted at the time of each census from 1911 to 1981. So some changes in population may be the result of changes in the constitutions of the areas; details can be found in the reports of the censuses. The cities shown do not include all urban areas with populations of 182 000 or more in 1981. Populations of Standard Regions and conurbations relate to approximately the same area throughout the period 1911 to 1981.
2. The statistics of area in square kilometers is for areas as constituted in 1971. The areas of urban and rural districts and of conurbations have not been measured since 1971, but there have been some changes in the areas of standard regions and cities.

3. Figures for Northern Ireland and the City of Belfast relate to the 1937 Census.
4. Figures for urban and rural districts in England and Wales and for the Conurbations are from the *Census 1981 Preliminary Report for Towns*.
   Figures for Scotland, standard regions, and cities (administrative districts) are persons present on census night from *Census 1981, Key Statistics for Local Authorities, Great Britain*.
   In Northern Ireland it is estimated that some 74 000 persons were not enumerated. These are included in the above figures. Some 32 000 of these were included in the Belfast figure.

Sources Office of Population Censuses and Surveys; General Register Office (Scotland); General Register Office (Northern Ireland).

2.9 Geographical distribution of Home population: mid-year estimates[1]

Thousands

	1973	1974	1975	1976	1977	1978	1979	1980	1981	1982	1983
England and Wales	49 459	49 468	49 470	49 459	49 440	49 442	49 508	49 603	49 634	49 601	49 654
Scotland	5 212	5 217	5 206	5 205	5 196	5 179	5 167	5 153	5 180	5 167	5 150
Northern Ireland	1 539	1 540	1 539	1 541	1 543	1 546	1 552	1 558	1 564	1 567	1 573
Standard regions of England and Wales											
North	3 152	3 154	3 153	3 154	3 149	3 134	3 130	3 128	3 118	3 107	3 100
Yorkshire and Humberside	4 923	4 927	4 928	4 924	4 921	4 920	4 921	4 923	4 918	4 910	4 908
East Midlands	3 723	3 745	3 762	3 774	3 787	3 798	3 818	3 838	3 853	3 852	3 860
East Anglia	1 751	1 772	1 793	1 814	1 825	1 842	1 864	1 882	1 895	1 911	1 925
South East	17 133	17 067	17 015	16 976	16 945	16 939	16 952	16 993	17 010	17 006	17 042
Greater London	*7 362*	*7 264*	*7 179*	*7 089*	*7 012*	*6 947*	*6 888*	*6 851*	*6 806*	*6 766*	*6 754*
South West	4 205	4 230	4 257	4 280	4 300	4 313	4 335	4 361	4 381	4 398	4 424
West Midlands	5 180	5 188	5 185	5 178	5 175	5 175	5 179	5 185	5 186	5 180	5 176
North West	6 619	6 600	6 581	6 560	6 538	6 517	6 498	6 477	6 460	6 431	6 410
Wales	2 773	2 785	2 795	2 799	2 801	2 804	2 810	2 816	2 814	2 807	2 808
Metropolitan counties											
Tyne and Wear	1 200	1 196	1 192	1 188	1 182	1 172	1 166	1 162	1 155	1 150	1 145
South Yorkshire	1 328	1 328	1 325	1 323	1 320	1 318	1 316	1 316	1 317	1 313	1 310
West Yorkshire	2 089	2 088	2 087	2 082	2 078	2 074	2 072	2 069	2 067	2 063	2 059
West Midlands	2 794	2 785	2 768	2 747	2 729	2 710	2 694	2 684	2 673	2 666	2 658
Greater Manchester	2 724	2 710	2 694	2 680	2 668	2 654	2 641	2 628	2 619	2 605	2 598
Merseyside	1 626	1 609	1 597	1 586	1 571	1 556	1 543	1 531	1 522	1 510	1 501
London boroughs and county districts (with about 275 000 or more population)											
Tyne and Wear											
Newcastle-upon-Tyne	303	301	299	297	295	292	290	288	284	281	281
Sunderland	291	292	293	295	296	296	296	297	297	300	299
South Yorkshire											
Sheffield	572	570	565	562	559	555	551	549	548	546	543
Doncaster	284	285	287	287	287	288	288	290	291	289	290
West Yorkshire											
Leeds	746	745	743	739	735	730	726	721	718	716	714
Bradford	464	464	464	463	463	463	462	463	465	465	464
Kirklees	376	378	378	377	377	376	377	377	377	377	377
Wakefield	306	307	309	310	310	311	313	314	314	314	312
Greater London											
Croydon	335	333	330	328	326	325	324	322	321	322	321
Barnet	308	305	303	301	299	297	296	295	295	295	294
Bromley	307	304	302	300	299	299	298	298	298	298	299
Ealing	303	300	298	295	292	291	288	283	282	282	284
Lambeth	304	300	296	288	282	270	263	257	253	248	245
Wandsworth	299	294	290	283	278	273	269	266	262	259	258
Avon											
Bristol	427	426	423	418	414	409	405	402	401	400	399
West Midlands											
Birmingham	1 094	1 083	1 068	1 056	1 046	1 037	1 029	1 025	1 021	1 017	1 013
Coventry	334	335	335	332	330	328	326	323	319	317	316
Sandwell	327	325	323	320	317	314	312	310	310	309	307
Dudley	298	299	300	299	299	299	299	300	301	301	301
Greater Manchester											
Manchester	525	512	501	494	486	477	470	465	463	459	458
Wigan	305	308	309	310	311	312	311	310	310	309	308
Stockport	294	292	290	289	289	291	292	291	290	290	289
Merseyside											
Liverpool	579	566	557	551	542	534	527	521	517	510	502
Wirral	353	350	348	346	345	343	341	341	341	339	338
Sefton	309	308	307	306	304	304	303	302	300	299	300
Humberside											
Kingston-upon-Hull	285	285	284	283	281	278	277	276	274	271	269
Leicestershire											
Leicester	285	285	285	282	281	280	280	281	283	282	282
Nottinghamshire											
Nottingham	297	296	292	287	284	282	279	277	278	278	277
South Glamorgan											
Cardiff	289	288	286	285	284	283	282	282	281	280	280
City of Glasgow local government district	924	905	881	856	832	810	794	782	774	762	751
City of Edinburgh local government district	473	475	470	467	464	457	455	453	446	444	441
City of Dundee local government district	196	196	195	194	193	192	191	189	185	183	181
City of Aberdeen local government district	213	212	210	210	208	209	209	209	212	213	214
Belfast	415	374	368	368	358	354	351	346	330	325	323

1. Revised series estimates, 1971–80; revised in the light of the 1981 Census.

Sources Office of Population Censuses and Surveys; General Register Office
(Scotland); General Register Office (Northern Ireland)

2.10 Migration into and out from the United Kingdom
Analysis by occupation and sex[1,2,3]

Thousands

	Total			Professional			Manual and Clerical			Not gainfully employed[4]		
	Persons	Males	Females	Persons	Males	Females	Persons	Males	Females	Persons	Males	Females
Immigrants												
1973	196	104	91	47	33	14	57	31	26	92	40	51
1974	184	104	80	48	34	14	46	30	16	90	39	51
1975	197	102	95	49	28	20	50	31	19	98	42	56
1976	191	100	91	52	37	15	41	23	18	98	40	58
1977	163	88	74	43	29	14	37	22	15	82	37	46
1978	187	96	91	46	33	13	33	19	14	109	44	64
1979	195	103	91	53	36	16	35	21	14	107	46	61
1980	174	92	82	44	32	12	32	19	14	97	41	56
1981	153	83	71	45	32	13	24	14	10	85	37	48
1982	202	100	101	44	35	9	38	18	20	120	48	73
1983	202	107	95	55	40	15	36	21	15	111	46	64
Emigrants												
1973	246	124	122	51	33	19	87	53	34	108	39	69
1974	269	141	128	62	40	23	97	60	37	110	42	68
1975	238	126	112	60	43	18	73	44	29	104	39	65
1976	210	118	93	70	50	20	56	36	20	84	31	53
1977	209	117	91	66	49	17	62	39	23	81	30	51
1978	192	108	85	56	39	16	56	36	20	81	33	48
1979	189	106	82	58	43	15	52	30	22	79	34	45
1980	229	134	95	65	49	16	62	42	20	102	43	59
1981	233	133	100	67	50	17	60	38	22	105	44	61
1982	259	135	124	67	48	19	66	37	29	126	50	76
1983	185	90	95	51	32	18	36	19	16	99	38	60
Balance												
1973	−50	−20	−30	−4	−	−4	−30	−21	−9	−16	+1	−17
1974	−85	−37	−48	−14	−5	−9	−51	−30	−22	−20	−3	−17
1975	−41	−24	−17	−12	−14	+2	−23	−13	−10	−6	+3	−9
1976	−19	−18	−1	−18	−13	−5	−15	−13	−1	+14	+9	+5
1977	−46	−29	−17	−23	−20	−3	−24	−16	−8	+1	+7	−6
1978	−5	−12	+6	−10	−7	−3	−24	−17	−7	+28	+12	+16
1979	+6	−3	+9	−5	−6	+1	−17	−9	−8	+28	+12	+16
1980	−55	−42	−14	−20	−16	−4	−30	−23	−6	−5	−2	−3
1981	−79	−50	−29	−22	−19	−4	−37	−24	−13	−20	−8	−13
1982	−57	−34	−23	−23	−13	−10	−29	−19	−10	−6	−2	−3
1983	+17	+17	−	+5	+8	−3	−	+1	−1	+12	+8	+4

1. Estimates are derived from the International Passenger Survey (IPS), a sample survey covering the principal air and sea routes between the United Kingdom and overseas but excluding routes to and from the Irish Republic.
2. An immigrant is defined as a person who has resided abroad for a year or more and on entering has declared the intention to reside in the United Kingdom for a year or more; and *vice versa* for an emigrant.
3. Type of occupation is that followed prior to migration.
4. Includes housewives, students, children and retired persons.

Source Office of Population Censuses and Surveys

2.11 Migration into and out from the United Kingdom
Analysis by nationality and country of last or next residence[1, 2]

Thousands

	All migrants	Commonwealth citizens									Foreign		
		Total	Country of last or next residence										
			Commonwealth								Foreign		
			All	Australia	Canada	New Zealand	Africa	Bangla-desh, India, Sri Lanka	Caribbean[3]	Other	All	European Com-munity[4]	Rest of Europe[4]
Immigrants													
1973	196	127	99	31	11	7	22	11	5	12	29	7	4
1974	184	122	90	23	7	10	18	11	4	17	32	10	4
1975	197	138	101	26	7	10	21	13	5	18	37	12	4
1976	191	136	94	24	7	8	18	15	4	17	42	15	2
1977	163	112	75	20	7	8	14	11	4	11	37	9	4
1978	187	123	82	18	6	9	13	19	5	12	41	12	2
1979	195	135	90	16	6	9	16	19	5	19	45	9	5
1980	174	109	68	12	5	6	11	14	4	15	41	14	3
1981	153	100	65	10	5	4	11	18	3	12	36	11	3
1982	202	139	65	10	6	4	14	17	2	11	74	38	6
1983	202	140	83	18	6	6	18	13	4	17	57	20	5
Emigrants													
1973	246	204	139	55	28	25	12	5	7	6	65	21	9
1974	269	228	156	63	36	28	13	4	6	6	73	19	7
1975	238	197	108	29	36	14	13	3	4	8	89	17	10
1976	210	166	90	32	22	9	11	4	3	10	76	17	5
1977	209	172	92	32	18	8	16	4	3	10	81	19	13
1978	192	152	74	25	14	9	10	4	2	10	78	21	8
1979	189	154	75	23	18	8	9	4	3	10	78	22	7
1980	229	181	98	35	19	10	12	4	3	14	83	18	8
1981	233	193	105	45	22	10	10	2	3	13	88	15	7
1982	259	219	111	45	19	10	11	5	5	17	108	30	4
1983	185	148	72	28	6	6	9	4	3	16	77	21	7
Balance													
1973	− 50	− 77	− 40	− 24	− 17	− 18	+ 10	+ 6	− 3	+ 6	− 37	− 14	− 5
1974	− 85	− 106	− 66	− 40	− 29	− 18	+ 6	+ 7	− 2	+ 11	− 40	− 9	− 3
1975	− 41	− 58	− 7	− 3	− 29	− 5	+ 8	+ 10	+ 1	+ 10	− 52	− 5	− 7
1976	− 19	− 29	+ 4	− 7	− 15	− 1	+ 7	+ 12	−	+ 8	− 33	− 2	− 3
1977	− 46	− 60	− 17	− 12	− 12	−	− 1	+ 7	+ 1	+ 1	− 43	− 10	− 9
1978	− 5	− 29	+ 9	− 7	− 8	−	+ 3	+ 15	+ 2	+ 3	− 37	− 9	− 5
1979	+ 6	− 19	+ 16	− 7	− 12	+ 1	+ 7	+ 15	+ 2	+ 10	− 33	− 12	− 2
1980	− 55	− 71	− 30	− 24	− 14	− 4	−	+ 9	+ 2	+ 2	− 42	− 4	− 4
1981	− 79	− 93	− 41	− 35	− 17	− 5	+ 1	+ 16	−	−	− 52	− 3	− 4
1982	− 57	− 81	− 46	− 34	− 13	− 6	+ 4	+ 12	− 3	− 6	− 35	+ 8	+ 2
1983	+ 17	− 8	+ 12	− 10	+ 1	−	+ 9	+ 9	+ 2	+ 1	− 20	− 1	− 2

1. Estimates are derived from the International Passenger Survey (IPS), a sample survey covering the principal air and sea routes between the United Kingdom and overseas but excluding routes to and from the Irish Republic.
2. An immigrant is defined as a person who has resided abroad for a year or more and on entering has declared the intention to reside in the United Kingdom for a year or more; and *vice versa* for an emigrant.
3. Including Guyana and Belize.
4. Including Greece with European Community from 1981.

Source Office of Population Censuses and Surveys.

2.11 *(continued)* Migration into and out from the United Kingdom
Analysis by nationality and country of last or next residence[1,2]

Thousands

Commonwealth citizens (*continued*)					Alien citizens							
Country of last or next residence (*continued*)					Total	Country of last or next residence						
Foreign (*continued*)						Common-wealth	Foreign					
United States of America	Rest of America	Republic of South Africa	Pakistan	Other		All	All	European Com-munity[4]	United States of America	Pakistan	Other[4]	
												Immigrants
6	–	7	1	4	68	4	65	17	15	5	28	1973
7	2	5	1	4	62	1	60	19	12	4	25	1974
6	2	7	2	5	59	2	57	11	10	4	31	1975
6	2	8	3	6	55	1	54	10	10	9	26	1976
5	1	11	2	5	50	2	48	9	7	10	22	1977
6	1	10	3	8	64	1	63	12	9	16	25	1978
5	1	9	3	13	60	2	58	13	8	11	25	1979
7	2	3	2	10	64	3	61	10	10	9	32	1980
7	1	2	3	9	53	3	50	12	10	7	22	1981
8	2	8	3	8	63	3	60	15	11	8	26	1982
11	1	5	4	10	62	2	60	11	14	8	27	1983
												Emigrants
11	1	11	2	10	42	2	39	11	9	2	17	1973
11	2	20	1	12	41	3	38	10	8	1	18	1974
12	2	28	2	18	41	2	39	11	10	–	18	1975
11	2	20	2	19	45	1	44	14	10	1	19	1976
11	1	7	1	30	36	1	35	10	10	1	14	1977
14	2	4	1	28	41	2	39	11	11	1	17	1978
17	2	5	1	25	35	1	34	7	10	1	17	1979
19	3	11	1	24	48	2	47	16	10	–	20	1980
16	3	22	1	25	40	1	38	14	9	–	15	1981
15	2	25	1	30	40	3	37	7	14	–	16	1982
17	–	8	1	21	37	2	35	8	15	–	13	1983
												Balance
−5	−1	−5	−1	−6	+27	+1	+25	+6	+6	+3	+11	1973
−5	–	−15	–	−8	+21	−2	+23	+9	+5	+3	+6	1974
−6	–	−22	–	−12	+17	–	+18	–	–	+4	+14	1975
−4	–	−12	+2	−14	+10	–	+11	−4	–	+8	+7	1976
−5	–	+4	+1	−25	+14	–	+14	−1	−3	+9	+8	1977
−9	−1	+6	+2	−20	+23	–	+24	+1	−1	+16	+8	1978
−11	−1	+3	+2	−12	+25	+1	+24	+6	−1	+10	+9	1979
−12	−1	−8	+1	−14	+16	+1	+14	−6	–	+9	+12	1980
−9	−1	−20	+2	−16	+13	+2	+12	−2	+1	+6	+7	1981
−7	–	−17	+1	−22	+23	–	+23	+8	−4	+8	+11	1982
−6	+1	−3	+3	−11	+25	–	+25	+3	–	+8	+14	1983

1. Estimates are derived from the International Passenger Survey (IPS), a sample survey covering the principal air and sea routes between the United Kingdom and overseas but excluding routes to and from the Irish Republic.
2. An immigrant is defined as a person who has resided abroad for a year or more and on entering has declared the intention to reside in the United Kingdom for a year or more; and *vice versa* for an emigrant.
3. Including Guyana and Belize.
4. Including Greece with European Community from 1981.

Source Office of Population Censuses and Surveys.

2.12 Acceptances for settlement by nationality

Number of persons

Geographical region and nationality	All acceptances for settlement				
	1979	1980	1981	1982	1983
All nationalities	69 670	69 750	59 060	53 870	53 460
Europe					
European Community Nationals[1]					
Belgium	140	90	70	60	70
Denmark	190	150	150	150	140
France	690	610	440	490	520
Germany (Federal Republic)	780	580	520	640	680
Greece	350	300	220	220	200
Italy	1 140	980	660	660	600
Luxembourg	10	–	–	–	–
Netherlands	550	430	250	410	460
European Community	3 860	3 140	2 310	2 640	2 680
Other Western Europe					
Austria	120	120	110	100	110
Cyprus	950	780	580	1 180[3]	560[3]
Finland	130	160	120	120	130
Malta	210	180	190	210	200
Norway	180	200	190	180	230
Portugal	960	850	640	460	390
Spain	1 070	720	590	510	480
Sweden	310	280	260	290	330
Switzerland	230	220	170	170	170
Turkey	540	560	570	520	580
Yugoslavia	160	120	120	100	140
Other Western Europe	4 850	4 200	3 540	3 830	3 310
Eastern Europe					
Bulgaria	10	10	10	10	10
Czechoslovakia	20	40	20	20	30
German Democratic Republic	50	20	–	10	10
Hungary	50	40	40	40	20
Poland	640	650	620	500	390
Romania	20	20	10	20	20
USSR	50	60	40	40	40
Eastern Europe	850	830	730	630	520
Europe	9 550	8 180	6 580	7 100	6 520
Americas					
Argentina	80	90	90	80	80
Barbados	90	100	80	60	40
Brazil	130	110	120	140	140
Canada	1 100	920	880	940	1 140
Chile	540	270	250	160	120
Colombia	600	400	310	180	180
Cuba	–	–	–	–	–
Guyana	280	240	220	180	190
Jamaica	600	590	440	320	310
Mexico	60	60	60	60	70
Peru	60	40	40	60	50
Trinidad and Tobago	160	150	150	150	170
USA	3 540	3 420	3 510	3 350	3 940
Uruguay	20	20	10	20	–
Venezuela	70	60	70	60	70
West Indies Associated States[2]	160	170	90	60	40
Americas	7 490	6 630	6 330	5 820	6 530
Africa					
Algeria	110	80	120	100	100
Egypt	550	410	400	390	380
Ethiopia	80	70	30	20	50
Ghana	400	370	340	450	560
Kenya	600	490	430	490	640

Geographical region and nationality	All acceptances for settlement				
	1979	1980	1981	1982	1983
Africa—continued					
Libya	70	110	100	90	100
Mauritius	610	580	510	520	520
Morocco	260	190	200	130	150
Nigeria	360	310	250	300	360
Sierra Leone	80	70	50	60	60
Somalia	20	20	40	20	20
South Africa	1 310	920	850	800	840
Sudan	80	40	60	50	50
Tanzania	400	340	280	320	320
Tunisia	90	60	50	50	50
Uganda	60	80	40	50	100
Zambia	170	140	80	80	90
Zimbabwe	240	260	220	200	280
Africa	5 490	4 550	4 060	4 120	4 670
Asia					
Indian Sub-Continent					
Bangladesh	3 920	5 210	5 810	7 020	4 870
India	9 270	7 930	6 590	5 410	5 380
Pakistan	10 940	9 080	8 970	7 750	6 440
Indian Sub-Continent	24 130	22 220	21 370	20 180	16 690
Middle East					
Iran	1 140	1 260	1 380	1 500	1 980
Iraq	240	310	330	400	430
Israel	320	350	330	260	310
Jordan	120	140	120	110	150
Kuwait	–	–	–	–	–
Lebanon	150	150	270	190	260
Saudi Arabia	20	40	20	20	30
Syria	80	60	90	80	100
Middle East	2 070	2 310	2 560	2 580	3 280
Remainder of Asia					
China	150	180	160	170	160
Indonesia	40	70	50	60	60
Japan	630	690	900	930	1 010
Malaysia	550	580	660	700	780
Philippines	1 560	1 790	1 760	960	680
Singapore	110	100	120	130	140
Sri Lanka	920	770	790	790	920
Thailand	400	230	220	210	260
BDTC Hong Kong[4]	1 510	1 710	1 450	1 070	1 050
Remainder of Asia	5 860	6 130	6 120	5 020	5 070
Asia	32 060	30 670	30 050	27 780	25 040
Australasia					
Australia	3 160	3 240	2 440	2 410	2 680
New Zealand	2 700	2 720	2 060	1 800	1 980
Australasia	5 870	5 960	4 500	4 220	4 660
British Overseas Citizens	4 040	3 030	2 780	2 720	3 280
Other countries not elsewhere specified[5]	2 310	3 350	870	650	820
Stateless[5]	2 880	7 390	3 890	1 450	1 930
All nationalities	69 670	69 750	59 060	53 870	53 460
Foreign	36 600	38 330	31 280	26 080	26 560
Commonwealth	33 070	31 420	27 780	27 800	26 910
Old Commonwealth	6 970	6 880	5 380	5 160	5 800
New Commonwealth and Pakistan	37 050	33 620	31 370	30 380	27 550
Foreign excluding Pakistan	25 650	29 250	22 310	18 330	20 120

1. Greece joined the EC on 1 January 1981.
2. The composition of the West Indies Associated States has changed with the independence of each of the constituent countries. After independence, their countries have been included in 'other countries not elsewhere specified'.
3. Includes 600 Cypriots accepted for settlement under the special concessions announced on 29 April 1982.
4. British Dependant Territories Citizens.
5. Includes refugees from South-East Asia.

Source Home Office

2.13 Marriages

Number

	1973	1974	1975	1976	1977	1978	1979	1980	1981	1982	1983
United Kingdom											
Marriages	453 665	436 346	430 678	406 024	403 938	416 373	416 927	418 446	397 846	387 021	389 316
Persons marrying per 1 000 home population	16.2	15.6	15.4	14.5	14.5	14.9	14.9	15.0	14.1	13.4	13.8
Civil condition											
Bachelors	366 302	348 359	339 883	315 476	309 307	314 463	315 137	314 849	297 589	288 408	..
Divorced men	66 016	68 136	71 446	71 945	76 732	84 637	85 255	87 663	85 141	92 508	..
Widowers	21 347	19 851	19 349	18 603	17 899	17 273	16 535	15 934	15 116	14 503	..
Spinsters	368 982	350 891	342 366	317 833	312 892	317 537	318 786	319 088	302 354	293 068	..
Divorced women	63 250	65 707	68 930	69 664	73 340	81 560	81 846	83 376	80 755	80 148	..
Widows	21 433	19 748	19 382	18 527	17 706	17 276	16 295	15 982	14 737	13 805	..
Males											
Under 21 years	74 984	71 639	67 393	61 980	59 877	58 536	55 867	52 644	46 197	41 544	..
21–24	165 750	155 655	152 241	139 858	137 206	139 394	140 399	141 776	133 522	127 833	..
25–29	102 148	100 086	100 265	95 345	92 745	95 975	97 614	98 831	96 062	96 194	..
30–34	34 696	35 348	36 682	37 195	41 794	45 954	47 331	48 104	46 873	45 266	..
35–44	32 740	32 675	33 764	32 675	33 710	36 996	37 964	39 427	39 366	41 111	..
45–54	20 625	20 082	19 523	18 597	18 668	19 615	19 063	19 360	18 333	18 297	..
55 and over	22 722	20 861	20 810	20 374	19 938	19 903	18 689	18 304	17 493	16 787	..
Females											
Under 21 years	167 686	159 863	154 212	142 191	138 994	137 971	133 554	127 542	114 540	104 642	..
21–24	138 091	130 751	128 847	119 916	119 149	124 514	128 444	133 309	129 565	128 446	..
25–29	64 812	63 954	64 380	62 448	61 117	63 161	64 589	65 818	65 131	66 293	..
30–34	24 084	24 853	26 346	26 258	29 143	32 568	33 487	34 064	32 786	31 306	..
35–44	25 309	25 646	26 014	25 741	26 669	29 152	29 622	30 699	30 493	31 795	..
45–54	18 305	17 351	16 717	15 513	15 477	15 770	14 981	15 011	14 091	13 857	..
55 and over	15 378	13 928	14 162	13 957	13 389	13 237	12 250	12 003	11 240	10 682	..
England and Wales											
Marriages	400 435	384 389	380 620	358 567	356 954	368 258	368 853	370 022	351 973	342 166	344 334
Persons marrying per 1 000 home population	16.3	15.6	15.5	14.6	14.5	15.0	15.0	15.0	14.2	13.8	13.9
Civil condition											
Bachelors	318 585	302 271	296 017	274 431	269 046	273 719	273 986	274 140	259 106	250 999	251 845
Divorced men	62 389	64 080	66 985	67 207	71 546	78 844	79 812	81 396	79 099	78 040	79 678
Widowers	19 461	18 038	17 618	16 929	16 362	15 695	15 055	14 486	13 768	13 127	12 811
Spinsters	321 101	304 626	298 217	276 544	272 215	276 385	277 166	277 826	263 368	255 171	256 214
Divorced women	59 550	61 660	64 655	65 063	68 493	76 099	76 822	77 595	75 147	74 418	75 909
Widows	19 784	18 103	17 748	16 960	16 246	15 774	14 865	14 601	13 458	12 577	12 211
Males[1]											
Under 21 years	63 719	60 602	56 788	51 975	49 961	49 007	46 863	44 062	38 660	34 809	31 216
21–24	144 475	135 213	132 766	121 798	119 365	121 213	121 739	123 080	115 924	110 972	110 537
25–29	90 582	88 662	89 419	85 002	82 713	85 668	86 982	88 067	85 391	85 333	88 470
30–34	31 274	31 898	33 282	33 716	38 118	41 909	43 308	43 854	42 696	41 084	41 402
35–44	30 049	29 967	30 946	29 970	31 074	34 169	35 119	36 323	36 312	37 712	39 882
45–54	19 074	18 635	18 044	17 163	17 204	17 998	17 667	17 842	16 862	16 812	17 389
55 and over	21 262	19 412	19 375	18 943	18 519	18 294	17 175	16 794	16 128	15 444	15 438
Females[1]											
Under 21 years	145 948	138 860	133 883	123 395	120 091	119 535	115 709	110 288	99 246	90 669	84 125
21–24	120 466	113 459	112 509	104 516	104 152	108 758	111,964	116 618	113 149	112 314	115 641
25–29	57 657	56 998	57 715	55 813	54 774	56 617	57 851	58 767	58 183	58 932	62 288
30–34	21 819	22 577	23 923	23 939	26 710	29 908	30 852	31 259	30 122	28 510	29 194
35–44	23 070	23 404	23 881	23 519	24 500	26 786	27 374	28 258	28 011	29 240	30 381
45–54	16 984	16 047	15 492	14 336	14 251	14 464	13 771	13 709	12 842	12 596	13 007
55 and over	14 491	13 044	13 217	13 049	12 476	12 190	11 332	11 123	10 420	9 905	9 698

1. The figures for England and Wales include an assumed distribution of 'Age not stated'.

Source Office of Population Censuses and Surveys

2.13 Marriages
Scotland, Northern Ireland
(continued)

Number

	1973	1974	1975	1976	1977	1978	1979	1980	1981	1982	1983
Scotland											
Marriages	42 018	41 174	39 191	37 543	37 288	37 811	37 860	38 501	36 237	34 942	34 962
Persons marrying per 1 000 population	*16.1*	*15.8*	*15.1*	*14.4*	*14.4*	*14.6*	*14.7*	*14.9*	*14.1*	*13.5*	*13.6*
Civil condition											
Bachelors	36 997	35 781	33 551	31 690	31 099	31 044	31 571	31 472	29 622	28 357	27 765
Divorced men	3 383	3 805	4 162	4 418	4 863	5 419	5 016	5 777	5 462	5 416	6 111
Widowers	1 638	1 588	1 478	1 435	1 326	1 348	1 273	1 252	1 153	1 169	1 086
Spinsters	37 077	35 920	33 758	31 875	31 455	31 417	31 989	31 968	30 103	28 736	28 185
Divorced women	3 504	3 816	4 039	4 338	4 570	5 125	4 652	5 355	5 065	5 163	5 755
Widows	1 437	1 438	1 394	1 330	1 263	1 269	1 219	1 178	1 069	1 043	1 022
Males											
Under 21 years	9 263	9 003	8 495	8 010	7 892	7 504	7 098	6 798	5 930	5 190	4 491
21–24	16 578	15 922	15 020	14 119	13 952	13 935	14 553	14 700	13 736	12 986	12 806
25–29	8 808	8 818	8 208	8 014	7 728	7 910	8 108	8 263	8 273	8 215	8 590
30–34	2 611	2 710	2 636	2 736	2 948	3 246	3 201	3 448	3 362	3 333	3 503
35–44	2 185	2 208	2 346	2 225	2 252	2 391	2 378	2 639	2 524	2 818	3 021
45–54	1 319	1 249	1 258	1 229	1 286	1 414	1 198	1 354	1 243	1 259	1 375
55 and over	1 254	1 264	1 228	1 210	1 230	1 411	1 324	1 299	1 169	1 141	1 176
Females											
Under 21 years	17 485	16 826	16 017	14 895	14 874	14 264	13 969	13 575	12 019	10 752	9 685
21–24	13 548	13 413	12 509	11 957	11 724	12 193	12 813	13 091	12 847	12 439	12 627
25–29	5 433	5 323	5 126	5 168	4 954	5 054	5 181	5 476	5 347	5 594	6 105
30–34	1 788	1 840	1 908	1 858	1 982	2 208	2 124	2 326	2 175	2 251	2 394
35–44	1 856	1 861	1 765	1 879	1 886	2 025	1 919	2 127	2 086	2 166	2 320
45–54	1 133	1 130	1 044	1 007	1 069	1 157	1 046	1 147	1 070	1 083	1 165
55 and over	775	781	822	779	799	910	808	759	693	657	666
Northern Ireland											
Marriages	11 212	10 783	10 867	9 914	9 696	10 304	10 214	9 923	9 636	9 913	..
Persons marrying per 1 000 population	*14.4*	*13.9*	*14.2*	*12.8*	*12.6*	*13.4*	*13.2*	*12.8*	*12.3*	*12.6*	..
Civil condition											
Bachelors	10 720	10 307	10 315	9 355	9 162	9 700	9 580	9 237	8 861	9 052	..
Divorced men	244	251	299	320	323	374	427	490	580	654	..
Widowers	248	225	253	239	211	230	207	196	195	207	..
Spinsters	10 804	10 345	10 391	9 414	9 222	9 735	9 631	9 294	8 883	9 161	..
Divorced women	196	231	236	263	277	336	372	426	543	567	..
Widows	212	207	240	237	197	233	211	203	210	185	..
Males											
Under 21 years	2 002	2 034	2 110	1 995	2 024	2 025	1 906	1 784	1 607	1 545	..
21–24	4 697	4 520	4 455	3 941	3 889	4 246	4 107	3 996	3 862	3 875	..
25–29	2 758	2 606	2 638	2 329	2 304	2 397	2 524	2 501	2 398	2 646	..
30–34	811	740	764	743	728	799	822	802	815	849	..
35–44	506	500	472	480	384	436	467	465	530	581	..
45–54	232	198	221	205	178	203	198	164	228	215	..
55 and over	206	185	207	221	189	198	190	211	196	202	..
Females											
Under 21 years	4 253	4 177	4 312	3 901	4 029	4 172	3 876	3 679	3 275	3 221	..
21–24	4 077	3 879	3 829	3 443	3 273	3 563	3 667	3 600	3 569	3 693	..
25–29	1 722	1 633	1 539	1 467	1 389	1 490	1 557	1 575	1 601	1 767	..
30–34	477	436	515	461	451	452	511	479	489	545	..
35–44	383	381	368	343	283	341	329	314	396	389	..
45–54	188	174	181	170	157	149	164	155	179	178	..
55 and over	112	103	123	129	114	137	110	121	127	120	..

Sources General Register Office (Scotland); General Register Office (Northern Ireland)

2.14 Divorce
England and Wales, Scotland

Number

	1973	1974	1975	1976	1977	1978	1979	1980	1981	1982	1983
England and Wales											
Decrees absolute, granted:											
Number	106 003	113 500	120 522	126 694	129 053	143 667	138 706	148 301	145 713	146 698	147 479
Rate per 1 000 married population[1]	*8.4*	*9.0*	*9.6*	*10.1*	*10.4*	*11.6*	*11.2*	*12.0*	*11.9*	*12.0*	*12.2[4]*
Duration of marriage:											
0–4 years	16 148	18 534	20 569	22 437	23 506	25 807	25 883	28 517	28 640	30 262	31 097
5–9 years	31 083	33 643	36 157	38 247	38 790	43 228	42 190	45 152	43 808	42 499	42 041
10–14 years	20 036	21 120	22 671	23 736	24 000	27 207	26 373	28 620	28 242	28 737	28 432
15–19 years	13 895	14 738	15 637	16 238	16 061	17 918	17 124	18 541	18 499	18 855	19 103
20 years and over	24 841	25 465	25 488	26 036	26 696	29 507	27 136	27 471	26 499	26 301	26 769
Not Stated									25	44	37
Age of wife at marriage											
16–19 years	40 459	43 323	46 501	48 784	49 170	54 484	52 550	55 946	54 424	54 067	52 547
20–24 years	47 951	51 399	54 184	56 452	57 153	63 319	60 523	64 786	63 034	62 955	63 382
25–29 years	10 096	10 630	11 306	12 138	12 545	14 259	14 118	15 060	15 281	15 714	16 351
30–34 years	3 564	3 740	3 912	4 231	4 535	5 203	5 187	5 638	5 813	6 317	7 092
35–39 years	1 665	1 864	1 894	2 137	2 341	2 637	2 690	2 893	3 091	3 312	3 502
40–44 years	953	1 028	1 171	1 203	1 390	1 528	1 572	1 672	1 757	1 975	2 081
45 years and over	1 315	1 516	1 554	1 749	1 919	2 237	2 066	2 306	2 313	2 358	2 524
Age of wife at divorce											
16–24 years	13 524	12 565	14 159	15 265	16 989	19 471	19 639	20 905	20 095	19 987	19 440
25–29 years	26 482	28 548	30 508	31 101	30 115	33 149	31 892	34 308	33 299	32 995	32 695
30–34 years	18 607	20 877	22 711	25 353	26 384	29 659	29 137	31 765	31 104	30 023	28 958
35–39 years	14 247	15 669	16 733	17 497	17 701	19 840	19 457	21 436	22 459	24 567	25 673
40–44 years	10 495	11 606	12 289	13 063	13 135	15 183	14 473	15 423	15 276	15 587	16 336
45 years and over	22 648	24 235	24 122	24 415	24 729	26 365	24 108	24 464	23 455	23 495	24 340
Not Stated									25	44	37
Divorces in which there were:											
No children	26 318	28 870	30 962	33 729	37 818	43 065	41 805	45 334	42 292	42 174	42 458
1 or more children	79 685	84 630	89 560	92 965	91 235	100 602	96 901	102 967	103 421	104 524	105 021
Scotland											
Decrees absolute, granted[2]:											
Number	6 670	6 745	7 795	8 129	8 568	8 411	8 833	10 528	9 894	11 288	13 238
Rate per 1 000 married population	*2.7*	*2.7*	*3.1*	*3.2*	*3.4*	*3.4*	*3.6*	*4.3*	*4.0*	*4.6*	*5.5*
Duration of marriage:											
0–4 years	1 319	1 364	1 598	1 849	1 741	1 563	1 457	1 807	1 699	1 991	2 267
5–9 years	2 083	2 141	2 478	2 490	2 418	2 441	2 612	3 134	3 014	3 493	4 008
10–14 years	1 315	1 255	1 519	1 487	1 457	1 430	1 728	2 090	1 944	2 272	2 419
15–19 years	895	947	1 046	1 049	1 146	972	1 115	1 359	1 224	1 401	1 655
20 years and over	1 058	1 038	1 154	1 254	1 806	1 997	1 921	2 138	2 013	2 131	2 889
Age of wife at marriage:											
16–20 years	4 079	4 110	4 721	4 913	4 967	4 684	5 042	5 988	5 584	6 423	7 089
21–24 years	1 811	1 825	2 132	2 187	2 365	2 365	2 408	2 935	2 769	3 159	3 813
25–29 years	519	475	564	612	709	740	787	902	853	929	1 218
30–34 years	126	152	168	201	218	264	249	314	293	322	470
35–39 years	57	61	97	81	130	128	130	150	167	184	252
40–44 years	24	49	51	62	67	66	68	78	86	105	144
45 years and over	54	73	62	73	92	103	100	161	142	127	178
Age not stated										39	74
Age of wife at divorce:											
16–24 years	1 478	1 535	1 712	1 909	1 755	1 638	1 468	1 702	1,525	1 831	1 909
25–29 years	1 748	1 728	2 083	2 116	2 047	1 923	2 126	2 625	2 428	2 820	3 154
30–34 years	1 211	1 170	1 402	1 419	1 412	1 379	1 663	2 027	2 012	2 285	2 494
35–39 years	865	890	1 043	1 022	1 094	991	1 129	1 431	1 345	1 543	1 850
40–44 years	584	624	724	734	774	771	875	1 053	1 000	1 112	1 382
45 years and over	784	798	831	929	1 466	1 648	1 525	1 690	1 584	1 658	2 375
Age not stated										39	74
Actions[3] in which there were											
No children	1 836	1 977	2 301	2 463	3 260	3 836	3 756	4 325	4 148	4 603	6 774
1 or more children	5 641	5 573	6 377	6 508	5 923	4 946	5 401	6 622	6 099	7 079	6 863

1. In England and Wales 'married population' refers to married couples i.e. rate per 1 000 married couples.
2. For divorces under pre-1976 legislation these figures relate only to persons who were married in Scotland, and obtained their decree of divorce from the Court of Session.

3. These Actions relate to all persons divorced or separated in Scotland, irrespective of the country of marriage.
4. Provisional.

Sources Office of Population Censuses and Surveys; General Register Office (Scotland); Scottish Courts Administration

2.15 Divorce proceedings
England and Wales

Number

	1973	1974	1975	1976	1977	1978	1979	1980	1981	1982	1983
Dissolution of marriage[1]											
Petitions filed[2]	115 048	129 993	138 048	143 698	167 074	162 450	162 867	170 882	169 076	173 452	168 428
On grounds of:											
Adultery	32 261	35 736	37 650	39 231	43 095	43 257	44 092	47 919	47 250	48 013	47 127
Desertion	7 626	6 712	5 847	5 263	6 113	5 495	4 449	4 482	3 745	3 079	2 449
Behaviour	30 468	37 012	42 869	46 238	62 579	56 333	60 846	64 882	66 937	72 320	69 849
Separation (2 years and consent)	24 203	30 201	33 085	34 173	36 399	40 167	38 714	39 761	38 479	37 704	36 930
Separation (5 years)	16 593	16 445	13 987	14 572	14 586	14 959	12 957	12 510	11 689	11 389	11 325
Adultery and desertion	594	414	44	36	343	238	84	72	9	26	20
Adultery and behaviour	2 113	2 367	2 923	2 912	2 925	1 450	1 219	888	717	714	575
Desertion and behaviour	830	740	87	76	317	113	92	51	44	70	33
Other	360	366	1 556	1 197	717	438	414	317	206	137	120
By husbands	38 792	41 002	41 651	42 866	44 411	46 844	45 589	48 893	46 225	46 473	45 153
By wives	76 256	88 991	96 397	100 832	122 663	115 606	117 278	121 989	122 851	126 979	123 275
Decrees nisi granted	106 522	117 150	122 397	130 616	136 086	151 533	139 503	150 385	147 226	147 763	149 187
Decrees absolute granted	105 199	110 753	117 665	125 910	125 440	141 777	137 256	145 669	144 051	144 984	144 133
Nullity of marriage[3]											
Petitions filed[2]	875	949	1 080	1 116	1 095	1 117	994	1 110	1 050	921	887
By husbands	415	382	459	479	448	432	384	546	426	399	319
By wives	460	567	621	637	647	685	610	564	624	522	568
Decrees nisi granted	759	785	831	954	1 003	959	810	929	894	803	819
Decrees absolute granted	804	685	623	772	940	836	729	789	774	846	770
Judicial separation											
Petitions filed[2]	430	696	936	1 601	1 980	2 611	3 650	5 423	6 036	7 480	7 430
By husbands	20	48	52	63	137	239	322	482	605	836	883
By wives	410	648	884	1 538	1 843	2 372	3 328	4 941	5 431	6 644	6 547
Decrees granted	190	246	323	584	761	1 228	1 640	2 560	3 334	4 026	4 854

1. Excluding petitions in which divorce is asked for in alternative to nullity.
2. The breakdown of petitions filed is based on actual figures for The Principal Registry of the Family Division together with grossed up figures, based on a two month sample, from the county courts.
3. Including cases in which dissolution is asked for in the alternative.

Source Lord Chancellor's Department

2.15 Divorce proceedings
Scotland, Northern Ireland
(continued)

Scotland
Number

	1973	1974	1975	1976	1977	1978	1979	1980	1981	1982	1983
Divorce											
Actions in which final judgment given	7 475	7 550	8 677	8 971	9 182	8 782	9 149	10 947	10 247	11 682	13 637
On grounds of[4]:											
Adultery	2 806	2 768	3 134	3 228	1 590	202	57	16	6	2	–
Desertion	1 332	1 243	1 380	1 290	464	36	10	4	–	–	–
Insanity	3	5	10	10	5	–	–	–	–	–	–
Cruelty	3 334	3 533	4 153	4 441	2 348	392	117	32	8	2	–
Sodomy	–	1	–	2	–	–	–	–	–	–	–
On grounds of[5]:											
Adultery	–	–	–	–	942	1 342	1 533	2 013	1 749	1 926	1 844
Desertion	–	–	–	–	438	403	243	311	242	252	207
Adultery and behaviour	–	–	–	–	3	1	–	2	1	4	7
Behaviour	–	–	–	–	1 782	3 010	3 638	4 456	4 382	5 096	4 900
2 years non-cohabitation	–	–	–	–	564	1 623	1 964	2 519	2 470	2 844	4 250
5 years non-cohabitation	–	–	–	–	1 046	1 773	1 587	1 594	1 389	1 556	2 428
At instances of: Husbands	2 015	1 964	2 092	2 109	2 398	2 377	2 372	2 805	2 584	2 833	3 847
Wives	5 460	5 586	6 585	6 862	6 784	6 405	6 778	8 142	7 663	8 849	9 790
Divorce granted	7 104	7 173	8 298	8 662	8 812	8 448	8 829	10 522	9 889	11 275	13 235
Separation											
Action in which final judgment given	2	–	1	–	1	–	1	–	–	–	–
Separation granted	2	–	1	–	–	–	1	–	–	–	–
Duration of marriages where divorce or separation granted											
Under 1 year	3	6	9	13	14	17	8	5	9	9	3
1–2 years	142	100	278	256	173	142	110	149	146	173	140
2–5 years	1 205	1 230	1 658	1 664	1 592	1 424	1 330	1 644	1 542	1 801	2 121
5–10 years	2 228	2 339	2 596	2 636	2 464	2 461	2 632	3 149	3 014	3 490	4 008
10–20 years	2 382	2 377	2 542	2 754	2 720	2 398	2 856	3 447	3 169	3 671	4 074
20 years and over	1 146	1 121	1 216	1 339	1 849	2 006	1 893	2 128	2 009	2 131	2 880
Actions[6] in which there were:											
Children of marriage	5 641	5 573	6 377	6 508	5 923	4 946	5 399	6 622	6 099	7 079	6 363
No children	1 836	1 977	2 301	2 463	3 260	3 836	3 751	4 325	4 148	4 603	6 774

4. Prior to the Divorce (Scotland) Act 1976.
5. The grounds given show the allegations made—divorce is granted on the grounds of irretrievable breakdown of marriage under the Divorce (Scotland) Act 1976.
6. Divorce and separation.

Northern Ireland
Number

	1973	1974	1975	1976	1977	1978	1979	1980	1981	1982	1983
Petitions filed											
Nullity of marriage	6	11	9	13	2	10	6	9	9	5	–
Divorce	460	464	572	690	632	714	872	1 620	1 645	1 734	1 577
Judicial separation	–	–	–	–	–	–	–	4	2	2	9

Sources Scottish Courts Administration; High Court of Justice (Northern Ireland)

2.16 Births
Annual averages or calendar years

	Live births										Still-births	
	By sex				By legitimacy			Rates			Thousands	Rate per 1 000 births (including still-births)
	Thousands			Males born per 1 000 females	Thousands		Illegitimate as percentage of all live births	Total per 1 000 population[2]	Total per 1 000 women aged 15–44[2]	Legitimate per 1 000 married women aged 16–44		
	Total	Males	Females		Legitimate	Illegitimate						
United Kingdom												
1900–02	1 095	558	537	1 037	1 049	47	4.3	28.6	115.1	240.7	..	..
1910–12	1 037	528	508	1 039	989	47	4.5	24.6	99.4	202.5	..	..
1920–22	1 018	522	496	1 052	968	49	4.8	23.1	93.0	..	..	..
1930–32	750	383	367	1 046	713	36	4.8	16.3	66.5	..	..	..
1940–42	723	372	351	1 062	685	38	5.3	15.0	..	..	..	..
1950–52	803	413	390	1 061	763	40	5.0	16.0	73.7	..	..	..
1960–62	946	487	459	1 063	892	55	5.8	17.9	90.3	..	..	..
1970–72	880	453	427	1 064	808	72	8.2	15.8	82.5	..	12	13
1980–82	735	377	358	1 053	641	93	12.7	13.0	62.5	..	5	7
1967	962	495	467	1 059	884	78	8.1	17.6	90.2	..	15	15
1968	947	487	460	1 059	869	78	8.2	17.2	88.9	..	14	14
1969	920	473	447	1 059	845	75	8.1	16.7	86.4	..	12	13
1970	904	465	439	1 059	831	73	8.0	16.3	84.8	..	12	13
1971	902	464	438	1 059	827	74	8.2	16.1	84.4	..	12	13
1972	834	430	404	1 065	764	70	8.4	14.9	77.8	..	10	12
1973	780	402	377	1 067	714	66	8.4	13.9	72.2	..	9	12
1974	737	380	358	1 060	674	64	8.7	13.2	68.0	..	8	11
1975	698	359	338	1 062	635	63	9.0	12.5	64.0	..	7	11
1976	676	347	328	1 058	614	61	9.0	12.0	61.3	..	7	10
1977	657	338	319	1 060	594	63	9.6	11.7	58.9	..	6	9
1978	687	353	334	1 059	618	68	10.0	12.2	60.8	86.3	6	8
1979	735	378	356	1 061	656	78	10.6	13.1	64.1	91.9	6	8
1980	754	386	368	1 050	667	87	11.5	13.4	64.9	93.6	6	7
1981	731	375	356	1 054	640	91	12.5	13.0	62.2	..	5	7
1982	719	369	350	1 054	618	101	14.1	12.8	60.5	..	5	6
1983[1]	721	370	351	1 055	610	111	15.2	12.8	60.2	..	4	6
Great Britain												
1900–02	1 064	542	522	1 038	1 019	45	4.2	28.7	115.7	239.4	..	..
1910–12	1 006	513	493	1 040	960	46	4.6	24.7	99.3	201.0	..	..
1920–22	987	506	482	1 050	939	48	4.9	23.1	92.6	183.8	..	..
1930–32	724	370	354	1 046	689	35	4.8	16.1	66.0	127.0	..	..
1940–42	696	357	338	1 056	659	37	5.3	14.9	62.1	102.5	26	36
1950–52	774	398	376	1 059	736	38	4.9	15.8	72.9	108.4	18	23
1960–62	914	470	443	1 061	860	54	5.9	17.8	89.8	126.3	18	19
1970–72	849	437	412	1 061	777	71	8.4	15.7	82.1	110.5	11	13
1980–82	707	363	344	1 053	616	91	12.9	12.9	61.8	90.0	5	7
1967	928	478	451	1 059	852	77	8.2	17.4	89.5	122.3	14	15
1968	914	470	444	1 058	837	77	8.4	17.1	88.2	119.7	13	14
1969	888	457	431	1 059	814	74	8.3	16.5	85.7	115.9	12	13
1970	872	448	423	1 059	800	71	8.2	16.2	84.2	114.4	12	13
1971	870	448	422	1 060	797	73	8.4	16.0	83.7	113.1	11	13
1972	804	414	390	1 063	735	69	8.6	14.8	77.1	103.9	10	12
1973	750	387	363	1 067	686	65	8.6	13.8	71.5	96.7	9	12
1974	710	365	345	1 060	647	63	8.9	13.1	67.3	91.4	8	11
1975	671	346	326	1 062	610	61	9.1	12.4	63.3	86.5	7	10
1976	649	334	315	1 059	589	60	9.2	11.9	60.6	83.8	6	10
1977	632	325	307	1 060	570	61	9.7	11.6	58.2	81.3	6	9
1978	661	340	321	1 061	594	67	10.1	12.1	60.1	85.0	6	8
1979	706	364	343	1 061	630	76	10.8	12.9	63.4	90.3	6	8
1980	725	371	354	1 050	640	85	11.7	13.2	64.2	92.0	5	7
1981	704	361	343	1 054	614	89	12.7	12.8	61.5	88.4	5	7
1982	692	355	337	1 055	593	99	14.3	12.6	59.9	87.6	4	6
1983[1]	694	357	338	1 056	585	109	15.7	12.7	59.6	..	4	6

1. Provisional.
2. Rates are based on a new series of population estimates which use a new definition and population base taking into account the 1981 Census results.

Sources Office of Population Censuses and Surveys; General Register Office (Scotland); General Register Office (Northern Ireland)

2.17 Live births by age of mother
England and Wales

	1973	1974	1975	1976	1977	1978	1979	1980	1981[1]	1982	1983
	Number										
Age of mother: all ages	675 953	639 885	603 445	584 270	569 259	596 418	638 028	656 234	634 492	625 931	629 134
Under 20	73 270	68 724	63 507	57 943	54 477	55 984	59 143	60 754	56 570	55 435	54 059
20–24	223 675	208 084	190 198	182 210	174 544	182 580	193 209	201 541	194 500	192 322	191 852
25–29	243 753	235 593	225 990	220 712	207 916	210 598	222 102	223 438	215 760	211 905	214 078
30–34	91 800	89 132	88 379	90 791	100 807	113 077	125 664	129 908	126 590	120 758	120 996
35–39	34 178	30 308	28 147	26 117	25 527	27 937	31 394	33 893	34 210	38 992	41 277
40–44	8 649	7 496	6 653	5 999	5 534	5 719	5 978	6 075	6 170	5 886	6 210
45 and over	628	548	571	498	454	523	538	625	690	633	662
	Rates per 1 000 women[2]										
All ages	71.3	67.2	63.0	60.4	58.1	60.1	63.3	64.2	61.3	59.9	59.7
Under 20	43.9	40.5	36.4	32.2	29.4	29.4	30.3	30.4	28.1	27.4	26.9
20–24	130.2	123.2	114.1	109.3	103.7	106.9	111.3	112.7	105.3	101.6	98.5
25–29	134.0	128.0	121.9	118.7	117.5	122.6	131.2	133.6	129.1	126.4	126.4
30–34	63.1	59.9	58.0	57.2	58.6	63.1	69.0	70.5	68.6	69.1	71.5
35–39	24.5	21.5	19.9	18.6	18.2	19.5	21.3	22.3	21.7	22.8	23.1
40–44	6.1	5.4	4.8	4.4	4.1	4.2	4.3	4.3	4.4	4.2	4.4
45 and over	0.4	0.4	0.4	0.3	0.3	0.4	0.4	0.5	0.5	0.5	0.5

1. Age-group figures based on ten per cent sample of live births.
2. Rates are based on a new series of population estimates which use a new definition and population base taking into account the 1981 Census results. The rates for women of all ages, under 20 and 45 and over are based upon the populations of women 15–44, 15–19 and 45–49 respectively.

Source Office of Population Censuses and Surveys

2.18 Live births by age of mother
Scotland

	1973	1974	1975	1976	1977	1978	1979	1980	1981	1982	1983
	Number										
Age of mother: all ages	74 392	70 093	67 943	64 895	62 342	64 295	68 366	68 892	69 054	66 196	65 078
15–19[1]	8 940	8 784	8 267	7 514	6 978	7 084	7 152	7 226	6 871	6 886	6 341
20–24	25 232	23 689	22 700	21 340	20 559	21 006	21 977	22 565	23 020	21 837	21 296
25–29	24 718	23 631	23 579	23 293	21 566	21 992	23 610	23 201	23 140	22 115	22 086
30–34	10 341	9 475	9 169	9 024	9 697	10 697	11 745	12 111	12 118	11 324	11 204
35–39	4 109	3 422	3 237	2 897	2 702	2 759	3 139	3 104	3 234	3 405	3 529
40–44	968	887	762	656	630	532	584	556	554	550	529
45 and over	42	62	56	32	41	25	30	27	27	26	22
Age not stated	42	143	173	139	169	200	129	102	90	53	71
	Rates per 1 000 women										
15–44	73.36	68.06	66.09	62.32	59.42	60.54	63.79	63.64	63.75	59.69	58.85
15–19	44.61	42.80	39.86	35.61	32.51	32.62	32.55	32.52	30.81	30.30	28.72
20–24	138.25	128.47	124.06	114.69	108.38	108.96	111.95	112.65	115.10	103.44	100.93
25–29	141.91	131.78	128.92	124.39	119.45	123.78	133.18	130.54	133.17	122.42	121.15
30–34	68.64	61.88	59.83	57.95	58.09	62.08	66.81	67.30	66.49	64.74	65.44
35–39	27.23	22.61	21.47	19.37	18.16	18.44	20.78	20.49	21.00	20.60	20.64
40–44	6.23	5.78	5.06	4.39	4.24	3.58	3.92	3.73	3.69	3.71	3.54
45–49	0.26	0.39	0.36	0.21	0.27	0.16	0.20	0.18	0.60	0.18	0.15

1. Includes births to mothers aged less than 15.

Source General Register Office (Scotland)

2.19 Deaths: analysis by age and sex
United Kingdom
Annual averages or calendar years

Number

	All ages[1]	Under 1 year	1 – 4	5 – 9	10 – 14	15 – 19	20 – 24	25 – 34	35 – 44	45 – 54	55 – 64	65 – 74	75 – 84	85 and over
Males														
1900 – 02	340 664	87 242	37 834	8 429	4 696	7 047	8 766	19 154	24 739	30 488	37 610	39 765	28 320	6 563
1910 – 12	303 703	63 885	29 452	7 091	4 095	5 873	6 817	16 141	21 813	28 981	37 721	45 140	29 397	7 283
1920 – 22	284 876	48 044	19 008	6 052	3 953	5 906	6 572	13 663	19 702	29 256	40 583	49 398	34 937	7 801
1930 – 32	284 249	28 840	11 276	4 580	2 890	5 076	6 495	12 327	16 326	29 376	47 989	63 804	45 247	10 022
1940 – 42	314 643	24 624	6 949	3 400	2 474	4 653	4 246	11 506	17 296	30 082	57 076	79 652	59 733	12 900
1950 – 52	307 312	14 105	2 585	1 317	919	1 498	2 289	5 862	11 074	27 637	53 691	86 435	79 768	20 131
1960 – 62	318 850	12 234	1 733	971	871	1 718	1 857	3 842	8 753	26 422	63 009	87 542	83 291	26 605
1970 – 72	335 166	9 158	1 485	1 019	802	1 778	2 104	3 590	7 733	24 608	64 898	105 058	82 905	30 027
1980 – 82[2]	330 495	4 829	774	527	652	1 999	1 943	3 736	6 568	19 728	54 159	105 155	98 488	31 936
1967	315 461	10 254	1 690	1 005	848	1 967	1 976	3 519	8 253	24 152	64 683	92 230	77 244	27 640
1968	333 594	10 319	1 753	1 030	807	1 788	1 974	3 386	8 220	24 481	66 381	98 937	84 089	30 429
1969	337 800	9 894	1 713	998	800	1 808	1 999	3 595	8 116	25 167	68 265	104 219	82 325	28 901
1970	334 355	9 713	1 556	978	773	1 752	2 131	3 585	7 836	24 399	66 657	103 589	81 996	29 390
1971	328 537	9 366	1 439	1 055	834	1 802	2 091	3 524	7 735	24 242	63 657	102 139	81 183	29 470
1972	342 605	8 393	1 460	1 024	801	1 779	2 092	3 661	7 629	25 184	64 379	109 448	85 535	31 220
1973	338 788	7 783	1 438	978	790	1 819	2 213	3 953	7 530	25 434	61 970	108 871	85 172	30 837
1974	337 263	7 180	1 307	858	775	1 895	1 968	3 820	7 448	25 864	59 703	110 718	84 491	31 236
1975	335 006	6 392	1 139	829	842	1 871	2 018	3 845	7 006	24 630	58 581	110 126	86 653	31 074
1976	341 910	5 706	1 036	798	769	1 978	1 994	3 867	6 976	23 663	59 703	112 234	90 710	32 476
1977	329 924	5 350	918	744	702	1 892	1 947	3 864	6 752	22 787	57 214	108 677	88 569	30 508
1978	336 395	5 220	866	726	729	2 067	2 055	3 944	6 912	22 439	57 381	110 384	92 574	31 098
1979	339 568	5 447	748	708	707	2 042	1 969	4 012	6 868	21 828	56 944	110 172	96 026	32 097
1980	332 370	5 174	792	609	659	2 022	1 940	3 786	6 698	20 577	55 176	107 089	96 301	31 547
1981	329 145	4 759	771	517	666	2 008	1 919	3 761	6 544	19 740	53 770	104 950	97 881	31 859
1982[2]	329 971	4 555	760	456	632	1 966	1 971	3 661	6 462	18 867	53 531	103 426	101 281	32 403
Females														
1900 – 02	322 058	68 770	36 164	8 757	5 034	6 818	8 264	18 702	21 887	25 679	34 521	42 456	34 907	10 099
1910 – 12	289 608	49 865	27 817	7 113	4 355	5 683	6 531	15 676	19 647	24 481	32 813	46 453	37 353	11 828
1920 – 22	274 772	35 356	17 323	5 808	4 133	5 729	6 753	14 878	18 121	24 347	34 026	48 573	45 521	14 203
1930 – 32	275 336	21 072	9 995	3 990	2 734	4 721	5 931	12 699	15 373	24 695	39 471	59 520	56 250	18 886
1940 – 42	296 646	17 936	5 952	2 743	2 068	4 180	5 028	11 261	14 255	23 629	42 651	70 907	71 377	24 658
1950 – 52	291 597	10 293	2 098	880	625	1 115	1 717	5 018	8 989	18 875	37 075	75 220	92 848	36 844
1960 – 62	304 871	8 887	1 334	627	522	684	811	2 504	6 513	16 720	36 078	73 118	105 956	51 117
1970 – 72	322 968	6 666	1 183	654	459	718	900	2 110	5 345	15 594	36 177	75 599	109 539	68 024
1980 – 82[2]	330 269	3 561	585	355	425	733	772	2 099	4 360	12 206	32 052	72 618	117 760	82 743
1967	301 249	7 821	1 317	624	506	814	863	2 111	5 840	15 359	35 373	71 005	101 744	57 872
1968	322 404	7 429	1 379	669	498	703	835	2 166	5 744	15 610	36 806	74 936	110 101	65 528
1969	321 737	7 189	1 280	579	423	714	918	2 125	5 874	15 824	37 725	77 206	108 385	63 495
1970	321 030	7 002	1 181	648	467	662	957	2 118	5 501	15 527	36 652	76 033	108 485	65 798
1971	316 541	6 798	1 129	649	493	721	866	2 105	5 267	15 358	35 621	73 502	107 056	66 976
1972	331 333	6 198	1 238	665	416	770	878	2 107	5 267	15 897	36 260	77 261	113 076	71 300
1973	330 904	5 646	1 060	610	455	803	847	2 166	5 145	15 822	34 733	77 067	113 393	73 157
1974	330 096	5 172	981	581	503	736	805	2 070	5 038	15 972	34 342	76 929	112 492	74 475
1975	327 471	4 798	860	540	405	751	813	2 211	4 897	15 054	33 904	75 459	112 838	74 941
1976	338 889	4 070	735	516	484	724	786	2 264	4 737	14 912	34 468	76 950	118 246	79 997
1977	325 219	3 933	720	431	450	750	839	2 148	4 583	13 905	33 395	74 573	113 872	75 620
1978	330 782	3 908	715	480	497	818	823	2 343	4 719	13 914	33 353	75 433	115 730	78 049
1979	336 009	4 026	617	428	462	701	738	2 244	4 544	13 667	33 274	75 610	118 859	80 839
1980	329 149	3 938	596	409	442	771	811	2 157	4 460	12 583	32 349	73 672	116 461	80 500
1981	328 829	3 402	599	352	424	738	737	2 083	4 309	12 275	31 625	72 476	117 458	82 351
1982[2]	332 830	3 342	561	304	410	689	767	2 057	4 312	11 759	32 183	71 705	119 362	85 379

1. In some years the totals include a small number of persons whose age was not stated.
2. Provisional.

Sources Office of Population Censuses and Surveys; General Register Office (Scotland); General Register Office (Northern Ireland)

2.19
(continued)
Deaths: analysis by age and sex
England and Wales
Annual averages or calendar years

	All ages[1]	Under 1 year	1–4	5–9	10–14	15–19	20–24	25–34	35–44	45–54	55–64	65–74	75–84	85 and over
Males														
1900–02	288 886	76 095	32 051	7 066	3 818	5 611	7 028	15 869	21 135	26 065	31 600	33 568	23 835	5 144
1910–12	257 253	54 678	24 676	5 907	3 348	4 765	5 596	13 603	18 665	24 820	32 217	38 016	24 928	6 036
1920–22	240 605	39 796	15 565	5 151	3 314	4 901	5 447	11 551	17 004	25 073	34 639	42 025	29 685	6 455
1930–32	243 147	23 331	9 099	3 844	2 435	4 354	5 580	10 600	14 041	25 657	41 581	54 910	39 091	8 624
1940–42	268 876	19 393	5 616	2 834	2 051	3 832	3 156	9 484	14 744	25 983	50 058	68 791	51 779	11 158
1950–52	266 879	11 498	2 131	1 087	778	1 248	1 947	4 990	9 489	23 815	46 948	75 774	69 496	17 677
1960–62	278 369	10 157	1 444	812	742	1 523	1 624	3 278	7 524	22 813	54 908	77 000	73 180	23 364
1970–72	293 934	7 818	1 259	860	677	1 524	1 788	3 079	6 637	21 348	56 667	92 389	73 365	26 522
1980–82	290 352	4 168	657	452	555	1 716	1 619	3 169	5 590	16 909	47 144	92 485	87 338	28 551
1967	277 178	8 673	1 427	851	708	1 749	1 718	3 003	7 118	20 981	56 632	81 430	68 428	24 460
1968	293 213	8 705	1 492	868	677	1 544	1 715	2 897	7 096	21 287	58 139	87 104	74 657	27 032
1969	296 561	8 331	1 484	839	662	1 574	1 727	3 083	6 952	21 937	59 763	91 925	72 822	25 462
1970	293 053	8 269	1 315	816	649	1 551	1 836	3 089	6 717	21 162	58 099	91 037	72 625	25 888
1971	288 359	7 974	1 228	916	690	1 538	1 771	3 046	6 683	21 046	55 699	89 802	71 907	26 059
1972	300 389	7 210	1 235	847	693	1 482	1 757	3 103	6 511	21 837	56 202	96 329	75 564	27 619
1973	296 546	6 599	1 203	817	677	1 510	1 836	3 336	6 455	21 923	53 976	95 605	75 300	27 309
1974	295 315	6 137	1 095	720	649	1 582	1 666	3 241	6 222	22 388	51 883	97 331	74 770	27 631
1975	294 174	5 430	983	677	692	1 584	1 697	3 229	5 935	21 337	51 088	96 934	76 879	27 709
1976	300 058	4 879	876	676	639	1 660	1 663	3 245	5 928	20 449	52 048	98 654	80 348	28 993
1977	289 773	4 519	769	635	598	1 620	1 599	3 270	5 695	19 600	49 855	95 873	78 528	27 212
1978	295 505	4 513	739	628	619	1 776	1 761	3 325	5 849	19 307	49 976	97 194	82 067	27 751
1979	297 862	4 731	641	602	605	1 727	1 649	3 426	5 822	18 607	49 586	96 764	85 091	28 611
1980	291 869	4 471	668	517	546	1 745	1 613	3 203	5 710	17 693	48 053	94 188	85 300	28 162
1981	289 022	4 119	651	447	573	1 734	1 576	3 181	5 535	16 889	46 858	92 189	86 774	28 496
1982	290 166	3 914	652	391	546	1 669	1 668	3 122	5 526	16 144	46 521	91 079	89 940	28 994
1983	289 419	3 654	604	391	514	1 580	1 635	3 071	5 581	15 632	47 315	88 622	91 531	29 289
Females														
1900–02	269 432	60 090	30 674	7 278	4 010	5 265	6 497	15 065	18 253	21 474	28 424	35 307	29 118	7 977
1910–12	242 079	42 642	23 335	5 883	3 519	4 522	5 256	12 742	16 363	20 611	27 571	38 489	31 363	9 782
1920–22	229 908	29 178	14 174	4 928	3 456	4 719	5 533	12 244	15 142	20 580	28 633	41 010	38 439	11 871
1930–32	233 915	16 929	8 013	3 338	2 293	3 969	5 039	10 716	13 022	21 190	33 798	50 844	48 531	16 234
1940–42	253 702	14 174	4 726	2 265	1 695	3 426	4 198	9 470	12 093	20 413	36 814	60 987	61 891	21 550
1950–52	252 176	8 367	1 727	732	520	893	1 365	4 131	7 586	16 161	31 875	65 087	81 154	32 579
1960–62	266 849	7 409	1 103	527	444	591	700	2 147	5 576	14 389	31 083	63 543	93 548	45 789
1970–72	284 181	5 677	1 020	562	396	620	806	1 814	4 585	13 417	31 222	65 817	96 952	61 293
1980–82	290 026	3 064	511	301	365	635	670	1 821	3 740	10 420	27 606	63 023	103 676	74 194
1967	265 338	6 593	1 147	535	438	710	755	1 843	5 032	13 328	30 657	61 832	90 324	52 144
1968	283 541	6 277	1 195	573	430	624	740	1 870	4 894	13 420	31 796	65 168	97 651	58 903
1969	282 817	6 060	1 075	498	352	634	810	1 856	5 065	13 602	32 596	67 219	96 021	57 029
1970	282 141	5 998	1 011	538	401	570	849	1 802	4 715	13 292	31 577	66 219	95 917	59 252
1971	278 903	5 746	976	568	419	631	787	1 836	4 528	13 274	30 760	64 017	94 958	60 403
1972	291 500	5 288	1 073	579	367	658	783	1 804	4 512	13 686	31 330	67 215	99 980	64 225
1973	290 932	4 808	896	510	393	681	740	1 876	4 362	13 611	29 872	67 137	100 293	65 753
1974	289 977	4 322	827	505	442	630	688	1 785	4 291	13 828	29 471	66 992	99 398	66 798
1975	288 667	4 058	716	463	354	632	711	1 921	4 180	13 053	29 192	65 822	100 000	67 565
1976	298 458	3 455	593	451	417	623	671	1 939	4 041	12 806	29 605	67 107	104 673	72 077
1977	286 155	3 322	614	373	394	616	702	1 870	3 883	11 929	28 828	64 903	100 536	68 185
1978	290 396	3 368	607	417	421	691	710	2 042	4 004	11 911	28 607	65 411	102 058	70 149
1979	295 157	3 447	527	368	386	622	635	1 938	3 868	11 671	28 624	65 646	104 807	72 618
1980	289 516	3 428	518	349	373	667	696	1 861	3 771	10 757	27 857	64 087	102 728	72 424
1981	288 868	2 902	529	302	368	650	642	1 821	3 742	10 513	27 211	62 762	103 554	73 872
1982	291 695	2 861	485	253	353	588	672	1 781	3 708	9 990	27 751	62 221	104 745	76 287
1983	290 189	2 727	489	269	332	629	597	1 655	3 708	9 786	27 792	59 913	104 844	77 448

1. In some years the totals include a small number of persons whose age was not stated.

Source Office of Population Censuses and Surveys

2.19
(continued)

Deaths: analysis by age and sex
Scotland
Annual averages or calendar years

Number

	All ages[1]	Under 1 year	1–4	5–9	10–14	15–19	20–24	25–34	35–44	45–54	55–64	65–74	75–84	85 and over
Males														
1900–02	40 224	9 189	4 798	1 083	672	1 069	1 292	2 506	2 935	3 591	4 597	4 531	3 117	834
1910–12	35 981	7 510	3 935	962	595	826	910	1 969	2 469	3 325	4 356	5 113	3 182	813
1920–22	34 649	6 757	2 847	710	489	747	791	1 616	2 128	3 314	4 785	5 624	3 928	911
1930–32	32 476	4 426	1 771	610	365	568	706	1 352	1 848	2 979	5 095	6 906	4 839	1 010
1940–42	36 384	3 973	1 011	449	321	668	888	1 643	2 090	3 348	5 728	8 556	6 317	1 337
1950–52	32 236	1 949	349	175	105	200	265	693	1 267	3 151	5 574	8 544	8 094	1 871
1960–62	32 401	1 578	222	121	102	146	185	456	1 013	2 986	6 682	8 505	7 980	2 425
1970–72	32 446	944	168	119	93	178	233	396	875	2 617	6 641	10 176	7 383	2 624
1980–82	31 723	451	80	56	71	206	233	423	776	2 280	5 601	10 152	8 804	2 591
1967	30 554	1 158	195	117	104	176	200	431	928	2 554	6 683	8 700	6 893	2 415
1968	32 146	1 156	217	128	103	190	210	387	935	2 633	6 770	9 484	7 354	2 579
1969	32 631	1 099	174	121	109	184	216	401	936	2 564	6 946	9 851	7 381	2 649
1970	32 538	1 010	186	125	90	161	232	403	891	2 604	6 923	9 987	7 266	2 660
1971	31 585	988	155	100	114	197	242	371	832	2 588	6 427	9 945	7 134	2 492
1972	33 215	833	162	133	76	176	226	413	902	2 658	6 573	10 596	7 748	2 719
1973	32 954	841	171	117	76	175	225	381	839	2 789	6 435	10 693	7 603	2 609
1974	32 722	748	148	97	83	202	183	403	953	2 739	6 205	10 757	7 505	2 699
1975	32 168	669	113	112	104	195	216	411	838	2 634	5 994	10 727	7 617	2 538
1976	32 983	568	110	84	97	204	212	448	811	2 621	6 109	10 926	8 146	2 647
1977	31 280	585	103	81	75	181	236	432	817	2 494	5 835	10 173	7 802	2 466
1978	32 432	479	87	63	78	211	210	479	854	2 508	5 888	10 734	8 299	2 542
1979	32 884	490	79	79	71	219	215	442	805	2 599	5 851	10 804	8 543	2 687
1980	31 669	481	93	65	78	190	223	421	778	2 316	5 628	10 248	8 571	2 577
1981	31 700	435	71	50	66	208	250	439	816	2 330	5 506	10 193	8 788	2 548
1982	31 801	436	77	53	69	220	225	410	733	2 195	5 669	10 015	9 052	2 647
1983	31 196	380	67	53	65	185	178	406	764	2 131	5 769	9 414	9 204	2 580
Females														
1900–02	39 891	7 143	4 477	1 162	747	1 058	1 246	2 625	2 732	3 130	4 485	5 273	4 305	1 508
1910–12	36 132	5 854	3 674	981	618	836	910	2 149	2 473	2 909	3 960	5 636	4 588	1 552
1920–22	34 449	5 029	2 602	687	489	711	889	1 947	2 266	2 828	4 157	5 587	5 443	1 814
1930–32	32 377	3 319	1 602	527	339	568	666	1 508	1 812	2 731	4 380	6 630	6 178	2 117
1940–42	33 715	2 852	921	373	283	595	656	1 382	1 672	2 528	4 630	7 674	7 613	2 536
1950–52	31 525	1 432	284	115	84	185	293	714	1 127	2 188	4 204	8 157	9 310	3 431
1960–62	30 559	1 107	170	80	63	72	87	287	762	1 897	4 115	7 752	9 991	4 177
1970–72	30 978	694	118	69	46	73	74	231	608	1 769	4 036	7 823	10 112	5 324
1980–82	32 326	337	49	37	44	74	73	213	493	1 456	3 565	7 781	11 333	6 871
1967	28 969	866	128	75	58	81	89	195	656	1 681	3 875	7 426	9 255	4 584
1968	31 165	814	139	74	49	60	72	234	667	1 787	4 078	7 850	10 075	5 266
1969	31 190	803	156	56	58	66	85	212	647	1 817	4 168	8 014	10 003	5 105
1970	31 102	704	129	82	50	77	92	244	632	1 804	4 108	7 814	10 158	5 209
1971	30 029	734	107	64	60	64	62	214	590	1 720	4 000	7 603	9 686	5 125
1972	31 802	644	117	62	29	79	67	234	602	1 783	4 001	8 052	10 493	5 639
1973	31 591	571	105	77	46	91	80	224	604	1 796	3 890	7 930	10 355	5 822
1974	32 018	578	109	59	48	73	90	217	613	1 741	3 979	8 037	10 440	6 034
1975	30 957	499	104	56	33	84	77	228	580	1 625	3 792	7 750	10 250	5 879
1976	32 270	391	86	48	49	69	88	235	567	1 708	3 916	7 961	10 795	6 357
1977	31 014	419	73	45	41	97	100	214	557	1 578	3 671	7 761	10 628	5 830
1978	32 691	351	73	37	61	93	86	236	598	1 651	3 871	8 208	11 028	6 398
1979	32 863	388	69	37	58	59	81	247	551	1 635	3 776	8 045	11 309	6 608
1980	31 630	350	51	41	44	77	90	222	547	1 511	3 587	7 673	10 988	6 449
1981	32 128	345	46	35	43	68	69	213	453	1 414	3 556	7 935	11 144	6 807
1982	33 221	317	50	35	45	78	60	203	479	1 444	3 552	7 735	11 867	7 356
1983	32 258	266	51	33	33	67	76	201	504	1 317	3 568	7 558	11 340	7 244

1. In some years the totals include a small number of persons whose age was not stated.

Source General Register Office (Scotland)

2.19
(continued)

Deaths: analysis by age and sex
Northern Ireland
Annual averages or calendar years

Number

	All ages[1]	Under 1 year	1 – 4	5 – 9	10 – 14	15 – 19	20 – 24	25 – 34	35 – 44	45 – 54	55 – 64	65 – 74	75 – 84	85 and over
Males														
1900 – 02	11 554	1 958	985	280	206	367	446	779	669	832	1 413	1 666	1 368	585
1910 – 12	10 469	1 697	841	222	152	282	311	569	679	836	1 148	2 011	1 287	434
1920 – 22	9 622	1 491	596	191	150	258	334	496	570	869	1 159	1 749	1 324	435
1930 – 32	8 626	1 083	406	126	90	154	209	375	437	740	1 313	1 988	1 317	388
1940 – 42	9 383	1 258	322	117	102	153	202	379	462	751	1 290	2 305	1 637	405
1950 – 52	8 197	658	105	55	36	50	77	179	318	671	1 169	2 117	2 178	583
1960 – 62	8 080	499	67	38	27	49	48	108	216	623	1 419	2 037	2 131	816
1970 – 72	8 786	396	58	40	32	76	83	115	221	643	1 590	2 493	2 157	881
1980 – 82[2]	8 420	211	37	20	26	77	92	144	202	539	1 414	2 518	2 346	795
1966	8 659	465	83	40	24	59	65	94	240	603	1 566	2 333	2 145	942
1967	7 729	423	68	37	36	42	58	85	207	617	1 368	2 100	1 923	765
1968	8 235	458	44	34	27	54	49	102	189	561	1 472	2 349	2 078	818
1969	8 608	464	55	38	29	50	56	111	228	666	1 556	2 443	2 122	790
1970	8 764	434	55	37	34	40	63	93	228	633	1 635	2 565	2 105	842
1971	8 593	404	56	39	30	67	78	107	220	608	1 531	2 392	2 142	919
1972	9 001	350	63	44	32	121	109	145	216	689	1 604	2 523	2 223	882
1973	9 288	343	64	44	37	134	152	236	236	722	1 559	2 573	2 269	919
1974	9 226	295	64	41	43	111	119	176	273	737	1 615	2 630	2 216	906
1975	8 664	293	43	40	46	92	105	205	233	659	1 499	2 465	2 157	827
1976	8 869	259	50	38	33	114	119	174	237	593	1 546	2 654	2 216	836
1977	8 871	246	46	28	29	91	112	162	240	693	1 524	2 631	2 239	830
1978	8 458	228	40	35	32	80	84	140	209	624	1 517	2 456	2 208	805
1979	8 822	226	28	27	31	96	105	144	241	622	1 507	2 604	2 392	799
1980	8 832	222	31	27	35	87	104	162	210	568	1 495	2 653	2 430	808
1981	8 423	205	49	20	27	66	93	141	193	521	1 406	2 568	2 319	815
1982[2]	8 004	205	31	12	17	77	78	129	203	528	1 341	2 332	2 289	762
Females														
1900 – 02	12 735	1 537	1 013	317	277	495	521	1 012	902	1 075	1 612	1 876	1 484	614
1910 – 12	11 397	1 369	808	249	218	325	365	785	811	961	1 282	2 328	1 402	494
1920 – 22	10 415	1 149	547	193	188	299	331	687	713	939	1 236	1 976	1 639	518
1930 – 32	9 044	824	380	125	102	184	226	475	539	774	1 293	2 046	1 541	535
1940 – 42	9 229	910	305	105	90	159	174	409	490	688	1 207	2 246	1 873	572
1950 – 52	7 896	494	87	33	21	37	59	173	276	526	996	1 976	2 384	834
1960 – 62	7 463	371	61	20	15	21	24	70	175	434	880	1 823	2 417	1 151
1970 – 72	7 809	295	45	23	17	25	20	65	152	408	919	1 959	2 475	1 407
1980 – 82[2]	7 917	160	26	17	17	23	29	65	127	329	881	1 813	2 752	1 678
1966	7 782	383	57	19	19	32	27	60	171	420	863	1 924	2 482	1 324
1967	6 942	362	42	14	10	23	19	73	152	350	841	1 747	2 165	1 144
1968	7 698	338	45	22	19	19	23	62	183	403	932	1 918	2 375	1 359
1969	7 730	326	49	25	13	14	23	57	162	405	961	1 973	2 361	1 361
1970	7 787	300	41	28	16	15	16	72	154	431	967	2 000	2 410	1 337
1971	7 609	318	46	17	14	26	17	55	149	364	861	1 882	2 412	1 448
1972	8 031	266	48	24	20	33	28	69	153	428	929	1 994	2 603	1 436
1973	8 381	267	59	23	16	31	27	66	179	415	971	2 000	2 745	1 582
1974	8 101	272	45	17	13	33	27	68	134	403	892	1 900	2 654	1 643
1975	7 847	241	40	21	18	35	25	62	137	376	920	1 887	2 588	1 497
1976	8 161	224	56	17	18	32	27	90	129	398	947	1 882	2 778	1 563
1977	8 050	192	33	13	15	37	37	64	143	398	896	1 909	2 708	1 605
1978	7 695	189	35	26	15	34	27	65	117	352	875	1 814	2 644	1 502
1979	7 989	191	21	23	18	20	22	59	125	361	874	1 919	2 743	1 613
1980	8 003	160	27	19	25	27	25	74	142	315	905	1 912	2 745	1 627
1981	7 833	155	24	15	13	20	26	49	114	348	858	1 779	2 760	1 672
1982[2]	7 914	164	26	16	12	23	35	73	125	325	880	1 749	2 750	1 736

1. In some years the totals include a small number of persons whose age was not stated.
2. Provisional.

Source General Register Office (Northern Ireland)

2.20 Deaths analysed by cause
England and Wales

Number

	Code numbers[1]	1979	1980	1981	1982	1983
Total deaths		593 019	581 385	577 890	581 861	579 608
Deaths from natural causes[2]		571 866	561 089	558 102	562 251	560 599
Infectious and parasitic diseases	001 – 139	2 273	2 239	2 102	2 116	2 043
Cholera	001	–	–	–	–	1
Typhoid fever	002.0	2	1	2	3	1
Shigellosis and amoebiasis	004, 006	8	5	8	4	7
Enteritis and other diarrhoeal diseases	008 – 009	176	141	149	134	119
Tuberculosis of respiratory system	010 – 012	490	474	432	454	375
Other tuberculosis, including late effects	013 – 018, 137	446	429	332	296	324
Plague	020	–	–	–	–	–
Diphtheria	032	–	–	–	1	–
Whooping cough	033	7	6	5	14	5
Streptococcal sore throat and scarlatina	034	7	3	4	3	2
Meningococcal infection	036	97	71	85	70	70
Acute poliomyelitis	045	–	–	–	–	–
Smallpox	050	–	1[3]	–	–	–
Measles	055	17	26	15	13	16
Louse-borne typhus and other rickettsioses	080 – 083	1	–	–	–	1
Malaria	084	6	8	2	10	7
Syphilis	090 – 097	76	59	55	46	47
Neoplasms	140 – 239	129 638	130 566	131 691	132 448	134 270
Malignant neoplasm of stomach	151	11 305	10 900	10 652	10 211	10 502
Malignant neoplasm of trachea, bronchus and lung	162	34 760	35 168	34 727	34 832	35 572
Malignant neoplasm of breast	174 – 175	12 174	12 245	12 597	12 492	12 759
Malignant neoplasm of uterus	179 – 182	3 598	3 576	3 537	3 512	3 464
Leukaemia	204 – 208	3 298	3 340	3 349	3 462	3 481
Benign neoplasms and neoplasms of unspecified nature	210 – 229, 239	1 065	1 011	1 240	1 532	956
Endocrine, nutritional and metabolic diseases and immunity disorders	240 – 279	6 462	6 440	6 195	5 963	6 153
Diabetes mellitus	250	4 809	4 781	4 626	4 534	4 516
Nutritional deficiencies	260 – 269	91	105	124	91	107
Diseases of blood and blood-forming organs	280 – 289	1 729	1 672	1 588	1 588	1 512
Anaemias	280 – 285	1 252	1 163	1 134	1 035	949
Mental disorders	290 – 319	3 211	3 308	3 441	3 757	4 142
Diseases of nervous system and sense organs	320 – 389	6 934	6 483	6 975	7 558	7 624
Meningitis	320 – 322	285	277	266	286	281
Diseases of the circulatory system	390 – 459	298 436	290 395	286 258	284 246	282 815
Acute rheumatic fever	390 – 392	3	4	2	4	1
Chronic rheumatic heart disease	393 – 398	3 396	3 248	3 120	2 904	2 884
Hypertensive disease	401 – 405	6 506	5 588	5 413	5 160	4 725
Ischaemic heart disease	410 – 414	155 647	154 371	155 196	154 605	156 550
Diseases of pulmonary circulation and other forms of heart disease	415 – 429	36 419	34 645	32 751	32 259	30 529
Cerebrovascular disease	430 – 438	74 378	71 443	69 651	69 028	67 785
Diseases of the respiratory system	460 – 519	85 925	83 405	83 507	88 111	86 633
Influenza	487	838	514	626	716	796
Pneumonia	480 – 486	54 376	53 704	54 057	56 529	55 513
Bronchitis, emphysema	490 – 492	21 627	19 255	17 530	17 297	15 410
Asthma	493	1 477	1 480	1 603	1 577	1 645
Diseases of the digestive system	520 – 579	16 255	16 140	16 447	16 456	15 838
Ulcer of stomach and duodenum	531 – 533	4 361	4 418	4 457	4 608	4 259
Appendicitis	540 – 543	222	179	164	155	136
Hernia of abdominal cavity and other intestinal obstruction	550 – 553, 560	2 114	1 999	1 959	1 908	1 861
Chronic liver disease and cirrhosis	571	2 186	2 218	2 212	2 152	2 184
Diseases of the genito-urinary system	580 – 629	7 913	7 735	7 970	8 132	7 830
Nephritis, nephrotic syndrome and nephrosis	580 – 589	4 380	4 482	4 766	4 950	4 742
Hyperplasia of prostate	600	818	722	749	694	621
Complications of pregnancy, childbirth and the puerperium	630 – 676	74	70	57	42	54
Abortion	630 – 639	9	13	10	6	8
Diseases of the skin and subcutaneous tissue	680 – 709	439	473	516	493	505
Diseases of the musculo-skeletal system and connective tissue	710 – 739	3 047	3 104	3 112	3 224	3 241
Congenital anomalies	740 – 759	3 498	3 404	3 039	3 037	2 944
Certain conditions originating in the perinatal period	760 – 779	3 424	3 148	2 659	2 464	2 422
Birth trauma, hypoxia, birth asphyxia and other respiratory conditions	767 – 770	1 921	1 731	1 445	1 336	1 268
Signs, symptoms and ill-defined conditions	780 – 799	2 608	2 507	2 545	2 616	2 573
Deaths by violence[2]	E800 – E999	21 153	20 296	19 788	19 610	19 009
All accidents	E800 – E929	14 846	14 032	..[4]	13 297	12 823
Motor vehicle accidents	E810 – E825	5 855	5 831	..[4]	5 310	5 146
Suicide and self-inflicted injury	E950 – E959	4 195	4 321	4 419	4 279	4 279
All other external causes	E930 – E949 } E960 – E999 }	2 112	1 943	..[4]	2 034	1 907

1. Code numbers refer to the Ninth Revision of the *International Statistical Classification of Diseases, Injuries and Causes of Death* introduced in 1979.
2. Within certain main categories only selected causes of death are shown.
3. Occurred 1978, but not registered until 1980.

4. Industrial action by registration officers in 1981 has meant that information normally supplied by coroners about accidental and violent deaths, with the exception of suicides, is not available, and therefore no comparable figures can be compiled for these categories for 1981.

Source Office of Population Censuses and Surveys

2.20

Deaths analysed by cause
Scotland

(*continued*)

Number

	Code numbers[1]	1979	1980	1981	1982	1983
Total deaths		65 747	63 299	63 828	65 022	63 454
Deaths from natural causes[2]		62 360	60 129	60 749	61 940	60 612
Infectious and parasitic diseases	001–139	285	292	284	283	279
Cholera	001	–	–	–	–	–
Typhoid fever	002.0	–	–	1	–	–
Shigellosis and amoebiasis	004,006	–	–	1	–	1
Enteritis and other diarrhoeal diseases	008–009	27	13	12	12	12
Tuberculosis of respiratory system	010–012	64	61	68	50	48
Other tuberculosis, including late effects	013–018, 137	63	59	54	65	52
Plague	020	–	–	–	–	–
Diphtheria	032	–	–	–	–	–
Whooping cough	033	1	–	1	2	–
Streptococcal sore throat and scarlatina	034	–	1	–	–	–
Meningococcal infection	036	8	10	5	10	–
Acute poliomyelitis	045	–	–	–	–	–
Smallpox	050	–	–	–	–	–
Measles	055	–	6	2	2	4
Louse-borne typhus and other rickettsioses	080–083	–	–	–	–	–
Malaria	084	1	–	–	1	–
Syphilis	090–097	6	6	6	2	4
Neoplasms	140–239	14 094	13 865	14 083	14 247	14 377
Malignant neoplasm of stomach	151	1 125	1 088	1 095	1 057	1 003
Malignant neoplasm of trachea, bronchus and lung	162	4 115	3 951	4 114	4 116	4 178
Malignant neoplasm of breast	174–175	1 183	1 217	1 182	1 236	1 271
Malignant neoplasm of uterus	179–182	374	320	328	331	359
Leukaemia	204–208	304	312	285	302	307
Benign neoplasms and neoplasms of unspecified nature	210–229, 239	148	134	111	130	122
Endocrine, nutritional and metabolic diseases and immunity disorders	240–279	875	768	872	818	779
Diabetes mellitus	250	647	559	652	591	558
Nutritional deficiencies	260–269	26	19	30	19	16
Diseases of blood and blood-forming organs	280–289	220	181	170	162	164
Anaemias	280–285	152	115	106	102	94
Mental disorders	290–319	568	576	561	640	629
Diseases of nervous system and sense organs	320–389	727	691	749	728	801
Meningitis	320–322	43	36	27	25	35
Diseases of the circulatory system	390–459	34 568	32 854	33 214	33 279	32 243
Acute rheumatic fever	390–392	3	1	1	3	–
Chronic rheumatic heart disease	393–398	413	334	318	336	306
Hypertensive disease	401–405	571	513	484	498	430
Ischaemic heart disease	410–414	18 447	17 885	18 453	18 633	18 335
Diseases of pulmonary circulation and other forms of heart disease	415–429	3 436	3 035	2 845	2 907	2 782
Cerebrovascular disease	430–438	9 636	9 140	9 190	8 996	8 594
Diseases of the respiratory system	460–519	6 874	6 788	6 546	7 528	7 253
Influenza	487	59	117	54	235	178
Pneumonia	480–486	3 780	3 824	3 676	4 195	4 037
Bronchitis, emphysema	490–492	1 835	1 558	1 365	1 390	1 081
Asthma	493	153	152	143	196	163
Diseases of the digestive system	520–579	2 016	2 094	2 185	2 116	2 077
Ulcer of stomach and duodenum	531–533	430	489	482	491	481
Appendicitis	540–543	19	24	20	13	14
Hernia of abdominal cavity and other intestinal obstruction	550–553, 560	226	202	188	207	207
Chronic liver disease and cirrhosis	571	431	406	450	422	431
Diseases of the genito-urinary system	580–629	801	817	871	933	892
Nephritis, nephrotic syndrome and nephrosis	580–589	452	446	519	572	557
Hyperplasia of prostate	600	77	61	40	36	41
Complications of pregnancy, childbirth and the puerperium	630–676	7	10	13	6	8
Abortion	630–639	1	1	1	–	2
Diseases of the skin and subcutaneous tissue	680–709	40	51	43	51	57
Diseases of the musculo-skeletal system and connective tissue	710–739	282	225	264	245	262
Congenital anomalies	740–759	383	341	297	293	298
Certain conditions originating in the perinatal period	760–779	401	359	324	324	245
Birth trauma, hypoxia, birth asphyxia and other respiratory conditions	767–770	228	202	183	173	143
Signs, symptoms and ill-defined conditions	780–799	219	217	273	287	248
Deaths by violence[2]		3 387	3 170	3 079	3 082	2 842
All accidents	E800–E929	2 542	2 299	2 254	2 245	2 085
Motor vehicle accidents	E810–E825	862	743	725	741	644
Suicide and self-inflicted injuries	E950–E959	494	515	516	561	505
All other external causes	{ E930–E949 / E960–E999 }	351	356	309	267	252

1. Code numbers refer to the Ninth Revision of the *International Statistical Classification of Diseases, Injuries and Causes of Death* introduced in 1979.
2. Within certain main categories only selected causes of death are shown.

Source General Register Office (Scotland)

2.20 Deaths analysed by cause
Northern Ireland

(*continued*)

Number

	Code numbers[1]	1979	1980	1981	1982[3]
Total deaths		16 811	16 835	16 256	15 918
Deaths from natural causes[2]		15 694	15 812	15 400	15 109
Infectious and parasitic diseases	001–139	62	67	74	72
Cholera	001	–	–	–	–
Typhoid fever	002.0	–	–	–	–
Shigellosis and amoebiasis	004,006	1	–	–	–
Enteritis and other diarrhoeal diseases	008–009	1	2	2	–
Tuberculosis of respiratory system	010–012	19	22	18	10
Other tuberculosis, including late effects	013–018, 137	7	14	4	2
Plague	020	–	–	–	–
Diphtheria	032	–	–	–	–
Whooping cough	033	–	–	–	–
Streptococcal sore throat and scarlatina	034	1	–	–	–
Meningococcal infection	036	2	–	2	2
Acute poliomyelitis	045	–	–	–	–
Smallpox	050	–	–	–	–
Measles	055	2	2	2	–
Louse-borne typhus and other rickettsioses	080–083	–	–	–	–
Malaria	084	–	–	–	–
Syphilis	090–097	2	1	1	2
Neoplasms	140–239	3 020	3 066	3 063	3,102
Malignant neoplasm of stomach	151	324	298	259	272
Malignant neoplasm of trachea, bronchus and lung	162	672	676	689	690
Malignant neoplasm of breast	174–175	266	293	296	269
Malignant neoplasm of uterus	179–182	73	70	83	89
Leukaemia	204–208	93	98	85	99
Benign neoplasms and neoplasms of unspecified nature	210–229, 239	52	44	40	28
Endocrine, nutritional and metabolic diseases and immunity disorders	240–279	121	184	137	117
Diabetes mellitus	250	87	137	103	93
Nutritional deficiencies	260–269	–	5	3	–
Diseases of blood and blood-forming organs	280–289	35	58	45	30
Anaemias	280–285	23	42	30	23
Mental disorders	290–319	36	44	37	29
Diseases of nervous system and sense organs	320–389	193	193	192	189
Meningitis	320–322	10	11	10	8
Diseases of the circulatory system	390–459	9 140	8 839	8 655	8 093
Acute rheumatic fever	390–392	2	4	5	2
Chronic rheumatic heart disease	393–398	93	74	66	67
Hypertensive disease	401–405	163	157	121	95
Ischaemic heart disease	410–414	4 923	4 858	4 909	4 563
Diseases of pulmonary circulation and other forms of heart disease	415–429	1 251	1 122	1 068	1 028
Cerebrovascular disease	430–438	2 305	2 217	2 111	1 982
Diseases of the respiratory system	460–519	2 029	2 255	2 111	2 364
Influenza	487	28	27	24	15
Pneumonia	480–486	147	1 332	1 263	1 523
Bronchitis, emphysema	490–492	450	415	334	301
Asthma	493	42	55	45	48
Diseases of the digestive system	520–579	392	465	421	442
Ulcer of stomach and duodenum	531–533	97	112	121	112
Appendicitis	540–543	3	5	4	5
Hernia of abdominal cavity and other intestinal obstruction	550–553, 560	44	61	46	37
Chronic liver disease and cirrhosis	571	59	72	65	71
Diseases of the genito-urinary system	580–629	267	267	286	293
Nephritis, nephrotic syndrome and nephrosis	580–589	174	151	193	206
Hyperplasia of prostate	600	19	38	18	11
Complications of pregnancy, childbirth and the puerperium	630–676	1	2	1	2
Abortion	630–639	1	1	–	1
Diseases of the skin and subcutaneous tissue	680–709	7	7	14	13
Diseases of the musculo-skeletal system and connective tissue	710–739	31	40	48	26
Congenital anomalies	740–759	168	162	134	150
Certain conditions originating in the perinatal period	760–779	163	140	146	137
Birth trauma, hypoxia, birth asphyxia and other respiratory conditions	767–770	94	69	77	49
Signs, symptoms and ill-defined conditions	780–799	29	27	36	50
Deaths by violence[2]		1 117	1 023	859	809
All accidents	E800–E929	901	784	602	591
Motor vehicle accidents	E810–E825	311	289	228	225
Suicide and self-inflicted injuries	E950–E959	76	81	90	93
All other external causes	E930–E949, E960–E999	140	158	167	125

1. Code numbers refer to the Ninth Revision of the *International Statistical Classification of Diseases, Injuries and Causes of Death* introduced in 1979.
2. Within certain main categories only selected causes of death are shown.
3. Provisional.

Source General Register Office (Northern Ireland)

2.21 Infant and maternal mortality

	Deaths of infants under 1 year of age per thousand live births												Maternal deaths per thousand live births[2]			
	United Kingdom			England and Wales[1]			Scotland			Northern Ireland						
	Total	Males	Females	Total	Males	Females	Total	Males	Females	Total	Males	Females	United Kingdom	England and Wales	Scotland	Northern Ireland
1900–02	142	156	128	146	160	131	124	136	111	113	123	103	4.71	4.67	4.74	6.03
1910–12	110	121	98	110	121	98	109	120	97	101	110	92	3.95	3.67	5.65	5.28
1920–22	82	92	71	80	90	69	94	106	82	86	95	77	4.37	4.03	6.36	5.62
1930–32	67	75	58	64	72	55	84	94	73	75	83	66	4.54	4.24	6.40	5.24
1940–42	59	66	51	55	62	48	77	87	66	80	89	70	3.29	2.74	4.50	3.79
1950–52	30	34	26	29	33	25	37	42	32	40	45	36	0.88	0.79	1.09	1.09
1960–62	22	25	19	22	24	19	26	30	22	27	30	24	0.36	0.36	0.37	0.43
1970–72	18	20	16	18	20	15	19	22	17	22	24	20	0.17	0.17	0.17	0.10
1980–82	12	13	10	11	13	10	12	13	10	13[3]	15[3]	12[3]	0.09[3]	0.09[3]	0.14	0.06[3]
1937	61.1	68.4	53.4	57.7	64.7	50.2	80.3	89.6	70.5	77.5	83.5	71.2	3.72	3.51	4.83	5.00
1938	55.5	62.3	48.4	52.8	59.7	45.6	69.5	76.6	62.1	75.1	79.1	70.9	3.62	3.37	4.87	5.32
1939	53.6	60.0	46.8	50.6	56.4	44.4	68.5	77.5	59.0	70.5	80.9	59.6	3.42	3.25	4.49	3.80
1940	61.0	69.3	52.3	56.8	64.3	48.8	78.3	90.3	65.7	85.9	94.8	76.3	3.03	2.78	4.39	4.22
1941	63.3	71.2	55.0	60.0	67.5	52.2	82.7	93.3	71.6	76.6	85.4	66.9	3.20	2.90	4.89	4.17
1942	52.9	59.2	46.2	50.6	56.5	44.3	69.3	77.9	60.2	76.4	86.7	65.4	2.78	2.57	4.21	2.97
1943	51.9	57.8	45.6	49.1	54.7	43.2	65.2	73.0	57.0	78.2	87.0	68.6	2.57	2.37	3.83	3.17
1944	47.6	52.9	41.9	45.4	50.4	40.1	65.0	73.0	56.4	67.4	73.7	60.8	2.14	1.99	3.05	3.07
1945	48.8	54.6	42.6	46.0	51.4	40.3	56.2	64.7	47.3	68.1	72.7	63.1	1.99	1.85	2.86	2.69
1946	42.7	48.1	37.0	42.9	48.3	37.1	53.8	60.0	47.3	54.0	61.5	46.0	1.59	1.47	2.26	2.32
1947	43.7	49.0	38.1	41.4	46.3	36.2	55.8	62.9	48.2	53.0	60.8	44.9	1.32	1.20	2.10	1.86
1948	36.0	40.6	31.2	33.9	38.1	29.5	44.7	51.3	37.7	45.6	53.1	37.6	1.12	1.05	1.60	1.52
1949	34.1	38.3	29.6	32.4	36.5	28.0	41.4	46.2	36.3	45.2	48.6	41.6	1.04	1.00	1.32	1.31
1950	31.2	35.0	27.2	29.6	33.4	25.7	38.6	43.0	33.8	40.5	43.9	36.9	0.93	0.89	1.15	1.11
1951	31.1	35.1	26.9	29.7	33.6	25.5	37.4	42.2	32.4	41.2	44.5	37.7	0.82	0.78	1.09	1.09
1952	28.8	32.3	25.1	27.6	30.9	24.1	35.2	39.3	30.8	38.8	45.1	32.1	0.74	0.69	1.02	1.08
1953	27.6	30.8	24.2	26.8	29.8	23.6	30.8	34.7	26.6	37.6	43.4	31.4	0.74	0.72	0.95	0.59
1954	26.4	29.6	22.8	25.4	28.7	22.0	31.0	34.9	26.9	33.0	36.9	28.9	0.68	0.66	0.76	0.73
1955	25.8	28.9	22.5	24.9	28.1	21.5	30.4	33.2	27.4	32.4	34.6	29.9	0.60	0.61	0.46	0.83
1956	24.4	27.6	21.0	23.8	26.9	20.4	28.6	32.6	24.4	28.9	30.9	26.6	0.54	0.53	0.54	0.58
1957	24.0	26.7	21.0	23.1	25.8	20.3	28.6	32.6	24.4	28.9	30.5	27.2	0.48	0.46	0.47	1.10
1958	23.4	26.2	20.4	22.5	25.3	19.6	27.7	30.9	24.3	28.1	31.3	24.6	0.46	0.44	0.53	0.56
1959	23.1	25.5	20.5	22.2	24.5	19.8	28.4	32.0	24.5	28.4	29.4	27.4	0.39	0.39	0.36	0.55
1960	22.4	25.1	19.5	21.8	24.5	18.9	26.4	29.7	22.9	27.2	30.0	24.2	0.39	0.39	0.35	0.44
1961	22.1	24.5	19.6	21.4	23.9	18.8	25.8	29.3	22.3	27.5	32.9	21.7	0.35	0.34	0.37	0.53
1962	22.4	25.3	19.3	21.7	24.5	18.7	26.5	31.0	21.7	26.5	27.6	25.7	0.36	0.36	0.40	0.31
1963	21.7	24.3	19.0	21.1	23.7	18.4	25.6	28.7	22.2	27.0	28.5	25.3	0.30	0.28	0.38	0.42
1964	20.6	22.9	18.0	19.9	22.2	17.5	24.0	26.8	21.1	26.3	30.5	21.9	0.25	0.26	0.23	0.17
1965	19.6	22.1	17.0	19.0	21.5	16.4	23.1	25.5	20.6	25.1	27.1	22.8	0.32	0.26	0.38	0.32
1966	19.6	22.0	17.1	19.0	21.4	16.5	23.2	25.8	20.4	25.5	26.8	24.1	0.26	0.26	0.25	0.18
1967	18.8	20.7	16.8	18.3	20.3	16.3	21.0	23.3	18.6	23.5	24.6	22.3	0.21	0.21	0.23	0.24
1968	18.7	21.2	16.2	18.3	20.7	15.8	20.8	23.6	17.7	24.0	26.7	21.1	0.23	0.24	0.15	0.27
1969	18.6	20.9	16.1	18.0	20.3	15.6	21.1	23.6	18.4	24.0	27.9	20.7	0.19	0.19	0.14	0.15
1970	18.5	20.9	15.9	18.2	20.5	15.7	19.6	22.4	16.6	22.9	26.2	19.4	0.18	0.19	0.19	–
1971	17.9	20.2	15.5	17.5	19.8	15.1	19.9	22.2	17.4	22.7	24.5	20.8	0.17	0.17	0.16	0.19
1972	17.5	19.5	15.4	17.2	19.3	15.0	18.8	20.7	16.8	20.5	22.5	18.4	0.15	0.15	0.17	0.10
1973	17.2	19.3	15.0	16.9	18.9	14.7	19.0	21.8	16.0	21.0	22.7	19.2	0.14	0.13	0.22	0.17
1974	16.8	18.9	14.4	16.3	18.6	13.9	18.9	20.9	16.9	20.8	21.1	20.6	0.14	0.13	0.23	0.22
1975	16.0	17.7	14.2	15.7	17.5	13.9	17.2	19.1	15.2	20.4	21.7	19.0	0.12	0.13	0.09	0.04
1976	14.5	16.4	12.4	14.3	16.2	12.2	14.8	17.0	12.5	18.3	19.1	17.5	0.13	0.13	0.15	0.11
1977	14.1	15.8	12.3	13.8	15.4	12.0	16.1	18.3	13.8	17.2	18.7	15.6	0.13	0.13	0.21	0.04
1978	13.3	14.8	11.7	13.2	14.7	11.6	12.9	14.5	11.2	15.9	17.3	14.5	0.10	0.11	0.06	–
1979	12.9	14.4	11.3	12.8	14.4	11.1	12.8	13.9	11.8	14.8	15.6	13.9	0.11	0.12	0.10	0.04
1980	12.2	13.4	10.6	12.0	13.3	10.7	12.1	13.6	10.4	13.4	15.1	11.5	0.11	0.11	0.15	0.07
1981	11.2	12.7	9.5	11.1	12.6	9.4	11.3	12.3	10.2	13.2	14.7	11.6	0.09	0.09	0.19	0.04
1982	11.0	12.3	9.5	10.8	12.2	9.4	11.4	12.9	9.8	13.6	14.8	12.4	0.07	0.07	0.09	0.07
1983	10.1	11.3	8.9	10.1	11.3	8.9	9.9	11.3	8.5	12.1	13.9	10.1	0 09[3]	0.09	0.12	0.15

1. From 1937 to 1956 death rates are based on the births to which they relate in the current and preceding years.
2. Deaths in pregnancy and childbirth.
3. Provisional.

Sources Office of Population Censuses and Surveys; General Register Office (Scotland); General Register Office (Northern Ireland)

2.21

Infant mortality
Analysis by sex and age of infant

(*continued*)

Deaths per 1 000 live births

	1973	1974	1975	1976	1977	1978	1979	1980	1981	1982	1983
Total											
United Kingdom:											
Under 1 day	5.7	5.3	5.1	4.8	4.4	3.8	3.8	3.5	3.0	2.9[1]	2.6[1]
1 day and under 1 week	4.1	4.3	4.2	3.8	3.5	3.4	3.1	2.8	2.3	2.3[1]	2.1[1]
1 week and under 4 weeks	1.6	1.7	1.7	2.0	1.6	1.6	1.5	1.5	1.4	1.2[1]	1.2[1]
4 weeks and under 1 year	5.8	5.4	5.1	5.1	4.6	4.5	4.6	4.4	4.4	4.6[1]	4.3[1]
England and Wales:											
Under 1 day	5.5	5.2	5.0	4.7	4.2	3.7	3.7	3.4	2.9	2.8	2.6
1 day and under 1 week	4.0	4.2	4.1	3.5	3.5	3.4	3.0	2.8	2.3	2.2	2.1
1 week and under 4 weeks	1.6	1.7	1.7	1.5	1.6	1.6	1.5	1.5	1.4	1.2	1.2
4 weeks and under 1 year	5.7	5.3	5.0	4.6	4.5	4.5	4.6	4.4	4.4	4.6	4.3
Scotland:											
Under 1 day	6.5	6.0	5.8	5.0	5.6	4.1	4.2	3.9	3.0	3.2	2.6
1 day and under 1 week	4.5	4.9	4.2	3.8	3.9	3.3	3.1	2.6	2.4	2.6	2.3
1 week and under 4 weeks	1.7	1.9	1.7	1.5	1.7	1.4	1.4	1.3	1.5	1.4	1.0
4 weeks and under 1 year	6.3	6.1	5.4	4.5	4.8	4.1	4.2	4.3	4.4	4.2	4.1
Northern Ireland:											
Under 1 day	8.2	6.1	5.9	6.1	5.3	5.4	5.0	4.2	3.9	3.6[1]	3.2[1]
1 day and under 1 week	4.3	5.7	5.6	5.8	3.9	3.6	3.0	2.8	2.7	2.9[1]	2.5[1]
1 week and under 4 weeks	1.9	1.9	1.6	1.3	1.5	1.4	1.4	1.6	1.7	1.3[1]	1.6[1]
4 weeks and under 1 year	6.3	7.1	7.3	5.0	6.5	5.4	5.4	5.4	4.9	5.9[1]	4.8[1]
Males											
United Kingdom:											
Under 1 day	6.4	6.1	5.6	5.5	5.0	4.3	4.3	3.9	3.4	3.3[1]	2.8[1]
1 day and under 1 week	4.8	4.8	4.6	4.5	4.0	3.7	3.5	3.0	2.7	2.6[1]	2.4[1]
1 week and under 4 weeks	1.7	1.7	1.7	2.0	1.8	1.7	1.6	1.5	1.6	1.3[1]	1.3[1]
4 weeks and under 1 year	6.4	6.2	5.7	5.7	5.1	5.0	4.9	4.9	5.0	5.1[1]	4.8[1]
England and Wales:											
Under 1 day	6.2	6.1	5.5	5.5	4.8	4.2	4.2	3.8	3.4	3.3	2.8
1 day and under 1 week	4.7	4.7	4.6	4.1	3.9	3.7	3.6	3.1	2.7	2.5	2.3
1 week and under 4 weeks	1.7	1.7	1.7	1.5	1.8	1.7	1.6	1.5	1.6	1.3	1.3
4 weeks and under 1 year	6.3	6.1	5.6	5.2	5.0	5.1	5.0	4.8	4.9	5.1	4.8
Scotland:											
Under 1 day	7.4	6.8	6.7	5.7	6.7	5.0	4.7	4.9	3.3	3.6	2.9
1 day and under 1 week	5.5	5.5	4.7	4.7	4.5	3.7	3.4	2.7	2.4	3.1	2.4
1 week and under 4 weeks	1.9	1.9	1.8	1.5	1.9	1.6	1.6	1.5	1.4	1.4	0.8
4 weeks and under 1 year	7.0	6.7	5.9	5.1	5.3	4.2	4.2	4.5	5.3	4.7	5.2
Northern Ireland:											
Under 1 day	9.8	6.4	6.2	6.4	5.2	5.8	5.4	4.9	4.4	3.7[1]	3.4[1]
1 day and under 1 week	4.5	5.3	6.1	6.5	4.9	3.8	3.2	2.6	2.7	3.3[1]	3.4[1]
1 week and under 4 weeks	2.0	2.0	1.5	1.2	1.8	1.6	1.2	1.6	1.7	1.4[1]	2.0[1]
4 weeks and under 1 year	6.3	7.4	7.9	4.9	6.8	6.1	5.7	6.1	6.0	6.4[1]	5.1[1]
Females											
United Kingdom:											
Under 1 day	4.9	4.4	4.4	4.0	3.7	3.3	3.2	2.9	2.5	2.5[1]	2.4[1]
1 day and under 1 week	3.3	3.7	3.7	3.1	3.0	3.0	2.6	2.4	2.0	1.9[1]	1.8[1]
1 week and under 4 weeks	1.5	1.7	1.6	2.0	1.5	1.4	1.3	1.4	1.2	1.1[1]	1.0[1]
4 weeks and under 1 year	5.2	4.6	4.4	4.5	4.1	4.0	4.1	3.9	3.8	4.0[1]	3.7[1]
England and Wales:											
Under 1 day	4.8	4.3	4.4	3.9	3.6	3.3	3.2	2.9	2.5	2.4	2.4
1 day and under 1 week	3.3	3.6	3.6	2.8	3.0	3.0	2.5	2.4	1.9	1.9	1.8
1 week and under 4 weeks	1.5	1.6	1.6	1.5	1.5	1.5	1.3	1.4	1.2	1.1	1.0
4 weeks and under 1 year	5.1	4.5	4.3	4.0	4.0	3.9	4.1	3.9	3.8	4.0	3.7
Scotland:											
Under 1 day	5.5	5.3	4.9	4.3	4.5	3.2	3.7	2.8	2.7	2.7	2.4
1 day and under 1 week	3.4	4.3	3.7	2.8	3.4	2.8	2.7	2.4	2.4	2.0	2.1
1 week and under 4 weeks	1.5	1.8	1.6	1.5	1.6	1.1	1.2	1.1	1.6	1.4	1.1
4 weeks and under 1 year	5.6	5.5	4.9	3.9	4.3	4.0	4.1	4.1	3.6	3.7	3.0
Northern Ireland:											
Under 1 day	6.5	5.9	5.6	5.8	5.4	5.0	4.5	3.4	3.4	3.5[1]	3.0[1]
1 day and under 1 week	4.2	6.1	5.1	5.1	2.8	3.4	2.9	1.9	2.8	2.5[1]	1.4[1]
1 week and under 4 weeks	1.9	1.9	1.7	1.4	1.1	1.3	1.5	1.6	1.6	1.1[1]	1.2[1]
4 weeks and under 1 year	6.3	6.7	6.5	5.1	6.3	4.7	5.0	4.6	3.7	5.3[1]	4.4[1]

1. Provisional.

Sources   Office of Population Censuses and Surveys; General Register Office
(Scotland); General Register Office (Northern Ireland)

2.22 Death rates per 1 000 population[1]
Analysis by age and sex
United Kingdom

	All ages	0–4	5–9	10–14	15–19	20–24	25–34	35–44	45–54	55–64	65–74	75–84	85 and over
Males													
1900–02	18.4	57.0	4.1	2.4	3.7	5.0	6.6	11.0	18.6	35.0	69.9	143.6	289.6
1910–12	14.9	40.5	3.3	2.0	3.0	3.9	5.0	8.0	14.9	29.8	62.1	133.8	261.5
1920–22	13.5	33.4	2.9	1.8	2.9	3.9	4.5	6.9	11.9	25.3	57.8	131.8	259.1
1930–32	12.9	22.3	2.3	1.5	2.6	3.3	3.5	5.7	11.3	23.7	57.9	134.2	277.0
1940–42	..	..	..	..	..	..	..	..	..	..	..	..	..
1950–52	12.6	7.7	0.7	0.5	0.9	1.4	1.6	3.0	8.5	23.2	55.2	127.6	272.0
1960–62	12.5	6.4	0.5	0.4	0.9	1.1	1.1	2.5	7.4	22.2	54.4	123.4	251.0
1970–72	12.4	4.6	0.4	0.4	0.9	1.0	1.0	2.4	7.3	20.9	52.9	116.3	246.1
1980–82	12.1	3.2	0.3	0.3	0.8	0.9	0.9	1.9	6.3	18.2	46.7	107.1	224.9
1965	12.2	5.3	0.5	0.4	1.0	1.0	1.1	2.5	7.5	21.8	53.6	118.9	245.2
1966	12.4	5.3	0.5	0.4	1.0	1.1	1.1	2.5	7.4	21.8	54.0	121.6	261.0
1967	11.8	4.8	0.4	0.4	1.0	1.0	1.0	2.4	7.1	20.9	51.7	113.5	240.1
1968	12.4	4.9	0.4	0.4	0.9	0.9	1.0	2.4	7.2	21.4	54.1	123.2	265.5
1969	12.5	4.8	0.4	0.4	0.9	0.9	1.0	2.4	7.4	21.9	55.5	119.8	250.4
1970	12.3	4.8	0.4	0.4	0.9	1.0	1.0	2.3	7.2	21.4	54.0	119.0	253.4
1971	12.2	4.7	0.4	0.4	0.9	1.0	1.0	2.4	7.3	20.6	52.3	118.2	251.0
1972	12.6	4.4	0.4	0.4	0.9	1.0	1.0	2.4	7.5	21.0	53.8	119.8	248.0
1973	12.4	4.2	0.4	0.3	0.9	1.1	1.0	2.3	7.4	20.8	51.9	117.5	240.9
1974	12.3	4.2	0.4	0.3	0.9	1.0	1.0	2.3	7.4	20.6	51.6	115.3	240.3
1975	12.2	3.7	0.4	0.3	0.9	1.0	1.0	2.2	7.3	19.9	50.5	115.2	237.2
1976	12.5	3.5	0.3	0.3	0.9	1.0	1.0	2.2	7.2	20.1	51.0	117.5	246.0
1977	12.1	3.5	0.3	0.3	0.9	1.0	1.0	2.1	7.0	19.2	49.0	110.7	229.4
1978	12.3	3.4	0.3	0.3	0.9	1.0	1.0	2.1	7.0	19.3	49.3	111.8	232.0
1979	12.4	3.8	0.3	0.3	0.9	1.0	1.0	2.1	6.9	19.2	48.8	112.0	236.0
1980	12.1	3.4	0.3	0.3	0.8	0.9	0.9	2.0	6.5	18.7	47.2	108.6	227.0
1981	12.3	3.2	0.3	0.3	0.9	0.9	1.0	2.0	6.4	18.4	47.5	110.6	239.5
1982	12.0	2.9	0.3	0.3	0.8	0.9	0.9	1.8	6.1	17.9	46.4	106.4	225.0
Females													
1900–02	16.3	47.9	4.3	2.6	3.5	4.3	5.8	9.0	14.4	27.9	59.3	127.0	262.6
1910–12	13.3	34.0	3.3	2.1	2.9	3.4	4.4	6.7	11.5	23.1	50.7	113.7	234.0
1920–22	11.9	26.9	2.8	1.9	2.8	3.4	4.1	5.6	9.3	19.2	45.6	111.5	232.4
1930–32	11.5	17.7	2.1	1.5	2.4	2.9	3.3	4.6	8.3	17.6	43.7	110.1	246.3
1940–42	..	..	..	..	..	..	..	..	..	..	..	..	..
1950–52	11.2	6.0	0.5	0.4	0.7	1.0	1.4	2.3	5.3	12.9	35.5	98.4	228.8
1960–62	11.2	4.9	0.3	0.3	0.4	0.5	0.8	1.8	4.5	11.0	30.8	87.3	218.5
1970–72	11.3	3.6	0.3	0.2	0.4	0.4	0.6	1.6	4.5	10.5	27.5	76.7	196.1
1980–82	11.4	2.3	0.2	0.2	0.3	0.4	0.5	1.3	3.9	9.9	24.8	67.2	179.5
1965	10.9	4.2	0.3	0.3	0.4	0.5	0.7	1.8	4.5	10.6	29.0	80.2	199.0
1966	11.2	4.1	0.3	0.3	0.4	0.5	0.7	1.8	4.5	10.5	29.2	82.2	206.7
1967	10.6	3.9	0.3	0.3	0.4	0.4	0.6	1.7	4.3	10.2	27.6	76.0	192.8
1968	11.3	3.8	0.3	0.3	0.4	0.4	0.7	1.7	4.4	10.6	28.7	80.9	215.6
1969	11.3	3.7	0.3	0.2	0.4	0.4	0.6	1.8	4.5	10.8	29.1	78.1	203.2
1970	11.2	3.6	0.3	0.2	0.4	0.4	0.6	1.7	4.5	10.5	28.3	77.0	205.0
1971	11.1	3.6	0.3	0.2	0.4	0.4	0.6	1.6	4.4	10.4	26.9	76.6	209.1
1972	11.5	3.5	0.3	0.2	0.4	0.4	0.6	1.6	4.6	10.7	27.8	78.2	197.3
1973	11.5	3.2	0.3	0.2	0.4	0.4	0.6	1.6	4.5	10.5	27.1	76.5	192.5
1974	11.4	3.1	0.3	0.2	0.4	0.4	0.6	1.6	4.5	10.6	26.7	74.8	191.0
1975	11.3	3.0	0.2	0.2	0.4	0.4	0.6	1.5	4.4	10.4	26.0	73.4	188.3
1976	11.7	2.6	0.2	0.2	0.3	0.4	0.6	1.5	4.4	10.4	26.5	75.2	198.0
1977	11.3	2.7	0.2	0.2	0.4	0.4	0.5	1.5	4.2	10.1	25.5	71.0	183.1
1978	11.5	2.8	0.2	0.2	0.4	0.4	0.6	1.5	4.3	10.1	25.7	70.5	184.5
1979	11.6	2.8	0.2	0.2	0.3	0.4	0.6	1.4	4.3	10.2	25.6	70.8	187.1
1980	11.4	2.7	0.2	0.2	0.3	0.4	0.5	1.3	4.0	10.0	25.0	67.7	181.3
1981	11.6	2.5	0.2	0.2	0.3	0.4	0.5	1.3	3.9	10.0	25.5	70.4	190.6
1982	11.5	2.3	0.2	0.2	0.3	0.4	0.5	1.2	3.8	9.9	24.8	66.8	179.4

1. 1973 to 1980 incorporates the revised England and Wales figures, but old series Scotland and Northern Ireland.

Sources Office of Population Censuses and Surveys; General Register Office (Scotland); General Register Office (Northern Ireland)

2.23 Life tables[1]

United Kingdom / England and Wales

Age x	United Kingdom Interim Life Table, 1978–80 Males l_x	e^o_x	Females l_x	e^o_x	England and Wales Interim Life Table, 1981–83 Males l_x	e^o_x	Females l_x	e^o_x
0	100 000	70.2	100 000	76.2	100 000	71.3	100 000	77.2
5	98 364	66.3	98 689	72.2	98 598	67.3	98 913	73.0
10	98 208	61.4	98 583	67.3	98 469	62.4	98 821	68.1
15	98 065	56.5	98 482	62.4	98 332	57.5	98 727	63.2
20	97 635	51.8	98 315	57.5	97 950	52.7	98 575	58.3
25	97 179	47.0	98 125	52.6	97 541	47.9	98 409	53.4
30	96 743	42.2	97 888	47.7	97 136	43.1	98 202	48.5
35	96 250	37.4	97 574	42.9	96 673	38.3	97 913	43.6
40	95 507	32.7	97 060	38.1	96 036	33.5	97 463	38.8
45	94 288	28.1	96 200	33.4	94 930	28.9	96 710	34.1
50	92 074	23.7	94 748	28.9	92 955	24.4	95 404	29.5
55	88 132	19.6	92 322	24.5	89 500	20.3	93 243	25.1
60	81 877	15.9	88 727	20.4	83 625	16.5	89 824	21.0
65	72 503	12.6	83 324	16.6	74 777	13.1	84 651	17.1
70	59 670	9.7	75 514	13.0	62 471	10.2	77 202	13.5
75	43 556	7.4	64 180	9.8	46 697	7.8	66 297	10.3
80	26 456	5.6	48 520	7.2	29 566	5.8	51 216	7.5
85	12 540	4.1	29 878	5.1	14 554	4.4	32 535	5.4

Scotland / Northern Ireland

Age x	Scotland Interim Life Table, 1981–83 Males l_x	e^o_x	Females l_x	e^o_x	Northern Ireland Interim Life Table, 1981–83 Males l_x	e^o_x	Females l_x	e^o_x
0	10 000	69.3	10 000	75.5	100 000	70.0	100 000	76.0
5	9 858	65.3	9 890	71.3	98 259	66.2	98 670	72.0
10	9 842	60.4	9 879	66.4	98 119	61.3	98 548	67.1
15	9 827	55.5	9 869	61.4	97 956	56.4	98 470	62.1
20	9 784	50.7	9 854	56.5	97 508	51.7	98 318	57.2
25	9 735	46.0	9 838	51.6	96 901	47.0	98 097	52.3
30	9 682	41.2	9 816	46.7	96 355	42.2	97 841	47.5
35	9 623	36.5	9 781	41.9	95 692	37.5	97 519	42.6
40	9 536	31.8	9 726	37.1	94 936	32.8	97 074	37.8
45	9 380	27.2	9 630	32.5	93 598	28.2	96 272	33.1
50	9 114	23.0	9 471	28.0	91 427	23.8	94 914	28.5
55	8 670	19.0	9 195	23.7	87 488	19.7	92 554	24.2
60	7 954	15.5	8 770	19.8	81 152	16.1	88 595	20.1
65	6 962	12.4	8 158	16.1	71 667	12.9	83 052	16.3
70	5 649	9.6	7 250	12.8	59 096	10.1	75 122	12.7
75	4 079	7.4	6 035	9.8	43 866	7.7	63 355	9.6
80	2 464	5.6	4 507	7.3	27 043	5.9	46 804	7.1
85	1 126	4.3	2 752	5.3	13 244	4.5	27 813	5.2

1. Column l_x shows the number who would survive to exact age x, out of 100 000 or 10 000 born, who were subject throughout their lives to the death rates experienced in the three year period indicated.
Column e^o_x is 'the expectation of life', that is, the average future lifetime which would be lived by a person aged exactly x if likewise subject to the death rates experienced in the three year period indicated. (See introductory note on page 5.)

Sources Government Actuary's Department; General Register Office (Scotland)

3 Social Conditions

Government expenditure on social services and housing

The following tables of general government expenditure on the social services and housing in the United Kingdom comprise a summary table followed by separate tables for each of the social services and housing. The definition of government expenditure used in these tables follows that in Table 9.4 of *United Kingdom National Accounts 1984 Edition,* the CSO Blue Book, and covers both current and capital expenditure of the central government (including the National Insurance Fund) and local authorities. The housing table also includes the capital expenditure of public corporations concerned with housing. As in the Blue Book government expenditure is measured after deducting fees and charges for services. Expenditure on administration includes the cost of common services (accommodation, stationery and printing, superannuation, etc.) some of which is not directly borne by the departments administering each service. Transfers from one part of government to another have been eliminated to avoid double counting. The figures relate to years ended 31 March. Figures for the latest two years are the most recent estimates available and are subject to revision.

It should be noted that the figures no longer include imputed rents for the use of fixed assets owned and used by general government. In the Blue Book imputed rents have been replaced by capital consumption. Capital consumption, however, cannot be allocated to individual services and is therefore not included in these tables.

The following notes give brief descriptions of each of the main services shown in the tables.

Education

This covers expenditure by the Education Departments, local education authorities and the University Grants Committee on education in schools, training colleges, technical institutions and universities. It includes expenditure on school meals and milk.

The education statistics in Table 3.2 are provided by the Department of Education and Science. They are not normally able to provide a full set of estimates, from their sources, for the latest two financial years. The CSO has in the past made estimates for these years from a variety of sources but, following a review of the accuracy of these estimates, it has been decided that they do not give a reliable guide to the final outcome and have therefore been withdrawn.

National health service

This covers expenditure by central government on hospital and community health, family practitioner and other health services. The expenditure by local authorities on the provision of health centres, health visiting, home nursing, ambulance services, vaccination and immunisation, etc., was transferred to central government on 1 April 1974. Only the net costs of providing these services are included in total government expenditure, receipts from patients being shown separately.

Personal social services

This covers local authority expenditure on the aged, handicapped and homeless, child care, care of mothers and young children, mental health, domestic help, etc. Also included are central government grants to voluntary approved schools.

Welfare foods

This covers the cost of providing welfare foods at reduced prices to children and expectant mothers. Only the net costs of providing these services are included in the total government expenditure, payments by the recipients of the services being shown separately.

Social security benefits

This is entirely central government expenditure and comprises both benefits under the national insurance schemes and non-contributory benefits and allowances, administered by the Department of Health and Social Security. The analysis by type of supplementary benefit is not exact; the estimates are derived from average numbers in receipt of benefit and average amounts paid.

Housing

The table shows, in addition to government expenditure on housing, the capital expenditure of public corporations and the total expenditure of the public sector on housing. The government expenditure figures cover subsidies paid by the Housing Departments towards the provision of housing by local authorities, new town development corporations and housing associations; subsidies by local authorities to their housing revenue accounts; rent rebates for tenants of housing owned by local authorities and new towns; rent allowances for tenants of privately-owned housing; grants to persons for the reduction of mortgage interest payments; capital expenditure on the provision of houses for letting; capital grants to housing associations; grants by local authorities towards the cost of conversion and improvement of privately-owned houses; net lending by the central government and local authorities for private house purchase and improvement and loans for first time purchases. The public corporations' figures cover capital expenditure on the provision of houses for letting and lending by the Housing Corporation to housing associations.

Social Security

Tables 3.12 to 3.16, 3.20 to 3.28 give details of contributors and beneficiaries under the National Insurance and Industrial Injury Acts, supplementary benefits and war pensions.

There are three types of contributor:

Class 1   Employed persons, that is, persons working for employers. Their contributions are paid partly by themselves and partly by their employers. They are covered for all benefits.

Class 2   Self-employed persons, that is, persons working on their own account. They are covered for all benefits other than unemployment and industrial injuries.

Class 3   Non-employed persons, that is, persons who do not work for gain. They are covered for benefits other than unemployment, sickness, industrial injuries and maternity allowances.

Class 4   Payable, in addition to Class 2 by self-employed persons, and the amount payable is proportionate to profits or gains in any one year.

An employer must pay a contribution for every employee whose earnings exceed a base level. Most employed persons pay the full employee's contribution, but retirement pensioners working for an employer do not and some married women and some widows who are working need not, unless they so wish, contribute except for industrial injuries benefit. Thus the total numbers in the analysis by benefit for which the contributions were payable are less than the total numbers in the analysis by class of contributor.

Sickness benefit (Tables 3.17 to 3.19)

The population at risk for sickness benefit is the working population apart from men over age 65 and women over age 60 who are retirement pensioners and all men over 70 and women over 65, members of the Armed Forces, mariners while at sea, most non-industrial civil servants and Post Office employees (who do not normally claim sickness benefit until an illness has lasted six months) and married women and certain widows who have chosen not to be insured for sickness benefit (about three-quarters of all married women in employment have chosen not to pay flat-rate contributions).

(continued on page 43)

Fatal injuries at work (Table 3.36)
Under new reporting regulations introduced on 1 January 1981, most fatal injuries at or resulting from work activities are reported to HSC enforcement authorities. It is thought that the 1981 figures are more comprehensive than earlier statistics, particularly for those sectors not formally covered by previous reporting requirements i.e. 'new entrants' which prior to 1981 were reported on a voluntary basis. The total is therefore not comparable with earlier years and includes injuries to members of the public and the self-employed as well as employees.

3.1 Summary of government expenditure on social services and housing
Years ended 31 March

£ million

	1973/74	1974/75	1975/76	1976/77	1977/78	1978/79	1979/80	1980/81	1981/82	1982/83	1983/84
Education[1]	4 236	5 528	7 021	7 852	8 281	9 123	10 511	12 855	13 905	14 857	..
National health service	3 055	4 095	5 470	6 249	6 896	7 835	9 195	11 944	13 267	14 437	15 376
Personal social services	565	782	1 095	1 264	1 375	1 575	1 972	2 468	2 673	2 945	3 164
Welfare foods	11	9	15	19	23	27	29	35	52	70	86
Social security benefits	5 723	7 171	9 749	11 575	13 844	16 474	19 444	23 508	28 905	32 391	33 991
Housing	2 620	4 480	4 694	5 194	5 090	5 429	6 658	7 025	5 196	5 652	6 977
Total government expenditure	16 210	22 065	28 044	32 153	35 509	40 463	47 809	57 835	63 998	70 352	..
Current expenditure	13 271	17 739	23 651	27 672	31 455	36 357	43 002	52 842	60 106	66 183	..
Capital expenditure	2 939	4 326	4 393	4 481	4 054	4 106	4 807	4 993	3 892	4 169	..
Total government expenditure	16 210	22 065	28 044	32 153	35 509	40 463	47 809	57 835	63 998	70 352	..
Central government	10 070	13 531	18 001	21 523	24 577	28 601	33 767	41 601	47 518	52 536	..
Local authorities	6 140	8 534	10 043	10 630	10 932	11 862	14 042	16 234	16 480	17 816	..
Total government expenditure	16 210	22 065	28 044	32 153	35 509	40 463	47 809	57 835	63 998	70 352	..

1. Includes school meals and milk

Source Central Statistical Office

3.2 Government expenditure on education
Years ended 31 March

£ million

	1972/73	1973/74	1974/75	1975/76	1976/77	1977/78	1978/79	1979/80	1980/81	1981/82	1982/83[3]
Current expenditure											
Nursery schools	10	12	18	25	31	30	33	43	52	57	63
Primary schools	747	840	1 201	1 536	1 711	1 833	2 030	2 321	2 840	3 093	3 255
Secondary schools	866	1 009	1 451	1 873	2 126	2 320	2 609	2 956	3 695	4 143	4 435
Special schools	83	98	139	187	221	248	296	350	443	500	543
Further and adult education[1]	369	416	580	753	926	1 020	1 112	1 301	1 591	1 812	1 987
Training of teachers: tuition	80	89	116	126	58	58	56	64	78	83	93
Universities[1]	348	390	464	578	681	724	826	981	1 264	1 277	1 322
Other education expenditure	130	151	208	270	307	330	347	405	516	553	599
Related current expenditure:											
Training of teachers: residence	22	25	30	31	10	9	9	12	15	15	18
School health[2]	43	48	5	9	10	11	13	16	20	23	27
Meals and milk	151	203	297	383	455	434	467	508	479	480	499
Youth service and physical training	33	40	51	72	80	87	102	121	148	169	192
Maintenance grants and allowances to pupils and students	156	166	206	284	336	364	436	520	630	702	759
Transport of pupils	48	55	70	100	117	131	155	181	215	234	253
Miscellaneous expenditure	2	6	–	–	–	–	2	2	2	3	3	4
Selective employment tax	41	–	–	–	–	–	–	–	–	–	–
Value added tax paid by local authorities	–	29	56	65	66	71	69	106	105	110	125
Total current expenditure	3 128	3 578	4 892	6 293	7 135	7 672	8 562	9 887	12 094	13 254	14 174
Capital expenditure											
Nursery schools	2	3	3	12	11	6	5	6	6	4	4
Primary schools	154	191	168	175	168	124	118	132	174	136	128
Secondary schools	215	248	249	268	268	263	238	235	274	233	239
Special schools	15	21	24	35	35	23	15	18	26	22	21
Further and adult education	63	68	70	85	89	80	74	93	129	108	139
Training of teachers	10	10	9	6	3	1	1	3	2	2	3
Universities	87	82	82	106	104	78	84	106	117	117	116
Other education expenditure	4	4	3	3	2	3	5	7	10	10	13
Related capital expenditure	30	32	27	37	37	31	21	24	23	19	20
Total capital expenditure	580	658	636	728	717	609	561	624	761	651	683
Total expenditure											
Central government	605	670	781	980	1 099	1 058	1 161	1 394	1 779	1 797	1 955
Local authorities	3 103	3 566	4 747	6 041	6 753	7 223	7 962	9 117	11 076	12 108	12 902
Total government expenditure	3 708	4 236	5 528	7 021	7 852	8 281	9 123	10 511	12 855	13 905	14 857
Gross domestic product at market prices	66 620	74 836	89 364	112 171	130 783	151 451	172 518	206 419	237 373	259 803	283 855
Expenditure as a percentage of GDP	5.6	5.7	6.2	6.3	6.0	5.5	5.3	5.1	5.4	5.4	5.2

1. Including tuition fees.
2. From 1 April 1974 expenditure on the school health service is included in the national health service.
3. Provisional.

Sources Department of Education and Science; Central Statistical Office

3.3 Government expenditure on the national health service
Years ended 31 March

£ million

	1973/74	1974/75	1975/76	1976/77	1977/78	1978/79	1979/80	1980/81	1981/82	1982/83	1983/84[5]
Current expenditure											
Central government:											
Hospitals and Community health services[1]:											
Running expenses[2]	1 774	2 662	3 687	4 182	4 662	5 241	6 168	8 162	9 033	9 700	10 305
Family practitioner services:											
General medical services	228	265	341	384	406	463	570	754	866	973	1 055
Pharmaceutical services[2]	313	440	485	618	745	880	986	1 213	1 394	1 599	1 769
General dental services[2]	147	204	239	265	273	330	400	494	562	629	692
General ophthalmic services[2]	35	51	76	79	80	90	107	123	148	238	192
Administration	86	157	211	245	266	297	365	450	474	488	513
less Payments by patients:											
Hospital services	− 19	− 20	− 25	− 32	− 33	− 34	− 42	− 57	− 69	− 72	− 77
Pharmaceutical services	− 29	− 32	− 27	− 27	− 27	− 28	− 49	− 88	− 107	− 125	− 136
Dental services	− 34	− 39	− 37	− 47	− 61	− 65	− 78	− 106	− 132	− 163	− 192
Ophthalmic services	− 18	− 21	− 21	− 26	− 27	− 30	− 33	− 34	− 38	− 45	− 59
Total	− 100	− 112	− 110	− 132	− 148	− 157	− 202	− 285	− 346	− 405	− 464
Departmental administration	36	43	54	62	68	71	88	109	121	130	144
Other services	52	83	82	123	134	154	191	236	183	206	226
Local authority health services[3]:											
Running expenses[4]	188	–	–	–	–	–	–	–	–	–	–
Total current expenditure	2 759	3 793	5 065	5 826	6 486	7 369	8 673	11 256	12 435	13 558	14 432
Capital expenditure											
Central government	271	302	405	423	410	466	522	688	832	879	944
Local authorities[3]	25	–	–	–	–	–	–	–	–	–	–
Total capital expenditure	296	302	405	423	410	466	522	688	832	879	944
Total expenditure											
Central government	2 842	4 095	5 470	6 249	6 896	7 835	9 195	11 944	13 267	14 437	15 376
Local authorities[3]	213	–	–	–	–	–	–	–	–	–	–
Total government expenditure	3 055	4 095	5 470	6 249	6 896	7 835	9 195	11 944	13 267	14 437	15 376

1. Including the school health service from 1 April 1974, previously included in education.
2. Before deducting payments by patients.
3. On 1 April 1974 Local authority health services became the responsibility of Central government, and from that date are included under the heading Community health services.
4. After deducting payments by patients.
5. Provisional.

Source Central Statistical Office

3.4 Government expenditure on welfare services[1]
Years ended 31 March

£ million

	1973/74	1974/75	1975/76	1976/77	1977/78	1978/79	1979/80	1980/81	1981/82	1982/83	1983/84
Personal social services											
Central government current expenditure	19	30	49	61	69	67	90	112	99	102	108
Local authorities current expenditure:											
Running expenses	449	644	919	1 081	1 206	1 388	1 701	2 092	2 327	2 566	2 787
Value added tax paid by local authorities	14	20	25	28	28	38	79	141	136	165	164
Capital expenditure	83	88	102	94	72	82	102	123	111	112	105
Total	565	782	1 095	1 264	1 375	1 575	1 972	2 468	2 673	2 945	3 164
Welfare foods service											
Central government current expenditure on welfare foods (including administration)	12	10	16	19	23	27	29	35	52	70	86
less Receipts from the public	−1	−1	−1	–	–	–	–	–	–	–	–
Total	11	9	15	19	23	27	29	35	52	70	86

1. School meals and milk is included in Table 3.2.

Source Central Statistical Office

3.5 Government expenditure on social security benefits
Years ended 31 March

£ million

	1973/74	1974/75	1975/76	1976/77	1977/78	1978/79	1979/80	1980/81	1981/82	1982/83	1983/84
Central government current expenditure											
National insurance:											
Retirement pensions	2 815	3 661	4 898	5 777	6 739	7 736	9 008	10 773	12 392	13 845	14 716
Lump sums to pensioners	79	90	–	–	–	–	98	100	103	105	106
Widows' benefits and guardians' allowances	254	323	409	451	485	525	585	663	718	753	801
Unemployment benefit	182	227	473	582	655	659	681	1 328	1 758	1 550	1 540
Sickness benefit	325	372	460	538	636	688	657	651	671	537	338
Invalidity benefit	255	339	475	596	740	892	1 048	1 212	1 441	1 673	1 926
Maternity benefit	44	48	57	84	96	126	146	172	181	157	173
Death grant	14	14	15	15	16	16	16	17	17	17	18
Injury benefit	35	36	40	47	51	53	48	47	45	48	–
Disablement benefit	92	116	152	175	200	226	255	294	329	359	383
Industrial death benefit	14	18	23	26	30	33	37	43	48	52	56
Statutory sick pay	–	–	–	–	–	–	–	–	–	–	505
War pensions	164	204	258	283	310	341	375	424	479	504	533
Family benefits:											
Child benefit	359	359	554	567	906	1 869	2 931	3 052	3 497	3 796	4 159
One parent benefit	–	–	–	–	–	–	–	63	78	93	110
Family income supplement	14	14	14	20	28	27	31	48	73	103	136
Maternity grants	–	–	–	–	–	–	–	–	–	15	19
Supplementary benefits:											
Old persons	284	318	407	486	567	694	760	930	1 454	1 487	755
Unemployed persons	150	200	388	578	729	755	770	1 182	2 091	3 422	3 468
Sick persons	96	118	131	133	158	167	197	227	393	445	450
Other persons in need	185	237	308	389	472	491	529	644	1 145	1 145	1 261
Other non-contributory benefits:											
Old persons' pensions	29	32	36	38	38	40	38	41	42	43	42
Lump sums to pensioners	3	3	–	–	98	101	6	5	5	5	6
Attendance allowance	38	66	102	134	151	178	215	257	348	435	515
Invalid care allowance	–	–	–	2	3	4	5	6	7	9	11
Mobility allowance	–	–	–	9	21	48	81	128	177	241	309
Invalidity pension	–	–	12	37	48	75	91	105	134	167	189
Administration	292	376	537	608	667	730	836	1 096	1 279	1 385	1 466
Total government expenditure	5 723	7 171	9 749	11 575	13 844	16 474	19 444	23 508	28 905	32 391	33 991

Source Central Statistical Office

3.6 Government and other public sector expenditure on housing
Years ended 31 March

£ million

	1973/74	1974/75	1975/76	1976/77	1977/78	1978/79	1979/80	1980/81	1981/82	1982/83	1983/84
Government expenditure											
Current expenditure											
Central government											
housing subsidies:											
to local authorities	299	579	749	987	1 025	1 207	1 533	1 689	1 065	567	474
to public corporations	40	62	112	156	203	233	287	310	320	296	275
to housing associations	4	7	11	15	17	23	24	29	40	50	120
Local authorities											
housing subsidies	89	177	217	185	188	267	413	537	553	582	651
Grants under rent rebate scheme	173	213	249	319	378	389	440	547	493	1 087	1 837
Grants under rent allowance scheme	26	36	43	73	79	90	98	108	61	85	510
Grants under the option mortgage scheme	51	75	109	140	152	141	181	222	254	299	–
Other grants for mortgage interest relief	16	–	–	–	–	–	–	–	–	–	
Administration, etc.	20	31	46	72	85	82	123	162	112	191	298
Total current expenditure	718	1 180	1 536	1 947	2 127	2 432	3 099	3 604	2 898	3 157	4 165
Capital expenditure											
Investment in housing by local authorities	1 144	1 879	2 114	2 156	1 938	1 724	1 789	1 445	314	60	664
Capital grants to housing associations	1	1	135	422	539	614	577	579	586	718	1 170
Improvement grants	164	176	79	76	80	99	144	177	239	483	1 017
Net lending for house purchase	356	824	290	52	– 42	54	398	282	484	257	– 242
Capital grants to public corporations	1	–	3	3	4	3	8	15	14	17	23
Net lending to public corporations	236	420	537	538	444	503	643	923	661	960	180
Total capital expenditure	1 902	3 300	3 158	3 247	2 963	2 997	3 559	3 421	2 298	2 495	2 812
Total expenditure											
Central government	802	1 440	1 729	2 509	2 676	3 028	3 607	4 216	3 398	3 581	2 272
Local authorities	1 818	3 040	2 965	2 685	2 414	2 401	3 051	2 809	1 798	2 071	4 705
Total government expenditure	2 620	4 480	4 694	5 194	5 090	5 429	6 658	7 025	5 196	5 652	6 977
Public corporations' capital expenditure											
Investment in housing	134	187	312	353	293	241	276	283	215	227	227
Net lending to private sector	52	133	111	53	8	21	113	340	355	364	19
Total	186	320	423	406	301	262	389	623	570	591	246
Total public sector expenditure[1]	2 569	4 380	4 577	5 059	4 943	5 185	6 396	6 710	5 091	5 266	7 020

1. Total government expenditure *less* grants and loans to public corporations
plus public corporations' capital expenditure.

Source Central Statistical Office

3.7 Stock of dwellings
Great Britain

	1973	1974	1975	1976	1977	1978	1979	1980	1981	1982	1983
Estimated annual gains and losses (Thousands)											
Gains: New construction	294.1	269.5	313.0	315.2	303.3	279.8	242.1	233.0	197.4	170.6	189.4
Other	12.2	11.8	10.2	9.4	8.8	11.7	12.4	11.5	8.7	9.7	15.2
Losses: Slum clearance	83.3	55.1	61.8	55.8	49.2	39.1	36.3	31.8	35.4	28.5	20.0
Other	20.4	14.0	18.0	15.0	12.2	11.0	11.0	8.8	13.4	13.2	9.3
Net gain	202.6	212.2	243.4	253.8	250.7	241.4	207.2	203.9	157.3	138.6	175.3
Stock at end of year [1]	19 415	19 627	19 870	20 124	20 374	20 615	20 822	21 025	21 178	21 317	21 494
Estimated tenure distribution at end of year (percentage)											
Owner occupied	52.3	52.7	53.0	53.3	53.6	54.1	54.6	55.4	57.4	58.9	60.2
Rented: From local authorities and new towns	30.5	30.8	31.3	31.7	31.9	32.0	31.9	31.6	30.3	29.2	28.4
From Housing associations [2]	17.2	16.5	15.7	15.0	14.5	13.9	13.5	13.0	2.1	2.2	2.3
From private owners including other tenures									10.1	9.6	9.1

Note: For statistical purposes the stock estimates are expressed to the nearest thousand, but should not be regarded as accurate to the last digit.
1. Figures from 1981 to 1983 are estimates based on 1981 census data and are not strictly comparable with the earlier figures which are based on the 1971 census.

2. Prior to April 1981, separate estimates for housing associations were not available but were included with those for 'Rented from private owners including other tenures'.

Sources Department of the Enviroment; Welsh Office; Scottish Development Department

3.8 Renovations
Great Britain

Number of dwellings

	1973	1974	1975	1976	1977	1978	1979	1980	1981	1982	1983 [5]
England											
Local authorities and new towns [1]	110 053	73 494	36 163	38 983	37 551	60 871	75 967	77 275	52 931	57 722	85 953
Housing associations [2]	3 201	3 952	4 603	13 388	18 789	13 056	17 173	14 832	11 288	17 286	13 854
Private owners: grants paid [3]	165 958	192 348	85 393	68 718	56 955	57 578	65 359	74 465	68 941	104 028	230 218
All	279 212	269 794	126 159	121 089	113 295	131 505	158 499	166 572	133 160	179 036	330 025
Wales											
Local authorities [4]	7 874	3 820	943	18	..	..	218	..	..	..	..
Housing associations [2]	18	21	14	–	511	237	218	252	694	1 009	1 235
Private owners: grants paid [3]	18 248	24 728	7 336	6 568	7 017	5 931	6 119	7 342	7 100	10 989	27 451
All	26 140	28 569	8 293	6 586	7 528	6 168	6 337	7 594	7 794	11 998	28 686
Scotland											
Local authorities and new towns [4]	70 147	43 814	24 734	35 760	56 402	44 770	34 838	22 282	26 065	50 027	37 954
Housing associations [2]	132	159	461	156	330	1 447	2 703	2 787	1 833	2 717	..
Private owners: grants paid [3]	15 437	28 713	9 424	7 206	7 051	6 840	8 719	13 420	18 036	23 839	41 631
All	85 716	72 686	34 619	43 122	63 783	53 057	46 260	38 489	45 934	76 583	..
Great Britain											
Local authorities and new towns [1, 4]	188 074	121 128	61 840	74 761	93 953	105 641	110 805	99 557	78 996	107 749	123 907
Housing associations [2]	3 351	4 132	5 078	13 544	19 630	14 740	20 094	17 871	13 815	21 012	..
Private owners: grants paid [3]	199 643	245 789	102 153	82 492	71 023	70 349	80 197	95 227	94 077	138 856	299 300
All	391 068	371 049	169 071	170 797	184 606	190 730	211 096	212 655	186 888	267 617	..

1. Work approved up to 1977: work completed from 1978 onwards. Figures for new towns are not available from 1st quarter 1978 to 1st quarter 1980 inclusive. From 1981 including improvement for sale.
2. Work approved under specific housing association legislation. Figures for England and Wales are of work completed from 1978 onwards.
3. Including grants paid to housing associations under private owner grant legislation. Figures from 4th quarter 1980 include a small number of grants to

both private and public tenants.
4. Work approved in Wales and Scotland. Figures of Welsh housing revenue account dwelling renovations are not available from 1976 onwards.
5. Provisional.

Sources Department of the Environment; Welsh Office; Scottish Development Department

3.9 Slum clearance: dwellings demolished or closed

Number

	1972	1973	1974	1975	1976	1977	1978	1979	1980/81	1981/82	1982/83 [5]
England and Wales: total [1]	70 234	66 786	43 513	51 127	48 964	43 465	34 835	30 426	29 547	24 652	17 221
Demolished: In clearance areas	55 956	54 674	37 871	41 772	38 581	34 134	26 670	23 747	22 971	20 143	14 470
Elsewhere	7 458	6 406	2 689	3 939	4 482	3 361	2 614	2 472	3 572	2 503	1 933
Closed [2]	6 820	5 706	2 953	5 416	5 901	5 970	5 551	4 207	3 004	2 006	818
Scotland [3]: total	18 518	16 479	11 615	10 658	6 881	5 763	4 307	5 573	5 814	4 969	3 698
Unfit [4]	16 151	14 872	10 271	9 964	5 524	5 047	3 739	4 001	4 017	2 704	2 506
Other [2]	2 367	1 607	1 344	694	1 357	716	568	1 572	1 797	2 265	1 192

1. From 1980/81 slum clearance statistics for England are collected on a financial year basis.
2. Excluding dwellings previously reported closed.
3. Action under the Housing Acts, Town and Country Planning Acts and other specific statutory powers and other action. Unfit houses comprise houses dealt with since 25 August 1969 as failing to meet the tolerable standard

introduced by the Housing (Scotland) Act 1969 and houses dealt with under earlier statutory provisions as being unfit for human habitation.
4. Figures from 1979 are for below tolerable standard.
5. Provisional.

Sources Department of the Environment; Welsh Office; Scottish Development Department

3.10 Permanent dwellings completed

Number

	United Kingdom				England and Wales			
	Total	For local housing authorities[1]	For private owners	Other[2]	Total	For local housing authorities[1]	For private owners	Other[2]
1963	307 714	123 903	177 787	6 024	270 655	97 015	168 242	5 398
1964	383 192	154 754	221 264	7 174	336 505	119 468	210 432	6 605
1965	391 234	164 957	217 162	9 115	347 181	133 024	206 246	7 911
1966	396 009	176 871	208 647	10 491	349 480	142 430	197 502	9 548
1967	415 455	199 749	204 208	11 498	362 898	159 347	192 940	10 611
1968	425 835	187 984	226 068	11 783	371 726	148 049	213 273	10 404
1969	378 324	180 958	185 916	11 450	324 165	139 850	173 377	10 938
1970	362 226	176 926	174 342	10 958	307 266	134 874	162 084	10 308
1971	364 475	154 894	196 313	13 268	309 776	117 215	179 998	12 563
1972	330 936	120 431	200 755	9 750	287 294	93 635	184 622	9 037
1973	304 637	102 604	191 080	10 953	264 047	79 289	174 413	10 345
1974	279 582	121 017	145 177	13 388	241 173	99 423	129 626	12 124
1975	321 936	150 526	154 528	16 882	278 694	122 857	140 381	15 456
1976	324 769	151 824	155 229	17 716	278 660	124 152	138 477	16 031
1977	314 093	143 250	143 905	26 938	276 011	121 246	128 688	26 077
1978	288 603	112 340	152 166	24 097	254 001	96 752	134 578	22 671
1979	251 805	88 485	144 055	19 265	220 722	77 192	125 306	18 224
1980	240 364	88 229	130 571	21 564	213 273	78 261	114 761	20 251
1981	204 126	68 143	116 381	19 602	177 354	58 219	101 803	17 332
1982	176 629	39 828	123 781	13 020	154 123	33 298	109 577	11 248
1983	197 531	38 902	142 979	15 650	171 591	31 409	126 370	13 812

	Scotland				Northern Ireland			
	Total	For local housing authorities[1]	For private owners	Other[2]	Total	For local housing authorities[1]	For private owners	Other[2]
1963	28 217	21 164	6 622	431	8 842	5 724	2 923	195
1964	37 171	29 156	7 662	353	9 516	6 130	3 170	216
1965	35 116	26 584	7 553	979	8 937	5 349	3 363	225
1966	36 029	27 515	7 870	644	10 500	6 926	3 275	299
1967	41 458	33 222	7 498	738	11 099	7 180	3 770	149
1968	41 989	32 011	8 720	1 258	12 120	7 924	4 075	121
1969	42 628	33 932	8 326	370	11 531	7 176	4 213	142
1970	43 126	34 360	8 220	546	11 834	7 692	4 038	104
1971	40 783	28 577	11 614	592	13 916	9 102	4 701	113
1972	31 992	19 593	11 835	564	11 650	7 203	4 298	149
1973	30 033	17 349	12 215	469	10 557	5 966	4 452	139
1974	28 336	16 182	11 239	915	10 073	5 412	4 312	349
1975	34 323	22 784	10 371	1 168	8 919	4 885	3 776	258
1976	36 527	21 154	13 704	1 669	9 582	6 518	3 048	16
1977	27 320	14 328	12 132	860	10 762	7 676	3 085	1
1978	25 759	9 907	14 443	1 409	8 843	5 681	3 145	17
1979	23 782	7 857	15 175	750	7 301	3 436	3 574	291
1980	20 611	7 455	12 242	914	6 480	2 513	3 568	399
1981	20 015	7 065	11 021	1 929	6 757	2 859	3 557	341
1982	16 432	3 716	11 532	1 184	6 074	2 814	2 672	588
1983	17 765	3 449	13 039	1 277	8 175	4 044	3 570	561

1. Including the Commission for the New Towns and new towns development corporations, the Scottish Special Housing Association, the Northern Ireland Housing Trust and the Northern Ireland Housing Executive.
2. Dwellings provided or authorised by government departments for the families of police, prison staffs, the armed forces and certain other services. Including housing associations other than the Scottish Special Housing Association and the Northern Ireland Housing Trust.

Sources   Department of the Environment; Welsh Office; Scottish Development Department; Department of the Environment (Northern Ireland)

3.11 National Insurance Fund
Years ended 31 March

£ thousand

	1975/76	1976/77	1977/78	1978/79	1979/80	1980/81	1981/82	1982/83
Receipts								
Total	9 629 362	11 886 250	13 944 796	15 584 802	17 790 825	21 200 352	22 726 368	24 103 243
Opening balance	1 947 516	2 278 663	3 237 234	3 927 423	4 197 180	4 752 533	5 177 647	4 194 593
Contributions	6 326 712	7 902 009	8 742 376	9 187 766	10 643 821	12 813 167	14 354 078	16 663 862
Consolidated Fund supplement	1 157 789	1 416 709	1 569 251	2 016 974	2 394 600	2 906 900	2 490 200	2 642 891
Income from investments	197 141	288 557	395 582	452 400	554 940	628 004	608 233	514 038
Other receipts	204	312	353	239	284	99 748	96 210	87 859
Expenditure								
Total	7 350 699	8 649 016	10 017 373	11 387 622	13 038 292	16 022 705	18 531 775	19 938 638
Total benefits	6 977 042	8 263 053	9 612 366	10 940 284	12 534 704	15 263 350	17 676 334	19 073 084
Unemployment	472 911	581 977	654 962	659 960	680 622	1 328 374	1 758 436	1 550 329
Sickness	440 439	514 049	606 449	655 222	617 064	618 416	643 782	514 251
Invalidity	475 013	595 641	740 308	892 508	1 048 343	1 211 978	1 441 266	1 672 580
Maternity	57 150	84 160	95 820	125 700	146 300	172 400	180 600	157 100
Widows' pensions	406 800	448 800	482 750	523 100	582 700	660 700	715 700	751 204
Guardians' allowances[1]	1 810 }	2 340	2 230	2 010	2 010	2 330	2 340	2 240
Child's special allowance	300 }							
Retirement pensions	4 892 274	5 772 847	6 733 047	7 754 282	9 003 744	10 767 868	12 387 182	13 844 825
Death grants	15 428	15 347	15 554	16 330	16 462	16 641	17 245	17 335
Injury	39 970	46 715	51 552	52 620	47 497	46 869	49 173	47 564
Disablement	147 761	171 022	195 524	221 132	250 279	289 173	323 517	353 326
Death	23 020	26 130	29 720	32 820	36 930	43 120	48 280	52 430
Pensioners' lump sum payments					97 953	100 381	103 413	104 500
Other benefits	4 166	4 025	4 450	4 600	4 800	5 100	5 400	5 400
Payments in lieu of benefits foregone[2]	19 157	23 753	29 615	32 749	39 946	32 312	26 223	31 176
Other payments	5 736	4 521	6 646	6 053	4 457	4 629	391	287
Administration	348 764	357 689	368 746	408 536	459 185	622 976	732 927	749 321
Transfers to Northern Ireland						99 438	95 900	84 770
Accumulated funds	2 278 663	3 237 234	3 927 423	4 197 180	4 752 533	5 177 647	4 194 593	4 164 605

1. Including figures of Child's special allowance for Northern Ireland.
2. Payments to the Post Office Consolidated and Trading Funds.

Sources Department of Health and Social Security; Department of Health and
Social Services (Northern Ireland)

3.12 National Insurance Acts: persons for whom contributions were payable
Persons who paid contributions in a tax year ending April[1]

Millions

	Total			Men			Married women			Single, widowed and divorced women		
	1980	1981	1982[4]	1980	1981	1982[4]	1980	1981	1982[4]	1980	1981	1982[4]
Total[2]	25.89	25.00	23.42	16.14	15.63	14.56	6.31	5.99	5.64	3.44	3.39	3.22
Class 1 Standard rate	20.71	20.32	19.46	14.56	14.08	13.27	2.98	3.12	3.19	3.17	3.13	3.01
Contracted in	10.30	10.02	9.53	6.65	6.35	5.88	1.76	1.85	1.91	1.89	1.82	1.74
Contracted out	8.95	9.13	9.01	6.92	6.95	6.79	1.02	1.10	1.13	1.02	1.09	1.09
Mixed contracted in/out	1.46	1.17	0.93	0.99	0.77	0.60	0.20	0.17	0.15	0.26	0.22	0.18
Class 1 Reduced rate	3.46	2.98	2.50				3.27	2.80	2.35	0.19	0.18	0.15
Mixed Class 1 Standard and Reduced rate	0.02	0.02	0.06				0.01	0.01	0.01	0.05	0.01	0.01
Class 2	1.38	1.40	1.18	1.30	1.31	1.10	0.04	0.05	0.04	0.04	0.04	0.04
Mixed Class 1 and Class 2	0.23	0.20	0.16	0.21	0.18	0.14	0.01	0.01	0.01	0.01	0.01	0.01
Class 3[3]	0.09	0.08	0.06	0.07	0.06	0.05	0.01	0.01	0.01	0.02	0.01	0.01

1. The tax year commences on 6 April and ends on 5 April of the year
following. The years shown at the head of the column refer to the end of
the tax year. Persons who paid any contributions at any time in the tax year
are shown.
2. Not all figures agree because of rounding.

3. Persons who paid a mixture of Class 3 contributions and others are not
included in 'Class 3' but are shown according to the type of the additional
contribution.
4. Provisional.

Source Department of Health and Social Security

3.13 Weekly rates of principal social security benefits

£

	1974 July	1975 April	1975 Nov.	1976 Nov.	1977 Nov.	1978 Nov.	1979 Nov.	1980 Nov.	1981 Nov.	1982 Nov.	1983 Nov.
Unemployment benefit[1]:											
Men, single women and widows	8.60	9.80	11.10	12.90	14.70	15.75	18.50	20.65	22.50	25.00	27.05
Married women (normal rate)	6.05	6.90	7.80	9.20	10.50	15.75	20.65	22.50	25.00	25.00	27.05
Boys and girls under 18 years of age	4.75	9.80	11.10	12.90	14.70	15.75	18.50	20.65	22.50	25.00	27.05
Sickness benefit[1]:											
Men, single women and widows	8.60	9.80	11.10	12.90	14.70	15.75	18.50	20.65	22.50	25.00	25.95
Married women (normal rate)	6.05	6.90	7.80	9.20	10.50	15.75	18.50	20.65	22.50	25.00	25.95
Boys and girls under 18 years of age	4.75	9.80	11.10	12.90	14.70	15.75	18.50	20.65	22.50	25.00	25.95
Invalidity benefit:											
Invalidity pension	10.00	11.60	13.30	15.30	17.50	19.50	23.30	26.00	28.35	31.45	32.60
Invalidity allowance:											
High rate	2.05	2.40	2.80	3.20	3.70	4.15	4.90	5.45	6.20	6.90	7.15
Middle rate	1.30	1.50	1.70	2.00	2.30	2.60	3.10	3.45	4.00	4.40	4.60
Low rate	0.65	0.75	0.85	1.00	1.15	1.30	1.55	1.75	2.00	2.20	2.30
Attendance allowance:											
Higher rate	8.00	9.20	10.60	12.20	14.00	15.60	18.60	21.65	23.65	26.25	27.20
Lower rate	5.35	6.20	7.10	8.15	9.30	10.40	12.40	14.45	15.75	17.50	18.15
Mobility allowance[2]				5.00	7.00	10.00	12.00	14.50	16.50	18.30	19.00
Maternity benefit:											
Maternity allowance for insured women	8.60	9.80	11.10	12.90	14.70	15.75	18.50	20.65	22.50	25.00	25.95
Death grant[3]	30.00	30.00	30.00	30.00	30.00	30.00	30.00	30.00	30.00	30.00	30.00
Guardian's allowance	4.90	5.65	6.50	7.45	7.40	6.35	7.10	7.50	7.70	7.95	7.60
Widow's benefit:											
Widow's pension	10.00	11.60	13.30	15.30	17.50	19.50	23.30	27.15	29.60	32.85	34.05
Widowed mother's allowance	10.00	11.60	13.30	15.30	17.50	19.50	23.30	27.15	29.60	32.85	34.05
Addition for first child	4.90	5.65	6.50	7.45	7.40	6.35	7.10	7.50	7.70	7.95	7.60
Addition for second child	4.00	4.15	5.00	5.95	6.90	6.35	7.10	7.50	7.70	7.95	7.60
Addition for each other child	3.90	4.15	5.00	5.95	6.90	6.35	7.10	7.50	7.70	7.95	7.60
Retirement pension:[4]											
Single person	10.00	11.60	13.30	15.30	17.50	19.50	23.30	27.15	29.60	32.85	34.05
Married couple	16.00	18.50	21.20	24.50	28.00	31.20	37.30	43.45	47.35	52.55	54.50
Non-contributory retirement pension:											
Man or woman	6.00	6.90	7.90	9.20	10.50	11.70	14.00	16.30	17.75	19.70	20.45
Married woman	3.70	4.30	4.90	5.60	6.30	7.05	8.40	9.80	10.65	11.80	12.25
Industrial injuries benefit:											
Injury benefit	11.35	12.55	13.85	15.65	17.45	18.50	21.25	23.40	25.25	27.75	[6]
Disablement pension at 100 per cent rate	16.40	19.00	21.80	25.00	28.60	31.90	38.00	44.30	48.30	53.60	55.60
Widow's or widower's pension	10.55	12.15	13.85	15.85	18.05	20.05	23.85	27.70	30.15	33.40	34.60
Increase for dependants[5]:											
One adult	5.30	6.10	6.90	8.00	9.10	9.75	11.45	12.75	13.90	15.45	16.00
First child	2.70	3.10	3.50	4.05	3.50	1.85	1.70	1.25	0.80	0.30	0.15
Second child	1.80	1.60	2.00	2.55	3.00	1.85	1.70	1.25	0.80	0.30	0.15
Each additional child	1.70	1.60	2.00	2.55	3.00	1.85	1.70	1.25	0.80	0.30	0.15

1. From 7 April 1975 the lower rate of unemployment benefit and of sickness benefit has been discontinued and persons under the age of 18 are entitled to the appropriate adult rate.
2. Mobility Allowance was introduced from 1 January 1976 at the £5.00 rate.
3. Death grant is not payable in respect of the death of a person who on 4 July 1948 was aged 65 or over (man) and 60 and over (women).
4. Retirement pensioners over 80 receive 25p addition.
5. An allowance for one adult dependent is payable, where appropriate, with unemployment benefit, sickness benefit, retirement pension, injury benefit, certain disablement pensions and, maternity allowance. Allowances for dependent children are payable with any of these benefits. The rates of increases of benefit for the children of widowed mothers are at higher rates than those for the children of other beneficiaries. Changes in these increases take effect from the same date as the main benefit.
6. Injury benefit ceased on 6.4.83. —1982 was last uprating.

Source Department of Health and Social Security

3.13 Weekly rates of principal social security benefits

(continued)

£

	1974 July	1975 April	1975 Nov.	1976 Nov.	1977 Nov.	1978 Nov.	1979 Nov.	1980 Nov.	1981 Nov.	1982 Nov.	1983 Nov.
Child benefit[7]:											
First child					1.00	3.00	4.00	4.75	5.25	5.85	6.50
Second child	0.90	1.50	1.50	1.50	1.50	3.00	4.00	4.75	5.25	5.85	6.50
Third and each subsequent child	1.00	1.50	1.50	1.50	1.50	3.00	4.00	4.75	5.25	5.85	6.50
Family income supplement (maximum awards payable):											
Families with 1 child	5.50	5.50	7.00	8.50	9.50	10.50	13.50	17.00	18.50	21.00	22.00
Families with 2 children	5.50	5.50	7.50	9.00	10.50	11.50	14.50	18.50	20.00	23.00	24.00
Families with 3 children	7.00[13]	7.00[13]	8.00	9.50	11.50	12.50	15.50	20.00	21.50	25.00	26.00
For each additional child			0.50	0.50	1.00	1.00	1.00	1.50	1.50	2.00	2.00
War pension:											
Ex-private (100 per cent assessment)	16.40	19.00	21.80	25.00	28.60	31.90	38.00	44.30	48.30	53.60	55.60
War widow	13.00	15.00	17.20	19.80	22.70	25.30	30.20	35.30	38.45	42.70	44.25
Supplementary benefits[8,9]											
Weekly scale rate of requirements[10]											
Married couple[11]											
Ordinary rate	13.65	15.65	17.75	20.65	23.55	25.25	29.70	34.60	37.75	41.70	43.50
Long-term rate	16.35	18.85	21.55	24.85	28.35	31.55	37.65	43.45	47.35	52.30	54.55
Single householder[12]											
Ordinary rate	8.40	9.60	10.90	12.70	14.50	15.55	18.30	21.30	23.25	25.70	26.80
Long-term rate	10.40	12.00	13.70	15.70	17.90	19.90	23.70	27.15	29.60	32.70	34.10
Non-householder aged:											
21 or over											
Ordinary rate	6.70	7.65	8.70	10.15	11.60	12.45	14.65	17.05	18.60	20.55	21.45
Long-term rate	8.40	9.65	11.00	12.60	14.35	15.95	18.95	21.70	23.65	26.15	27.25
18−20											
Ordinary rate	6.70	7.65	8.70	10.15	11.60	12.45	14.65	17.05	18.60	20.55	21.45
Long-term rate	8.40	9.65	11.00	12.60	14.35	15.95	18.95	21.70	23.65	26.15	27.25
16−17											
Ordinary rate	5.15	5.90	6.70	7.80	8.90	9.55	11.25	13.10	14.30	15.80	16.50
Long-term rate									18.15	20.05	20.90
Increase for children aged:											
13−15	4.35	4.95	5.60	6.50	7.40	7.95	9.35	10.90	11.90	13.15	13.70
11−12	3.55	4.05	4.60	5.35	6.10	6.55	7.70	10.90	11.90	13.15	13.70
5−10	2.90	3.30	3.75	4.35	4.95	5.30	6.25	7.30	7.90	8.75	9.15
Under 5	2.40	2.75	3.10	3.60	4.10	4.40	5.20	7.30	7.90	8.75	9.15

7. Child benefit replaced family allowance from 5 April 1977.
8. From October 1973 the long-term addition has been incorporated in the long-term rate: persons aged 80 years and over are entitled to a further 25p.
9. Supplementary pension is paid to people over age 65 (men) or 60 (women). Supplementary allowance is paid to people below those ages.
10. Scale rates for requirement other than for rent, which is allowed for in addition. There is in addition a special scale rate for a person aged 16 years and over who is registered blind or whose wife is registered blind.
11. Including couples as man and wife.
12. Including any single person who is directly responsible for rent.
13. Maximum award payable regardless of number of children. From July 1975 this was changed to increased steps for each additional child.

Source Department of Health and Social Security

3.14 National Insurance contributions from 6 April 1977

	Class 1												Others	
	Lower earnings limit (LEL)		Upper earnings limit (UEL)		Percentage of earnings									
	No contribution liability if earnings are below		Weekly/monthly up to		Standard rate[1]			Reduced rate[2]			Employers contribution only[3]			
Date from	Weekly	Monthly	Weekly	Monthly	Employee	Employer	Total	Employee	Employer	Total		Class 2	Class 3
	£	£	£	£	%	%	%	%	%	%	%	£	£
6 April 1977	15.00	65.00	105.00	455.00	5.75	10.75	16.5	2.0	10.75	12.75	10.75		
Classes 2 and 3													
Men												2.66	2.45
Women												2.55	2.45
6 April 1978													
Not contracted out	17.50	75.83	120.00	520.00	6.5	12.0[5]	18.5[5]	2.0	12.0[5]	14.0[5]	12.0[5]		
Contracted out (i) (ii)	17.50	75.83	120.00	520.00									
(i) on earnings up to LEL plus					6.5+	12.0[5]+	18.5[5]+	2.0+	12.0[5]	14.0[5]+	12.0[5]+		
(ii) on earnings between LEL and UEL					4.0	7.5[5]	11.5[5]	2.0	7.5[5]+	9.5[5]	7.5[5]		
Classes 2 and 3[4]												1.90	1.80
6 April 1979													
Not contracted out	19.50	84.50	135.00	585.00	6.5	13.5[5]	20.0[5]	2.0	13.5[5]	15.5[5]	13.5[5]		
Contracted out (i) (ii)	19.50	84.50	135.00	585.00									
(i) on earnings up to LEL plus					6.5+	13.5[5]+	20.0[5]+	2.0+	13.5[5]+	15.5[5]+	13.5[5]+		
(ii) on earnings between LEL and UEL					4.0	9.0[5]	13.0[5]	2.0	9.0[5]	11.0[5]	9.0[5]		
Classes 2 and 3[4]												2.10	2.00
6 April 1980													
Not contracted out	23.00	99.67	165.00	715.00	6.75	13.7[5]	20.45[5]	2.0	13.7[5]	15.7[5]	13.7[5]		
Contracted out (i) (ii)	23.00	99.67	165.00	715.00									
(i) on earnings up to LEL plus					6.75+	13.7[5]+	20.45[5]+	2.0+	13.7[5]+	15.7[5]+	13.7[5]+		
(ii) on earnings between LEL and UEL					4.25	9.2[5]	13.45[5]	2.0	9.2[5]	11.2[5]	9.2[5]		
Classes 2 and 3[4]												2.50	2.40
6 April 1981													
Not contracted out	27.00	117.00	200.00	866.67	7.75	13.7[5]	21.45[5]	2.75	13.7[5]	16.45[5]	13.7[5]		
Contracted out (i) (ii)	27.00	117.00	200.00	866.67									
(i) on earnings up to LEL plus					7.75+	13.7[5]+	21.45[5]+	2.75+	13.7[5]+	16.45[5]+	13.7[5]+		
(ii) on earnings between LEL and UEL					5.25	9.2[5]	14.45[5]	2.75	9.2[5]	11.95[5]	9.2[5]		
Classes 2 and 3[4]												3.40	3.30
6 April 1982													
Not contracted out	29.50	127.83	220.00	953.33	8.75	12.2[5]	20.95[5]	3.2	12.2[5]	15.4[5]	12.2[5]		
Contracted out (i) (ii)	29.50	127.83	220.00	953.33									
(i) on earnings up to LEL plus					8.75+	12.2[5]+	20.95[5]+	3.2+	12.2[5]+	15.4[5]+	12.2[5]+		
(ii) on earnings between LEL and UEL					6.25	7.7[5]	13.95[5]	3.2	7.7[5]	10.9[5]	7.7[5]		
Classes 2 and 3[4]												3.75	3.65
6 April 1983													
Not contracted out	32.50	140.83	235.00	1 018.33	9.0	11.95[5]	20.95[5]	3.85	11.95[5]	15.8[5]	11.95[5]		
Contracted out (i) (ii)	32.50	140.83	235.00	1 018.33									
(i) on earnings up to LEL plus					9.00	11.95[5]+	20.95[5]+	3.85+	11.95[5]+	15.8[5]+	11.95[5]+		
(ii) on earnings betweeen LEL and UEL					6.85	7.85[5]	14.70[5]	3.85	7.85[5]	11.7[5]	7.85[5]		
Classes 2 and 3[4]												4.40	4.30
6 April 1984													
Not contracted out	34.00	147.33	250.00	1 083.33	9.00	11.45[5]	20.45[5]	3.85	11.45[5]	15.30[5]	11.45[5]		
Contracted out (i) (ii)	34.00	147.33	250.00	1 083.33									
(i) on earnings up to LEL plus					9.00+	11.45[5]+	20.45[5]+	3.85+	11.45[5]+	15.30[5]+	11.45[5]		
(ii) on earnings between LEL and UEL					6.85	7.35[5]	14.20[5]	3.85	7.35[5]	11.20[5]	7.35[5]		
Classes 2 and 3[4]												4.60	4.50

1. For employees who are under pension age (65 men/60 women), (or who, prior to 6 April 1978 were under age 70 men/65 women and not treated as retired for National Insurance purposes) but excluding those married women or widows who are liable for contributions at the reduced rate.
2. For employees who are married women or widows and liable for contributions at the reduced rate.
3. Prior to 6 April 1978 for employees who had reached pension age and had retired or were treated as having retired for National Insurance purposes and from 6 April 1978 for all employees over pension age. Applicable also to employees who had made other arrangements to pay Class 1 contributions.
4. Amalgamation of basic contributions of Class 2 and 3 payable by both men and women was introduced from 6 April 1978.
5. Includes 2 per cent National Insurance surcharge under the National Insurance Surcharge Act 1976. The employers contribution was raised by a further 1.5 per cent from 2 October 1978 when the surcharge was increased to 3.5 per cent. From 2 August 1982 the surcharge was reduced to 2 per cent, from 6 April 1983 reduced to 1.5 per cent and from 1 August 1983 reduced to 1.0 per cent.

Source Department of Health and Social Security

3.15 Social Security Acts: number of persons receiving benefit
At 31 December

Thousands

Persons receiving:	1973	1974	1975	1976	1977	1978	1979	1980	1981	1982	1983
Unemployment benefit[1]	261	272	464	617	589	561	503	753	1 206[9]	1 041	987
Sickness and invalidity benefit[2,3]	1 064	1 064	1 037	45[8]	1 068	1 180	1 238	1 197	1 156[10]	1 198	1 202
Maternity grant	709	681	667	658	622	638	674	680	587[11]	670	..
Death grant[4]	534	557	575	580	581	597	607	606	604[11]	611	..
Guardians' allowances	5.7	5.8	5.7	5.6	5.0	5.0	4.9	4.6	4.4	4.1	3.9
Widows' benefits[5]	561	547	527	501	500	473	467	15[8]	433	426	420
National Insurance retirement pensions:											
Total	7 993	8 144	8 324	8 510	8 637	8 785	8 936	9 108	9 291	9 386	9 528
Males	2 781	2 846	2 918	3 015	3 069	3 135	3 199	3 241	3 280	3 280	3 284
Females	5 212	5 298	5 406	5 495	5 568	5 650	5 737	5 866	6 010	6 105	6 244
Non contributory retirement pensions:											
Total	119	105	98	85	78	69	60	56	51	48	45
Males	18	14	12	11	9	7	6	6	6	6	6
Females	101	90	88	74	68	62	54	50	45	42	39
Injury benefit[3,6]	59	60	46	1.3	47	51	51	43	36	36	30
Industrial disablement pensions At 30 September	206	207	203	205	205	204	202	201	197	194	5.1[8]
Child benefit[3,7]											
Families receiving allowance	4 595	4 606	4 603	4 592	7 506	7 390	7 410	7 397	7 352	7 261	7 140[12]
Family income supplement	107	79	67	85	97	89	89	106	143	179	13[8]
Supplementary benefits At November/December	2 772	2 778	2 897	3 049	3 106	3 048	2 970	3 247	3 873	4 432	4 509
War pensions	464	447	430	413	397	382	367	355	341	327	314

1. Great Britain figures are from Annual Statistical enquiry from 1983. For Northern Ireland figures are an average of two six-monthly figures.
2. Average of twelve monthly figures commencing on the first Monday in June up to 1982 and from first Monday in April thereafter. A relatively small number of claims do not result in the payment of benefit but are included here because they indicate notified incapacity for work.
3. Includes overseas cases.
4. Grants paid in year.
5. Excluding widows' allowances paid during the first twenty-six weeks of widowhood the number of such allowances does not exceed 35 000 in a six month period.

6. Excludes overseas cases in 1978.
7. From April 1977 child benefit replaced family allowance.
8. Northern Ireland only.
9. February 1981 data for Great Britain only, due to industrial action.
10. April to August inclusive missing due to industrial action. Average of six monthly figures for Northern Ireland.
11. Estimated.
12. Provisional.

Sources Department of Health and Social Security; Department of Health and Social Services (Northern Ireland)

3.16 Unemployed claimants analysed by benefit entitlement

Thousands

	1975		1976[1]	1977		1978		1979		1980		1981[2]		1982		1983	
	May	Nov.	May	May	Nov.	May	Nov.	May	Nov.	May	Nov.	May	Nov.	May	Nov.	May	Nov.
Males																	
Total	701	894	988	985	1 029	986	923	860	860	986	1 428	73	77	1 988	2 182	2 163	2 117
Flat-rate benefit payable—total	346	444	486	429	434	404	363	332	333	431	705	32	25	720	701	683	613
Flat-rate benefit only	124	156	175	151	156	154	136	134	126	162	245	..	10	393	463	451	414
Flat-rate benefit and earnings-related supplement[3]	132	177	179	159	167	145	144	119	134	172	311	..	8	97[3]	[3]	–	–
Flat-rate benefit, earnings-related supplement and supplementary allowance[3]	18	27	27	26	20	19	17	18	17	24	44	..	2	34[3]	[3]	–	–
Flat-rate benefit and supplementary allowance	72	84	104	95	91	85	65	61	56	73	105	..	5	196	239	232	199
Supplementary allowance only	227	305	357	414	428	423	415	390	378	397	522	39	50	998	1 156	1 260	1 284
No flat-rate benefit or supplementary allowance[4]	128	145	146	142	168	160	145	139	149	157	200	2	2	270	324	220	221
Females																	
Total	146	235	264	304	381	361	349	306	357	386	560	30	33	699	802	817	888
Flat-rate benefit payable—total	73	109	131	137	155	151	156	145	162	193	279	18	16	301	309	319	325
Flat-rate benefit only	40	60	74	77	84	92	91	89	96	116	160	..	11	232	279	288	295
Flat-rate benefit and earnings-related supplement[3]	25	38	43	44	57	46	53	45	54	64	101	..	5	40[3]	[3]	–	–
Flat-rate benefit, earnings-related supplement and supplementary allowance[3]	2	2	4	3	3	2	2	2	3	3	4	..	–	4[3]	[3]	–	–
Flat-rate benefit and supplementary allowance	6	9	10	12	11	11	9	8	8	10	14	..	1	25	32	30	30
Supplementary allowance only	38	75	77	104	143	120	134	109	126	121	187	9	14	272	343	353	401
No flat-rate benefit or supplementary allowance[4]	35	51	56	64	82	90	60	54	69	72	95	3	3	126	149	146	162

Note: Figures are based on a five per cent sample except those for May 1976 which are based on a four per cent sample for Great Britain. For Northern Ireland figures are based on a twenty per cent sample.

1. Because of industrial action at local offices of the Employment Services Agency the figures for November 1976 are not available.
2. 1981 figures are for Northern Ireland only. Due to industrial action 1981 figures for Great Britain are not available.
3. Earnings related supplement was abolished from 2 January 1982, but continued in payment for certain transitional cases up to 30 June 1982, when it finally ceased.
4. Prior to November 1978 figures for non-recipients of benefit include non-claimants; from November 1978 only claimants for benefit or credit are included.

Sources Department of Health and Social Security; Department of Health and Social Services (Northern Ireland)

3.17 Sickness and invalidity benefit
Claimants analysed by age and duration of spell
At beginning of June/At end of statistical year[1]

Thousands

Age at 31 May/31 March[2]	1973	1974	1975	1976	1977	1978	1979	1980	1981	1982	1983[3]
Males											
All durations: All ages	775	802	764	832	839	891	891	849	834	901	874
Under 20	20	21	18	24	18	24	26	22	14	18	13
20–29	80	82	76	87	83	88	80	73	64	73	63
30–39	92	98	95	105	110	118	99	99	94	102	91
40–49	127	137	127	140	138	144	145	134	132	142	128
50–59	222	223	213	233	244	260	276	255	253	269	262
60–64	217	217	211	221	219	222	224	219	228	246	260
65 and over	19	23	26	22	29	35	41	49	49	53	56
Over six months: All ages	356	362	369	387	407	445	491	503	527	570	592
Under 20	1	1	1	2	1	1	2	2	1	2	2
20–29	9	9	11	13	11	12	13	13	18	17	17
30–39	20	20	21	25	27	33	31	34	39	41	42
40–49	45	47	48	54	55	61	65	67	73	80	81
50–59	115	117	118	124	131	147	171	165	168	179	184
60–64	151	150	150	154	157	160	172	174	181	200	211
65 and over	15	17	22	19	26	33	39	47	48	52	55
Females											
All durations: All ages	219	220	211	208	206	243	254	261	249	297	271
Under 20	25	21	20	22	19	24	19	20	11	14	11
20–29	59	62	62	58	54	62	69	66	56	65	57
30–39	25	26	28	28	29	37	40	43	48	60	50
40–49	36	37	34	37	36	46	47	50	51	63	59
50–59	70	69	63	60	63	71	74	76	77	86	87
60 and over	4	4	4	4	4	5	6	6	6	8	7
Over six months: All ages	89	87	85	81	86	98	106	112	122	140	150
Under 20	1	1	1	2	1	2	2	1	1	1	1
20–29	8	9	8	9	10	10	13	14	15	17	19
30–39	9	8	10	10	11	12	14	17	19	24	24
40–49	19	19	19	17	18	20	21	22	27	33	34
50–59	49	46	44	40	43	50	51	52	55	59	66
60 and over	3	3	3	3	3	4	5	5	5	7	7

Note Figures for Great Britain are based on a 2½ per cent sample from 1969/70 to 1974/75, on a 2 per cent sample from 1975/76 to 1977/78 and on a 1 per cent sample thereafter. Figures for Northern Ireland are based on a 20 per cent sample.

1. For Great Britain commencing on first Monday in June up to 1982 and first Monday in April thereafter.
2. Prior to 1983, date was at 31 May.
3. Great Britain only; data for Northern Ireland not available due to computer problems.

Sources Department of Health and Social Security; Department of Health and Social Services (Northern Ireland)

3.18 Sickness and invalidity benefit[1]: days of certified incapacity
Analysis by age at end of period
Years starting on first Monday in June

Millions

	1971/72	1972/73	1973/74	1974/75[2]	1976/77[2]	1977/78	1978/79	1979/80	1980/81	1981/82	1982/83
Males: All ages	248.0	259.0	259.6	253.0	265.4	282.7	298.0	285.2	272.2	280.5	281.4
Under 20	6.0	6.4	5.9	5.7	6.3	6.9	7.2	6.4	5.0	4.8	4.3
20–29	25.3	27.4	26.5	26.6	27.0	29.2	30.3	26.5	23.5	23.0	20.7
30–39	28.8	30.5	31.2	30.9	34.0	37.1	36.2	34.7	32.4	31.9	30.0
40–49	41.6	43.2	43.0	41.9	43.4	46.0	48.2	45.5	42.3	44.1	42.8
50–59	67.7	70.6	70.7	68.1	73.9	79.5	87.8	81.4	76.9	79.3	80.7
60–64	65.1	66.2	66.7	63.9	64.7	65.6	68.3	67.7	68.4	73.9	79.0
65 and over	13.5	14.7	15.4	16.0	16.1	18.3	20.0	23.1	23.8	23.4	24.1
Females: All ages	71.0	73.4	71.7	69.9	69.0	83.4	87.3	87.6	86.3	91.7	93.9
Under 20	7.3	7.8	6.9	6.1	6.2	6.9	7.1	6.4	4.6	4.0	3.4
20–29	19.3	21.4	21.6	21.0	19.0	21.0	25.1	23.1	21.7	21.3	20.2
30–39	7.4	7.8	8.0	8.7	9.8	12.1	13.4	15.2	15.3	17.7	18.0
40–49	11.5	11.5	11.3	11.3	11.8	15.2	15.2	15.8	16.9	19.0	20.0
50–59	22.6	21.8	21.0	20.1	20.0	25.7	23.7	24.0	24.7	25.9	28.5
60 and over	2.8	3.1	2.9	2.6	2.3	2.5	2.8	3.2	3.1	3.8	3.8

See *note* to Table 3.17.
1. Invalidity benefit was introduced on 23 September 1971.
2. Figures for 1975/76 are not available.

Sources Department of Health and Social Security, Department of Health and Social Services (Northern Ireland)

3.19 Sickness and invalidity benefit: days of certified incapacity in statistical year
Analysis by cause of incapacity
Great Britain
Year starting on first Monday in April[1]

Millions

Diagnostic groups according to the *International Classification of Diseases, Injuries and Causes of Death* (9th Revision)	ICD number	1979/80	1980/81	1981/82	1982/83
Males					
All causes		275.6	263.2	271.2	271.7
All causes except influenza		271.9	259.9	267.7	267.6
Infective and parasitic diseases	001 – 139	8.3	6.9	6.9	5.7
Tuberculosis	010 – 018	1.5	1.3	1.5	1.5
Neoplasms	140 – 239	2.1	2.1	2.7	3.0
Endocrine, nutritional and metabolic diseases	240 – 279	4.2	4.3	4.3	5.1
Diseases of blood and blood-forming organs	280 – 289	0.7	0.7	0.7	0.6
Mental disorders	290 – 319	29.6	30.6	32.7	33.6
Diseases of nervous system and sense organs	320 – 389	17.0	17.3	17.8	19.0
Diseases of circulatory system	390 – 459	53.6	52.8	56.4	58.2
Hypertensive disease	401 – 405	9.0	8.6	9.2	9.5
Ischaemic heart disease	410 – 414	24.6	24.8	27.0	29.1
Diseases of respiratory system	460 – 519	46.5	41.1	40.5	38.2
Influenza	487	3.7	3.3	3.5	4.1
Bronchitis, emphysema and asthma excluding acute bronchitis	490 – 493	28.2	25.4	24.4	23.1
Diseases of digestive system	520 – 579	14.4	12.8	12.7	12.5
Diseases of genito-urinary system	580 – 629	3.1	3.2	3.5	3.4
Diseases of skin and subcutaneous tissue	680 – 709	3.7	3.2	3.0	2.7
Diseases of musculo-skeletal system and connective tissue	710 – 739	42.8	42.7	44.3	46.1
Arthritis, except arthritis of back	710 – 716	14.7	14.2	15.4	16.7
Rheumatism, except rheumatic fever and rheumatism of back	725 – 729	4.6	4.0	3.8	3.6
Congenital anomalies	740 – 759	0.3	0.2	0.3	0.4
Symptoms and ill-defined conditions	780 – 799	19.2	18.1	17.1	16.2
Accidents, poisonings and violence	800 – 999	29.9	27.1	28.1	26.8
Females					
All causes		83.0	82.1	87.3	89.3
All causes except influenza		81.5	80.5	85.5	87.0
Infective and parasitic diseases	001 – 139	4.2	3.5	3.6	3.0
Tuberculosis	010 – 018	0.3	0.2	0.2	0.2
Neoplasms	140 – 239	0.5	0.5	0.7	1.0
Endocrine, nutritional and metabolic diseases	240 – 279	1.3	1.4	1.7	1.5
Diseases of blood and blood-forming organs	280 – 289	0.7	0.6	0.4	0.5
Mental disorders	290 – 319	14.6	15.2	17.8	18.7
Diseases of nervous system and sense organs	320 – 389	5.0	5.5	5.7	5.8
Diseases of circulatory system	390 – 459	5.3	5.4	6.0	6.9
Hypertensive disease	401 – 405	1.3	1.5	1.7	2.0
Ischaemic heart disease	410 – 414	1.4	1.4	1.6	1.9
Diseases of respiratory system	460 – 519	11.5	10.4	10.4	9.5
Influenza	487	1.6	1.6	1.9	2.3
Bronchitis, emphysema and asthma excluding acute bronchitis	490 – 493	3.2	3.0	3.0	3.1
Diseases of digestive system	520 – 579	3.7	3.2	3.2	3.4
Diseases of genito-urinary system	580 – 629	4.3	4.4	4.5	4.5
Diseases of pregnancy, childbirth and puerperium	630 – 676	4.1	3.2	3.0	3.1
Diseases of skin and subcutaneous tissue	680 – 709	1.4	1.1	1.1	1.0
Diseases of musculo-skeletal system and connective tissue	710 – 739	11.4	12.6	13.6	15.2
Arthritis, except arthritis of back	710 – 716	4.1	4.4	4.7	5.2
Rheumatism, except rheumatic fever and rheumatism of back	725 – 729	1.7	1.6	1.6	1.6
Congenital anomalies	740 – 759	0.2	0.4	0.4	0.3
Symptoms and ill-defined conditions	780 – 799	8.6	8.5	8.7	8.4
Accidents, poisonings and violence	800 – 999	6.1	5.9	6.6	6.4

Note: Figures are based on a 1 per cent sample.
1. Prior to 1982/83, date was June.

Source Department of Health and Social Security

3.20 Widow's benefit (excluding widow's allowance [1]):
Number in payment analysed by type of benefit and age of widow

Thousands

	November								September		
	1973	1974	1975 [2]	1976	1977	1978	1979	1980 [3]	1981	1982	1983
All widow's benefit (excluding widow's allowance)											
All ages	560	546	524	501	486	473	467	15	433	426	420
Under 30	3	3	3	3	3	3	3	–	3	3	3
30–39	17	18	17	17	17	17	17	1	18	18	19
40–49	85	82	80	79	78	77	75	3	70	71	69
50–59	315	310	306	304	309	316	320	9	293	289	283
60 and over	142	134	117	98	79	61	54	2	50	46	47
Widowed mother's allowance – with dependant children											
All ages	106	104	103	102	99	95	91	5	84	79	75
Under 30	3	3	3	3	3	3	3	–	2	3	3
30–39	17	17	17	16	16	16	16	1	16	17	17
40–49	47	45	45	45	43	42	40	2	36	34	32
50–59	37	36	36	36	35	33	32	2	29	27	24
60 and over	2	2	2	2	2	–	1	–	1	–	1
Widowed mother's allowance – without dependent children											
All ages	31	32	32	32	33	33	33	1	34	35	35
30–39	1	1	1	1	1	1	1	–	1	2	2
40–49	8	9	9	9	9	10	11	–	11	12	12
50–59	19	19	19	20	20	21	21	1	20	21	19
60 and over	3	3	3	3	3	1	1	–	1	1	1
Widow's pension											
All ages	317	301	279	257	243	235	231	7	208	203	203
40–49	2	1	1	1	–	–	–	–	–	–	–
50–59	184	178	173	170	174	179	184	5	165	163	162
60 and over	131	122	105	86	69	55	47	2	43	40	41
Age-related widow's pension [4]											
All ages	102	105	110	110	110	110	111	3	109	109	108
40–49	27	27	26	26	25	25	24	1	24	25	26
50–59	70	72	78	79	80	82	83	2	80	79	77
60 and over	5	6	6	6	5	4	5	–	5	5	5
Widow's basic pension [4]											
All ages	5	4									
30–39	–	–									
40–49	1	1									
50–59	4	4									
60 and over	–	–									

1. This is an especially high rate of benefit which is payable for the first 26 weeks of widowhood, provided that the widow is under pensionable age (age 60) or, if she is over that age, provided that her husband was not entitled to retirement pension.
2. Estimated.
3. Northern Ireland data only, Great Britain figures not available due to computer error.

4. From 1975 figures for widow's basic pension are included in Age-related widow's pension.

Sources Department of Health and Social Security; Department of Health and Social Services (Northern Ireland)

3.21 Family allowances/Child benefits [1]
At 31 December

Thousands

	1973	1974	1975	1976	1977	1978	1979	1980	1981	1982	1983 [3]
Families receiving allowances: total	4 595	4 606	4 603	4 592	7 338	7 390	7 409	7 397	7 352	7 261	216
With 1 child					2 787	2 887	2 951	2 987	2 996	2 986	74
2 children [2]	2 784	2 844	2 899	2 961	3 011	3 032	3 051	3 055	3 048	3 016	74
3 children [2]	1 165	1 153	1 144	1 122	1 086	1 059	1 032	1 005	977	947	40
4 children [2]	427	414	388	359	327	302	278	260	247	234	17
5 or more children [2]	218	195	172	150	126	110	98	90	84	79	11

1. From April 1977 Family allowance has been replaced by Child benefit which is payable for all children in the family, including the first or only child.
2. Until 1976 including the elder or eldest child for whom no allowance was payable, but excluding children over the age limit.
3. Northern Ireland only. Great Britain figures not available due to industrial action by computer staff.

Sources Department of Health and Social Security; Department of Health and Social Services (Northern Ireland)

3.22 Contributory and non-contributory retirement pensions
Numbers in payment analysed by age group[1]

Thousands

	At 31 December					At 30 November					
	1973	1974	1975	1976	1977	1978	1979	1980	1981	1982	1983
Men: Total all ages	2 799	2 861	2 930	3 016	3 078	3 142	3 205	3 248	3 286	3 286	3 285
Age groups:											
65–69	1 060	1 084	1 120	1 151	1 168	1 171	1 171	1 170	1 157	1 130	1 072
Percentage	*37.9*	*37.9*	*38.2*	*38.2*	*37.9*	*37.3*	*36.5*	*36.0*	*35.2*	*34.4*	*32.6*
70–74	878	900	916	951	960	982	1 003	1 019	1 026	1 034	1 043
Percentage	*31.4*	*31.5*	*31.3*	*31.5*	*31.2*	*31.3*	*31.3*	*31.4*	*31.2*	*31.5*	*31.8*
75–79	482	498	512	531	561	587	614	629	653	661	684
Percentage	*17.2*	*17.4*	*17.5*	*17.6*	*18.2*	*18.7*	*19.2*	*19.4*	*19.9*	*20.1*	*20.8*
80–84	249	251	255	259	259	267	279	289	304	315	334
Percentage	*8.9*	*8.8*	*8.7*	*8.6*	*8.4*	*8.5*	*8.7*	*8.9*	*9.3*	*9.6*	*10.2*
85–89	103	99	98	99	102	103	105	109	113	113	117
Percentage	*3.7*	*3.5*	*3.3*	*3.3*	*3.3*	*3.3*	*3.3*	*3.4*	*3.4*	*3.4*	*3.6*
90 and over	27	29	30	25	28	31	32	32	34	34	35
Percentage	*1.0*	*1.0*	*1.0*	*0.8*	*0.9*	*1.0*	*1.0*	*1.0*	*1.0*	*1.0*	*1.1*
Women: Total all ages	5 313	5 390	5 491	5 499	5 635	5 712	5 791	5 911	6 057	6 148	6 247
Age groups:											
60–64	813	820	849	877	879	862	852	945	1 007	1 110	1 210
Percentage	*15.3*	*15.2*	*15.5*	*15.9*	*15.6*	*15.1*	*14.7*	*16.0*	*16.5*	*18.1*	*19.4*
65–69	1 387	1 396	1 403	1 407	1 426	1 421	1 423	1 417	1 410	1 367	1 293
Percentage	*26.1*	*25.9*	*25.6*	*25.6*	*25.3*	*24.9*	*24.6*	*24.0*	*23.3*	*22.2*	*20.7*
70–74	1 235	1 273	1 289	1 304	1 327	1 344	1 361	1 358	1 373	1 377	1 378
Percentage	*23.2*	*23.6*	*23.5*	*23.7*	*23.5*	*23.5*	*23.5*	*23.0*	*22.7*	*22.4*	*22.1*
75–79	917	933	953	965	973	1 009	1 040	1 055	1 085	1 095	1 122
Percentage	*17.3*	*17.3*	*17.4*	*17.6*	*17.3*	*17.7*	*18.0*	*17.8*	*17.9*	*17.8*	*18.0*
80–84	584	582	598	590	626	638	658	670	690	701	727
Percentage	*11.0*	*10.8*	*10.9*	*10.7*	*11.1*	*11.2*	*11.4*	*11.3*	*11.4*	*11.4*	*11.6*
85–89	273	280	287	266	292	314	326	336	348	351	362
Percentage	*5.1*	*5.2*	*5.2*	*4.8*	*5.2*	*5.5*	*5.6*	*5.7*	*5.8*	*5.7*	*5.8*
90 and over	104	106	113	91	113	124	130	130	144	146	155
Percentage	*2.0*	*2.0*	*2.1*	*1.7*	*2.0*	*2.2*	*2.2*	*2.2*	*2.4*	*2.4*	*2.5*

1. Including pensions payable to persons residing overseas.

Sources Department of Health and Social Security; Department of Health and Social Services (Northern Ireland)

3.23 Family income supplement[1]
At 31 December

Thousands

	1973	1974	1975	1976	1977	1978	1979	1980	1981	1982	1983
Families receiving supplements:											
total	107	79	67	85	97	89	89	105	143	179	215
Two-parent families: total	61	41	35	49	58	51	43	51	78	105	133
With 1 child	11	7	7	10	11	9	7	10	15	21	28
2 children	14	9	8	13	16	14	12	15	25	36	47
3 children	13	9	7	11	14	13	12	14	19	26	32
4 children	10	8	6	8	9	8	7	7	11	13	15
5 children	6	4	4	4	5	4	3	3	4	5	6
6 or more children	6	5	4	4	3	3	2	3	3	3	3
One-parent families: total	45	39	33	36	40	38	46	54	65	74	83
With 1 child	29	23	19	20	22	21	24	29	34	40	46
2 children	10	9	8	9	11	10	14	17	21	24	28
3 or more children	6	6	5	6	6	6	7	8	9	9	10

1. For weekly rates of Family income supplement see Table 3.13.

Sources Department of Health and Social Security; Department of Health and Social Services (Northern Ireland)

3.24 Supplementary benefits: number of beneficiaries receiving weekly payment
On a day in November/December

Thousands

	1973	1974	1975	1976[1]	1977	1978	1979	1980	1981	1982	1983[4]
All supplementary benefits	2 772	2 778	2 897	3 049	3 106	3 048	2 970	3 247	3 873	4 432	175
All supplementary pensions	1 903	1 866	1 734	1 742	1 794	1 795	1 779	1 750	1 793	1 836	54
Retirement pensioners and national insurance widows over 60	1 796	1 761	1 632	1 639	1 684	1 680	1 675	1 642	1 693	1 747	48
Others over pension age	107	106	103	104	110	115	104	108	101	88	6
All supplementary allowances	869	911	1 162	1 307	1 313	1 255	1 191	1 496	2 080	2 596	121
Unemployed with contributory benefit	50	76	140	684	132	97	83	182	242	293	8
Unemployed without contributory benefit	212	240	426		573	535	516	719	1 142	1 505	74
Sick and disabled with contributory benefit[2]	122	98	80	80	77	73	58	216	73	90	8
Sick and disabled without contributory benefit	173	175	174	175	164	161	160		160	162	5
National insurance widows under 60	56	44	32	30	24	24	21	17	18	22	2
One-parent families not included in the above categories[3]	233	250	283	310	317	330	314	325	379	427	13
Miscellaneous	24	27	27	28	26	35	37	39	67	98	11

1. Because of industrial action in some unemployment benefit offices at the time of the supplementary benefit annual statistical inquiry, in December 1976, it was not possible to obtain the usual information on unemployed claimants. As a result 1976 figures for unemployed cases, total supplementary allowance and total supplementary benefit cases are estimated.

2. Includes claimants in receipt of non-contributory invalidity pensions.
3. From 1975 the figures relate to one-parent families headed by a man also.
4. Northern Ireland only. Due to industrial action figures for Great Britain are not available.

Sources Department of Health and Social Security; Department of Health and Social Services (Northern Ireland)

3.25 Supplementary benefits
On a day in November/December

Thousands

	1973	1974	1975	1976[1]	1977	1978	1979	1980	1981	1982	1983[2]
Number of regular weekly payments	2 772	2 778	2 897	3 049	3 106	3 048	2 970	3 247	3 873	4 432	174
Total number of persons provided for	4 188	4 254	4 620	4 922	4 976	4 814	4 576	5 105	5 145	7 388	340
Number of dependants	1 415	1 477	1 723	1 874	1 869	1 766	1 607	1 858	1 877	2 956	166
Wives	571	559	587	639	640	613	587	653	659	1 055	49
Total children under 16 years	824	896	1 108	1 202	1 192	1 116	985	1 165	1 177	1 826	111
Under 5 years	248	276	347	351	344	318	294	812	822	1 272	77
5–10 years	328	355	444	485	482	442	384				
11–12 years	104	112	134	156	151	148	124	354	356	554	34
13–15 years	144	153	182	210	215	207	183				
Other dependants 16 years and over	20	21	29	34	36	36	35	39	41	75	6

1. Estimated figures for Great Britain—see footnote 1 to Table 3.24.
2. Northern Ireland only. Due to industrial action figures for Great Britain are not available

Sources Department of Health and Social Security; Department of Health and Social Services (Northern Ireland)

3.26 Supplementary benefits: average weekly amounts of benefit
Great Britain
November or December

£

	1973	1974	1975	1976[3]	1977[2]	1978	1979	1980	1981	1982[3]	1983[4]
All supplementary benefits	4.71	6.68	9.24	..[2]	13.01	13.56	15.48	19.51	25.08	23.58	
All supplementary pensions	2.79	4.27	5.52	6.61	7.65	8.33	9.57	11.91	15.31	10.76	
Retirement pensioners and national insurance widows over 60	2.47	3.85	4.93	5.92	6.83	7.40	8.51	10.63	14.01	9.39	
Others over pension age	8.54	11.83	15.50	18.17	20.83	22.55	27.25	32.13	37.82	38.77	
All supplementary allowances	8.98	11.68	14.87	..[2]	20.43	21.17	24.47	28.55	33.64	32.77	
Unemployed with contributory benefit	4.02	5.06	6.98	..[2]	9.19	9.40	10.65	15.84	19.88	19.19	
Unemployed without contributory benefit	11.79	13.84	16.69	..[2]	22.12	22.95	25.79	29.22	34.71	34.82	
Sick and disabled with contributory benefit	2.53	3.86	5.69	7.08	8.12	8.37	10.04	14.36	16.33	14.45	
Sick and disabled without contributory benefit	8.43	10.83	12.05	13.92	16.29	17.01	20.24	24.26	27.17	26.74	
National insurance widows under 60	2.74	4.33	6.01	7.29	8.58	8.70	11.07	14.55	17.84	14.59	
One-parent families not included in other groups[1]	12.59	16.25	21.05	24.72	27.77	27.03	31.03	38.78	44.45	39.86	
Miscellaneous	10.16	14.08	17.61	20.25	22.54	24.12	28.58	34.18	41.52	41.48	

Northern Ireland
November or December

£

	1973	1974	1975	1976	1977	1978	1979	1980	1981	1982	1983[5]
All supplementary benefits	5.40	6.45	9.33	11.19	13.62	14.35	16.42	20.64	24.58	29.23	25.79
All supplementary pensions	3.08	3.73	4.95	5.86	6.95	7.84	9.08	10.46	12.82	14.53	9.87
Retirement pensioners and national insurance widows over 60	2.07	2.39	3.25	4.02	4.93	5.83	6.73	7.97	10.19	11.78	6.74
Others over pension age	8.19	10.29	13.68	15.90	18.97	20.69	25.27	28.95	32.99	36.84	35.63
All supplementary allowances	8.97	10.59	14.25	16.66	19.82	20.53	23.45	28.41	31.48	36.61	32.85
Unemployed with contributory benefit	2.87	3.15	4.71	5.76	6.99	8.00	9.94	16.03	20.66	21.53	15.49
Unemployed without contributory benefit	13.26	14.22	17.64	20.49	23.90	24.28	27.15	31.39	33.66	38.92	35.93
Sick and disabled with contributory benefit	1.94	2.11	3.29	5.13	6.35	7.07	8.88	12.72	13.00	15.12	12.54
Sick and disabled without contributory benefit	8.32	10.31	13.15	15.29	18.04	19.63	23.18	28.18	30.69	33.56	31.75
National insurance widows under 60	2.25	2.59	3.62	4.83	4.92	6.11	8.94	9.56	13.55	14.31	9.32
One-parent families not included in other groups[1]	13.00	15.37	20.10	24.15	26.97	25.79	29.35	36.45	40.75	48.08	38.78
Miscellaneous	8.46	11.23	14.16	16.69	20.86	21.64	24.11	29.41	35.43	41.83	36.93

1. From 1975 the figures relate to one-parent families headed by a man also.
2. Not available because of estimated figure for unemployed cases—see footnote 1 to Table 3.24.
3. From 22 November 1982, the majority of local authority tenants received housing requirements through Housing benefit—hence average weekly amounts of benefit have been affected.
4. Great Britain data not available due to industrial action by computer staff.
5. From November 1983 the majority of local authority tenants received housing requirements through Housing Benefit hence average weekly amounts of benefit have been affected.

Sources Department of Health and Social Security; Department of Health and Social Services (Northern Ireland)

3.27 Supplementary benefits: recipients of regular weekly payments
By household category
On a day in November/December

Thousands

	1973	1974	1975	1976[1]	1977	1978	1979	1980	1981	1982	1983[3]
All cases	2 772	2 778	2 897	3 049	3 106	3 048	2 970	3 247	3 873	4 432	175
All householders	2 384	2 358	2 354	2 423	2 528	2 504	2 424	2 553	2 968	3 318	119
Lone person	1 248	1 256	1 229	1 271	1 353	1 343	1 319	1 380	1 510	1 652	..
Man and wife only	346	327	291	312	317	318	323	317	368	425	..
Household includes dependent children but not adults other than spouse	241	267	351	395	413	399	363	} 539	} 1 091	1 245	..
Household includes dependent children and non-dependent adults	80	77	86	94	96	98	86				
Household includes non-dependent adults but no dependent children	469	433	396	353	348	344	332	318			
All other categories	388	418	544	615	579	544	547	694	902	1 111	55
Living as members of another person's household	306	339	450	518	477	443	442	578	774	970	53
Paying an inclusive charge for board and lodging	22	19	23	24	25	27	25	31	38	55	1
Local authority Part III accommodation or other comparable homes	40	42	47	45	45	47	48	54	53	51	1
Hospital in-patients	6	6	6	7	6	7	7	6	5	4	–
Others[2]	13	14	16	21	25	18	24	24	31	31	–

1. Great Britain figures estimated see footnote 1 to Table 3.24.
2. Mainly persons paying for accommodation only and living in hostels and lodging houses.
3. Northern Ireland only; Great Britain data not available due to industrial action by computer staff.

Sources Department of Health and Social Security; Department of Health and Social Services (Northern Ireland)

3.28 War pensions
Estimated number of pensioners
At 31 March in each year

Thousands

	1974	1975	1976	1977	1978	1979	1980	1981	1982	1983	1984
Total	458.85	441.75	424.65	407.50	391.65	377.25	362.45	349.36	336.19	323.40	310.34
Disablement— 1914 war; 1939 war and later service	341.60	329.45	317.35	305.50	294.20	283.45	273.00	263.66	253.86	244.50	234.60
Widows and dependants— 1914 war; 1939 war and later service	117.25	112.30	107.30	102.00	97.45	93.80	89.45	85.70	82.34	78.90	75.74

Source Department of Health and Social Security

3.29 Hospital and family practitioner services
England and Wales

	Unit	1974	1975	1976	1977	1978	1979	1980	1981	1982	1983 England	1983 Wales
Hospital services												
In-patients:												
Staffed beds at 31 December	Thousands	427	419	412	404	395	388	383	380	378	349	23
Average daily occupation of beds:												
All departments	,,	341	332	330	325	318	311	307	304	298	276	18
Psychiatric departments	,,	148	143	140	136	131	129	125	122	119	110	6
Persons on waiting lists	,,	553	626	644	637	716	726	678	658	787	703	40
Discharges or deaths	,,	5 501	5 296	5 593	5 688	5 700	5 750	6 036	6 135	6 090	6 019	393
Out-patients[1]												
New cases	,,	16 994	16 179	17 224	17 455	17 769	17 873	18 146	18 489	18 782	18 261	1 063
Total attendances	,,	48 763	50 141	47 997	49 027	49 635	49 921	50 994	51 656	51 950	50 123	2 945
Staff: at 30 September												
Medical, dental[2]	Number	27 831	29 326	30 169	30 991	31 977	33 269	34 298	35 112	35 640	34 286	2 075
Professional, technical[2,3]	,,	40 117	49 724	57 602	57 471	60 706	63 630	65 630	69 049	71 258	..	4 161
Nursing and midwifery[3,4]												
Whole-time	,,	339 858	371 629	378 371	377 620	385 960	393 822	405 922	422 759	425 055	..	25 981
Part-time	,,											
Administrative: clerical[2,4,5,6]	,,	81 696	97 596	104 388	104 930	106 637	108 999	111 709	115 179	115 240	..	6 481
Blood transfusion[2]	,,	2 885										
Maintenance, domestic[2,4,7]	,,	202 838	206 670	213 409	212 738	212 722	212 320	213 878	214 679	212 998	..	15 104
Family practitioner services												
Medical services:												
Doctors on the list[8]	Number	21 510	21 667	21 837	22 100	22 363	22 696	23 184	23 701	24 217	23 254	1 465
Number of patients per doctor	,,	2 372	2 355	2 342	2 322	2 302	2 277	2 238	2 193	2 147	2 116	1 975
Paid to doctors	£ million	221.2	285.7	332.8	369.7	412.1	493.3	658.6	776.5	878.5	908.9	51.6
Pharmaceutical services:												
Prescriptions dispensed	Million	295.4	303.4	315.2	318.5	330.9	328.2	327.0	323.4	335.3	315.3	24.6
Payments to pharmacists[9]	£ million	293.9	387.5	485.6	596.5	708.3	795.9	966.6	1 103.7	1 268.8	1 307.9	97.6
Payment by patients	,,	23.5	23.0	23.4	23.2	24.2	35.0	62.5	81.3	94.5	95.7	6.9
Paid out of public funds	,,	268.9	364.5	462.2	573.3	684.1	760.9	904.1	1 022.4	1 174.3	1 212.1	90.7
Average total cost per prescription	£	0.995	1.277	1.541	1.873	2.140	2.425	2.956	3.413	3.784	4.148	3.970
Dental services:												
Dentists on the list[10] at 30 September	Number	11 528	11 737	12 054	12 360	12 517	12 750	13 039	13 473	13 936	13 672	702
Courses of treatment completed and emergency cases[11]	Thousands	25 785	27 087	27 501	28 276	28 428	28 538	30 072	30 502	31 468	30 506	1 581
Payments to dentists	£ million	147.5	191.4	217.6	238.5	263.1	320.2	410.5	478.3	536.5	553.1	28.4
Payments by patients	,,	32.0	32.2	40.1	50.1	57.4	66.5	93.8	115.9	141.9	154.1	6.9
Paid out of public funds	,,	115.5	159.2	177.5	188.4	205.7	253.7	316.7	362.4	394.6	399.0	22.6
Average gross cost per course and case	£	5.7	7.1	7.9	8.4	9.3	11.2	13.7	15.7	17.0	18.13	18.50
General ophthalmic services:												
Sight tests, given[12]	Thousands	7 481	7 861	8 181	7 856	8 308	8 593	8 795	8 932	9 192	9 039	519
Pairs of glasses paid for	,,	5 199	5 949	5 196	4 902	4 786	4 975	5 148	5 226	5 200	4 847	329
Cost of services (gross)	£ million	35.5	61.5	64.5	73.0	77.5	88.8	108.0	125.2	141.4	226.1[14]	13.8[15]
Payments by patients	,,	16.9	17.0	21.9	24.3	26.1	28.4	30.6	33.1	38.9	41.6	2.5
Paid out of public funds:												
For sight testing	,,	12.5	24.7	25.8	27.3	30.3	33.6	40.8	45.4[13] }	87.8[14]	175.8[14]	{ 6.7
For dispensing	,,	6.1	19.8	16.8	19.4	17.0	17.5	18.2	24.7[13] }			{ 5.2

1. At consultant and general practitioner clinics and accident and emergency departments.
2. Total whole-time equivalents. Whole-time equivalents of consultants known to have maximum part-time contracts counted as one. Excluding doctors holding locum appointments, hospital practitioners, general practitioners participating in Hospital Staff Funds and part-time medical/dental officers (clinical assistants), but including medically qualified staff in mass radiography units and blood transfusion service for England and for Wales.
3. Including for Wales, community health care and hospital staff.
4. Including for Wales, headquarters staff of hospital boards. Figures at 31 March. Nursing and Midwifery figures for Wales for 1978 and 1979 show whole-time equivalent, not number.
5. Including staff at regional hospital board headquarters.
6. Includes Area health authorities headquarters staff, Welsh health technical services organisation (WHTSO) staff, family practitioner committees (FPC) staff and community health care staff.
7. Including for Wales, maintenance and architectural, engineering, surveying staff and ancillary, hospital, community health care and ambulance staff.
8. Principals providing unrestricted services as at 1 October.
9. The cost of prescriptions dispensed during the calendar year as certified by the Pricing authorities.
10. All assistants are included.
11. Number scheduled for payment.
12. Number of sight tests paid for by FPCs in the period and not those carried out.
13. England figures contain an element of arrears payments.
14. Figures contain an element of arrears payments which cannot be apportioned between sight testing and dispensing.
15. Welsh figures contain an element of arrears payments.

Sources Department of Health and Social Security; Welsh Office

3.30 Hospital and primary care services
Scotland

	Unit	1973	1974	1975	1976	1977	1978	1979	1980	1981	1982	1983
Hospital services												
In-patients:												
Average allocated staffed beds[1]	Thousands	61.8	61.5	60.7	59.8	59.1	58.8	58.3	57.9	57.9	57.6	57.4
Average occupied beds:[1]												
All departments	,,	51.5	51.5	50.6	50.2	49.8	49.5	48.7	48.4	48.1	47.8	47.3
Mental and mentally deficient	,,	24.1	23.8	23.4	23.0	22.7	22.3	21.8	21.3	21.0	20.7	20.6
Discharges or deaths[1,2]	,,	706	718	697	743	737	749	738	774	793	794	785
Out-patients[1,3]:												
New cases	,,	1 782	1 819	1 812	1 882	1 920	1 961	1 961	1 999	2 033	2 047	2 027
Total attendances	,,	4 770	5 061	5 000	5 136	5 128	5 183	5 203	5 321	5 434	5 440	5 384
Medical and dental staff[4,5]:												
Whole-time	Number	3 797	3 915	4 027	4 107	4 220	4 293	4 446	4 456	4 479	4 584	4 657
Part-time	,,	1 167	1 185	1 221	1 245	1 221	1 218	1 280	1 267	1 465	1 362	1 420[10]
Professional and technical staff[4]:												
Whole-time	,,	5 250	5 240	5 604	5 816	5 998	6 267	6 460	6 615	6 812	6 902	7 071
Part-time	,,	1 126	1 222	1 329	1 317	1 289	1 244	1 357	1 378	1 415	1 404	1 400[10]
Nursing and midwifery staff[4]:												
Whole-time	,,	31 968	31 804	33 659	34 489	34 484	35 368	36 594	37 977	40 218	40 810	41 328
Part-time	,,	18 395	20 564	23 620	23 462	23 030	23 311	23 800	23 974	24 407	24 420	24 068[10]
Administrative and clerical staff[4]:												
Whole-time	,,	4 302	4 622	4 883	5 259	5 105	5 027	5 106	5 158	5 310	5 400	5 533
Part-time	,,	1 110	1 365	1 605	1 791	1 846	1 838	1 894	1 927	2 066	2 155	2 274[10]
Domestic, transport, etc. staff[4]:												
Whole-time	,,	19 218	19 917	19 957	19 916	19 804	18 970	17 742	17 481	17 465	17 259	16 854
Part-time	,,	11 799	13 087	13 940	14 311	14 535	14 914	14 946	15 211	15 661	16 152	16 296
Cost of services (gross)[6]	£ million	238.8	308.1	396.9	456.8	518.5	628.7	749.3	964.3	1 117.9	1 212.6	1 290.2
Payments by patients[6]	,,	0.9	0.9	0.9	0.9	0.9	0.8	0.9	1.0	1.2	1.1	1.3
Payments out of public funds[6]	,,	237.9	307.2	396.0	455.9	517.6	627.9	748.4	963.3	1 116.7	1 211.5	1 288.9
Primary care services												
Medical services												
Doctors on the list[7]:												
Principals	Number	2 699	2 745	2 797	2 820	2 839	2 884	2 921	2 959	3 001	3 040	3 106
Assistants	,,	51	46	29	31	40	34	22	28	29	32	31
Average number of patients per principal doctor	,,	2 001	1 973	1 939	1 928	1 905	1 875	1 857	1 835	1 804	1 778	1 739
Payments to doctors	£ million	23.6	26.2	34.3	40.4	43.7	49.0	59.3	76.7	90.7	102.2	110.8
Pharmaceutical services												
Prescriptions dispensed	Million	29.7	30.7	31.3	33.4	33.0	34.5	34.3	34.3	33.9	35.0	35.7
Payments to pharmacists (gross)[8]	£ million	28.3	33.6	44.1	56.6	62.8	81.1	90.1	111.1	126.7	144.4	161.1
Average gross cost per prescription	£	0.954	1.097	1.409	1.695	2.079	2.341	2.625	3.242	3.741	4.128	4.514
Dental services												
Dentists on list[9]	Number	1 067	1 117	1 128	1 133	1 164	1 188	1 207	1 251	1 294	1 362	1 407
Number of courses of treatment completed	Thousands	2 182	2 279	2 345	2 363	2 419	2 419	2 460	2 549	2 595	2 672	2 742
Payments to dentists (gross)	£ million	11.5	14.2	18.5	20.4	22.2	25.0	29.9	36.6	41.4	46.1	50.9
Payments by patients	,,	2.7	3.0	3.1	4.0	5.3	5.8	6.9	9.5	12.0	15.3	17.9
Payments out of public funds	,,	8.8	11.2	15.4	16.4	16.9	19.2	23.0	27.1	29.4	30.8	32.9
Average gross cost per course	£	5.3	6.2	7.8	8.6	9.2	10.4	12.2	14.3	15.9	17.3	18.5
General ophthalmic services												
Number of sight tests given	Thousands	614	644	668	714	673	688	722	727	736	761	816
Number of pairs of glasses supplied	,,	451	509	590	543	522	489	522	546	552	568	570
Cost of services (gross)	£ million	2.7	3.4	5.8	7.0	6.9	7.4	8.7	10.0	12.1	18.3	17.5
Payments by patients	,,	1.4	1.6	1.9	2.6	2.4	2.6	2.6	2.8	3.1	3.6	4.3
Payments out of public funds: For sight testing and dispensing	,,	1.3	1.8	3.9	4.4	4.5	4.8	6.1	7.2	9.0	14.7	13.2

1. In year to 30 September 1983 is to 31 March and is provisional.
2. Includes transfers out from 1976 onwards.
3. At out-patient and accident and emergency departments.
4. At 30 September.
5. Figures exclude officers holding honorary and locum appointments. Part-time includes maximum part-time and GP hospital appointments.
6. Estimated from financial year figures.
7. At 1 October.
8. For prescriptions dispensed in calendar year by all general practice pharmacists and appliance suppliers.
9. Assistants are excluded.
10. Provisional.

Source Common Services Agency for the Scottish Health Service

3.31 Hospital and general health services
Northern Ireland

	Unit	1974	1975	1976	1977	1978	1979	1980	1981	1982	1983
Hospital services											
In-patients:											
Beds available[1]	Number	17 504	17 266	17 236	17 221	17 093	17 126	17 060	17 023	9	16 978
Average daily occupation of beds	Per cent	*80.3*	*79.5*	*80.6*	*79.7*	*79.8*	*79.9*	*79.8*	*78.4*	9	*78.4*
Discharges or deaths	Thousands	224	220	231	231	237	241	246	249	9	258
Out-patients[2]:											
New cases	,,	559	563	589	592	608	618	628	637	9	685
Total attendances	,,	1 544	1 518	1 589	1 590	1 639	1 670	1 736	1 746	9	1 891
General health services											
Medical services											
Doctors (principals) on the list[3]	Number	744	741	742	734	735	747	764	790	813	838
Number of patients per doctor[4]	,,	2 107	2 105	2 140	2 163	2 189	2 165	2 097	2 032	1 981	1 951
Payments to doctors	£ thousand	6 642	8 741	10 401	11 146	12 310	14 392	19 325	22 923	24 854	28 539
Pharmaceutical services											
Prescription forms dispensed	Thousands	7 032	7 163	7 458	7 458	7 802	7 809	7 866	7 886	8 077	8 389
Number of prescriptions	,,	11 207	11 430	11 986	12 162	12 591	12 589	12 682	12 691	13 067	13 593
Payments to pharmacists (gross)	£ thousand	12 471	15 958	20 447	25 114	29 326	32 814	40 812	47 699	55 454	61 883
Payments by patients	,,	787	771	799	808	831	1 202	2 112	2 596	2 807	2 936
Payments out of public funds	,,	11 684	15 187	19 648	24 306	28 495	31 612	38 700	45 102	52 646	58 947
Average gross cost per prescription	£	1.113	1.396	1.706	2.065	2.329	2.607	3.22	3.76	4.24	4.55
Dental services											
Dentists on the list[1]	Number	320	310	309	310	309	319	336	342	363	377
Number of courses of treatment completed	Thousands	666	684	681	680	688	682	726	752	775	812
Payments to dentists (gross)	£ thousand	4 817	6 168	6 798	6 984	8 232	9 788	12 733	14 669	15 333	16 952
Payments by patients	,,	796	759	806	925	1 067	1 250	1 781	2 252	2 679	3 034
Payments out of public funds	,,	4 021	5 409	5 993	6 058	7 166	8 539	10 952	12 417	12 654	13 917
Average gross cost per course	£	7.2	9.0	10.0	10.3	12.0	14.3	17.5	19.5	19.8	20.9
Ophthalmic services											
Number of sight tests given[5]	Thousands	147	156	149	154	158	162	170	168	161	207
Number of optical appliances supplied	,,	126	142	135	129	132	135	146	144	143	168
Cost of service (gross)[6]	£ thousand	769	1 376	1 429	1 786	1 902	2 146	2 688	3 085	3 315	6 242
Payments by patients	,,	381	445	584	552	620	655	716	756	908	1 210
Payments out of public funds	,,	388	932	845	1 234	1 281	1 491	1 971	2 329	2 407	5 031
Health and social services[7]											
Medical and dental staff											
Whole-time	Number	1 280	1 464	1 483	1 585	1 711	1 810	1 864	1 874	1 935	1 988
Part-time	,,	709	697	706	721	711	726	725	697	661	660
Nursing and midwifery staff											
Whole-time	,,	11 872	12 254	12 439	12 912	13 269	13 523	14 082	14 971	15 391	15 376
Part-time	,,	4 048	4 558	4 121	4 242	4 676	5 288	5 704	5 857	5 811	5 722
Administrative and clerical staff											
Whole-time	,,	3 681	3 975	3 990	4 171	4 416	4 586	4 661	4 786	4 833	4 933
Part-time	,,	632	673	702	760	867	952	971	1 009	1 071	1 113
Professional and technical staff											
Whole-time	,,	1 658	1 683	1 786	1 888	2 051	2 080	2 121	2 157	2 172	2 261
Part-time	,,	366	361	375	371	397	414	445	437	442	419
Social services staff (excluding casual home helps)											
Whole-time	,,	2 015	2 264	2 465	2 751	2 956	3 199	3 402	3 554	3 728	3 717
Part-time	,,	493	601	625	708	799	959	1 009	1 086	1 180	1 240
Ancillary and other staff											
Whole-time	,,	8 189	8 582	8 887	9 218	9 355	9 357	9 432	9 574	9 608	9 279
Part-time	,,	3 086	3 306	3 755	4 063	4 358	4 535	4 644	4 949	5 174	5 238
Cost of services (gross)[8]	£ thousand	112 454	158 663	191 649	215 595	248 848	302 901	381 276	438 533	474 189	507 484
Payments by recipients	,,	1 745	2 098	2 543	3 064	3 564	4 223	4 978	5 924	7 066	7 747
Payments out of public funds	,,	110 709	156 565	189 106	212 531	245 284	298 677	376 298	432 609	467,123	499 737

1. Average during year.
2. At out-patient and casualty departments.
3. At 31 March.
4. At 1 July.
5. Excluding sight tests given in hospitals and under the school health service.
6. Figures from 1977 include payments of VAT and superannuation.

7. Manpower figures refer to 31 December. From 1981, figures for medical and dental staff included some joint appointees, information for whom is not held on the computer payroll.
8. Figures relate to the cost of the hospital, community health, and personal social services, and have been estimated from financial year data.
9. Data not available due to industrial action.

Source Department of Health and Social Services (Northern Ireland)

3.32 Health and personal social services: manpower summary
Great Britain
At 30 September each year

Number or whole-time equivalent

	1973	1974	1975	1976	1977	1978	1979	1980	1981	1982	1983
Health service staff and practitioners: total	843 119	859 468	914 068	945 877	950 498	966 584	983 983	1 008 200	1 045 504	1 056 807	..
Regional and area health authorities/boards and boards of governors staff: total[1]	794 028	809 681	863 347	894 294	898 127	913 539	929 816	952 415	988 273	997 633	..
Medical staff: total	33 329	34 338	36 217	37 257	38 224	39 256	40 571	41 729	42 566	43 161	43 939
Hospital medical staff: total[2,3]	30 594	31 486	33 017	33 909	34 821	35 815	37 102	38 235	39 012	39 618	40 382
Consultant and Senior hospital medical officer with allowance[4]	11 086	11 477	11 793	12 230	12 400	12 726	13 004	13 482	13 777	14 017	14 349
Associate specialist	1 039	1 065	1 106	1 072	1 069	1 013	1 020	1 039	1 014	1 035	1 019
Senior registrar	2 248	2 327	2 419	2 530	2 639	2 688	2 808	2 933	3 046	3 079	3 187
Registrar	5 661	5 626	6 036	6 165	6 266	6 479	6 613	6 764	6 787	6 995	7 099
Junior hospital medical officer	3	..	..	..	..	..	..	..	..	..	..
Senior house officer including Post registration House officer[5]	7 361	7 762	8 396	8 966	9 325	9 668	10 285	10 590	10 904	11 023	1 137
Pre-registration House officer	2 941	2 996	3 051	2 824	3 022	3 149	3 291	3 355	3 419	3 411	3 553
Other staff[6]	254	233	216	122	100	91	81	71	66	58	37
Community health medical staff[7,8]	2 735	2 852	3 200	3 348	3 403	3 442	3 469	3 494	3 554	3 543	3 557
Dental staff: total	2 535	2 745	2 935	2 957	3 019	3 101	3 146	3 141	3 202	3 245	3 227
Hospital dental staff: total[2]	943	996	1 057	1 078	1 118	1 153	1 210	1 220	1 250	1 288	1 288
Consultant and Senior hospital dental officer with allowance[4]	358	376	384	398	419	433	452	471	477	485	489
Associate specialist	65	59	78	83	86	74	76	91	91	101	103
Senior registrar	96	91	109	109	108	112	111	100	108	106	112
Registrar	145	152	167	160	175	190	206	204	199	211	210
Senior house officer	102	134	132	150	157	174	182	186	196	197	202
Dental house officer	135	152	159	158	157	154	170	159	170	180	166
Other staff[6]	43	33	28	20	16	16	12	10	10	8	5
Community health dental staff[7,8]	1 592	1 749	1 878	1 879	1 901	1 948	1 936	1 921	1 952	1 957	1 939
Nursing and midwifery staff: total[9]	370 595	377 633	405 817	414 961	415 694	424 304	433 490	448 824	474 497	481 873	..
Qualified nurses and midwives	185 119	189 567	202 464	213 225	219 900	226 904	233 249	240 462	256 921	265 109	..
Student and pupil nurses and midwives	95 321	93 285	95 461	98 961	94 939	92 433	91 043	91 983	96 255	97 044	..
Other nursing and midwifery staff	84 246	90 219	103 679	99 822	99 675	104 154	108 582	115 808	120 991	119 504	..
Nursing cadets	5 910	4 563	4 212	2 953	1 181	813	616	571	330	216	..
Professional and technical (excluding works) staff[7,10]	53 552	52 828	57 025	63 539	65 405	68 650	72 097	74 153	77 887	80 299	..
Works and maintenance staff	26 656	27 445	29 457	30 042	30 493	30 867	31 243	32 166	32 977	32 971	..
Administrative and clerical staff[7,11,12]	87 406	94 798	105 781	112 982	113 757	115 107	118 078	120 492	124 426	124 863	..
Ambulance officers, ambulancemen/women and other ambulance staff	19 164	19 255	20 425	20 170	20 383	20 707	20 223	20 934	21 435	21 590	..
Ancillary and other staff	200 791	200 639	205 690	212 386	211 153	211 547	210 969	210 976	211 284	209 631	..

1. Common Service Agency Staff in Scotland are included from 1974 onwards.
2. Figures exclude locums, hospital practitioners, general practitioners participating in Hospital Staff funds and part-time medical/dental officers (clinical assistants).
3. Includes staff working in Blood Transfusion Centres and Mass Radiography Units.
4. Figures for senior hospital medical and dental officers with allowance have been combined with those for consultants. Due to rounding, the figures given here may differ slightly from the sum of those published in earlier volumes.
5. For 1972–1975 figures for Post-registration House officers are included with Pre-registration House officers, Senior House officers are shown separately.
6. Figures for 'Other Staff' include Senior hospital medical/dental officers without allowance.

7. Figures for 1972 and 1973 exclude community health staff in Scotland.
8. Includes community health doctors and dentists, school health service doctors and dentists and up to 1973, Regional Hospital Boards' administrative medical staff (doctors only); figures for the school health service 1972 and 1973 relate to 31 December. Figures from 1974 exclude occasional sessional staff for whom no whole-time equivalent was collected. From 1976 locum and temporary staff are excluded.
9. Figures relate to 31 December for community health staff in Scotland for 1972 and 1973.
10. Hospital social workers are included up to 1973—responsibility for these staff was transferred to Local Authority Social Service on 1 April 1974.
11. Figures exclude ambulance officers.
12. Includes Family Practitioner Service administrative and clerical staff.

Source Department of Health and Social Security

3.32

(*continued*)

Health and personal social services: manpower summary
Great Britain
At 30 September each year

Number or whole-time equivalent

	1973	1974	1975	1976	1977	1978	1979	1980	1981	1982	1983
Family Practitioner Committee services:											
Practitioners: total	45 691	45 985	46 688	47 439	48 283	48 978	50 011	51 381	52 897	54 263	..
General medical practitioners[13]:											
total	25 583	25 844	26 128	26 418	26 810	27 227	27 696	28 414	29 252	29 806	30 422[18]
Unrestricted principals	23 965	24 255	24 464	24 657	24 939	25 245	25 614	26 141	26 702	27 256	27 825[18]
Restricted principals	374	338	340	323	315	296	276	257	238	227	204[18]
Assistants	640	526	442	450	435	391	345	312	315	301	317[18]
Trainees	604	725	882	988	1 121	1 295	1 461	1 704	1 997	2 022	2 076[18]
General dental practitioners: total	12 520	12 704	12 921	13 254	13 564	13 740	13 989	14 316	14 803	15 305	15 769
Principals	12 124	12 383	12 620	13 015	13 359	13 573	13 845	14 173	14 671	15 181	15 646
Assistants	396	321	301	239	205	167	144	143	132	124	123
Ophthalmic medical practitioners[14]	980	918	943	948	949	913	918	938	963	957	973
Ophthalmic opticians[14]	5 219	5 141	5 184	5 218	5 235	5 246	5 680	5 511	5 540	5 608	5 697
Dispensing opticians[14]	1 392	1 378	1 509	1 601	1 725	1 862	2 027	2 200	2 338	2 460	2 558
Dental Estimates Board staff[15]:											
total	1 417	1 484	1 598	1 611	1 588	1 577	1 565	1 682	1 626	1 603	..
Professional and technical staff	5	6	4	6	6	1	1	1	1	1	..
Administrative and clerical staff	1 366	1 431	1 548	1 557	1 538	1 533	1 521	1 639	1 579	1 556	..
Ancillary and other staff	46	48	46	48	44	43	43	42	46	46	..
Prescription Pricing Authority/ Prescription Pricing Division staff/Welsh Pricing Committee[16]:											
total	1 983	2 318	2 435	2 533	2 501	2 490	2 591	2 722	2 708	2 583	..
Administrative and clerical staff	1 940	2 275	2 386	2 475	2 448	2 434	2 534	2 661	2 645	2 526	..
Ancillary and other staff	42	43	49	58	53	56	57	61	63	57	..
Personal social services staff[17]	151 162	166 197	179 070	183 894	187 930	192 160	193 614	199 529	200 945	203 883	

13. Figures relate to 1 October.
14. Figures relate to 31 December.
15. The figures for the Dental Estimates Board in Scotland for 1972 and 1973 are numbers instead of whole-time equivalents. The figures for England relate to 31 December for 1975.
16. The Prescription Pricing Authority in England is synonymous with the Prescription Pricing Division in Scotland. Figures for the Prescription Pricing Division relate to 30 November and are numbers instead of whole-time equivalents.
17. Figures are for England only.
18. Provisional.

Source Department of Health and Social Security

3.33 NHS hospitals: selected diagnoses of in-patients treated in non-psychiatric departments (excluding maternity)[1]
Great Britain

Thousands

Diagnostic group	Code numbers[2]	1979	1980	1981
All causes: total	001 – 999	4 961.1	5 167.9	5 355.7
Males		2 376.4	2 461.4	2 549.5
Females		2 584.7	2 706.5	2 806.2
Tuberculosis: total	010 – 018	10.9	10.3	9.2
Males		6.6	6.5	5.7
Females		4.3	3.8	3.5
Malignant neoplasms: total	140 – 208	417.0	433.8	451.5
Males		211.3	217.4	226.1
Females		205.7	216.4	225.4
Benign and unspecified neoplasms: total	210 – 239	95.3	96.7	97.8
Males		26.8	27.0	28.6
Females		68.5	69.7	69.2
Endocrine, metabolic and nutritional diseases and immunity disorders: total	240 – 279	96.9	100.4	101.3
Males		38.1	40.2	40.4
Females		58.8	60.2	60.9
Diseases of nervous system: total	320 – 359	103.5	109.5	114.9
Males		48.9	52.0	55.0
Females		54.6	57.5	59.9
Diseases of the heart, including rheumatic fever and hypertensive disease: total	390 – 429	337.1	346.1	359.9
Males		194.4	198.7	206.9
Females		142.7	147.4	153.0
Other diseases of circulatory system: total	430 – 459	248.7	262.3	271.3
Males		124.4	128.4	131.1
Females		124.3	133.9	140.2
Diseases of respiratory system: total	460 – 519	410.4	444.1	459.3
Males		232.8	249.4	260.7
Females		177.6	194.7	198.6
Diseases of digestive system: total	520 – 579	550.8	578.1	595.8
Males		293.9	310.6	316.6
Females		256.9	267.5	279.2
Diseases of urinary system: total	580 – 599	96.3	101.5	106.4
Males		52.0	55.8	57.9
Females		44.3	45.7	48.5
Deliveries and disorders of pregnancy, childbirth and puerperium: Females	630 – 676	157.2	159.1	159.6
Diseases of musculo-skeletal system: total	710 – 739	239.0	271.8	292.2
Males		107.8	123.1	130.4
Females		131.2	148.7	161.8
Fractures, dislocations and sprains: total	800 – 848	215.8	209.8	218.7
Males		113.7	108.8	112.0
Females		102.1	101.0	106.7
Other injuries and reactions: total	850 – 999	419.0	412.4	428.4
Males		237.1	232.5	243.0
Females		181.9	179.9	185.4
Other causes: total		1 563.2	1 632.0	1 689.4
Males		688.5	711.0	735.1
Females		874.7	921.0	954.3

1. Data for the eighth revision of the *International Classification of Diseases, Injuries and Causes of Death*, last appeared in *Annual Abstract of Statistics* No. 119, 1983 edition.

2. Code numbers refer to the Ninth Revision (1975) of the *International Classification of Diseases, Injuries and Causes of Death.* World Health Organisation.

Sources Department of Health and Social Security; Office of Population Censuses and Surveys; Welsh Office; Scottish Health Service

3.34 Notifications of infectious diseases

Number

	1973	1974	1975	1976	1977	1978	1979	1980	1981	1982	1983
United Kingdom											
Diphtheria	2	3	12	2	3	–	–	5	2	4	4
Typhoid and paratyphoid fevers	283	239	302	294	327	353	313	307	277	253	269
Scarlet fever	12 968	11 087	10 235	10 731	11 903	10 239	10 815	12 936	8 024	8 415	7 609
Whooping cough	2 754	18 259	9 923	4 392	18 129	70 508	33 200	22 873	21 459	70 868	21 589
Smallpox	6	–	–	–	–	2					
Dysentery	9 308	9 705	9 375	7 354	8 332	5 486	4 037	3 595	3 699	3 256	6 039
Tuberculosis: total	12 935	12 535	12 612	11 786	11 172	11 221	10 721	10 486	9 292	8 449	7 792
Respiratory	10 182	9 645	9 649	9 150	8 507	8 357	8 015	7 779	6 817	6 696	6 138
Other	2 753	2 890	2 963	2 636	2 665	2 864	2 706	2 697	2 475	1 906	1 764
Acute poliomyelitis[1]	7	8	4	15	18	3	8	3	2	4	5
England and Wales[2]											
Diphtheria	2	3	11	2	2	–	293	5	2	4	4
Typhoid and paratyphoid fevers	256	206	280	283	296	331	293	290	254	234	259
Scarlet fever	12 034	10 401	9 487	9 712	10 769	9 169	9 585	11 116	7 148	7 601	6 539
Measles	152 482	109 602	143 024	55 498	173 342	124 064	77 363	139 485	52 975	94 195	103 700
Whooping cough	2 437	16 225	8 910	3 907	17 475	65 956	30 816	21 131	19 395	65 810	19 340
Smallpox	6	–	–	–	–	2					
Dysentery	8 032	8 207	7 915	6 217	6 202	4 332	2 786	2 708	3 398	2 850	5 003
Food poisoning	7 059	6 225	8 863	9 051	7 922	9 739	11 060	10 071	9 925	14 242	17 726
Ophthalmia neonatorum	366	316	265	222	239	228	235	278	210	201	208
Tuberculosis[3, 4] total	11 156	10 677	10 818	10 098	9 520	9 682	9 266	9 142	8 128	7 406	6 800
Respiratory[5]	8 710	8 102	8 208	7 712	7 121	7 078	6 807	6 670	5 859	5 827	5 317
Other[5]	2 446	2 575	2 610	2 386	2 399	2 604	2 459	2 472	2 269	1 732	1 593
Acute poliomyelitis[1]	5	6	3	13	16	3	8	3	2	2	4
Acute encephalitis (infective and post infective)	171	108	126	102	103	154	79	91	58	71	56
Acute meningitis: total	2 103	2 222	2 635	1 896	1 339	1 697	1 427	1 796	1 393	1 271	1 226
Meningococcal	1 067	1 296	863	718	500	500	525	509	464	410	428
Scotland											
Diphtheria	–	–	1	–	1	–	–	–	–	–	–
Typhoid and paratyphoid fevers	27	32	15	10	29	20	18	17	20	18	10
Erysipelas	126	34	33	97	94	78	90	99	87	76	75
Scarlet fever	579	422	430	712	821	766	818	1 343	592	552	734
Measles	15 733	7 515	5 619	12 436	8 626	8 953	10 324	6 646	4 698	10 581	6 193
Whooping cough	126	1 691	813	371	943	3 500	1 885	1 366	1 385	4 224	1 870
Smallpox	–	–	–	–	–	–	–	–	–	–	–
Dysentery	1 138	1 301	1 206	907	2 015	1 076	1 052	854	204	261	871
Food poisoning	1 094	829	1 413	2 023	1 563	2 319	1 937	1 836	2 934	3 038	2 632
Ophthalmia neonatorum	48	40	65	60	37	33		27	38	45	86
Pneumonia[6]	2 425	2 007	..	..	..	..	..	..	..	..	..
Puerperal fever and pyrexia	26	8	6	5	11	10	5	2	9	4	6
Tuberculosis[7] total	1 483	1 612	1 582	1 483	1 465	1 322	1 224	1 138	972	902	829
Respiratory	1 230	1 344	1 270	1 265	1 226	1 093	1 014	943	799	762	692
Other	253	268	312	218	239	229	210	195	173	140	137
Acute poliomyelitis[1]	2	1	1	2	–	–	–	–	–	1	1
Northern Ireland											
Diphtheria	–	–	–	–	–	–	–	–	–	–	–
Typhoid and paratyphoid fevers	–	1	7	1	2	2	2	–	3	1	–
Scarlet fever	355	264	318	307	313	304	412	477	284	262	336
Whooping cough	191	343	200	114	311	1 052	499	376	679	834	379
Smallpox	–	–	–	–	–	–	–	–	–	–	–
Dysentery	138	197	254	230	115	78	199	33	72	145	165
Tuberculosis: total	296	246	212	205	187	217	231	206	190	141	163
Respiratory	242	199	171	173	160	186	194	176	159	107	129
Other	54	47	41	32	27	31	37	30	31	34	34
Acute poliomyelitis[1]	–	1	–	–	2	–	–	–	–	1	–

1. Including acute polioencephalitis.
2. The figures show the corrected number of notifications, incorporating revisions of diagnosis, either by the notifying medical practitioner or by the medical superintendent of the infectious diseases hospital. Cases notified in Port Health Districts are excluded.
3. Formal notifications of new cases only.
4. The figures for 1982 and 1983 exclude chemoprophylaxis. The numbers of chemoprophylaxis cases reported were 597 and 354 respectively.

5. In 1982 and 1983 categories overlap and therefore cases will be included in respiratory and other tuberculosis (totals of 153 and 110 respectively).
6. Acute primary and acute influenzal. Ceased to be notifiable from 1975.
7. From 1974, figures include cases of tuberculosis not notified before death. Prior to 1974 recording practice may or may not have included such cases, as notifications.

Sources Office of Population Censuses and Surveys; Common Services Agency for the Scottish Health Service; General Register Office (Northern Ireland)

3.35 Industrial diseases in Great Britain

	1973	1974	1975	1976	1977	1978	1979	1980	1981	1982	1983[2]
Cases reported: total	488	411	475	506	470	338	260	221	122	97	62
Lead poisoning	58	36	27	31	12	14	8	11	3	4	1
Other poisoning	21	21	42	45	27	19	17	8	7	6	3
Anthrax	1	2	1	3	3	1	–	–	–	–	–
Epitheliomatous ulceration	9	12	11	7	15	12	4	5	3	–	–
Chrome ulceration	117	71	69	65	120	65	36	39	16	18	9
Compressed air illness	2	1	16	34	–	–	–	1	–	–	9
Gassing[1]	280	268	309	321	293	227	195	157	93	69	40
Deaths reported: total	6	9	6	4	4	2	5	4	4	–	1
Lead poisoning	–	–	–	–	1	–	–	–	–	–	–
Other poisoning	–	1	–	1	–	–	–	–	–	–	–
Anthrax	–	–	–	–	–	–	–	–	–	–	–
Epitheliomatous ulceration	1	2	–	–	2	–	1	–	–	–	–
Chrome ulceration	–	–	–	–	–	1	–	–	–	–	–
Compressed air illness	–	–	–	–	–	–	–	–	–	–	–
Gassing[1]	5	6	6	3	1	1	4	4	4	–	1

1. Figures include persons injured in gassing accidents, deaths are also included in Table 3.36.
2. Provisional.

Source Health and Safety Executive

3.36 Fatal injuries[1] at work
Standard Industrial Classification 1968

Number

		1981	1982	1983[6]
I	Agriculture, forestry and fishing	69	66	64
II	Mining and quarrying[2]	61	73	46
III	Food, drink and tobacco	10	10	23
IV	Coal and petroleum products	3	3	1
V	Chemicals and allied industries	8	6	11
VI	Metal manufacture	19	27	13
VII	Mechanical engineering	12	19	18
VIII	Instrument engineering	–	–	–
IX	Electrical engineering	1	8	3
X	Shipbuilding and marine engineering	13	8	4
XI	Vehicles	6	5	8
XII	Metal goods not elsewhere specified	11	11	4
XIII	Textiles	6	7	5
XIV	Leather, leather goods and fur	–	–	–
XV	Clothing and footwear	3	1	5
XVI	Bricks, pottery, glass, cement, etc.	5	11	4
XVII	Timber, furniture, etc.	7	9	10
XVIII	Paper, printing and publishing	5	6	6
XIX	Other manufacturing industries	10	2	6
	Total: all manufacturing industries	119	133	121
XX	Construction	129	131	148
XXI	Gas, electricity and water	10	14	12
XXII	Transport and communication	52	59	89
XXIII	Distributive trades	12	11	15
XXIV	Insurance, banking, finance and business services	–	3	–
XXV	Professional and scientific services	25	16	19
XXVI	Miscellaneous service	30	47	43
XXVII	Public administration and defence	19	17	22
	Unclassified[3]	50	33	47
	Total reported to Enforcement Authorities	576	603	626
Reported to other authorities under:				
Merchant Shipping (Returns of Births and Deaths) Regulations:[4]		44	49	25
(a) Seamen				
(b) Fishermen:				
	Deep sea trawlers (over 80 ft. in length)	3	3	5
	Other fishing vessels	22	14	1
	Total fishermen	25	17	6
Total Merchant Shipping, etc. Regulations		69	66	31
Civil aviation (various legislation)[5]		7	6	1
Total reported to other authorities		76	72	32
Total reported to all authorities		652	675	658

Footnotes see page 71.   Sources Health and Safety Executive; Department of Energy; Department of Transport; Department of Trade; Civil Aviation Authority

3.37 Private households with usual residents: Census 1981
number of families and family type by selected tenures of households in permanent buildings and with no car

Number of families in household and family type	All households	Selected tenures of households in permanent buildings			With no car
		Owner occupied	Rented		
			From council or new town	Unfurnished	
Great Britain					
All households	1 949 341	1 084 545	607 085	114 553	768 474
Households with no family	516 171	222 685	174 084	53 066	365 946
One person	423 980	178 732	152 025	44 603	322 613
Two or more persons	92 191	43 953	22 059	8 463	43 333
Households with one family	1 416 132	852 256	426 900	60 909	397 726
Married couple family	1 252 564	787 622	345 521	52 289	310 261
With no children	498 920	306 319	133 694	31 371	162 350
With at least one dependent child	595 088	387 713	158 577	15 342	117 754
With non-dependent child(ren) only	158 556	93 590	53 250	5 576	30 157
Lone parent family	163 568	64 634	81 379	8 620	87 465
With at least one dependent child	91 582	31 859	49 605	3 825	53 815
With non-dependent child(ren) only	71 986	32 775	31 774	4 795	33 650
Households with two or more families	17 038	9 604	6 101	578	4 802
England and Wales					
All households	1 770 745	1 022 529	509 678	107 279	681 914
Households with no family	469 089	208 665	148 560	49 763	329 447
One person	384 915	167 373	129 989	41 836	290 990
Two or more persons	84 174	41 292	18 571	7 927	38 457
Households with one family	1 286 201	804 662	356 095	56 972	348 387
Married couple family	1 139 273	743 572	286 554	48 887	271 792
With no children	458 406	290 246	113 575	29 478	145 770
With at least one dependent child	537 926	364 711	129 228	14 201	100 570
With non-dependent child(ren) only	142 941	88 615	43 751	5 208	25 452
Lone parent family	146 928	61 090	69 541	8 085	76 595
With at least one dependent child	83 057	30 327	43 270	3 613	47 667
With non-dependent child(ren) only	63 871	30 763	26 271	4 472	28 928
Households with two or more families	15 455	9 202	5 023	544	4 080
Scotland					
All households	178 596	62 016	97 407	7 274	86 560
Households with no family	47 082	14 020	25 524	3 303	36 499
One person	39 065	11 359	22 036	2 767	31 623
Two or more persons	8 017	2 661	3 488	536	4 876
Households with one family	129 931	47 594	70 805	3 937	49 339
Married couple family	113 291	44 050	58 967	3 402	38 469
With no children	40 514	16 073	20 119	1 893	16 580
With at least one dependent child	57 162	23 002	29 349	1 141	17 184
With non-dependent child(ren) only	15 615	4 975	9 499	368	4 705
Lone parent family	16 640	3 544	11 838	535	10 870
With at least one dependent child	8 525	1 532	6 335	212	6 148
With non-dependent child(ren) only	8 115	2 012	5 503	323	4 722
Households with two or more families	1 583	402	1 078	34	722

Note Figures are based on a ten per cent sample.

Source Office of Population, Censuses and Surveys; General Register Office (Scotland)

Table 3.36 (*contd.*)
See *Note* on page 43.
1. Includes injuries to employees and non-employees i.e. the self-employed and members of the public.
2. Includes figures for the oil and gas industry collected under the Minerals Working (Offshore Installations) Act 1971.
3. Mainly local authorities for which an industrial breakdown is not available.
4. The numbers of fatal accidents include deaths of the crew of vessels registered in the United Kingdom resulting from casualties to vessels and accidents on board (excluding homicide and suicide) and the presumed deaths of crew members missing at sea.
5. Fatal accidents at home and overseas to employees of air transport operators and other commercial aviation concerns in the United Kingdom.
6. Provisional.

3.38 Parliamentary elections

Thousands

	5 July 1945	23 Feb 1950	25 Oct 1951	26 May 1955	8 Oct 1959	15 Oct 1964	31 Mar 1966	18 June 1970[1]	28 Feb 1974	10 Oct 1974	3 May 1979	9 June 1983
United Kingdom												
Number of electors	33 240	34 412	34 919	34 852	35 397	35 894	35 957	39 615	40 256	40 256	41 573	42 704
Average — electors per seat	51.9	55.1	55.9	55.3	56.2	57.0	57.1	62.9	63.4	63.4	65.5	65.7
Number of votes cast	25 095	28 771	28 597	26 760	27 863	27 657	27 265	28 345	31 340	29 189	31 221	30 671
As percentage of electorate	75.5	83.6	81.9	76.8	78.7	77.1	75.8	71.5	77.9	72.5	75.1	71.8
England and Wales												
Number of electors	28 992	30 177	30 626	30 591	31 109	31 610	31 695	34 931	35 509	35 509	36 695	37 708
Average — electors per seat	52.4	55.1	56.5	55.9	56.9	57.8	57.9	63.9	64.3	64.3	66.5	67.2
Number of votes cast	21 950	25 483	25 356	23 570	24 619	24 384	24 116	24 877	27 735	25 729	27 609	27 082
As percentage of electorate	75.7	84.4	82.8	77.0	79.1	77.1	76.1	71.2	78.1	72.5	75.2	71.8
Scotland												
Number of electors	3 407	3 370	3 421	3 388	3 414	3 393	3 360	3 659	3 705	3 705	3 837	3 934
Average — electors per seat	46.0	47.5	48.2	47.7	48.1	47.8	47.3	51.5	52.2	52.2	54.0	54.6
Number of votes cast	2 423	2 727	2 778	2 543	2 668	2 635	2 553	2 688	2 887	2 758	2 917	2 825
As percentage of electorate	71.1	80.9	81.2	75.1	78.1	77.6	76.0	73.5	77.9	74.5	76.0	71.8
Northern Ireland												
Number of electors	841	865	872	873	875	891	902	1 025	1 042	1 042	1 041	1 061
Average — electors per seat	64.7	72.1	72.5	72.8	72.9	74.2	75.2	85.4	86.8	86.8	86.8	62.4
Number of votes cast	722	561	463	647	576	638	596	779	718	702	696	765
As percentage of electorate	85.9	64.9	53.1	74.1	65.8	71.7	66.1	76.0	68.9	67.4	66.9	72.1
Number of Members of Parliament elected:	640	625	625	630	630	630	630	630	635	635	635	650
Conservative	212	297	320	344	364	303	253	330	296	276	339	396
Labour	393	315	295	277	258	317	363	287	301	319	268	209
Liberal	12	9	6	6	6	9	12	6	14	13	11	17
Social Democratic Party	–	–	–	–	–	–	–	–	–	–	–	6
Scottish National Party	–	–	–	–	–	–	–	1	7	11	2	2
Plaid Cymru	–	–	–	–	–	–	–	–	2	3	2	2
Other[2]	23	4	4	3	2	1	2	6	15	13	13	18

1. The Representation of the Peoples Act 1969 lowered the minimum voting age from 21 to 18 years with effect from 16 February 1970.
2. The Speaker is included in Other.

Sources Home Office; Scottish Home and Health Department; Northern Ireland Office

3.39 Parliamentary by-elections

	June 1970 – Feb 1974	Previous[1] General Election June 1970	March 1974 – Oct 1974	Previous[1] General Election Feb 1974	Oct 1974 – May 1979	Previous[1] General Election Oct 1974	May 1979 – June 1983	Previous[1] General Election May 1979	June 1983 – June 1984	Previous[1] General Election June 1983
Number of by-elections	30		1		30		20		6	
Votes recorded										
By party (*percentages*)										
Conservative	34.2	44.8	11.1	12.2	45.1	32.0	23.8	33.7	32.3	45.9
Labour	40.5	42.2	62.6	66.1	36.6	44.8	25.7	35.2	28.8	27.2
Liberal[2]	15.3	6.0	12.5	14.8	10.9	17.3	9.0	8.0	21.3	13.8
Social Democratic Party[2]	–	–	–	–	–	–	14.2	–	14.4	11.5
Plaid Cymru	1.2	0.3	–	–	–	–	0.5	0.4	1.4	1.2
Scottish National Party	3.5	1.1	–	–	2.7	2.6	1.7	1.4	–	–
Other	5.4	5.6	13.7	6.9	4.7	3.3	25.1[3]	21.2[3]	1.9	0.4
Total votes recorded										
(*percentages*)	100.0	100.0	100.0	100.0	100.0	100.0	100.0	100.0	100.0	100.0
(*thousands*)	1 028	1 210	15	36	1 058	1 288	715	852	255	293

1. Votes recorded in the same seats in the previous General Election.
2. The Social Democratic Party was launched on 26 March 1981. An SDP candidate contested a Parliamentary seat for the first time in the by-election held at Warrington on 16 July 1981. From that date, the Liberal and Social Democratic Parties contested 19 by-elections with only one of the parties putting up a candidate in each.

3. The proportions of votes recorded for 'other' is high because 3 of the 20 by-elections were in Northern Ireland. Two were in the same constituency, Fermanagh and South Tyrone, and as votes recorded at both by-elections have been included, votes recorded for the 1979 General Election have been included twice in the previous General Election column.

Source Home Office

4 Law enforcement

There are differences in the legal and judicial systems of England and Wales, Scotland and Northern Ireland which make it impossible to provide tables covering the United Kingdom as a whole in this section. These differences concern the classification of offences, the meaning of certain terms used in the statistics and the effects of the several Criminal Justice Acts.

Court proceedings and police cautions

The statistical basis of the tables of court proceedings is broadly similar in England and Wales, Scotland and Northern Ireland; the tables show the number of persons found guilty, recording a person under the heading of the principal offence of which he is found guilty, excluding additional findings of guilt at the same proceedings. A person found guilty at a number of separate court proceedings is included more than once. In Scotland not all cases in which a charge is proved lead to a formal conviction or finding of guilt; these cases are those in summary procedure in which the accused receives an absolute discharge or a probation order.

The statistics on offenders cautioned covers only those who, on admission of guilt were given a formal caution by, or on the instructions of, a senior police officer as an alternative to prosecution; written warnings by the police for motoring offences and persons

paying fixed penalties for certain motoring offences are excluded. There are no statistics on cautioning available for Northern Ireland.

From 1979 a new offence classification and tabulation procedure was introduced to reflect the changes in the mode of trial introduced by Part III of the Criminal Law Act 1977 in July 1978. Figures for 1977 and 1978 are given on the new basis to enable comparisons to be made with 1979 to 1983. Figures for 1969 to 1978 on the old basis last appeared in *Annual Abstract of Statistics* No 118, 1982 edition. Indictable offences cover offences for which a defendant may be tried at the Crown Court; summary offences cover offences for which the defendant may only be tried at a Magistrates' Court. Since 29 March 1982 the courts have had the power to suspend between one quarter and three quarters of a sentence of imprisonment of six months for up to two years.

Section 45 of the Criminal Justice (Scotland) Act 1980 was implemented on 15 November 1983; this introduced unified custodial sentencing for under 21 offenders and abolished borstal training.

In Northern Ireland non-indictable offences are dealt with at Magistrates' Courts where some indictable offences may also be tried. The majority of indictable offences are, however, tried at Crown Courts. The Crown Court system was introduced in Northern Ireland in April 1979; prior to this date the County Courts and Assizes system was equivalent to the Crown Court in England and Wales.

4.1 Notifiable[1] offences recorded by the police
England and Wales

Thousands

	1973	1974	1975	1976	1977	1978	1979	1980[2]	1981[2]	1982[2]	1983[2]
Total[3]	1 657.7	1 963.4	2 105.6	2 135.7	2 636.5	2 561.5	2 536.7	2 688.2	2 963.8	3 262.4	3 247.0
Violence against the person	61.3	63.8	71.0	77.7	82.2	87.1	95.0	97.2	100.2	108.7	111.3
Sexual offences[4]	25.7	24.7	23.7	22.2	21.3	22.4	21.8	21.1	19.4	19.7	20.4
Burglary	393.2	483.8	521.9	515.5	604.1	565.7	549.1	622.6	723.2	810.6	813.4
Robbery	7.3	8.7	11.3	11.6	13.7	13.1	12.5	15.0	20.3	22.8	22.1
Theft and handling stolen goods[5]	998.9	1 189.9	1 267.7	1 285.7	1 487.5	1 441.3	1 416.1	1 463.5	1 603.2	1 755.9	1 705.9
Fraud and forgery	110.7	117.2	123.1	119.9	120.6	122.2	118.0	105.2	106.7	123.1	121.8
Criminal damage[3]	52.8	67.1	78.5	93.0	297.4	306.2	320.5	359.5	386.7	417.8	443.3
Other offences[5, 6]	7.8	8.2	8.4	10.1	9.7	3.5	3.7	4.1	4.1	3.8	8.7

1. These offences were referred to in 1978 and earlier years as 'Indictable offences recorded by the police'.
2. Figures for 1980 onwards are not comparable with those for previous years because of changes to improve the consistency of recording of multiple, continuous and repeated offences.
3. Offences of criminal damage value £20 and under are not included before 1977; in 1983 there were 176 100 such offences.

4. Includes from the beginning of 1983 offences of 'Gross indecency with a child' (511 offences).
5. Offences of abstracting electricity are included in 'Other offences' up to and including 1977 and in 'Theft and handling stolen goods' from 1978.
6. Includes from the beginning of 1983 offences of 'Trafficking in controlled drugs' (4 994 offences).

Source   Home Office

4.2 Police Forces: authorised establishment and strength
United Kingdom
End of year

Number

	1973	1974	1975	1976	1977	1978	1979	1980	1981	1982	1983
England and Wales											
Regular police											
Authorised establishment[1]	112 168	114 637	116 007	116 880	116 980	117 668	118 322	118 930	120 008	120 125	120 447
Strength[1]:											
Men	94 874	96 068	99 923	101 042	98 935	99 134	102 360	105 563	107 379	108 517	108 519
Women	4 337	4 706	5 773	6 997	7 789	8 477	9 394	10 355	10 702	10 935	10 995
Seconded[2]:											
Men	1 333	1 263	1 375	1 368	1 400	1 386	1 477	1 430	1 424	1 419	1 407
Women	67	65	67	69	77	78	78	75	70	80	82
Additional constables[3]:											
Men	259	196	201	144	97	85	114	96	90	89	84
Women	–	–	–	–	–	1	2	1	1	1	2
Special constables											
Enrolled strength:											
Men	23 443	22 050	20 743	19 046	16 923	14 636	13 513	12 438	11 813	11 932	11 743
Women	1 889	2 118	2 268	2 370	2 329	2 316	2 447	2 629	2 791	3 228	3 588
Scotland											
Regular police[4]											
Authorised establishment:											
Men	11 690	12 400	12 564 }	13 163	13 144	13 162	13 148	13 187	13 195	13 205	13 261
Women	543	577	581 }								
Strength[5]:											
Men	10 920	11 143	11 656	11 442	11 069	11 477	12 280	12 419	12 379	12 433	12 435
Women	488	532	676	737	763	746	786	771	749	719	713
Central service[5, 6]:											
Men	47	49	53	55	52	51	56	60	54	55	65
Women	4	3	3	2	3	4	4	5	2	2	2
Seconded[5, 7]:											
Men	125	124	85	99	78	72	72	69	78	73	68
Women	8	5	3	7	8	5	3	2	5	4	3
Additional regular police											
Authorised establishment[4]	44	44	44	157	174	179	126	72	67	62	60
Strength	44	44	44	138	174	176	148	71	66	62	60
Part-time auxiliaries[8]											
Strength:											
Men	3 909	3 810	3 563	3 266	3 102	2 974	2 944	2 807	2 612	2 528	2 439
Women	140	153	161	158	162	164	184	198	202	208	204
Northern Ireland											
Royal Ulster Constabulary											
Strength:											
Men	4 172	4 283	4 549	4 811	5 140	5 495	5 938	6 224	6 622	7 017	7 328
Women	219	282	353	442	552	615	676	711	712	701	675
Royal Ulster Constabulary											
Reserve Strength:											
Men	2 299	3 392	4 089	3 964	3 965	3 904	3 823	4 123	4 350	4 385	4 105
Women	215	468	730	733	721	704	690	629	520	455	388

1. Total of establishments of individual forces *plus* the Metropolitan Regional
   Crime Squad and additional constables in the Metropolitan Police.
2. Regional Crime Squads, other inter-force units and officers on central service.
3. Excluding additional constables in the Metropolitan Police Force.
4. From 1976, officers employed at ports, airports and oil related industries are
   no longer included in 'Regular police' but included in 'Additional regular
   police'.
5. 'Strength' includes central service and seconded police.
6. Instructors at Training Establishments, etc. formerly shown as secondments.
7. Scottish Crime Squad, Officers on courses, etc.
8. Including special constables (enrolled strength).

Sources Home Office; Scottish Home and Health Department; Northern Ireland
Office

4.3 Offenders found guilty: by offence group
Magistrates' courts and the Crown Court
England and Wales

Thousands

	1977	1978	1979	1980	1981	1982	1983
Offenders[1] of all ages found guilty				Indictable offences			
Total	429.3	414.2	412.3	455.4	464.6	475.1	461.0
Violence against the person:							
Murder	0.1	0.1	0.1	0.2	0.1	0.1	0.1
Manslaughter	0.2	0.2	0.3	0.3	0.3	0.2	0.2
Wounding	40.8	40.8	46.2	50.0	48.7	49.6	49.5
Other offences of violence against the person	1.5	1.5	1.9	1.9	1.7	1.7	1.6
Sexual offences	7.0	7.5	7.4	8.0	6.9	6.6	6.4
Burglary	70.1	69.0	59.1	68.1	76.4	76.5	72.7
Robbery	3.2	3.4	3.2	3.5	4.1	4.4	4.0
Theft and handling stolen goods	233.7	226.3	220.6	233.6	232.2	238.7	224.9
Fraud and forgery	20.8	19.9	20.9	24.9	25.7	24.9	25.6
Criminal damage	8.9	9.5	9.2	11.4	11.8	11.4	12.1
Other offences (excluding motoring)	15.0	15.8	21.6	27.9	29.0	31.2	33.4
Motoring offences	28.0	20.2	21.8	25.7	27.7	29.8	30.5
				Summary offences			
Total	1 526.8	1 462.5	1 485.8	1 756.3	1 640.1	1 555.9	1 634.5
Assaults	11.1	11.6	12.4	12.2	11.2	11.1	10.7
Betting and gaming	1.3	0.7	0.8	0.8	0.5	0.5	0.6
Breach of local or other regulations	17.2	16.8	16.9	19.2	15.8	14.7	14.4
Intoxicating Liquor Laws:							
Drunkenness	99.9	98.0	105.6	109.5	97.2	96.4	96.2
Other offences	7.3	8.0	8.9	8.6	6.5	4.9	4.5
Education Acts	4.1	3.7	3.5	3.7	3.0	2.9	2.5
Game Laws	2.1	1.9	1.8	1.7	1.9	1.7	1.9
Labour Laws	0.8	0.8	0.6	0.4	0.4	0.3	0.2
Summary offences of criminal damage and							
malicious damage	31.5	33.3	36.2	38.6	37.8	36.6	38.6
Offences by prostitutes	3.8	3.7	3.0	3.4	4.1	5.8	10.4
Railway offences	16.2	15.1	15.0	18.1	17.4	15.4	15.9
Revenue Laws	94.0	62.2	63.6	83.3	73.6	72.7	107.8
Motoring offences (summary)	1 122.6	1 088.9	1 079.8	1 294.1	1 210.5	1 128.0	1 161.7
Vagrancy Acts	4.2	4.2	3.8	3.9	2.9	2.0	1.6
Wireless Telegraphy Acts	45.2	40.8	33.7	44.7	49.6	61.9	67.5
Other summary offences	65.5	72.8	100.2	114.2	107.5	100.7	99.7
Persons aged under 17 found guilty[2]				Indictable offences			
Total	89.0	89.7	81.9	90.3	86.6	81.8	73.3
Violence against the person	5.7	6.0	6.6	7.4	7.3	7.3	6.7
Sexual offences	0.7	0.6	0.7	0.7	0.6	0.6	0.6
Burglary	29.2	28.8	22.6	25.6	25.8	23.0	21.2
Robbery	0.9	0.9	0.7	0.8	1.0	1.0	0.8
Theft and handling stolen goods	47.3	47.8	45.2	48.3	44.6	42.9	38.0
Fraud and forgery	1.0	1.0	1.0	1.1	1.1	0.9	0.8
Criminal damage	2.6	2.8	2.6	3.3	3.1	2.8	2.9
Other offences (excluding motoring)	0.3	0.3	0.5	0.6	0.7	0.7	0.6
Motoring offences	1.3	1.5	2.0	2.5	2.4	2.5	1.9
				Summary offences			
Total	33.7	35.1	34.5	37.8	31.7	28.3	27.1
Highway Acts and motoring summary offences:							
Offences with pedal cycles	2.2	2.3	2.7	3.1	2.4	2.1	2.2
Other	13.9	14.4	13.1	15.0	15.5	11.2	10.9
Breach of local or other regulations	1.0	1.0	1.1	1.4	0.9	0.8	0.8
Summary offences of criminal damage and							
malicious damage	6.8	7.0	6.8	7.5	7.1	6.0	6.2
Railway offences	1.3	1.5	1.6	1.6	0.7	0.7	0.7
Other summary offences	8.5	8.9	9.2	9.2	5.1	7.5	6.5

1. Includes 'Companies', etc. (see Tables 4.5 and 4.6).
2. Figures for persons aged under 17 are included in the totals for all offenders
above.

Source Home Office

4.4 Offenders cautioned: by offence group
England and Wales

Thousands

	1977	1978	1979	1980	1981	1982	1983
Offenders[1] of all ages cautioned			Indictable offences				
Total	111.2	103.0	96.8	100.9	103.9	111.3	114.9
Violence against the person	4.3	4.4	4.7	5.1	5.6	6.5	7.0
Sexual offences	3.1	3.0	2.8	2.9	2.8	2.7	2.9
Burglary	12.6	11.1	10.0	11.3	11.5	11.2	12.0
Robbery	0.1	0.1	0.1	0.1	0.1	0.2	0.2
Theft and handling stolen goods	85.5	79.1	75.0	77.0	79.2	85.9	86.9
Fraud and forgery	1.5	1.3	1.2	1.4	1.4	1.4	1.6
Criminal damage	2.0	2.1	2.0	2.0	2.1	1.9	2.4
Other offences (excluding motoring)	2.1	1.8	1.0	1.1	1.2	1.5	2.1
			Summary offences				
Total	38.1	38.4	39.7	45.0	50.0	49.2	50.6
Assaults	0.1	0.1	0.1	0.1	0.2	0.2	0.2
Betting and gaming	0.1	0.1	0.2	0.2	0.2	0.1	0.1
Breach of local or other regulations	1.2	1.1	1.1	1.2	1.3	1.2	1.2
Intoxicating Liquor Laws:							
Drunkenness	0.6	0.5	0.6	0.7	0.7	0.8	2.1
Other offences	2.3	2.4	2.5	3.0	3.0	2.8	2.2
Education Acts	[3]	[3]	[3]	[3]	[3]	[3]	[3]
Game Laws	0.2 [3]	0.2 [3]	0.2 [3]	0.1 [3]	0.2	0.2	0.2
Labour Laws					[3]	[3]	[3]
Summary offences of criminal damage and malicious damage	6.0	6.1	5.9	7.4	8.5	9.2	10.1
Offences by prostitutes	3.8	5.4	5.3	6.2	7.9	7.9	7.3
Railway offences	0.1	0.1	0.1	0.1	0.1	0.1	0.1
Revenue Laws	1.6	1.1	1.4	1.2	1.4	1.6	1.4
Highway Act offences	9.0	8.8	9.8	11.7	14.0	12.4	12.9
Vagrancy Acts	0.3	0.3	0.2	0.3	0.2	0.2	0.2
Wireless Telegraphy Acts	—	—	—	[3]	[3]	[3]	[3]
Other summary offences	12.8	11.8	12.3	12.7	12.4	12.5	12.7
Persons aged under 17 cautioned[2]			Indictable offences				
Total	95.2	87.5	82.2	85.5	87.6	93.0	94.6
Violence against the person	2.9	2.9	3.1	3.4	3.8	4.4	4.8
Sexual offences	1.3	1.3	1.3	1.4	1.4	1.4	1.5
Burglary	12.2	10.8	9.7	11.0	11.2	10.7	11.5
Robbery	0.1	0.1	0.1	0.1	0.1	0.1	0.2
Theft and handling stolen goods	75.4	69.2	65.2	66.6	68.2	73.2	73.2
Fraud and forgery	1.0	0.8	0.8	0.9	0.8	0.8	0.9
Criminal damage	1.9	2.0	1.9	1.8	1.9	1.8	2.2
Other offences (excluding motoring)	0.4	0.4	0.1	0.2	0.3	0.4	0.5
			Summary offences				
Total	16.7	15.9	16.0	18.9	20.6	19.8	20.8
Highway Acts offences:							
Offences with pedal cycles	4.3	4.3	4.7	5.3	5.4	4.8	5.0
Other	0.8	0.8	0.7	0.8	1.6	0.8	0.7
Breach of local or other regulations	0.7	0.6	0.6	0.7	0.6	0.6	0.6
Summary offences of criminal damage and malicious damage	5.3	5.2	5.0	6.5	7.5	8.0	8.7
Railway offences	0.1	0.1	0.1	0.1	0.1	0.1	0.1
Other summary offences	5.5	4.9	4.9	5.5	5.5	5.4	5.6

1. Includes 'Companies', etc. (see Tables 4.5 and 4.6).
2. Figures for persons aged under 17 are included in the figures for all offenders above.
3. Less than 50.

Source Home Office

4.5 Offenders found guilty of offences: by sex and age
Magistrates' courts and the Crown Court
England and Wales

Thousands

	1977	1978	1979	1980	1981	1982	1983
Males		Indictable offences					
All ages	356.6	350.5	349.2	386.6	397.9	407.7	397.0
10 and under 14 years	19.2	18.6	16.1	16.9	15.1	13.6	11.6
14 and under 17 years	59.7	60.8	56.6	63.5	62.3	59.5	54.4
17 and under 21 years	89.7	91.5	93.8	106.1	113.9	119.6	115.3
21 years and over	188.0	179.6	182.7	200.0	206.6	215.1	215.8
		Summary offences					
All ages	1 364.3	1 294.7	1 314.8	1 547.3	1 437.1	1 358.8	1 411.7
10 and under 14 years	3.2	3.2	3.2	3.2	2.7	2.2	2.2
14 and under 17 years	28.3	29.7	29.0	32.2	27.0	24.5	23.5
17 and under 21 years	175.0	181.6	193.0	227.7	215.8	213.2	212.2
21 years and over	1 157.8	1 080.2	1 089.6	1 284.3	1 191.6	1 118.9	1 173.8
Females		Indictable offences					
All ages	67.7	65.5	62.7	67.8	65.5	66.1	62.7
10 and under 14 years	2.5	2.3	2.0	2.0	1.8	1.7	1.3
14 and under 17 years	7.6	8.0	7.2	7.8	7.5	7.0	6.1
17 and under 21 years	12.6	12.6	13.0	14.7	14.6	15.1	14.8
21 years and over	45.0	42.6	40.5	43.3	41.6	42.3	40.5
		Summary offences					
All ages	139.7	144.0	145.9	181.01	175.6	169.4	190.4
10 and under 14 years	0.1	0.2	0.1	0.2	0.1	0.1	0.1
14 and under 17 years	2.1	2.0	2.1	2.2	1.8	1.5	1.4
17 and under 21 years	11.5	11.8	12.2	14.8	14.7	14.8	16.7
21 years and over	126.0	130.0	131.5	163.8	158.9	153.1	172.3
Companies, etc.							
Indictable offences	0.5	0.4	0.4	1.1	1.2	1.3	1.4
Summary offences	23.7	25.0	25.0	28.0	27.4	29.1	32.4

Source Home Office

4.6 Offenders cautioned by the police: by sex and age
England and Wales

Thousands

	1977	1978	1979	1980	1981	1982	1983
Males		Indictable offences					
All ages	86.3	79.6	69.1	73.3	75.1	78.5	82.7
10 and under 14 years	42.2	36.3	31.1	31.9	32.2	31.6	32.0
14 and under 17 years	33.3	32.7	28.9	31.7	32.6	35.4	37.5
17 and under 21 years	3.4	3.5	3.0	3.2	3.4	3.8	4.4
21 years and over	7.4	7.1	6.1	6.5	6.9	7.7	8.7
		Summary offences					
All ages	24.7	23.4	30.2	33.8	36.8	36.2	38.2
10 and under 14 years	3.1	2.7	5.1	5.6	6.3	5.9	6.3
14 and under 17 years	7.3	7.0	9.5	11.4	12.4	12.0	12.4
17 and under 21 years	2.6	2.7	3.2	3.6	4.5	4.6	4.6
21 years and over	11.7	11.0	12.4	13.2	13.7	13.7	14.9
Females		Indictable offences					
All ages	30.8	29.4	27.6	27.7	28.8	32.9	32.2
10 and under 14 years	14.2	13.0	11.9	11.3	11.5	12.8	12.0
14 and under 17 years	10.7	10.7	10.3	10.6	11.3	13.2	13.1
17 and under 21 years	0.7	0.7	0.7	0.7	0.8	1.0	1.1
21 years and over	5.2	5.0	4.7	5.0	5.2	5.9	6.1
		Summary offences					
All ages	7.5	9.0	9.5	11.1	13.1	13.0	12.4
10 and under 14 years	0.3	0.2	0.4	0.5	0.5	0.5	0.6
14 and under 17 years	0.8	0.8	1.0	1.4	1.5	1.4	1.6
17 and under 21 years	2.2	2.9	2.8	3.3	3.9	3.7	3.1
21 years and over	4.2	5.1	5.3	5.9	7.3	7.3	7.1
Companies, etc.							
Indictable offences	—	—	—	1	1	1	1
Summary offences	0.1	0.1	0.1	0.1	0.1	0.1	0.1

1. Less than 50.

Source Home Office

4.7 Sentence or order passed on offenders sentenced for indictable offences: by sex
Magistrates' courts and the Crown Court
England and Wales

Percentages

	1977	1978	1979	1980	1981	1982	1983
Males							
Total number of offenders (thousands) = 100 per cent	356.9	350.8	349.5	387.9	399.2	409.6	399.2
Sentence or order							
Absolute discharge	0.6	0.6	0.6	0.6	0.6	0.6	0.6
Conditional discharge	10.4	9.8	9.1	9.3	9.9	10.2	10.5
Probation order	4.3	4.1	4.5	5.0	5.4	5.5	6.0
Supervision order	3.8	3.6	3.6	3.7	3.3	3.1	2.8
Fine	50.6	50.0	49.8	48.1	45.0	44.0	43.0
Community service order	2.7	3.2	3.6	4.7	5.9	6.5	7.5
Attendance centre order	2.5	2.9	2.9	3.2	3.4	3.5	2.9
Detention centre order	2.9	3.2	3.1	3.0	3.2	3.1	0.5
Care order	1.3	1.3	1.0	1.0	0.8	0.7	3.6
Borstal training/Youth custody[1]	2.2	2.3	2.1	2.1	2.1	2.0	
Imprisonment							
Fully suspended[2]	7.7	7.7	7.6	7.4	7.6	7.7	6.7
Partly suspended[3]						0.3	0.9
Unsuspended[4]	9.8	10.3	10.7	10.6	11.3	11.7	10.4
Other sentence or order	1.1	1.1	1.2	1.2	1.1	1.2	1.2
Females							
Total number of offenders (thousands) = 100 per cent	67.7	65.5	62.7	67.8	65.4	66.0	62.7
Sentence or order							
Absolute discharge	1.0	0.9	0.8	0.8	0.8	0.8	0.8
Conditional discharge	20.2	19.4	18.8	19.1	20.8	21.7	22.3
Probation order	11.3	11.4	12.6	14.0	14.9	15.2	15.8
Supervision order	3.6	3.6	3.7	3.7	3.5	3.2	2.5
Fine	53.4	53.5	52.0	49.8	46.2	45.0	44.0
Community service order	0.8	1.1	1.4	1.7	1.9	2.3	2.6
Attendance centre order	–	–	0.2	0.5	0.7	0.8	0.8
Detention centre order	–	–	–	–	–	–	–
Care order	1.3	1.3	1.0	1.0	0.9	0.6	0.5
Borstal training/Youth custody[1]	0.5	0.5	0.5	0.6	0.4	0.3	0.9
Imprisonment							
Fully suspended[2]	4.5	4.9	5.1	5.0	5.3	5.7	5.0
Partly suspended[3]						0.2	0.6
Unsuspended[4]	2.4	2.7	2.9	3.0	3.4	3.5	3.2
Other sentence or order	0.8	0.7	1.0	0.9	0.9	0.9	1.0

1. Following the Criminal Justice Act 1982, borstal training was abolished with effect from 24 May 1983 and replaced by youth custody.
2. Up until 1982 this was known as Suspended sentence.
3. Introduced on 29 March 1982.
4. Up until 1982 this was known as Immediate imprisonment.

Source Home Office

4.8 Receptions into prison[1]: by number of previous convictions
England and Wales

Number of receptions

	1973	1974	1975	1976	1977	1978	1979	1980	1981	1982[2]	1983[2,3]
Number of previous convictions:											
Males: total	26 071	27 138	30 667	32 914	33 906	34 832	36 412	38 016	43 388	46 779	42 716
None	1 527	1 361	1 915	2 028	2 135	1 936	1 634	1 731	1 518	1 773	1 848
1–2 sentences	2 089	1 983	2 309	2 511	2 516	2 500	2 484	2 685	3 002	3 164	2 969
3–5 sentences	4 198	4 261	4 804	5 079	5 401	5 399	5 652	6 092	7 161	7 312	6 104
6–10 sentences	7 604	7 744	8 631	8 960	9 177	9 470	9 412	9 665	11 152	11 845	10 048
11 or more sentences	7 836	8 152	9 221	10 280	10 893	11 011	11 340	11 905	13 343	14 057	13 632
Previous conviction information not recorded	2 817	3 637	3 787	4 056	3 784	4 516	5 890	5 938	7 212	8 628	8 115
Females: total	1 136	1 112	1 351	1 614	1 839	2 000	2 109	2 265	2 533	2 692	2 349
None	157	147	226	259	231	240	156	155	177	176	271
1–2 sentences	62	55	71	120	152	149	148	172	234	261	273
3–5 sentences	126	100	118	204	285	279	293	322	423	445	419
6–10 sentences	172	142	135	230	279	253	287	331	434	443	401
11 or more sentences	111	110	94	125	207	189	196	195	267	322	294
Previous conviction information not recorded	508	558	707	676	685	890	1 029	1 090	998	1 045	691

1. Receptions into Prison Department custody under sentence of imprisonment without the option of a fine.
2. 1982 and 1983 data are not comparable because of the Criminal Justice Act 1982.
3. Youth custody for offenders aged 15 to 20 replaced imprisonment on 24 May 1983.

Source Home Office

4.9 Receptions and average population in custody
England and Wales

Number

	1973	1974	1975	1976	1977	1978	1979	1980	1981	1982[4]	1983[4]
Receptions											
Type of inmate											
Untried	46 144	51 422	53 450	45 285	44 471	39 757	41 394	40 145	47 169	48 474	47 496[5]
Convicted, unsentenced	23 770	23 683	25 911	24 194	22 561	21 071	22 565	21 771	24 085	23 268	19 585[5]
Remanded for medical examination[1]	2 959	2 782	3 292	2 637	2 220	1 810	2 003	1 760	1 568	1 357	..
Others	20 811	20 901	22 619	21 557	20 341	19 261	20 562	20 011	22 517	21 911	..
Sentenced	51 777	56 478	64 313	68 479	69 898	72 311	74 079	75 896	88 110	94 377	93 414
Immediate imprisonment[2]											
Up to 18 months	19 642	20 677	23 387	25 300	27 436	28 280	29 981	31 964	37 456	40 978	36 696
Over 18 months up to 4 years	6 391	6 440	7 344	7 742	6 933	7 164	7 114	6 929	7 039	6 849	6 772
Over 4 years (including life)	1 174	1 133	1 287	1 486	1 376	1 388	1 426	1 388	1 426	1 644	1 597
Imprisoned in default of payment of a fine	10 406	12 622	14 417	15 911	16 040	16 442	17 044	15 938	21 153	24 492	23 241
Youth custody[2]	—	—	—	—	—	—	—	—	—	—	10 411
Borstal training[2]	6 054	6 455	7 675	7 596	7 250	7 399	6 912	7 357	7 459	7 219	2 839
Detention centre	8 110	9 151	10 203	10 444	10 863	11 638	11 602	12 320	13 577	13 195	11 858
Non-criminal prisoners	5 550	4 812	5 423	5 900	6 198	5 882	5 309	4 743	4 735	4 715	4 050
Immigration Act 1971	1 521	846	715	1 037	1 396	1 305	1 168	1 137	907	963	872
Others[3]	4 029	3 966	4 708	4 863	4 802	4 577	4 141	3 606	3 828	3 752	3 178
Average population											
Grand total	36 774	36 867	39 820	41 443	41 570	41 796	42 220	42 264[6]	43 311	43 707	43 462
Untried	2 792	3 213	3 573	3 303	3 539	3 849	4 019	3 921	4 804	5 362	6 002
Convicted, unsentenced	1 821	1 868	2 036	1 787	1 742	1 782	2 113	1 872	2 101	2 023	1 649
Remanded for medical examination[1]	196	181	224	174	145	130	139	129	138	173	118
Others	1 625	1 687	1 812	1 613	1 597	1 652	1 974	1 743	1 963	1 850	1 531
Sentenced	31 665	31 396	33 733	35 838	35 659	35 561	35 591	35 981	36 022	35 928	35 486
Imprisonment[2]											
Up to 18 months	10 235	9 873	11 164	12 318	12 547	12 679	12 729	12 940	13 380	13 857	12 941
Over 18 months up to 4 years	9 986	9 564	9 816	10 433	10 130	9 724	9 788	9 647	9 158	8 966	8 881
Over 4 years (including life)	4 610	4 837	4 897	5 125	5 398	5 576	5 707	5 794	5 643	5 704	5 878
Youth custody[2]	—	—	—	—	—	—	—	—	—	—	4 389
Borstal training[2]	5 307	5 409	6 006	6 206	5 798	5 692	5 464	5 596	5 674	5 288	1 704
Detention centre	1 527	1 713	1 850	1 756	1 786	1 890	1 903	2 004	2 167	2 113	1 693
Non-criminal prisoners	496	390	478	515	630	604	497	490	384	394	323
Immigration Act 1971	160	77	96	121	221	206	166	166	116	113	141
Others[3]	336	313	382	394	409	398	331	324	268	281	183

1. Under Sec. 26, Magistrates' Courts Act 1952 or Sec. 30, Magistrates' Courts Act 1980.
2. Youth custody for offenders aged 15 to 20 replaced borstal training and imprisonment on 24 May 1983.
3. Mainly persons failing to comply with money orders.

4. 1982 and 1983 data are not comparable because of the Criminal Justice Act 1982.
5. Provisional.
6. Including approved places.

Source Home Office

4.10 Prison population serving sentences: analysis by age and offence

Number

	Total	Age in years							
		14–16	17–20	21–24	25–29	30–39	40–49	50–59	60 and over
At 30 June 1981									
Offence									
Males									
Total	35 549	1 637	9 268	7 255	5 847	7 093	3 059	1 128	262
Violence against the person	6 606	211	1 607	1 382	1 159	1 402	594	216	35
Sexual offences	1 506	10	193	220	232	415	270	125	41
Burglary	11 067	881	3 767	2 380	1 669	1 623	552	169	26
Robbery	2 453	62	611	612	458	521	155	30	4
Theft, handling, fraud and forgery	8 983	378	2 053	1 636	1 423	1 969	990	422	112
Other offences	3 720	52	663	786	732	926	394	134	33
Offence not known	1 214	43	374	239	174	237	104	32	11
Females									
Total	1 120	29	258	235	188	236	132	35	7
Violence against the person	191	8	45	39	32	39	20	6	2
Sexual offences	5	–	–	–	–	3	2	–	–
Burglary	115	8	57	22	10	9	7	2	–
Robbery	42	4	14	8	7	5	3	1	–
Theft, handling, fraud and forgery	502	8	102	105	78	115	74	17	3
Other offences	198	1	28	37	49	53	22	6	2
Offence not known	67	–	12	24	12	12	4	3	–
At 30 June 1982									
Offence									
Males									
Total	35 011	1 500	8 983	7 362	5 951	6 859	3 017	1 081	258
Violence against the person	6 451	180	1 527	1 367	1 178	1 365	593	194	47
Sexual offences	1 390	17	169	182	219	382	273	113	35
Burglary	10 900	798	3 639	2 406	1 735	1 606	522	161	33
Robbery	2 489	69	607	650	482	483	171	26	1
Theft, handling, fraud and forgery	8 214	353	1 910	1 577	1 298	1 707	883	392	94
Other offences	3 816	51	688	777	735	970	428	130	37
Offence not known	1 751	32	443	403	304	346	147	65	11
Females									
Total	989	15	187	219	197	229	96	40	6
Violence against the person	157	6	30	27	31	34	22	6	1
Sexual offences	5	–	–	–	1	4	–	–	–
Burglary	82	2	31	18	13	11	6	1	–
Robbery	51	4	15	10	7	11	4	–	–
Theft, handling, fraud and forgery	424	2	77	107	74	96	40	24	4
Other offences	204	–	25	46	52	57	17	6	1
Offence not known	66	1	9	11	19	16	7	3	–
At 30 June 1983									
Offence									
Males									
Total	34 395	1 302	7 999	7 796	6 167	6 878	3 022	972	259
Violence against the person	6 596	188	1 408	1 503	1 244	1 383	616	212	42
Sexual offences	1 410	21	134	208	241	376	271	123	36
Burglary	10 553	645	3 315	2 587	1 832	1 527	498	120	29
Robbery	2 496	41	521	693	527	499	183	28	4
Theft, handling, fraud and forgery	7 882	320	1 647	1 593	1 308	1 714	873	329	98
Other offences	4 054	51	638	847	782	1 131	444	124	37
Offence not known	1 404	36	336	365	233	248	137	36	13
Females									
Total	1 043	25	209	210	194	246	103	48	8
Violence against the person	181	7	37	38	28	41	21	6	3
Sexual offences	5	–	1	–	2	1	1	–	–
Burglary	106	8	41	19	12	13	11	2	–
Robbery	47	–	10	17	8	10	–	2	–
Theft, handling, fraud and forgery	433	9	87	73	89	108	40	25	2
Other offences	222	1	25	49	45	64	24	11	3
Offence not known	49	–	8	14	10	9	6	2	–

Source Home Office

4.11 Expenditure on prisons
England and Wales
Years ended 31 March

£ thousand

	1972/73	1973/74	1974/75	1975/76	1976/77	1977/78	1978/79	1979/80	1980/81	1981/82	1982/83
Current expenditure											
Total gross current expenditure	76 752	87 758	126 160	174 087	193 517	215 357	256 934	316 256	400 907	457 016	513 196
Central charges and cost of staff in establishments	58 556	66 490	88 684	124 924	135 610	151 390	186 611	227 447	295 395	338 777	382 192
General supplies and operations	9 797	11 869	16 191	21 574	26 762	29 663	30 400	39 430	45 026	53 222	59 164
Prison industries	5 408	6 216	9 387	10 695	12 438	13 933	16 111	20 483	20 764	22 285	23 711
Prisoners' welfare	2 058	2 215	4 027	6 177	6 152	7 359	7 950	9 854	12 575	13 065	15 322
Prisoners' earnings	933	968	1 180	1 671	1 960	2 217	2 488	2 786	3 092	3 648	3 967
Home Office administration	–	–	6 691	9 046	10 595	10 795	13 374	16 256	24 055	26 019	28 840
Current receipts											
Proceeds from sale of manufactures, surplus stocks, etc.	6 689	7 160	8 753	10 480	9 887	10 069	10 567	13 572	14 722	13 006	15 059
Total net current expenditure	70 063	80 598	117 407	163 607	183 630	205 288	246 367	302 684	386 185	444 010	498 137
Capital expenditure											
New buildings, plant, etc.	14 326	18 675	22 013	31 791	27 729	26 999	26 071	25 906	33 571	31 915	46 157
Maintenance, repairs, rentals, etc.	4 061	4 498	5 322	7 449	8 494	10 248	12 828	15 736	18 128	22 499	28 302
Total capital expenditure	18 387	23 173	27 335	39 240	36 223	37 247	38 899	41 642	51 699	54 414	74 459
Emergency arrangements[1]	–	–	–	–	–	–	–	–	17 220	4 201	–
Total net expenditure	88 450	103 771	144 742	202 847	219 853	242 535	285 266	344 326	455 104	502 625	572 597

1. This was the cost of setting up and maintaining camps during the prison officers' dispute from October 1980 to February 1981. The costs cannot be attributed to individual groups.

Source Home Office

4.12 Crimes and offences recorded by the police
Scotland

Thousands

	1973	1974	1975	1976	1977	1978	1979	1980	1981	1982	1983
Total crimes and offences	504.3	537.1	574.5	598.3	641.3	640.8	674.0	724.7	744.7	762.5	799.6
Total crimes	207.8	233.6	281.5	317.9	363.4	335.0	346.7	364.6	408.2	435.1	448.3
Non-sexual crimes of violence against the person	7.6	7.9	9.0	9.7	10.0	9.9	10.0	11.1	12.2	12.1	13.0
Assault, etc.	2.7	2.7	3.3	3.3	3.2	3.4	3.5	4.4	4.5	4.5	5.0
Handling offensive weapons	2.3	2.0	1.6	1.7	1.9	1.8	2.0	2.3	2.9	2.7	3.1
Robbery	2.1	2.6	3.5	4.2	4.2	3.9	3.8	3.7	4.2	4.2	4.2
Other	0.5	0.6	0.6	0.6	0.8	0.9	0.7	0.7	0.6	0.7	0.8
Crimes involving indecency	4.5	4.1	4.3	4.3	4.4	4.7	4.7	5.2	4.8	5.0	5.5
Sexual assault	0.9	0.9	1.0	1.1	1.1	1.3	1.3	1.3	1.3	1.1	1.3
Lewd and libidinous practices	2.5	2.2	2.4	2.3	2.3	2.5	2.4	2.5	2.2	2.3	2.5
Other	1.2	0.9	0.9	0.9	1.0	0.9	1.0	1.5	1.3	1.6	1.8
Crimes involving dishonesty	160.5	186.3	227.3	254.9	290.2	262.6	269.2	279.8	320.0	340.1	342.5
Housebreaking	47.3	56.1	72.0	79.8	91.2	75.7	76.6	78.4	95.7	106.3	108.5
Theft by opening lockfast places	16.5	18.8	25.4	29.7	34.5	32.4	33.5	36.6	47.3	49.2	50.7
Theft of a motor vehicle	19.6	24.5	29.8	32.7	37.3	34.7	35.1	32.2	32.5	33.0	30.0
Shoplifting	} 65.9	75.1	86.2	96.7	110.6	103.6	105.9	{ 24.1	22.6	24.3	24.0
Other theft								86.2	97.4	101.8	101.5
Fraud	6.7	7.4	8.8	10.8	10.8	10.1	12.0	15.9	16.9	17.2	17.3
Other	4.5	4.5	5.1	5.2	5.8	6.2	6.1	6.3	7.7	8.3	10.5
Fire-raising, malicious and reckless conduct	30.9	30.8	36.5	43.8	53.1	51.1	56.1	60.1	61.7	66.0	73.1
Fire-raising	1.1	1.2	1.6	1.7	2.4	2.5	2.6	2.8	3.0	3.4	3.7
Malicious and reckless conduct	29.8	29.6	34.9	42.1	50.7	48.7	53.5	57.3	58.7	62.6	69.4
Other crimes	4.2	4.4	4.5	5.2	5.6	6.6	6.7	8.3	9.5	11.9	14.3
Total offences	296.5	303.5	293.0	280.4	278.0	305.8	327.3	360.1	336.5	327.4	351.3
Miscellaneous offences	117.6	120.2	119.6	115.7	117.2	121.9	123.3	123.2	118.2	115.4	114.8
Petty assault	21.7	22.9	25.3	26.4	27.6	28.0	29.5	28.2	27.6	28.5	30.3
Breach of the peace	44.5	47.1	47.8	44.7	44.7	47.7	50.4	53.9	53.6	53.0	51.3
Drunkenness	17.8	19.4	19.8	19.0	17.1	17.9	18.6	18.2	16.5	15.8	15.0
Other	33.6	30.8	26.7	25.5	27.7	28.2	24.9	22.9	20.4	18.1	18.1
Motor vehicle offences	178.9	183.3	173.4	164.7	160.8	183.9	204.0	236.9	218.3	212.0	236.5
Reckless and careless driving	20.4	20.4	20.5	22.1	21.3	22.7	23.3	25.0	24.4	24.0	25.4
Drunk driving	14.8	15.6	14.7	12.6	12.4	14.7	15.5	15.9	13.8	14.0	15.4
Speeding	31.9	34.3	33.9	26.6	21.4	30.7	38.3	46.8	33.9	29.3	37.7
Unlawful use of a motor vehicle	50.5	52.3	48.6	52.3	52.2	58.3	64.5	76.0	79.3	86.6	90.7
Vehicle defect offences	28.1	27.1	23.0	21.2	20.0	20.6	22.0	24.4	25.1	26.1	29.4
Other	33.2	33.6	33.3	29.9	33.4	37.0	40.2	48.8	41.9	32.1	38.0

Source Scottish Home and Health Department

4.13 Persons proceeded against
Scotland

Number of persons

	1972	1973	1974	1975	1976	1977	1978	1979	1980	1981	1982
Total crimes and offences	215 697	234 801	241 146	237 249	224 247	212 836	228 142	223 250	264 844	246 295	235 452
Total crimes	39 154	38 308	42 336	44 590	46 960	48 726	50 472	46 462	53 374	58 767	68 622
Non-sexual crimes of violence	3 175	3 277	3 229	3 127	3 121	2 804	3 190	2 876	3 491	3 299	4 740
Homicide	129	134	119	124	163	161	135	118	137	116	132
Serious assault	1 417	1 295	1 222	1 278	1 228	958	1 343	1 142	2 006	1 861	2 451
Handling offensive weapons	960	1 211	1 085	885	867	785	858	815	366	460	1 035
Robbery	431	362	420	468	573	595	571	494	657	610	843
Other Violence	238	275	383	372	290	305	283	307	325	252	279
Crimes of indecency	1 484	1 426	1 354	1 298	1 223	1 201	1 061	828	1 161	1 340	1 799
Sexual assault	206	199	232	190	185	198	221	180	189	182	178
Lewd and libidinous practices	547	594	563	544	485	447	462	417	455	439	420
Other indecency	731	633	559	564	553	556	378	231	517	719	1 201
Crimes of dishonesty	29 753	27 907	31 555	34 195	36 338	38 647	39 295	36 019	41 058	44 255	49 824
Housebreaking	6 609	5 375	6 066	6 520	7 047	7 952	8 074	6 744	8 061	8 847	11 297
Theft by opening lockfast places	1 855	1 612	1 666	1 740	1 639	1 792	1 869	1 633	2 275	2 510	3 351
Theft of or from motor vehicle	3 483	3 737	4 493	4 916	5 072	5 179	5 140	4 194	4 678	4 002	4 427
Shoplifting[1]	2 636	2 543	2 903	3 238	3 351	3 556	3 637	3 481	4 588	5 693	5 581
Other theft[1]	10 866	10 540	11 812	12 986	13 666	14 464	14 842	14 307	14 741	16 135	17 595
Fraud	2 019	2 138	2 375	2 744	3 258	3 241	3 074	3 162	3 254	3 586	4 005
Other dishonesty	2 285	1 962	2 240	2 051	2 305	2 463	2 659	2 498	3 461	3 482	3 568
Damage	2 808	3 422	3 912	3 706	3 731	3 574	4 073	3 874	5 080	6 087	6 441
Fire-raising	105	108	125	95	88	135	149	118	170	185	194
Malicious and reckless conduct	2 703	3 314	3 787	3 611	3 643	3 439	3 924	3 756	4 910	5 902	6 247
Other Crime	1 934	2 276	2 286	2 264	2 547	2 500	2 853	2 865	3 584	3 786	5 818
Total Offences	176 543	196 493	198 810	192 659	177 287	164 110	177 670	176 788	210 470	187 528	166 830
Miscellaneous offences	79 825	90 346	91 648	88 842	84 802	79 595	83 027	79 440	87 540	84 127	75 182
Petty assault	9 427	11 678	12 687	12 930	12 651	12 027	13 085	12 874	13 394	13 231	12 639
Breach of the peace	33 408	38 748	39 639	38 870	37 207	35 031	36 554	34 335	37 663	39 697	36 798
Drunkenness	13 801	16 316	17 752	18 045	16 999	14 627	14 828	15 531	14 459	11 579	10 033
Other miscellaneous offences	23 189	23 604	21 570	18 997	17 945	17 910	18 560	16 700	22 024	19 620	15 712
Motor vehicle offences	96 718	106 147	107 162	103 817	92 485	84 515	94 643	97 348	122 930	103 401	91 648
Reckless and careless driving	10 596	11 699	11 977	12 462	13 185	12 083	12 156	10 509	12 380	10 470	8 955
Drunk driving	10 671	12 208	12 928	12 419	10 353	9 387	11 337	11 636	12 779	11 440	10 666
Speeding	26 341	30 052	31 533	31 609	26 690	20 804	24 161	24 797	37 557	27 296	20 466
Unlawful use of vehicle	17 784	18 823	18 109	17 118	18 105	18 812	21 472	23 404	29 363	27 066	28 291
Vehicle defect offences	11 582	13 301	13 723	11 961	10 525	9 415	9 299	9 571	10 526	10 024	8 356
Other motor vehicle offences	19 744	20 064	18 892	18 248	13 627	14 014	16 218	17 431	20 325	17 085	14 914

1. Only since 1980 has shoplifting been distinguished from 'Other theft'. Figures
   for earlier years in this table are estimated. In subsequent tables, no separate
   figure is given for shoplifting for 1979 and earlier years.

Source Scottish Home and Health Department

4.14 Persons called to trial
Scotland

Number of persons

	1972	1973	1974	1975	1976	1977	1978	1979	1980	1981	1982
Court procedure											
Solemn	3 271	2 954	2 979	3 313	3 461	3 737	3 399	3 129	4 097	3 443	4 357
High Court	481	446	471	502	456	493	461	422	576	467	576
Sheriff Court (remit to High Court)					121	111	68	96	101	85	94
Sheriff Court (other Solemn)	2 790	2 508	2 508	2 811	2 884	3 133	2 870	2 611	3 420	2 891	3 687
Summary	207 992	225 736	232 025	227 856	216 264	205 461	221 281	216 403	257 265	238 563	228 690
Sheriff Court	123 353	133 577	142 679	140 612	135 990	135 997	148 398	137 201	172 403	143 379	137 575
District Court	–	–	–	51 625	63 854	57 637	62 178	68 780	72 839	81 272	75 458
Stipendiary Magistrate Court					16 420	11 827	10 705	10 422	12 023	13 912	15 657
Police/Burgh Court	77 008	82 046	78 100	31 758	–	–	–	–	–	–	–
Justice of Peace Court	7 631	10 113	11 246	3 861	–	–	–	–	–	–	–
Total called to trial	211 263	228 690	235 004	231 169	219 725	209 198	224 680	219 532	261 362	242 006	233 047

Source Scottish Home and Health Department

4.15 Persons with charge proved
Scotland

Number of persons

Main penalty	1972	1973	1974	1975	1976	1977	1978	1979	1980	1981	1982
Absolute discharge	1 441	1 575	1 587	1 598	1 574	1 204	1 203	1 036	1 078	939	792
Admonition or caution	18 303	19 814	21 163	21 251	21 540	20 434	20 498	20 040	23 568	23 101	22 010
Probation	3 084	2 998	2 854	2 695	2 584	2 364	2 654	2 090	2 410	2 639	2 682
Remit to children's hearing	359	399	367	279	314	183	128	91	90	99	49
Community service order	–	–	–	–	–	–	–	220	329	1 099	1 950
Fine	167 959	184 116	187 230	182 634	170 659	162 110	175 352	175 515	208 096	187 308	173 856
Compensation order	–	–	–	–	–	–	–	–	–	363	909
Guardianship order	6	4	7	3	7	5	7	5	6	3	4
Prison	8 276	6 905	7 597	7 275	6 771	6 562	7 195	6 014	7 053	7 060	8 995
Young offenders' institution	2 132	1 842	1 876	1 990	1 821	1 639	1 821	1 564	1 851	1 719	2 243
Borstal training	893	765	799	881	906	825	934	715	715	691	955
Detention centre	1 141	991	1 037	1 057	889	967	1 051	622	921	949	1 140
Detention of child	205	264	257	234	249	231	170	120	101	77	88
Insane and hospital order	190	164	173	112	111	97	108	53	45	48	45
Total persons with charge proved	203 989	219 837	224 947	220 009	207 425	196 621	211 121	208 085	246 263	226 095	215 718

Source Scottish Home and Health Department

4.16 Persons with charge proved
Scotland

Number of persons

	1972	1973	1974	1975	1976	1977	1978	1979	1980	1981	1982
Males	182 786	196 619	201 410	195 796	184 712	174 501	187 386	185 719	218 354	199 327	191 184
Under 16	2 093	2 438	2 236	1 830	1 712	1 412	1 353	887	924	822	642
16 to 20	45 541	50 045	51 927	51 672	51 545	50 509	54 601	52 159	61 683	60 013	59 423
21 to 30	55 967	59 774	60 537	58 664	55 055	51 361	54 870	55 228	65 121	60 583	60 513
Over 30	79 185	84 362	86 710	83 630	76 400	71 219	76 562	77 445	90 626	77 909	70 606
Females	19 818	21 574	21 881	22 890	21 576	20 532	21 356	19 896	24 948	24 313	22 151
Under 16	114	140	135	118	110	104	90	60	93	73	25
16 to 20	3 286	3 871	4 243	4 224	3 952	3 618	3 999	3 589	4 316	4 595	4 170
21 to 30	5 433	5 740	5 530	5 949	6 026	5 564	5 751	5 492	7 024	7 047	6 794
Over 30	10 985	11 823	11 973	12 599	11 488	11 246	11 516	10 755	13 515	12 598	11 162
Males and females	202 604	218 193	223 291	218 686	206 288	195 033	208 742	205 615	243 302	223 640	213 335
Under 16	2 207	2 578	2 371	1 948	1 822	1 516	1 443	947	1 017	895	667
16 to 20	48 827	53 916	56 170	55 896	55 497	54 127	58 600	55 748	65 999	64 608	63 593
21 to 30	61 400	65 514	66 067	64 613	61 081	56 925	60 621	60 720	72 145	67 630	67 307
Over 30	90 170	96 185	98 683	96 229	87 888	82 465	88 078	88 200	104 141	90 507	81 768
Companies	1 385	1 644	1 656	1 323	1 137	1 588	2 379	2 470	2 961	2 455	2 383
Total persons with charge proved	203 989	219 837	224 947	220 009	207 425	196 621	211 121	208 085	246 263	226 095	215 718

Source Scottish Home and Health Department

4.17 Penal establishments: average daily population and receptions
Scotland

Number

	1973	1974	1975	1976	1977	1978	1979	1980	1981	1982	1983
Average daily population											
Total	4 810	4 689	4 951	4 884	4 871	5 062	4 585	4 860	4 518	4 891	5 052
Male	4 656	4 539	4 783	4 709	4 704	4 893	4 433	4 713	4 383	4 755	4 917
Female	154	150	168	175	167	169	152	147	135	136	135
Analysis by type of custody											
Remand	597	645	740	746	706	728	691	705	746	844	863
Persons under sentence: total	4 207	4 036	4 206	4 133	4 161	4 331	3 891	4 152	3 769	4 047	4 189
Adult prisoners											
direct sentence	2 428	2 321	2 362	2 376	2 388	2 559	2 318	2 441	2 379	2 540	2 635
in default of fine	192	234	281	259	232	256	236	309	177	179	176
in default of compensation order									–	1	2
Young offenders											
direct sentence	674	634	646	596	613	628	597	610	547	587	566
in default of fine	31	35	48	63	54	53	57	77	54	54	50
in default of compensation order									–	–	–
Borstal inmates	683	623	658	664	673	608	508	521	451	493	569
Detention centre inmates	164	157	171	138	141	157	99	140	122	142	136
Persons recalled from											
supervision/licence	22	22	24	24	26	29	44	34	33	42	42
Others	13	10	16	13	34	41	32	20	6	7	9
Persons sentenced by court martial	5	7	4	3	3	2	2	2	2	2	5
Civil prisoners	1	1	1	2	1	1	1	1	1	1	1
Receptions to penal establishments											
Total[1]											
Remand	16 132	16 831	17 324	16 210	16 296	16 640	14 400	13 864	13 550	16 072	15 286
Male	15 392	15 977	16 419	15 463	15 444	15 775	13 636	13 151	12 791	15 265	14 400
Female	740	854	905	747	852	865	764	713	759	807	886
Persons under sentence: total	18 419	19 354	19 674	18 106	17 540	17 574	14 447	16 933	15 539	20 522	20 183
Male	17 660	18 545	18 773	17 197	16 769	16 753	13 792	16 250	14 863	19 749	19 276
Female	759	809	901	909	771	821	655	683	676	773	907
Imprisoned:											
directly	7 043	7 343	7 286	6 953	6 910	7 179	5 905	6 763	6 311	7 992	7 925
in default of fine	6 569	7 176	7 076	6 314	5 972	5 775	5 072	6 125	5 635	7 773	7 572
in default of compensation order									1	8	2
Sentenced to young offenders institution:											
directly	1 748	1 689	1 821	1 656	1 541	1 560	1 315	1 329	1 221	1 542	1 463
in default of fine	1 284	1 456	1 575	1 467	1 454	1 376	955	1 264	1 120	1 679	1 757
in default of compensation order									–	1	1
Sentenced to borstal training	755	667	828	810	716	706	570	573	490	630	544
Sentenced to detention centre	975	963	1 043	837	879	919	591	834	729	862	889
Recalled to Young Offenders Institutions/from Borstal supervision	45	51	49	58	65	59	39	44	31	33	28
Other sentences	–	9	8	11	3	–	–	1	1	2	2
Persons sentenced by court martial	16	11	7	2	5	6	3	8	10	10	12
Civil prisoners	10	16	16	26	5	20	11	15	14	13	15

1. Total receptions cannot be calculated by adding together receptions in each
   category because there is double counting. This arises because when a
   person is received on remand and then under sentence in relation to the
   same set of charges, he is counted in both categories.

Source Scottish Home and Health Department

4.18 Expenditure on penal establishments
Scotland
Years ended 31 March

£ thousand

	1972/73	1973/74	1974/75	1975/76	1976/77	1977/78	1978/79	1979/80	1980/81	1981/82	1982/83[1]
Central charges and costs of staff	6 328	7 701	10 199	15 031	15 675	18 492	20 804	25 268	31 565	35 955	40 661
Inmate maintenance	972	1 232	1 383	1 786	2 084	2 407	1 686	2 043	4 267	4 630	5 048
Materials for production and training	597	692	1 303	1 440	1 489	1 432	2 034	2 194	2 605	2 076	2 627
Miscellaneous	265	360	533	851	1 201	1 222	2 135	2 823	1 490	1 807	2 139
Maintenance of establishments	358	412	458	683	839	1 112	1 622	1 898	2 469	3 273	3 971
Capital expenditure	1 623	3 438	3 646	3 912	6 854	2 049	1 963	2 010	4 410	5 339	4 752
Cost of central administration	565	663	735	983	1 197	1 192	1 185	1 453	1 547	1 865	1 954
Total	10 708	14 498	18 257	24 686	29 339	27 906	31 429	37 689	48 353	54 945	61 152
Receipts from sales, etc.	958	1 341	1 758	2 167	1 878	1 927	2 188	2 917	2 769	2 050	2 583
Net total	9 750	13 157	16 499	22 519	27 461	25 979	29 241	34 772	45 584	52 895	58 569
Average daily number of inmates	5 190	4 707	4 668	4 766	4 832	4 892	5 038	4 616	4 822	4 455	5 036

1. Provisional

Source   Scottish Home and Health Department

4.19 Offences known to police, proceedings taken and results of proceedings
Northern Ireland

Number

	1973	1974	1975	1976	1977	1978	1979	1980	1981	1982	1983
Offences known to police[1]	32 057	33 314	37 239	39 914	45 571	46 499	49 975	52 384	59 157	62 020	63 984
Indictable offences[2]											
Persons proceeded against	3 772	5 037	5 385	5 261	5 603	5 140	7 054	6 998	9 136	10 510	9 007
Tried in Courts of Summary Jurisdiction	2 663	3 072	3 549	3 534	3 679	3 308	5 150	5 469	7 368	8 518	7 138
Tried at Crown Courts	1 109	1 965	1 836	1 727	1 924	1 832	1 904	1 529	1 768	1 992	1 869
Results of proceedings:											
Found guilty	3 528	4 524	4 986	4 857	5 230	4 803	6 593	6 566	7 932	8 244	8 317
Absolute discharge	96	118	77	79	83	71	119	150	204	178	115
Probation order	265	335	440	467	430	325	502	571	638	600	580
Conditional discharge	443	728	779	688	704	850	1 070	1 026	1 289	1 403	1 461
Committed to training schools	149	181	175	216	201	164	274	262	270	181	187
Fine	764	1 111	1 020	1 105	1 074	1 009	1 540	1 692	1 811	1 904	2 000
Sentenced to:											
Borstal training[3]	50	76	114	120	123	122	160	56			
Imprisonment[4]	1 041	1 351	1 362	1 297	1 572	1 217	1 460	1 320	1 724	1 813	1 806
Suspended sentence	603	601	894	764	944	950	1 196	1 112	1 354	1 491	1 488
Otherwise dealt with	117	23	125	121	99	95	272	377	642	674	680
Non-indictable offences[2]											
Persons proceeded against	33 672	35 023	38 143	41 636	44 226	47 593	46 177	46 480	32 033	33 555	34 687
Tried in Courts of Summary Jurisdiction	33 672	35 023	38 143	41 636	44 226	47 593	46 177	46 480	32 033	33 555	34 687
Results of proceedings:											
Found guilty	30 994	32 215	35 454	38 836	41 119	44 296	42 036	40 608	30 181	31 505	32 444
Absolute discharge	860	977	968	1 345	1 308	1 321	1 345	1 647	1 482	1 555	1 290
Probation order	208	231	259	260	247	203	255	283	201	169	157
Conditional discharge	1 145	1 383	1 477	1 573	1 821	1 009	1 768	1 284	1 037	1 201	1 134
Committed to training schools	105	48	61	123	146	119	193	194	94	98	77
Fine	27 408	28 543	31 441	34 130	34 730	39 675	35 423	34 888	20 029	21 072	22 220
Sentenced to:											
Borstal training[3]	7	9	23	22	33	27	32	47			
Imprisonment[4, 5]	1 110	917	1 162	1 163	1 687	1 714	1 943	1 526	1 745	1 704	1 844
Otherwise dealt with	151	107	63	220	1 147	228	1 077	739	5 593	5 706	5 722

1. Offences known to the police consist mainly of indictable offences and include some hybrid offences. Hybrid offences are offences which may be tried either on indictment or summarily.
2. From 1972 to 1974 hybrid offences dealt with summarily were included under indictable offences. From 1975 to 1981 they were included under non-indictable offences; for 1982 they are included under indictable offences.

3. Borstal training ceased in October 1980.
4. Includes those awarded periods of detention in the young offenders centre.
5. Includes those awarded suspended sentences.

Source   Northern Ireland Office

4.20 Persons found guilty: analysis by type of offence
Northern Ireland

Number

	1973	1974	1975	1976	1977	1978	1979	1980	1981	1982	1983
All offences	34 522	36 739	40 432	43 686	46 348	49 093	48 629	47 174	38 113	39 749	40 762
Indictable offences[1]	3 528	4 524	4 973	4 850	5 229	4 797	6 593	6 566	7 932	8 244	8 317
Burglary and robbery	791	1 376	1 511	1 721	1 831	1 603	2 020	2 192	2 556	2 514	2 619
Fraud[2]	169	161	265	250	275	252	379	424	499	513	382
Theft and unauthorised taking	1 072	1 274	1 482	1 491	1 459	1 520	2 132	2 273	2 842	3 023	2 962
Handling stolen goods	215	197	208	180	216	205	334	324	390	390	406
Sexual offences	84	115	116	91	105	95	108	131	128	119	124
Offences against the person: total	355	516	630	501	551	479	717	573	629	769	771
Murder	18	26	73	52	74	46	59	23	34	21	15
Manslaughter	11	9	13	18	33	19	32	13	22	22	13
Wounding	122	444	440	381	417	385	620	521	545	681	698
Other offences against the person	204	37	104	50	27	29	6	16	28	45	45
Other offences	842	885	761	616	792	643	903	649	888	916	1 053
Non-indictable offences[1]	30 994	32 215	35 459	38 836	41 119	44 296	42 036	40 608	30 181	31 505	32 444
Assaults	903	996	1 268	1 444	1 585	1 450	1 484	1 386	1 231	1 454	1 555
Betting and gaming	52	6	10	6	11	49	69	41	21	81	104
Local and Police Regulations	2 659	2 571	3 079	3 273	3 017	2 912	3 113	2 833	3 017	3 038	3 212
Intoxicating Liquor Laws:											
Drunkenness	241	250	308	385	311	360	354	374	284	259	317
Other offences	754	480	674	683	889	725	642	541	473	433	567
Education Acts	330	246	333	313	437	436	199	341	–	–	–
Game Laws	7	4	4	4	2	1	2	–	2	7	15
Labour Laws	290	245	253	202	295	147	218	87	1	5	1
Malicious damage	490	627	662	706	660	670	925	956	973	739	767
Offences by prostitutes	4	–	–	3	4	–	–	17	5	8	34
Railway offences	14	6	3	10	4	22	–	17	–	3	–
Revenue Laws	1 554	2 340	2 001	2 040	2 591	2 905	2 344	2 055	45	45	71
Traffic offences	21 831	22 577	24 568	27 433	26 533	29 266	28 140	28 640	22 585	23 459	24 145
Vagrancy Acts	22	24	23	14	42	45	17	40	26	355	22
Wireless Telegraphy Acts	225	103	157	268	156	97	116	85	1	–	–
Other offences	1 618	1 740	2 116	2 052	4 582	5 211	4 413	3 195	1 517	1 599	1 634

1. From 1972 to 1974 hybrid offences dealt with summarily were included under indictable offences. From 1975 to 1981 they were included under non-indictable offences. For 1982 they are included under indictable offences.

2. Including offences in connection with bankruptcy.

Source Northern Ireland Office

4.21 Juveniles found guilty of offences[1]
Northern Ireland

Number

	1973	1974	1975	1976	1977	1978	1979	1980	1981	1982	1983
Juveniles found guilty											
All offences	2 210	2 505	2 714	2 722	2 794	2 432	2 646	2 580	2 176	2 052	1 784
Indictable offences[2]	702	988	1 091	1 042	1 120	952	1 259	1 214	1 251	1 132	1 009
Theft and unauthorised taking	150	233	305	266	257	284	352	368	421	379	296
Burglary and robbery	381	593	594	611	664	514	693	709	657	518	532
Handling stolen goods	38	23	27	26	34	29	63	51	57	49	45
Sexual offences	9	4	4	6	11	10	4	9	8	7	5
Fraud	5	2	15	10	14	13	12	15	20	12	12
Offences against the person	6	31	60	31	49	27	51	32	24	39	28
Other offences	113	102	86	92	91	75	84	30	64	128	91
Non-indictable offences[2]	1 508	1 517	1 623	1 680	1 674	1 480	1 387	1 366	925	920	775
Assaults	123	108	141	153	144	137	137	110	80	100	124
Offences against the Education Act	102	113	140	167	117	109	48	91			–
Offences connected with motor vehicles	503	638	670	662	628	582	531	668	354	374	247
Malicious damage	150	153	246	203	248	175	295	176	158	123	139
Disorderly behaviour	451	409	322	332	332	296	229	199	225	258	168
Other offences	179	96	104	163	205	181	147	122	108	65	97
Disposal by Courts											
Total dealt with	2 210	2 505	2 714	2 722	2 794	2 432	2 646	2 580	2 176	2 052	1 784
Absolute discharge	155	134	166	170	170	141	109	93	53	84	76
Conditional discharge	569	819	892	823	837	775	887	675	548	667	572
Placed on probation	284	341	478	404	370	301	389	400	412	354	275
Fine	870	956	814	821	832	714	539	667	395	306	310
Remand home order	70	23	18	42	33	19	40	46	47	10	23
Training school order	182	175	205	267	263	171	369	385	296	248	232
Borstal training[3]	55	29	47	40	43	99	68	22			
Otherwise dealt with	25	28	94	155	246	212	245	292	425	383	296

1. Persons under 17 years of age.
2. From 1972 to 1974 hybrid offences dealt with summarily were included under indictable offences. From 1975 to 1981 they were included under non-indictable offences; for 1982 they are included under indictable offences.

3. Borstal institutions closed down in October 1980.

Source Northern Ireland Office

4.22 Prisons, Young Offenders Centres and Borstal institutions: receptions and average population[1]
Northern Ireland

Number

	1973	1974	1975	1976	1977	1978	1979	1980	1981	1982	1983
Receptions											
Reception of untried prisoners[2]	1 463	1 455	1 928	1 902	2 135	1 667	1 680	1 550	2 354	2 159	2 175
Reception of sentenced prisoners:											
Imprisonment without the option of a fine[3]	1 638	1 731	1 692	1 670	1 929	1 623	1 590	976	1 148	1 198	1 156
Imprisonment in default of payment of a fine	261	205	263	277	317	306	315	214	348	415	620
Total	1 899	1 936	1 955	1 947	2 246	1 929	1 905	1 190	1 496	1 613	1 776
Reception into Young Offenders Centres:[1]											
Detention without the option of a fine								533	755	632	651
Detention in default of payment of a fine								80	135	207	305
Total								613	890	839	956
Other receptions											
Sentenced to Borstal training[4]	61	86	109	130	135	127	150	58			
Civil committals	105	100	149	137	128	83	88	74	68	43	22
Persons detained or interned	511	313	11	–	–	–	–	–	–	–	–
Other receptions	9	15	–	2	3	–	–	–	–	–	–
Total	686	514	269	269	266	210	238	132	68	43	22
Daily average population											
Total	2 067	2 602	2 687	2 530	2 566	2 813	2 691	2 489	2 521	2 481	2 453
Unconvicted[5]	373	498	402	664	656	603	400	361	424	428	430
Internees and detainees	527	568	264	–	–	–	–	–	–	–	–
Convicted	1 167	1 536	2 021	1 866	1 910	2 210	2 291	2 128	2 097	2 053	2 023

1. 1980 is the first full year of operation of the Young Offenders Centres.
2. Prior to 1975, figures for receptions of untried prisoners exclude those sentenced to imprisonment in the same year.
3. Includes those detained under Section 73 of the Children and Young Persons (NI) Act 1968.
4. Borstal institutions closed down in October 1980.
5. Prisoners on remand or awaiting trial and prisoners committed by civil process.

Source Northern Ireland Office

5 Education

In general the education services of the United Kingdom are not subject to detailed central control. Standards are maintained by an Inspectorate with advisory functions having access to all institutions except the universities and related bodies. Within this framework detailed control is exercised by local education authorities or by various forms of independent governing bodies, in association with the teaching staff. In all sectors, such matters as engaging teachers and selection of textbooks and curricula are part of these detailed local responsibilities.

The four government departments dealing with education statistics are:

Department of Education and Science:
which deals with all sectors of education in England, and with the Government's responsibilities towards universities in Great Britain.
Welsh Office, Education Department:
which deals with schools and (from April 1978) higher and further education in Wales, excluding matters connected with universities and with the qualifications, probation, remuneration, superannuation and misconduct of teachers.
Scottish Education Department:
schools and further education in Scotland.
Department of Education, Northern Ireland:
schools, further education and universities in Northern Ireland.

The University Grants Committee advises the education departments in Great Britain and in Northern Ireland on the needs of the universities and is concerned with plans for their development.

Statistics for the separate systems obtaining in England, Wales, Scotland and Northern Ireland are collected and processed separately in accordance with the particular needs of the responsible Departments and, particularly where there are structural differences, the assembly of statistics covering the United Kingdom as a single unit presents considerable problems and in some fields is impossible at present.

Stages of education

There are three stages of education: primary (including nursery), secondary, and further (including higher) education. The first two stages are compulsory for all children between the ages of five and sixteen years (fifteen before 1972/73); and the transition from primary to secondary education is usually made between ten and a half and twelve years. The third stage of education is voluntary and includes all education provided after full-time schooling ends.

Primary education

Primary education includes three age ranges: nursery, under five years of age; infant, five to seven or eight years; and junior, seven or eight to eleven or twelve years. The great majority of public sector primary schools take both boys and girls in mixed classes. In Scotland the distinction between infant and primary schools is generally not made.

Middle schools

In England middle schools take children from first schools and generally lead on, in turn, to comprehensive upper schools. They cover varying age ranges between eight and fourteen. Depending on their individual age range they are deemed either primary or secondary by Order of the Secretary of State for Education and Science or (for age range nine to thirteen) by choice of the local education authority. Wales has only one middle school, Scotland has two.

Secondary education

Provision of secondary education in an area may include any combination of types of schools. The pattern is a reflection of historical circumstance and of the policy adopted by the local education authority. There is a growing trend to comprehensive schools, on a variety of patterns as to forms of organisation and the age range of the pupils attending. In their 'pure' form, comprehensive schools admit pupils without reference to ability and aptitude, and cater for all the children in a neighbourhood. Over 80 per cent of secondary education in England is provided in comprehensive schools. Scotland has some schools which are part comprehensive/part selective; these are comprehensive in intake but selective as regards level of courses offered (typically not beyond 'O' grade).

Special schools, both day and boarding, provide education for handicapped children who cannot be educated satisfactorily in an ordinary school. Hospital special schools provide education for children who are spending a period in hospital.

Further education

The term 'further education' may be used in a general sense to cover all education after the period of compulsory education. More commonly it excludes those staying on at secondary school, and those studying at universities, or at colleges of education (teacher training) in Scotland and Northern Ireland. Following the reorganisation of teacher training in England and Wales from 1976 the former colleges of education that did not merge with a university department of education, have been included with other further education establishments in England and Wales.

Higher education

The term 'higher education' includes all students in universities, and colleges of education in Scotland and Northern Ireland, together with students in further education colleges on courses leading to advanced level qualifications, i.e. qualifications above General Certificate of Education 'A' levels, Scottish Certificate of Education 'H' grade, and Ordinary National Diploma or Ordinary National Certificate. This will include all teacher training courses.

5.1 Number of schools[1] or departments by type and establishments of higher and further education
Academic years[2]

	1970/71	1975/76	1977/78	1978/79	1979/80	1980/81	1981/82	1982/83
United Kingdom: Public sector								
Nursery	723	1 040	1 180	1 213	1 236	1 251	1 254	1 259
Primary[3]	26 799	26 981	26 928	26 850	26 764	26 504	26 072	25 755
Secondary[3]	6 010	5 625	5 599	5 585	5 571	5 542	5 506	5 437
Non-maintained[3, 4]	3 096	2 760	2 781	2 761	2 654	2 640	2 635	2 637
Special[5]	1 204	1 913	2 006	2 018	2 016	2 011	1 994	1 989
Universities (including Open University)	46	46	46	46	46	46	46	46
Polytechnics and other major establishments, vocational further education colleges and colleges of education								
Public sector[6]	1 038	889	763	751	746	744	729	729
Assisted[7]	110	95	76	67	63	62	58	57
Adult education centres (England and Wales)	6 502	7 260	6 345	5 303	4 926	4 628	4 318	4 542
England: Public sector								
Nursery	454	564	593	593	596	588	582	575
Primary	21 083	21 394	21 372	21 309	21 242	21 018	20 650	20 384
Secondary	4 984	4 728	4 711	4 694	4 680	4 654	4 622	4 553
Non-maintained	2 754	2 442	2 480	2 459	2 351	2 342	2 340	2 344
Special	983	1 545	1 591	1 599	1 597	1 593	1 571	1 562
Universities (including Open University)	35	35	35	35	35	35	35	35
Polytechnics	25	29	29	29	29	29	29	29
Other major establishments								
Maintained and assisted	687	573	500	488	481	468	459	450
Grant-aided	78	66	49	40	36	35	34	33
Adult education centres	5 061	5 976	5 280	4 527	4 309	4 067	3 747	3 958
Wales: Public sector								
Nursery	44	67	70	70	69	69	64	64
Primary	1 990	1 959	1 940	1 930	1 925	1 908	1 873	1 844
Secondary	311	254	251	244	241	239	241	238
Non-maintained	74	71	67	71	71	72	71	73
Special	36	73	74	74	75	73	73	71
Universities	1	1	1	1	1	1	1	1
Polytechnics	1	1	1	1	1	1	1	1
Other major establishments								
Maintained and assisted	59	54	46	45	46	44	43	43
Grant-aided	3	2	1	1	1	1	1	1
Adult education centres	1 441	1 284	1 065	776	617	561	571	584
Scotland: Public sector								
Nursery	201	373	464	489	503	515	527	537
Primary	2 497	2507	2 525	2 532	2 530	2 522	2 499	2 489
Secondary	510	439	433	443	445	444	439	442
Non-maintained[4]	173	160	150	144	144	138	136	132
Special[5]	159	264	310	319	320	319	324	330
Universities	8	8	8	8	8	8	8	8
Vocational further education colleges								
Education authority								
Day	85	70	69	69	69	65	64	67
Evening	146	132	89	90	91	109	105	111
Central institutions	13	14	14	14	14	14	14	14
Voluntary bodies	4	1	–	–	–	–	–	–
Colleges of education	10	10	10	10	10	10	7	7
Northern Ireland: Public sector								
Nursery	24	36	53	61	68	79	81	83
Primary[3]	1 229	1 121	1 091	1 079	1 067	1 056	1 050	1 038
Secondary[3]	205	204	204	204	205	205	204	204
Non-maintained[3]	95	87	87	87	88	88	88	88
Special	26	30	31	26	24	26	26	26
Universities	2	2	2	2	2	2	2	2
Colleges of education	4	3	3	3	3	3	3	3
Ulster Polytechnic	–	1	1	1	1	1	1	1
Further education colleges	33	28	27	27	27	26	26	26

1. Schools (excluding independent) in Scotland and Northern Ireland with more than one department have been counted once for each department.
2. Schools are counted at January except for Scotland (session 1974–75 onwards) and Wales (1977–78 onwards) when the count is at September. Further education establishments are counted at 1 November—England and Wales, October—Scotland and Northern Ireland. University establishments at 31 December.
3. The secondary and preparatory departments of assisted and public sector grammar schools in Northern Ireland have been counted as separate schools.
4. Including for Scotland grant-aided nursery, primary and secondary schools/departments and independent schools.
5. Education authority and grant-aided special schools/departments for Scotland.
6. Polytechnics and maintained and assisted colleges in England and Wales, education authority colleges in Scotland, Northern Ireland Polytechnic, Stranmillis College of Education and education authority/education and library board colleges in Northern Ireland.
7. Direct grant colleges in England and Wales, central institutions, voluntary bodies and colleges of education in Scotland, voluntary colleges of education in Northern Ireland (St. Mary's College and St. Joseph's College).

Source Education Departments

5.2 Pupils in school by age and sex: number and as a percentage of the population
All schools
At January[1]

	1974	1975	1976	1977	1978	1979	1980[2]	1980[3]	1981	1982[4]	1983
Age at the beginning of January											
Number (thousands)											
United Kingdom	11 130	11 222	11 301	11 320	11 222	11 091	10 892	10 892	10 633	10 367	10 094
England	9 120	9 189	9 258	9 278	9 196	9 094	8 933	8 933	8 720	8 502	8 276
Wales	563	569	576	577	573	567	558	558	545	531	519
Scotland	1 078	1 093	1 094	1 092	1 081	1 059	1 034	1 034	1 005	975	945
Northern Ireland	370	371	374	374	372	371	367	367	363	359	354
Boys and girls											
2–4[5]	509	532	576	569	557	573	585	804	792	794	823
5–10	5 614	5 549	5 453	5 374	5 247	5 090	4 908	4 959	4 752	4 542	4 302
11	928	942	965	950	936	921	908	919	903	869	879
12–14	2 631	2 710	2 768	2 835	2 857	2 853	2 808	2 822	2 777	2 727	2 660
Total 2–14	9 682	9 733	9 762	9 727	9 597	9 437	9 209	9 503	9 225	8 932	8 664
15	832	841	876	897	922	937	960	943	940	924	903
16	400	429	432	455	458	468	468	266	280	306	312
17	163	167	175	181	186	186	192	160	168	181	188
18 and over	54	53	56	60	60	63	63	19	21	24	27
Boys											
14	435	452	462	475	482	495	487	488	481	475	465
15	426	432	449	459	472	479	492	483	481	472	462
16	205	219	222	232	232	236	234	130	136	149	152
17	85	86	91	94	96	95	97	83	85	91	94
18 and over	31	31	32	34	34	35	34	12	13	14	15
Girls											
14	412	430	439	452	460	471	463	464	457	450	442
15	406	409	427	437	450	458	468	461	459	452	440
16	195	210	211	223	225	232	234	136	144	157	161
17	78	80	84	87	90	91	95	78	82	90	93
18 and over	23	23	24	26	26	28	28	8	8	10	12
As a percentage of population[6]											
Boys and girls											
2–4	*19.4*	*20.9*	*23.7*	*24.9*	*25.8*	*27.8*	*29.4*	*40.8*	*40.2*	*39.5*	*39.4*
5–10	*100.9*	*100.9*	*100.7*	*100.1*	*100.2*	*100.1*	*100.3*	*104.3*	*99.9*	*99.7*	*100.6*
11	*100.7*	*100.6*	*101.5*	*100.1*	*100.4*	*100.2*	*100.3*	*103.6*	*101.8*	*100.7*	*102.5*
12–14	*100.2*	*100.4*	*100.2*	*100.1*	*100.1*	*100.2*	*100.2*	*103.3*	*101.6*	*101.2*	*100.5*
15	*98.7*	*98.7*	*100.0*	*99.8*	*99.4*	*99.7*	*99.5*	*100.0*	*99.6*	*99.9*	*98.3*
16	*48.5*	*50.8*	*50.6*	*51.9*	*50.8*	*50.8*	*49.7*	*28.0*	*29.5*	*32.4*	*33.2*
17	*20.3*	*20.2*	*20.7*	*21.2*	*21.2*	*20.7*	*20.8*	*17.1*	*17.9*	*19.0*	*19.5*
18 and over[7]	*6.9*	*6.6*	*6.7*	*7.2*	*7.0*	*7.2*	*7.0*	*2.1*	*2.3*	*2.6*	*2.8*
Boys											
14	*99.5*	*100.4*	*99.7*	*100.0*	*100.0*	*100.1*	*100.2*	*102.7*	*101.3*	*101.1*	*101.2*
15	*98.4*	*98.5*	*99.5*	*99.7*	*99.2*	*99.7*	*99.4*	*99.8*	*99.3*	*99.4*	*98.2*
16	*48.4*	*50.4*	*50.5*	*51.4*	*50.3*	*49.9*	*48.5*	*26.7*	*27.9*	*30.7*	*31.4*
17	*20.6*	*20.4*	*21.0*	*21.4*	*21.3*	*20.5*	*20.5*	*17.3*	*17.8*	*18.7*	*19.1*
18 and over[7]	*7.8*	*7.4*	*7.5*	*7.9*	*7.6*	*7.7*	*7.3*	*2.5*	*2.7*	*2.9*	*3.2*
Girls											
14	*99.8*	*101.5*	*100.0*	*100.1*	*100.1*	*100.1*	*100.0*	*103.1*	*101.6*	*100.6*	*101.1*
15	*99.0*	*98.8*	*100.5*	*99.9*	*99.5*	*99.8*	*99.6*	*100.4*	*100.0*	*100.1*	*98.5*
16	*48.7*	*51.2*	*50.6*	*52.4*	*51.3*	*51.6*	*50.9*	*29.4*	*31.1*	*34.1*	*35.2*
17	*20.0*	*20.0*	*20.5*	*21.0*	*21.1*	*20.8*	*21.2*	*17.1*	*18.1*	*19.3*	*19.9*
18 and over[7]	*6.0*	*5.8*	*5.9*	*6.4*	*6.3*	*6.6*	*6.4*	*1.8*	*1.9*	*2.2*	*2.5*

1. In Scotland with effect from the 1974/75 session and in Wales from 1977 the school census date was advanced to September whereas that for the rest of the United Kingdom remains at January. References to 1975 onwards reflect Scottish figures at the previous September (the same academic session).
2. Age at beginning of January for 1980.
3. Age at 31 August from 1980 onwards.
4. For non-maintained schools in England, pupils' ages have been estimated.
5. Each part-time pupil (aged 2–4, but also small numbers aged 5 in Scotland attending nursery schools) has been counted as one.
6. The Registrars General estimates of Home population have sometimes been slightly below the number of children found to have attended school.
7. As a percentage of the 18 years age-group.

Sources Department of Education and Science; Welsh Office; Scottish Education Department; Department of Education for Northern Ireland

5.3 Numbèr of pupils and teachers: pupil/teacher ratios
At January[1]

Thousands

	1973	1974	1975	1976	1977	1978	1979	1980	1981	1982	1983
All schools or departments											
Total											
Pupils											
Full-time and full-time											
equivalent of part-time	10 006.7	10 422.7	10 501.8	10 575.9	10 586.2	10 490.2	10 353.9	10 754.6	10 509.2	10 218.9	9 934.5
Teachers[2]	475.0	501.1	518.7	531.6	537.4	538.7	543.4	588.5	578.1	566.5	558.5
Pupils per teacher:											
United Kingdom[3]	21.1	20.8	20.2	19.9	19.7	19.5	19.1	18.3	18.2	18.0	17.8
England	21.0	20.8	20.3	20.0	19.8	19.6	19.2	18.4	18.2	18.1	17.9
Wales	20.9	20.6	20.0	19.7	19.6	19.5	19.0	18.6	18.5	18.5	18.3
Scotland	20.6	20.2	19.5	18.7	18.4	18.3	17.7	17.0	16.9	16.9	16.8
Northern Ireland[3]	23.5	23.0	22.5	22.1	20.9	19.9	19.6	19.0	18.9	18.9	18.7
Public sector schools or departments											
Nursery											
Pupils											
Full-time and full-time											
equivalent of part-time	40.1	43.3	44.5	47.1	50.2	53.2	54.7	54.9	55.5	55.8	56.3
Teachers[2]	1.6	1.8	2.0	2.1	2.3	2.4	2.5	2.5	2.6	2.6	2.6
Pupils per teacher	25.1	23.9	22.2	22.1	21.8	22.5	22.1	21.6	21.5	21.6	21.8
Primary											
Pupils											
Full-time and full-time											
equivalent of part-time	6 031.8	6 037.5	5 987.5	5 940.3	5 834.6	5 675.7	5 513.6	5 317.1	5 087.3	4 870.0	4 659.0
Teachers[2]	236.0	242.2	247.8	249.5	246.4	242.1	241.2	237.0	227.8	218.7	211.1
Pupils per teacher	25.6	24.9	24.2	23.8	23.7	23.4	22.9	22.4	22.3	22.3	22.1
Secondary											
Pupils											
Full-time and full-time											
equivalent of part-time	3 801.3	4 205.4	4 332.0	4 448.4	4 558.9	4 617.5	4 643.1	4 636.2	4 606.3	4 558.5	4 493.6
Teachers[2, 3]	224.7	243.3	254.1	264.1	271.9	276.8	281.8	283.4	281.6	278.5	277.0
Pupils per teacher	16.9	17.3	17.0	16.8	16.8	16.7	16.5	16.4	16.4	16.4	16.2
Special											
Pupils											
Full-time and full-time											
equivalent of part-time	133.5	136.5	137.7	140.0	142.5	143.8	142.4	148.7[4]	146.7[4]	144.4[4]	142.2[4]
Teachers[2]	12.7	13.8	14.7	15.8	16.8	17.4	18.0	19.5[4]	19.5[4]	19.5[4]	19.4[4]
Pupils per teacher	10.5	9.9	9.3	8.9	8.5	8.3	7.9	7.6[4]	7.5[4]	7.4[4]	7.3[4]

1. In Scotland with effect from the 1974/75 session and in Wales from 1977 the school census date was advanced to September whereas that for the rest of the United Kingdom remains at January. References to 1975 onwards reflect Scottish figures at the previous September (the same academic session).
2. Figures of teachers and of pupil/teacher ratios take account of the full-time equivalent of part-time teachers.
3. Excluding one technical intermediate school in Northern Ireland, in 1973 and 1974. These schools were conducted in association with institutions of further education; the last of them closed in June 1974.
4. Including assisted special schools.

Sources Department of Education and Science; Welsh Office; Scottish Education Department; Department of Education for Northern Ireland

5.4 Numbers of public sector and assisted special schools; full-time pupils and teachers
At January[1]

	1973	1974	1975	1976	1977	1978	1979	1980	1981	1982	1983
Hospital schools[2]											
Schools: total	160	160	164	166	159	155	150	149	145	135	128
Public sector	151	152	157	159	154	150	145	145	141	132	125
Assisted	9	8	7	7	5	5	5	4	4	3	3
Full-time pupils (thousands)	9.9	9.7	9.9	9.7	9.2	8.8	8.1	7.8	7.3	6.7	6.2
Teachers (thousands)[3]											
Full-time teachers	1.0	1.1	1.1	1.2	1.2	1.3	1.3	1.2	1.2	1.1	1.0
Other special schools or departments											
Schools: total	1 640	1 680	1 706	1 747	1 826	1 851	1 875	1 875	1 875	1 868	1 870
Public sector	1 522	1 562	1 586	1 627	1 707	1 733	1 759	1 760	1 763	1 759	1 763
Assisted	118	118	120	120	119	118	116	115	112	109	107
Day	1 194	1 226	1 230	1 276	1 357	1 375	1 384	1 412	1 412	1 412	1 393
Boarding	446	454	476	471	469	476	491	463	463	456	477
Full-time pupils (thousands): total	132.9	136.1	137.0	139.5	142.4	143.8	143.3	140.7	139.2	137.3	135.5
Blind and partially sighted	3.6	3.6	3.8	3.9	3.9	3.8	3.8	3.7	3.5	3.3	3.2
Deaf and partially hearing	6.7	6.8	7.0	6.8	6.6	6.4	6.1	5.6	5.3	5.0	4.7
Delicate and physically handicapped	16.8	17.0	18.4	18.9	19.0	18.8	18.6	18.0	17.3	16.8	16.2
Maladjusted	10.9	12.0	14.0	14.4	14.6	14.6	14.3	15.0	14.7	14.5	14.8
Educationally sub-normal and mentally handicapped[4]	91.0	91.8	84.0	86.3	90.8	93.5	94.2	92.1	92.8	92.9	92.2
Epileptic	1.4	1.6	2.3	2.4	2.2	2.0	2.0	1.9	1.8	1.6	1.6
Speech defect	2.4	3.1	6.9	6.2	4.8	4.1	3.7	3.5	3.1	2.5	2.3
Autistic[5]	..	0.3	0.5	0.5	0.6	0.6	0.6	0.6	0.7	0.6	0.6
Teachers (thousands)											
Full-time teachers	12.3	13.3	14.2	15.2	16.2	16.9	17.4	17.6	17.7	17.7	17.7
Full-time equivalent of part-time teachers	0.6	0.6	0.6	0.6	0.7	0.6	0.7	0.7	0.7	0.7	0.7

1. In Scotland with effect from the 1974/75 session and in Wales from 1977 the school census date was advanced to September whereas that for the rest of the United Kingdom remains at January. References to 1975 onwards reflect Scottish figures at the previous September (the same academic session).
2. England, Wales and Northern Ireland only.
3. Excluding part-time teachers in hospital schools, full-time equivalent in 1983 was 57.
4. In 1975 a change was made in the method of recording the major handicap of pupils attending educationally sub-normal (severe) special schools in England and Wales and for the first time a number of them (6,908) were returned within a category other than 'educationally sub-normal'.
5. England and Wales only.

Sources Department of Education and Science; Welsh Office; Scottish Education Department; Department of Education for Northern Ireland

5.5 Pupils leaving school by sex and highest qualification held
Academic years

Thousands

	1973/74	1974/75	1975/76	1976/77	1977/78	1978/79	1979/80	1980/81[1]	1981/82[1]	1982/83[1]
Boys and girls										
Total school leavers	790	804	823	868	888	900	915	865	885	902
Leavers with GCE 'A' level/SCE 'H' grade passes										
2 or more 'A', 3 or more 'H'	103	104	109	113	117	117	121	122	128	131
1 'A', 1 or 2 'H'	31	31	31	33	32	31	33	32	35	37
Leavers with GCE 'O' level/CSE/SCE 'O' grades alone										
5 or more A – C awards/CSE grade 1 [2]	68	67	68	78	81	83	85	81	87	91
1 – 4 A – C awards/CSE grade 1 [2]	189	201	209	228	232	241	242	228	234	244
No higher grades										
1 or more other grades [3]	398	402	406	416	427	427	434	{ 284	287	293
No GCE/SCE or CSE qualifications								{ 119	113	105
Boys										
Total school leavers	405	411	423	445	457	461	469	442	451	460
Leavers with GCE 'A' level/SCE 'H' grade passes										
2 or more 'A', 3 or more 'H'	57	57	61	63	64	64	64	65	66	68
1 'A', 1 or 2 'H'	15	14	15	16	15	15	16	15	17	17
Leavers with GCE 'O' level/CSE/SCE 'O' grades alone										
5 or more A – C awards/CSE grade 1 [2]	31	30	31	36	38	38	39	37	40	42
1 – 4 A – C awards/CSE grade 1 [2]	92	97	101	110	110	116	115	109	112	116
No higher grades										
1 or more other grades	211	212	216	220	230	228	234	{ 149	151	155
No GCE/SCE or CSE qualifications								{ 68	64	62
Girls										
Total school leavers	384	393	400	424	432	439	446	423	434	442
Leavers with GCE 'A' level/SCE 'H' grade passes										
2 or more 'A', 3 or more 'H'	46	47	49	51	52	54	58	57	62	63
1 'A', 1 or 2 'H'	16	17	16	17	17	17	17	17	19	20
Leavers with GCE 'O' level/CSE/SCE 'O' grades alone										
5 or more A – C awards/CSE grade 1 [2]	37	37	38	42	43	45	45	44	47	49
1 – 4 A – C awards/SCE grade 1 [2]	98	104	108	118	122	125	127	120	122	128
No higher grades										
1 or more other grades	187	189	190	196	198	199	200	{ 135	136	138
No GCE/SCE or CSE qualifications								{ 51	48	44

1. Great Britain only.
2. 'O' grades in Scotland (from 1973) and 'O' levels in England, Wales and Northern Ireland (from 1975) have been awarded in bands A to E; awards in bands A to C can be regarded as equivalent to what were previously rated as passes.
3. From 1973/74 the numbers of pupils who left school in Great Britain with no GCE/SCE or CSE qualifications were as follows:

thousands

1973/74	1974/75	1975/76	1976/77	1977/78	1978/79	1979/80	1980/81	1981/82	1982/83
172	166	152	147	146	135	132	119	113	105

Sources Department of Education and Science; Welsh Office; Scottish Education Department; Department of Education for Northern Ireland

5.6 Numbers and percentages continuing education aged 16 and over by age, sex and type of course
Men and women
1982 – 83

Home students

	Total 16 and over	Age at 31 August 1982						
		Total 16 – 18	16	17	18	19 – 20	21 – 24	25 and over
Number in thousands								
Total population[1]		2 851	940	961	950	1 822	3 392	
Full-time and sandwich students								
Schools	527	524	312	188	24	3	–	–
Further education								
Non-advanced	412	342	175	114	52	28	17	26
Advanced[2]	249	44	1	4	40	98	66	41
Universities	273	53	–	5	48	123	73	24
of which Undergraduates	242	53	–	5	48	123	54	13
Postgraduates	30	–	–	–	–	–	18	12
Total full-time and sandwich students	1 460	962	488	310	164	252	155	91
of which Higher education	521	97	1	9	87	221	138	65
Part-time students in education beyond compulsory school age								
Advanced courses								
University (excluding Open University)	35	–	–	–	–	1	6	28
Open University	74	–	–	–	–	–	6[4]	68[5]
Other higher education establishments								
Day students	148	11	–	1	9	39	42	55
Evening students	47	1	–	–	–	3	11	32
Total part-time advanced courses	305	12	–	1	10	43	66	184
Non-advanced courses in further education establishments								
Day students	616	286	83	105	98	92	42	196
Evening students[3]	2 182	258	94	90	74	134	369	1 423
Total part-time students	3 102	556	178	196	182	269	475	1 802
As percentage of population								
Full-time and sandwich students								
Schools		18.4	33.2	19.5	2.5	0.2	–	
Further education								
Non-advanced		12.0	18.6	11.9	5.5	1.5	0.5	
Advanced		1.6	0.1	0.4	4.2	5.4	1.9	
Universities		1.8	–	0.5	5.0	6.8	2.1	
of which Undergraduates		1.8	–	0.5	5.0	6.7	1.6	
Postgraduates		–	–	–	–	–	0.5	
Total full-time and sandwich students		33.8	52.0	32.3	17.2	13.8	4.6	
of which Higher education		3.4	0.1	0.9	9.2	12.1	4.1	
Part-time students in education beyond compulsory school age								
Advanced courses								
University (excluding Open University)		–	–	–	–	0.1	0.2	
Open University		–	–	–	–	–	0.2	
Other higher education establishments								
Day students		0.4	–	0.1	1.0	2.2	1.3	
Evening students		–	–	–	0.1	0.2	0.3	
Total part-time advanced courses		0.4	–	0.1	1.1	2.4	1.9	
Non-advanced courses in further education establishments								
Day students		10.0	8.9	10.9	10.3	5.0	1.2	
Evening students		9.1	10.0	9.4	7.8	7.4	10.8	
Total part-time students		19.5	18.9	20.4	19.1	14.8	14.0	

1. Based on Registrars General mid-year estimates for 1982.
2. Including teacher training except for that in universities.
3. Including estimated age detail for 1 576 thousand students aged 16 years or more in adult education centres, but excluding 207 thousand such students aged under 16. Excluding 468 thousand students on courses run by Responsible Bodies for whom age detail was not available.
4. Including a few students aged under 21.
5. Including some postgraduate and associate students aged under 25.

Sources Department of Education and Science; Welsh Office; Scottish Education Department; Department of Education for Northern Ireland

5.7 Students in further education by mode of study[1]
Autumn term

Thousands

	1972	1973	1974	1975	1976	1977	1978	1979[2]	1980	1981	1982
Major establishments											
Full-time[3]	424	421	446	495	508	499	498	495	510	564	603
Sandwich	45	46	48	52	56	59	62	65	68	74	83
Part-time day	789	787	812	830	789	790	846	836	820	806	787
Evening	825	843	841	860	773	739	778	698	694	692	720
Total	2 083	2 097	2 147	2 237	2 126	2 087	2 184	2 094	2 092	2 136	2 193
Adult education centres (England and Wales only)	1 591	1 730	1 841	1 982	1 797	1 708	2 005	1 849	1 645	1 609[4]	1 632

1. Excluding students on non-vocational courses in Scotland and Northern Ireland.
2. In previous years this time series was based on ages as at 31 December, for this year the basis has been changed to 31 August.
3. Including from 1977, teacher training colleges of education in Scotland and Northern Ireland.
4. In 1982 contains 163 thousand men and 177 thousand women aged 18 years and under and 346 thousand men and 946 thousand women aged 19 years and over.

Sources Department of Education and Science; Welsh Office; Scottish Education Department; Department of Education for Northern Ireland

5.8 Full-time students from abroad
(i) Enrolments by type of course, sex and country, in the universities and public sector and assisted establishments of further education.
Autumn 1982

Thousands

	Advanced			Non-advanced		Men	Women	Total
	Postgraduate level	First degree level or equivalent	Other	GCE/SCE and CSE	Other			
Europe								
Cyprus	0.1	0.6	0.1	–	0.1	0.6	0.3	0.9
Germany, West	0.2	0.9	0.1	–	–	0.6	0.6	1.2
Greece	1.1	0.9	0.2	0.2	0.1	1.9	0.5	2.4
Ireland, Republic of	0.2	0.2	0.1	–	0.1	0.4	0.2	0.6
Norway	0.1	0.5	–	–	–	0.5	0.1	0.6
Other	0.9	1.6	0.3	0.1	0.4	1.8	1.3	3.1
Australasia								
Australia	0.3	–	–	–	–	0.2	0.1	0.3
New Zealand	0.1	–	–	–	–	0.1	0.1	0.2
Other	–	–	–	–	–	0.1	–	0.1
Africa								
Algeria	0.4	0.1	–	–	–	0.4	0.1	0.5
Ghana	0.2	0.1	0.1	–	0.1	0.4	0.1	0.5
Kenya	0.2	0.3	0.1	0.1	0.1	0.5	0.2	0.7
Libya	0.2	0.1	0.2	–	0.5	0.9	–	1.0
Mauritius	–	0.2	–	–	–	0.2	0.1	0.3
Nigeria	1.7	1.3	0.9	0.1	0.6	3.5	1.0	4.5
South Africa	0.1	0.1	–	–	–	0.2	0.1	0.3
Tanzania	0.2	0.1	0.1	–	–	0.4	0.1	0.5
Zimbabwe	0.1	0.3	0.1	–	0.1	0.5	0.1	0.6
Other	1.3	0.9	0.5	0.1	0.3	2.6	0.5	3.1
The Americas								
Canada	0.3	0.2	–	–	–	0.4	0.2	0.5
USA	0.9	1.2	–	–	0.1	1.2	1.1	2.3
Venezuela	0.1	0.1	–	–	–	0.2	0.1	0.3
Other	1.1	0.4	0.1	–	0.1	1.2	0.6	1.8

Sources Department of Education and Science; Welsh Office; Scottish Education Department; Department of Education for Northern Ireland.

5.8
(continued)

Full-time students from abroad

(i) Enrolments by type of course, sex and country, in the universities and public sector and assisted establishments of further education.
Autumn 1982

Thousands

	Advanced			Non-advanced		Men	Women	Total
	Postgraduate level	First degree level or equivalent	Other	GCE/SCE and CSE	Other			
Asia								
Hong Kong	0.6	3.3	0.4	1.1	0.3	4.2	1.6	5.7
Brunei	0.1	0.5	0.2	–	0.2	0.8	0.3	1.0
Indonesia	0.1	0.1	–	–	–	0.2	0.1	0.2
India	0.4	0.1	1.0	–	0.1	0.5	0.1	0.6
Iran	0.3	1.0	0.3	0.2	0.3	2.4	0.4	2.8
Iraq	1.3	0.3	0.1	0.2	0.2	1.9	0.3	2.2
Jordan	0.1	0.4	0.6	0.1	0.1	0.7	0.1	0.7
Malaysia	0.8	4.5	0.1	0.4	0.2	4.5	2.0	6.5
Pakistan	0.3	0.1	0.1	–	0.1	0.5	0.1	0.5
Singapore	0.3	0.7	0.2	–	–	0.7	0.3	1.0
Sri Lanka	0.2	0.2	0.1	–	0.1	0.5	0.1	0.6
Turkey	0.1	0.1	–	–	–	0.3	0.1	0.3
Thailand	0.1	0.1	0.4	–	0.1	0.2	0.1	0.3
Other	2.1	1.3	–	0.2	0.8	4.1	0.8	4.9
UK treated as overseas	0.5	0.6	–	–	–	0.8	0.3	1.1
Stateless/Unknown	–	–	–	–	–	0.1	–	0.1
All countries [1]	16.7	22.4	6.4	3.1	5.1	40.0	13.7	53.7
Foreign	10.0	8.6	3.0	1.1	2.9	19.3	6.4	25.6
Commonwealth	6.7	13.8	3.4	2.0	2.2	20.7	7.4	28.1

(ii) Entrants and enrolments by grouped country of domicile in the universities and public sector and assisted establishments of further education.

Thousands

	Entrants						
	1975–76[2]	1977–78[2]	1978–79[2]	1979–80	1980–81	1981–82	1982–83
European Community	2.0	1.9	2.0	1.9	3.0	3.0	3.6
Europe	..	5.2	5.1	4.7	4.1	3.9	4.9
OPEC	11.6	14.1	12.6	10.8	9.4	8.0	6.9
Commonwealth	23.6	24.0	23.5	23.2	18.1	15.7	13.6
Non-Commonwealth	23.1	24.8	24.6	21.6	17.3	14.9	14.7
Developing countries	39.3	40.1	38.9	37.5	29.5	24.5	22.0
All countries [1,3]	46.7	48.8	48.1	44.9	35.6	30.7	28.3
of which							
Advanced	26.8	29.1	28.7	26.4	23.8	24.5	23.0
Non-advanced	19.9	18.8	18.9	18.5	11.8	6.2	5.3

	Enrolments						
	1975–76[2]	1977–78[2]	1978–79[2]	1979–80	1980–81	1981–82	1982–83
European Community	2.6	3.0	3.1	3.0	5.3	5.3	6.4
Europe	..	9.1	9.0	8.6	8.3	7.5	8.8
OPEC	17.1	23.2	22.3	19.8	17.4	15.1	12.5
Commonwealth	39.8	44.0	44.5	43.0	38.7	32.7	28.0
Non-Commonwealth	35.0	41.2	41.2	40.0	32.3	27.8	25.6
Developing countries	62.2	71.5	71.4	68.6	60.9	50.4	43.9
All countries [1,3]	74.8	85.1	85.8	82.9	71.2	60.6	53.8
of which							
Advanced	48.1	56.0	57.0	56.2	51.6	49.4	45.6
Non-advanced	26.8	27.5	27.1	26.7	19.7	11.2	8.2

1. Excluding UK students classified as students from abroad. In 1982–83 there were 557 entrants and 1 095 enrolments.
2. Great Britain data.
3. Numbers in grouped countries do not sum to all overall student numbers due to overlap.

Sources Department of Education and Science; Welsh Office; Scottish Education Department; Department of Education for Northern Ireland.

5.9 Students in education by type of course, mode of study, sex and subject group[1]
Home and overseas students

Academic year 1982–83   Thousands

	Postgraduate level		Undergraduate level or equivalent		Other higher education		Total higher education	Non-advanced further education[2]		All students Full-time[3]		Part-time[4]
	Full-time[3]	Part-time[4]	Full-time[3]	Part-time[4]	Full-time[3]	Part-time[4]		Full-time[3]	Part-time[4]	Home-	Home- and over-seas	Home
Male												
Subject group												
1. Education	6.0	5.2	6.5	2.9	2.5	5.1	28.2	2.0	14.5	15.6	17.0	27.7
2. Medicine, dentistry and health	2.3	2.0	17.3	0.1	0.9	3.1	25.8	1.2	5.6	19.7	21.7	10.8
3. Engineering and technology	6.9	4.0	54.8	3.2	19.1	61.4	149.4	70.7	313.2	135.5	151.5	381.8
4. Agriculture, forestry and veterinary science	0.9	0.3	3.3	–	1.4	0.1	6.0	6.9	16.5	11.8	12.5	16.9
5. Science	8.7	4.3	55.1	2.4	6.4	8.1	84.9	5.5	15.7	70.5	75.7	30.4
6. Administrative, business and social studies	7.9	10.0	56.7	3.9	14.4	42.5	135.4	18.7	51.4	89.0	97.7	107.8
7. Architecture and other professional and vocational subjects	1.9	1.3	8.3	0.5	4.3	2.6	19.0	17.4	28.8	29.7	32.0	33.2
8. Languages, literature and area studies	1.5	1.2	11.8	0.5	0.1	0.5	15.5	2.0	28.8	14.3	15.4	30.9
9. Arts other than languages	1.2	1.7	12.9	0.7	0.6	0.1	17.1	0.2	0.3	14.2	14.8	2.7
10. Music, drama, art and design	1.0	0.5	12.2	0.3	2.8	0.2	17.0	10.7	12.1	26.0	26.7	13.1
11. GCE, SCE and CSE	–	–	–	–	–	–	–	45.6	91.3	43.4	45.6	91.3
12. Other	–	–	–	–	–	–	0.1	10.1	67.8	10.1	10.2	67.8
All subjects	38.2	30.6	239.0	14.5	52.6	123.6	498.5	190.9	645.9	480.0	520.8	814.5
Female												
Subject group												
1. Education	7.6	3.6	20.5	4.4	3.2	6.8	46.1	2.0	43.9	32.4	33.3	58.7
2. Medicine, dentistry and health	1.4	1.2	16.2	0.2	4.5	4.8	28.2	19.6	13.5	40.6	41.6	20.0
3. Engineering and technology	0.6	0.3	4.4	0.1	1.4	1.4	8.3	5.0	12.9	10.3	11.4	14.7
4. Agriculture, forestry and veterinary science	0.3	0.1	2.0	–	0.4	0.1	3.0	1.5	3.4	4.2	4.3	3.6
5. Science	2.4	1.4	28.0	0.8	2.4	4.0	39.0	2.7	10.2	33.1	35.4	16.5
6. Administrative, business and social studies	4.4	3.3	44.7	2.2	12.8	21.4	88.7	74.2	136.9	131.9	136.0	163.8
7. Architecture and other professional and vocational subjects	1.0	0.5	5.9	0.2	4.6	0.7	12.9	41.9	82.0	52.6	53.4	83.5
8. Languages, literature and area studies	1.2	1.3	27.0	1.1	0.9	1.1	32.7	3.8	45.7	31.7	33.0	49.2
9. Arts other than languages	0.5	0.7	16.3	1.0	0.8	0.2	19.5	0.2	0.4	17.4	17.8	2.3
10. Music, drama, art and design	0.9	0.4	18.5	0.5	3.4	0.3	23.9	14.5	21.8	36.2	37.2	23.0
11. GCE, SCE and CSE	–	–	–	–	–	–	–	56.4	131.6	55.5	56.4	131.6
12. Other	–	–	0.2	–	0.1	–	0.3	9.4	160.3	9.7	9.7	160.3
All subjects	20.1	12.9	183.7	10.6	34.4	40.8	302.5	231.3	662.9	455.5	469.5	727.1
Persons												
Subject group												
1. Education	13.5	8.9	27.0	7.2	5.7	11.9	74.3	4.0	58.4	48.0	50.3	86.5
2. Medicine, dentistry and health	3.7	3.2	33.5	0.3	5.4	7.9	54.0	20.8	19.3	60.3	63.4	30.7
3. Engineering and technology	7.5	4.4	59.2	3.3	20.5	62.8	157.7	75.6	326.1	145.8	162.8	396.5
4. Agriculture, forestry and veterinary science	1.1	0.4	5.4	–	1.9	0.2	9.0	8.5	19.9	16.0	16.8	20.5
5. Science	11.1	5.7	83.0	3.2	8.7	12.1	123.9	8.2	25.9	103.5	111.1	46.9
6. Administrative, business and social studies	12.3	13.3	101.4	6.2	27.2	63.8	224.2	92.9	188.2	220.9	233.8	271.5
7. Architecture and other professional and vocational subjects	2.9	1.8	14.2	0.7	8.9	3.3	31.9	59.3	110.9	82.4	85.3	116.7
8. Languages, literature and area studies	2.7	2.5	38.8	1.6	1.0	1.6	48.2	5.9	74.5	46.1	48.4	80.1
9. Arts other than languages	1.7	2.4	29.1	1.6	1.4	0.3	36.5	0.4	0.7	31.6	32.6	5.0
10. Music, drama, art and design	1.8	0.9	30.7	0.8	6.2	0.5	40.9	25.1	33.9	62.2	63.9	36.1
11. GCE, SCE and CSE	–	–	–	–	–	–	–	102.1	222.9	98.9	102.1	222.9
12. Other	–	–	0.2	–	0.1	–	0.4	19.5	228.1	19.8	19.9	228.1
All subjects	58.3	43.5	422.7	25.0	87.0	164.4	801.0	422.3	1 308.8	935.4	990.3	1 541.6[5]

1. Excluding data for pupils at schools and for the Open University for which subject detail in this format is not available.
2. Including 608.4 thousand students in all modes in England, Wales and Northern Ireland who are taking unspecified courses.
3. Including sandwich students.
4. Day and evening.
5. Including 1.0 thousand part-time students from abroad in Scotland.

Source Education Departments

5.10 Degrees and classes of degree and national diplomas and certificates by subject of study,[1] sex and awarding body in the year ended 31 December 1982[2]

Number of persons

	Education	Medicine, dentistry and health	Engineering and technology	Agriculture, forestry and veterinary science	Science	Administrative, business and social studies	Architecture and other professional and vocational studies	Language, literature and area studies	Arts other than languages	Music, drama, art and design	Modular courses	All students	Men
Higher degree													
University[3]	2 445	1 417	3 221	583	4 645	4 848	561	1 392	752	209	–	20 073	14 864
CNAA	36	17	195	–	411	221	88	12	32	215	–	1 227	..
Total	2 481	1 434	3 416	583	5 056	5 069	649	1 404	784	424	–	21 300	..
Higher diplomas and certificates													
University	7 225	530	362	62	353	2 165	384	163	112	141	–	11 497	5 936
CNAA	149	122	77	–	111	332	396	47	7	48	–	1 289	684
Total	7 374	652	439	62	464	2 497	780	210	119	189	–	12 786	6 620
First degree University[3]													
First class honours	39	261	1 014	59	1 658	582	45	480	230	59	–	4 427	3 189
Second class honours	880	1 581	5 989	878	9 753	14 438	742	7 279	3 494	1 044	–	46 078	26 265
Other honours	162	503	1 804	157	3 472	2 013	127	1 265	826	135	–	10 464	7 242
Pass or ordinary	496	4 326	1 401	354	1 908	1 711	281	279	852	51	–	11 659	7 387
CNAA													
First class honours	80	14	168	–	170	117	39	34	57	457	34	1 170	695
Second class honours	1 187	369	1 563	–	2 111	5 200	742	922	1 336	3 544	693	17 667	9 999
Third class honours	131	29	323	–	355	825	120	85	138	522	84	2 612	1 747
Pass or ordinary	2 131	366	2 354	–	724	1 273	620	77	111	104	115	7 875	5 110
Total	5 106	7 449	14 616	1 448	20 151	26 159	2 716	10 421	7 044	5 916	926	101 952	61 634
First university diplomas and certificates	437	231	734	–	688	385	172	100	161	11	–	2 919	1 919
CNAA diplomas and certificates	2 092	–	–	–	–	1 653[5]	–	–	–	–	–	3 745	2 357
Higher national diploma[4]	–	–	2 698	557	521	–	883	–	–	–	–	4 659	..
Higher national certificate[4]	–	185	401	–	472	–	–	–	–	–	–	1 058	..
TEC/SCOTEC higher certificate/diploma[4]	–	615	12 372	–	1 216	–	297	–	–	–	–	14 500	11 400[4]
BEC/SCOTBEC higher certificate/diploma	–	–	–	–	–	6 564	204	–	–	–	–	6 768	..
Total[2]	–	800	15 471	557	2 209	6 564	1 384	–	–	–	–	26 985	..
Total higher education[2]	17 490	10 566	34 676	2 650	28 568	42 327	5 701	12 135	8 108	6 540	926	169 687	..
Ordinary national diploma[4]	–	–	819	924	–	–	39	–	–	–	–	1 782	..
Ordinary national certificate[4]	–	–	11	–	147	–	1	–	–	–	–	159	..
TEC/SCOTEC ordinary certificate/diploma[4]	–	201	32 645	1 270	3 029	34	1 184	–	–	808	–	39 171	29 021[4]
BEC/SCOTBEC ordinary certificate/diploma[4]	–	–	–	–	–	29 253	1 737	–	–	–	–	30 990	..
Total	–	201	33 475	2 194	3 176	29 287	2 961	–	–	808	–	72 102	..
Grand Total	17 490	10 767	68 151	4 844	31 744	71 614	8 662	12 135	8 108	7 348	926	241 789	..
Men[4]													
University higher degrees	1 607	895	2 960	456	3 673	3 440	364	792	550	127	–	14 864	14 864
Higher diplomas and certificates	3 306	395	405	55	377	1 474	340	97	73	98	–	6 620	6 620
First degrees	1 736	4 312	13 793	956	13 675	15 734	1 679	3 409	3 361	2 574	405	61 634	61 634
First university diplomas and certificates	211	43	669	–	535	182	143	30	104	2	–	1 919	1 919
CNAA diplomas and certificates	901	–	–	–	–	1 456[5]	–	–	–	–	–	2 357	2 357

1. Teacher training results are shown in table 5.2. However these overlap with results shown here.
2. Excluding professional qualifications, from both the public and private sectors.
3. Excluding Open University degrees for which subject detail in this format is not available. These numbered 48 higher degrees, 1 241 honours degrees (670 men) and 6 440 ordinary degrees (3 321 men).
4. Data by sex are not available for CNAA higher degrees, teacher training, higher national diplomas/certificates, SCOTEC, BEC, SCOTBEC diplomas/certificates, ordinary and higher.
5. Diploma in Management Studies which is equivalent to First Degree.

Source Education Departments

5.11 Lecturers and teachers by type of establishment, sex and graduate status
percentage trained

(i) Full-time

	1977–78		1978–79		1979–80		1980–81		1981–82			1982–83		
	All 000s	% Graduate[1]	All 000s	% Graduate	All 000s	% Graduate	All 000s	% Graduate	All 000s	% Graduate	% Graduates trained[2]	All 000s	% Graduate	% Graduates trained[2]
United Kingdom														
Males														
Schools														
Public sector														
Primary[3]	52	18.6	51	20.3	50	21.8	48	23.6	46	25.6	94.7	45	27.5	95.1
Secondary	154	52.1	155	53.9	155	55.7	154	57.5	153	59.4	84.9	152	61.2	85.7
Non-maintained[4]	19	72.2	19	74.3	20	77.6	20	77.9	20	79.8	..	21	79.9	..
Special	6	18.9	7	20.3	6	22.3	6	24.5	6	26.9	91.3	6	29.3	92.2
All schools[4]	231	45.3	232	47.3	231	49.4	229	51.2	227	53.4	..	224	55.2	..
Establishments of further education[5]	66	43.2	66	43.7	70	42.9	70	43.2	70	43.5	46.6	71	43.7	46.8
Universities[6]	30	99.5	30	99.5	31	99.5	30	98.9	30	98.8	..	28	98.9	..
All establishments[7]	330	49.7	332	51.1	336	52.4	332	53.8	329	55.3	..	325	56.4	..
Females														
Schools														
Public sector														
Primary[3]	184	10.1	183	11.5	181	13.2	174	14.6	167	16.0	93.9	162	17.4	94.5
Secondary	121	42.5	124	44.7	127	46.9	127	49.3	126	51.5	87.8	126	53.8	88.5
Non-maintained[4]	18	40.9	19	45.1	20	50.5	23	50.4	20	50.8	..	20	52.8	..
Special	13	14.2	13	16.2	13	18.0	13	20.4	13	22.8	92.6	13	24.9	93.1
All schools[4]	336	23.6	340	25.7	341	28.1	336	30.3	327	32.1	..	321	34.2	..
Establishments of further education[5]	16	41.4	16	42.2	19	40.7	19	41.5	20	42.2	56.1	21	43.0	57.4
Universities[6]	3	98.9	4	98.9	4	98.7	4	98.5	4	98.7	..	3	98.6	..
All establishments[7]	357	25.0	361	27.1	366	29.5	361	31.5	352	33.3	..	347	35.4	..
England and Wales														
All schools														
Males	203	43.4	205	45.3	204	47.6	202	49.6	200	51.9	76.7	198	53.9	85.8
Females	288	23.0	291	25.1	292	27.8	288	30.1	280	32.1	82.4	276	34.3	89.7
Scotland														
All schools[8]														
Males	20	66.2	20	66.4	20	66.7	20	67.4	20	67.9	..	19	68.2	..
Females	37	28.9	37	29.4	38	29.8	37	30.7	35	31.3	..	34	32.3	..
Northern Ireland														
All schools														
Males	7	48.7	7	49.8	7	51.8	7	53.7	7	55.6	..	7	56.8	..
Females	12	26.3	12	29.0	12	31.0	12	33.4	12	35.6	..	11	37.3	..

(ii) Part-time

	1977–78		1978–79		1979–80		1980–81		1981–82			1982–83		
	All 000s	% Graduate[1]	All 000s	% Graduate	All 000s	% Graduate	All 000s	% Graduate	All 000s	% Graduate	% Graduates trained	All 000s	% Graduate	% Graduates trained
Great Britain[9]														
Persons	37	..	38	..	..	..	..	..	..	..	..	..	..	..
Persons—full-time equivalent	17	..	18	..	39	..	40	..	40	..	..	40	..	..
Schools[8]	17	..	18	..	18	..	18	..	18	..	..	17	..	..
Establishments of further education[2]	..	..	..	..	21	..	23	..	23	..	..	23	..	..

1. Including estimate for schools in Scotland.
2. England and Wales only. Percentage graduates trained partly estimated.
3. Including nursery schools.
4. Excluding independent schools in Scotland and, in 1979–80, Wales. Percentage graduates in 1979–80 are estimated for non-maintained schools in England.
5. Including teacher training.
6. Excluding 672 male and female professors and lecturers and 5 121 part-time tutorial and counselling staff employed by the Open University at January 1983.
7. Totals include a number of teachers in England and Wales classified as miscellaneous who are not shown above. The numbers in 1982–83 were 2 065 men and 1 728 women.
8. Excluding independent schools.
9. Excluding universities.

Source Education Departments

5.12 Initial training of teachers by sex, type of course and stage
Men and Women

Thousands

	1972	1973	1974	1975	1976	1977	1978	1979	1980	1981	1982
Admissions to courses of initial training[1]											
University Departments of Education											
Courses for graduates	5.3	5.0	4.8	5.0	5.0	5.2	5.2	5.1	5.7	5.7	4.9
Courses for non-graduates	0.2	0.3	0.4	0.5	0.6	0.3	0.7	0.6	0.6	0.5	0.7
Total	5.6	5.3	5.2	5.5	5.6	5.5	5.9	5.7	6.2	6.2	5.5
Other institutions											
Courses for graduates	8.1	8.0	7.1	7.8	6.9	5.6	6.1	6.4	7.0	6.8	5.2
Courses for non-graduates	44.9	42.0	37.7	34.4	23.5	16.7	13.1	11.2	8.7	9.1	9.7
Total	53.0	49.9	44.8	42.2	30.4	22.4	19.2	17.6	15.7	15.9	15.0
Students on initial training courses[2]											
University Departments of Education											
Courses for graduates	5.4	5.1	4.9	5.0	5.0	5.3	5.1	5.1	5.7	5.7	4.9
Courses for non-graduates	0.5	0.5	0.7	0.9	1.1	1.2	2.0	1.9	2.0	2.2	2.3
Total	5.8	5.6	5.5	6.0	6.1	6.5	7.1	7.0	7.7	7.9	7.2
Other institutions											
Courses for graduates	8.1	8.0	7.1	7.9	6.9	5.9	5.2	6.5	7.0	6.8	5.2
Courses for non-graduates	122.3	120.0	113.4	105.3	88.2	64.3	45.6	35.1	28.0	25.9	25.0
Total	130.4	127.9	120.5	113.2	95.0	70.2	50.8	41.6	35.1	32.7	30.3
Students successfully completing courses of initial training[3]											
University Departments of Education											
Courses for graduates	5.0	5.1	4.8	4.5	4.8	4.9	4.7	4.9	4.8	5.4	5.4
Courses for non-graduates	0.1	0.2	0.2	0.3	0.4	0.2	0.4	0.8	0.6	0.6	0.6
Total	5.1	5.3	5.0	4.8	5.1	5.1	5.0	5.7	5.5	6.0	6.0
Other institutions											
Courses for graduates	6.2	7.4	7.3	6.5	7.2	5.8	5.7	6.2	6.2	6.6	6.3
Courses for non-graduates[4]	37.7	36.4	36.5	35.8	34.0	27.8	27.5	19.8	13.1	9.6	8.5
Total	43.9	43.8	43.7	42.2	41.2	33.5	33.2	26.0	19.4	16.2	14.8

1. Calendar year.
2. October/November of year shown.
3. Academic year ending in year shown.
4. Including students in England and Wales who failed their B.Ed degree course
   but have received qualified teacher status.

Sources Department of Education and Science; Welsh Office; Scottish Education Department; Department of Education for Northern Ireland

5.13 Full-time teaching and research staff at universities[1]
Academic years

Number

	Professors	Readers and senior lecturers	Lecturers and assistant lecturers	Other	Total	Percentage annual change
1968/69	3 051	5 170	17 485	948	26 654	*3.2*
1969/70	3 200	5 368	17 989	983	27 540	*3.3*
1970/71	3 432	5 646	18 606	983	28 667	*4.1*
1971/72	3 492	6 034	19 215	914	29 655	*3.5*
1972/73	3 649	6 475	19 651	969	30 744	*3.7*
1973/74	3 753	6 972	19 698	1 031	31 454	*2.3*
1974/75	3 906	7 398	19 883	914	32 101	*2.1*
1975/76	3 989	7 617	19 722	880	32 208	*0.3*
1976/77	4 124	7 877	20 022	712	32 735	*1.6*
1977/78	4 164	8 163	19 980	677	32 984	*0.8*
1978/79	4 225	8 454	20 302	714	33 695	*2.2*
1979/80	4 337	8 734	20 518	661	34 250	*1.6*
1980/81	4 382	8 809	20 460	646	34 297	*0.1*
1981/82	4 351	8 777	20 045	562	33 735	*− 1.6*
1982/83	4 017	8 284	18 885	456	31 642	*− 6.2*

1. Full-time teaching and research staff in post wholly financed from general
   university funds excluding the Open University.

Source University Grants Committee

5.14 Students at universities[1,2]
Academic years

Number

	1972/73	1973/74	1974/75	1975/76	1976/77	1977/78	1978/79	1979/80	1980/81	1981/82	1982/83
Full-time students											
Total full-time students[3]	246 813	251 226	257 684	268 714	279 321	288 135	295 923	300 526	306 614	308 394	303 965
of which											
Total overseas students	22 007	24 880	27 974	31 539	34 075	35 494	36 839	35 177	31 275	28 365	27 520
Total postgraduate students	46 906	47 625	48 606	50 626	51 052	49 674	49 990	48 536	48 439	47 674	46 232
Total women students	76 298	80 396	85 323	90 641	95 574	100 222	105 265	110 509	115 691	118 840	119 381
Overseas students as a percentage of total	8.9	9.9	10.9	11.7	12.2	12.3	12.4	11.7	10.2	9.2	9.1
Postgraduate students as a percentage of total	19.0	19.0	18.9	18.8	18.3	17.2	16.9	16.2	15.8	15.5	15.2
Women students as a percentage of total	30.9	32.0	33.1	33.7	34.2	34.8	35.6	36.8	37.7	38.5	39.3
At undergraduate level											
Total[4]	199 907	203 601	209 078	218 088	228 269	238 461	245 933	251 990	258 175	260 720	257 733
Men	134 749	135 006	136 278	140 812	146 626	152 067	154 996	155 987	157 335	156 685	152 869
Women	65 158	68 595	72 800	77 276	81 643	86 394	90 937	96 003	100 840	104 035	104 864
From United Kingdom											
Total	191 067	193 424	197 198	203 843	212 247	221 125	227 708	234 379	242 771	246 965	244 506
Men	127 998	127 283	127 239	130 099	134 561	139 083	141 598	143 320	146 162	146 886	143 580
Women	63 069	66 141	69 959	73 744	77 686	82 042	86 110	91 059	96 609	100 079	100 926
From overseas											
Total	8 840	10 177	11 875	14 244	16 021	17 336	18 225	17 611	15 404	13 755	13 227
Men	6 751	7 723	9 034	10 712	12 064	12 984	13 398	12 667	11 173	9 799	9 289
Women	2 089	2 454	2 841	3 532	3 957	4 352	4 827	4 944	4 231	3 956	3 938
At postgraduate level											
Total[5]	46 906	47 625	48 606	50 626	51 052	49 674	49 990	48 536	48 439	47 674	46 232
Men	35 766	35 824	36 083	37 261	37 121	35 846	35 662	34 030	33 588	32 869	31 715
Women	11 140	11 801	12 523	13 365	13 931	13 828	14 328	14 506	14 851	14 805	14 517
From United Kingdom											
Total	33 739	32 922	32 506	33 331	32 998	31 516	31 376	30 970	32 568	33 064	31 939
Men	24 820	23 642	22 856	23 178	22 580	21 356	20 885	20 120	21 072	21 354	20 527
Women	8 919	9 280	9 650	10 153	10 418	10 160	10 491	10 850	11 496	11 710	11 412
From overseas											
Total	13 167	14 703	16 099	17 295	18 054	18 158	18 614	17 566	15 871	14 610	14 293
Men	10 946	12 182	13 226	14 083	14 541	14 490	14 777	13 910	12 516	11 515	11 188
Women	2 221	2 521	2 873	3 212	3 513	3 668	3 837	3 656	3 355	3 095	3 105
Part-time students											
Total part-time students	23 556	24 388	25 373	26 317	27 337	28 679	29 553	31 412	33 311	34 613	34 942
At undergraduate level											
Total	3 449	3 504	3 405	3 815	3 812	4 169	4 086	4 381	4 779	5 258	5 450
Men	2 054	1 977	1 839	1 967	1 944	2 086	2 068	2 223	2 421	2 476	2 496
Women	1 395	1 527	1 566	1 848	1 868	2 083	2 018	2 158	2 358	2 782	2 954
At postgraduate level											
Total	20 107	20 884	21 968	22 502	23 525	24 510	25 467	27 031	28 532	29 355	29 492
Men	16 155	16 475	17 113	17 314	17 911	18 156	18 638	19 373	20 143	20 352	20 072
Women	3 952	4 409	4 855	5 188	5 614	6 354	6 829	7 658	8 389	9 003	9 420

1. Excluding the Open University.
2. Overseas students are defined by fee-paying status. From 1980/81 most European Community students paid home fees and are therefore excluded from the overseas figures.
3. Excluding students on courses not at undergraduate or postgraduate level.
4. Including 5 students in 1974/5 and 1 student in 1975/6 whose fee paying status was not known.
5. Including 1 student in 1974/5 whose fee paying status was not known.

Source University Grants Committee

5.15 Students at universities[1]

New admissions, taking courses, and numbers of full-time students by country of home residence and university residence
Academic years

Number

		1972/73	1973/74	1974/75	1975/76	1976/77	1977/78	1978/79	1979/80	1980/81	1981/82	1982/83
New students admitted												
(full-time only)												
Men		45 163	44 657	46 598	49 355	50 687	52 359	52 870	51 997	52 214	50 646	48 387
Women		22 894	24 341	26 143	27 467	28 598	30 463	32 014	33 906	34 613	33 879	33 452
Students taking courses												
(full and part-time)												
Men		188 724	189 282	191 313	197 354	203 602	208 155	211 364	211 613	213 487	212 382	207 152
Women		81 645	86 332	91 744	97 677	103 056	108 659	114 112	120 325	126 438	130 625	131 755
Full-time students:												
Total	Men	170 515	170 830	172 361	178 073	183 747	187 913	190 658	190 017	190 923	189 554	184 584
	Women	76 298	80 396	85 323	90 641	95 574	100 222	105 265	110 509	115 691	118 840	119 381
Advanced	Men	35 766	35 824	36 083	37 261	37 121	35 846	35 662	34 030	33 588	32 869	31 715
	Women	11 140	11 801	12 523	13 365	13 931	13 828	14 328	14 506	14 851	14 805	14 517
First degree	Men	132 622	132 974	134 372	138 775	144 469	150 122	152 711	153 852	155 601	154 991	151 299
	Women	63 765	66 996	71 119	75 534	79 825	84 371	88 789	94 041	99 107	102 416	103 201
First diploma	Men	402	346	408	457	349	267	301	360	281	275	178
	Women	211	232	239	225	224	299	201	173	119	123	93
Others	Men	1 725	1 686	1 498	1 580	1 808	1 678	1 984	1 775	1 453	1 419	1 392
	Women	1 182	1 367	1 442	1 517	1 594	1 724	1 947	1 789	1 614	1 496	1 570
Part-time students:												
Total	Men	18 209	18 452	18 952	19 281	19 855	20 242	20 706	21 596	22 564	22 828	22 568
	Women	5 347	5 936	6 421	7 036	7 482	8 437	8 847	9 816	10 747	11 785	12 374
Advanced	Men	16 155	16 475	17 113	17 314	17 911	18 156	18 638	19 373	20 143	20 352	20 072
	Women	3 952	4 409	4 855	5 188	5 614	6 354	6 829	7 658	8 389	9 003	9 420
First degree	Men	1 127	1 056	1 054	1 293	1 335	1 440	1 392	1 503	1 644	1 699	1 770
	Women	563	552	612	926	1 015	1 143	1 095	1 200	1 378	1 751	1 972
First diploma	Men	27	85	21	19	20	80	30	61	84	70	52
	Women	77	87	82	85	70	93	43	52	64	48	26
Occasional	Men	900	836	764	655	589	566	646	659	693	707	674
	Women	755	888	872	837	783	847	880	906	916	983	956
Country of home residence:[2]												
United Kingdom		222 637	223 835	227 789	235 491	243 372	250 673	257 065	262 527	270 442	273 443	270 323
Foreign and Commonwealth countries		24 176	27 391	29 895	33 222	35 949	37 462	38 858	37 999	36 172	34 951	33 642
University residence[3, 4]												
Colleges and hostels:	Men	68 078	71 978	74 980	80 695	83 087	86 227	87 162	86 911	87 766	88 974	87 196
	Women	31 738	35 432	37 668	41 143	43 062	45 718	47 736	50 557	52 728	53 542	54 569
Lodgings:	Men	69 582	66 160	63 577	62 635	63 780	65 519	67 592	67 983	69 131	68 016	66 566
	Women	30 149	29 730	30 776	30 872	32 462	33 963	36 577	37 881	40 568	42 838	42 949
At home:	Men	28 672	27 766	27 970	28 567	29 308	29 065	28 947	28 173	27 758	26 156	25 340
	Women	12 226	12 776	14 002	15 254	16 134	16 257	16 658	17 343	18 029	17 674	17 715

1. Excluding the Open University.
2. Stateless and unknown domicile included in the overseas figure.
3. Including those students on courses 'not of university standard', but not those sandwich students undertaking the industrial part of their training away from the university or college at the time of the student count, which is the end of the autumn term (31 December).
4. Excludes students whose type of residence is other than those listed or unknown.

Source University Grants Committee

5.16 Universities[1]: courses taken by full-time students
Academic years

Number

	1972/73	1973/74	1974/75	1975/76	1976/77	1977/78	1978/79	1979/80	1980/81	1981/82	1982/83
Education:											
Men	4 795	4 969	5 116	5 601	5 223	5 537	5 713	5 437	5 797	5 767	5 225
Women	4 473	4 888	5 455	5 696	5 760	6 152	6 534	7 153	7 160	7 426	6 869
Medicine, dentistry and health:											
Men	17 254	17 931	18 332	18 627	19 171	19 407	19 633	19 553	19 368	18 970	18 408
Women	8 233	9 029	9 760	10 379	10 908	11 343	11 954	12 657	13 280	13 796	14 440
Engineering and technology:											
Men	35 734	34 837	34 508	35 378	37 515	39 066	40 202	40 494	40 850	40 701	39 945
Women	1 158	1 250	1 399	1 539	1 837	2 145	2 457	2 759	3 102	3 405	3 748
Agriculture, forestry and veterinary science:											
Men	3 607	3 598	3 673	3 896	4 081	4 089	4 271	4 310	4 185	4 203	4 059
Women	1 018	1 091	1 167	1 372	1 495	1 693	1 858	2 050	2 113	2 208	2 258
Science:											
Men	46 085	45 274	44 897	45 342	45 883	46 741	47 650	47 875	48 694	48 887	48 651
Women	15 328	15 686	16 331	16 840	17 391	18 125	18 973	20 015	21 229	22 166	22 551
Social administration and business studies:											
Men	34 902	36 074	37 276	39 865	41 876	42 642	42 947	43 027	43 249	42 581	40 940
Women	17 295	18 650	20 147	21 966	23 666	24 867	26 295	27 609	29 259	29 877	30 261
Architecture and other professional and vocational subjects:											
Men	3 650	3 705	4 014	4 138	4 166	4 263	4 158	3 928	3 904	3 831	3 721
Women	999	1 103	1 293	1 498	1 613	1 653	1 777	1 853	1 993	1 996	2 054
Language, literature and area studies:											
Men	12 335	12 256	12 241	12 521	12 777	12 836	12 804	12 610	12 411	12 187	11 616
Women	16 495	17 066	17 749	18 754	19 661	20 766	21 772	23 067	24 021	24 347	23 958
Arts other than languages, music, drama and visual arts:											
Men	12 153	12 186	12 302	12 702	13 048	13 332	13 280	12 783	12 465	12 427	12 019
Women	11 299	11 633	12 021	12 593	13 239	13 478	13 645	13 346	13 534	13 619	13 242

1. Excluding the Open University.

Source University Grants Committee

5.17 Universities[1]: degrees and diplomas obtained by full-time students
Academic years[2]

Number

		1971/72	1973[2]	1974	1975	1976	1977	1978	1979	1980	1981	1982
Degrees												
Total: Men		45 497	46 532	48 304	49 770	50 150	52 251	55 307	55 869	57 245	58 507	58 947
Women		17 567	19 030	20 365	22 011	23 305	25 149	26 822	28 525	29 830	31 584	33 754
First degrees—honours:	Men	28 522	28 557	29 159	29 377	29 813	31 195	33 095	34 085	35 127	36 018	36 696
	Women	12 922	13 730	14 630	15 273	16 479	17 685	19 004	20 193	21 344	22 563	24 273
First degrees—ordinary:	Men	7 307	6 914	7 579	7 312	7 064	7 496	7 631	7 611	7 704	7 743	7 387
	Women	3 031	3 276	3 444	3 686	3 693	4 008	3 927	4 093	3 975	4 218	4 272
Higher degrees:	Men	9 668	11 061	11 566	13 081	13 273	13 560	14 581	14 173	14 414	14 746	14 864
	Women	1 614	2 024	2 291	3 052	3 133	3 456	3 891	4 239	4 511	4 803	5 209
Diplomas and certificates:	Men	6 157	6 623	7 559	8 109	7 979	7 576	7 238	7 379	7 044	7 260	7 572
	Women	4 703	4 902	5 273	5 541	5 692	5 597	5 290	5 509	5 754	6 015	6 208

1. Excluding the Open University.
2. From 1973 the figures relate to a calendar year.

Source University Grants Committee

5.18 Scientific research: postgraduate awards and special grants
At 1 October in each year

	1973	1974	1975	1976	1977	1978	1979	1980[1]	1981	1982	1983
Special research grants											
Number of new awards	2 225	2 289	2 390	2 316	2 179	2 492	2 645	4 394	2 462	2 355	2 609
Number current: total	4 031	4 155	4 386	4 270	4 115	4 434	7 023	5 056	5 024	5 056	5 376
Biological sciences	660	679	710	605	625	653	1 007	720	752	754	713
Biotechnology											95[3]
Chemistry/enzyme chemistry	559	569	529	544	525	563	982	670	668	618	572
Computing science	39	58	92	95	80	78	104				
Mathematics	84	76	82	84	73	77	146	73	66	94	136
Chemical engineering	179	174	163	161	147	139	155	–	–	–	–
Control engineering	31	33	37	39	44	44	63	–	–	–	–
Electrical and systems engineering	188	209	221	224	204	185	217	–	–	–	–
Aeronautical and mechanical engineering	256	267	278	258	223	190	208	–	–	–	–
Civil and transport engineering	113	123	144	152	147	148	177	–	–	–	–
Manufacturing technology	85	81	81	102	97	91	118	–	–	–	–
Materials	–	351	357	345	299	302	462	344	381	346	335
Physics (other than nuclear)	455	437	422	371	320	308	497	357	339	331	508
Nuclear physics	63	70	78	74	86	102	202	98	117	143	143
Astronomy	79	94 ⎫									
Space	52	60 ⎬	217	236	287	364	691	397	388	371	355
Radio	13	15 ⎭									
Information science	84	35	88	60	84	77	94	82	63	87	78
Geology and geophysics	169	183	178	172	162	171	181	186	183	178	167
Social sciences	500	531	588	575	453	542	578	506	319	324	381
Neutron beam	34	36	39	35	81	78	102	70	77	71	66
Polymer science/engineering	76	–	–	–	–	–	156	114	117	106	90
Laser facility	–	–	–	–	–	–	–	14	13	14	26
Science based archeology	–	–	–	–	–	–	–	25	22	22	25
Synchroton radiation facility	–	–	–	–	–	–	–	51	73	77	98
Engineering processes	–	–	–	–	–	–	–	224	229	225	212
Environment	–	–	–	–	–	–	–	160	172	197	236
Information engineering	–	–	–	–	–	–	–	320	370	378	489
Machines and power	–	–	–	–	–	–	–	277	341	349	357
Marine technology	–	–	–	–	–	–	–	55	61	73	84
Teaching company	–	–	–	–	–	–	–	38	65	98	146
Energy	–	–	–	–	–	–	–	27	39	47	52
Joint SERC/ESRC[2]	–	–	–	–	–	–	–	19	31	25	28
Other grants	41	74	82	138	178	323	883	229	138	128	84
Total expenditure on grants (years beginning 1 April) (£ thousand)	21 072	21 578	26 742	33 665	33 486	38 057	52 438	67 567	73 769	80 082	83 824
Postgraduate awards											
Studentships:											
Number of new awards	5 719	5 933	5 899	5 827	6 118	5 849	5 295	5 207	4 791	4 501	5 814
Number current: total	11 003	11 014	11 173	11 158	11 529	11 726	11 405	11 173	10 622	10 132	11 278
Biological sciences/Biology	1 378	1 505	1 633	1 743	1 832	1 918	1 996	1 989	1 924	1 861	1 820
Biotechnology											112[3]
Chemical engineering	342	309	269	257	259	273	250	–	–	–	–
Chemistry/enzyme chemistry	1 430	1 468	1 464	1 431	1 444	1 476	1 523	1 534	1 488	1 456	1 464
Electrical engineering	577	527	502	487	431	458	437	–	–	–	–
Aeronautical and mechanical engineering	421	361	349	313	336	334	319	–	–	–	–
Civil and transport engineering	464	418	408	398	401	368	376	–	–	–	–
Manufacturing technology	112	125	116	105	111	111	125	–	–	–	–
Materials	–	453	461	450	432	395	401	412	434	477	515
Total technology	4	15	39	44	75	90	98	–	–	–	81
Geology and geophysics	441	447	444	459	463	479	462	473	498	499	496
Mathematics	829	767	778	719	692	655	640	614	587	531	562
Physics	1 099	1 119	1 128	1 102	1 050	1 031	993	572	521	519	534
Computing science	289	258	264	257	272	291	329	–	–	–	–
Social sciences	2 880	2 966	2 997	3 037	3 285	3 383	2 938	2 348	1 758	1 727	1 689
Control engineering	74	68	78	92	82	70	82	–	–	–	–
Polymer science/engineering	77	–	–	–	–	–	–	–	27	26	20
Information science	47	48	51	52	51	51	53	81	51	53	1 130

1. The Science Research Council became the Science and Engineering Research Council from mid – 1981, incorporating additional classifications.
2. The Social Science Research Council became the Economic and Social Research Council on 1 January 1984.
3. Previously included in Other.

Sources Science and Engineering Research Council; Natural Environment Research Council; Economic and Social Research Council; The British Library Research and Development Department; Department of Education and Science

5.18
(continued)

Scientific research: postgraduate awards and special grants
At 1 October in each year

	1973	1974	1975	1976	1977	1978	1979	1980 [1]	1981	1982	1983
Postgraduate awards *(continued)*											
Neutron beam	–	–	–	–	–	–	–	5	9	9	7
Science base archeology	–	–	–	–	–	–	–	24	27	29	31
Astronomy, space and radio	–	–	–	–	–	–	–	248	246	232	249
Nuclear physics	–	–	–	–	–	–	–	179	176	178	180
Engineering processes	–	–	–	–	–	–	–	370	368	349	360
Environment	–	–	–	–	–	–	–	261	535	323	316
Information engineering	–	–	–	–	–	–	–	770	829	731	667
Machines and power	–	–	–	–	–	–	–	583	415	406	398
Marine technology	–	–	–	–	–	–	–	76	92	95	107
Energy	–	–	–	–	–	–	–	42	42	43	58
Joint SERC/ESRC [2]	–	–	–	–	–	–	–	313	288	267	201
Other	152	160	192	212	313	343	383	279	307	321	281
Fellowships:											
Number of new awards	102	107	114	104	107	105	108	109	118	96	128
Number current	180	210	233	238	245	224	234	264	291	275	282
Bursaries:											
Number of new awards	582	526	458	450	261	267	184	200	159	127	144
Number current	754	730	641	661	458	341	238	235	178	133	155
Total expenditure on awards (years beginning 1 April) (£ thousand)	11 457	13 613	17 354	21 591	30 449	34 656	37 914	54 930	47 064	49 083	55 322

1. The Science Research Council became the Science and Engineering Research Council from mid – 1981, incorporating additional classifications.
2. The Social Science Research Council became the Economic and Social Research Council on 1 January 1984.

Sources Science and Engineering Research Council; Natural Environment Research Council; Economic and Social Research Council; The British Library Research and Development Department; Department of Education and Science

5.19 Student awards
New and current, by type

Thousands

	1972–73	1973–74	1974–75	1975–76	1976–77	1977–78	1978–79	1979–80	1980–81	1981–82	1982–83
New awards											
All new awards[1]	207.5	203.2	203.9	222.0	227.2	223.7	235.2[5]	241.0[5]	243.4[5]	264.7[5]	267.3[5]
Postgraduate awards:											
Made by education departments and the research councils[1]	8.3	8.5	8.0	8.6	9.7[5]	10.2[5]	10.3[5]	10.5[5]	10.4[5]	9.3[5]	9.1[5]
Local education authorities[2]	1.4	1.5	1.5	1.9	1.9	2.1	2.4	2.2	2.2	2.4	3.0
Undergraduate and non-graduate awards at university[1]	59.7	59.8	61.7	64.4	68.6	69.8[5]	71.7[5]	72.9[5]	74.5[5]	73.2[5]	70.2
Teacher training awards[1]	53.8	51.9	47.2	46.7	36.7	26.5	24.0	23.5	21.2	21.5	19.7
Other awards: Including further education first degree and comparable courses,[3] other further education courses, state scholarships and adult education bursaries[4]	56.9	57.2	61.1	66.6	70.3	70.2	71.7	73.7	79.6	91.6	96.4
Lesser value awards[1]	27.4	24.3	24.4	33.8	40.1	45.0	55.2[5]	58.3[5]	55.5[5]	66.7[5]	63.9[5]
Current awards											
All current awards	494.6	485.6	491.1	508.6	520.1	521.5	529.4	536.8	545.7	586.2	604.3
Postgraduate awards:											
Made by education departments and the research councils	17.2	17.0	16.9	17.7	18.5	19.2	19.6	19.2	19.0	18.1	17.8
Local education authorities[2]	1.6	1.7	1.7	2.1	2.1	2.3	2.6	2.4	2.3	2.5	3.1
Undergraduate and non-graduate awards at university	186.2	186.7	188.7	193.0	204.6	211.9	218.5	224.6	231.1	237.1	232.2
Teacher training awards	137.2	132.7	125.0	121.4	104.2	79.7	61.4	50.1	44.1	41.4	37.6
Other awards: Including further education first degree and comparable courses,[3] other further education courses, state scholarships and adult education bursaries[4]	117.4	119.0	126.4	129.6	136.9	147.9	154.4	160.5	171.8	193.2	212.1
Lesser value awards	35.0	28.5	32.4	44.8	53.8	60.5	72.9	80.1	77.3	93.8	101.5

1. Data refers to calendar years during the period 1972–73 to 1974–75 (inclusive).
2. Postgraduate course awards made under Section 2 of the Education Act 1962 (excluding initial teacher training) in England and Wales (includes estimated numbers of new awards prior to 1975/76).
3. 'Comparable courses' are courses at establishments of further education which have been designated under the University and other Awards regulations, 1965, as comparable to first degree courses.
4. The adult education bursary scheme commenced in September 1975 and operates in England, Wales and Scotland.
5. United Kingdom estimate based upon data for England, Wales and Northern Ireland.

Sources Department of Education and Science; Welsh Office; Scottish Education Department; Department of Education for Northern Ireland

6. Employment

6.1 Distribution of total working population
At mid-June each year

Thousands

United Kingdom	1973	1974	1975	1976	1977	1978	1979	1980	1981	1982[1]	1983[1]
Total working population[2]	25 613	25 658	25 877	26 094	26 209	26 342	26 609	26 819[4]	26 718	26 757	26 776[5]
Males	16 245	16 068	16 162	16 262	16 217	16 214	16 218	16 310[4]	16 338	16 282	16 165[5]
Females	9 368	9 589	9 715	9 831	9 992	10 128	10 392	10 509[4]	10 380	10 474	10 611[5]
Unemployed	557	528	838	1 266	1 359	1 343	1 234	1 513[4]	2 395	2 770	2 984[5]
Males	476	456	698	986	1 021	986	888	1 072[4]	1 775	2 043	2 145[5]
Females	81	72	140	280	339	357	346	441[4]	620	727	839[5]
Employed labour force[2]	25 057	25 130	25 039	24 828	24 849	24 999	25 375	25 306	24 323	23 987	23 792
Males	15 769	15 613	15 463	15 276	15 196	15 228	15 330	15 238	14 562	14 239	14 020
Females	9 288	9 517	9 575	9 552	9 653	9 770	10 045	10 068	9 761	9 748	9 771
HM Forces[3]	361	345	336	336	327	318	314	323	334	324	322
Males	346	331	321	321	313	303	299	307	317	309	306
Females	15	14	15	15	14	15	15	16	17	15	16
Self-employed persons (with or without employees)[2]	2 032	1 996	1 993	1 949	1 904	1 904	1 903	2 011	2 118	2 190	2 260
Males	1 650	1 622	1 607	1 564	1 521	1 536	1 552	1 625	1 698	1 716	1 733
Females	382	374	386	385	383	367	351	386	420	474	528
Total employees in employment[2]	22 664	22 789	22 710	22 543	22 619	22 777	23 158	22 972	21 870	21 473	21 210
Males	13 773	13 660	13 536	13 392	13 363	13 389	13 479	13 306	12 547	12 215	11 982
Females	8 891	9 129	9 174	9 152	9 256	9 388	9 679	9 666	9 323	9 259	9 228
of whom											
Total, index of production industries	9 911	9 894	9 506	9 254	9 260	9 215	9 233	8 918	8 069	7 657	7 320
Total, all manufacturing industries	7 862	7 908	7 524	7 281	7 328	7 290	7 258	6 939	6 222	5 912	5 642
Great Britain											
Total working population[2]	25 041	25 079	25 283	25 486	25 598	25 716	25 970	26 176[4]	26 076	26 117	26 136[5]
Males	15 869	15 694	15 781	15 874	15 831	15 824	15 826	15 916[4]	15 942	15 891	15 775[5]
Females	9 172	9 385	9 502	9 613	9 767	9 892	10 144	10 260[4]	10 134	10 226	10 361[5]
Unemployed	529	502	803	1 215	1 303	1 282	1 175	1 444[4]	2 299	2 664	2 871[5]
Males	455	436	672	950	980	942	847	1 024[4]	1 706	1 967	2 062[5]
Females	74	66	131	265	323	340	328	420[4]	593	697	809[5]
Employed labour force[2]	24 512	24 577	24 481	24 271	24 295	24 434	24 795	24 731	23 777	23 453	23 265
Males	15 414	15 258	15 109	14 924	14 851	14 882	14 979	14 892	14 236	13 924	13 713
Females	9 098	9 319	9 371	9 348	9 444	9 553	9 816	9 839	9 541	9 529	9 552
HM Forces[3]	361	345	336	336	327	318	314	323	334	324	322
Males	346	331	321	321	313	303	299	307	317	309	306
Females	15	14	15	15	14	15	15	16	17	15	16
Self-employed persons (with or without employees)[2]	1 969	1 935	1 933	1 888	1 843	1 843	1 842	1 950	2 057	2 129	2 199
Males	1 589	1 563	1 549	1 506	1 465	1 478	1 499	1 567	1 640	1 658	1 675
Females	380	372	384	382	378	364	343	383	417	471	525
Total employees in employment[2]	22 182	22 297	22 213	22 048	22 126	22 274	22 639	22 458	21 386	21 000	20 744
Males	13 478	13 363	13 240	13 097	13 076	13 100	13 186	13 018	12 278	11 957	11 733
Females	8 705	8 933	8 973	8 951	9 050	9 173	9 453	9 440	9 107	9 044	9 011
of whom											
Total, index of production industries	9 692	9 675	9 297	9 054	9 067	9 024	9 041	8 737	7 910	7 512	7 183
Total, all manufacturing industries	7 693	7 737	7 365	7 131	7 183	7 147	7 113	6 804	6 100	5 803	5 539

Note: Because the figures have been rounded independently totals may differ from the sum of the components. Also the totals may include some employees whose industrial classification could not be ascertained.

1. Figures for 1982 and 1983 may be subject to future revision.
2. Estimates for working population and employed labour force from September 1981 and employees in employment from December 1981 include an allowance for underestimation. See article on page 319 of *Employment Gazette,* July 1984.
3. HM Forces figures, provided by the Ministry of Defence, represent the total number of UK service personnel, male and female, in HM Regular Forces, wherever serving and including those on release leave.
4. The figures are affected by the introduction in Great Britain of fortnightly payment of unemployment benefit. This is estimated to have resulted in an artificial increase of 20 000 (13 000 males and 7 000 females) in the count of the unemployed and therefore a corresponding reduction should be made when comparing the 1980 figures with those of earlier years.
5. From April 1983, the figures of unemployment reflect the effects of the provisions in the Budget for some men aged 60 and over who no longer have to sign on at an unemployment office.

Source Department of Employment.

6.2 Employees in employment

Analysis by industry based on the Standard Industrial Classification 1980

At June in each year

Thousands

	SIC 1980[1,2]	United Kingdom					Great Britain				
		1979	1980	1981	1982	1983	1979	1980	1981	1982	1983
All industries and services		23 158	22 972	21 870	21 473	21 210	22 639	22 458	21 386	21 000	20 744
Agriculture, forestry and fishing	0	368	361	352	354	349	359	352	343	345	339
Index of production and construction industries	1–5	9 234	8 918	8 069	7 657	7 320	9 041	8 737	7 910	7 512	7 183
Index of production industries	1–4	7 980	7 666	6 930	6 598	6 303	7 825	7 520	6 799	6 480	6 192
of which, manufacturing industries	*2–4*	*7 258*	*6 940*	*6 221*	*5 912*	*5 641*	*7 113*	*6 804*	*6 100*	*5 803*	*5 539*
Service industries	6–9	13 556	13 693	13 450	13 462	13 541	13 239	13 370	13 132	13 143	13 222
Agriculture, forestry and fishing	0	368	361	352	354	349	359	352	343	345	339
Agriculture and horticulture	010	347	340	332	334	328	339	332	324	326	320
Energy and water supply	1	722	726	709	686	662	712	716	699	676	653
Coal extraction and solid fuels	111	298	297	285	270	256	298	297	285	270	256
Deep coal mines	1113	..	..	..	..	..	..	..	..	262	247
Extraction of mineral oil, natural gas	130	..	..	..	..	..	..	..	..	28	30
Mineral oil processing	140	33	33	30	27	24	33	32	30	27	24
Nuclear fuel production	152	..	..	..	..	..	..	..	..	16	16
Electricity	161	..	..	..	..	..	..	..	..	162	159
Gas	162	..	..	..	..	..	..	..	..	103	101
Water supply	170	62	66	68	67	65	60	64	66	65	63
Other mineral and ore extraction, etc.	2	1 127	1 067	934	884	821	1 110	1 051	922	874	811
Metal manufacturing	22	..	..	..	..	..	..	..	..	252	225
Iron and steel	221	..	..	..	..	..	..	..	..	116	100
Steel tubes	222	..	..	..	..	..	..	..	..	33	30
Steel drawing, cold rolling, cold forming	223	..	..	..	..	..	..	..	..	29	28
Non-ferrous metals	224	..	..	..	..	..	..	..	..	74	67
Aluminium and aluminium alloys	2245	..	..	..	..	..	..	..	..	29	27
Copper, brass and other copper alloys	2246	..	..	..	..	..	..	..	..	27	23
Extraction of metaliferous ores and minerals nes	21/23	..	..	..	..	..	..	..	..	41	42
Non-metallic mineral products	24	279	265	233	220	202	273	260	229	215	198
Structural clay	241	..	..	..	..	..	..	..	..	18	18
Cement, lime and plaster	242	..	..	..	..	..	..	..	..	15	14
Building products of concrete, cement, etc.	243	..	..	..	..	..	..	..	..	42	40
Asbestos goods	244	..	..	..	..	..	..	..	..	12	10
Abrasive products and working of stone, etc.	245/246	..	..	..	..	..	..	..	..	19	17
Glass and glassware	247	..	..	..	..	..	..	..	..	53	50
Refractory and ceramic goods	248	..	..	..	..	..	..	..	..	57	50
Chemical industry	25	..	..	..	351	334	..	..	..	349	331
Basic industrial chemicals	251	..	..	..	..	..	..	..	..	133	123
Inorganic chemicals except industrial gases	2511	..	..	..	..	..	..	..	..	64	61
Paints, varnishes and printing ink	255	..	..	..	..	..	..	..	..	33	32
Specialised industrial products	256	..	..	..	..	..	..	..	..	49	47
Pharmaceutical products	257	..	..	..	..	..	..	..	..	81	81
Soap and toilet preparations	258	..	..	..	..	..	..	..	..	40	37
Specialised household products	259	..	..	..	..	..	..	..	..	14	13
Man made fibres	26	..	..	..	18	16	..	..	..	16	15
Metal goods, engineering and vehicles	3	3 380	3 267	2 919	2 772	2 650	3 338	3 226	2 880	2 737	2 618
Metal goods nes	31	519	493	417	403	380	516	490	414	401	378
Ferrous metal foundries	3111	..	..	..	..	..	..	..	..	59	54
Non-ferrous metal foundries	3112	..	..	..	..	..	..	..	..	18	17
Forging, pressing and stamping	312	..	..	..	..	..	..	..	..	32	29
Bolts, nuts, springs, etc.	313	..	..	..	..	..	..	..	..	51	47
Metal doors, windows, etc.	314	..	..	..	..	..	..	..	..	19	18
Hand tools and finished metal goods	316	..	..	..	..	..	..	..	..	222	213
Mechanical engineering	32	1 022	997	899	855	796	1 011	986	889	847	789
Industrial plant and steelwork	320	..	..	..	..	..	..	..	..	81	74
Agricultural machinery and tractors	321	..	..	..	..	..	..	..	..	42	39
Metal-working machine tools, etc.	3221	..	..	..	..	..	..	..	..	37	31
Engineers' small tools	3222	..	..	..	..	..	..	..	..	54	47
Textile machinery	323	..	..	..	..	..	..	..	..	12	11
Machinery for food, etc., industries	324	..	..	..	..	..	..	..	..	45	42
Mining machinery, etc.	325	..	..	..	..	..	..	..	..	92	87
Mechanical lifting and handling equipment	3255	..	..	..	..	..	..	..	..	54	53
Mechanical power transmission equipment	326	..	..	..	..	..	..	..	..	36	31
Machinery for printing, etc., industries	327	..	..	..	..	..	..	..	..	30	29
Other machinery and mechanical equipment	328	..	..	..	..	..	..	..	..	392	371
Internal combustion engines except road vehicles, etc.	3281	..	..	..	..	..	..	..	..	53	45
Compressors and fluid power equipment	3283	..	..	..	..	..	..	..	..	53	53
Refrigerating machinery, space heating, ventilation	3284	..	..	..	..	..	..	..	..	42	42
Ordnance, small arms and ammunition	329	..	..	..	..	..	..	..	..	27	27

1. Division, class or activity heading.
2. The data on SIC 1968 classification was last published in *Annual Abstract of Statistic No. 120, 1984 editiion.*

Sources Department of Employment; Department of Manpower Services (Northern Ireland)

6.2
Employees in employment
Analysis by industry based on the Standard Industrial Classification 1980
(*continued*)   At June in each year

Thousands

	SIC 1980[1,2]	United Kingdom					Great Britain				
		1979	1980	1981	1982	1983	1979	1980	1981	1982	1983
Office machinery, data processing equipment	33	..	..	..	76	75	..	..	..	75	75
Electrical and electronic engineering	34	..	..	..	648	648	..	..	..	642	641
Insulated wires and cables	341	..	..	..	..	..	..	..	..	38	38
Basic electrical equipment	342	..	..	..	..	..	..	..	..	120	118
Industrial equipment, batteries, etc.	343	..	..	..	..	..	..	..	..	95	92
Telecommunication equipment	344	..	..	..	..	..	..	..	..	199	200
Telegraph and telephone appliances and equipment	3441	..	..	..	..	..	..	..	..	57	56
Radio and electronic capital goods	3443	..	..	..	..	..	..	..	..	86	88
Components other than active components	3444	..	..	..	..	..	..	..	..	30	31
Other electronic equipment	345	..	..	..	..	..	..	..	..	123	126
Domestic-type electric appliances	346	..	..	..	..	..	..	..	..	42	43
Electric lighting equipment and electrical equipment installation	347, 348	..	..	..	..	..	..	..	..	25	25
Motor vehicles and parts	35	436	415	359	321	309	433	412	355	318	306
Motor vehicles and engines	351	..	..	..	..	..	..	..	..	112	111
Bodies, trailers and caravans	352	..	..	..	..	..	..	..	..	56	55
Parts	353	..	..	..	..	..	..	..	..	151	140
Other transport equipment	36	446	421	380	356	335	432	407	365	343	323
Shipbuilding and repairing	361	..	..	..	..	..	..	..	..	119	114
Railway and tramway vehicles	362	..	..	..	..	..	..	..	..	42	36
Cycles, motor cycles and other vehicles	363, 365	..	..	..	..	..	..	..	..	9	10
Aerospace equipment	364	..	..	..	..	..	..	..	..	173	163
Instrument engineering	37	128	124	112	112	109	126	123	111	111	108
Measuring, precision instruments, etc.	371	..	..	..	..	..	..	..	..	58	59
Medical and surgical equipment	372	..	..	..	..	..	..	..	..	20	20
Optical precision instruments, etc.	373	..	..	..	..	..	..	..	..	24	22
Clocks, watches, etc.	374	..	..	..	..	..	..	..	..	9	7
Other manufacturing industries	4	2 751	2 607	2 367	2 256	2 170	2 666	2 528	2 298	2 192	2 109
Food, drink and tobacco	41/42	739	730	688	669	642	715	707	666	649	623
Meat and meat products, organic oils and fats	411/412	..	..	..	..	..	..	..	..	103	103
Bacon curing and meat processing	4122	..	..	..	..	..	..	..	..	61	60
Milk and milk products	413	..	..	..	..	..	..	..	..	44	43
Fruit and vegetable processing	414	..	..	..	..	..	..	..	..	36	34
Fish processing	415	..	..	..	..	..	..	..	..	14	14
Bread, biscuits and flour confectionery	419	..	..	..	..	..	..	..	..	141	134
Sugar and sugar by-products	420	..	..	..	..	..	..	..	..	9	9
Cocoa, chocolate, sugar confectionery, etc.	421	..	..	..	..	..	..	..	..	67	64
Animal feeding stuffs and miscellaneous food	416/418/ 422/423	..	..	..	..	..	..	..	..	92	90
Spirit distilling and compounding	424	..	..	..	..	..	..	..	..	25	21
Brewing and malting, cider and perry	426, 427	..	..	..	..	..	..	..	..	63	60
Soft drinks	428	..	..	..	..	..	..	..	..	26	25
Tobacco	429	..	..	..	..	..	..	..	..	29	27
Textiles	43	395	345	289	270	251	376	329	276	258	240
Woollen and worsted	431	..	..	..	..	..	..	..	..	49	44
Cotton and silk	432	..	..	..	..	..	..	..	..	42	39
Hosiery and other knitted goods	436	..	..	..	..	..	..	..	..	89	84
Textile finishing	437	..	..	..	..	..	..	..	..	30	28
Carpets, etc.	438	..	..	..	..	..	..	..	..	18	17
Other textiles	433, 434, 435,439	..	..	..	..	..	..	..	..	30	28
Leather and leather goods	44	..	..	..	26	25	..	..	..	26	25
Footwear and clothing	45	..	..	..	307	290	..	..	..	291	276
Footwear	451	..	..	..	..	..	..	..	..	53	50
Clothing, hats, gloves and fur goods	453, 456	..	..	..	..	..	..	..	..	211	199
Mens and boys tailored outerwear	4532	..	..	..	..	..	..	..	..	36	33
Womens and girls tailored outerwear	4533	..	..	..	..	..	..	..	..	25	23
Work clothing and mens and boys jeans	4534	..	..	..	..	..	..	..	..	19	18
Womens and girls light outerwear, lingerie, etc.	4536	..	..	..	..	..	..	..	..	76	73
Household textiles, etc.	455	..	..	..	..	..	..	..	..	27	26
Timber and wooden furniture	46	254	240	220	204	207	249	235	216	200	203
Saw-milling, planing, semi-finished wood products	461, 462	..	..	..	..	..	..	..	..	30	30
Builders carpentry and joinery	463	..	..	..	..	..	..	..	..	36	40
Articles of wood, cork, etc.	464/465/466	..	..	..	..	..	..	..	..	30	29
Wooden and upholstered furniture, etc.	4671	..	..	..	..	..	..	..	..	80	81
Shop and office fitting	4672	..	..	..	..	..	..	..	..	25	24

1. Division, class or activity heading.
2. The data on SIC 1968 classification was last published in *Annual Abstract of Statistics No. 120, 1984 edition.*

Sources Department of Employment; Department of Manpower Services (Northern Ireland)

6.2

Employees in employment

Analysis by industry based on the Standard Industrial Classification 1980

(*continued*)   At June in each year

Thousands

	SIC 1980[1,2]	United Kingdom					Great Britain				
		1979	1980	1981	1982	1983	1979	1980	1981	1982	1983
Paper, printing and publishing	47	553	547	517	505	494	547	541	512	499	489
Pulp, paper and board	471	..	..	..	..	..	..	..	..	42	39
Conversion of paper and board	472	..	..	..	..	..	..	..	..	112	107
Packaging products of board	4725	..	..	..	..	..	..	..	..	48	46
Printing and publishing	475	..	..	..	..	..	..	..	..	346	343
Printing and publishing of newspapers	4751	..	..	..	..	..	..	..	..	98	99
Printing and publishing of books etc.	4752/4753	..	..	..	..	..	..	..	..	39	39
Rubber and plastics	48	247	230	205	192	180	240	223	198	185	175
Rubber products, tyre repair, etc.	481, 482	..	..	..	..	..	..	..	..	73	65
Processing of plastics	483	..	..	..	..	..	..	..	..	113	110
Other manufacturing	49	107	100	88	83	80	106	99	88	83	80
Jewellery and coins	491	..	..	..	..	..	..	..	..	16	15
Photo/cinematographic processing	493	..	..	..	..	..	..	..	..	14	15
Toys and sports goods	494	..	..	..	..	..	..	..	..	27	27
Other manufacturing nes	492, 495	..	..	..	..	..	..	..	..	26	23
Construction	5	1 253	1 252	1 138	1 059	1 016	1 216	1 216	1 112	1 033	991
Construction and repair of buildings, demolition work	500/501	..	..	..	..	..	..	..	..	577	556
Civil engineering	502	..	..	..	..	..	..	..	..	196	179
Installation of fixtures and fittings	503	..	..	..	..	..	..	..	..	165	163
Building completion	504	..	..	..	..	..	..	..	..	95	93
Distribution, hotels, catering, repairs	6	4 252	4 317	4 167	4 177	4 208	4 173	4 238	4 092	4 102	4 134
Wholesale distribution	61	889	915	888	899	908	867	893	868	880	890
Agricultural and textile raw materials, etc.	611	..	..	..	..	..	..	..	..	31	31
Fuels, ores, metals, etc.	612	..	..	..	..	..	..	..	..	107	105
Timber and building materials	613	..	..	..	..	..	..	..	..	124	128
Motor vehicles and parts	6148	..	..	..	..	..	..	..	..	44	44
Machinery, industrial equipment, vehicles	6149	..	..	..	..	..	..	..	..	94	94
Household goods, hardware, ironmongery	615	..	..	..	..	..	..	..	..	55	55
Textiles, clothing, footwear, etc.	616	..	..	..	..	..	..	..	..	39	39
Food, drink and tobacco	617	..	..	..	..	..	..	..	..	252	247
Pharmaceutical and medical goods	618	..	..	..	..	..	..	..	..	28	30
Other wholesale distribution	619	..	..	..	..	..	..	..	..	107	117
Dealing in scrap and waste materials	62	..	..	..	19	19	..	..	..	19	19
Commission agents	63	..	..	..	18	18	..	..	..	18	18
Retail distribution	64/65	2 174	2 175	2 090	2 057	2 079	2 133	2 134	2 051	2 018	2 040
Food	641	..	..	..	..	..	..	..	..	561	566
Confectioners, tobacconists, etc.	642	..	..	..	..	..	..	..	..	156	157
Dispensing and other chemists	643	..	..	..	..	..	..	..	..	123	123
Clothing	645	..	..	..	..	..	..	..	..	146	153
Footwear and leather goods	646	..	..	..	..	..	..	..	..	58	61
Furnishing fabrics, etc.	647	..	..	..	..	..	..	..	..	22	24
Household goods, hardware, ironmongery	648	..	..	..	..	..	..	..	..	172	176
Motor vehicles and parts	651	..	..	..	..	..	..	..	..	188	189
Filling stations	652	..	..	..	..	..	..	..	..	77	81
Books, stationery, office supplies	653	..	..	..	..	..	..	..	..	68	66
Other specialised distribution	654	..	..	..	..	..	..	..	..	103	103
Mixed retail businesses	656	..	..	..	..	..	..	..	..	345	342
Hotels and catering	66	950	979	950	982	975	938	966	937	969	962
Restaurants, snack bars, cafes, etc.	661	..	..	..	..	..	..	..	..	188	185
Public houses and bars	662	..	..	..	..	..	..	..	..	235	234
Night clubs and licensed clubs	663	..	..	..	..	..	..	..	..	142	141
Canteens and messes	664	..	..	..	..	..	..	..	..	124	113
Hotel trade	665	..	..	..	..	..	..	..	..	236	237
Other tourist, etc. accommodation	667	..	..	..	..	..	..	..	..	43	53
Repair of consumer goods and vehicles	67	204	211	204	201	209	199	207	200	198	206
Motor vehicles	671	..	..	..	..	..	..	..	..	170	175
Footwear, leather and other consumer goods	672, 673	..	..	..	..	..	..	..	..	28	31
Transport and communication	7	1 473	1 483	1 423	1 373	1 332	1 452	1 462	1 403	1 354	1 313
Railways	71	184	183	177	169	162	183	182	176	168	161
Other inland transport	72	457	454	416	404	400	450	447	410	398	394
Scheduled road passenger transport	721	..	..	..	..	..	..	..	..	190	189
Road haulage	723	..	..	..	..	..	..	..	..	192	187
Other inland transport nes	722, 726	..	..	..	..	..	..	..	..	17	18
Sea transport	74	..	..	..	59	49	..	..	..	58	49
Air transport	75	55	57	56	47	43	55	56	55	47	43
Supporting services to transport	76	116	117	111	103	98	115	115	110	102	97
Inland transport	761	..	..	..	..	..	..	..	..	17	17
Sea transport	763	..	..	..	..	..	..	..	..	50	45
Air transport	764	..	..	..	..	..	..	..	..	35	35
Miscellaneous transport and storage	77	164	165	159	155	147	162	164	157	153	146
Postal services	7901	..	..	..	..	..	..	..	..	197	197
Telecommunications	7902	..	..	..	..	..	..	..	..	231	227

1. Division, class or activity heading.
2. The data on SIC 1968 classification was last published in *Annual Abstract of Statistics No. 120, 1984 edition.*

Sources Department of Employment; Department of Manpower Services (Northern Ireland)

6.2
(continued)
Employees in employment
Analysis by industry based on the Standard Industrial Classification 1980
At June in each year

Thousands

	SIC 1980[1,2]	United Kingdom					Great Britain				
		1979	1980	1981	1982	1983	1979	1980	1981	1982	1983
Banking, finance, insurance, etc.	8	1 663	1 714	1 739	1 783	1 837	1 638	1 688	1 714	1 758	1 811
Banking and finance	81	449	464	473	481	501	441	456	466	473	493
Banking and bill discounting	814	..	..	..	..	..	..	..	..	364	377
Other financial institutions	815	..	..	..	..	..	..	..	..	108	116
Insurance, except social security	82	219	218	227	227	232	216	215	224	224	230
Business services	83	798	832	848	882	905	788	821	838	872	895
Auxiliary to banking and finance	831	..	..	..	..	..	..	..	..	19	21
Auxiliary to insurance	832	..	..	..	..	..	..	..	..	66	68
House and estate agents	834	..	..	..	..	..	..	..	..	83	78
Professional services nes	837	..	..	..	..	..	..	..	..	172	178
Advertising	838	..	..	..	..	..	..	..	..	37	39
Computer services	8394	..	..	..	..	..	..	..	..	54	55
Business services nes	8395	..	..	..	..	..	..	..	..	155	166
Central offices not allocable	8396	..	..	..	..	..	..	..	..	45	42
Renting of movables	84	..	..	..	89	92	..	..	..	88	91
Construction machinery, etc.	842	..	..	..	..	..	..	..	..	39	39
Consumer goods	846	..	..	..	..	..	..	..	..	26	28
Transport and movables nes	841, 843, 848, 849	..	..	..	..	..	..	..	..	22	24
Owning and dealing in real estate	85	..	..	..	105	106	..	..	..	102	102
Other services	9	6 168	6 179	6 122	6 129	6 164	5 976	5 982	5 923	5 930	5 963
Public administration and defence	91	1 721	1 669	1 625	1 593	1 600	1 670	1 618	1 574	1 542	1 547
National government service nes	9111	..	..	..	..	..	..	..	..	407	406
Local government services nes	9112	..	..	..	..	..	..	..	..	594	605
Justice	912	..	..	..	..	..	..	..	..	50	51
Police	913	..	..	..	..	..	..	..	..	189	191
Fire services	914	..	..	..	..	..	..	..	..	60	61
National defence	915	..	..	..	..	..	..	..	..	138	132
Social security	919	..	..	..	..	..	..	..	..	104	102
Sanitary services	92	280	303	280	278	290	276	299	276	275	287
Refuse disposal, etc.	921	..	..	..	..	..	..	..	..	86	84
Cleaning services	923	..	..	..	..	..	..	..	..	188	203
Education	93	1 647	1 630	1 604	1 595	1 599	1 591	1 574	1 548	1 539	1 543
Research and development	94	113	119	121	119	118	113	118	120	118	117
Medical and other health services	95	1 229	1 254	1 289	1 323	1 339	1 186	1 209	1 243	1 276	1 292
Hospitals, nursing homes, etc.	951	..	..	..	..	..	..	..	..	1 051	1 060
Other medical care institutions	952	..	..	..	..	..	..	..	..	118	120
Medical practices	953	..	..	..	..	..	..	..	..	52	56
Dental practices	954	..	..	..	..	..	..	..	..	35	36
Other health services	955, 956	..	..	..	..	..	..	..	..	20	20
Other services	96	545	578	589	601	625	518	550	560	571	595
Social welfare, etc.	961	..	..	..	..	..	..	..	..	470	492
Tourist and other services	969	..	..	..	..	..	..	..	..	37	37
Recreational and cultural services	97	430	435	432	441	414	422	427	424	433	406
Film production, authors, etc.	971, 976	..	..	..	..	..	..	..	..	29	25
Radio, television, theatres, etc.	974	..	..	..	..	..	..	..	..	69	71
Libraries, museums, art galleries, etc.	977	..	..	..	..	..	..	..	..	65	62
Sport and other recreational services	979	..	..	..	..	..	..	..	..	270	248
Personal services	98	200	188	180	177	176	196	184	177	174	173
Laundries, dyers and dry cleaners	981	..	..	..	..	..	..	..	..	62	62
Laundries	9811	..	..	..	..	..	..	..	..	43	44
Hairdressing and beauty parlours	982	..	..	..	..	..	..	..	..	90	89
Personal services nes	989	..	..	..	..	..	..	..	..	23	23

1. Division, class or activity heading.
2. The data on SIC 1968 classification was last published in *Annual Abstract of Statistics No. 120. 1984 edition.*

Sources Department of Employment; Department of Manpower Services
(Northern Ireland)

6.3 Males employed in engineering industries
Analysis by broad occupational category and industry[1]
Great Britain
At April 1983

Thousands

Industry based on the Standard Industrial Classification 1980[2]	All employees	Managerial, administrative, technical and clerical	Foremen[3]	Craftsmen (production and maintenance)	All other production and other occupations	All apprentices[5]	Craft apprentices[5]	Others being trained[4,5]
Metal manufacturing	51.04	10.21	3.31	7.41	30.11	0.71	0.65	0.77
Iron and steel industry	0.98	0.21	0.05	0.16	0.56	0.01	0.01	–
Steel tubes	12.20	2.43	0.87	1.84	7.06	0.17	0.15	0.36
Drawing, cold rolling and cold forming of steel	6.70	1.37	0.41	0.91	4.00	0.04	0.03	0.08
Non-ferrous metals industry	31.16	6.19	1.98	4.49	18.49	0.49	0.47	0.33
Manufacturing of metal goods nes (excluding Foundries)	174.18	37.34	10.95	35.49	90.40	3.96	3.27	2.30
Forging, pressing, stamping	27.15	4.86	1.76	5.32	15.21	0.49	0.41	0.10
Bolts, nuts, etc; springs, non-precision chains, metals treatment	27.70	5.71	1.99	4.35	15.65	0.41	0.34	0.30
Metal doors, windows, etc.	17.46	4.83	0.96	2.69	8.98	0.25	0.18	0.58
Hand tools and finished metal goods	101.87	21.94	6.24	23.14	50.56	2.81	2.34	1.33
Mechanical engineering	513.76	153.39	25.44	160.48	174.45	19.14	15.45	6.02
Industrial plant and steelwork	64.74	19.76	3.21	21.97	19.79	2.68	2.03	0.58
Agricultural machinery and tractors	26.33	7.45	1.08	3.98	13.82	0.52	0.37	0.21
Metal-working machine tools and engineers' tools	51.20	12.73	2.50	20.83	15.14	2.07	1.78	0.74
Textile machinery	7.06	1.79	0.37	2.77	2.13	0.21	0.20	0.01
Machinery for food, chemical and related industries; process engineering contractors	25.58	9.56	1.29	9.13	5.61	1.30	1.16	0.46
Mining machinery, construction and mechanical handling equipment	74.25	23.40	3.41	24.74	22.70	2.95	2.33	0.89
Mechanical power transmission equipment	22.77	5.48	1.27	5.40	10.61	1.04	0.79	0.73
Machinery for the printing, paper, wood, leather, rubber, glass and related industries, laundry and dry cleaning machinery	17.79	6.61	0.90	6.24	4.04	0.67	0.65	0.09
Other machinery and mechanical equipment	218.36	64.72	11.12	63.15	79.37	7.11	5.58	2.26
Ordnance, small arms and ammunition	5.68	1.88	0.29	2.28	1.24	0.59	0.56	0.06
Manufacture of office machinery and data processing equipment	57.43	41.19	1.62	3.00	11.62	1.19	0.23	1.43
Electrical and electronic engineering	345.06	155.41	17.83	52.41	119.41	11.87	5.07	7.13
Insulated wires and cables	26.48	8.06	1.51	3.13	13.78	0.54	0.32	0.52
Basic electrical equipment	76.05	28.71	3.52	19.44	24.38	3.12	1.70	1.28
Electrical equipment for industrial use, and batteries and accumulators	43.92	19.49	2.22	6.50	15.71	1.55	0.62	0.85
Telecommunications equipment, electrical measuring equipment, electronic capital goods and passive electronics components	119.02	68.42	6.00	14.65	29.96	4.84	1.52	2.75
Other electronic equipment	41.12	21.45	2.44	4.30	12.92	1.09	0.37	1.11
Domestic-type electric appliances	26.51	5.25	1.19	2.58	17.49	0.41	0.28	0.49
Electric lamps and other electric lighting equipment	11.93	4.02	0.95	1.80	5.16	0.33	0.26	0.13
Electrical equipment installation	0.02	–	–	0.01	–	–	–	–
Manufacture of motor vehicles and parts thereof	243.18	48.71	11.30	42.71	140.46	5.90	4.45	2.42
Motor vehicles and their engines	158.33	30.39	7.14	28.06	92.74	3.97	3.07	1.14
Motor vehicle bodies, trailers and caravans	13.50	1.96	0.68	2.21	8.65	0.04	0.03	0.02
Motor vehicle parts	71.36	16.36	3.48	12.44	39.08	1.89	1.34	1.26
Manufacture of other transport equipment	189.57	72.60	7.59	66.90	42.48	12.14	8.60	2.00
Shipbuilding and repairing	0.06	0.02	0.01	0.01	0.03	–	–	–
Railway and tramway vehicles	36.79	6.17	0.89	18.65	11.09	3.48	3.28	0.20
Cycles and motor cycles	4.59	1.02	0.20	0.37	3.00	0.06	0.06	0.44
Aerospace equipment manufacturing and repairing	147.89	65.35	6.48	47.86	28.21	8.60	5.26	1.33
Other vehicles	0.24	0.05	0.01	0.02	0.15	–	–	0.03
Instrument engineering	49.58	24.19	2.33	8.68	14.38	1.42	0.86	0.65
Measuring, checking and precision instruments and apparatus	27.93	15.55	1.33	4.63	6.41	0.87	0.49	0.46
Medical and surgical equipment and orthopaedic appliances	5.91	1.98	0.33	1.54	2.07	0.10	0.06	0.04
Optical precision instruments and photographic equipment	12.84	5.57	0.47	1.92	4.88	0.32	0.18	0.08
Clocks, watches and other timing devices	2.90	1.09	0.19	0.59	1.03	0.13	0.12	0.07
All other engineering industries nes	13.08	7.91	0.45	1.32	3.40	0.35	0.10	0.27
Total	1 636.87	550.93	80.82	378.40	626.72	56.69	38.68	23.00

1. This occupational survey is carried out by the EITB in April every year on a sample basis. All the figures in this table are estimates based on this survey and other EITB data. For information about the detailed methods used please contact the Statistics Section, EITB, 41 Clarendon Road, Watford, Herts: Watford (0923) 44322.

2. Only that part of each industry which is in scope to the EITB is included in the figures.
3. Except works and other senior foremen and office supervisors, who are included in the preceding column.
4. Excluding canteen staff and seafarers.
5. Included in the previous columns.

Source Engineering Industry Training Board (EITB)

6.3
(continued)

Females employed in engineering industries
Analysis by broad occupational category and industry[1]
Great Britain
At April 1983

Thousands

Industry based on the Standard Industrial Classification 1980[2]	All employees	Managerial, administrative, technical and clerical	Foremen[3]	Craftsmen (production and maintenance)	All other production and other occupations	All apprentices[5]	Craft apprentices[5]	Others being trained[4,5]
Metal manufacturing	9.29	4.78	0.02	0.01	4.48	0.01	–	0.15
Iron and steel industry	0.13	0.09	–	–	0.03	–	–	–
Steel tubes	2.21	1.20	–	–	1.00	0.01	–	0.03
Drawing, cold rolling and cold forming of steel	2.79	0.86	0.01	0.01	1.91	–	–	0.05
Non-ferrous metals industry	4.17	2.62	0.01	–	1.54	–	–	0.06
Manufacturing of metal goods nes (excluding Foundries)	58.08	20.91	0.40	0.10	36.68	0.07	0.03	0.98
Forging, pressing, stamping	8.65	2.63	0.05	0.01	5.97	0.01	–	0.04
Bolts, nuts, etc. springs, non-precision chains, metals treatment	9.25	3.77	0.03	0.04	5.41	0.01	0.01	0.05
Metal doors, windows, etc.	3.54	2.27	0.01	–	1.25	–	–	0.18
Hand tools and finished metal goods	36.65	12.24	0.30	0.05	24.05	0.05	0.03	0.72
Mechanical engineering	80.64	56.67	0.20	0.19	23.59	0.27	0.02	1.33
Industrial plant and steelwork	6.09	5.31	0.01	0.01	0.77	0.03	–	0.16
Agricultural machinery and tractors	2.30	2.02	–	–	0.27	0.05	–	0.03
Metal-working machine tools and engineers' tools	8.96	5.68	0.02	0.03	3.23	0.03	–	0.12
Textile machinery	1.04	0.68	–	–	0.35	–	–	0.01
Machinery for food, chemical and related industries; process engineering contractors	4.20	3.46	–	0.01	0.72	0.01	–	0.12
Mining machinery, construction and mechanical handling equipment	9.02	8.06	–	0.01	0.95	0.02	–	0.23
Mechanical power transmission equipment	4.07	2.11	0.02	–	1.93	0.02	–	0.04
Machinery for the printing, paper, wood, leather, rubber, glass and related industries, laundry and dry cleaning machinery	2.80	2.33	–	–	0.46	0.01	–	0.02
Other machinery and mechanical equipment	41.03	26.39	0.14	0.10	14.40	0.08	–	0.60
Ordnance, small arms and ammunition	1.15	0.63	0.01	0.02	0.48	0.04	0.02	–
Manufacture of office machinery and data processing equipment	20.09	12.90	0.16	0.09	6.95	0.08	–	0.82
Electrical and electronic engineering	167.35	57.01	2.31	0.59	107.44	0.63	0.07	3.59
Insulated wires and cables	9.38	3.53	0.09	–	5.76	0.02	–	0.24
Basic electrical equipment	25.47	9.54	0.26	0.05	15.63	0.13	0.03	0.44
Electrical equipment for industrial use, and batteries and accumulators	17.86	7.12	0.18	0.08	10.49	0.08	–	0.36
Telecommunications equipment, electrical measuring equipment, electronic capital goods and passive electronics components	63.24	22.10	1.20	0.38	39.55	0.29	0.03	1.70
Other electronic equipment	28.36	7.96	0.43	0.07	19.91	0.08	–	0.51
Domestic-type electric appliances	12.30	4.57	0.06	0.01	7.66	0.01	–	0.17
Electric lamps and other electric lighting equipment	10.73	2.20	0.08	–	8.44	0.01	–	0.17
Electrical equipment installation	–	–	–	–	–	–	–	–
Manufacture of motor vehicles and parts thereof	27.59	13.58	0.08	0.09	13.84	0.12	0.03	0.58
Motor vehicles and their engines	11.47	6.73	0.05	0.03	4.67	0.07	0.01	0.16
Motor vehicle bodies, trailers, caravans	1.02	0.63	0.01	0.05	0.34	0.01	0.01	–
Motor vehicle parts	15.10	6.23	0.02	0.01	8.84	0.04	–	0.42
Manufacture of other transport equipment	23.56	17.79	0.05	0.10	5.61	0.44	0.04	0.44
Shipbuilding and repairing	0.01	0.01	–	–	–	–	–	–
Railway and tramway vehicles	2.29	1.65	–	–	0.63	0.02	–	0.06
Cycles and motor cycles	1.19	0.42	0.01	–	0.77	–	–	0.08
Aerospace equipment manufacturing and repairing	20.02	15.68	0.05	0.10	4.19	0.42	0.03	0.30
Other vehicles	0.06	0.04	–	–	0.01	–	–	–
Instrument engineering	17.46	8.53	0.15	0.10	8.69	0.06	0.02	0.24
Measuring, checking and precision instruments and apparatus	9.76	4.75	0.10	0.06	4.84	0.04	–	0.14
Medical and surgical equipment and orthopaedic appliances	1.80	1.00	0.01	0.01	0.78	–	–	–
Optical precision instruments and photographic equipment	3.09	2.22	0.01	0.01	0.85	0.02	0.01	0.04
Clocks, watches and other timing devices	2.81	0.56	0.03	0.01	2.21	0.01	0.01	0.05
All other engineering industries nes	2.65	2.10	0.01	0.01	0.53	0.03	–	0.07
Total	406.72	194.27	3.37	1.27	207.81	1.71	0.21	8.20

1. This occupational survey is carried out by the EITB in April every year on a sample basis. All the figures in this table are estimates based on this survey and other EITB data. For information about the detailed methods used please contact the Statistics Section, EITB, 41 Clarendon Road, Watford, Herts: Watford (0923) 44322.

Source Engineering Industry Training Board (EITB)

2. Only that part of each industry which is in scope of EITB is included in the figures.
3. Except works and other senior foremen and office supervisors, who are included in the preceding column.
4. Excluding canteen staff and seafarers.
5. Included in the previous columns.

6.4 Administrative, technical and clerical workers in manufacturing industries[1]
Analysis by industry based on Standard Industrial Classification 1980[2]
Great Britain

Percentage

	Division/class SIC 1980	1981	1982	1983
All manufacturing industries	2–4	29.3	30.5	28.7
Minerals and ores extraction other than fuels	2	31.8	33.0	31.6
Metal manufacturing	22	27.4	27.8	26.5
Non-metallic mineral products	24	23.7	25.3	23.3
Chemical industry	25	40.2	41.8	40.4
Metal goods, engineering and vehicles	3	32.9	34.4	32.6
Metal goods nes	31	24.3	25.3	23.1
Mechanical engineering	32	33.9	35.2	33.3
Office machinery, data processing equipment	33	52.6	64.0	46.9
Electrical and electronic engineering	34	37.8	39.4	37.5
Motor vehicles and parts	35	24.9	24.4	24.9
Other transport equipment	36	33.7	35.3	35.7
Instrument engineering	37	37.0	36.2	34.0
Other manufacturing industries	4	23.8	24.9	23.0
Food, drink and tobacco	41/42	23.2	22.9	21.9
Textiles	43	18.7	19.8	18.6
Leather and leather goods	44	17.9	18.1	19.0
Footwear and clothing	45	15.2	16.7	14.4
Timber and wooden furniture	46	24.4	25.5	21.5
Paper, printing and publishing	47	32.8	34.9	32.7
Rubber and plastics	48	24.1	26.8	24.6
Other manufacturing	49	21.3	22.6	22.7

1. Expressed as percentage of total number of employees at September.
2. Analysis based on Standard Industrial Classification 1968 last published in *Annual Abstract of Statistics No. 120 1984 Edition.*

Source Department of Employment

6.5 Number of workers employed in agriculture[1]
At June in each year[2]

Thousands

	Regular workers					Seasonal or casual workers[4]			All workers			Salaried managers[4]
	Total[3]	Whole-time		Part-time		Total	Male	Female	Total[3]	Male	Female[3]	
		Male	Female[4]	Male	Female							
1976	290.4	188.8	24.6	34.7	42.2	79.6	45.0	34.6	370.0	268.5	101.4	7
1977	274.5	184.0	19.6	36.5	34.3	95.9	54.3	41.6	370.3	274.8	95.5	8
1978	264.7	177.0	18.5	35.7	33.5	100.9	58.0	42.9	365.6	270.7	94.9	8
1979	252.7	168.7	18.3	33.2	32.5	96.9	56.0	40.9	349.6	257.9	91.7	8
1980	244.1	162.6	17.3	32.3	31.9	100.7	57.2	43.4	344.7	252.1	92.7	8
1981	236.7	157.7	16.7	31.5	30.7	97.0	57.1	39.9	333.8	246.4	87.4	8
1982	232.2	154.6	16.0	31.9	29.7	98.7	57.3	41.5	331.0	243.8	87.2	8
1983	228.3	152.2	15.5	31.3	29.4	97.9	56.9	41.0	326.2	240.3	85.9	8

1. Figures exclude school children.
2. Figures from 1977 onwards include estimates for minor holdings not surveyed at the June census in England and Wales.
3. Small adjustments made retrospectively to 1981 and 1982 following 1983 census of minor holdings in England.
4. Great Britain only.

Source Ministry of Agriculture, Fisheries and Food

6.6 Rates of unemployment[1]
Analysis by standard regions

Percentages

Annual averages	1974	1975	1976	1977	1978	1979	1980	1981	1982	1983
United Kingdom	2.6	4.0	5.5	5.9	5.7	5.3	6.8	10.4	12.1	12.9
Great Britain	2.5	3.9	5.4	5.7	5.6	5.2	6.7	10.2	11.9	12.7
North	4.6	5.8	7.2	8.0	8.6	8.3	10.4	14.7	16.5	17.7
Yorkshire and Humberside	2.5	3.8	5.3	5.5	5.7	5.4	7.3	11.4	13.2	14.1
East Midlands	2.2	3.5	4.5	4.8	4.7	4.4	6.1	9.6	10.9	11.8
East Anglia	1.9	3.3	4.7	5.1	4.9	4.2	5.3	8.3	9.7	10.2
South East	1.5	2.6	4.0	4.3	3.9	3.4	4.2	7.0	8.5	9.3
South West	2.6	4.6	6.2	6.5	6.2	5.4	6.4	9.2	10.6	11.2
West Midlands	2.1	3.9	5.5	5.5	5.3	5.2	7.3	12.5	14.7	15.6
North West	3.4	5.2	6.7	7.0	6.9	6.5	8.5	12.7	14.7	15.8
Wales	3.7	5.5	7.1	7.6	7.7	7.3	9.4	13.5	15.4	15.9
Scotland	3.8	5.0	6.7	7.7	7.7	7.4	9.1	12.4	14.0	14.9
Northern Ireland	5.4	7.4	9.5	10.5	11.0	10.7	12.8	16.8	18.7	20.2

1. Numbers of unemployed claimants expressed as a percentage of the estimated total number of employees.

Sources Department of Employment; Department of Economic Development (Northern Ireland)

6.7 Civil Service staff[1]
Analysis by ministerial responsibility
At 1 April in each year

Full-time equivalents[2] (thousands)

	1974	1975	1976	1977	1978	1979	1980	1981	1982	1983	1984
Total civil and defence departments	692.0	701.4	747.6	745.6	735.7	732.3	704.9	689.6	666.4	648.9	624.0
of which Non-industrials	*511.8*	*524.1*	*568.5*	*571.1*	*567.3*	*565.8*	*547.5*	*539.9*	*528.0*	*518.5*	*504.3*
Industrials	*180.2*	*177.3*	*179.1*	*174.4*	*168.4*	*166.5*	*157.4*	*149.7*	*138.4*	*130.4*	*119.7*
Total civil departments	425.0	434.8	481.4	486.9	485.3	484.6	465.1	460.0	449.4	440.0	424.8
Agriculture, Fisheries and Food	15.5	15.8	16.1	15.5	14.6	14.5	14.3	13.6	13.1	12.7	12.1
Chancellor of the Exchequer's Departments:[3, 4, 5]	111.7	119.8	126.8	129.3	128.9	128.2	119.0	114.9	121.0	117.4	112.4
Customs and Excise	24.8	28.4	29.4	29.3	28.8	28.8	27.2	26.8	26.2	25.4	25.1
Inland Revenue	69.8	74.2	80.3	83.9	85.2	84.6	78.3	75.6	74.0	73.1	69.8
Department for National Savings	13.6	13.3	13.4	12.2	10.9	10.8	10.4	10.0	9.1	8.3	8.0
Treasury and others	3.5	3.9	3.7	3.9	4.0	4.0	3.1	2.5	11.7	10.6	9.5
Education and Science[6]	3.9	4.0	4.1	4.0	3.7	3.7	3.7	3.6	3.5	3.5	2.4
Employment	28.3	19.2	47.7	52.5	53.7	53.6	50.7	53.8	58.7	57.9	56.4
Energy	–	1.3	1.4	1.3	1.3	1.3	1.3	1.2	1.1	1.1	1.1
Environment[7, 8, 9, 10]	74.0	75.2	77.5	61.5	57.3	56.0	51.7	47.0	42.1	39.4	36.6
Foreign and Commonwealth[11]	12.4	12.6	12.5	12.4	12.1	12.1	11.6	11.4	11.1	11.1	10.0
Home[11, 12]	28.7	30.7	32.3	32.6	33.2	33.5	34.1	35.4	34.6	35.1	36.4
Industry[13]	–	10.4	10.1	9.7	9.5	9.5	9.1	8.8	8.3	7.7	–
Scotland[14, 15]	12.0	12.3	13.2	13.0	13.5	13.7	13.6	13.6	13.4	13.1	12.8
Social Services	86.0	91.5	95.8	98.3	99.5	100.9	98.9	100.1	98.0	96.4	92.6
Trade[13, 16]	20.5	9.5	10.3	10.0	9.7	9.6	9.4	9.3	8.9	8.9	–
Trade and Industry[12, 13]	–	–	–	–	–	–	–	–	–	–	14.7
Transport[8, 16]	–	–	–	13.6	14.5	13.9	13.5	13.7	13.0	13.0	14.2
Wales	1.2	1.3	1.5	1.6	2.5	2.6	2.5	2.3	2.3	2.2	2.2
Other civil departments[3]	30.7	31.1	32.1	31.5	31.3	31.4	31.7	31.3	20.2	20.5	20.9
Total Ministry of Defence	267.1	266.6	266.2	258.7	250.4	247.7	239.8	229.6	216.9	208.9	199.2

1. The figures include non-industrial and industrial staff but exclude casual or seasonal staff (normally recruited for short periods of not more than twelve months) and employees of the Northern Ireland Government.
2. Part-time employees are counted as half units.
3. The responsibilities for the Paymaster General's Office transferred from the Chancellor of the Exchequer's Departments to 'Other civil departments' on 1 July 1979 (868 staff) and are now included with 'Other civil departments'. The Treasury Solicitor was reclassified to 'Other civil departments' on 1 April 1981.
4. Certain Civil Service Department (CSD) divisions, along with responsibility for CISCO, HMSO, COI and the Government Actuary's Department, were transferred to the Chancellor of the Exchequer (9 873 staff in all) on 7 December 1981. From the same date the Management and Personnel Office became responsible for CSD's work on efficiency and personnel management, recruitment and training (1 378 staff).
5. On 1 April 1982, responsibility for the HMSO binderies was transferred to the British Libraries Board, and in Scotland, to the National Library of Scotland. A total of 160 staff have been excluded from the manpower count.
6. As of 1 April 1984 the Victoria and Albert and the Science Museum became non-manpower count bodies, they have been accorded Trustee status – around 1 100 staff are involved.
7. From 1 October 1980, certain staff in PSA (1 276 involved) have been excluded from the manpower count.
8. With effect from 1 April 1981, some 765 non-industrial Environment/ Transport common services staff employed on work for the Department of Transport and previously counted in the Department of the Environment, were instead included in the former's figures.

9. With effect from 1 April 1982, the Department of the Environment transferred to the Countryside Commission, 96 staff formerly on secondment to it; and hived-off the Hydraulics Research Station with its 244 staff. A total of 340 staff have been excluded from the manpower count.
10. From 1 April 1984 approximately 1 100 staff of the Directorate of Historic Monuments and Ancient buildings have been transferred to a new Commission outside the manpower count.
11. From 1 April 1984 responsibility for the Passport Office was passed to the Home Office from the Foreign and Commonwealth Office (around 950 staff involved).
12. 279 non-industrial staff employed in the Radio Regulatory Department of the Home Office were transferred to the Department of Trade and Industry in June 1983.
13. Following the general election in June 1983 the former Departments of Trade and Industry merged.
14. Departments of the Secretary of State for Scotland and the Lord Advocate.
15. The State Hospital Carstairs was hived off on 31 March 1984, around 400 staff were involved.
16. Some 1 454 non-industrial staff employed in the Aviation and Shipping divisions of the Department of Trade were transferred in June 1983 to the Department of Transport.

Source HM Treasury

6.8 Unemployed in Great Britain[1]

Thousands

	Average of monthly counts	January	February	March	April	May	June	July	August	September	October	November	December
Total													
1972	799	894	896	898	876	803	741	736	771	773	749	737	717
1973	566	742	692	660	625	573	529	512	524	504	488	477	469
1974	571	583	584	575	562	521	502	522	597	592	587	600	631
1975[2]	902	718	735	746	779	788	803	904	1 046	1 048	1 056	1 081	1 117
1976	1 250	1 216	1 214	1 194	1 188	1 177	1 215	1 328	1 372	1 330	1 258	1 250	1 257
1977	1 345	1 331	1 307	1 270	1 272	1 224	1 303	1 452	1 472	1 450	1 368	1 353	1 339
1978	1 321	1 405	1 365	1 320	1 309	1 246	1 282	1 401	1 429	1 351	1 274	1 245	1 222
1979[3]	1 234	1 312	1 308	1 261	1 203	1 161	1 175	1 279	1 277	1 226	1 206	1 199	1 201
1980	1 591	1 311	1 325	1 313	1 353	1 340	1 444	1 657	1 763	1 806	1 832	1 929	2 011
1981[4]	2 422	2 178	2 218	2 239	2 279	2 312	2 299	2 414	2 488	2 643	2 668	2 668	2 663
1982	2 809	2 791	2 766	2 718	2 714	2 695	2 664	2 744	2 790	2 950	2 935	2 951	2 985
1983	2 988	3 109	3 085	3 059	3 053	2 934	2 871	2 904	2 893	3 044	2 974	2 965	2 961
Males													
1972	683	769	770	771	751	689	638	632	653	657	634	622	608
1973	483	628	586	560	531	490	455	439	446	429	417	409	405
1974	488	499	501	496	482	451	436	450	503	498	499	509	536
1975[2]	736	604	618	626	653	660	672	738	828	831	840	863	897
1976	969	971	968	952	948	936	950	1 004	1 028	998	953	957	965
1977	1 004	1 017	1 001	976	976	940	980	1 052	1 066	1 050	1 002	996	994
1978	966	1 045	1 020	990	976	932	942	998	1 012	961	916	901	894
1979[3]	887	963	967	935	891	854	847	891	888	855	849	850	859
1980	1 129	936	950	942	972	963	1 024	1 145	1 222	1 260	1 294	1 383	1 460
1981	1 773	1 583	1 622	1 647	1 682	1 710	1 706	1 775	1 820	1 909	1 932	1 942	1 953
1982	2 056	2 047	2 032	1 999	2 000	1 988	1 967	2 012	2 037	2 127	2 127	2 148	2 186
1983[5]	2 134	2 271	2 253	2 236	2 221	2 115	2 062	2 059	2 041	2 116	2 076	2 072	2 081
Females													
1972	116	125	126	127	125	114	103	104	118	117	115	115	109
1973	83	113	106	100	94	83	74	73	78	74	71	68	64
1974	83	84	83	79	80	70	66	72	95	94	88	91	95
1975[2]	166	114	117	120	126	129	131	166	218	217	216	218	220
1976	281	245	246	242	240	241	265	324	344	333	305	293	292
1977	341	313	305	294	296	284	323	401	406	400	366	357	345
1978	355	359	345	330	332	314	340	404	417	390	358	343	328
1979[3]	347	349	341	326	312	307	328	389	389	372	357	350	342
1980	461	375	375	371	382	377	420	512	542	547	538	547	552
1981	649	594	596	593	598	601	593	639	669	735	736	726	710
1982	753	743	734	718	714	707	697	733	753	823	808	803	798
1983[5]	854	838	832	823	833	819	809	844	852	927	898	892	880

1. New basis (claimants), article in *Employment Gazette,* December 1982, page S 20 refers.
2. From October 1975 onwards the day of the count was changed from Monday to Thursday. Adjustments to take into account amendments—in respect of the numbers unemployed on the statistical date—notified during the four days following the date of the count were discontinued.
3. The figures for 1979 are affected by the introduction of fortnightly payment of benefit in October 1979 (see page 1151 of *Employment Gazette* November 1979).
4. The recorded unemployment figures for July to October 1981 are overstated by about 20,000 (net) as the result of industrial action at benefit offices.
5. From April 1983 the figures reflect the efforts of the provisions in the Budget for some men aged 60 and over who no longer have to sign at an unemployment office.

Source Department of Employment

6.9 Unemployed in Northern Ireland
Claimant based

Thousands

	Annual averages	January	February	March	April	May	June	July	August	September	October	November	December
1973	29.5	34.9	33.9	32.9	31.5	29.3	28.3	29.9	28.6	27.4	25.6	25.6	26.0
1974	28.1	28.5	28.3	27.0	26.1	24.9	25.6	30.1	29.6	29.4	28.3	29.6	30.1
1975	39.2	31.9	32.8	32.3	34.4	35.0	35.3	42.8	44.5	44.7	45.3	46.0	45.7
1976	51.8	49.0	48.2	47.7	47.2	48.8	50.7	57.0	58.4	57.2	53.0	52.5	52.4
1977	57.9	55.3	54.1	53.0	53.8	53.5	56.4	65.0	65.1	63.6	58.4	58.1	58.2
1978	62.3	61.0	60.0	59.1	61.3	59.1	61.3	69.5	70.3	67.6	61.4	58.2	58.3
1979	61.8	61.3	61.4	59.6	58.0	58.1	59.6	68.3	68.0	66.0	61.5	59.7	60.2
1980	74.5	63.0	63.5	62.7	64.7	64.2	68.7	79.7	83.0	84.2	84.8	86.5	88.6
1981	98.0	93.5	94.3	94.3	93.5	95.9	95.9	97.9	98.0	105.4	103.9	101.8	101.2
1982	108.3	105.8	104.7	103.2	104.2	105.1	105.8	108.2	109.0	115.8	113.7	112.2	112.3
1983	117.1	116.2	114.7	113.7	116.4	115.0	113.4	117.1	117.0	123.7	119.8	119.7	118.4
1984		112.2	112.5	120.8	120.1								

Source Department of Economic Development (Northern Ireland)

6.10 Employment vacancies unfilled in Great Britain[1]

Thousands

	January	February	March	April	May	June	July	August	September	October	November	December
Numbers notified to jobcentres[2]												
1973	185	219	244	273	301	323	337	335	353	365	363	348
1974	285	267	267	298	324	336	330	303	307	299	271	237
1975	199	181	178	173	164	159	143	136	141	129	113	101
1976	87	97	107	117	122	125	127	128	139	138	129	122
1977	118	132	143	154	164	167	161	156	159	167	158	153
1978	157	170	184	202	214	226	217	212	231	240	230	219
1979	214	215	226	249	266	275	259	246	252	245	229	203
1980	185	178	175	174	176	164	132	118	119	108	93	83
1981	81	83	90	99	106	102	96	96	104	106	100	91
1982	92	98	105	115	122	123	114	111	114	119	110	101
1983	102	109	120	140	147	156	156	159	170	172	159	139
1984	132	133	142	154	168	171	166	160				
Numbers notified to careers offices[2]												
1973	47	55	62	72	86	96	117	123	124	121	114	108
1974	92	85	86	101	106	111	122	104	92	76	66	53
1975	44	41	43	41	37	35	37	27	27	26	24	20
1976	18	18	21	24	29	28	26	25	26	23	21	18
1977	17	17	23	25	32	27	21	20	21	19	18	17
1978	17	19	24	25	33	31	28	27	30	29	27	27
1979	25	23	28	34	41	37	34	31	31	28	24	21
1980	19	18	19	19	24	19	16	12	9	8	5	4
1981	4	4	4	4	7	6	5	5	5	5	4	3
1982	4	5	6	6	9	8	6	6	6	6	5	5
1983	5	5	6	7	11	9	8	7	8	8	7	6
1984	6	7	7	8	10	12	10	9				

1. About one third of all vacancies are notified to jobcentres. These could include some that are suitable for young persons and similarly vacancies notified to careers offices could include some for adults. Because of possible duplication the two series should not be added together. The figures represent only the number of vacancies notified by employers and remaining unfilled on the day of the count.

2. The figures for October 1974 to January 1975 and November 1976 to January 1977 include estimates.

Source Department of Employment

6.11 Employment vacancies unfilled in Northern Ireland[1]

Number

	January	February	March	April	May	June	July	August	September	October	November	December
1973	3 345	4 041	4 400	5 033	5 326	5 229	5 056	5 274	6 106	6 270	6 180	6 061
1974	5 852	5 860	6 150	6 441	6 683	6 479	6 624	6 391	6 375	6 445	5 909	5 227
1975	4 856	5 355	4 843	4 682	4 259	4 280	3 568	3 580	3 443	3 306	3 063	2 756
Adults												
1976	2 039	2 271	2 126	2 330	2 430	2 219	2 005	1 823	2 303	2 058	1 935	1 720
1977	1 835	1 795	1 808	1 815	1 802	2 029	1 994	2 046	2 092	2 134	1 986	1 786
1978	1 757	1 907	1 929	1 810	1 863	1 941	1 713	1 604	1 608	1 460	1 366	1 155
1979	1 098	1 160	1 237	1 489	1 558	1 517	1 398	1 314	1 388	1 318	1 210	1 109
1980	1 054	1 177	1 289	1 228	1 284	1 334	1 001	993	825	759	669	639
1981	595	603	619	732	728	741	714	735	791	811	859	795
1982	752	847	875	900	937	957	1 022	1 079	1 123	1 207	1 072	1 019
1983	1 017	1 037	1 160	1 171	1 237	1 380	1 351	1 334	1 298	1 203	1 070	1 113
1984	1 109	1 203	1 294	1 331	1 543	1 779	1 756	1 746				
Young Persons												
1976	583	641	644	693	652	547	532	548	710	570	491	489
1977	518	495	543	462	607	565	400	474	567	508	427	345
1978	364	359	303	349	344	338	307	316	505	406	341	278
1979	243	252	261	286	306	240	261	294	308	250	228	182
1980	170	187	165	164	163	164	149	135	182	123	109	64
1981	71	64	66	109	61	62	54	82	135	158	120	124
1982	136	190	167	158	170	190	157	162	221	206	214	210
1983	193	208	243	295	340	282	240	227	309	352	371	330
1984	309	330	377	394	469	595	542	576				

1. The figures refer to vacancies notified to the Employment Service Jobmarkets of the Department of Economic Development

Source Department of Economic Development (Northern Ireland)

6.12 Number of temporarily stopped workers
Great Britain

Number

	Average of monthly counts	January	February	March	April	May	June	July	August	September	October	November	December
Total													
1973	11 095	9 461	11 251	12 172	10 408	11 312	21 566	4 397	6 539	13 566	9 139	15 336	7 994
1974[1,2]	173 145	914 889	744 870	101 823	13 431	21 884	8 912	10 271	15 577	19 740	23 855	29 345	..
1975[1,2,3]	60 830	..	57 231	83 828	72 657	91 097	79 687	57 424	60 747	56 326	37 843	38 990	33 298
1976[1,4]	23 878	41 512	39 333	30 773	26 245	21 139	19 669	13 777	12 622	17 214	16 491	..	..
1977	17 535	14 907	19 551	46 361	15 377	18 044	6 884	9 569	9 596	18 402	23 139	16 392	12 196
1978	10 330	15 469	13 596	16 930	11 664	7 095	9 113	10 920	4 177	8 651	9 431	7 293	9 619
1979	12 265	17 990	39 854	19 918	8 949	7 542	5 490	5 824	3 783	6 985	15 491	10 404	4 953
1980	17 372	8 879	35 198	34 105	22 410	8 818	9 542	13 531	9 844	13 836	18 563	17 217	16 526
1981	16 835	22 524	22 642	19 898	20 439	14 820	13 085	12 594	12 472	12 904	14 911	19 542	16 187
1982[4]	18 158	29 395	27 424	24 967	20 064	15 676	12 221	12 290	12 218	13 458	13 865		
1982[5]	14 983										14 985	13 819	16 144
1983	12 799	17 765	22 163	17 605	16 043	14 913	10 934	12 327	7 913	7 698	9 218	8 562	8 441
Males													
1973	9 977	8 825	10 263	11 096	9 414	9 777	18 681	3 859	5 773	11 967	8 586	14 221	7 258
1974[1]	..	..	..	..	12 195	19 877	8 164	9 350	14 198	17 990	19 578	24 300	..
1975[1,2,3]	48 949	..	45 002	70 440	57 984	74 422	64 303	46 964	51 486	44 313	28 199	29 949	25 381
1976[1,4]	18 732	30 186	31 201	24 840	20 972	17 174	15 922	10 859	9 657	12 446	14 060	..	..
1977	15 303	11 814	17 942	41 905	13 942	16 291	5 983	8 338	7 042	14 933	20 707	14 184	10 551
1978	9 045	13 551	12 161	13 802	10 320	6 127	7 890	9 759	3 633	8 177	8 197	6 364	8 559
1979	10 698	15 900	35 947	17 871	7 782	6 156	4 942	4 165	2 940	5 938	14 155	8 508	4 072
1980	14 479	7 406	33 012	29 975	17 544	7 106	7 584	11 112	7 725	10 780	14 775	13 546	13 179
1981	13 399	18 616	18 690	16 006	15 672	12 046	10 370	9 739	9 642	9 817	11 661	15 939	12 586
1982[4]	13 945	24 034	21 036	19 594	15 443	11 813	9 054	9 022	8 904	9 449	11 097		
1982[5]	12 199										12 325	11 672	12 599
1983	10 262	14 559	18 175	13 636	12 724	11 611	8,830	9 586	6 154	6 294	7 896	6 613	7 064
Females													
1973	1 118	636	988	1 076	994	1 535	2 885	538	766	1 599	553	1 115	736
1974[1]	..	..	..	..	1 236	2 007	748	921	1 379	1 750	4 277	5 045	..
1975[1,2,3]	11 880	..	12 229	13 388	14 673	16 675	15 384	10 460	9 261	12 013	9 644	9 041	7 917
1976[1,4]	5 146	11 326	8 132	5 933	5 273	3 965	3 747	2 918	2 965	4 768	2 431	..	..
1977	2 232	3 093	1 609	4 456	1 435	1 753	901	1 231	2 554	3 469	2 432	2 208	1 645
1978	1 285	1 918	1 435	3 128	1 344	968	1 223	1 161	544	474	1 234	929	1 060
1979	1 567	2 090	3 907	2 047	1 167	1 386	548	1 659	843	1 047	1 336	1 896	881
1980	2 894	1 473	2 186	4 130	4 866	1 712	1 958	2 419	2 119	3 056	3 788	3 671	3 347
1981	3 436	3 908	3 952	3 892	4 767	2 774	2 715	2 855	2 830	3 087	3 250	3 603	3 601
1982[4]	4 213	5 361	6 388	5 373	4 621	3 863	3 167	3 268	3 314	4 009	2 768		
1982[5]	2 784										2 660	2 147	3 545
1983	2 537	3 206	3 988	3 969	3 319	3 302	2 104	2 741	1 759	1 404	1 322	1 949	1 377

1. In January, February and March 1974, the numbers of temporarily stopped were affected by the energy crises. Separate information for males and females was not collected in January, February and March 1974. Because of industrial action by some staff in the Department of Employment group, figures for October and November 1974 do not include West Midlands and no count was made in December 1974, January 1975, November and December 1976.
2. Averages are for eleven months.
3. In October 1975 the day of the count was changed from Monday to Thursday.
4. Averages are for ten months.
5. Computerised count of claimants. Averages are for three months.

Source Department of Employment

6.13 Number of temporarily stopped workers
Northern Ireland

Number

	Annual averages	January	February	March	April	May	June	July	August	September	October	November	December
Total													
1973	485	606	664	719	1 147	764	522	272	192	225	170	273	269
1974	1 829	6 609	2 654	979	284	2 401	1 227	370	300	643	1 201	3 853	1 426
1975	1 936	3 592	2 174	2 540	3 108	1 883	1 460	2 340	1 134	1 372	1 155	1 322	1 146
1976	1 040	1 744	1 987	1 346	1 036	743	1 067	967	867	795	715	689	518
1977	2 433	837	818	553	736	19 398	415	303	313	904	2 623	1 459	839
1978	863	679	721	703	934	2 142	2 241	397	213	310	475	942	593
1979	780	2 085	1 839	504	874	227	444	405	151	390	503	1 463	470
1980	827	880	1 089	828	1 127	647	710	716	672	707	856	884	807
1981[1]	1 074	1 087	1 576	1 395	977	979	1 045	1 265	859	775	981	947	1 011
1982	1 508	2 314	1 465	1 773	1 751	1 255	1 786	1 202	1 100	1 438	1 379	1 369	1 266
1983	1 179	1 800	2 155	1 620	1 281	1 082	997	874	740	820	827	933	1 018
Males													
1973	273	405	433	289	413	446	252	160	139	189	121	215	211
1974	970	2 285	1 574	474	217	1 701	1 094	244	206	327	776	2 086	650
1975	919	1 720	1 037	1 201	1 736	835	550	774	469	592	638	775	698
1976	513	927	1 060	582	431	374	485	345	376	399	458	438	276
1977	2 000	574	564	353	512	17 083	320	151	230	538	1 941	1 182	555
1978	685	355	482	531	397	2 013	2 055	234	128	233	416	841	533
1979	666	1 908	1 672	398	638	203	386	318	119	287	416	1 270	374
1980	628	622	949	608	857	553	457	397	507	527	705	746	609
1981[1]	845	861	1 382	1 118	708	811	826	927	686	671	772	681	694
1982	962	1 646	1 026	1 157	928	826	1 090	804	704	871	852	833	805
1983	802	1 164	1 378	911	800	702	693	615	536	661	670	710	778
Females													
1973	213	201	231	430	734	318	270	112	53	36	49	58	58
1974	859	4 324	1 080	505	67	700	133	126	94	316	425	1 767	776
1975	1 017	1 872	1 137	1 339	1 372	1 048	910	1 566	665	780	517	547	448
1976	527	817	927	764	605	369	582	622	491	396	257	251	242
1977	433	263	254	200	224	2 315	95	152	83	366	682	277	284
1978	178	324	239	172	537	129	186	163	85	77	59	101	60
1979	114	177	167	106	236	24	58	87	32	103	87	193	96
1980	199	258	140	220	270	94	253	319	165	180	151	138	198
1981[1]	230	226	194	227	269	168	219	338	173	104	209	266	317
1982	546	668	439	616	823	429	696	398	396	567	527	536	461
1983	377	636	777	709	481	380	304	259	204	159	157	223	240

1. April to July 1981 include estimates for some personnel involved in an industrial dispute.

Source Department of Economic Development (Northern Ireland)

6.14 Industrial stoppages[1]
Number of stoppages and workers involved

Standard Industrial Classification 1968	1979	1980	1981	1982
Numbers of stoppages beginning in each year				
Analysis by industry				
All industries and services[2]	2 080	1 330	1 338	1 528
Mining and quarrying	309	310	305	404
Metals, engineering, shipbuilding				
and vehicles	848	380	434	473
Textiles	42	25	26	41
Clothing and footwear	27	10	13	14
Construction	170	103	59	45
Transport and communication	180	158	157	167
All other industries and services	521	352	353	396
Workers directly and indirectly involved in				
these stoppages: total (thousands)	4 583	842	1 499	2 103
Analysis by industry				
Mining and quarrying	54	87	98	225
Metals, engineering, shipbuilding				
and vehicles	2 025	367	410	686
Textiles	13	6	3	7
Clothing and footwear	7	1	2	4
Construction	301	30	12	10
Transport and communication	250	112	81	481
All other industries and services	1 934	239	893	690
Analysis by duration of stoppage				
Not more than 5 days	579	342	750	692
Over 5 but not more than 10 days	191	154	72	90
Over 10 but not more than 20 days	1 662	101	132	141
Over 20 but not more than 30 days	127	19	61	35
Over 30 but not more than 50 days	461	17	7	12
Over 50 days	1 564	209	477	1 133

Standard Industrial Classification 1980	1982	1983
Numbers of stoppages beginning in each year		
Analysis by industry		
All industries and services[2]	1 528	1 352
Coal, coke, mineral oil and natural gas	407	359
Metals, engineering and vehicles	472	369
Textiles, footwear and clothing	48	40
Construction	44	45
Transport and communication	167	150
All other industries and services	401	394
Workers directly and indirectly involved in		
these stoppages: total (thousands)	2 103	571
Analysis by industry		
Coal, coke, mineral oil and natural gas	228	137
Metals, engineering and vehicles	684	226
Textiles, footwear and clothing	9	7
Construction	10	7
Transport and communication	481	48
All other industries and services	690	147
Analysis by duration of stoppage		
Not more than 5 days	692	281
Over 5 but not more than 10 days	90	68
Over 10 but not more than 20 days	141	75
Over 20 but not more than 30 days	35	37
Over 30 but not more than 50 days	12	67
Over 50 days	1 133	87

Working days lost as a result of stoppages

Thousands

Standard Industrial Classification 1968	1979	1980	1981	1982
Working days lost through stoppages which				
began in year[3]	29 051	11 965	4 244	5 276
Analysis by workers involved:				
Under 100 workers	302	184	175	148
100 and under 250 workers	603	252	241	236
250 and under 500 workers	779	316	375	312
500 and under 1 000 workers	1 089	466	536	426
1 000 and under 2 500 workers	1 497	734	589	511
2 500 and under 5 000 workers	1 486	317	250	303
5 000 workers and over	23 295	9 696	2 078	3 340
Working days lost through all stoppages				
in progress[4]				
Analysis by industry				
All industries and services	29 474	11 964	4 266	5 313
Mining and quarrying	128	166	237	374
Metals, engineering, shipbuilding				
and vehicles	20 390	10 155	1 731	1 457
Textiles	72	36	20	45
Clothing and footwear	38	8	19	21
Construction	834	281	86	44
Transport and communication	1 419	253	359	1 675
All other industries and services	6 594	1 065	1 814	1 697

Standard Industrial Classification 1980	1982	1983
Working days lost through stoppages		
which began in year[3]	5 276	3 981
Analysis by workers involved:		
Under 100 workers	148	158
100 and under 250 workers	236	251
250 and under 500 workers	312	330
500 and under 1 000 workers	426	435
1 000 and under 2 500 workers	511	517
2 500 and under 5 000 workers	303	559
5 000 workers and over	3 304	1 732
Working days lost through all stoppages		
in progress[4]		
Analysis by industry		
All industries and services	5 313	3 754
Coal, coke, mineral oil and natural gas	380	591
Metals, engineering and vehicles	1 457	1 420
Textiles footwear and clothing	61	32
Construction	41	68
Transport and communication	1 675	295
All other industries and services	1 699	1 348

1. Excluding stoppages involving fewer than 10 workers or lasting less than one day except any in which the aggregate number of working days lost exceeded 100. There may be some under-recording of small or short stoppages; this would have much more effect on the total of stoppages than of working days lost.
2. Some stoppages which affected more than one industry group have been counted under each of the industries but only once in the totals.
3. The figures for working days lost include days lost in subsequent years where the stoppages extended into the following calendar year.
4. This analysis shows the total working days lost *within* each year as a result of stoppages in progress in that year whether beginning in that or an earlier year.

Source Department of Employment

6.15

Economic activity: 1981[1]
Great Britain
All residents

Thousands

	Total	Age last birthday							
		Under 20	20–24	25–34	35–44	45–54	55–59	60–64	65 and over
Males: total population (aged 16 and over)	19 929	1 821	2 004	3 835	3 250	3 011	1 542	1 310	3 155
Total economically inactive (aged 16 and over)	4 430	645	218	110	71	109	130	333	2 815
Students	896	627	193	60	13	4	—	—	—
Retired	2 923	—	—	—	3	10	28	181	2 702
Permanently sick	512	8	13	31	43	86	98	147	85
Other	99	10	11	18	12	9	5	5	28
Total economically active	15 499	1 177	1 787	3 725	3 180	2 902	1 412	977	340
Self-employed (included above)	1 840	23	103	435	496	407	160	120	95
In employment	13 736	949	1 492	3 326	2 902	2 648	1 263	822	333
Working full-time	13 374	933	1 476	3 299	2 881	2 625	1 243	788	130
Working part-time	362	17	17	27	21	24	20	33	203
Out of employment	1 763	227	294	399	278	253	149	156	7
Seeking work	1 595	222	285	374	246	214	122	129	5
Temporarily sick	168	5	9	25	32	39	27	27	3
Females: total population (aged 16 and over)	21 687	1 746	1 954	3 797	3 223	3 039	1 625	1 474	4 830
Total economically inactive (aged 16 and over)	11 809	760	602	1 733	1 112	1 032	776	1 144	4 651
Students	862	672	139	34	13	4	—	—	—
Retired	1 785	—	—	—	3	10	38	298	1 437
Permanently sick	357	6	11	26	33	62	58	31	130
Other	8 806	82	451	1 673	1 064	958	680	815	3 083
Total economically active	9 878	986	1 352	2 064	2 110	2 007	849	330	179
Self-employed (included above)	457	5	23	100	128	107	43	26	26
In employment	9 146	814	1 196	1 909	2 014	1 912	802	324	174
Working full-time	5 602	776	1 092	1 163	975	1 013	417	117	50
Working part-time	3 543	38	104	746	1 039	899	385	207	125
Out of employment	732	172	157	155	96	95	47	6	5
Seeking work	645	165	147	139	79	72	36	4	3
Temporarily sick	88	7	10	16	17	22	11	2	2

1. During the week before the census (5 April 1981). For definition of terms used see *Census 1981, Definitions, Great Britain* (HMSO 1981).

Sources Office of Population Censuses and Surveys; General Register Office (Scotland)

6.16 Size of manufacturing units 1982

	Total	Analysis by number of employees					
		20 – 49	50 – 99	100 – 199	200 – 499	500 – 999	1 000 or more
Number of units							
All manufacturing industries	34 585	16 375	7 481	5 057	3 677	1 227	768
Extraction and preparation of metalliferous ores and metal manufacturing	986	356	229	156	136	60	49
Extraction of minerals not elsewhere specified and manufacture of non-metallic mineral products	1 751	875	390	221	182	58	25
Chemical industry and production of man-made fibres	1 396	478	312	244	202	91	69
Manufacture of metal goods not elsewhere specified	3 715	2 069	814	479	256	75	22
Mechanical engineering	5 490	2 921	1 042	719	508	190	110
Manufacture of office machinery and data processing equipment	157	50	45	20	25	5	12
Electrical and electronic engineering	2 478	879	521	392	371	186	129
Manufacture of motor vehicles and parts thereof	1 049	414	209	151	127	75	73
Manufacture of other transport equipment	699	255	141	107	71	34	91
Instrument engineering	718	327	182	111	73	16	9
Food, drink and tobacco manufacturing industries	3 138	1 228	651	495	494	176	94
Textile industry	1 985	705	502	426	298	44	10
Manufacture of leather and leather goods	300	174	72	45	9	–	–
Footwear and clothing industries	2 969	1 474	685	483	284	38	5
Timber and wooden furniture industries	2 206	1 354	481	249	101	20	1
Manufacture of paper and paper products; printing and publishing	3 349	1 716	677	476	338	99	43
Processing of rubber and plastics	1 533	709	373	209	170	51	21
Other manufacturing industries	666	391	155	74	32	9	5
Number of employees (thousands)							
All manufacturing industries	5 352.8	505.6	521.7	703.6	1 131.8	840.9	1 649.1
Extraction and preparation of metalliferous ores and metal manufacturing	251.5	11.2	16.0	22.5	42.0	41.5	118.2
Extraction of minerals not elsewhere specified and manufacture of non-metallic mineral products	218.5	26.7	27.2	30.2	56.8	38.9	38.7
Chemical industry and production of man-made fibres	315.0	15.0	22.2	34.5	63.6	62.2	117.6
Manufacture of metal goods not elsewhere specified	350.7	64.6	55.9	65.4	79.0	54.3	31.5
Mechanical engineering	744.4	90.8	72.4	100.4	160.3	127.1	193.5
Manufacture of office machinery and data processing equipment	37.3	1.5	3.0	2.8	8.2	3.8	17.9
Electrical and electronic engineering	600.2	27.4	35.9	54.5	115.4	126.6	240.3
Manufacture of motor vehicles and parts thereof	399.9	12.7	14.8	20.8	40.3	54.5	256.8
Manufacture of other transport equipment	373.9	7.9	10.0	14.6	22.1	23.8	295.5
Instrument engineering	86.9	10.1	12.6	15.2	23.5	11.0	14.4
Food, drink and tobacco manufacturing industries	599.3	38.0	45.8	69.9	155.0	120.7	170.0
Textile industry	248.4	22.3	35.7	59.3	85.6	30.1	15.4
Manufacture of leather and leather goods	18.8	5.1	5.1	5.9	2.7	–	–
Footwear and clothing industries	273.9	44.2	48.5	67.2	82.9	24.5	6.6
Timber and wooden furniture industries	154.1	40.9	33.6	34.6	31.0	12.8	1.2
Manufacture of paper and paper products; printing and publishing	421.4	53.1	46.8	66.2	103.5	68.9	83.0
Processing of rubber and plastics	203.4	22.1	25.8	29.5	50.1	34.0	42.0
Other manufacturing industries	55.2	11.9	10.4	10.1	10.0	6.1	6.6

Notes

(i) The analysis follows the Classes of the *Standard Industrial Classification 1980*.

(ii) Units in the 1 to 19 employment size band have been excluded from the table. The information relating to these smaller units is of doubtful reliability as they are generally excluded from BSO inquiries.

(iii) The employment information is drawn from BSO production inquiries (in particular the Annual Census of Production and the quarterly inquiries into manufacturers' sales) and relates generally to 1980.

Source Business Statistics Office

6.16 Size of manufacturing units 1983

	Total	Analysis by number of employees					
		20 – 49	50 – 99	100 – 199	200 – 499	500 – 999	1 000 or more
Number of units							
All manufacturing industries	33 145	16 000	7 238	4 732	3 397	1 120	658
Extraction and preparation of metalliferous ores and metal manufacturing	931	344	224	146	126	50	41
Extraction of minerals not elsewhere specified and manufacture of non-metallic mineral products	1 693	855	384	208	175	53	18
Chemical industry and production of man-made fibres	1 355	477	306	223	196	96	57
Manufacture of metal goods not elsewhere specified	3 555	2 027	801	408	239	62	18
Mechanical engineering	5 194	2 841	989	635	475	161	93
Manufacture of office machinery and data processing equipment	153	53	39	23	20	9	9
Electrical and electronic engineering	2 419	881	524	376	357	172	109
Manufacture of motor vehicles and parts thereof	988	400	202	147	113	61	65
Manufacture of other transport equipment	669	249	129	106	62	39	84
Instrument engineering	692	330	171	110	56	17	8
Food, drink and tobacco manufacturing industries	3 068	1 216	638	502	458	171	83
Textile industry	1 915	705	503	410	243	44	10
Manufacture of leather and leather goods	277	162	65	38	12	–	–
Footwear and clothing industries	2 740	1 354	647	441	259	36	3
Timber and wooden furniture industries	2 111	1 296	471	229	100	14	1
Manufacture of paper and paper products; printing and publishing	3 252	1 713	639	456	321	84	39
Processing of rubber and plastics	1 522	713	369	223	157	44	16
Other manufacturing industries	611	384	137	51	28	7	4
Number of employees (thousands)							
All manufacturing industries	4 872.5	495.9	505.4	660.2	1 044.4	770.0	1 396.5
Extraction and preparation of metalliferous ores and metal manufacturing	220.3	11.0	15.6	21.2	39.9	34.9	97.6
Extraction of minerals not elsewhere specified and manufacture of non-metallic mineral products	200.3	26.3	26.9	28.4	54.5	36.1	28.0
Chemical industry and production of man-made fibres	289.6	15.2	21.7	31.1	61.0	66.8	93.8
Manufacture of metal goods not elsewhere specified	311.7	63.7	55.3	55.7	71.1	43.5	22.4
Mechanical engineering	676.2	88.6	69.6	87.3	148.6	109.3	172.8
Manufacture of office machinery and data processing equipment	34.3	1.6	2.6	3.1	6.5	7.0	13.6
Electrical and electronic engineering	543.4	27.6	36.3	53.1	111.8	118.2	196.4
Manufacture of motor vehicles and parts thereof	328.6	12.3	14.3	20.7	36.4	43.5	201.4
Manufacture of other transport equipment	353.0	7.9	9.1	14.8	19.3	27.1	274.8
Instrument engineering	80.5	10.3	11.8	15.4	17.7	11.0	14.3
Food, drink and tobacco manufacturing industries	566.1	37.7	45.0	70.8	143.2	118.1	151.4
Textile industry	229.2	22.2	35.2	57.8	71.3	29.2	13.5
Manufacture of leather and leather goods	17.3	4.7	4.6	4.6	3.4	–	–
Footwear and clothing industries	249.8	40.1	45.8	62.0	74.4	23.8	3.8
Timber and wooden furniture industries	144.1	39.0	32.3	32.0	30.4	9.2	1.2
Manufacture of paper and paper products; printing and publishing	392.5	53.8	44.7	63.9	99.3	58.4	72.4
Processing of rubber and plastics	189.9	22.2	25.5	31.7	47.3	29.0	34.2
Other manufacturing industries	45.8	11.7	9.2	6.8	8.5	4.7	5.0

Notes
(i) The analysis follows the Classes of the *Standard Industrial Classification 1980.*
(ii) Units in the 1 to 19 employment size band have been excluded from the table. The information relating to these smaller units is of doubtful reliability as they are generally excluded from BSO inquiries.
(iii) The employment information is drawn from BSO production inquiries (in particular the Annual Census of Production and the quarterly inquiries into manufacturers' sales) and relates generally to 1981.

Source Business Statistics Office

6.17 Average weekly earnings and hours of full-time manual workers
At October in each year

| | Standard Industrial Classification 1968 | | | | | | | | | | |
	1973	1974	1975	1976	1977	1978	1979	1980	1981	1982	1983
Average weekly earnings[1] (£)											
Manufacturing and certain other industries:											
Men (aged 21 and over)	40.92	48.63	59.58	66.97	72.89	83.50	96.94	..	..	..	..
Women (aged 18 and over)	21.16	27.01	34.19	40.61	44.31	50.03	58.24	..	..	..	..
Males on adult rates	..	..	..	..	..	..	..	113.06	125.58	137.06	149.13
Females on adult rates	..	..	..	..	..	..	..	68.73	76.44	83.96	91.18
Manufacturing industries:											
Men (aged 21 and over)	41.52	49.12	59.74	67.83	73.56	84.77	98.28	..	..	..	..
Women (aged 18 and over)	21.15	27.05	34.23	40.71	44.45	50.08	58.44	..	..	..	..
Males on adult rates	..	..	..	..	..	..	..	111.64	123.23	134.26	147.23
Females on adult rates	..	..	..	..	..	..	..	68.40	75.71	83.17	90.29
Average weekly hours worked[2]											
Manufacturing and certain other industries:											
Men (aged 21 and over)	45.6	45.1	43.6	44.0	44.2	44.2	44.0	..	..	..	..
Women (aged 18 and over)	37.7	37.4	37.0	37.4	37.4	37.4	37.4	..	..	..	..
Males on adult rates	..	..	..	..	..	..	..	43.0	43.0	42.9	43.3
Females on adult rates	..	..	..	..	..	..	..	37.5	37.7	38.0	38.2
Manufacturing industries:											
Men (aged 21 and over)	44.7	44.0	42.7	43.5	43.6	43.5	43.2	..	..	..	..
Women (aged 18 and over)	37.5	37.2	36.8	37.2	37.2	37.2	37.2	..	..	..	..
Males on adult rates	..	..	..	..	..	..	..	41.9	42.0	42.0	42.6
Females on adult rates	..	..	..	..	..	..	..	37.3	37.5	37.8	38.1

Note: From 1981 surveys have excluded workers on short-time.

1. The figures represent the average earnings, including bonus, overtime, etc., and before deduction of income tax or insurance contributions, in one week in the month indicated. Administrative and clerical workers and other salaried persons have been excluded. Certain qualifications including explanations of the change of definitions are given in a full account of the survey relating to October 1980, published in the *Employment Gazette* for March 1981.
2. The figures include overtime and correspond with those for average earnings.

Source Department of Employment

6.18 Average weekly and hourly earnings and hours
Great Britain
New Earnings Survey
April of each year

	All industries					Manufacturing industries[3]				
	Average weekly earnings[1]		Average hours[2]	Average hourly earnings[1,2]		Average weekly earnings[1]		Average hours[2]	Average hourly earnings[1,2]	
				including overtime pay and overtime hours	excluding overtime pay and overtime hours				including overtime pay and overtime hours	excluding overtime pay and overtime hours
	Including those whose pay was affected by absence	Excluding those whose pay was affected by absence				Including those whose pay was affected by absence	Excluding those whose pay was affected by absence			
	£	£		p	p	£	£		p	p
All full-time men[4]										
1977	76.8	78.6	43.0	181.1	181.5	76.1	78.5	43.8	177.7	177.1
1978	86.9	89.1	43.1	204.3	204.9	87.3	90.0	44.0	202.9	202.2
1979	98.8	101.4	43.2	232.2	232.4	100.5	103.7	44.2	233.1	231.8
1980	121.5	124.5	42.7	288.2	287.6	120.3	124.3	43.4	284.1	281.8
1981	136.5	140.5	41.7	332.0	331.2	131.3	137.1	42.0	323.5	320.8
1982[3]	151.5	154.5	41.7	365.6	364.6	{ 148.8	152.6	42.2	357.0	354.0
						{ 147.9	151.8	42.3	354.2	351.4
1983	163.8	167.5	41.5	399.1	398.0	158.6	163.3	42.2	383.0	380.0
Full-time manual men[4]										
1977	69.5	71.5	45.7	156.5	154.3	71.8	74.2	45.6	162.6	160.0
1978	78.4	80.7	46.0	175.5	172.8	81.8	84.7	45.8	184.8	181.8
1979	90.1	93.0	46.2	201.2	197.5	94.5	97.9	46.0	212.8	208.7
1980	108.6	111.7	45.4	245.8	240.5	111.2	115.2	45.0	255.5	250.0
1981	118.4	121.9	44.2	275.3	269.1	119.3	124.7	43.5	286.0	279.8
1982[3]	131.4	133.8	44.3	302.0	294.7	{ 134.8	138.1	43.8	315.1	307.9
						{ 134.4	137.8	43.9	313.7	306.7
1983	140.3	143.6	43.9	326.5	319.0	142.8	147.4	43.7	336.7	329.2
Full-time non-manual men[4]										
1977	88.4	88.9	38.7	227.2	227.9	88.2	88.9	39.2	223.4	223.8
1978	99.9	100.7	38.7	257.1	257.9	102.4	103.0	39.4	258.1	258.9
1979	112.1	113.0	38.8	288.6	289.5	116.8	117.7	39.6	293.8	294.7
1980	140.4	141.3	38.7	360.8	361.3	143.6	144.8	39.4	362.3	362.0
1981	161.2	163.1	38.4	419.1	419.7	159.6	161.8	38.8	411.9	411.5
1982[3]	177.9	178.9	38.2	462.5	462.3	{ 180.1	181.4	38.8	457.9	457.0
						{ 178.5	179.8	38.9	453.4	452.5
1983	193.7	194.9	38.4	503.4	502.9	193.2	194.6	39.1	491.6	491.0
All full-time women[5]										
1977	50.0	51.0	37.5	134.0	133.9	44.9	46.4	38.7	120.0	119.6
1978	55.4	56.4	37.5	148.2	148.0	51.3	52.8	38.8	136.1	135.4
1979	61.8	63.0	37.5	166.0	165.7	57.9	60.0	38.8	154.6	153.7
1980	77.3	78.8	37.5	207.0	206.4	70.3	72.8	38.7	187.3	186.1
1981	89.3	91.4	37.2	241.8	241.2	78.1	81.5	38.4	211.6	210.6
1982[3]	97.5	99.0	37.1	263.1	262.1	{ 87.1	89.7	38.5	232.1	230.4
						{ 86.8	89.4	38.5	231.4	229.7
1983	106.9	108.8	37.2	288.5	287.5	94.5	97.6	38.6	251.8	250.1
Full-time manual women[5]										
1977	42.2	43.7	39.4	111.2	110.7	43.0	45.0	39.8	113.4	112.7
1978	48.0	49.4	39.6	125.3	124.4	49.3	51.2	39.9	128.5	127.5
1979	53.4	55.2	39.6	139.9	138.7	55.4	57.9	39.9	145.4	144.2
1980	65.9	68.0	39.6	172.1	170.4	66.4	69.5	39.8	174.5	172.8
1981	72.1	74.5	39.4	189.8	188.2	72.5	76.3	39.6	192.8	191.4
1982[3]	78.3	80.1	39.3	205.0	202.7	{ 79.9	82.9	39.6	209.5	207.1
						{ 79.6	82.6	39.6	208.9	206.6
1983	85.6	87.9	39.3	224.3	222.0	86.7	90.3	39.7	227.3	224.9

1. The figures are gross before deductions. Generally they exclude the value of earnings in kind, but include payments such as overtime (except where otherwise stated), bonus, commission and shift premiums for the pay period.
2. The estimates given relate to employees for whom normal basic hours were reported and for whom total hours and hourly earnings could, therefore, be calculated.

3. Results for manufacturing industries for 1977-81 inclusive and the first row of figures for 1982 relate to orders III to XIX inclusive of the 1968 Standard Industrial Classification (SIC). Results for manufacturing industries for 1983 and the second row of figures for 1982 relate to divisions 2, 3 and 4 of the 1980 SIC.
4. Men aged 21 and over.
5. Women aged 18 and over.

Source Department of Employment

6.18 (continued) Average weekly and hourly earnings and hours
Great Britain
New Earnings Survey
April of each year

	All industries					Manufacturing industries[3]				
	Average weekly earnings[1]		Average hours[2]	Average hourly earnings[1,2]		Average weekly earnings[1]		Average hours[2]	Average hourly earnings[1,2]	
				including overtime pay and overtime hours	excluding overtime pay and overtime hours				including overtime pay and overtime hours	excluding overtime pay and overtime hours
	Including those whose pay was affected by absence	Excluding those whose pay was affected by absence				Including those whose pay was affected by absence	Excluding those whose pay was affected by absence			
	£	£		p	p	£	£		p	p
Full-time non-manual women[5]										
1977	53.4	53.8	36.7	143.8	143.7	48.1	48.4	37.1	130.1	129.8
1978	58.5	59.1	36.7	158.1	157.9	54.9	55.2	37.2	148.0	147.5
1979	65.3	66.0	36.7	176.8	176.6	62.3	62.8	37.2	168.5	168.0
1980	82.0	82.7	36.7	221.2	220.7	76.7	77.1	37.3	205.8	204.9
1981	95.6	96.7	36.5	259.7	259.2	86.4	87.3	37.1	234.2	233.4
1982[3]	104.3	104.9	36.5	283.0	282.2	97.2	97.6	37.2	260.3	259.0
						97.0	97.4	37.2	259.8	258.5
1983	114.2	115.1	36.5	310.0	309.0	105.5	106.2	37.2	283.3	281.9
Full-time adults[4,5]										
1977	68.7	70.2	41.3	168.0	167.5	68.9	71.3	42.7	165.8	164.3
1978	77.3	79.1	41.4	188.6	187.9	78.8	81.5	42.8	188.7	187.0
1979	87.4	89.6	41.5	213.6	212.4	90.4	93.7	43.0	216.7	214.2
1980	107.7	110.2	41.1	264.8	262.8	108.4	112.4	42.3	263.3	259.8
1981	121.6	124.9	40.3	305.1	303.2	118.6	124.3	41.2	299.0	295.6
1982[3]	134.1	136.5	40.2	334.6	332.1	134.0	138.0	41.3	329.6	325.4
						133.3	137.2	41.4	327.2	323.1
1983	145.4	148.3	40.0	365.1	362.5	143.2	148.0	41.4	354.1	349.9
Full-time adults[6]										
1977	67.8	69.3	41.3	165.7	165.1	68.0	70.4	42.7	163.8	162.3
1978	76.3	78.1	41.4	186.1	185.3	77.8	80.5	42.8	186.5	184.7
1979	86.2	88.4	41.5	210.7	209.3	89.1	92.5	43.0	213.9	211.3
1980	106.3	108.7	41.1	261.1	259.0	106.9	110.9	42.3	259.8	256.2
1981	119.8	123.1	40.3	300.4	298.4	116.8	122.5	41.2	294.7	291.2
1982[3]	132.1	134.5	40.2	329.3	326.7	132.0	135.9	41.3	324.6	320.3
						131.2	135.2	41.4	322.3	318.2
1983	143.2	146.1	40.1	359.5	356.8	141.2	146.0	41.4	349.1	344.8
Full-time youths and boys[7]										
1977	42.4	43.0	41.7	103.3	101.9	43.5	44.5	42.1	105.8	103.9
1978	48.1	48.7	41.9	116.3	114.3	49.8	50.9	42.3	120.5	118.0
1979	54.4	55.2	41.8	132.4	129.9	57.0	58.3	42.5	137.4	134.1
1980	66.5	67.2	41.4	162.1	159.1	68.2	70.0	41.8	167.7	163.7
1981	73.7	74.3	40.9	181.9	179.0	75.0	76.4	41.1	185.8	182.4
1982[3]	81.9	82.4	40.8	202.1	198.3	83.7	84.7	41.1	206.4	202.0
						83.2	84.3	41.2	205.0	200.7
1983	86.8	87.7	40.7	216.5	212.9	88.7	90.5	41.4	219.5	215.1
Full-time girls[8]										
1977	28.7	29.1	38.4	75.9	75.7	30.3	31.0	39.1	79.1	78.9
1978	31.4	31.8	38.3	83.3	83.0	33.8	34.7	39.0	88.9	88.6
1979	35.9	36.6	38.3	95.7	95.2	38.1	39.6	39.2	101.1	100.6
1980	46.6	47.1	38.2	123.7	123.0	46.9	47.9	39.1	122.4	121.8
1981	50.3	50.6	37.9	134.0	133.4	51.8	52.7	38.8	136.1	135.7
1982[3]	53.4	53.9	38.0	142.5	141.7	53.6	55.2	39.0	141.7	140.5
						53.6	55.3	39.1	141.9	140.7
1983	54.7	55.7	38.0	147.2	146.4	56.0	58.4	39.1	149.8	148.9

1. The figures are gross before deductions. Generally they exclude the value of earnings in kind, but include payments such as overtime (except where otherwise stated), bonus, commission and shift premiums for the pay period.
2. The estimates given relate to employees for whom normal basic hours were reported and for whom total hours and hourly earnings could, therefore, be calculated.
3. Results for manufacturing industries for 1977-81 inclusive and the first row of figures for 1982 relate to orders III to XIX inclusive of the 1968 Standard Industrial Classification (SIC). Results for manufacturing industries for 1983 and the second row of figures for 1982 relate to divisions 2, 3 and 4 of the 1980 SIC.

4. Men aged 21 and over.
5. Women aged 18 and over.
6. Males and females aged 18 and over.
7. Under 21 years.
8. Under 18 years.

Source Department of Employment

6.19 Average earnings index: all employees
Great Britain

Analysis by industry based on Standard Industrial Classification 1980

January 1980 = 100

Unadjusted

	Annual averages	January	February	March	April	May	June	July	August	September	October	November	December
Whole economy (Divisions 0 – 9)													
1980	111.4	100.0[1]	102.6[1]	105.9[1]	107.1	109.2	112.5	113.3	114.0	117.9	116.0	117.8	120.8
1981	125.8	118.2	119.3	121.2	121.9	123.5	126.0	126.9	129.0	129.4	130.0	131.4	133.1
1982	137.6	131.2	132.8	134.6	134.5	136.5	138.3	140.7	138.8	138.7	139.6	142.4	143.6
1983	149.2	142.6	145.4	146.1	146.0	148.3	149.7	151.7	150.4	150.5	151.7	152.8	155.1
Manufacturing industries (Revised definition Divisions 2 – 4)													
1980	109.1	100.0	101.2	104.4	105.7	108.3	111.6	112.5	110.8	111.7	112.2	115.2	116.1
1981	123.6	115.7	117.3	118.9	118.4	121.0	124.5	125.4	126.0	126.2	128.6	130.8	130.8
1982	137.4	131.1	131.8	134.4	134.8	137.5	138.8	139.2	137.6	137.9	140.0	142.5	143.2
1983	149.7	142.9	143.7	145.1	146.7	149.2	150.2	151.2	149.9	150.9	153.3	156.5	157.0
Production industries (Revised definition Divisions 1 – 4)													
1980	109.4	100.0	101.1	105.5	106.1	108.6	111.7	112.7	111.1	111.9	112.5	115.2	115.9
1981	124.1	116.4	117.8	119.9	119.1	121.5	125.2	126.2	126.3	126.6	128.9	130.9	130.9
1982	138.2	131.6	133.7	135.2	135.2	137.8	139.6	140.1	138.4	138.7	139.9	143.7	144.0
1983	150.0	143.5	144.1	145.9	147.4	149.3	150.4	151.8	150.4	151.4	154.1	155.7	155.9

Seasonally adjusted

	Annual averages	January	February	March	April	May	June	July	August	September	October	November	December
Whole economy (Divisions 0 – 9)													
1980	111.4	101.1[1]	103.7[1]	105.9[1]	107.7	109.2	111.4	112.2	114.1	118.0	116.2	117.3	119.6
1981	125.8	119.7	120.7	121.3	122.6	123.6	124.8	125.8	128.9	129.5	130.2	130.8	131.7
1982	137.6	132.8	134.3	134.7	135.4	136.7	137.0	139.5	138.6	138.9	139.8	141.7	142.0
1983	149.2	144.5	147.2	146.3	147.0	148.6	148.2	150.3	150.2	150.7	152.0	152.1	153.4
Manufacturing industries (Revised definition Divisions 2 – 4)													
1980	109.1	100.5	101.9	104.3	106.1	107.3	110.0	111.5	111.9	112.8	113.0	114.5	115.5
1981	123.6	116.5	118.2	118.9	119.2	120.0	122.6	124.2	126.9	127.4	129.4	129.9	130.2
1982	137.4	132.0	132.8	134.4	136.0	136.5	136.7	137.8	138.4	139.3	140.9	141.6	142.7
1983	149.8	144.0	144.8	145.0	148.1	148.2	147.8	149.7	150.8	152.4	154.4	155.6	156.6
Production industries (Revised definition Divisions 1 – 4)													
1980	109.3	100.6	101.8	105.1	106.3	107.5	110.2	111.6	112.1	113.1	113.4	114.5	115.5
1981	124.1	117.3	118.7	119.4	119.7	120.5	123.5	124.8	127.3	127.9	129.9	130.0	130.5
1982	138.2	132.6	134.7	134.6	136.1	136.9	137.6	138.5	139.3	140.2	141.1	142.8	143.8
1983	150.0	144.6	145.2	145.3	148.5	148.4	148.2	150.0	151.3	153.0	155.4	154.7	155.8

Note: The seasonal adjustment factors currently used for the SIC 1980 series are based on data up to December 1982 with data prior to January 1980 from the corresponding SIC 1968.

1. The figures reflect abnormally low earnings owing to the effects of national disputes.

Source Department of Employment

6.19 (continued) Average earnings index: all employees
Great Britain
Analysis by industry based on Standard Industrial Classification 1980

January 1980 = 100

	Agri- culture and forestry [1]	Coal and coke	Mineral oil and natural gas	Elec- tricity, gas, other energy and water supply	Metal process- ing and manu- factur- ing [2]	Mineral extrac- tion and manu- factur- ing	Chemi- cals and man- made fibres	Mech- anical engin- eering	Elec- trical and elect- ronic engin- eering	Motor vehicles and parts	Other trans- port equip- ment	Metal goods and instru- ments	Food, drink and tobacco	Tex- tiles
SIC 1980 Class	(01–02)	(11–12)	(14)	(15–17)	(21–22)	(23–24)	(25–26)	(32)	(33–34)	(35)	(36)	(31,37)	(41–42)	(43)
1980 Annual averages	117.7	106.1	104.4	116.2	[2]	109.2	109.8	106.9	109.0	100.5	111.4	103.7	109.0	107.3
1981	131.8	118.6	119.8	133.5	124.9	121.6	124.8	117.3	123.4	111.4	124.0	116.8	123.8	120.2
1982	144.2	131.1	135.8	147.8	137.3	136.8	138.9	130.6	139.2	125.3	137.3	129.3	136.7	131.7
1983	157.5	134.7	147.8	159.2	150.7	148.5	152.0	142.3	152.9	138.6	143.2	140.3	149.6	143.5
1983 January	138.0	141.3	146.3	146.2	140.9	141.2	143.7	135.1	147.0	133.9	138.5	133.5	142.2	137.9
February	145.2	139.5	146.1	145.9	140.4	141.9	145.0	136.0	147.1	134.6	139.5	134.1	142.6	139.0
March	145.1	139.0	146.1	156.0	141.8	142.7	143.3	138.1	150.1	134.7	143.7	137.3	144.1	140.6
April	155.1	136.5	147.3	158.9	146.2	144.9	146.2	138.8	150.6	133.7	142.7	136.4	146.6	141.7
May	151.0	131.2	146.3	158.2	147.4	146.5	149.4	141.7	152.2	139.0	144.0	141.0	149.4	144.0
June	156.7	133.7	148.6	160.1	147.6	152.3	150.3	143.2	154.0	139.0	144.5	139.2	150.9	144.6
July	167.2	135.4	156.7	164.9	166.3	147.7	151.9	143.4	154.8	140.1	141.5	140.3	151.1	145.1
August	162.7	135.5	149.0	161.8	151.7	149.7	157.1	141.8	152.8	137.1	137.9	140.7	149.7	143.7
September	178.0	137.0	150.9	162.6	152.1	151.3	152.9	143.2	153.3	137.8	142.4	142.1	150.8	145.5
October	173.6	140.1	143.9	169.7	163.8	150.2	153.1	145.3	157.5	139.8	146.1	144.1	152.0	146.6
November	160.4	123.9	140.9	165.1	154.3	156.8	164.7	148.6	156.8	146.0	150.6	147.9	155.5	147.2
December	156.7	123.6	151.9	161.5	155.8	156.6	166.1	152.8	158.7	147.2	147.4	146.6	159.7	146.1

	Leather, foot- wear and clothing	Timber and wooden furniture	Paper products printing and publish- ing	Rubber, plastics and other manu- factur- ing	Con- struction	Distri- bution and repairs	Hotels and catering	Trans- port and com- muni- cation [3]	Bank- ing, finance and insur- ance	Public adminis- tration	Edu- cation and health	Other ser- vices [4]	Whole econ- omy [2]
SIC 1980 Class	(44–45)	(46)	(47)	(48–49)	(50)	(61–65, 67)	(66)	(71–72, 75–77, 79)	(81–82 84pt.)	(91– 92pt.)	(93,95)	(97pt.– 98pt.)	
1980 Annual averages	107.6	105.9	110.4	107.6	111.5	107.2	107.9	108.4	112.7	114.2	123.8	113.4	111.4
1981	121.4	115.2	128.3	121.1	125.8	120.3	120.4	120.6	128.9	129.6	140.8	128.0	125.8
1982	134.1	126.9	142.8	134.0	137.6	132.6	127.6	132.2	144.6	140.0	147.9	143.8	137.6
1983	145.2	139.9	156.6	144.0	148.0	143.6	137.9	144.3	157.5	149.5	163.6	156.0	149.2
1983 January	141.2	141.7	146.4	137.6	140.7	138.6	130.9	135.2	145.8	143.9	159.9	149.7	142.6
February	143.0	143.8	147.3	139.3	142.3	138.9	131.6	137.6	148.9	144.9	175.7	148.3	145.4
March	144.2	133.9	149.7	139.6	147.9	140.0	132.8	140.3	164.3	146.2	161.3	150.3	146.1
April	143.7	138.3	156.4	141.3	145.5	142.3	133.1	142.3	150.9	147.0	156.2	149.9	146.0
May	146.0	138.5	156.3	145.2	145.7	147.3	136.7	141.4	158.2	150.7	158.1	152.1	148.3
June	146.2	134.7	159.3	144.2	150.7	143.3	137.1	144.4	162.0	150.2	163.2	154.5	149.7
July	145.4	138.5	157.7	144.6	149.7	144.7	139.1	150.6	157.4	150.6	169.2	156.1	151.7
August	145.0	143.7	157.3	143.3	148.0	143.3	139.7	145.4	156.3	150.8	168.7	163.3	150.4
September	145.1	141.2	159.9	146.1	148.6	144.4	141.0	147.3	153.3	151.7	162.6	157.9	150.5
October	146.3	141.2	162.2	147.2	150.3	143.4	141.2	146.3	155.9	153.0	163.8	158.0	151.7
November	147.7	151.0	163.4	151.0	152.9	145.6	140.4	149.5	159.3	152.4	161.2	166.9	152.8
December	148.8	132.8	163.1	148.2	153.7	151.3	150.6	151.2	177.8	152.1	162.8	165.3	155.1

See *Note* on page 127.

1. England and Wales only.
2. Because of a dispute in the steel industry, insufficient information is available to enable reliable indices for 'Metal processing and manufacturing' to be calculated but the best possible estimates have been used in the compilation of the indices for manufacturing and whole economy. The index series for this group has a base of April 1980 = 100.
3. Excluding sea transport.
4. Excluding private domestic and personal services.

Source Department of Employment

6.20 Gross weekly and hourly earnings of full-time adults[1]
Great Britain
New Earnings Survey
April of each year

		Gross weekly earnings[2]					Gross hourly earnings[2, 3]				
		Lowest decile	Lower quartile	Median	Upper quartile	Highest decile	Lowest decile	Lower quartile	Median	Upper quartile	Highest decile
		£	£	£	£	£	p	p	p	p	p
All men	1975	37.5	45.3	55.9	70.1	88.2	89.4	105.2	128.0	161.4	212.5
	1976	44.5	53.5	65.8	82.7	104.9	106.1	124.8	151.6	191.9	258.7
	1977	49.3	58.9	72.3	90.8	114.0	116.9	136.6	165.1	207.7	277.6
	1978	54.8	66.1	82.0	102.6	129.5	130.1	152.3	186.1	236.5	316.6
	1979	61.9	75.4	93.9	117.5	147.3	147.8	174.2	213.5	271.2	357.2
	1980	74.7	90.7	113.3	143.4	183.1	178.4	212.5	260.8	335.7	447.8
	1981	82.9	100.9	126.5	163.8	212.1	201.1	238.8	298.0	392.2	531.1
	1982	89.7	109.9	139.1	180.5	233.8	217.5	260.5	327.8	433.3	587.9
	1983	96.3	118.4	150.3	195.0	255.0	234.6	281.5	356.1	473.0	648.6
Manual men	1975	36.8	44.1	53.2	64.5	76.9	86.4	100.5	118.0	139.7	164.1
	1976	43.6	51.8	62.1	75.1	90.1	102.6	118.4	139.1	164.2	191.9
	1977	48.1	56.7	68.2	82.1	98.5	112.8	129.8	151.4	178.0	206.4
	1978	53.4	63.3	76.8	93.1	112.2	125.5	143.5	169.1	199.7	233.8
	1979	60.3	72.1	88.2	107.8	131.1	141.7	163.3	193.8	229.1	270.0
	1980	71.8	86.3	105.0	129.0	156.7	170.1	198.5	234.8	278.8	330.5
	1981	79.6	94.5	114.2	139.9	172.0	190.7	221.0	261.9	314.4	374.7
	1982	85.5	102.4	125.2	154.6	191.0	206.1	241.2	287.7	345.7	412.6
	1983	91.2	110.2	134.8	165.4	204.5	221.5	259.3	310.1	375.2	450.5
Non-manual men	1975	38.7	47.9	61.8	80.2	103.1	99.1	122.5	158.1	209.6	281.4
	1976	46.2	57.5	73.9	96.4	123.7	118.3	146.9	190.1	256.7	345.6
	1977	51.5	63.5	81.1	104.4	133.3	131.4	161.3	206.7	274.8	364.8
	1978	57.7	72.0	91.8	117.4	150.4	147.8	182.7	234.9	309.7	408.7
	1979	65.7	81.8	103.6	131.9	169.0	169.2	209.3	266.9	346.5	452.2
	1980	80.3	100.4	127.7	163.8	215.0	206.2	256.8	330.2	432.3	568.1
	1981	91.5	115.5	148.9	192.8	248.3	235.0	295.5	383.7	507.7	676.2
	1982	98.9	125.4	162.5	210.5	275.2	254.4	325.4	423.6	559.8	739.8
	1983	106.3	136.2	176.1	230.3	300.2	273.9	351.5	458.1	608.5	808.5
		Percentage					Percentage				
As percentages of the corresponding median											
All men	1975	*67.0*	*81.0*	*100.0*	*125.3*	*157.6*	*69.8*	*82.2*	*100.0*	*126.1*	*166.0*
	1976	*67.6*	*81.3*	*100.0*	*125.6*	*159.5*	*69.9*	*82.3*	*100.0*	*126.6*	*170.6*
	1977	*68.1*	*81.4*	*100.0*	*125.6*	*157.7*	*70.8*	*82.7*	*100.0*	*125.8*	*168.2*
	1978	*66.8*	*80.6*	*100.0*	*125.1*	*157.9*	*69.9*	*81.8*	*100.0*	*127.0*	*170.1*
	1979	*66.0*	*80.3*	*100.0*	*125.1*	*156.9*	*69.3*	*81.6*	*100.0*	*127.1*	*167.3*
	1980	*65.9*	*80.1*	*100.0*	*126.5*	*161.6*	*68.4*	*81.5*	*100.0*	*128.7*	*171.7*
	1981	*65.6*	*79.8*	*100.0*	*129.5*	*167.7*	*67.5*	*80.1*	*100.0*	*131.6*	*178.2*
	1982	*64.5*	*79.0*	*100.0*	*129.8*	*168.1*	*66.4*	*79.5*	*100.0*	*132.2*	*179.4*
	1983	*64.1*	*78.8*	*100.0*	*129.8*	*169.7*	*65.9*	*79.1*	*100.0*	*132.8*	*182.2*
Manual men	1975	*69.2*	*82.8*	*100.0*	*121.3*	*144.4*	*73.2*	*85.1*	*100.0*	*118.4*	*139.0*
	1976	*70.2*	*83.4*	*100.0*	*120.8*	*144.9*	*73.8*	*86.1*	*100.0*	*118.1*	*138.0*
	1977	*70.6*	*83.1*	*100.0*	*120.3*	*144.4*	*74.5*	*85.7*	*100.0*	*117.5*	*136.3*
	1978	*69.4*	*82.4*	*100.0*	*121.2*	*146.0*	*74.2*	*84.9*	*100.0*	*118.1*	*138.3*
	1979	*68.3*	*81.7*	*100.0*	*122.2*	*148.5*	*73.1*	*84.3*	*100.0*	*118.2*	*139.3*
	1980	*68.4*	*82.2*	*100.0*	*122.9*	*149.2*	*72.4*	*84.5*	*100.0*	*118.7*	*140.7*
	1981	*69.7*	*82.8*	*100.0*	*122.5*	*150.6*	*72.8*	*84.4*	*100.0*	*120.1*	*143.1*
	1982	*68.3*	*81.8*	*100.0*	*123.5*	*152.6*	*71.6*	*83.8*	*100.0*	*120.2*	*143.4*
	1983	*67.7*	*81.8*	*100.0*	*122.7*	*151.7*	*71.4*	*83.6*	*100.0*	*121.0*	*145.3*
Non-manual men	1975	*62.6*	*77.5*	*100.0*	*129.6*	*166.7*	*62.7*	*77.5*	*100.0*	*132.6*	*178.1*
	1976	*62.5*	*77.8*	*100.0*	*130.5*	*167.5*	*62.2*	*77.2*	*100.0*	*135.0*	*181.8*
	1977	*63.6*	*78.4*	*100.0*	*128.8*	*164.5*	*63.6*	*78.0*	*100.0*	*132.9*	*176.5*
	1978	*62.9*	*78.4*	*100.0*	*127.9*	*163.9*	*62.9*	*77.8*	*100.0*	*131.8*	*174.0*
	1979	*63.4*	*79.0*	*100.0*	*127.3*	*163.0*	*63.4*	*78.4*	*100.0*	*129.8*	*169.4*
	1980	*62.9*	*78.6*	*100.0*	*128.2*	*168.3*	*62.4*	*77.8*	*100.0*	*130.9*	*172.0*
	1981	*61.4*	*77.6*	*100.0*	*129.5*	*166.8*	*61.2*	*77.0*	*100.0*	*132.3*	*176.3*
	1982	*60.9*	*77.2*	*100.0*	*129.6*	*169.4*	*60.1*	*76.8*	*100.0*	*132.2*	*174.7*
	1983	*60.4*	*77.3*	*100.0*	*130.8*	*170.4*	*59.8*	*76.7*	*100.0*	*132.8*	*176.5*

1. Men aged 21 and over; women aged 18 and over.
2. Of those whose pay for the survey pay period was not affected by absence. The figures are gross before deductions. Generally they exclude the value of earnings in kind, but include payments such as overtime, bonus, commission, and shift premiums for the pay period.
3. Including overtime hours and overtime pay, of persons for whom normal basic hours were reported and for whom hourly earnings could, therefore, be calculated.

Source Department of Employment

6.20
(continued)

Gross weekly and hourly earnings of full-time adults [1]
Great Britain
New Earnings Survey
April of each year

		Gross weekly earnings [2]					Gross hourly earnings [2, 3]				
		Lowest decile	Lower quartile	Median	Upper quartile	Highest decile	Lowest decile	Lower quartile	Median	Upper quartile	Highest decile
		£	£	£	£	£	p	p	p	p	p
All women	1975	23.0	27.8	34.1	42.7	56.2	61.1	73.5	89.2	111.9	153.2
	1976	28.0	34.0	42.4	53.3	70.3	74.4	90.2	110.9	139.2	194.5
	1977	32.2	38.6	46.9	58.5	76.1	85.9	101.6	122.5	152.1	203.9
	1978	35.8	42.6	51.8	65.0	83.6	95.7	111.8	135.6	168.9	223.6
	1979	40.6	47.9	58.4	72.8	92.6	108.4	125.8	152.2	189.2	250.9
	1980	49.5	58.8	72.4	91.2	116.7	131.5	153.7	188.9	238.9	317.7
	1981	55.9	66.3	82.2	106.7	141.9	148.0	174.9	216.3	278.5	385.8
	1982	60.2	71.7	90.0	116.5	152.0	160.2	190.4	237.4	306.1	418.0
	1983	65.6	78.7	98.8	128.3	166.2	174.1	208.1	260.4	337.7	459.6
Manual women	1975	21.2	25.8	31.0	37.1	43.8	56.1	67.7	79.6	93.3	108.0
	1976	26.0	31.7	38.4	45.9	53.9	70.1	84.0	98.6	115.3	132.7
	1977	29.9	35.5	42.6	50.3	58.7	79.7	94.8	108.9	125.7	143.7
	1978	33.7	39.6	47.6	57.0	67.1	90.1	105.4	121.4	141.8	163.3
	1979	37.5	44.1	53.3	63.7	74.9	102.1	116.4	135.2	158.4	182.8
	1980	45.6	53.8	64.7	78.1	92.9	122.5	140.2	165.1	194.8	226.3
	1981	49.7	58.8	71.4	86.2	102.5	135.2	153.6	182.5	216.3	252.5
	1982	53.0	62.8	76.7	92.4	110.5	144.2	165.9	197.2	234.4	270.5
	1983	57.9	68.5	84.1	101.8	122.2	155.8	179.9	215.6	255.9	300.6
Non-manual women	1975	23.9	28.8	35.9	45.7	61.6	63.8	77.0	95.2	122.1	173.2
	1976	28.8	35.3	44.2	56.9	76.4	76.4	94.6	118.1	152.2	220.5
	1977	33.5	40.2	49.2	62.4	81.4	89.0	106.4	130.2	164.9	226.7
	1978	37.1	44.2	53.9	68.7	88.8	98.6	117.0	142.8	181.9	249.3
	1979	42.3	49.7	60.8	76.9	97.8	111.5	132.1	161.2	205.4	277.4
	1980	51.4	61.0	75.7	96.6	122.3	137.2	162.4	201.2	258.3	345.9
	1981	58.7	69.5	87.0	114.9	150.3	156.3	185.9	231.9	304.2	421.4
	1982	63.4	75.9	95.6	124.7	158.8	169.6	203.8	255.7	335.3	454.0
	1983	69.1	83.0	104.7	137.9	172.4	183.8	222.7	280.5	369.2	498.3

As percentages of the corresponding median		Percentage					Percentage				
All women	1975	*67.4*	*81.5*	*100.0*	*125.2*	*164.4*	*68.5*	*82.4*	*100.0*	*125.4*	*171.7*
	1976	*66.1*	*80.2*	*100.0*	*125.9*	*165.9*	*67.1*	*81.4*	*100.0*	*125.6*	*175.5*
	1977	*68.6*	*82.1*	*100.0*	*124.7*	*162.1*	*70.1*	*83.0*	*100.0*	*124.1*	*166.4*
	1978	*69.1*	*82.2*	*100.0*	*125.3*	*161.4*	*70.5*	*82.5*	*100.0*	*124.5*	*164.9*
	1979	*69.4*	*82.1*	*100.0*	*124.7*	*158.6*	*71.2*	*82.6*	*100.0*	*124.4*	*164.8*
	1980	*68.4*	*81.3*	*100.0*	*126.1*	*161.3*	*69.6*	*81.4*	*100.0*	*126.5*	*168.2*
	1981	*68.0*	*80.6*	*100.0*	*129.8*	*172.6*	*68.5*	*80.9*	*100.0*	*128.8*	*178.4*
	1982	*66.9*	*79.7*	*100.0*	*129.4*	*169.0*	*67.5*	*80.2*	*100.0*	*128.9*	*176.1*
	1983	*66.4*	*79.7*	*100.0*	*129.9*	*168.3*	*66.9*	*79.9*	*100.0*	*129.7*	*176.5*
Manual women	1975	*68.4*	*83.3*	*100.0*	*119.6*	*141.4*	*70.5*	*85.1*	*100.0*	*117.3*	*135.8*
	1976	*67.8*	*82.6*	*100.0*	*119.6*	*140.6*	*71.1*	*85.2*	*100.0*	*117.0*	*134.5*
	1977	*70.3*	*83.3*	*100.0*	*118.3*	*137.8*	*73.2*	*81.0*	*100.0*	*115.4*	*131.9*
	1978	*70.8*	*83.2*	*100.0*	*119.6*	*140.9*	*74.2*	*86.8*	*100.0*	*116.8*	*134.5*
	1979	*70.4*	*82.8*	*100.0*	*119.5*	*140.6*	*75.5*	*86.1*	*100.0*	*117.3*	*135.3*
	1980	*70.5*	*83.1*	*100.0*	*120.7*	*143.6*	*74.2*	*84.9*	*100.0*	*118.0*	*137.0*
	1981	*69.6*	*82.4*	*100.0*	*120.7*	*143.6*	*74.1*	*84.1*	*100.0*	*118.6*	*138.3*
	1982	*69.2*	*81.9*	*100.0*	*120.5*	*144.1*	*73.1*	*84.1*	*100.0*	*118.8*	*137.2*
	1983	*68.8*	*81.5*	*100.0*	*121.1*	*145.3*	*72.3*	*83.4*	*100.0*	*118.7*	*139.4*
Non-manual women	1975	*66.5*	*80.3*	*100.0*	*127.2*	*171.5*	*67.1*	*80.9*	*100.0*	*128.2*	*181.9*
	1976	*65.1*	*79.9*	*100.0*	*128.6*	*172.9*	*64.7*	*80.1*	*100.0*	*128.9*	*186.7*
	1977	*68.1*	*81.7*	*100.0*	*126.8*	*165.6*	*68.3*	*81.7*	*100.0*	*126.7*	*174.1*
	1978	*68.8*	*81.9*	*100.0*	*127.4*	*164.7*	*69.1*	*82.0*	*100.0*	*127.4*	*174.6*
	1979	*69.5*	*81.8*	*100.0*	*126.4*	*160.7*	*69.2*	*81.9*	*100.0*	*127.4*	*172.1*
	1980	*67.9*	*80.6*	*100.0*	*127.6*	*161.6*	*68.2*	*80.7*	*100.0*	*128.4*	*172.0*
	1981	*67.5*	*79.9*	*100.0*	*132.1*	*172.7*	*67.4*	*80.2*	*100.0*	*131.2*	*181.7*
	1982	*66.4*	*79.4*	*100.0*	*130.5*	*166.2*	*66.3*	*79.7*	*100.0*	*131.2*	*177.6*
	1983	*66.1*	*79.3*	*100.0*	*131.7*	*164.8*	*65.5*	*79.4*	*100.0*	*131.6*	*177.7*

1. Men aged 21 and over; women aged 18 and over.
2. Of those whose pay for the survey pay period was not affected by absence. The figures are gross before deductions. Generally they exclude the value of earnings in kind, but include payments such as overtime, bonus, and commission and shift premiums for the pay period.
3. Including overtime hours and overtime pay, of persons for whom normal basic hours were reported and for whom hourly earnings could, therefore, be calculated.

Source Department of Employment

6.21 Gross weekly and hourly earnings of full-time adults[1]
Northern Ireland
April of each year

		Gross weekly earnings[2]					Gross hourly earnings[2]				
		Lowest decile	Lower quartile	Median	Upper quartile	Highest decile	Lowest decile	Lower quartile	Median	Upper quartile	Highest decile
		£	£	£	£	£	p	p	p	p	p
All men	1975	33.4	39.7	49.9	64.0	80.2	80.9	93.6	113.3	140.1	175.6
	1976	41.1	48.7	61.5	79.2	103.2	99.3	115.7	140.7	172.1	218.7
	1977	44.1	52.5	65.0	83.5	107.3	107.6	123.7	147.8	181.4	228.5
	1978	47.9	57.6	74.4	95.7	123.6	117.7	135.7	166.7	206.2	263.1
	1979	53.7	65.5	84.3	112.7	145.3	130.6	153.6	190.7	239.3	318.6
	1980	64.8	79.1	103.5	134.3	176.6	158.7	188.6	234.0	304.9	379.1
	1981	73.4	90.1	114.8	152.9	210.3	178.5	212.3	264.3	347.0	439.6
	1982	79.6	97.5	125.5	163.5	225.8	193.3	229.8	291.8	385.4	507.9
	1983	83.9	102.3	133.2	175.6	240.0	208.7	246.4	307.1	410.9	518.3
Manual men	1975	33.1	38.4	46.3	57.7	69.3	79.7	89.4	105.2	125.6	145.5
	1976	40.5	46.6	57.1	72.2	88.7	97.4	109.6	129.8	153.0	175.1
	1977	43.8	51.0	60.5	73.9	90.3	106.4	119.3	139.1	163.2	186.5
	1978	47.4	55.3	68.5	83.1	103.9	116.4	129.3	154.3	186.3	217.3
	1979	52.5	61.9	77.5	97.3	124.8	127.7	144.0	174.4	208.3	243.6
	1980	63.2	75.1	92.0	120.1	147.6	153.9	178.0	213.8	257.3	318.1
	1981	71.3	83.7	103.4	128.5	157.0	175.2	203.3	241.4	294.7	348.1
	1982	75.6	90.4	111.0	137.1	164.8	187.4	218.2	262.1	308.9	371.1
	1983	80.5	94.8	117.4	146.4	174.6	201.1	232.0	276.5	334.7	392.1
Non-manual men	1975	34.1	43.9	59.6	75.4	94.8	87.9	110.8	140.3	178.8	231.4
	1976	43.8	54.3	71.7	97.0	128.1	112.5	138.8	174.0	225.3	317.0
	1977	45.3	58.2	77.5	101.3	129.3	115.5	144.3	180.0	230.6	316.5
	1978	50.5	65.7	86.0	113.9	150.5	130.0	159.6	202.6	261.1	345.5
	1979	58.6	72.3	96.4	128.8	163.9	146.8	179.9	232.5	303.3	387.8
	1980	69.6	91.1	119.1	161.8	210.6	172.5	222.7	291.6	366.4	472.1
	1981	78.8	105.9	143.3	196.8	262.9	200.2	257.3	348.6	445.8	573.4
	1982	91.1	118.4	154.5	210.2	305.9	224.8	293.0	392.9	501.7	694.0
	1983	97.0	124.2	165.6	225.0	290.7	241.1	305.1	419.3	514.7	680.3

As percentages of the corresponding median

		Percentage					Percentage				
All men	1975	66.9	79.5	100.0	128.4	160.9	71.4	82.6	100.0	123.7	155.0
	1976	66.9	79.2	100.0	128.7	167.7	70.5	82.2	100.0	122.3	155.4
	1977	67.8	80.9	100.0	128.6	165.1	72.8	83.7	100.0	122.7	154.6
	1978	64.4	77.4	100.0	128.6	166.0	70.6	81.4	100.0	123.7	157.8
	1979	63.7	77.8	100.0	133.7	172.4	68.5	80.6	100.0	125.5	167.1
	1980	62.6	76.5	100.0	129.7	170.7	67.8	80.6	100.0	130.3	162.0
	1981	63.9	78.5	100.0	133.2	183.2	67.5	80.4	100.0	131.3	166.3
	1982	63.4	77.7	100.0	130.2	179.9	66.2	78.8	100.0	132.1	174.1
	1983	63.0	76.8	100.0	131.8	180.2	68.0	80.2	100.0	133.8	168.8
Manual men	1975	71.5	83.0	100.0	124.7	149.7	75.8	85.0	100.0	119.4	138.3
	1976	70.9	81.5	100.0	126.4	155.4	75.0	84.4	100.0	117.8	134.9
	1977	72.5	84.3	100.0	122.3	149.3	76.5	85.8	100.0	117.4	134.1
	1978	69.1	80.7	100.0	121.3	151.7	75.4	83.8	100.0	120.7	140.8
	1979	67.7	79.8	100.0	125.5	161.0	73.2	82.6	100.0	119.5	139.7
	1980	68.7	81.6	100.0	130.6	160.4	72.0	83.2	100.0	120.3	148.8
	1981	69.0	81.0	100.0	124.3	151.8	72.6	84.2	100.0	122.1	144.2
	1982	68.1	81.5	100.0	123.5	148.5	71.5	83.3	100.0	117.9	141.6
	1983	68.5	80.7	100.0	124.7	148.7	72.7	83.9	100.0	121.0	141.8
Non-manual men	1975	57.2	73.6	100.0	126.5	159.2	62.6	79.0	100.0	127.4	165.0
	1976	61.0	75.8	100.0	135.3	178.7	64.6	79.8	100.0	129.5	182.2
	1977	58.4	75.0	100.0	130.7	166.7	64.2	80.2	100.0	128.1	175.8
	1978	58.7	76.4	100.0	132.4	174.9	64.1	78.8	100.0	128.9	170.5
	1979	60.7	75.0	100.0	133.6	169.9	63.2	77.4	100.0	130.5	166.8
	1980	58.4	76.4	100.0	135.8	176.8	59.2	76.4	100.0	125.7	161.9
	1981	54.9	73.9	100.0	137.3	183.4	57.4	73.8	100.0	127.9	164.5
	1982	58.9	76.6	100.0	136.0	198.0	57.2	74.6	100.0	127.7	176.6
	1983	58.6	75.0	100.0	135.9	175.5	57.5	72.8	100.0	122.7	162.3

1. Men aged 21 and over; women aged 18 and over.
2. Those whose pay in the survey period was not affected by absence. Weekly earnings figures refer to April in each year and are gross before deductions excluding, generally, the value of incomes in kind, but including bonus and commission payments for the pay period.

Source Department of Economic Development (Northern Ireland)

6.21
(*continued*)

Gross weekly and hourly earnings of full-time adults [1]
Northern Ireland
April of each year

		Gross weekly earnings [2]					Gross hourly earnings [2]				
		Lowest decile	Lower quartile	Median	Upper quartile	Highest decile	Lowest decile	Lower quartile	Median	Upper quartile	Highest decile
		£	£	£	£	£	p	p	p	p	p
All women	1975	20.9	26.2	31.9	40.5	54.3	55.0	67.4	81.5	101.0	122.4
	1976	26.9	33.6	42.1	52.9	73.7	70.0	87.0	105.1	129.6	162.9
	1977	30.9	37.3	46.1	57.3	78.6	79.2	95.0	114.7	139.8	171.2
	1978	34.1	40.7	49.7	63.3	82.8	88.8	104.9	124.4	151.8	188.8
	1979	39.0	45.4	55.8	72.1	97.6	100.4	114.2	137.4	169.5	212.5
	1980	45.9	54.8	68.7	87.5	118.1	117.6	140.6	172.3	210.4	271.0
	1981	51.2	62.3	78.9	105.1	145.3	132.9	160.2	198.5	245.0	316.8
	1982	54.7	67.3	85.0	112.6	157.7	138.2	169.3	212.2	267.4	339.7
	1983	60.9	73.4	95.4	126.8	166.8	160.7	188.5	235.7	297.8	390.0
Manual women	1975	19.5	24.1	29.9	35.3	41.5	52.7	61.9	75.8	87.8	104.6
	1976	26.1	31.0	38.4	46.3	54.5	69.3	82.7	97.2	111.4	131.3
	1977	28.8	33.9	40.6	48.2	56.4	75.8	88.3	102.7	121.4	142.9
	1978	33.5	38.3	45.7	55.9	66.4	89.2	99.4	115.4	137.8	162.5
	1979	36.5	42.2	50.5	60.7	71.8	96.0	109.2	127.3	147.6	172.5
	1980	43.5	50.2	60.4	75.1	88.4	113.5	130.2	156.8	185.2	211.0
	1981	48.3	56.9	69.2	84.1	100.9	130.1	147.9	177.5	209.8	247.4
	1982	52.6	61.1	72.8	90.6	112.3	136.9	156.3	187.3	226.1	274.3
	1983	55.9	65.7	77.5	95.5	115.1	147.0	169.1	198.6	241.3	291.5
Non-manual women	1975	22.3	28.1	34.9	43.9	63.0	58.9	72.3	88.6	107.8	151.4
	1976	27.4	35.8	44.9	58.3	80.8	70.3	91.0	115.5	141.7	187.9
	1977	33.1	39.4	49.8	65.3	85.5	83.5	99.9	123.3	149.3	188.6
	1978	34.8	42.3	52.0	66.7	90.3	88.3	108.9	129.8	159.9	202.4
	1979	40.8	48.0	59.6	80.2	100.0	103.6	120.0	146.5	186.3	234.5
	1980	49.5	58.6	73.8	97.7	125.6	126.8	145.9	184.0	226.4	303.5
	1981	53.1	64.4	84.4	116.9	158.2	135.0	166.3	210.8	264.8	361.3
	1982	57.7	72.0	90.5	124.1	160.3	139.2	177.9	229.4	281.9	371.3
	1983	66.1	81.9	103.6	141.3	176.4	170.1	207.0	256.5	332.5	434.4

As percentages of the corresponding median		Percentage					Percentage				
All women	1975	65.6	82.0	100.0	127.0	170.2	67.4	82.6	100.0	123.8	150.1
	1976	63.9	79.8	100.0	125.6	175.0	66.6	82.7	100.0	123.3	154.9
	1977	67.0	81.1	100.0	124.3	170.8	69.0	82.8	100.0	121.9	149.2
	1978	68.5	81.8	100.0	127.2	166.4	71.4	84.4	100.0	122.1	151.8
	1979	70.0	81.5	100.0	129.4	175.1	73.0	83.1	100.0	123.4	154.6
	1980	66.8	79.7	100.0	127.3	171.9	68.2	81.6	100.0	122.2	157.3
	1981	64.9	78.9	100.0	133.2	184.0	66.9	80.7	100.0	123.4	159.6
	1982	64.4	79.1	100.0	132.5	185.4	65.1	79.8	100.0	126.0	160.1
	1983	63.9	77.0	100.0	132.9	174.9	68.2	80.0	100.0	126.4	165.5
Manual women	1975	65.2	80.7	100.0	118.3	139.1	69.6	81.7	100.0	115.8	138.0
	1976	68.0	80.9	100.0	120.8	142.2	71.2	85.1	100.0	114.6	135.1
	1977	71.0	83.5	100.0	118.7	138.8	73.9	86.0	100.0	118.2	139.2
	1978	73.5	83.9	100.0	122.3	145.4	77.3	86.1	100.0	119.4	140.8
	1979	72.2	83.6	100.0	120.2	142.2	75.4	85.7	100.0	115.9	135.5
	1980	71.9	83.1	100.0	124.3	146.2	72.4	83.0	100.0	118.1	134.6
	1981	69.8	82.2	100.0	121.5	145.8	73.3	83.3	100.0	118.2	139.4
	1982	72.2	83.8	100.0	124.4	154.1	73.1	83.4	100.0	120.7	146.5
	1983	72.1	84.8	100.0	123.2	148.5	74.0	85.2	100.0	121.5	146.8
Non-manual women	1975	63.9	80.5	100.0	125.7	180.4	66.5	81.6	100.0	121.6	170.8
	1976	61.0	79.8	100.0	129.9	180.2	60.9	78.8	100.0	122.7	162.7
	1977	66.5	79.1	100.0	131.1	171.8	67.7	81.1	100.0	121.1	153.0
	1978	67.0	81.4	100.0	128.3	173.7	68.0	83.9	100.0	123.2	155.9
	1979	68.6	80.6	100.0	134.7	167.8	70.7	81.9	100.0	127.1	160.1
	1980	67.1	79.4	100.0	132.5	170.2	68.9	79.3	100.0	123.0	164.9
	1981	62.9	76.3	100.0	138.5	187.4	64.0	78.9	100.0	125.6	171.4
	1982	63.7	79.6	100.0	137.0	177.1	60.7	77.5	100.0	122.9	161.9
	1983	63.8	79.1	100.0	136.4	170.3	66.3	80.7	100.0	129.6	169.4

1. and 2. See footnotes on page 131.

Source   Department of Economic Development (Northern Ireland)

6.22 Average earnings by age group of full-time employees whose pay for the survey pay-period was not affected by absence

Great Britain

New Earnings Survey April 1983

	Gross weekly earnings								Average hourly earnings excluding overtime pay[1]	Average weekly hours[1]	
	Average		As percentage of the median			As percentage of the median		Percentage earning under £75			
	Total	Overtime pay	Lowest decile	Lower quartile	Median	Upper quartile	Highest decile			Total	Normal basic
	£	£			£				p		
All full-time males											
Under 18	61.0	3.0	64.6	80.4	56.6	123.6	156.0	80.0	149.7	40.4	38.9
18 to 20	95.0	6.2	68.0	81.3	88.4	125.1	157.1	29.7	230.1	40.8	38.7
21 to 24	126.1	10.0	67.9	81.6	118.3	123.5	150.8	6.4	301.4	41.1	38.4
25 to 29	151.5	12.4	67.1	81.7	142.4	122.3	152.3	2.3	361.2	41.4	38.2
30 to 39	178.9	13.4	64.2	79.3	164.5	126.9	161.7	1.2	427.2	41.4	38.1
40 to 49	184.3	13.6	63.5	78.2	163.8	131.8	173.0	1.2	437.5	41.7	38.2
50 to 59	170.1	11.9	64.7	78.8	149.3	132.1	176.3	1.9	404.9	41.4	38.3
60 to 64	150.1	11.0	67.9	80.6	133.4	127.8	166.3	3.0	352.3	41.6	38.6
18 and over	163.3	12.1	61.8	77.8	146.9	130.6	171.1	3.8	387.6	41.4	38.3
21 and over	167.5	12.5	64.1	78.8	150.3	129.8	169.7	2.2	398.0	41.5	38.3
All ages	161.6	12.0	60.5	77.2	145.7	131.0	171.7	5.0	383.6	41.4	38.3
Full-time manual males											
Under 18	61.7	3.5	64.0	79.3	57.1	124.2	157.0	78.4	148.8	40.9	39.2
18 to 20	97.4	7.4	65.9	80.9	91.5	124.8	155.5	26.2	230.2	41.8	39.2
21 to 24	125.7	13.2	67.9	81.6	118.0	123.6	151.5	6.6	286.5	43.0	39.3
25 to 29	139.8	17.1	67.2	81.6	132.4	121.3	148.9	3.3	311.2	43.8	39.3
30 to 39	151.9	20.7	68.4	82.2	142.4	123.1	151.8	1.8	332.8	44.5	39.2
40 to 49	151.9	20.3	68.8	82.2	141.8	123.3	152.7	1.5	334.4	44.3	39.1
50 to 59	140.9	17.1	69.2	82.9	132.4	122.0	149.8	2.5	315.8	43.6	39.1
60 to 64	132.4	14.8	70.8	82.9	124.5	121.7	147.8	3.2	300.0	43.2	39.1
18 and over	140.1	17.3	65.7	80.6	131.9	123.5	152.9	4.5	312.4	43.8	39.2
21 and over	143.6	18.1	67.7	81.8	134.8	122.7	151.7	2.8	319.0	43.9	39.2
All ages	138.4	17.0	63.8	79.9	130.8	123.9	153.5	6.2	308.7	43.7	39.2
Full-time non-manual males											
Under 18	58.9	1.5	66.1	84.0	55.1	119.0	146.6	85.5	152.7	38.8	38.0
18 to 20	89.9	3.6	71.8	84.2	82.1	124.8	154.1	37.2	230.0	38.5	37.5
21 to 24	126.6	5.8	68.1	81.5	118.6	123.4	149.7	6.1	323.7	38.5	37.2
25 to 29	163.9	7.4	68.9	82.9	153.2	123.1	152.8	1.1	421.0	38.7	37.1
30 to 39	203.7	6.8	65.6	81.3	187.6	125.5	160.3	0.8	528.6	38.3	37.0
40 to 49	221.7	5.8	61.0	77.6	201.3	128.4	168.7	0.8	580.0	38.3	37.0
50 to 59	208.6	5.2	58.8	75.9	186.4	132.7	176.3	1.2	540.9	38.3	37.1
60 to 64	180.1	4.5	63.0	76.9	157.1	131.8	176.5	2.6	455.6	38.6	37.5
18 and over	190.7	6.0	57.7	75.8	173.1	131.2	171.3	3.0	490.7	38.4	37.1
21 and over	194.9	6.1	60.4	77.3	176.1	130.8	170.4	1.5	502.9	38.4	37.1
All ages	189.6	6.0	56.8	75.5	172.4	131.3	171.5	3.6	487.7	38.4	37.1
All full-time females											
Under 18	55.7	0.9	65.3	81.5	53.7	119.4	144.1	88.4	146.4	38.0	37.6
18 to 20	78.2	1.4	71.4	86.2	75.4	117.0	138.3	49.3	206.4	37.8	37.3
21 to 24	97.8	2.2	71.4	83.1	93.7	119.6	140.4	20.6	258.8	37.6	36.9
25 to 29	117.2	2.3	65.8	80.8	112.3	122.9	144.2	10.9	314.9	36.8	36.2
30 to 39	121.8	2.3	63.1	77.5	111.4	133.7	163.6	13.8	324.1	36.8	36.2
40 to 49	117.5	2.1	65.5	79.8	104.4	138.8	171.9	16.5	311.6	37.0	36.3
50 to 59	112.5	1.8	66.2	80.8	100.5	131.6	173.5	18.5	296.5	37.2	36.6
60 to 64	109.1	1.8	62.8	78.7	100.3	124.3	170.3	20.7	290.0	37.2	36.6
18 and over	108.8	2.0	66.4	79.7	98.8	129.9	168.3	20.7	287.5	37.2	36.6
21 and over	113.3	2.1	66.1	80.2	103.5	129.6	164.4	16.4	300.2	37.1	36.5
All ages	107.3	2.0	64.8	79.0	97.5	130.2	169.8	22.6	283.2	37.2	36.6
Full-time manual females											
Under 18	57.4	1.3	61.2	79.1	54.5	123.9	152.2	84.1	145.4	39.5	38.9
18 to 20	74.9	2.2	67.8	84.0	71.5	120.8	145.3	56.9	188.2	39.6	38.8
21 to 24	86.9	3.6	70.9	81.9	83.1	122.0	145.0	36.7	216.1	39.9	38.7
25 to 29	92.0	3.0	70.3	83.3	87.5	121.9	149.9	28.9	230.5	39.4	38.4
30 to 39	91.9	4.1	66.8	81.8	87.0	122.8	148.5	30.8	230.3	39.4	38.1
40 to 49	91.7	4.0	70.6	82.5	87.2	119.9	144.9	30.0	231.9	39.3	37.9
50 to 59	88.5	3.2	70.0	82.3	85.1	119.8	141.3	32.6	226.2	39.0	37.9
60 to 64	81.0	2.7	69.9	82.3	79.8	121.1	137.7	39.7	211.7	38.7	37.6
18 and over	82.9	3.4	68.8	81.5	84.1	121.1	145.3	35.3	222.0	39.3	38.2
21 and over	89.7	3.6	69.8	82.3	85.6	121.1	145.1	32.3	226.8	39.3	38.1
All ages	86.7	3.4	67.6	80.7	83.2	121.5	146.0	37.2	218.9	39.3	38.2

1. The estimates given relate to employees for whom normal basic hours were reported and for whom total hours and hourly earnings could, therefore, be calculated.

Source Department of Employment

6.22
(continued)

Average earnings by age group of full-time employees whose pay for the survey pay-period was not affected by absence

Great Britain
New Earnings Survey April 1983

	Gross weekly earnings								Average hourly earnings excluding overtime pay[1]	Average weekly hours[1]	
	Average		As percentage of the median			As percentage of the median		Per-centage earning under £75			
	Total	Overtime pay	Lowest decile	Lower quartile	Median	Upper quartile	Highest decile			Total	Normal basic
	£	£			£				p		
Full-time non-manual females											
Under 18	54.9	0.7	*67.2*	*82.5*	53.3	*117.7*	*140.0*	90.4	146.8	37.3	37.0
18 to 20	79.1	1.2	*73.2*	*86.9*	76.4	*116.3*	*136.5*	47.2	211.8	37.2	36.9
21 to 24	100.0	1.9	*72.3*	*83.8*	96.2	*118.6*	*138.4*	17.3	268.1	37.1	36.6
25 to 29	121.2	2.2	*67.1*	*82.1*	116.4	*121.2*	*142.3*	8.0	329.5	36.4	35.9
30 to 39	129.6	1.9	*62.9*	*77.4*	120.7	*129.7*	*157.7*	9.4	351.9	36.1	35.6
40 to 49	128.2	1.2	*64.2*	*78.2*	115.4	*139.1*	*166.0*	10.9	349.3	35.9	35.6
50 to 59	124.2	1.1	*65.6*	*80.7*	110.0	*138.8*	*172.9*	11.6	334.3	36.2	35.9
60 to 64	123.8	1.4	*67.2*	*82.3*	110.0	*131.5*	*170.0*	10.8	332.0	36.4	36.1
18 and over	115.1	1.6	*66.1*	*79.3*	104.7	*131.7*	*164.8*	16.2	309.0	36.5	36.1
21 and over	120.4	1.7	*66.5*	*80.3*	109.7	*131.2*	*161.7*	11.6	324.8	36.4	35.9
All ages	113.5	1.6	*64.6*	*78.6*	103.6	*131.7*	*165.8*	18.1	304.6	36.5	36.1

1. The estimates given relate to employees for whom normal basic hours were reported and for whom total hours and hourly earnings could, therefore, be calculated.

Source Department of Employment

6.23

Trade unions[1,2]
At end of year

	1972	1973	1974	1975	1976	1977	1978	1979	1980	1981	1982
Number of trade unions	507	519	507	501	473	481	462	456	438	421	410
Analysis by number of members:											
Under 100 members	83	84	80	80	69	74	72	73	69	69	80
100 and under 500	136	137	138	138	143	145	135	124	118	113	100
500 and under 1 000	45	52	52	54	47	45	48	47	45	45	48
1 000 and under 2 500	67	74	69	66	60	66	62	58	56	54	51
2 500 and under 5 000	56	51	52	45	45	41	37	43	39	37	37
5 000 and under 10 000	33	36	31	30	30	28	26	24	25	25	23
10 000 and under 15 000	13	11	11	11	8	10	9	7	7	4	3
15 000 and under 25 000	18	18	18	17	15	13	14	19	21	18	18
25 000 and under 50 000	18	18	17	20	17	18	19	17	19	17	15
50 000 and under 100 000	13	14	14	15	14	15	14	17	14	14	13
100 000 and under 250 000	14	13	14	14	14	15	15	16	15	14	11
250 000 and over	11	11	11	11	11	11	11	11	10	11	11
Membership[3] (Thousands)											
Total	11 359	11 456	11 764	12 193	12 386	12 846	13 112	13 289	12 952	12 182	11 594
Males	8 452	8 450	8 586	8 729	8 825	9 071	9 238	9 424	9 162	8 406	..[4]
Females	2 907	3 006	3 178	3 464	3 561	3 775	3 874	3 864	3 790	3 776	..[4]
Analysis by size of unions:											
Under 100 members	4	4	4	4	3	4	4	4	4	4	4
100 and under 500	36	35	36	35	36	37	34	30	28	28	25
500 and under 1 000	31	37	37	39	35	32	34	34	32	32	34
1 000 and under 2 500	101	114	107	105	99	109	103	93	88	86	79
2 500 and under 5 000	182	171	173	147	153	144	134	154	140	132	127
5 000 and under 10 000	221	238	201	200	201	178	169	158	167	167	154
10 000 and under 15 000	150	129	135	129	100	123	112	84	82	54	43
15 000 and under 25 000	333	335	343	327	296	256	267	364	392	354	364
25 000 and under 50 000	609	624	609	664	621	642	711	594	725	617	546
50 000 and under 100 000	912	997	948	1 045	997	1 015	947	1 004	1 024	978	975
100 000 and under 250 000	1 879	1 810	1 958	1 995	2 053	2 199	2 263	2 387	2 518	2 175	1 862
250 000 and over	6 901	6 963	7 213	7 503	7 790	8 107	8 335	8 424	7 752	7 555	7 380

1. The statistics relate to all organisations of employees with head offices in the United Kingdom—including those of salaried and professional workers, as well as those of manual wage-earners—which are known to include among their functions that of negotiating with employers with the object of regulating the conditions of employment of their members.
2. Figures are confined to organisations which appear to satisfy the statutory definition of trade union in section 28 of the Trade Union and Labour Relations Act 1974. This has had the effect of excluding 31 organisations which were previously regarded by the Department as trade unions e.g.

organisations representing members of the police service which are specifically excluded from the statutory definition by section 30 of the 1974 Act.
3. The figures of membership include the membership of branches in the Irish Republic and overseas but wholly exclude the membership of unions whose headquarters are situated outside the United Kingdom. A small number of people who are members of more than one union are included more than once in the figures, but the effect on the aggregates is relatively insignificant.
4. Not separately counted in 1982.

Source Department of Employment

7 Defence

This section includes figures on Defence expenditure, on the size and role of the Armed Forces and on related support activities.

Much of the material in this section can be found in Volume 2 of the *Statement on the Defence Estimates 1984* (*Defence Statistics*) (Cmnd. 9227 – II) (HMSO 1984).

Formation of the Armed Forces (Table 7.1). This table shows the number of units which comprise the 'teeth' elements of the Armed Forces and excludes supporting units. Greater detail for the current year is given in Volume I of the *Statement on the Defence Estimates 1984* Cmnd. 9227 – I).

Finance (Table 7.2). Expenditure covered by the Royal Ordnance Factories Trading Fund is excluded from 1975/76.

Service personnel (Tables 7.3 to 7.5 and 10). The Regular Forces consist entirely of volunteer members serving on a whole-time basis. The figures for females consist of all members of the Women's Services (i.e. WRNS, WRAC and WRAF) and female members of the Nursing Services. Certain male members of the RAF Medical Branch were transferred to the Princess Mary's RAF Nursing Service on 1 April 1980 and certain members of the RN Medical specialisation were transferred to the Queen Alexandra's Royal Naval Nursing Service on 1 April 1983 as a result of reorganisations. They continue to be shown in the male figures in Table 7.3 and are now included in the Nursing Services figures in Table 7.10. Certain professionally qualified female officers are not commissioned in the Women's Service, but in the appropriate branch or corps (i.e. medical, dental, legal, veterinary) and are not accounted for in the female figures. There were 115 such officers on 1 April 1984.

Locally Entered Personnel are recruited outside the United Kingdom for whole-time service in special formations with special conditions of service and normally restricted locations. The Brigade of Gurkhas is an example.

The Regular Forces are supported by Reserves and Auxiliary Forces. There are both regular and volunteer Reserves. Regular Reserves consist of former Service personnel with a Reserve liability. The Army General Reserve which consisted mainly of former National Servicemen, ceased to exist on 30 June 1974 when the relevant legislation expired. Volunteer Reserves are open to both former Service personnel and civilians. The call out liabilities of the various reserve forces differ in accordance with their roles.

All three Services run cadet forces for young people and the Combined Cadet Force, which is found in certain schools where education is continued to the age of 17 or above, may operate sections for any or all of the Services.

Deployment of Service personnel (Table 7.5). The source from which the individual national totals are compiled is different from that used to obtain the total United Kingdom strength and consequently the figures for England, Wales, Scotland and Northern Ireland do not add up to the United Kingdom figure. Royal Navy and Royal Marines personnel on board ship are included in the United Kingdom figure if the ship was in home waters on the situation date or otherwise against the appropriate overseas area. The overseas figures include personnel who are on loan to countries in the areas shown.

Service married accommodation and Defence land holdings (Table 7.6). Accommodation is provided for Service families in the United Kingdom and abroad, partly by building to approved standards and partly by renting accommodation. Permanent holdings in the United Kingdom include a small number of unfurnished hirings taken on from local authorities which are not recorded separately. Multiple hirings relate to accommodation built by private developers and leased by the Federal German Authorities and the Government of Gibraltar on behalf of British Forces.

The table also presents statistics of land and foreshore in the United Kingdom owned by the Ministry of Defence or over which it has limited rights under grants or licences. Land declared as surplus to Defence requirements is also included. At 1 April 1984 about 2 685 hectares were awaiting disposal by the Property Services Agency.

Civilian personnel (Table 7.7). This table gives the number of civilians employed by the Department at 1 April for each of the years, broken down into Management areas, viz Centre (those authorities not in the Service Departments, PE or the ROFs), Royal Dockyards, Other Navy, Army, Royal Air Force (including the Meteorological Office), Procurement Executive (PE) and Royal Ordnance Factories (ROFs). The attribution of civilian staff within the Ministry of Defence can change according to circumstances so that figures for successive years may not always be comparable.

During the period April 1983 to April 1984 there was a reduction of 3.4 thousand in non-industrial centre staff in the Royal Dockyards. This reduction was primarily due to the closure of Chatham Dockyard.

Some civilians from the United Kingdom serve tours of duty overseas. There were 5 437 such civilians serving abroad on 1 April 1984. Other civilian staff are engaged overseas to work locally as circumstances demand.

In addition Department of the Environment staff directly engaged on the Defence programme totalled 21 948 on 1 April 1984.

Energy consumption (Table 7.8). A new table is included showing Defence energy consumption.

Health (Tables 7.9 to 7.11). The Services operate a number of hospitals in this country and in areas abroad where there is a significant British military presence. These hospitals take as patients members of all three Services and their dependants; in addition the hospitals in the United Kingdom take civilian patients under arrangements agreed with the National Health Service. Medical support is also supplied by Service medical staff at individual units, ships and stations.

Sickness, medical discharges and deaths of UK Service personnel (Table 7.11). It should be noted that, whereas the Royal Navy and Royal Air Force content is for all cases of off-duty sickness lasting 2 days or more terminating in the year, that for the Army covers only those cases admitted to medical units (including hospitals) for 2 days or more.

Search and rescue (Table 7.12). This table covers incidents in which Rescue Co-ordinating Centres (RCCs) in the United Kingdom co-ordinated search and rescue (SAR) action in which elements of the Armed Forces were involved. The table also includes urgent medical incidents in which the Forces SAR facilities gave assistance (e.g. inter-hospital transfers).

Defence services and the civilian community (Table 7.13). The Ministry of Defence helps the civil community in a variety of ways, for example by providing assistance in time of natural disasters or other emergencies and by undertaking community projects which are of training value to the Services. In some cases facilities established primarily for defence purposes also provide benefits to the general public. Overall figures are not available, but the table presents information on a number of these activities and facilities.

Service assistance may be provided during an industrial dispute at the request of the civil ministries in order to maintain services essential to the life of the community (e.g. maintenance of emergency fire services in 1977/78).

The Royal Navy Fishery Protection squadron operates within the United Kingdom fishery limits on behalf of Fishery departments, who pay some of the running costs of the squadron.

The Hydrographer of the Navy is the national authority responsible for hydrographic and oceanographic surveys and nautical charting. The Admiralty chart series comprises some 3 400 basic charts and 600 latticed versions covering the whole world.

The Meteorological Office is the State Meteorological Service and forms part of the Ministry of Defence. It is responsible for the provision of meteorological services to the Royal Air Force and the Army. Services are provided on a repayment basis, principally for civil aviation and industry, and some free services are provided to the general public through the press and other media.

7.1 Formation of the Armed Forces
At 1 April

Number

	Unit[1]	1974	1975	1976	1977	1978	1979	1980	1981	1982	1983	1984
Royal Navy[2]												
Submarines	Vessels	25	24	22	24	24	22	23	22	22	21	22
Carriers and assault ships	Vessels	4	5	3	3	4	3	4	3	3	4	4
Cruisers and destroyers	Vessels	10	12	9	10	12	11	10	12	11	13	13
Frigates	Vessels	47	47	46	40	43	42	39	36	38	42	39
Mine counter-measure[3]	Vessels	42	40	37	34	35	35	35	32	33	36	34
Patrol ships and craft	Vessels	13	10	13	15	19	19	23	22	21	25	31
Fixed wing aircraft	Squadrons	3	3	3	3	3	–	2	3	3	3	3
	Flights	1	1	1	1	1	–	–	–	–	–	–
Helicopters	Squadrons	13	13	12	12	12	13	14	14	15	10	10
	Flights	40	39	40	41	47	49	43	47	49	68	57
Royal Marines	Commandos	4	4	4	3	4	4	4	4	3	3	3
Army[4]												
Royal Armoured Corps	Regiments	19	19	19	19	19	19	19	19	19	19	19
Royal Artillery	Regiments	27	26	26	21	22	22	22	22	22	22	22
Royal Engineers[5]	Regiments	14	13	13	10	10	9	10	11	11	12	12
Infantry[5]	Battalions	55	55	55	55	55	56	56	56	57	56	56
Special Air Service	Regiments	1	1	1	1	1	1	1	1	1	1	1
Army Air Corps[6]	Regiments	..	..	..	6	6	6	6	6	6	4	4
Royal Air Force[4]												
Strike/attack[7]	Squadrons	} 16	{ 13	13	14	14	14	15	15	12	10	11
Ground support[7]	Squadrons		6	6	5	5	5	5	5	5	5	5
Air defence	Squadrons	9	9	9	9	9	9	9	9	9	9	9
Maritime patrol[7]	Squadrons	}	{ 5	5	5	4	4	4	4	4	4	4
Reconnaissance[7]	Squadrons	} 12	{ 5	5	5	5	5	5	5	3	2	3
Airborne early warning[7]	Squadrons	}	{ 1	1	1	1	1	1	1	1	1	1
Transport[8]	Squadrons	18	18	11	10	10	10	10	9	10	11	11
Tankers	Squadrons	3	3	3	2	2	2	2	2	2	3	3
Search and rescue	Squadrons	3	3	3	3	3	3	3	3	3	3	3
Surface to air missiles	Squadrons	7	6	7	7	7	7	8	8	8	8	8
Ground defence	Squadrons	6	6	5	5	5	6	6	6	6	6	6

1. The number of personnel and the amount of equipment in each vessel, regiment, etc, varies according to the role currently assigned.
2. Excludes vessels undergoing major refit, conversion, or on stand-by, etc.
3. In 1981 4 ex-inshore minesweepers used for training are excluded.
4. Regular forces only.
5. Includes Gurkhas.

6. Prior to 1977 the Army Air Corps was not organised in regiments.
7. For the years to 1974 these categories were not readily divisible.
8. Includes helicopters.

Source Ministry of Defence

7.2 Defence budget: annual expenditure[1,2]

£ million

	1972/73	1973/74	1974/75	1975/76	1976/77	1977/78	1978/79	1979/80	1980/81	1981/82	1982/83
Total expenditure at outturn prices[3]	3 092	3 484	4 164	5 346	6 158	6 787	7 455	9 178	11 182	12 607	14 412
of which:											
Expenditure on personnel	1 552	1 694	2 026	2 530	2 864	3 021	3 293	3 912	4 556	5 058	5 455
Pay, etc. of Armed Forces	851	902	1 063	1 305	1 465	1 519	1 639	2 099	2 460	2 728	2 914
Retired pay, etc. of Armed Forces	157	186	200	255	316	361	432	459	503	624	680
Pay, etc. of civilian staff	544	606	763	970	1 083	1 141	1 222	1 354	1 593	1 706	1 861
Expenditure on equipment	1 023	1 153	1 302	1 792	2 138	2 565	2 984	3 640	4 885	5 638	6 297
Sea systems[4]	227	306	315	440	590	672	878	1 110	1 513	1 624	1 730
Land systems	151	182	249	413	486	612	601	740	904	1 101	1 353
Air systems	385	489	595	752	844	1 010	1 214	1 427	2 059	2 458	2 640
Other[5]	260	176	143	187	218	271	291	363	410	456	574
Other expenditure	517	637	836	1 024	1 156	1 201	1 178	1 625	1 741	1 910	2 659
Works, buildings and land[6]	215	266	314	394	463	462	405	599	623	664	832
Miscellaneous stores and services	302	371	522	630	693	739	773	1 026	1 118	1 246	1 827
Total expenditure at constant (1975/76) prices[3]	5 399	5 320	5 111	5 346	5 247	5 126	5 089	5 243	5 421	5 498	5 832

1. Expenditure as given in the annual Appropriation Accounts for the Defence Votes, Class XII for 1972/73 and 1973/74, and Class I for 1974/75 onwards.
2. Including expenditure of government departments other than the Ministry of Defence in years when these contributed to the Defence budget.
3. Because of changes in the responsibilities of the Ministry of Defence, expenditures in successive years are not necessarily comparable.
4. Prior to 1976/77 the dockyard services element of the sea systems expenditure was included under other equipment.

5. Including expenditure on guided weapons and electronic systems (£176.3 million in 1972/73 and £53.7 million in 1973/74) which is divided between the appropriate systems in later years.
6. Including pay of civilian staff employed in works and building.

Source Ministry of Defence

7.3 Defence manpower strengths
At 1 April[1]

Thousands

	1974	1975	1976	1977	1978	1979	1980	1981	1982	1983	1984
UK service personnel											
All services: total	349.3	338.3	336.6	330.5	320.7	315.0	320.6	333.8	327.6	320.6	325.9
Male	334.9	323.9	321.8	316.0	306.1	299.7	304.4	316.8	311.9	305.2	309.7
Female	14.4	14.5	14.8	14.5	14.6	15.3	16.2	16.9	15.7	15.4	16.2
Royal Navy: total	70.5	68.4	68.3	68.5	67.8	65.1	64.4	66.4	65.1	64.0	63.7
Male	66.9	64.6	64.4	64.6	63.8	61.2	60.5	62.3	61.1	60.1	59.8
Female	3.6	3.7	3.9	4.0	4.0	3.8	3.8	4.1	4.0	3.9	3.9
Royal Marines: total	7.8	7.9	7.8	7.7	7.5	7.4	7.6	7.9	7.9	7.8	7.6
Male	7.8	7.9	7.8	7.7	7.5	7.4	7.6	7.9	7.9	7.8	7.6
Army: total	171.7	167.1	169.8	167.3	160.8	156.2	159.0	166.0	163.2	159.1	161.5
Male	165.9	161.4	163.9	161.6	155.1	150.4	152.8	159.4	157.2	152.9	155.0
Female	5.8	5.7	5.9	5.8	5.7	5.8	6.3	6.6	6.0	6.1	6.6
Royal Air Force: total	99.2	95.0	90.7	86.9	84.6	86.3	89.6	93.5	91.5	89.8	93.1
Male	94.3	90.0	85.7	82.2	79.7	80.7	83.5	87.2	85.7	84.5	87.3
Female	5.0	5.1	5.0	4.8	4.9	5.6	6.1	6.3	5.8	5.4	5.7
Personnel Locally Entered overseas: total	9.2	9.3	9.1	8.5	8.4	8.4	8.2	9.7	10.1	10.1	9.6
Regular Reserves:[1] total	355.8	170.0	170.0	174.9	179.5	188.5	192.6	196.5	196.4	193.4	198.0
Royal Navy	27.7	27.9	27.4	27.9	26.3	28.4	27.0	26.8	24.7	23.9	23.5
Royal Marines	2.2	2.2	2.3	2.4	2.4	2.4	2.2	2.2	2.2	2.2	2.2
Army	115.1	108.2	107.3	111.2	118.5	127.0	133.1	137.5	140.2	138.3	143.2
Army General Reserve[2]	179.4	–	–	–	–	–	–	–	–	–	–
Royal Air Force	31.4	31.7	33.0	33.4	32.3	30.8	30.3	30.1	29.3	28.9	29.0
Volunteer Reserves and Auxilliary Forces: total[1]	69.7	69.1	70.6	75.2	75.3	73.5	77.0	83.9	86.3	87.3	85.7
Royal Navy	6.2	6.1	5.8	5.4	5.4	5.4	5.0	5.4	5.4	5.4	5.2
Royal Marines	0.8	0.9	1.0	0.9	1.0	0.9	0.9	0.9	1.1	1.1	1.0
Territorial Army	54.7	54.1	55.9	60.9	60.6	59.4	63.3	69.5	72.1	72.8	71.4
Ulster Defence Regiment	7.7	7.7	7.7	7.6	7.9	7.6	7.4	7.5	7.1	7.1	6.8
Home Service Force	–	–	–	–	–	–	–	–	–	0.3	0.3
Royal Air Force	0.3	0.3	0.3	0.3	0.4	0.3	0.5	0.6	0.6	0.6	1.0
Cadet Forces:[1, 3] total	130.5	129.4	137.3	141.6	142.2	140.0	141.5	144.1	144.6	142.0	141.2
Royal Navy	22.7	22.6	24.9	25.1	25.0	23.9	22.7	24.5	24.6	22.4	23.1
Army	66.3	65.0	69.8	72.7	73.4	72.6	74.6	75.1	74.1	74.5	73.8
Royal Air Force	41.6	41.8	42.6	43.7	43.8	43.5	44.1	44.4	45.9	45.1	44.3

1. A few of the figures for reserves and cadets were collected at irregular intervals and do not necessarily refer to 1 April; they are the latest figures available at that date.

2. The Army General Reserve ceased to exist on 30 June 1974 when the relevant legislation expired.
3. Combined Cadet Force cadets are included under the relevant service.

Source Ministry of Defence

7.4 Recruitment of UK Service personnel to each Service

Number

	1973/74	1974/75	1975/76	1976/77	1977/78	1978/79	1979/80	1980/81	1981/82	1982/83	1983/84
All Services: total	32 433	42 236	46 906	40 244	38 237	43 366	50 652	50 488	22 607	21 647	36 991
Male	27 722	36 852	41 686	36 390	34 188	38 774	46 206	46 693	21 188	19 342	33 760
Female	4 711	5 384	5 220	3 854	4 049	4 592	4 446	3 795	1 419	2 305	3 231
Royal Navy: total	6 895	8 282	8 910	8 195	7 167	6 791	8 526	9 088	3 805	3 584	4 785
Male	5 813	7 203	7 732	7 238	6 269	5 978	7 701	8 130	3 353	3 078	4 223
Female	1 082	1 079	1 178	957	898	813	825	958	452	506	562
Royal Marines: total	1 170	1 520	1 154	929	903	1 282	1 676	1 674	699	447	447
Male	1 170	1 520	1 154	929	903	1 282	1 676	1 674	699	447	447
Army: total	17 554	24 264	29 591	24 088	22 550	25 254	29 189	28 871	14 204	13 071	22 348
Male	15 310	22 041	27 238	22 344	20 868	23 528	27 164	27 241	13 603	11 679	20 811
Female	2 244	2 223	2 353	1 744	1 682	1 726	2 025	1 630	601	1 392	1 537
Royal Air Force: total	6 814	8 170	7 251	7 032	7 617	10 039	11 261	10 855	3 899	4 545	9 411
Male	5 429	6 088	5 562	5 879	6 148	7 986	9 665	9 648	3 533	4 138	8 279
Female	1 385	2 082	1 689	1 153	1 469	2 053	1 596	1 207	366	407	1 132

Source Ministry of Defence

7.5 Deployment of Service personnel
At 1 July

Thousands

	1973	1974	1975	1976	1977	1978	1979	1980	1981	1982	1983
UK Service personnel, Regular Forces: total	361.2	345.4	336.2	335.7	327.1	318.2	314.1	323.4	334.3	324.3	321.7
In United Kingdom	260.5	244.4	242.3	247.3	241.9	230.2	232.2	238.1	245.0	215.2	228.9
England[1]	215.2	202.0	200.3	203.3	202.8	192.7	192.6	200.0	207.7	195.9	195.1
Wales[1]	6.1	5.6	6.3	6.7	6.4	6.3	6.3	6.9	6.3	6.1	6.1
Scotland[1]	17.5	16.0	18.7	19.2	19.1	19.3	19.0	18.1	18.9	19.0	18.7
Northern Ireland[2]	18.9	18.5	15.6	15.7	14.7	14.4	13.6	11.9	11.6	10.9	10.2
Overseas	105.8	105.3	97.9	94.1	88.6	91.7	84.9	87.6	91.3	109.8	94.0
Federal Republic of Germany[3]	64.6	63.6	62.6	65.6	67.1	65.7	64.6	65.3	70.4	69.8	67.0
Elsewhere in Continental Europe[4]	7.0	7.0	7.0	6.1	6.8	5.9	5.7	5.7	6.1	6.2	6.1
Gibraltar	2.0	2.0	1.9	2.5	2.2	2.7	2.0	3.2	2.2	2.7	2.0
Malta	2.5	2.7	2.6	1.7	1.8	1.3	–	–	–	–	–
Cyprus	9.1	9.0	7.0	4.9	4.7	4.6	4.0	4.7	4.9	4.8	4.9
Elsewhere in Mediterranean, Near East and Gulf	3.0	5.8	5.2	1.7	0.5	0.4	0.4	0.4	1.4	1.1	0.3
Hong Kong	4.6	4.5	4.4	3.5	2.6	2.4	2.4	2.5	2.5	2.5	2.4
Singapore	2.2	2.1	2.1	–	–	–	–	–	–	–	–
Malaysia	0.1	0.1	–	–	–	–	–	–	–	–	–
Elsewhere in the Far East	2.6	3.3	1.7	0.3	0.3	0.3	1.8	1.7	0.3	0.3	0.7
Other locations[1,5]	8.3	5.3	3.5	7.8	2.6	8.4	3.9	4.1	3.5	22.4	10.5
Locally entered service personnel: total	9.1	9.2	9.3	8.9	8.4	8.3	8.3	9.2	10.0	9.9	10.0
United Kingdom	0.9	0.9	0.9	0.8	0.7	0.7	0.7	0.9	1.3	0.6	1.2
Gibraltar	0.1	0.1	0.1	0.1	0.1	0.1	0.1	0.1	0.1	0.1	0.1
Malta	0.8	0.7	0.6	0.6	0.5	0.4	–	–	–	–	–
Hong Kong	5.4	5.7	5.6	5.3	5.2	5.4	5.8	6.4	6.7	6.6	6.6
Brunei	0.8	0.8	0.8	0.8	0.8	0.8	0.8	0.8	0.8	0.8	0.8
Nepal	1.2	1.1	1.2	1.3	1.2	1.0	1.0	1.1	1.2	1.3	1.4
Other locations[6]	0.1	0.1	0.1	–	–	–	–	–	–	0.6	–

1. The 1982 England, Wales and Scotland national figures include personnel who were UK based but temporarily deployed in the South Atlantic. These have been included also in the Overseas numbers against 'Other locations'.
2. The figures for Northern Ireland include all personnel from other parts of the United Kingdom and the British Army of the Rhine who are serving on emergency tours of duty, but exclude the Ulster Defence Regiment.
3. Army personnel serving in Northern Ireland on emergency tours of duty but remaining under the command of the Commander-in-Chief British Army of the Rhine are included in these figures.
4. These figures include personnel stationed in Berlin and Sardinia.
5. These figures include Defence Attaches/Advisers and their staffs.
6. The 1982 figures comprise Gurkha troops serving in the Falkland Islands.

Source   Ministry of Defence

7.6 Service married accommodation and Defence land holdings

	1974	1975	1976	1977	1978	1979	1980	1981	1982	1983	1984
Married accommodation[1]	Thousand										
United Kingdom: total	101.6	102.6	102.4	98.3	97.9	95.4	92.7	88.7	87.5	87.0	85.9
Permanent holdings	95.8	97.6	98.4	95.5	96.7	94.7	92.4	88.3	87.2	86.6	85.7
Hirings	5.9	4.9	4.0	2.8	1.3	0.6	0.4	0.3	0.3	0.3	0.2
Overseas: total	49.2	47.3	47.2	47.6	47.4	46.7	46.5	46.4	45.9	46.0	46.2
Permanent holdings	22.9	22.8	21.1	21.6	21.5	21.2	21.1	21.4	21.4	21.4	21.4
Hirings[2]	26.3	24.5	26.1	26.1	25.8	25.6	25.4	25.0	24.5	24.6	24.8
Land holdings[3]	Thousand hectares										
United Kingdom											
Land: freehold	227.5	225.4	224.2	223.1	222.1	221.1	220.2	220.1	217.8	215.9	214.9
leasehold	16.5	15.5	11.9	11.9	12.0	11.9	11.9	11.9	11.9	11.9	11.6
Foreshore: freehold	12.8	12.8	13.2	13.2	13.2	13.3	13.2	13.2	13.2	13.1	13.1
leasehold	5.4	5.4	4.9	4.9	4.9	4.9	4.9	4.9	4.9	4.9	4.9
Rights	25.7	27.0	29.5	30.3	30.5	31.3	31.1	36.7	36.7	36.7	36.0
Defence land (freehold and leasehold)											
used for agricultural purposes	113.6	111.0	112.3	112.2	111.6	112.6	113.8	111.9	109.1	109.7	110.2
Used for grazing only	61.9	61.7	60.6	61.9	60.1	61.2	60.2	59.8	58.8	58.8	59.8
Full agricultural use	51.7	49.4	51.8	50.3	51.5	51.4	53.6	52.0	50.3	50.9	50.5

1. From 1978 onwards at 15 January each year. Before that the different Services collated information at different times, usually between 1 December in the preceding year and 1 March. Mobile accommodation was included for the Army and the RAF in the years 1974 and 1975.
2. Includes multiple hirings.
3. At 1 April each year. The figures include land taken over with the functions of the former Ministry of Aviation Supply.

Sources   Crown Suppliers; Ministry of Defence

7.7 Defence civilian manpower strengths
At 1 April

Thousands

	1975	1976	1977	1978	1979	1980	1981	1982	1983	1984
Ministry of Defence civilians: total[1]	316.7	310.8	300.9	290.4	285.9	276.2	264.9	251.7	242.7	232.5
UK based[2]	266.6	266.2	258.7	250.4	247.7	239.8	229.6	216.9	208.9	199.1
Non-industrial	130.2	130.1	125.9	122.2	120.6	118.5	113.5	108.1	105.6	103.2
Industrial	136.4	136.2	132.8	128.1	127.0	121.2	116.1	108.8	103.3	95.9
of which										
Centre										
Non-industrial	23.8	24.2	22.9	21.8	20.9	20.2	19.0	18.3	14.5	14.1
Industrial	0.7	0.7	0.7	0.7	0.6	0.6	0.6	0.6	0.6	0.5
Royal Dockyards										
Non-industrial	7.7	8.2	8.3	9.1	9.1	9.0	8.4	7.6	7.0	6.3
Industrial	25.5	25.6	25.5	25.3	25.0	24.2	23.6	22.4	20.7	18.0
Other Navy										
Non-industrial	14.3	14.2	14.1	13.9	13.8	14.0	13.7	13.1	14.5	14.3
Industrial	23.3	23.3	22.6	22.1	22.0	21.3	20.3	19.0	18.4	17.2
Army										
Non-industrial	28.8	28.4	27.6	26.9	26.7	25.7	24.7	23.9	24.2	23.6
Industrial	36.2	35.1	33.5	32.2	32.0	30.3	28.4	26.3	25.2	24.0
Air Force										
Non-industrial	16.6	16.2	15.5	14.5	14.4	14.1	14.0	13.4	13.5	13.4
Industrial	15.1	14.6	13.7	12.3	12.3	11.7	11.5	10.7	10.1	9.5
Procurement Executive										
Non-industrial	34.2	33.5	32.2	30.4	29.9	29.6	27.8	26.4	26.8	26.3
Industrial	21.4	20.6	19.5	18.4	17.9	17.4	16.8	15.9	14.9	14.0
Royal Ordnance Factories										
Non-industrial	4.9	5.3	5.4	5.7	5.9	5.9	5.8	5.4	5.1	5.2
Industrial	14.1	16.4	17.3	17.2	17.1	15.9	15.0	14.0	13.4	12.7
Locally engaged overseas	50.1	44.6	42.2	40.0	38.2	36.4	35.3	34.8	33.8	33.4
Non-industrial	14.6	12.7	11.9	11.5	11.2	11.0	10.9	10.7	10.5	10.4
Industrial	35.5	31.9	30.3	28.5	27.1	25.5	24.4	24.1	23.3	23.0

1. Two part-time employees are counted as one whole-time employee.
2. Including UK-based civilians serving overseas

Source Ministry of Defence

7.8 Defence energy consumption

Thousand tonnes of oil or oil equivalent

	1976–77	1977–78	1978–79	1979–80	1980–81	1981–82	1982–83	1983–84
All fuels	3 854	3 872	3 873	3 702	3 429	3 446	3 823	3 780
Royal Navy[1]	1 176	1 163	1 146	1 111	1 006	1 027	1 327	1 287
Army	757	744	788	722	669	654	638	654
Royal Air Force	1 466	1 502	1 478	1 453	1 355	1 344	1 471	1 426
Procurement Executive	287	281	279	248	241	244	228	235
Royal Ordnance Factories	170	183	181	169	158	177	158	178
Liquid fuels	2 884	2 898	2 873	2 747	2 480	2 492	2 877	2 760
Aviation fuel	1 096	1 127	1 091	1 083	1 010	1 000	1 157	1 104
Furnace oil	1 122	1 139	1 119	992	892	899	818	781
Diesel	544	517	551	566	482	496	800	777
Petrol	102	94	92	87	78	79	82	80
Other	20	21	21	20	19	19	19	19
Non-liquid fuels	971	974	1 000	955	947	953	946	1 020
Electricity	650	644	671	637	639	642	633	678
Gas	164	176	189	190	192	187	197	220
Solid fuel	156	153	139	128	115	124	116	123

1. Royal Navy figures include the Royal Dockyards.

Source Ministry of Defence.

7.9 Service hospitals

	1973	1974	1975	1976	1977	1978	1979	1980	1981	1982	1983
Average number of beds[1]											
United Kingdom	2 995	2 826	2 757	2 796	2 555	2 352	2 297	2 287	2 286	2 195	2 113
Overseas	1 625	1 599	1 637	1 432	1 422	1 351	1 243	1 231	1 269	1 252	1 262
Average percentage of beds occupied[2]											
United Kingdom	*70.0*	*70.7*	*70.7*	*63.3*	*64.1*	*63.4*	*67.0*	*65.8*	*64.2*	*61.5*	*61.6*
Overseas	..	..	..	*60.8*	*58.9*	*56.4*	*58.5*	*60.8*	*58.2*	*56.6*	*55.0*
In-patient admissions (thousands)											
United Kingdom:	80.0	77.4	78.2	77.7	73.2	68.3	72.3	76.0	75.9	71.3	71.3
Service personnel	33.6	32.6	32.2	31.9	30.5	28.4	27.4	28.2	28.6	27.0	27.5
Service dependants	22.2	20.0	19.7	18.8	15.8	14.5	14.4	14.6	14.4	14.1	13.1
NHS/Other	24.1	24.8	26.3	27.0	26.9	25.4	30.5	33.2	32.9	30.2	30.7
Overseas:[3]	47.9	48.7	47.9	45.3	45.5	43.5	42.1	43.8	42.3	42.7	43.6
UK Service personnel	13.2	14.5	13.8	13.8	12.8	12.6	12.4	13.2	12.7	13.6	14.3
Service dependants	29.8	28.1	26.4	25.3	24.7	23.3	20.8	21.8	21.5	23.2	22.9
Others	4.9	6.0	7.6	6.2	8.0	7.6	8.9	8.8	8.1	5.9	6.3
Average number of admissions per bed[2]											
United Kingdom	*26.7*	*27.4*	*28.4*	*27.8*	*28.7*	*29.1*	*31.5*	*33.2*	*33.1*	*32.5*	*33.7*
Overseas	*29.5*	*30.5*	*29.3*	*31.6*	*32.0*	*32.2*	*33.9*	*35.6*	*33.4*	*34.1*	*34.4*
Average days in hospital per patient											
United Kingdom	*9.6*	*9.5*	*9.1*	*8.3*	*8.2*	*8.0*	*7.8*	*7.2*	*7.1*	*6.9*	*6.7*
Overseas	..	..	..	*7.0*	*6.7*	*6.4*	*6.3*	*6.2*	*6.4*	*6.1*	*5.8*
Outpatient attendances (thousands)											
United Kingdom	..	..	..	..	..	..	366.3	377.5	401.4	399.7	375.2
Service personnel	..	..	..	..	..	..	115.4	118.4	133.0	134.3	125.0
Service dependants	..	..	..	..	..	..	71.0	69.3	67.9	65.1	59.7
NHS/others	..	..	..	..	..	..	179.9	189.8	200.5	200.2	190.5
Overseas	..	..	..	..	..	..	235.9	223.1	229.0	232.1	235.4
UK Service personnel	..	..	..	..	..	..	62.5	60.5	65.5	68.7	71.2
Service dependants	..	..	..	..	..	..	101.6	96.5	111.8	111.5	113.1
Others	..	..	..	..	..	..	71.8	66.1	51.7	51.9	51.2

1. Up to 1980, these are the numbers of approved beds. From 1981 they are the numbers of available beds.
2. Based on the numbers of beds as defined above.

3. Figures of admissions to Royal Navy hospitals are not comprehensive for 1973.

Source Ministry of Defence

7.10 Strength of uniformed medical staff[1]
At 1 April

Number

	1974	1975	1976	1977	1978	1979	1980	1981	1982	1983	1984
Qualified doctors: total	1 353	1 308	1 288	1 254	1 243	1 181	1 176	1 185	1 180	1 165	1 171
Royal Navy	311	298	291	283	286	282	272	290	295	285	289
Army	551	542	550	539	544	504	496	507	493	507	515
Royal Air Force	491	468	447	432	413	395	408	388	392	373	367
Qualified dentists: total	402	398	392	384	371	366	376	380	399	406	399
Royal Navy	99	93	93	93	90	91	95	98	101	101	92
Army	184	181	180	181	171	172	173	173	182	197	197
Royal Air Force	119	124	119	110	110	103	108	109	116	108	110
Nursing services:[2] total	2 882	2 790	2 654	2 772	2 719	2 686	2 917	3 012	2 976	2 963	2 928
QARNNS[3]	624	638	597	607	581	568	586	591	596	563	533
QARANC[4]	1 465	1 436	1 406	1 483	1 463	1 418	1 402	1 567	1 637	1 682	1 755
PMRAFNS[5]	793	716	651	682	675	700	929	854	743	718	640
Medical and dental support staff: total	6 644	6 593	6 156	5 991	5 870	5 807	5 575	5 655	5 808	5 879	5 989
Royal Navy	1 426	1 427	1 223	1 245	1 243	1 295	1 253	1 227	1 317	1 280	1 214
Army	3 363	3 355	3 188	3 158	3 108	3 002	2 893	2 982	3 051	3 177	3 334
Royal Air Force	1 855	1 811	1 745	1 588	1 519	1 510	1 429	1 446	1 440	1 422	1 441

1. Includes staff employed at units (including ships) and in hospitals.
2. Including trained personnel, and personnel undertaking 'on-the-job' training and held against established posts.
3. Queen Alexandra's Royal Naval Nursing Service. Includes male nurses from 1983.

4. Queen Alexandra's Royal Army Nursing Corps.
5. Princess Mary's Royal Air Force Nursing Service. Includes male nurses from 1980.

Source Ministry of Defence

7.11 Sickness, medical discharges and deaths of United Kingdom Service personnel[1]

	Code numbers[2]	1973	1974	1975	1976	1977	1978	1979	1980	1981	1982	1983[3]
Average strength: (Thousands)		356.8	341.6	334.5	333.1	327.1	319.3	316.1	325.2	333.8	325.0	322.4
Male		342.2	327.2	320.0	318.5	312.6	304.5	300.6	308.7	317.1	309.5	306.7
Female		14.6	14.4	14.5	14.6	14.5	14.8	15.5	16.5	16.7	15.5	15.7
Number of cases of sickness[4]												
All causes		70 172	65 181	61 915	66 448	55 944	58 199	55 184	55 070	53 186	52 349	51 367
Male		64 972	60 078	56 848	60 827	51 292	53 101	50 033	50 038	48 489	48 058	47 128
Female		5 200	5 103	5 067	5 621	4 652	5 098	5 151	5 032	4 697	4 291	4 239
All diseases	001 – 799	55 127	50 904	47 682	52 148	42 123	45 516	42 931	42 539	40 798	39 393	39 795
Infective and parasitic diseases	001 – 139	6 597	5 198	5 080	5 736	4 755	5 273	4 041	3 782	3 307	2 954	3 230
Neoplasms	140 – 239	830	760	656	773	672	608	566	501	543	604	638
Endocrine, nutritional and metabolic	240 – 279	591	562	534	520	475	397	371	391	464	406	390
Diseases of blood and blood forming organs	280 – 289	185	120	128	127	115	114	116	117	76	90	87
Mental disorders	290 – 319	2 173	2 145	1 813	1 698	1 464	1 276	1 440	1 457	1 307	1 108	1 157
Diseases of the nervous system and sense organs	320 – 389	1 727	1 623	1 457	1 444	1 252	1 237	1 266	1 221	1 181	1 113	1 113
Diseases of the circulatory system	390 – 459	2 257	2 187	1 947	2 890	1 828	1 770	1 682	1 661	1 416	1 505	1 631
Diseases of the respiratory system	460 – 519	16 529	15 090	14 031	17 285	11 273	14 862	12 185	11 683	10 007	9 560	8 930
Diseases of the digestive system	520 – 579	8 380	7 891	7 353	7 208	6 558	6 221	7 513	7 942	8 073	7 829	7 636
Diseases of the genito-urinary system	580 – 629	2 414	2 324	2 254	2 142	2 006	1 979	2 270	2 231	2 339	2 394	2 477
Complications of pregnancy, childbirth and the puerperium	630 – 676	129	117	111	120	143	162	185	215	267	207	152
Diseases of skin and subcutaneous tissue	680 – 709	3 003	2 733	2 456	2 524	2 340	2 256	2 151	2 242	2 250	2 144	2 052
Diseases of the musculoskeletal system and connective tissue	710 – 739	5 549	5 578	5 472	5 522	5 509	5 561	6 031	6 097	6 728	6 962	7 633
Congenital anomalies	740 – 759	332	359	342	295	310	342	311	320	366	265	280
Symptoms and ill-defined conditions	780 – 799	4 431	4 217	4 048	3 864	3 423	3 458	2 803	2 679	2 474	2 252	2 389
All injuries	800 – 999	12 936	11 731	11 467	11 443	11 112	9 979	9 822	10 303	10 097	10 670	9 439
Aircraft accident injuries[5]		218	144	164	155	144	142	160	114	127	119	133
Training and exercise injuries		615	487	521	521	491	491	695	956	1 104	930	1 256
Road traffic accident injuries[5]		2 430	1 986	1 732	1 840	1 775	1 601	1 594	1 770	1 735	1 691	1 317
Other injuries[5]		9 673	9 114	9 050	8 927	8 702	7 745	7 373	7 463	7 131	7 930	6 733
Supplementary classifications[6]	V01 – V82	2 109	2 546	2 766	2 857	2 709	2 704	2 431	2 228	2 291	2 286	2 133
Number of medical discharges												
All causes		2 796	2 571	1 822	1 749	1 691	1 632	1 386	1 004	877	799	796
Male		2 680	2 464	1 746	1 694	1 630	1 575	1 334	956	830	771	763
Female		116	107	76	55	61	57	52	48	47	28	33
All diseases	001 – 799	2 524	2 288	1 537	1 487	1 411	1 363	1 187	840	734	676	632
Mental disorders	290 – 319	987	812	443	374	345	191	174	158	125	106	113
Diseases of the nervous system and sense organs	320 – 389	360	318	249	281	264	273	272	197	175	150	156
Diseases of the musculoskeletal system	710 – 739	337	385	327	320	345	411	349	218	194	222	162
Other diseases	001 – 799 nes	840	773	518	512	457	488	392	267	240	198	201
All injuries	800 – 999	272	283	285	262	280	269	199	164	143	123	164
Number of deaths												
All causes		533	424	422	413	412	393	384	365	368	596	349
Male		522	419	414	405	404	387	378	362	362	592	345
Female		11	5	8	8	8	6	6	3	6	4	4
All diseases	001 – 799	160	156	181	169	165	125	133	118	136	119	129
Neoplasms	140 – 239	64	50	74	54	62	43	50	44	54	48	49
Heart and cerebrovascular diseases	390 – 438	68	75	80	83	75	57	59	56	65	56	63
Other diseases	001 – 799 nes	28	31	27	32	28	25	24	18	17	15	17
All injuries	800 – 999	373	268	241	244	247	268	251	247	232	477	220
Road traffic accident injuries		179	126	116	119	142	135	132	142	130	115	115
Other injuries		194	142	125	125	105	133	119	105	102	362	105

1. Regular Service personnel only. Includes all deaths whether occurring on or off duty.
2. Code numbers refer to the Ninth Revision (1979) of the *International Statistical Classification of Diseases, Injuries and Causes of Death*. Prior to 1979 the Eighth Edition (1967) was used and this may mean that some groups of diseases are not exactly comparable, the changes however are small.
3. Figures for the latest year are provisional.
4. Based upon spells of off-duty sickness lasting 2 days or more terminating during the year except for the Army, where the coverage is for admissions to medical units for 2 days or more.
5. Where an injury could be classified under more than one cause it is shown under the first listed cause.
6. Used where no classifiable diagnosis is reported or where the person is not sick, e.g. admissions for investigation, preventive measures or elective surgery.

Source Ministry of Defence

7.12 Search and rescue operations at home

Number

	1973	1974	1975	1976	1977	1978	1979	1980	1981	1982	1983
Incidents: total	816	1 028	1 245	1 316	1 206	1 373	1 268	1 070	1 097	1 116	1 146
Call outs[1]											
of helicopters[2]	768	1 147	1 345	1 535	1 206	1 317	1 309	1 082	1 165	1 169	1 222
of other aircraft	70	50	49	58	67	113	98	68	58	59	73
of marine craft[3]	14	7	4	7	7	11	2	9	6	3	2
of mountain rescue teams[3]	45	48	49	45	47	60	55	45	43	58	46
Persons assisted[4]**: total**	474	662	732	659	713	1 030	986	856	858	906	969
by helicopters	453	625	712	648	692	945	974	834	839	842	950
by marine craft[3]	6	7	–	–	3	6	–	1	–	1	1
by mountain rescue teams[3]	15	30	20	11	18	79	12	21	19	63	18

1. More than one element of the Search and Rescue services may be called out
   to a reported incident.
2. Prior to 1977 these figures are estimated numbers of journeys based on the
   reported flying hours and the average flight length.
3. Royal Air Force only.
4. Figures for persons assisted relate only to number of persons who were
   actually removed (alive) from a hazard or who were assisted in an urgent
   medical incident.

Source Ministry of Defence

7.13 Defence services and the civilian community

	1974	1975	1976	1977	1978	1979	1980	1981	1982	1983
Military aid to civil ministries during industrial disputes										
(Manweeks of Service personnel deployed)[1]	–	–	–	180 000	1 550	–	17 000	3	305	–
Fishery protection										
Vessels boarded[2]	..	..	..	1 702	1 637	1 563	1 508	1 548	1 869	2 102
Hydrographic services										
New charts produced	..	189	212	203	207	236	226	143	163	226
New editions of charts	..	174	193	250	289	353	254	300	372	277
Charts printed (millions)[3]	3.3	3.9	3.9	4.3	3.5	3.5	3.5	3.6	3.5	2.8
Meteorological services[1]										
For aviation (UK only)										
Meteorological briefings (thousands)	353	361	362	360	374	368	370	373	353	325
Forecasts (thousands)	1 738	1 811	1 868	1 956	2 131	2 124	1 761	1 704	1 795	1 940
For other than aviation										
Forecast inquiries answered (thousands)	1 851	1 847	1 897	2 051	2 222	2 253	2 008	2 008	1 794	1 715
Automatic telephone weather service (millions of calls)	16.4	16.8	16.9	21.5	29.0	25.6	26.4	30.6	24.6	25.1
Local radio stations for which Meteorological Office staff broadcast	12	13	12	16	18	19	22	24	30	41

1. Data relates to financial years (1 April – 31 March) commencing in the year
   shown.
2. Boardings by RN Fishery Protection Squadron only.
3. The figure for 1974 relates to the financial year ending 31 March 1975.

Sources Ministry of Defence; Ministry of Agriculture, Fisheries & Food

8 Production

Censuses of Production (*Table 8.1*)

The Census of Production provides summary information about the structure of industry in the United Kingdom. The results meet a wide range of needs for government, economic analysts and the business community at large. In official statistics the censuses are an important source for the national accounts and input-output tables, but they also provide weights for use in compiling the indexes of production and wholesale prices. Census results also enable the United Kingdom to meet the statistical requirements of the European Community.

In 1970 the earlier series of quinquennial censuses was replaced by a new system of production statistics. This took the form of a simplified annual census supplemented by a quarterly inquiry into manufacturing sales and an occasional purchases inquiry. During its early years the annual census covered in general all establishments with 25 or more employees, but this was reduced to 20 employees for the 1973 and subsequent censuses. For the 1978 and 1979 Censuses in 68 selected manufacturing industries, coverage of establishments in the 20 to 49 employment size band has been reduced to a 1 in 2 sample. A still wider use of sampling has been applied for most industries in the 1980 and subsequent censuses, with a 1 in 4 selection in the 20 to 49 employment size band and a 1 in 2 selection for the 50 to 99 employment size band. For industries with fewer records in the sample size bands, all establishments employing 20 or more receive a form.

Currently census results are published in the *Business Monitor* series and appear as 110 individual industry reports and a summary volume.

Index of output of the production industries – selected component indicators (*Table 8.2*)

Table 8.2 shows selected component series of the index of output of the production industries (see Table 14.6 and paragraphs 11 to 16 on pages 224/245). However, these component series do not include adjustments to correct mixed sales and production data to true production index numbers (see paragraph 13 on page 244) because they are at a too disaggregated level: consequently, they are not strictly comparable with index of output of the production industries aggregates shown in Table 14.6.

The weight shown against each component industry is proportional to its contribution to gross domestic product at factor cost in 1980, expressed as parts per thousand of the index of output of the production industries (revised definition comprising energy and water supply and manufacturing), which is shown in Table 14.6.

The coverage of the component series is in accordance with the *Standard Industrial Classification Revised 1980* (HMSO) to which reference should be made for details of the composition of each SIC(80) industrial Group.

8.1 Censuses of production: summary table
Standard Industrial Classification Revised 1980

	Estimates for all firms							
	Gross output (production)[1]	Gross value added	Stocks and work in progress		Capital expenditure *less* disposals	Wages and salaries	Average number of persons employed[2]	Gross value added per person employed
			At end of year	Change during year				
	£ million						Thousands	£
Production and construction								
Divisions 1 – 5[3]								
1979	204 038	72 655	..	5 736	10 038	39 657	8 899	8 165
1980	222 221	78 351	..	1 556	10 320	45 840	8 453	9 269
1981	225 386	79 819	..	..	9 720	47 205	7 603	10 498
1982	241 903	84 613	..	..	10 491	48 876	7 129	11 869
Production industries (Revised definition)								
Divisions 1 – 4[3]								
1979	180 635	64 200	38 709	5 661	9 327	33 782	7 562	8 490
1980	195 258	68 207	41 532	1 528	9 794	38 536	7 147	9 544
1981	199 419	70 312	42 802	1 768	9 201	39 025	6 406	10 975
1982	212 640	74 329	43 192	936	9 876	40 154	5 971	12 449
Manufacturing (Revised definition)								
Divisions 2 – 4								
1979	155 365	54 160	35 029	4 579	6 750	30 198	6 910	7 838
1980	163 913	57 131	36 599	573	6 507	34 154	6 495	8 796
1981	165 471	57 935	37 501	1 260	5 493	34 191	5 778	10 027
1982	175 657	60 799	37 521	229	5 514	35 050	5 360	11 342
Energy and water supply industries								
Division 1[3,4]								
1979	25 271	10 039	3 680	1 082	2 577	3 584	652	15 392
1980	31 345	11 076	4 933	955	3 287	4 381	652	16 999
1981	33 948	12 376	5 301	508	3 708	4 834	629	19 688
1982	36 983	13 530	5 671	706	4 362	5 103	610	22 178
Coal extraction, coke ovens and manufacture of solid fuels								
Classes 11 and 12								
1979	3 826	2 573	622	− 12	588	1 546	292	8 803
1980	4 578	3 166	906	284	709	1 847	289	10 936
1981	4 748	3 326	984	95	699	1 964	274	12 159
1982	4 958	3 398	1 012	25	730	2 018	262	12 988

See footnotes on page 146.

8.1
Censuses of production: summary table
Standard Industrial Classification Revised 1980
(continued)

	Estimates for all firms							
	Gross output (production)[1]	Gross value added	Stocks and work in progress		Capital expenditure *less* disposals	Wages and salaries	Average number of persons employed[2]	Gross value added per person employed
			At end of year	Change during year				
	£ million						Thousands	£
Extraction of mineral oil and natural gas								
Class 13[5]								
1979	6 458	5 729	..	64	2 057	130	16	353 660
1980	9 874	8 809	..	113	2 393	181	19	468 559
1981	13 621	12 068	..	68	2 882	238	20	597 431
1982	15 959	13 808	..	121	3 081	284	22	627 623
Mineral oil processing								
Class 14								
1979	9 945	2 348	1 561	681	298	152	24	97 273
1980	12 672	2 017	2 022	364	369	190	24	82 900
1981	12 874	1 772	1 985	87	412	204	23	75 584
1982	13 850	1 401	1 771	− 250	239	206	21	67 248
Other energy and water supply								
Classes 15 to 17[4]								
1979	11 500	5 119	1 498	413	1 691	1 887	336	15 242
1980	14 095	5 894	2 006	307	2 209	2 344	338	17 449
1981	16 326	7 279	2 332	325	2 597	2 666	332	21 947
1982	18 176	8 732	2 888	931	3 393	2 880	328	26 649
Extraction of minerals and ores other than fuels; manufacture of metals, mineral products and chemicals								
Division 2								
1979	34 091	10 403	6 832	1 069	2 028	5 198	1 046	9 950
1980	34 668	10 341	6 479	− 405	1 849	5 729	951	10 878
1981	34 920	10 565	6 508	133	1 459	5 637	823	12 831
1982	36 348	10 838	6 294	− 169	1 396	5 679	757	14 325
Extraction and preparation of metalliferous ores								
Class 21								
1979	26	15	4	−	4	9	2	9 857
1980	22	13	4	−	−	10	1	9 231
1981	21	12	3	− 1	1	9	1	8 866
1982	24	14	9	− 2	1	10	1	11 619
Metal manufacturing								
Class 22								
1979	10 430	2 305	2 646	276	497	1 703	347	6 635
1980	10 238	2 008	2 274	− 376	346	1 772	292	6 876
1981	9 751	2 167	2 214	− 2	292	1 655	238	9 086
1982	9 505	1 950	1 924	− 289	226	1 547	207	9 437
Extraction of minerals nes								
Class 23								
1979	681	332	45	11	65	114	24	14 114
1980	798	398	63	17	53	142	23	17 249
1981	799	422	65	−	41	139	21	19 824
1982	923	486	71	1	52	149	21	23 655
Manufacture of non-metallic mineral products								
Class 24								
1979	5 833	2 537	913	152	374	1 280	279	9 100
1980	6 388	2 772	1 024	108	405	1 411	260	10 677
1981	6 235	2 623	1 031	27	268	1 364	227	11 557
1982	6 886	2 814	1 038	9	286	1 419	211	13 334
Chemical industry								
Class 25								
1979	16 246	4 967	3 059	609	1 039	1 910	362	13 715
1980	16 529	5 008	2 998	− 109	1 003	2 218	350	14 294
1981	17 473	5 196	3 077	99	837	2 330	318	16 321
1982	18 397	5 456	3 154	134	814	2 433	303	17 997
Production of man-made fibres								
Class 26								
1979	875	246	165	22	49	182	32	7 673
1980	693	142	116	− 44	41	176	24	5 875
1981	642	146	117	10	20	140	17	8 566
1982	613	118	99	− 21	17	122	14	8 421
Metal goods, engineering and vehicles industries								
Division 3								
1979	57 542	23 915	17 776	2 135	2 531	14 543	3 184	7 510
1980	61 768	25 705	19 555	1 166	2 445	16 594	3 026	8 493
1981	61 341	25 377	20 452	913	2 149	16 465	2 680	9 467
1982	65 802	26 968	20 542	131	2 091	16 831	2 468	10 927
Manufacture of metal goods nes								
Class 31								
1979	8 266	3 430	1 591	207	362	2 065	498	6 885
1980	8 452	3 429	1 562	− 65	313	2 275	467	7 336
1981	7 826	3 205	1 459	− 69	220	2 138	400	8 020
1982	8 507	3 498	1 451	− 12	209	2 214	372	9 409

See footnotes on page 146.

8.1
(continued)

Censuses of production: summary table
Standard Industrial Classification Revised 1980

	Estimates for all firms							
	Gross output (production)[1]	Gross value added	Stocks and work in progress		Capital expenditure *less* disposals	Wages and salaries	Average number of persons employed[2]	Gross value added per person employed
			At end of year	Change during year				
	£ million						Thousands	£
Mechanical engineering Class 32								
1979	18 033	7 948	5 733	545	655	4 572	967	8 216
1980	19 170	8 434	6 002	210	631	5 178	911	9 259
1981	18 601	8 143	5 969	− 10	556	5 108	808	10 079
1982	19 668	8 340	6 025	69	559	5 192	732	11 385
Electrical and electronic engineering and manufacture of office machinery and data processing equipment Classes 33 and 34								
1979	12 982	5 656	3 656	456	514	3 214	740	7 647
1980	14 526	6 486	3 975	201	531	3 720	714	9 089
1981	14 741	6 495	4 112	78	541	3 802	634	10 238
1982	16 304	7 256	4 213	157	562	3 943	593	12 241
Manufacture of motor vehicles and parts thereof Class 35								
1979	10 977	3 664	2 561	327	689	2 388	491	7 459
1980	10 443	3 319	2 418	− 189	628	2 624	449	7 396
1981	10 164	3 207	2 268	− 110	474	2 397	369	8 680
1982	10 657	3 211	2 245	− 58	468	2 318	325	9 867
Manufacture of other transport equipment Class 36								
1979	5 742	2 548	3 776	557	249	1 872	384	6 640
1980	7 395	3 218	5 045	972	282	2 294	385	8 362
1981	8 262	3 555	6 092	1 014	311	2 509	377	9 431
1982	8 556	3 722	5 998	− 64	235	2 597	356	10 462
Instrument engineering Class 37								
1979	1 542	669	459	42	62	433	104	6 422
1980	1 782	819	553	38	59	502	101	8 112
1981	1 746	772	551	9	48	511	92	8 384
1982	2 110	942	610	39	59	568	90	10 496
Other manufacturing industries Division 4								
1979	63 731	19 842	10 421	1 374	2 191	10 457	2 680	7 404
1980	67 478	21 085	10 565	− 189	2 213	11 832	2 518	8 374
1981	69 210	21 993	10 541	215	1 885	12 090	2 274	9 671
1982	73 507	22 994	10 684	268	2 027	12 539	2 136	10 765
Food, drink and tobacco manufacturing industries Classes 41/42								
1979	30 192	6 799	4 328	487	901	2 895	727	9 355
1980	32 838	7 664	4 360	134	958	3 379	701	10 927
1981	34 843	8 424	4 502	150	881	3 624	657	12 825
1982	37 425	8 958	4 677	223	1 015	3 786	626	14 299
Textile industry Class 43								
1979	5 612	1 978	1 206	100	196	1 246	368	5 375
1980	5 140	1 804	1 069	− 146	142	1 233	315	5 731
1981	4 918	1 794	1 021	− 3	113	1 157	267	6 711
1982	5 068	1 812	1 014	−	128	1 170	248	7 313
Footwear and clothing industries and manufacture of leather and leather goods Classes 44 and 45								
1979	5 383	2 130	1 177	202	111	1 234	448	4 752
1980	5 247	2 072	1 116	− 104	92	1 351	413	5 015
1981	5 070	2 050	1 088	23	83	1 328	360	5 692
1982	5 207	2 040	1 059	7	92	1 334	328	6 209

See footnotes on page 146.

Source Business Statistics Office

8.1 Censuses of production: summary table
Standard Industrial Classification Revised 1980
(continued)

	Estimates for all firms							
	Gross output (production)[1]	Gross value added	Stocks and work in progress		Capital expenditure *less* disposals	Wages and salaries	Average number of persons employed[2]	Gross value added per person employed
			At end of year	Change during year				
	£ million						Thousands	£
Timber and wooden furniture industries Class 46								
1979	4 890	1 744	932	156	175	1 003	246	7 096
1980	5 216	1 756	1 040	− 17	163	1 151	237	7 412
1981	5 190	1 761	971	− 35	108	1 159	216	8 149
1982	5 598	1 848	966	11	114	1 207	206	8 953
Manufacture of paper and paper products; printing and publishing Class 47								
1979	10 738	4 533	1 450	214	516	2 609	533	8 506
1980	11 946	5 095	1 636	− 10	556	3 099	523	9 747
1981	12 422	5 384	1 673	89	462	3 257	484	11 133
1982	13 307	5 654	1 644	− 11	424	3 438	458	12 338
Processing of rubber and plastics Class 48								
1979	5 349	2 074	890	135	249	1 157	267	7 756
1980	5 636	2 139	899	− 31	262	1 293	250	8 556
1981	5 379	2 093	863	−	201	1 250	221	9 467
1982	5 562	2 177	873	24	204	1 286	205	10 618
Other manufacturing industries Class 49								
1979	1 567	584	436	80	42	313	91	6 424
1980	1 454	556	444	− 15	41	325	79	7 040
1981	1 388	487	424	− 10	36	315	69	7 063
1982	1 340	505	452	13	49	319	64	7 949
Construction Division 5								
1979	23 403	8 456	..	75	711	5 875	1 337	6 325
1980	26 963	10 143	..	28	526	7 304	1 306	7 764
1981	25 966	9 507	..	..	519	8 180	1 196	7 946
1982	29 264	10 284	..	..	615	8 723	1 158	8 879

Source Business Statistics Office

Note: Results of the Census of Production 1954 to 1979 on earlier Standard Industrial Classifications were last published in *Annual Abstract of Statistics* No. 119 1983 edition.

1. Figures for gross output include a substantial amount of duplication represented by the total value of partly manufactured goods sold by one industrial establishment to another. The extent of duplication varies from one census industry to another.
2. The figures include working proprietors but exclude outworkers.
3. Figures for mineral oil and natural gas not included.
4. Figures for stocks and work in progress exclude water undertakings and work in progress in the gas industry.
5. Figures for stocks and work in progress exclude goods on hand for sale.

8.2 Index of output of the production industries—selected component indicators[1]

Average 1980 = 100

	Group heading[2]	1980 Weights[3]	1974[4]	1975[4]	1976[4]	1977[4]	1978	1979	1980	1981	1982	1983
Coal extraction and solid fuels manufacture	111	40	92.9	108.8	100.9	98.0	97.0	97.0	100.0	97.5	93.4	89.6
Oil and gas extraction	130	123	0.1	0.3	16.2	47.4	68.9	98.7	100.0	110.3	125.6	137.6
Mineral oil processing	140	15	124.2	104.4	111.1	109.4	110.2	113.3	100.0	93.3	93.7	95.6
Iron and steel manufacture	221	7	165.7	140.2	151.0	153.6	155.0	165.4	100.0	120.5	114.9	119.2
Steel tubes	222	3	195.4	165.4	155.1	145.5	148.8	146.7	100.0	124.0	134.8	121.7
Drawing, cold rolling/forming of steel	223	4	135.8	118.3	130.3	126.9	125.2	124.7	100.0	97.5	94.9	96.1
Non-ferrous metals	224	11	109.6	103.6	105.2	105.1	103.3	105.7	100.0	96.8	90.5	91.7
Building products	241–246	23	126.3	118.2	113.6	108.3	108.8	108.9	100.0	88.3	90.4	94.8
Glass	247	7	107.6	98.5	102.7	104.6	108.3	110.6	100.0	91.8	89.8	92.7
Basic industrial chemicals	251	24	109.3	92.8	106.5	108.4	107.7	111.3	100.0	98.5	96.3	104.0
Paints, varnishes and printing ink	255	5	93.2	90.2	98.9	104.6	106.8	109.2	100.0	98.4	98.4	101.6
Chemical products mainly for industry	256	11	89.1	85.3	93.4	101.1	104.4	109.2	100.0	99.1	97.4	102.6
Pharmaceutical products	257	16	86.8	88.4	97.2	101.7	104.7	103.9	100.0	102.7	107.1	113.3
Soap and toilet preparations	258	7	91.5	88.9	94.2	97.4	104.6	103.6	100.0	98.7	101.7	107.1
Other household and office chemicals	259	3	95.6	79.6	84.8	94.4	101.9	109.1	100.0	90.6	90.9	94.8
Metal foundries	311	10	163.9	148.2	148.8	145.0	139.3	135.6	100.0	87.2	82.9	77.8
Forgings, pressings and stampings	312	6	158.1	148.2	139.4	138.5	124.0	119.5	100.0	87.5	87.6	83.1
Hand tools and finished metal goods	316	21	118.4	110.1	116.8	125.7	120.8	116.7	100.0	93.6	98.3	105.1
Industrial plant and steel work	320	15	104.7	103.8	105.0	103.0	99.4	109.5	100.0	99.4	105.5	103.5
Machine tools and engineers' tools	322	10	132.6	131.7	112.8	112.0	112.6	106.3	100.0	72.7	68.2	65.0
Machinery for classes 25, 41 and 42[5]	324	13	112.8	113.7	116.8	118.7	112.7	109.2	100.0	94.6	94.1	87.7
Mining, construction and handling machinery	325	14	107.5	118.9	111.5	109.6	108.1	108.9	100.0	83.0	82.0	75.0
Mechanical power transmission equipment	326	6	141.0	128.8	120.9	118.7	116.0	112.6	100.0	81.0	79.3	76.3
Other machinery and mechanical equipment	328	33	115.9	111.4	107.8	110.3	108.8	105.2	100.0	87.9	87.9	80.8
Ordnance, small arms and ammunition	329	4	65.1	71.4	84.1	89.3	103.4	92.7	100.0	92.8	106.6	120.4
Computers and office machinery	330	10	53.4	57.7	58.5	66.3	77.7	93.0	100.0	85.5	96.3	146.4
Basic electrical equipment	342	14	115.3	120.1	116.0	120.7	121.5	100.5	100.0	83.3	87.5	86.6
Electrical equipment for industrial use	343	9	107.3	104.4	105.9	110.3	115.0	113.5	100.0	81.1	86.1	86.1
Telecommunication equipment etc	344	31	82.2	78.6	78.3	81.4	84.8	93.2	100.0	99.6	103.7	108.4
Motor vehicles and their engines	351	18	150.1	126.9	126.1	127.8	124.1	114.6	100.0	80.2	77.2	81.1
Motor vehicle parts	353	20	107.5	105.3	106.6	121.0	116.6	117.7	100.0	88.3	85.3	88.0
Shipbuilding and repairing	361	10	127.3	128.5	124.2	123.1	113.8	106.5	100.0	104.2	110.4	112.5
Instrument engineering	370	10	96.3	97.5	95.3	97.6	103.5	102.2	100.0	101.4	94.9	96.1
Preparation of milk and milk products	413	8	83.2	84.1	88.2	96.5	101.4	100.7	100.0	100.6	104.7	106.3
Bread, biscuits and flour confectionery	419	13	105.3	103.2	101.4	102.0	99.2	101.5	100.0	101.1	99.9	98.6
Ice cream and chocolate/sugar confectionery	421	8	106.5	95.7	104.3	104.5	109.3	106.4	100.0	97.8	105.1	107.4
Animal feeding stuffs	422	5	86.9	87.1	94.2	93.4	95.4	99.1	100.0	98.6	106.2	107.1
Miscellaneous foods	423	11	96.2	94.1	97.0	92.7	96.4	96.5	100.0	98.7	103.5	106.9
Spirits	424	5	96.4	90.4	86.7	90.3	100.1	100.8	100.0	91.5	88.3	87.5
Brewing and malting	427	12	97.4	99.8	100.9	100.8	102.9	104.1	100.0	95.6	92.5	93.3
Soft drinks	428	5	71.5	80.5	88.1	85.8	92.8	101.7	100.0	93.9	96.4	107.8
Tobacco	429	8	94.2	91.8	92.2	90.9	98.1	97.3	100.0	97.2	90.3	90.5
Woollen and worsted	431	5	139.6	123.2	123.9	128.4	124.3	115.6	100.0	90.4	86.0	87.1
Hosiery and other knitted goods	436	7	109.6	106.5	112.5	112.9	110.6	108.3	100.0	96.0	93.4	93.7
Leather and leather goods	440	3	145.5	148.6	153.8	148.1	144.8	125.3	100.0	87.2	79.7	85.9
Footwear	451	5	117.1	111.8	110.5	116.4	115.3	114.3	100.0	88.4	85.6	86.6
Clothing, hats and gloves	453	17	100.7	101.7	98.0	104.6	108.3	110.7	100.0	91.3	89.7	90.4
Timber and related industries (excluding furniture)	461–466	11	126.9	121.4	129.8	118.3	116.6	117.3	100.0	91.7	94.4	102.4
Pulp, paper and board	471–472	22	123.4	99.5	104.2	107.7	109.6	111.5	100.0	92.8	88.4	90.2
Printing and publishing	475	45	101.3	92.0	92.9	97.3	99.8	104.9	100.0	95.2	92.4	91.7
Rubber products	481	11	100.7	98.5	107.7	111.3	113.7	113.0	100.0	86.6	78.9	78.6
Processing of plastics	483	17	95.8	85.2	95.1	102.3	106.5	110.6	100.0	95.0	94.5	102.9

1. These indices are components of the index of the output of the production industries (revised definition) (see Table 14.6) *however,* they do not include an adjustment to correct mixed sales and production data to true production index numbers: consequently, they are not strictly comparable with the index of output of the production industries series. See paragraphs 11 to 16 of the notes on pages 244 and 245.
2. The Group numbers are those of the Standard Industrial Classification 1980.

3. Parts per 1 000 of the index of output of the production industries (revised definition) shown in Table 14.6.
4. Figures for years prior to 1978 have been linked to data based on minimum list headings of the Standard Industrial Classification 1968 and are therefore only approximations.
5. Machinery for food, chemical and related industries; process engineering contractors.

Source Central Statistical Office.

8.3 Total inland energy consumption
Heat supplied basis

Million therms[1]

	1973	1974	1975	1976	1977	1978	1979	1980	1981	1982	1983
Inland energy consumption of primary fuels and equivalents	88 301	83 839	80 421	81 709	83 680	84 023	87 766	81 109	78 740	77 315	77 673
Coal[2]	33 043	29 090	29 264	29 780	29 878	29 107	31 288	29 084	28 926	26 978	27 229
Petroleum[3]	41 368	38 185	34 259	33 758	34 350	35 073	35 016	30 710	28 117	28 189	27 046
Nuclear and hydro-electricity[4]	2 785	3 281	2 985	3 408	3 761	3 567	3 678	3 536	3 677	4 218	4 708
Natural gas[5]	11 105	13 283	13 913	14 763	15 691	16 276	17 784	17 779	18 020	17 930	18 690
less Energy used by fuel producers and losses in conversion and distribution	27 267	25 555	24 545	24 382	25 147	24 896	26 071	24 572	23 819	23 036	23 494
Total consumption by final users	61 034	58 284	55 876	57 327	58 533	59 127	61 695	56 537	54 921	54 279	54 179
Analysed by type of fuel											
Coal (direct use)	8 064	7 544	6 420	6 019	6 154	5 738	6 004	5 103	4 748	4 831	4 640
Coke and breeze	3 859	3 396	2 934	3 182	2 866	2 652	2 889	1 578	2 039	1 850	1 945
Other solid fuel[6]	905	856	785	703	694	652	627	597	523	512	502
Coke oven gas	512	387	412	433	401	357	388	255	264	240	252
Natural gas (direct use)[7]	10 495	11 740	12 310	13 394	14 120	15 025	16 417	16 562	16 631	16 691	16 906
Electricity	7 502	7 287	7 262	7 359	7 522	7 676	8 028	7 653	7 521	7 371	7 486
Petroleum (direct use)	29 623	27 024	25 715	26 193	26 741	26 996	27 323	24 775	23 191	22 772	22 438
Other fuels (direct use)[8]	74	50	38	44	35	31	19	14	4	12	9
Analysed by class of consumer											
Agriculture	883	747	731	695	735	732	732	594	557	558	555
Iron and steel industry	6 596	5 567	4 916	5 327	4 929	4 662	5 025	2 867	3 249	2 934	2 924
Other industries	19 195	18 224	17 037	17 500	17 886	17 711	18 145	16 263	14 893	14 502	14 019
Railways	558	529	512	491	494	504	495	485	466	420	441
Road transport	9 974	9 712	9 507	9 922	10 176	10 697	10 925	11 042	10 722	11 035	11 376
Water transport	436	496	519	526	524	518	543	501	437	472	480
Air transport	1 908	1 675	1 723	1 777	1 857	2 005	2 074	2 081	1 993	1 982	2 022
Domestic	14 917	15 086	14 713	14 543	15 045	15 359	16 501	15 816	15 750	15 569	15 494
Public administration	3 558	3 317	3 228	3 456	3 696	3 657	3 792	3 546	3 504	3 441	3 447
Miscellaneous	3 009	2 931	2 990	3 090	3 191	3 282	3 463	3 342	3 350	3 366	3 421

1. Estimates of the gross calorific values used for converting the statistics for the various fuels to therms are given in the *Digest of United Kingdom Energy Statistics 1984*.
2. Including net trade and stock change in other solid fuels.
3. Refinery throughput of crude oil, *plus* net foreign trade and stock change in petroleum products. Liquid fuels derived from coal (which are included in coal consumption) and petroleum products not used as fuels (chemical feedstock, industrial and white spirits, lubricants, bitumen and wax) are excluded.
4. The figures for nuclear and hydro-electricity represent the notional thermal input of fossil fuel that would have been needed to produce the same quantities of electricity at the efficiency of contemporary conventional steam power stations.
5. Natural gas includes both indigenous and imported natural gas and colliery methane piped to the surface and consumed at collieries or sold.
6. Including briquettes, ovoids, Phurnacite, Coalite, Rexco, etc.
7. Figures for Natural gas include Town gas. For 1983 consumption of Town gas was 18m therms. Data for consumption of Town gas in previous years may be found in earlier editions of this publication.
8. Liquid fuels derived from coal.

Source Department of Energy

8.4 Coal: supply and demand

Million tonnes

	1973	1974	1975	1976	1977	1978	1979	1980	1981	1982	1983
Supply											
Production of deep-mined coal	120.1	100.0	117.4	110.3	107.1	107.5	107.8	112.4	110.5	106.2	101.7
Production of opencast coal	10.1	9.3	10.4	11.9	13.5	14.2	12.9	15.8	14.8	15.3	14.7
Total	130.2	109.3	127.8	122.2	120.6	121.7	120.7	128.2	125.3	121.5	116.4
Recovered slurry, fines, etc.	1.8	1.2	0.9	1.6	1.5	1.9	1.7	1.9	2.2	3.2	2.8
Imports	1.6	3.5	5.0	2.8	2.4	2.4	4.4	7.3	4.3	4.1	4.4
Total	133.6	114.0	133.7	126.6	124.5	126.0	126.8	137.4	131.8	128.8	123.6
Change in colliery stocks	+0.1	−3.7	+4.9	+0.4	−1.1	+1.6	−1.9	+5.3	+4.3	+0.2	+1.2
Change in stocks at opencast sites	−0.1	−1.2	−0.3	−0.3	+0.1	+1.1	−0.8	+2.4	+0.5	−0.4	+0.8
Total supply	133.6	118.9	129.1	126.5	125.5	123.3	129.5	129.7	127.0	129.0	121.6
Home consumption											
Electricity supply industry[1]	76.8	67.0	74.6	77.8	80.0	80.6	88.8	89.6	87.2	80.2	81.6
Gas supply industry	0.5	0.1	–	–	–	–	–	–	–	–	–
Coke ovens	21.9	18.5	19.1	19.4	17.4	15.0	15.1	11.6	10.8	10.4	10.4
Low temperature carbonization plants	2.2	2.6	2.5	2.0	2.0	1.9	1.7	1.9	1.4	1.3	1.2
Manufactured fuel plants	1.4	1.1	1.5	1.4	1.2	1.2	1.2	1.1	1.1	1.1	0.9
Railways	0.1	0.1	0.1	0.1	0.1	0.1	0.1	0.1	0.1	0.1	–
Collieries	1.4	1.3	1.2	1.1	1.1	1.0	0.8	0.7	0.6	0.5	0.5
Industry:											
Iron and steel	0.4	0.4	0.3	0.3	0.2	0.2	0.3	0.2	0.2	0.1	0.1
Other industries[2]	11.7	10.7	9.4	8.7	8.8	8.4	8.9	7.6	6.8	7.0	7.1
Agriculture	0.1	0.1	–	–	–	–	–	–	–	–	–
Domestic:											
House coal[3]	10.4	9.9	7.9	7.5	7.8	6.9	7.1	5.5	5.2	5.1	4.8
Anthracite and dry steam coal[3, 4]	1.8	1.7	1.7	1.4	1.5	1.5	1.6	1.7	1.6	1.8	1.7
Miners' coal	2.3	2.1	2.0	1.9	1.9	1.8	1.8	1.7	1.6	1.6	1.5
Public services	2.0	1.9	1.5	1.7	1.7	1.6	1.7	1.5	1.4	1.4	1.4
Miscellaneous	0.3	0.4	0.4	0.3	0.3	0.3	0.3	0.3	0.4	0.4	0.4
Total home consumption	133.3	117.9	122.2	123.6	124.0	120.5	129.4	123.5	118.4	111.0	111.5
Overseas shipments and bunkers	2.7	1.6	1.9	1.2	1.8	2.3	2.2	3.8	9.1	7.4	6.6
Total consumption and shipments	136.0	119.5	124.1	124.8	125.8	122.8	131.6	127.3	127.5	118.4	118.0
Change in distributed stocks[5]	−2.3	−1.2	+4.7	+1.9	−0.7	+0.3	−2.5	+2.1	−0.2	+10.3	+3.5
Balance[6]	−0.1	+0.6	+0.3	−0.2	+0.4	+0.2	+0.4	+0.3	−0.3	+0.3	–
Stocks at end of year[7]											
Distributed[5]	17.0	15.8	20.5	22.4	21.7	22.0	18.2	20.4	20.2	30.4	34.0
At collieries	7.7	4.0	8.9	9.3	8.2	9.9	7.8	13.1	17.4	17.7	18.9
At opencast sites	3.2	2.0	1.7	1.4	1.5	2.6	1.8	4.2	4.7	4.3	5.1
Total stocks	27.9	21.8	31.1	33.1	31.4	34.5	27.8	37.7	42.3	52.4	58.0

TIME SERIES. Figures relate to periods of 52 weeks.

1. Includes quantities used in the production of steam for sale.
2. From October 1973 the figures relate to colliery and opencast disposals to industry.
3. From April 1973 the figures relate to colliery and opencast disposals for the domestic market.
4. Including disposals of imports.
5. Great Britain. Stock change in 1973 and thereafter excludes industrial and domestic stocks.
6. This is the balance between supply and consumption, shipments and changes in known distributed stocks.
7. Stock change in 1973 is calculated on stocks at 30 December 1972. Figures for stocks at end of year for 1978 relate to position at 23 December. Stock change in 1979 is calculated on stocks at 30 December 1978. Figures for stocks at end of year for 1983 relate to position at 24 December.

Source Department of Energy

8.5 Coal: production[1]
Great Britain
Years ended March

Million tonnes

	1973/74[2]	1974/75	1975/76	1976/77	1977/78	1978/79	1979/80[3]	1980/81[3]	1981/82[3]	1982/83[3]	1983/84[3][4][5]
Total—Saleable mined coal	98.68	116.84	114.45	108.43	106.24	105.38	108.64	109.56	108.20	104.26	89.49
Scottish	8.96	10.12	9.82	9.15	8.41	8.09	8.03	7.74	7.22	6.62	5.27
North East	13.75	14.79	14.58	13.12	12.76	12.93	13.98	14.09	13.41	12.42	10.91
North Yorkshire	7.34	8.41	8.45	8.20	8.16	8.20	8.15	8.50	8.26	8.39	7.55
Doncaster	6.65	8.44	8.01	7.87	7.49	6.96	7.49	7.16	7.12	6.78	5.82
Barnsley	6.19	7.75	7.51	7.30	7.55	7.39	8.00	8.32	8.40	8.13	6.20
South Yorkshire	7.69	8.27	7.95	7.79	7.65	7.59	7.56	7.38	7.23	7.33	6.57
North Derbyshire	6.41	7.85	7.90	7.34	7.42	7.38	7.65	8.26	8.48	8.15	6.29
North Nottingham	9.18	11.01	10.76	10.65	11.08	11.01	11.86	11.97	12.26	12.36	11.60
South Nottingham	7.95	9.86	9.80	9.06	8.95	8.60	8.65	8.83	8.54	8.25	6.97
South Midlands	6.88	8.76	9.09	8.83	8.54	8.54	8.54	8.45	8.64	8.17	6.65
Western	10.20	12.78	12.12	11.34	10.77	10.94	11.10	11.19	11.08	10.78	9.08
South Wales	7.48	8.80	8.46	7.78	7.46	7.75	7.63	7.67	7.56	6.88	6.58

TIME SERIES. Figures relate to periods of 52 weeks.

1. Collieries operated by the National Coal Board. Excludes coal extracted in work on capital account (0.68 million tonnes in 1982/83).
2. Production was affected by a miners' strike in February/March 1974.

3. See footnote 2 to table 8.7.
4. Partly estimated.
5. Production was affected by a national overtime ban from 1st November 1983 and by wider industrial action from 12th March 1984.

Source Department of Energy

8.6 Coal: average number of wage-earners on colliery books[1]
Great Britain
Years ended March

Thousands

	1973/74	1974/75	1975/76	1976/77	1977/78	1978/79	1979/80	1980/81	1981/82	1982/83	1983/84
Total	252.0	246.0	247.1	242.0	240.5	234.9	232.5	229.8	218.5	207.7	191.5
Scottish	25.2	24.4	24.2	23.1	22.1	21.1	21.0	20.5	18.3	16.9	14.5
North East	40.6	37.7	36.6	35.4	34.9	34.4	33.5	32.9	30.4	27.6	24.5
North Yorkshire	15.1	14.9	15.4	15.3	15.5	15.6	15.8	15.4	14.8	14.4	13.6
Doncaster	16.5	16.8	17.2	17.1	17.2	16.6	16.7	16.7	15.9	15.0	13.9
Barnsley	16.4	16.6	16.7	16.5	16.6	15.9	15.8	15.6	15.1	15.0	14.3
South Yorkshire	18.2	17.9	18.0	17.8	17.8	17.3	17.1	16.9	16.3	15.5	14.7
North Derbyshire	13.2	12.6	12.6	12.4	12.5	12.3	12.1	12.3	12.0	11.8	11.1
North Nottingham	17.6	17.4	17.7	17.6	17.8	18.0	18.1	18.4	18.1	17.8	17.1
South Nottingham	15.4	15.4	15.8	15.7	16.1	15.9	15.9	15.8	15.3	14.8	13.7
South Midlands	14.7	15.1	16.1	16.0	16.2	16.2	16.5	16.8	16.1	15.2	13.6
Western	26.8	25.8	25.7	25.0	24.3	23.6	23.0	22.7	21.5	20.3	19.1
South Wales	32.3	31.4	31.1	30.1	29.5	28.0	27.0	25.8	24.8	23.4	21.5

1. Collieries operated by the National Coal Board.

Source Department of Energy

8.7 Coal: output per manshift[1]
Great Britain
Years ended March

Tonnes

	1973/74	1974/75	1975/76	1976/77	1977/78	1978/79	1979/80[2]	1980/81[2]	1981/82[2]	1982/83[2]	1983/84[2][3]
Total	2.15	2.29	2.28	2.21	2.19	2.24	2.31	2.32	2.40	2.44	2.43
Scottish	1.97	2.01	2.00	1.96	1.91	1.96	1.98	1.92	2.00	1.97	1.95
North East	1.83	1.90	1.96	1.85	1.83	1.86	2.07	2.07	2.07	2.09	2.23
North Yorkshire	2.69	2.64	2.63	2.57	2.56	2.57	2.50	2.68	2.80	3.01	3.11
Doncaster	2.41	2.58	2.46	2.45	2.30	2.27	2.29	2.18	2.27	2.30	2.31
Barnsley	2.15	2.34	2.29	2.26	2.31	2.44	2.56	2.62	2.71	2.64	2.36
South Yorkshire	2.40	2.27	2.21	2.19	2.17	2.25	2.24	2.17	2.22	2.35	2.47
North Derbyshire	2.67	2.95	3.01	2.82	2.84	2.90	2.99	3.21	3.33	3.30	2.90
North Nottingham	2.79	2.98	2.91	2.89	2.96	2.92	3.08	3.04	3.17	3.25	3.35
South Nottingham	2.72	2.93	2.94	2.75	2.67	2.60	2.64	2.68	2.68	2.69	2.55
South Midlands	2.45	2.65	2.62	2.60	2.47	2.50	2.45	2.36	2.52	2.51	2.41
Western	2.03	2.35	2.27	2.18	2.14	2.24	2.35	2.35	2.45	2.53	2.44
South Wales	1.28	1.35	1.37	1.32	1.29	1.41	1.40	1.46	1.47	1.47	1.57

1. Collieries operated by the National Coal Board.
2. From April 1980 the National Coal Board have reclassified certain drivages from revenue account (on which the calculation of output per manshift is based) to capital account. The figures for 1979/80 have been adjusted to this new basis. Figures on this basis prior to 1979/80 are not available.

3. Partly estimated.

Source Department of Energy

8.8 Fuel input and gas output; gas sales
Public supply

	1973	1974	1975	1976	1977	1978	1979	1980	1981	1982	1983
Fuel input to gas industry:	million tonnes										
Coal	0.5	0.1	–	–	–	–	–	–	–	–	–
Petroleum	1.8	1.0	0.5	0.2	0.1	0.1	0.1	0.1	0.1	0.1	0.1
	million therms										
Petroleum gases[1]	267	116	51	31	37	86	80	79	71	52	33
Natural gas	1 662	1 219	708	181	53	8	–	–	–	–	–
Coke oven gas	54	30	10	9	–	–	–	–	–	–	–
Total to gas works	2 934	1 866	991	307	137	145	114	106	100	85	61
Natural gas for direct supply	9 197	11 863	13 080	14 264	15 287	15 777	17 238	17 012	17 044	16 667	17 153
Total fuel input	12 131	13 729	14 071	14 571	15 424	15 922	17 352	17 118	17 144	16 752	17 214
Fuel input to gas industry	million tonnes of coal or coal equivalent										
Coal	0.5	0.1	–	–	–	–	–	–	–	–	–
Petroleum	3.0	1.8	0.8	0.3	0.2	0.2	0.1	0.1	0.1	0.1	0.1
Petroleum gases[1]	1.0	0.4	0.2	0.1	0.1	0.3	0.3	0.3	0.2	0.2	0.1
Natural gas	6.6	4.8	2.8	0.8	0.2	–	–	–	–	–	–
Coke oven gas	0.3	0.2	0.1	–	–	–	–	–	–	–	–
Total to gas works	11.4	7.3	3.9	1.2	0.5	0.5	0.4	0.4	0.3	0.3	0.2
Natural gas for direct supply	36.6	47.3	52.1	56.8	61.1	63.1	68.9	68.0	68.2	66.7	68.6
Total fuel input	48.0	54.6	56.0	58.0	61.6	63.6	69.3	68.4	68.5	67.0	68.8
Gas output and sales	million therms										
Gas output:											
Town gas	2 711	1 782	952	279	101	55	40	35	31	26	23
Natural gas supplied direcct[2]	9 197	11 863	13 081	14 273	15 309	15 858	17 303	17 076	17 108	16 719	17 186
Gross total available	11 908	13 645	14 033	14 552	15 410	15 913	17 343	17 111	17 139	16 745	17 209
Own use[3]	73	87	85	94	99	106	128	134	139	126	121
Statistical difference[4]	– 1 106	– 890	– 836	– 461	– 732	– 499	– 624	– 347	– 378	+ 38	– 244
Total sales	10 729	12 668	13 112	13 997	14 579	15 308	16 591	16 630	16 622	16 657	16 844
Analysis of gas sales											
Power stations	285	985	858	662	519	338	239	140	78	76	77
Final users:											
Iron and steel industry	396	395	371	438	485	446	538	451	409	365	342
Other industries	4 150	4 635	4 645	5 182	5 398	5 519	5 622	5 539	5 261	5 319	5 295
Domestic	4 815	5 384	5 891	6 194	6 590	7 261	8 225	8 439	8 764	8 719	8 871
Public Administration	512	540	597	687	746	814	908	948	966	1 003	1 050
Miscellaneous	571	729	750	834	841	930	1 059	1 113	1 144	1 175	1 210
Total final users	10 444	11 683	12 254	13 335	14 060	14 970	16 352	16 490	16 544	15 681	16 768
Total sales	10 729	12 668	13 112	13 997	14 579	15 308	16 591	16 630	16 622	16 657	16 844

1. Butane, propane, ethane and refinery tail gases.
2. Including substitute natural gas.
3. Used in works, offices, showrooms, etc.
4. Supply greater than recorded demand (–). Includes losses in distribution.

Source Department of Energy

8.9 Electricity: production and fuel used[1]

	1973	1974	1975	1976	1977	1978	1979	1980	1981	1982	1983
	GWh										
Electricity generated: total	259 503	251 115	251 952	255 610	262 746	267 491	280 177	267 087	260 422	256 090	261 082
England and Wales	225 237	218 848	219 249	222 124	226 994	231 411	242 127	230 940	224 315	220 505	226 324
South of Scotland Electricity Board	22 912	21 072	22 313	23 176	25 316	25 577	26 907	25 565	25 331	23 276	20 332
North of Scotland Hydro-Electric Board	5 165	5 340	4 514	4 269	4 243	4 176	4 471	4 205	4 640	6 312	8 395
Northern Ireland	5 486	5 206	5 187	5 351	5 492	5 627	5 977	5 673	5 445	5 346	5 384
Railway and transport authorities	703	649	689	690	701	700	695	704	691	651	647
Method of generation											
Steam plant (nuclear): total	23 658	29 395	26 518	32 419	36 417	33 339	34 604	33 462	34 043	40 001	45 776
England and Wales	21 416	26 928	23 940	28 298	30 703	28 459	29 669	26 552	26 706	30 970	35 534
South of Scotland Electricity Board	2 242	2 467	2 578	4 121	5 714	4 880	4 935	6 910	7 337	9 031	10 242
Steam plant (other): total	230 595	216 350	220 301	218 185	220 622	228 762	239 875	228 577	220 849	210 545	209 116
England and Wales	202 177	190 428	194 333	193 111	195 094	202 079	211 538	203 714	196 847	188 768	189 422
South of Scotland Electricity Board	20 408	18 293	19 484	18 779	19 253	20 398	21 657	18 309	17 663	13 896	9 811
North of Scotland Hydro-Electric Board	1 840	1 802	702	281	217	156	200	291	321	1 956	3 907
Northern Ireland	5 467	5 178	5 173	5 324	5 455	5 560	5 922	5 659	5 428	5 337	5 374
Railway and transport authorities	703	649	609	690	603	569	558	604	590	588	601
Gas turbines and oil engines: total	1 347	1 139	779	487	1 064	819	895	551	610	580	401
England and Wales	1 089	899	460	210	629	312	355	106	150	187	89
South of Scotland Electricity Board	52	16	9	8	40	6	4	2	3	7	1
North of Scotland Hydro-Electric Board	187	196	216	242	260	303	344	329	339	314	256
Northern Ireland	19	28	14	27	37	67	55	14	17	9	10
Railway and transport authorities	–	–	80	–	98	131	137	100	101	63	46
Hydro-electric plant other than pumped storage plant: total	3 235	3 534	3 201	3 138	3 330	3 388	3 628	3 309	3 917	3 884	3 892
England and Wales	188	245	172	153	223	210	243	234	258	221	217
South of Scotland Electricity Board	210	296	242	268	309	292	311	344	328	342	279
North of Scotland Hydro-Electric Board	2 837	2 993	2 787	2 717	2 798	2 886	3 074	2 731	3 331	3 321	3 397
Pumped storage plant: total	668	697	1 153	1 381	1 313	1 183	1 175	1 188	1 003	1 080	1 897
England and Wales	367	348	344	352	345	351	322	334	354	359	1 062
North of Scotland Hydro-Electric Board	301	349	809	1 029	968	832	853	854	649	721	835
	Thousand tonnes										
Fuel used											
Coal: total	76 514	66 856	74 324	77 570	79 311	80 627	88 539	89 348	87 038	79 816	81 439
England and Wales	67 941	59 397	65 471	68 817	70 343	71 928	79 562	80 546	78 439	72 833	76 314
South of Scotland Electricity Board	8 087	6 993	8 567	8 413	8 511	8 195	8 440	8 236	8 103	6 456	4 566
Northern Ireland	486	466	286	340	457	504	537	566	496	527	559
Coke and coke breeze: total	65	70	136	52	80	131	158	117	82	69	33
England and Wales	65	70	136	52	80	131	158	117	82	69	33
Oil: total	16 976	17 194	12 818	10 155	10 596	11 475	10 670	6 573	5 075	6 232	4 704
England and Wales	14 103	14 292	10 707	8 246	8 775	9 365	8 294	5 016	3 568	4 427	2 537
South of Scotland Electricity Board	1 000	1 100	448	363	456	755	925	202	150	127	75
North of Scotland Hydro-Electric Board	476	470	217	122	112	107	126	157	162	543	981
Northern Ireland	1 199	1 147	1 245	1 271	1 236	1 240	1 300	1 193	1 181	1 126	1 107
Railway and transport authorities	198	185	201	153	17	8	25	5	14	9	3
Natural gas[2]: total	1 136	3 924	3 419	2 639	2 067	1 352	955	557	313	304	311
England and Wales	1 136	3 924	3 419	2 548	1 745	1 012	644	218	–	1	1
Railway and transport authorities	–	–	–	91	322	340	311	339	313	303	309

1. Public electricity supply and railway and transport authorities.
2. Expressed in thousand tonnes of coal equivalent.

Sources   Department of Energy; Scottish Economic Planning Department;
Department of Economic Development (Northern Ireland)

8.10

Electricity: generating capacity of plant and demand[1]
Great Britain

	1973	1974	1975	1976	1977	1978	1979	1980	1981	1982	1983
Capacity of generating plant installed at end of year (Megawatt)	71 125	72 136	71 816	69 852	69 747	69 911	71 426	70 886	68 382	68 106	67 022
Simultaneous maximum load on generating stations during the year[2] (Megawatt)	44 883	46 526	46 677	47 902	48 605	50 144	49 582	48 284	48 561	47 333	47 396
Electricity generated (GWh)	253 314	245 260	246 076	249 569	256 553	261 164	273 505	260 710	254 286	250 093	255 052
Electricity supplied net (GWh)	235 222	227 459	228 372	230 743	237 341	242 723	254 232	242 377	237 045	232 817	236 296
System load factor[3] (Percentage)	56.9	56.9	56.8	55.7	56.6	56.1	59.4	58.0	56.0	57.1	58.0

1. Public supply stations only.
2. Maximum occurring near the end of the year, or early in the following year.
3. The system load factor is the average hourly quantity of electricity sent out during the year (including purchases from other sources) expressed as a percentage of the maximum potential demand nearest the end of the year or early the following year.

Source Department of Energy

8.11

Electricity: sales[1]
Great Britain

GWh

	1973	1974	1975	1976	1977	1978	1979	1980	1981	1982	1983
Total	220 591	213 902	213 499	216 282	220 904	225 346	235 644	225 053	221 621	217 096	220 352
Domestic and farm premises	93 279	94 545	90 817	86 737	87 720	87 662	91 506	87 907	86 201	84 601	84 640
Domestic and commercial[2]	2 879	2 692	2 612	2 514	2 447	2 426	2 144	2 197	2 129	2 014	1 979
Shops, offices and other commercial premises	34 894	31 778	34 859	36 294	38 685	41 183	44 114	44 539	45 359	46 134	49 019
Factories and other industrial premises	85 412	80 734	80 656	86 132	87 377	89 349	93 167	85 539	83 078	79 806	79 967
Public lighting	1 946	1 826	2 073	2 150	2 163	2 177	2 160	2 252	2 240	2 243	2 259
Traction	2 181	2 327	2 482	2 455	2 512	2 549	2 553	2 619	2 614	2 298	2 488

1. Public supply system.
2. Premises used for domestic and commercial purposes having a combined tariff.

Source Department of Energy

8.12 Indigenous production, refinery receipts, arrivals and shipments of oil[1]

Thousand tonnes

	1973	1974	1975	1976	1977	1978	1979	1980	1981	1982	1983
Total indigenous petroleum production[2]	373	410	1 567	12 171	38 265	54 006	77 854	80 468	89 481	103 218	114 917
Crude petroleum[3]:											
Refinery receipts total	114 032	113 478	92 273	98 384	92 260	96 759	98 325	87 457	76 665	76 749	76 395
Indigenous[4]	235	250	1 156	8 576	21 929	28 609	38 493	39 896	37 818	40 338	44 866
Other[5]	1 560	1 810	1 275	692	682	916	606	2 005	2 486	3 162	2 366
Net foreign arrivals[6]	112 237	111 418	89 842	89 116	69 649	67 234	59 226	45 556	36 361	33 249	29 163
Foreign trade											
Arrivals[6]	115 472	112 822	91 366	90 466	70 697	68 144	60 380	46 717	36 855	33 754	30 324
Shipments											
Indigenous	–	–	–	2 935	15 611	23 948	39 044	38 531	51 149	60 195	67 397
Other[7]	3 235	1 404	1 524	1 350	1 048	910	1 154	1 161	494	505	1 161
Petroleum products											
Foreign trade											
Arrivals[6]	18 300	14 537	12 786	10 709	13 049	11 586	12 035	9 246	9 402	12 524	9 907
Shipments[6]	17 404	14 631	13 924	15 988	14 294	13 536	13 359	14 598	12 793	13 585	14 674
Net arrivals[6]	+896	– 94	– 1 138	– 5 279	– 1 245	– 1 950	– 1 324	– 5 352	– 3 391	– 1 061	– 4 767
Bunkers[8]	5 499	4 759	3 444	3 569	2 829	2 623	2 671	2 457	2 073	2 583	2 019

1. The term indigenous is used in this table for convenience to include oil from the UK Continental Shelf as well as the small amounts produced on the mainland.
2. Crude oil *plus* condensates and petroleum gases derived at onshore treatment plants.
3. Includes process (partly refined) oils.
4. Includes condensate for distillation.
5. Mainly recycled products.

6. Foreign trade as recorded by the petroleum industry and may differ from figures published in *Overseas Trade Statistics.*.
7. Re-exports of imported crude which may include some indigenous oil in blend.
8. International marine bunkers.

Source Department of Energy

8.13 Throughput of crude and process oils and output of refined products from refineries[1]

Thousand tonnes

	1973	1974	1975	1976	1977	1978	1979	1980	1981	1982	1983
Throughput of crude and process oils	114 338	111 217	93 579	97 755	93 553	96 319	97 806	86 341	78 287	77 130	76 876
less: Refinery fuel[2]	7 053	6 946	6 031	6 313	6 176	6 352	6 490	6 265	5 445	5 549	5 297
Losses	1 331	1 211	901	1 158	1 039	811	733	849	836	834	652
Total output of refined products	105 954	103 060	86 647	90 284	86 338	89 156	90 583	79 227	72 006	70 747	70 927
Gases:											
Butane and propane	1 655	1 602	1 447	1 575	1 539	1 613	1 604	1 366	1 391	1 400	1 482
Other petroleum	394	272	151	158	142	147	168	92	75	75	56
Naphtha and other feedstock	6 607	6 448	3 968	4 583	4 488	4 626	5 242	3 541	3 406	3 492	3 550
Aviation spirit	63	14	16	26	41	37	67	60	57	44	–
Wide-cut gasoline	314	254	234	213	92	76	87	6	–	–	–
Motor spirit	14 842	14 520	13 940	15 232	14 805	15 958	16 111	16 609	17 140	19 134	21 053
Industrial and white spirits	150	150	94	109	96	81	89	73	115	115	134
Kerosene:											
Aviation turbine fuel	4 550	4 475	3 959	4 163	4 004	4 783	5 236	5 198	4 559	4 457	4 723
Burning oil	2 682	2 544	2 281	2 440	2 452	2 602	2 709	2 034	1 904	1 851	1 770
Vaporising oil	35	20	18	18	10	12	–	–	–	–	–
Gas/diesel oil	27 853	27 641	23 323	24 198	23 476	24 024	25 450	22 153	20 411	20 581	21 029
Fuel oil	42 026	40 022	32 711	32 695	30 481	30 518	28 600	23 700	19 069	15 808	13 483
Lubricating oils	1 477	1 455	1 141	1 310	1 380	1 203	1 330	1 250	1 063	990	936
Bitumen	2 225	2 129	2 099	1 897	1 882	1 886	2 065	1 928	1 735	1 862	1 798
Petroleum wax	86	99	67	81	86	91	98	86	82	71	56
Petroleum coke	995	1 415	1 198	1 586	1 364	413	452	481	505	492	499
Other products						1 086	1 275	650	494	375	358

1. Crude and process oils comprise all feedstocks, other than distillation benzines, for treatment at refinery plants. Refinery production does not cover further treatment of finished products for special grade such as in distillation plant for the preparation of industrial spirits.

2. Comprising 1 931 thousand tonnes gases, 2 516 thousand tonnes fuel oil and 850 thousand tonnes other products in 1983.

Source Department of Energy

8.14 Deliveries of petroleum products for inland consumption

Thousand tonnes

	1973	1974	1975	1976	1977	1978	1979	1980	1981	1982	1983
Total (including refinery fuel)	106 839	100 355	88 855	87 892	88 935	90 493	91 044	77 442	71 701	72 795	69 821
Total (excluding refinery fuel)	99 786	93 409	82 824	81 579	82 759	84 141	84 554	71 177	66 256	67 246	64 524
Gases:											
Butane and propane:											
For gas-works	261	72	53	46	26	28	32	31	34	39	35
Other uses	1 328	1 316	1 205	1 262	1 275	1 223	1 317	1 160	1 116	1 312	1 523
Other gases											
For gas-works	268	155	52	35	57	154	160	156	142	97	63
Other uses	–	–	–	–	–	–	–	–	–	154	307
Feedstock:											
For petroleum chemical plants	7 196	7 212	4 934	5 676	5 747	5 847	5 880	3 741	4 492	4 165	4 512
Naptha (LDF) for gasworks[1]	1 650	996	456	176	108	66	70	71	74	71	56
Aviation spirit	63	53	50	46	47	46	44	40	32	27	27
Wide-cut gasoline	72	63	32	2	6	5	3	3	2	3	2
Motor spirit: total	16 927	16 484	16 125	16 879	17 336	18 348	18 685	19 145	18 718	19 247	19 566
Dealers:											
5 star	2 669	1 998	1 572	1 338	694	161	21	–	–	–	–
4 star	8 249	9 162	9 522	10 620	12 117	14 101	14 872	15 393	15 041	15 656	16 107
3 star	2 033	1 846	1 717	1 621	1 388	1 112	859	590	410	257	166
2 star	2 996	2 579	2 384	2 400	2 220	2 052	2 023	2 181	2 286	2 483	2 431
Commercial consumers:											
5 star	148	113	93	67	50	37	5	–	–	–	–
4 star	471	448	503	525	555	601	645	706	719	616	621
3 star	94	87	93	93	99	103	101	132	118	103	99
2 star	267	251	241	215	213	181	159	143	144	132	142
Industrial and white spirits	234	207	202	188	177	195	200	170	174	175	196
Kerosene:											
Aviation turbine fuel	4 202	3 690	3 834	3 989	4 165	4 506	4 666	4 685	4 495	4 474	4 566
Burning oil	3 184	2 782	2 628	2 620	2 615	2 652	2 695	2 103	1 906	1 745	1 676
Vaporising oil	35	27	17	13	12	8	3	–	–	–	–
Gas/diesel oil:											
Derv fuel	5 658	5 518	5 414	5 594	5 711	5 875	6 057	5 854	5 549	5 731	6 192
Other	15 100	13 581	13 050	12 984	13 914	13 600	13 804	11 771	10 994	10 552	9 982
Fuel oil	39 447	36 810	30 470	27 825	27 772	28 233	27 487	19 157	15 645	16 191	12 511
Lubricating oils	1 185	1 045	992	1 010	1 029	1 021	1 030	896	837	827	818
Bitumen	2 458	2 241	2 089	1 867	1 847	1 887	1 977	1 826	1 666	1 956	1 987
Petroleum wax	76	90	64	79	74	84	79	71	64	56	57
Petroleum coke[2]	442	1 067	1 157	1 288	841	{ 115	115	100	98	128	142
Miscellaneous Products[2] }						{ 248	250	197	218	296	306

1. Including a small quantity supplied for use as fuel by other consumers.
2. Prior to 1978 estimated.

Source Department of Energy

8.15 Iron and steel
Summary of steel supplies, deliveries and stocks

Thousand tonnes

	1973	1974	1975	1976	1977	1978	1979	1980	1981	1982	1983
Total supply (ingot equivalent)	30 924	28 629	25 217	25 932	25 570	25 593	26 752	18 567	20 067	19 103	19 376
Home sources: total	27 065	23 314	19 990	20 547	20 685	20 801	21 806	12 487	15 712	14 113	14 986
Crude steel production	26 594	22 323	20 098	22 274	20 411	20 311	21 464	11 277	15 573	13 704	14 986
Re-usable material[1]	149	100	86	88	78	69	95	85	58	84	100
Producers' stock changes[2]	+322	+891	−194	−1 815	+196	+421	+247	+1 125	+81	+325	−100
Imported[3]: total	3 859	5 315	5 227	5 385	4 885	4 792	4 946	6 080	4 355	4 990	4 390
Ingots	19	18	19	8	3	7	6	7	5	2	2
Semi-finished	131	150	250	447	274	275	373	384	372	295	272
Finished	3 709	5 147	4 958	4 930	4 608	4 510	4 567	5 689	3 978	4 693	4 116
Distribution of supply (ingot equivalent)											
Exports[3]	5 604	4 323	4 152	4 687	5 597	5 569	5 802	3 443	5 170	4 470	5 130
Supply for home use	25 320	24 306	21 065	21 245	19 973	20 024	20 950	15 124	14 897	14 633	14 250
Estimated home consumption[4]	24 142	23 193	21 599	21 236	20 526	20 530	20 160	15 990	15 810	15 270	14 760
Net deliveries (actual tonnage)[5]	23 382	21 607	18 636	19 689	19 354	19 555	20 266	14 491	15 716	15 139	15 163
Exports[3]	4 030	3 116	2 985	3 517	4 243	4 216	4 399	2 601	3 779	3 361	3 925
Supply for home use	19 352	18 491	15 651	16 172	15 111	15 339	15 867	11 890	11 937	11 778	11 238
Stocks (end of period) (actual tonnage) Producers':											
Ingots and semi-finished steel	1 687	1 093	1 469	2 288	2 021	1 716	1 963	1 195	1 243	1 051	1 072
Finished steel[6]	1 600	1 392	1 229	1 894	1 960	1 901	1 879	1 655	1 560	1475	1 548
Consumers'[7]	4 440	4 960	4 525	4 373	4 147	3 814	3 640	2 870	2 330	2 104	1 740
Merchants'[7]	582	872	923	1 081	982	921	1 317	1 413	1 263	990	1 070

TIME SERIES. The figures relate to periods of 52 weeks (53 weeks in 1975 and 1981).

1. Currently mainly old rails for re-rolling.
2. Steel industry stocks of ingots, semi-finished and finished steel.
3. Based on statistics as shown in the *Overseas Trade Statistics of the United Kingdom.*
4. After allowing for changes in consumers' and merchants' stocks.
5. Finished steel, including that produced in the United Kingdom from imported ingots and semi-finished steel, and second-hand materials. Excluding deliveries of all material for conversion within the industry.
6. Excluding stocks of tubes, pipes, forgings and steel castings.
7. Finished steel produced in the United Kingdom and imported. Wire is excluded and replaced by the material for its manufacture.

Sources   Department of Trade and Industry: Iron and Steel Statistics Bureau

8.16 Iron and steel
Iron ore, manganese ore, pig iron and iron and steel scrap

Thousand tonnes

	1973	1974	1975	1976	1977	1978	1979	1980	1981	1982	1983
Iron ore											
Production: total	7 105	3 602	4 490	4 582	3 745	4 239	4 269	916	731	470	384
Jurassic	6 875	3 421	4 322	4 456	3 629	4 131	4 156	874	729	468	382
Hematite	230	181	168	126	116	108	113	42	2	2	2
Consumption: total	28 504	22 220	20 422	23 629	19 999	19 856	21 188	9 350	13 777	11 652	13 205
Home produced	7 064	3 951	4 709	4 992	3 973	4 477	4 268	875	923	527	448
Imported	21 440	18 269	15 713	18 637	16 026	15 379	16 919	8 475	12 854	11 125	12 756
Manganese ore											
Consumption	448	299	292	402	352	277	495	168	259	188	262
Pig iron (and blast furnace ferro-alloys)											
Average number of furnaces in blast during period	*45*	*40*	*35*	*36*	*32*	*29*	*26*	*9*	*11*	*11*	*11*
Production											
In blast furnaces: total	16 838	13 902	12 131	13 835	12 232	11 434	12 898	6 316	9 554	8 388	9 560
Steelmaking iron	15 830	13 075	11 265	13 123	11 533	10 942	12 432	6 099	9 395	8 279	9 400
Foundry iron	849	736	781	590	602	423	329	165	75	48	77
Spiegeleisen and ferro-manganese	159	91	85	122	97	69	137	52	84	61	83
In other processes											
Refined iron	181	213	207	189	168	167	132	97	63	53	68
Consumption of pig iron: total	16 993	13 872	12 369	13 761	12 591	11 856	13 203	6 373	9 651	8 312	9 618
In steel works and steel foundries	15 872	12 940	11 507	12 833	11 753	11 152	12 494	6 065	9 473	8 160	9 468
In iron foundries	1 121	932	862	928	838	704	709	308	178	152	150
Pig iron stocks (end of period)[1]	452	608	523	855	704	473	410	408	94	202	121
Iron and steel scrap[1]											
Receipts: total	18 939	17 565	16 308	17 555	15 427	15 185	15 369	[4]			
Bought[2]	9 388	9 540	8 737	9 465	7 559	7 911	7 928	[4]			
Circulating (arising in own works)	9 343	7 913	7 484	7 709	7 792	7 252	7 395	4 693	5 271	4 790	4 787
Imported	208	112	87	381	76	22	46	–	1	19	–
Consumption of iron and steel scrap: total	18 951	17 069	16 029	16 973	15 684	15 524	15 368	9 287	10 382	9 557	9 693
In steelworks and steel foundries	13 862	12 196	11 208	12 217	11 222	11 826	11 739	6 756	8 216	7 463	7 670
Other[3]	5 089	4 873	4 821	4 756	4 462	3 698	3 629	2 531	2 166	2 094	2 023
Stocks (end of period)	1 119	1 584	1 986	2 521	2 288	1 648	1 544	1 044	782	906	581

TIME SERIES. The figures relate to periods of 52 weeks (53 weeks in 1975 and 1981).

1. At blast furnaces, steel works, steel foundries, iron foundries and refined iron works.
2. Receipts of scrap bought in the home market and direct receipts from steel processing works.
3. At iron foundries, blast furnaces and refined iron works.
4. These figures are no longer being produced in this form.

Sources Department of Trade and Industry; Iron and Steel Statistics Bureau

8.17 Iron and steel
Number of furnaces and production of steel

	1973	1974	1975	1976	1977	1978	1979	1980	1981	1982	1983
Steel furnaces (Number in existence at end of period)[1]											
Total	546	535	535	520	512	471	431	399	400	353	286
Open hearth	107	97	86	78	63	21	2	–	–	–	–
Oxygen converters	30	25	22	23	23	21	21	16	14	14	14
Electric	391	396	407	401	408	414	396	380	384	339	272
Stock and tropenas	18	17	20	18	18	15	12	3	2	–	–
Production of crude steel (thousand tonnes)											
Total	26 594	22 323	20 098	22 274	20 411	20 311	21 464	11 277	15 573	13 705	14 986
by process											
Open hearth	8 453	6 189	4 446	4 026	3 279	1 764	1 163	–	–	–	–
Oxygen converters	12 814	10 846	10 064	11 470	10 843	11 336	12 894	6 689	10 535	9 036	10 496
Electric	5 293	5 258	5 562	6 756	6 269	7 200	7 385	4 579	5 038	4 669	4 490
Stock and tropenas	34	31	26	22	20	11	22	9	–	–	–
by cast method											
Cast to ingot	25 275	20 646	17 870	19 619	17 382	16 722	17 442	7 845	10 306	8 020	7 754
Continuously cast[2]	811	1 126	1 704	2 165	2 554	3 149	3 627	3 059	4 959	5 341	6 986
Steel for castings	507	551	524	489	475	441	395	373	308	344	247
by quality											
Non alloy steel	24 371	20 233	18 250	20 283	18 529	18 416	19 553	10 041	14 088	12 500	13 887
Alloy steel[3]	2 223	2 090	1 848	1 991	1 882	1 895	1 911	1 236	1 485	1 205	1 100
Production of iron castings and finished steel products (thousand tonnes)											
Iron castings	3 445	3 190	3 002	2 963	2 795	2 689	2 675	1 819	1 644	1 474	1 500
Finished steel products (All qualities)[4]											
Rods and bars for reinforcement (in coil and lengths)	877	746	762	1 116	948	1 037	982	709	711	675	814
Wire rods and other rods and bars in coil	2 027	1 800	1 472	1 658	1 676	1 708	1 779	1 004	1 169	1 011	1 040
Hot rolled bars in lengths[5]	1 805	1 904	1 572	1 621	1 608	1 608	1 638	1 081	1 039	936	807
Bright steel bars	738	706	520	544	558	522	486	353	331	300	292
Light sections other than rails[6]	563	528	503	472	351	311	351	268	246	175	177
Heavy and light rails and accessories	255	285	344	226	262	233	257	176	219	209	260
Other heavy sections[6]	2 291	2 050	1 766	1 784	1 815	1 907	1 907	1 336	1 856	1 621	1 712
Hot rolled plates and sheets in coil and lengths	9 692	7 923	6 151	7 223	6 945	6 816	7 525	3 863	6 181	5 535	5 810
Cold rolled plates and sheets in coil and lengths	5 085	4 195	2 990	3 865	3 852	3 734	3 928	1 873	3 081	2 964	3 208
Hot rolled strip[7]	1 665	1 121	1 031	1 264	1 134	1 126	1 113	414	249	267	300
Cold rolled strip[8]	604	572	371	466	461	455	429	306	300	290	303
Tinplate	1 281	1 132	979	1 118	1 176	1 126	1 108	597	876	883	884
Other coated sheet	978	870	466	751	709	779	1 012	556	838	921	1 027
Tubes and pipes	1 745	1 601	1 553	1 491	1 407	1 478	1 503	1 049	1 269	1 227	1 021
Tyres, wheels, axles and rolled rings	66	71	85	69	55	55	59	52	59	48	39
Forgings (other than drop forgings)	116	125	128	121	103	93	81	67	65	67	53
Castings	236	270	263	255	246	204	192	174	145	153	112

TIME SERIES. The figures relate to periods of 52 weeks (53 weeks in 1975 and 1981).

1. Includes steel furnaces at steel foundries.
2. Product weight of continuously cast semi-manufacturers.
3. Any steel containing, by weight, at least 0.50 per cent of silicon, or 1.60 per cent of manganese, or 0.30 per cent of chromium or nickel, or 0.10 per cent of tungsten or vanadium, or 0.08 per cent of molybdenum.
4. Includes material for conversion into products also listed in this table.
5. Includes all alloy sections and bars.
6. Excludes alloy.
7. Excludes stainless hot rolled strip.
8. Includes stainless hot rolled strip.

Source Department of Trade and Industry; Iron and Steel Statistics Bureau.

8.18 Non-ferrous metals

Thousand tonnes

	1973	1974	1975	1976	1977	1978	1979	1980	1981	1982	1983
Copper											
Production of refined copper:											
Primary	75.9	69.1	75.5	51.6	44.4	46.2	48.5	68.3	59.8	63.2	67.5
Secondary	95.0	91.0	76.0	85.7	77.8	79.4	73.2	93.0	76.3	71.0	76.8
Home consumption:											
Refined	541.2	496.9	450.5	457.6	512.0	501.6	498.8	409.2	333.1	355.4	358.0
Scrap (metal content)	177.5	164.1	124.4	147.3	131.0	146.8	117.6	121.2	128.0	128.4	109.6
Stocks (end of period)[1, 2]	26.8	36.8	93.9	116.7	118.7	120.9	92.5	82.0	62.0	69.3	75.8
Analysis of home consumption											
(Refined and scrap):[3] total	718.7	661.0	574.8	604.8	643.0	648.4	616.4	530.4	461.1	483.8	467.6
Wire[4]	321.5	298.1	263.8	273.5	305.5	300.4	288.3	255.7	215.2	226.0	227.0
Rods, bars and sections	122.3	106.7	80.4	88.0	91.3	93.3	86.6	65.7	56.3	58.8	58.9
Sheet, strip and plate	123.0	116.2	96.0	105.4	108.4	108.5	102.1	80.1	63.4	69.2	59.9
Tubes	92.6	81.3	79.3	83.7	83.9	90.8	88.0	78.1	77.2	80.8	80.1
Castings and miscellaneous	59.3	58.7	55.3	54.2	53.9	55.4	51.3	50.8	48.9	49.0	41.7
Zinc											
Slab zinc:											
Production	83.8	84.4	53.4	41.6	81.5	73.6	76.7	86.7	81.7	79.3	87.7
Home consumption	305.8	268.5	207.1	242.8	244.8	247.6	238.8	181.3	185.4	181.6	180.6
Stocks (end of period)	21.1	22.4	25.8	21.6	22.2	23.8	22.0	19.7	16.1	16.0	19.5
Other zinc (metal content):											
Consumption	89.5	84.6	69.2	67.9	70.3	72.1	72.9	62.3	56.1	57.8	54.4
Analysis of home consumption											
(slab and scrap): total	394.9	353.1	276.3	310.7	315.1	319.7	311.7	243.6	241.5	239.3	235.0
Brass	112.6	100.6	76.1	83.8	87.5	86.7	81.6	66.7	56.8	59.3	56.6
Galvanized products	102.1	92.3	74.1	84.0	80.9	85.1	89.1	69.1	80.1	83.5	86.6
Zinc sheet and strip	28.9	22.2	17.4	20.6	23.4	23.2	20.6	19.1	15.9	14.1	8.6
Zinc alloy die castings	79.6	69.8	52.2	61.9	62.7	65.9	62.1	37.7	40.1	37.5	39.7
Zinc oxide	42.3	38.3	28.7	33.7	32.4	29.8	29.9	26.6	21.5	18.7	20.6
Other products	29.5	29.8	27.7	26.6	28.2	29.1	28.3	24.4	27.1	26.2	23.0
Refined lead											
Production[5, 6]	265.1	276.9	241.3	341.9	351.1	345.8	368.3	324.8	333.4	306.2	322.2
Home consumption[6, 7]											
Refined lead	282.2	266.4	306.0	318.3	317.7	336.5	333.2	295.5	265.8	271.9	292.9
Scrap and remelted lead[6]	81.9	58.8	2.4	2.4	2.4	2.4	2.7	10.0	8.2	9.9	14.3
Stocks (end of period)[8]											
Lead bullion	14.0	9.1	10.2	26.5	38.9	53.4	68.4	115.7	94.6	13.6	14.8
Refined lead at consumers	11.2	20.6	15.0	19.7	20.9	24.1	23.4	19.7	21.3	25.7	28.1
In LME Warehouses (UK)	12.8	2.9	12.3	18.3	26.7	10.9	16.4	19.0	39.5	53.7	60.3
Analysis of home consumption											
(refined and scrap): total	364.1	325.2	308.4	320.7	320.1	338.9	335.9	305.5	274.0	281.8	307.1
Cables	45.8	44.4	36.5	33.5	31.1	31.0	26.6	21.7	19.4	20.9	19.2
Batteries (excluding oxides)	54.2	38.5	44.0	45.4	49.5	54.2	58.1	49.3	41.5	43.7	43.3
Oxides and compounds:											
Batteries	52.3	41.6	37.6	44.3	47.8	53.6	55.8	49.3	37.7	45.0	44.4
Other uses	91.5	91.7	84.2	88.8	86.3	96.3	91.8	81.9	75.9	73.5	74.7
Sheets and pipes	55.3	47.5	50.3	48.2	47.2	47.9	47.1	50.9	51.7	53.6	77.2
White lead	1.7	1.1	1.0	0.8	1.4	0.9	1.2	0.9	0.7	0.7	0.5
Solder	16.4	15.1	12.2	13.1	13.8	12.6	11.9	9.7	9.6	9.0	8.4
Alloys	18.6	17.2	14.0	14.1	13.4	13.4	12.6	11.9	7.1	7.9	11.2
Other uses	28.2	28.1	28.7	32.6	29.6	29.0	30.8	29.9	30.4	27.6	28.3
Tin											
Tin ore (metal content):											
Production	3.6	3.2	3.3	3.3	3.8	2.8	2.4	3.0	3.9	4.2	..
Stocks (end of period)	0.9	1.2	0.6	0.2	..	..	..	..	..	..	..
Tin metal[9]:											
Production[10]	23.1	15.4	15.0	13.7	13.9	11.2	11.4	11.4	12.9	13.6	..
Home consumption[10]	18.4	16.7	14.4	15.2	14.9	13.9	13.2	9.9	10.9	10.4	10.2
Exports and re-exports[11]	16.3	9.4	11.4	6.9	6.8	7.0	6.2	7.0	1.3	5.4	1.0
Stocks (end of period):											
Consumers	2.0	1.7	1.1	1.2	1.5	1.5	1.2	1.1	1.1	0.9	0.9
Merchants and others	2.5	0.8	2.3	0.9	..	..	..	..	..	..	..
Analysis of home consumption											
(excluding scrap): total	18.4	16.7	14.4	15.1	14.9	13.9	13.2	9.9	10.9	10.4	10.2
Tinplate	8.0	7.0	5.7	6.4	6.4	6.0	5.7	3.1	4.3	4.0	3.8
Alloys	5.9	5.5	5.1	4.9	4.7	4.7	4.2	3.6	3.4	3.4	3.2
Solder	1.6	1.4	1.1	1.0	1.1	0.8	1.0	0.9	1.0	0.8	0.9
Other uses	2.9	2.8	2.5	2.8	2.7	2.4	2.3	2.3	2.2	2.2	2.2
Primary aluminium[12]											
Production	251.6	293.1	308.3	334.5	349.7	346.2	359.5	374.4	339.2	240.8	252.5
Despatches to consumers	554.5	566.4	440.8	577.1	526.6	523.8	563.7	520.9	446.2	399.2	418.3

Sources Department of Trade and Industry; World Bureau of Metal Statistics

8.18 Non-ferrous metals
(continued)

Thousand tonnes

	1973	1974	1975	1976	1977	1978	1979	1980	1981	1982	1983
Secondary aluminium											
Production	209.6	206.6	176.2	205.8	200.8	193.7	176.7	162.1	148.0	114.6	128.3
Despatches to consumers	219.2	206.0	175.9	202.4	201.7	195.1	180.5	161.9	149.4	115.8	128.1
Exports	..	..	..	..	..	..	..	..	59.2	40.0	37.7
Fabricated aluminium											
Total despatches[13]	586.9	604.0	514.4	565.2	539.1	542.4	573.9	521.1	444.3	455.4	460.5
Rolled products[14]	223.0	231.7	181.1	217.0	203.8	189.4	209.5	199.4	165.8	173.7	174.9
Extrusions and tubes[15]	170.0	185.9	163.1	181.6	176.6	183.8	205.3	183.6	161.2	169.6	177.7
Wire products	43.5	48.6	45.5	41.8	34.8	35.0	38.2	33.3	31.6	31.9	29.2
Castings	146.6	134.2	120.6	121.1	121.6	131.9	118.9	101.9	83.3	78.3	77.0
Forgings	3.8	3.6	4.1	3.7	2.3	2.3	2.0	2.9	2.3	1.9	1.7
Foil products (Aluminium content)	42.7	44.8	36.2	39.8	39.0	39.7	41.3	40.4	37.8	18	18
Magnesium and magnesium alloys											
Production[16]	3.1	3.8	2.8	3.0	2.7	2.7	2.7	2.8	1.9	1.8	18
Consumption: total[17]	8.0	8.4	6.2	7.5	6.5	6.3	6.0	5.4	4.1	4.1	18
Refined nickel											
(including ferro-nickel) Production	36.8	35.7	37.3	33.1	23.2	21.4	18.9	19.3	23.2	7.3	23.2

1. Unwrought copper (electrolytic, fire refined and blister).
2. Reported stocks of refined copper held by consumers and those held in London Metal Exchange (LME) warehouses in the United Kingdom.
3. Copper content.
4. Consumption for high-conductivity copper and cadmium copper wire represented by consumption of wire rods, production of which for export is also included.
5. Lead reclaimed from secondary and scrap material and lead refined from bullion and domestic ores.
6. From 1975, figures for production and consumption of refined lead include antimonial lead, and for scrap and remelted lead, exclude secondary antimonial lead.
7. Including toll transactions involving fabrication.

8. Excluding government stocks.
9. Including production from imported scrap and residues refined on toll.
10. Primary and secondary metal.
11. Including re-exports on toll transactions.
12. Including primary alloys.
13. Includes wrought, cast and forged products, and excludes foil products.
14. Includes foil stock and excludes foil products.
15. Excluding forging bars, wirebars, and almost two-thirds of despatches of hot rolled rod.
16. Primary and remelt alloys.
17. Despatches to consumers of primary metal, primary and remelt alloys.
18. Data no longer obtainable.

Sources Department of Trade and Industry; World Bureau of Metal Statistics; Aluminium Federation

8.19 Cotton, man-made fibres and wool

	Unit	1973	1974	1975	1976	1977	1978	1979	1980	1981	1982	1983
Raw cotton[1]												
Imports	Thousand	171	93	113	122	104	101	99	69	48	54	50
Home consumption: total	tonnes	133	118	106	120	103	92	96	69	46	45	45
Cotton spinning	,,	126	111	99	113	96	92	96	69	46	45	45
Other uses	,,	6	7	7	7	7	..	..	..	..	..	..
Stocks (end of period)	,,	45	22	25	29	23	21	17	9	6	5	5
Cotton waste												
Imports	,,	30.9	22.4	24.0	25.1	20.3	24.7	29.0	26.5	22.6	30.2	28.9
Cotton linters												
Imports	,,	50.2	36.4	23.0	30.2	33.0	33.8	35.7	29.9	25.7	37.8	24.8
Man-made fibres[2]												
Production: total	,,	730.8	627.6	562.5	618.4	551.8	607.2	596.3	449.7	394.7	333.6	389.3
Continuous filament yarn	,,	305.6	271.0	246.5	270.7	239.3	240.6	230.6	162.6	126.3	89.3	102.6
Staple fibre	,,	425.3	356.6	316.0	347.7	312.5	366.6	365.7	287.2	268.4	244.3	286.6

Source Department of Trade and Industry

8.19 Cotton, man-made fibres and wool

(continued)

	Unit	1973	1974	1975	1976	1977	1978	1979	1980	1981	1982	1983
Cotton and man-made fibre yarn												
Production of single yarn:												
Cotton[3]	,,	93.3	80.6	76.5	91.4	84.4	79.0	79.0	61.3	42.5	42.3	40.9
Cotton mixture yarn	,,	35.2	36.1	30.9	26.5	27.4	26.8	27.4	18.4	15.5	15.6	17.1
Spun man-made fibre yarn	,,	52.8	47.6	40.9	45.3	45.1	43.7	41.9	31.2	25.5	26.5	28.2
Cotton waste yarn[4]	,,	22.2	20.7	17.9	15.5	13.7	12.3	11.8	10.8	8.5	8.7	9.0
Other waste yarn	,,	4.2	3.9	4.5	4.1	4.8	4.8	4.3	2.3	1.9	1.7	2.1
Production of doubled yarn	,,	82.1	74.7	68.4	69.4	69.8	60.6	58.0	49.1	39.8	34.1	30.6
Spindle activity[5]:												
Single yarn spindles:												
total (ring equivalent)	Millions	2.5	2.5	2.3	2.2	2.2	2.0	1.9	1.5	1.2	1.0	1.0
Doubling spindles	,,	0.4	0.4	0.3	0.3	0.3	0.3	0.3	0.2	0.2	0.1	0.1
Yarn consumed in cotton and man-made fibre weaving:												
Cotton and waste yarns	Thousand tonnes	78.3	67.5	62.6	68.1	63.2	58.5	58.6	45.5	35.9	35.8	36.2
Man-made fibres: total	,,	88.5	87.6	86.1	87.6	90.1	82.2	82.0	62.5	50.3	45.0	41.7
Continuous filament yarn	,,	67.3	66.6	67.0	71.6	72.6	63.5	62.6	50.7	39.4	35.0	31.9
Spun yarn	,,	21.3	21.0	19.1	15.9	17.5	18.7	19.4	11.8	10.9	10.0	9.8
Cotton and man-made fibre weaving												
Production of woven cloth:	Million linear metres											
Cotton		454	409	405	375	368	380	365	314	278	261	255
Man-made fibres	,,	389.4	390.6	398.8	385.8	395.7	377.8	385.6	298.9	229.9	204.8	176
Cotton/man-made fibre mixtures	,,	112.9	114.7	104.2	107.1	101.7	80.6	81.4	51.2	42.9	45.7	52.3
Loom activity												
Average number of looms running on cotton and man-made fibres	Thousands	49.9	48.9	42.8	39.1	37.5	34.4	32.9	26.2	19.8	16.9	14.7
Wool												
Virgin wool (clean weight):	Million kilo-grammes											
Production[6]		32	33	33	32	30	32	32	34	33	33	33
Imports	,,	108	88	94	114	97	105	86[1]	67	76[1]	71[1]	77
Exports[7]	,,	23	20	25	26	23	23	26[1]	25	27[1]	24[1]	26
Stocks at 31 August	,,	63	45	49	49	46	54	49	42	39	21	19
Consumption:												
Wool	,,	136.6	112.6	110.5	119.8	113.5	109.0	106.0	92.3	88.2	88.1	90.0
Hair	,,	12.5	8.0	8.0	10.2	9.4	8.6	7.6	6.4	6.6	5.9	6.6
Man-made fibres	,,	104.3	102.3	85.8	87.2	85.6	84.2	73.8	53.1	51.6	48.8	51.5
Other fibres[8]	,,	29.3	24.7	23.4	21.3	21.4	21.0	21.0	15.0	11.5	10.1	10.1
Tops												
Production: total	,,	118.1	98.7	91.2	103.8	97.6	91.8	78.9	65.8	70.1	66.5	70.3
Wool and hair	,,	62.2	43.9	46.8	56.5	52.3	48.7	43.6	39.1	38.7	37.3	38.5
Man-made fibres	,,	55.9	54.8	44.4	47.4	45.3	43.1	35.3	26.7	31.4	29.2	31.8
Stocks at 31 August	,,	9.7	8.0	5.5	7.0	6.7	8.3	7.4	6.3	5.9	..	..
Worsted yarns[9]:												
Deliveries	,,	88.6	76.5	67.0	72.4	72.8	69.0	60.5	52.8	51.6	53.4	55.6
Semi-worsted yarns[9]:												
Deliveries	,,	11.4	10.7	8.4	8.5	8.4	8.7	8.5	7.1	7.2	8.1	9.4
Woollen yarn[6]:												
Production	,,	135	123	112	108	106	106	105	81.2	72.0	53.4	56.2
Woven woollen and worsted fabrics[10]:	Million square metres											
Deliveries		192.4	174.7	151.4	143.1	150.1	144.1	137.8	118.2	96.7	100.3	94.0
Blankets:												
Deliveries	,,	30.6	28.1	24.7	22.8	22.2	22.0	18.2	15.0	9.9	9.4	8.3

TIME SERIES. Figures for consumption of raw cotton, and production and consumption of cotton and man-made, fibre yarn are for periods of 52 weeks (53 weeks in 1975, and 1980).

1. From 1978 figures for consumption of raw cotton are for calendar months.
2. Figures are based on returns from producers (excluding waste) and include all man-made fibres in commercial production.
3. Excluding waste yarns.
4. Yarns wholly of cotton waste, cotton yarn spun on condenser system and mixture yarns of cotton and cotton waste.
5. Average of numbers running in last week of each month. Waste spinning spindles are excluded.

6. Estimated.
7. Including imported wool and wool from imported skins, scoured, etc. in the United Kingdom.
8. Including noils, broken tops, wastes, mungo and shoddy.
9. Including all yarn spun on the worsted system.
10. Includes mixture and man-made fibre fabrics classified as wool or worsted, but excludes blankets.

Source Department of Trade and Industry

8.20 Packaging products of paper and board: manufacturers' sales[1]

£ thousand

	1973	1974	1975	1976	1977	1978	1979	1980	1981	1982	1983
Rigid boxes	35 633	49 415	47 956	54 203	65 019	72 430	79 285	63 492	59 838	60 158	63 622
Cartons	171 845	227 287	253 715	309 174	378 644	406 456	456 104	449 474	451 647	490 665	505 172
Fibreboard packing cases:											
Solid	15 506	22 586	21 219	26 030	30 289	33 222	36 547	34 356	30 990	28 989	29 313
Corrugated	197 896	298 593	293 255	360 980	410 795	442 716	525 017	512 001	513 777	529 413	558 480
Paper bags	33 448	46 649	50 470	56 732	64 456	64 969	73 969	58 063	55 858	57 145	48 916
Paper carrier bags	5 404	6 191	5 796	5 020	4 245	4 255	3 588	2 818	2 270	3 563	6 923
Paper sacks	52 285	80 599	77 627	96 637	105 722	109 830	131 337	115 961	114 680	120 987	119 401

1. Up to 1979 sales are by manufacturers employing 25 or more people, and
   from 1980 by those employing 75 or more in the case of board products or
   100 or more in the case of paper products.

Source Department of Trade and Industry

8.21 Woodpulp, paper and paper-making materials

Thousand tonnes

	1973	1974	1975	1976	1977	1978	1979	1980	1981	1982	1983
Woodpulp[1]											
Consumption	2 189.4	2 139.4	1 630.8	1 720.0	1 683.0	1 707.9	1 706.9	1 517.2	1 357.4	1 254.7	1 205.0
Stocks (end of period)	268.1	250.4	229.6	248.7	203.3	250.3	220.9	160.3	171.6	127.0	142.1
Other paper-making materials											
Total (paper equivalent):											
Consumption	2 187.5	2 206.8	1 834.7	2 147.9	2 168.1	2 090.7	2 266.8	2 052.2	1 815.3	1 772.0	1 752.0
Stocks (end of period)[2]	161.9	277.4	288.0	259.4	317.5	274.5	224.8	177.2	145.9	148.3	129.0
Homegrown pulpwood (including wood waste, chippings and rejected pitprops)											
Consumption	981.2	886.9	896.4	957.8	900.6	970.0	1 020.6	863.0	397.3	426.0	479.9
Stocks (end of period)[2]	87.4	225.4	194.4	149.0	230.9	136.5	118.4	89.1	73.0	28.4	27.9
Other vegetable fibre (including straw and esparto grass)											
Consumption	18.8	20.3	15.4	16.0	18.4	11.8	11.2	12.6	24.9	22.0	17.9
Stocks (end of period)[2]	7.3	8.8	8.6	6.1	6.5	7.7	7.3	3.0	5.9	4.5	3.5
Rags, waste ropes, etc.											
Consumption	44.0	41.8	36.2	37.9	36.8	32.3	25.8	16.3	3.0	6.1	8.2
Stocks (end of period)[2]	6.8	9.3	6.8	6.5	7.7	7.7	6.1	2.4	1.4	3.0	2.3
Waste paper											
Consumption	2 069.8	2 121.8	1 703.8	2 056.6	2 114.7	2 109.1	2 190.6	2 014.5	1 945.4	1 880.9	1 834.0
Stocks (end of period)[2]	134.7	195.5	241.7	228.4	262.3	252.8	203.8	165.8	135.4	157.4	135.8
Paper and board[3]											
Production: total	4 678.4	4 603.9	3 640.2	4 158.5	4 113.6	4 164.8	4 222.2	3 788.2	3 378.4	3 226.3	3 211.7
Paper: total	3 435.4	3 373.0	2 699.0	3 049.9	3 062.5	3 168.9	3 253.3	3 025.0	2 670.3	2 552.3	2.546.0
Newsprint	441.9	381.5	315.1	326.2	300.5	319.0	363.7	363.2	113.1	86.4	79.8
Other printings and writings	1 148.3	1 146.2	849.6	951.1	966.8	1 033.9	1 029.9	937.4	892.7	833.2	818.7
Food wrappings	65.8	60.9	44.8	54.0	49.6	45.4	44.5	36.7	37.8	33.3	26.4
Kraft wrappings	195.0	187.8	147.0	140.0	132.4	133.2	134.5	113.2	82.8	86.1	88.4
Other wrappings and packings	946.5	975.0	780.2	966.6	987.2	1 020.8	1 035.1	941.9	913.0	914.4	935.8
Household toilet papers and tissues	363.4	355.1	358.0	380.3	395.2	383.6	402.3	420.8	426.9	407.8	412.9
Other tissues	26.2	22.2	19.8	21.7	21.8	18.2	16.5	13.6	13.5	12.0	11.0
Industrial and special purpose papers	248.3	244.3	184.5	210.0	209.0	214.8	226.8	198.2	190.5	179.2	172.9
Board: total[3]	1 243.0	1 230.9	941.2	1 108.6	1 051.1	995.9	968.9	763.2	708.1	674.0	665.7
Packaging board	901.8	889.9	649.7	778.6	767.9	749.2	746.5	586.3	546.1	503.5	500.9
Industrial and special purposes board	242.8	229.3	204.2	228.0	212.8	192.5	177.7	135.8	116.8	124.9	121.9
Other board	98.4	111.7	87.3	102.0	70.4	54.2	44.7	41.1	45.2	45.6	42.9
Stocks (end of period): total[3, 4]	181.9	184.2	185.0	184.6	216.1	215.8	212.7	190.5	210.5	191.3	184.2
Paper	150.1	150.6	155.8	152.3	180.9	176.5	169.3	161.3	176.5	161.1	149.3
Boards	31.8	33.6	29.2	32.3	35.2	39.3	48.4	29.2	34.0	30.2	34.9

TIME SERIES. The figures relate to periods of 52 weeks (53 weeks in 1976 and 1982).

1. For paper-making and manufacture of cellulose wadding; woodpulp for manufacture of rayon and transparent cellulose film is not included.
2. Stocks held at pulp and paper mills only.
3. Excluding building board.
4. Stocks held by paper and board makers.

Source Department of Trade and Industry

8.22 Timber

Thousand cubic metres

	1973	1974	1975	1976	1977	1978	1979	1980	1981	1982	1983
Softwood											
Deliveries: total	10 048	7 751	6 669	7 646	6 678	7 008	7 355	6 519	6 077	6 832	7 512
Imported	9 746	7 483	6 428	7 348	6 369	6 709	7 053	6 131	5 649	6 237	6 895
Home grown[1,2]	302	268	241	298	309	299	302	388	428	595	617
Stocks (end of period):											
Imported	2 270	3 338	2 132	1 983	2 040	1 798	1 959	1 846	1 646	1 494	1 729
Hardwood											
Deliveries: total	1 452	979	941	1 000	973	1 012	1 113	874	802	814	1 031
Imported	1 294	843	815	839	813	842	964	766	717	740	951
Home grown[1,2]	158	136	126	161	160	170	149	108	85	74	80
Stocks (end of period):											
Imported	417	352	284	286	282	270	300	228	223	232	272
Imported plywood											
Deliveries	1 364	941	878	1 007	892	1 059	1 159	830	972	920	1 068
Stocks (end of period)	259	236	181	221	197	196	216	142	209	130	191
Mining timber											
Production: total	532.0	447.3	520.2	492.5	499.1	513.8	509.5	560.2	556.9	564.6	539.4
Sawn	355.3	310.6	365.9	344.4	355.2	373.5	372.3	407.6	407.2	428.3	415.2
Round	176.7	136.7	154.3	148.1	143.9	140.4	137.1	152.6	149.7	136.3	124.2
Consumption:											
Sawn	368.9	326.0	383.3	358.0	365.2	384.0	382.2	424.4	415.8	429.4	415.5
Round	325.2	262.8	289.5	255.5	233.0	215.1	202.0	214.6	198.1	175.9	149.6
Stocks (end of period):											
Sawn	36.3	79.4	61.3	49.3	58.7	55.2	57.2	70.3	54.2	64.7	61.2
Round	240.2	250.1	266.2	204.1	169.8	134.7	103.5	45.2	96.1	62.6	39.9
Wood chipboard											
Production[3]	195.8	241.4	354.8	451.6	369.8	366.5	597.9	606.7	524.7	514.6	518.5
Stocks (end of period)[3]	13.4	31.1	44.9	23.8	23.0	37.2	32.6	55.4	24.1	45.5	39.4

TIME SERIES. Figures for wood chipboard relate to periods of 52 weeks (53 weeks in 1976 and 1982).

1. Up to and including 1979 sales of home grown timber and of plywood are by firms employing 25 or more people and from 1980 by firms employing 35 or more people.

2. Home grown excludes mining timber and relates to sawn and planed only. From 1976, homegrown hardwood also excludes planed timber.
3. Up to and including 1978 woodchip board figures are in thousand tonnes.

Sources Department of Trade and Industry; Timber Trade Federation

8.23 Synthetic rubber, carbon black and rubber products[1]

	Unit	1976	1977	1978	1979	1980	1981	1982	1983
Synthetic rubber	Thousand tonnes								
UK manufactures sales									
Synthetic rubber: total	,,	..	..	..	..	..	160.2	175.6	196.4
Solid	,,	..	..	..	..	..	139.6	139.0	145.3
Latex	,,	..	..	..	..	..	81.1	102.2	107.7
Carbon black									
Production[2]	,,	213.7	193.2	198.9	199.9	172.3	152.5	3	
Rubber products	£ million								
UK manufactures sales									
Rubber products: total	,,	1 208.7	1 413.9	1 551.3	1 718.9	1 637.8	1 488.9	1 390.3	1 428.4
New tyres	,,	483.3	534.0	558.4	611.8	650.9	588.4	574.5	608.7
Retreads	,,	45.1	50.3	52.0	54.8	43.0	40.7	38.0	47.2
Tubes	,,	20.4	21.6	24.5	26.3	27.8	24.2	21.8	18.5
Belting	,,	75.3	87.4	90.1	104.5	118.9	103.1	114.0	104.4
Hose/tubing	,,	90.6	117.9	126.8	142.6	131.9	127.1	126.9	123.9
Other products	,,	494.0	602.7	699.5	778.9	665.6	605.2	515.1	525.7

1. Figures prior to 1981 for synthetic rubber/carbon black and rubber products relate to establishments with minimum employments levels of 25 persons. From 1981 minimum employments levels are 75 and 100 respectively; except for those establishments producing new tyres and tubes whose minimum employment level is 300 persons.

2. Including lamp and vegetable black; excluding acetylene and bone black.
3. Data no longer published.

Source Department of Trade and Industry

8.24 Fertilisers
Years ended 31 May

Thousand tonnes

	1973	1974	1975	1976	1977	1978	1979	1980	1981	1982	1983
Production[1]											
P_2O_5 (phosphate):											
Single superphosphate[2]	43	48	52	41	48	36	31	31	..	..	..
Basic slag[2]	71	37	28	40	29	26	30	30	..	..	..
Compounds[3]	2 786	2 837	2 674	2 855	2 770	3 083	2 797	3 289	..	..	..
Deliveries to UK agriculture											
N (nitrogen):											
Straight[2]	..	..	..	..	581	579	638	701	695	785	896
Compounds[2]	..	..	..	..	509	538	522	544	468	476	529
P_2O_5 (phosphate)[2]	370	456	337	355	377	388	394	394	372	379	407
K_2O (potash)[2]	437	473	455	414	385	393	395	425	388	407	467
Compounds[3]	2 288	3 211	2 471	2 746	3 077	3 062	3 024	3 200	2 819	2 913	3 259

1. Data no longer supplied by the Fertiliser Manufacturers' Association.
2. Nutrient content.
3. Total weight of compound fertilisers.

Source Department of Trade and Industry

8.25 Synthetic dyestuffs, colours, paint, varnish and allied products[1]

	Unit	1973[2]	1974	1975	1976	1977	1978	1979	1980	1981[1]	1982	1983
Dyestuffs and pigments	Thousand tonnes											
Finished synthetic dyestuffs	,,	38.0	53.6	43.2	52.0	53.7	48.3	53.2	46.2	42.6	42.4	42.1
Synthetic organic pigments	,,	12.6	15.6	11.8	16.7	16.9	15.8	15.7	13.0	10.5	9.8	11.9
Inorganic pigment colours	,,	22.2	23.4	16.5	22.3	21.3	19.7	20.3	17.0	13.2	11.9	13.6
Ochres and mineral colours	,,	13.4	20.2	17.0	22.8	26.6	27.9	21.5	16.0	..[6]	..	..
Titanium dioxide	,,	160.3	183.2	157.7	191.4	198.1	205.3	192.9	186.7	169.6	172.3	193.9
White lead	,,	1.7	1.5	1.2	1.1	0.9	0.8	0.5	0.4	..[6]	..	..
Paint, varnish and allied products												
Sales by larger establishments	Million litres											
All paints and varnishes: total	,,	569.0	556.4	558.2	585.2	612.0	630.4	660.0	596.0	524.5	533.1	548.0[7]
Emulsion paints	,,	152.6	145.6	150.1	170.1	174.4	184.9	183.1	173.4	160.8	171.5	178.7
Other water paints	,,	18.3	20.5	21.5	25.7	27.3	27.0	21.6	23.7	33.8	38.0	39.3
Cellulose based varnishes, lacquers and clear solutions and pigmented cellulose paints	,,	43.7	42.3	40.0	42.4	48.7	46.6	51.4	40.2	32.2	26.2	29.0
Varnishes, lacquers and stains (other than cellulose)	,,	6.5	6.0	4.9	5.5	6.5	7.8	10.5	8.9	8.4	9.4	10.0
Others[3]	,,	347.9	342.0	341.7	341.5	355.1	364.1	393.4	349.8	289.3	288.0	291.0[7]
Manufactured thinners (solvent mixtures), removers and strippers[4]	,,	62.4	58.2	50.4	52.3	54.7	58.8	71.8	66.3	60.1	57.0	60.9
Mastics and putty[5]	Mn. kilogrammes	96.6	89.2	57.3	65.0	57.4	65.9	64.3	65.1	64.0	73.5	76.2

1. Figures relate to sales by manufacturers in the United Kingdom employing 25 or more persons and from 1981 those with a minimum employment of 50.
2. Figures of dyestuffs and pigments in 1973 are for April to December only.
3. Including oil and/or synthetic based non-aqueous products, marine paints, and bituminous paints. Figures prior to 1981 include paste fillers.

4. Removers and strippers are excluded from 1975 to 1978 data.
5. Figures prior to 1975 include sealants (oil-based, preformed bituminous strips).
6. Data no longer published.
7. 1983 is an estimated figure.

Source Department of Trade and Industry

8.26 Inorganic chemicals

Thousand tonnes

	1973	1974	1975	1976	1977	1978	1979	1980	1981	1982	1983
Materials used for the manufacture of sulphuric acid											
Zinc concentrates:											
Consumption	201.4	202.9	156.8	129.3	208.4	178.5	215.8	242.6	188.7	210.1	237.2
Spent oxide:											
Consumption	27.5	8.9	10.3	12.0	11.1	12.5	9.3	10.6	7.6	6.1	6.6
Stocks (end of period)	61.1	6.6	6.3	7.3	7.8	4.7	3.1	0.9	0.8	8.1	7.4
Sulphur:											
Consumption											
(for acid production)[1]	1 163.2	1 166.0	977.8	1 056.4	1 078.6	1 104.0	1 106.9	1 058.6	926.0	805.0	823.2
Stocks (end of period)[1]	45.2	69.9	50.4	55.6	44.1	53.2	41.0	48.7	50.5	36.7	29.3
Sulphuric acid[2]											
Production	3 885.8	3 855.0	3 165.7	3 271.2	3 404.9	3 453.1	3 498.1	3 380.7	2 888.9	2 587.3	2 630.5
Consumption[3]: total	4 282.4	4 015.0	3 370.3	3 561.2	3 536.6	3 450.5	3 504.3	3 241.2	2 914.5	2 906.4	3 122.1
Fertilizers	1 359.7	1 300.8	1 229.5	1 097.4	1 057.1	1 096.3	1 072.0	1 042.8	824.2	769.5	857.1
All other chemical uses	1 755.2	1 735.0	1 390.4	1 691.5	1 780.5	1 652.4	1 719.3	1 571.7	1 383.8	1 856.6	1 998.5
Metallurgy	124.4	107.5	77.6	83.8	79.1	74.4	69.0	50.4	45.0	48.6	44.7
Textiles											
Other	1 043.2	871.7	672.8	688.5	619.9	627.4	644.0	576.3	661.5	621.4	665.0
Stocks (end of period)	150.2	168.2	174.6	172.3	162.2	174.8	139.3	145.0	151.2	122.3	139.8

1. Filter cake and boiler bottom are included.
2. As 100 per cent acid.
3. Including recovered acid.

Source Department of Trade and Industry

8.27 Organic chemicals: production[1]

Thousand tonnes[2]

	1973	1974	1975	1976	1977	1978	1979	1980	1981	1982	1983
Ethylene[3]	1 246.8	1 274.7	958.9	1 286.1	1 137.5	1 095.7	1 233.6	1 094.9	1 235.5	1 115.4	1 154.6
Propylene[3]	641.6	662.5	565.6	747.5	659.6	670.8	765.8	572.7	736.6	770.6	781.2
Butadiene[3]	216.7	212.0	169.0	230.2	221.7	209.4	227.1	191.9	207.9	228.8	237.7
Benzene[4]	768.1	695.6	581.8	928.0	844.6	790.7	1 056.3	825.5	751.9	569.5[9]	725.9[9]
Toluene[5]	293.0	252.0	183.8	273.1	212.9	199.5	293.7	170.1	179.0		
Formaldehyde[6]	126.9	135.0	110.2	132.7	146.1	131.6	137.8	123.9	113.0	107.2	102.6
Propyl alcohols	170.6	158.5	102.6	130.9	154.3	145.2	135.7	61.4	[10]		
Acetone	196.3	193.0	118.1	149.0	143.7	145.6	146.9	122.6	111.2	135.3	121.8
Phenol (synthetic)	184.9	196.1	131.8	184.6	168.1	169.1	178.6	..	109.7	140.8	143.2
Phthalic anhydride	100.4	98.0	68.8	..	98.2	90.9	94.4	46.3	61.1	73.0	[10]
Phthalates, organic[7]	110.2	111.2	97.1	106.4	116.0	127.2	..	..	..	..	..
Ethyl alcohol[8]	1 866.0	2 940.8	1 976.6	2 496.1	2 710.8	2 982.6	2 808.7	1 810.6	1 839.4	2 071.5	2 398.1
(Thousand hectolitres of alcohol)											

1. Figures relate to total production i.e. 'captive use' is included.
2. Except for Ethyl alcohol which is measured in thousand hectolitres of alcohol.
3. Produced from oil base, other than for use as fuel.
4. Includes production obtained by dealkylation of toluene (excludes production from coal).
5. Includes that used for the production of benzene, but excludes production from coal.
6. Including paraformaldehyde (expressed as 100 per cent formaldehyde).

7. Figures not available after 1978.
8. Industrial alcohol made from molasses and derived from other processes. The figures include a small quantity of beverage spirits produced by rectification of spirits distilled from molasses. In the financial year ended 31 March 1984 this amounted to about 14.85 thousand hectolitres of alcohol a month.
9. Figures suppressed for disclosure reasons.
10. No longer published in the *British Monitor* series.

Sources Department of Trade and Industry; HM Customs and Excise

8.28 Production of synthetic resins[1]

Thousand tonnes

	1973	1974	1975	1976	1977	1978	1979	1980	1981[2]	1982	1983
All synthetic resins	2 463.4	2 426.7	2 051.5	2 560.8	2 571.3	2 614.9	2 646.5	2 259.3	1 972.8	1 661.9	1 415.4
Products of condensation, poly-condensation and polyaddition	796.8	804.9	717.9	864.8	864.7	895.7	880.1	729.9	673.3	617.0	465.2
Alkyds (including styrenated alkyds and unsaturated polyesters):											
Solid and liquid alkyd resins including solutions, emulsions and dispersions (net resin content including oil but excluding solvent)	104.2	104.3	112.2	125.9	132.0	123.1	129.8	111.8	102.5	99.1	98.0
Unsaturated polyester resins (including reactive monomer, but excluding filler)	65.8	56.7	51.3	62.9	59.0	60.8	59.6	48.4	51.0	48.6	49.0
Aminoplastics:											
Alkylated resin solutions (actual weight including solvent)	11.4										
Solid resins Other liquid resins and solutions (actual weight including solvent)	132.3	140.4	121.9	172.1	178.4	167.2	164.5	164.8	155.1	139.4	141.8
Phenolics:											
Straight liquid resins, including aqueous solutions and dispersions (actual weight including water)	41.6	29.2	24.4	25.7	29.5	25.0	26.9	15.9	17.1	17.3	18.3
Straight resins, solid or in organic solution	24.4	23.6	17.8	20.9	22.5	22.3	21.6	20.7	18.3	20.2	21.7
Modified resins, including those in solution	7.1	6.5	4.5	6.6	5.9	5.7	6.2	4.6	4.1	3.8	3.6
Polyurethanes	47.1	59.5	57.3	69.9	78.9	81.5	85.2	73.2	75.0	83.9	95.1
Epoxide resins (net resin content excluding added non-reactive solvent and/or filler)	18.7	18.5	16.4	20.1	21.4	24.1	27.0	27.0	28.4	27.7	37.7
Other[3]	344.2	366.2	312.1	360.5	337.1	386.0	359.3	263.5	222.0	177.0	..[5]
Products of polymerisation and copolymerisation	1 537.0	1 487.9	1 227.8	1 583.9	1 597.2	1 611.1	1 665.2	1 323.4	1 207.7[4]	970.3[4]	889.2[4]
Acrylics:											
Latices, dispersions and solutions	20.0										
Moulding and extrusion compounds, cast sheet, cast rod and cast tube (based on methyl methacrylic monomer)	30.4	49.5	38.7	46.1	60.9	68.3	71.3	58.7	50.3	63.7	58.5
Polyolefines:											
Polyethylene	534.3	491.0	382.9	474.4	489.4	428.4	483.6	434.8	454.4	425.8	409.1
Polypropylene	166.7	210.9	169.7	250.7	248.2	292.3	263.4	190.4	197.5	221.4	229.9
Polyvinyl acetate, including solutions and dispersions (net resin content excluding plasticiser)	60.5	63.0	66.2	85.7	105.3	116.5	113.4	93.9	94.8	92.8	94.9
Polyvinyl chloride (including lattices, solutions and dispersions)	400.0	367.0	334.0	417.2	386.4	410.1	440.2	349.7	314.8	..[5]	..[5]
Styrene polymers and co-polymers:											
Non-toughened straight polystyrene resins, moulding and extrusion compounds	53.3	53.0	39.6	59.9	59.4	53.3	48.9	39.5	36.9	22.0	29.8
Toughened grades of resins, moulding and extrusion compounds	119.5	110.9	86.6	116.0	102.0	109.6	100.8	67.0	59.0	61.2	67.0
Other, including solutions, emulsions and dispersions, co-polymer resins and non-toughened co-polymer moulding and extrusion compounds but excluding styrene-butadiene copolymers	66.5	60.3	58.4	64.7	67.5	46.2	66.8	50.6	..[5]	..[5]	..[5]
Other	85.7	82.4	51.7	69.3	78.1	86.4	76.8	38.8	..[5]	83.4	..[5]
Cellulosics and other plastics and modified natural resins	129.6	134.0	105.8	112.1	109.4	108.1	101.2	93.6	91.8	74.6	61.0[4]
Regenerated cellulose film, including laminates	92.2	91.1	64.6	81.4	77.7	79.8	73.8	78.8	76.7	62.6	61.0
Other cellulosics and other plastics and modified natural resins (including casein, alginates and resin ester gums)	37.5	42.8	41.2	30.6	31.7	28.3	27.4	14.8	15.1	12.0	..[5]

1. Unless separately specified, all figures are in terms of net resin content and co-polymers are recorded against the heading for resins made from the major monomeric ingredient of the co-polymer.
2. From 1981 figures relate to establishments with a minimum employment level of 75. Previous figures were based on a minimum of 25 persons.
3. Include production of polymers and co-polymers of polyamide and polyester by firms classified to man-made fibre industry.
4. Totals do not include suppressed figures.
5. Data suppressed for disclosure reasons.

Source Department of Trade and Industry

8.29 Minerals: production
Great Britain

Thousand tonnes

	1975	1976	1977	1978	1979	1980	1981	1982	1983
Limestone[1]	91 033	83 797	81 500	83 839	86 655	72 423	62 850	69 114	75 753
Sandstone	10 163	10 115	9 015	10 026	10 519	9 788	9 611	10 803	12 199
Igneous rock	32 646	28 476	26 708	27 807	29 098	28 497	25 323	29 987	30 733
Clay/shale	27 545	25 812	23 250	25 473	21 644	19 825	18 799	20 323	22 403
Industrial sand	6 139	5 900	6 283	6 224	5 829	5 708	4 451	4 123	4 026
Chalk	17 320	15 740	15 780	16 321	15 945	13 732	11 756	11 616	12 430
Fireclay	1 606	1 464	1 499	1 404	1 710	1 217	992	850	689
Barium sulphate	51.5	49.8	56.8	54.4	45.5	53.9	63.3	81.1	36.0
Calcium fluoride	235.3	217.2	205.6	189.3	153.6	186.1	255.5	200.8	131.3
Copper	0.7	0.6	0.5	0.1	..	0.2	0.6	0.6	0.7
Lead	6.4	7.1	8.2	4.6	4.7	3.6	7.0	4.0	3.8
Tin	4.1	4.0	4.2	3.2	2.7	3.3	3.7	4.2	4.0
Zinc	4.0	4.9	7.5	2.7	0.6	4.4	10.9	10.2	8.9
Iron ore: crude	4 460	4 209	3 781	4 254	4 272	960	703	392	262
Iron ore: iron content	1 143	1 100	891	1 116	1 130	225	162	85	57
Calcspar	19	16	14	13	21	18	20	18	10
China clay (including ball clay)	3 220	3 847	4 343	4 199	4 444	3 964	3 508	3 358	3 346
Chert and flint	362	158	39	52	47	14	10	..	174
Fuller's earth	211	201	223	218	..	..	205	243	267
Lignite	1	1	1	8	..	..	..	..	1
Rock salt	754	611	905	1 311	1 590	1 746	1 350	2 209	1 316
Salt from brine	1 740	1 918	1 871	1 760	1 915	1 608	1 454	1 554	1 394
Salt in brine	5 136	5 477	5 426	4 239	4 315	3 800	3 916	3 874	3 601
Anhydrite	221	26	25	92	..	76	47	67	51
Dolomite[2]	2 315	3 314	2 556	..	2 937	14 060	13 936	13 727	14 983
Gypsum	3 258	3 324	3 236	3 230	..	3 371	2 897	2 674	2 916
Slate[3]	547	303	1 823	945	513	225	350	785	494
Soapstone and talc	..	..	15	18	17	17	18	19	16
Sand and gravel (land-won)	106 082	98 004	87 900	90 196	89 267	83 624	77 951	79 287	88 002
Sand and gravel (marine dredged)	11 097	11 948	11 328	12 159	13 488	12 534	11 501	11 919	12 797

1. Prior to 1980, includes dolomite for constructional uses.
2. Prior to 1980, figures relate to dolomite and high magnesium limestone for special uses only.
3. Includes waste used for constructional fill, and powder and granules used in manufacturing.

Source Business Statistics Office

Northern Ireland

Thousand tonnes

	1975	1976	1977	1978	1979	1980	1981	1982	1983
Chalk	604	598	473	410	320	317	..	..	
Clay and shale	249	265	295	..	..	..	..	..	
Sand and gravel	3 946	3 887	3 931	4 127	4 300	3 807	3 738	3 665	3 207
Basalt and igneous rock (other than granite)	9 325	8 642	8 812	7 443	7 080	6 179	5 449	6 151	6 140
Limestone	1 865	2 143	2 316	2 465	2 602	2 290	2 281	2 609	3 249
Grit and conglomerate	3 189	3 442	3 186	3 364	3 025	2 809	2 622	2 524	2 532
Diatomite	..	..	..	..	..	..	..	..	..
Granite	..	..	107	..	..	..	..	..	..
Sandstone	..	..	..	..	..	..	..	..	..
Rock salt	..	..	..	..	..	..	..	..	..

Source Department of Economic Development (Northern Ireland)

8.30 Building materials and components: production[1]
Great Britain

	Unit	1973	1974	1975	1976	1977	1978	1979	1980	1981	1982	1983
Building bricks (excluding refractory and glazed)[2]	Millions	7 183	5 575	5 046	5 406	5 067	4 842	4 887	4 562	3 725	3 517	3 806
Cement[3]	Thousand tonnes	19 986	17 781	16 891	15 780	15 457	15 916	16 140	14 805	12 729	12 962	13 396
Building sand[4,5]	,,	23 619	20 295	21 444	20 431	18 608	18 510	18 983	18 005	15 675	17 044	17 949
Concreting sand[5]	,,	37 587	32 468	32 667	31 118	27 483	29 164	29 455	26 699	25 427	25 242	26 109
Gravel[5,6]	,,	67 943	59 876	63 069	58 405	53 138	54 426	54 056	51 454	48 351	48 920	50 791
Manufactured lightweight aggregates[2,7]	Thousand m³	1 091	1 012	1 274	1 546	1 399	1 402	[14]				
Crushed rock aggregates:[8]	Thousand tonnes											
used as roadstone (coated)		20 308	18 435	17 146	14 577	14 374	13 910	14 413	14 366	13 179	13 800	..
roadstone (uncoated)	,,	54 246	49 122	41 216	37 548	35 756	37 807	41 785	42 896	35 949	39 198	..
fill and ballast	,,	30 481	33 737	34 301	29 973	29 227	31 131	31 722	31 619	31 049	37 129	..
concrete aggregate	,,	21 403	16 958	16 930	16 227	15 259	15 872	15 588	13 653	11 205	12 721	..
Ready mixed concrete[3]	Million m³	31.7	27.8	26.7	24.5	23.5	23.8	24.4	22.4	19.9	20.7	21.5
Asbestos cement products:	Thousand tonnes											
Corrugated sheets		433.9	406.0	291.9	301.7	313.4	309.0	330.0	284.5	219.4	217.7	206.0
Flat sheets	,,	46.8	48.4	41.7	49.2	45.6	45.4	27.6	17.0	11.4	13.2	10.3
All other products	,,	118.8	93.5	89.1	93.0	90.9	74.4	47.9	50.7	34.7	30.8	23.2
Clay roofing tiles[3,9]	Thousand m²	1 238	1 195	1 108	1 170	1 192	1 207	2 265	1 698	1 635	1 632	2 260[15]
Concrete roofing tiles[2]	,,	30 669	27 359	25 942	29 839	24 151	27 899	28 263	28 813	23 345	25 551	33 243
Concrete building blocks:[2]												
dense aggregate	,,	20 849	17 533	18 407	18 092	19 206	20 780	22 298	21 014	18 911	23 918	29 186
lightweight aggregate	,,	35 034	23 196	26 015	31 210	27 118	29 937	28 407	23 779	20 896	23 395	25 544
aerated concrete	,,	16 885	15 813	17 715	20 461	20 542	20 343	22 385	22 027	15 758	16 372	20 912
Concrete pipes[3,9,10]	Thousand tonnes	1 470	1 330	1 424	1 374	1 111	1 158	1 063	692	648	694	744
Pitch fibre pipes and conduits	,,	30.1	24.5	16.8	17.4	13.1	11.0	[14]				
Roofing slates	,,	17.0	18.0	17.4								
Slates (damp-proof course)	,,	0.9	0.6	0.5	15.8	14.3	15.0	14.5	17.7	16.3	22.7	18.4
Gypsum (excluding anhydrite)	,,	3 689	3 115	3 206	3 148	3 136	3 144	3 396	3 264	2 667	2 566	2 978
Plaster	,,	1 125	1 038	1 047	1 053	988	975	949	960	775	764	855
Plasterboard	Thousand m²	112 801	110 861	104 396	116 999	101 827	114 120	113 961	111 132	101 987	106 147	118 807
Hardboard and insulation board[3,9]	Thousand tonnes	35.3	29.3	24.6	30.2	31.3	31.4	30.8	29.5	[14]		
Unglazed floorquarries[3,9]	Thousand m²	1 325	1 241	1 146	1 019	1 155	1 273	1 220	1 123	1 007	949	1 013[15]
Unglazed tiles[3,9]	,,	1 840	1 906	1 704	1 769	1 900	2 025	2 099	2 332	2 085	1 357	1 151[15]
Glazed tiles[3,9]	,,	17 142	16 376	14 212	15 448	15 375	15 939	[14]				
Cast iron pipes and fittings[3,11,12]	Thousand tonnes	43	40	40	50	38	43	34	[14]			
Pressure pipes and fittings[3,12]	,,	350	340	291	267	222	278	278	[14]			
Copper tubing[3,13]	,,	79	66	64	73	73	80	79	69	68	72	74

1. The figures are summaries of returns made by manufacturers and producers. They represent total production and not merely the quantities available for building purposes.
2. From 1975 figures include additional sites. The change has had the following effects: Building bricks production increased by 1 per cent; concrete building blocks production increased by an average of 11.0 per cent; manufactured lightweight aggregate 24 per cent and concrete roofing tiles production increased by less than 1 per cent.
3. United Kingdom.
4. Including sand used in the production of sand lime bricks.
5. From 1975 the figures relate to production derived from the Annual Minerals Raised Inquiries. These include additional sites not covered by the quarterly inquiries on which data prior to 1975 is based. From 1979 figures represent volume sold, not production.
6. Figures include hoggin, concrete aggregate, other purposes (excluding fill) and fill.
7. Including aglite, foamed slag, leca, lytag and solite.
8. From 1979 figures represent volume sold, not production.
9. Figures represent volume sold, not production.
10. From 1974 figures relate to manufacturers' sales by firms employing 11 or more persons. From 1975 figures relate to manufacturers' sales by firms employing 25 or more persons.
11. Including rainwater, hot water and soil pipes and gutters.
12. 1975 was a 53-week year.
13. Figures relate to the production of copper tubes for all purposes including those used in the construction industry.
14. Series discontinued.
15. Provisional.

Sources Department of the Environment; Business Statistics Office; Department of Trade and Industry; World Bureau of Metal Statistics

8.31 Construction: value of output in Great Britain

£ million

	1973	1974	1975	1976	1977	1978	1979	1980	1981	1982	1983
All work: total	8 613	9 733	11 077	12 176	13 309	15 702	18 871	22 052	21 547	22 540	24 343
New work: total	6 128	6 804	7 724	8 477	8 972	10 313	11 722	13 055	12 354	12 629	13 396
New housing: total	2 485	2 536	2 963	3 521	3 545	4 124	4 384	4 296	3 738	3 920	4 849
For public sector	849	1 100	1 453	1 760	1 717	1 749	1 711	1 711	1 222	1 021	1 120
For private sector	1 636	1 436	1 510	1 761	1 828	2 375	2 673	2 585	2 516	2 899	3 729
Other new work: total	3 643	4 268	4 761	4 956	5 427	6 189	7 338	8 760	8 616	8 709	8 546
For public sector	1 814	2 001	2 347	2 568	2 603	2 764	3 068	3 524	3 572	3 671	3 729
For private sector: total	1 829	2 267	2 414	2 388	2 824	3 425	4 270	5 236	5 044	5 038	4 817
Industrial	825	1 050	1 150	1 187	1 512	1 802	2 351	2 806	2 382	2 087	1 850
Commercial	1 004	1 217	1 264	1 201	1 312	1 623	1 919	2 430	2 662	2 951	2 967
Repair and maintenance: total	2 485	2 929	3 353	3 699	4 337	5 389	7 148	8 997	9 193	9 911	10 948
Housing	1 255	1 474	1 625	1 755	2 069	2 571	3 601	4 480	4 568	4 970	5 622
Public other work	860	974	1 208	1 338	1 528	1 854	2 269	2 920	3 026	3 285	3 548
Private other work	370	481	520	606	740	964	1 278	1 597	1 599	1 656	1 777

Note:
(i) Output by contractors, including unrecorded estimates by small firms and self-employed workers, and by the public sectors' direct labour departments classified to construction in the *Standard Industrial Classification, Revised 1980.*

Source Department of the Environment

8.32 Construction: value of new orders obtained by contractors[1]
Great Britain

£ million

	1973	1974	1975	1976	1977	1978	1979	1980	1981	1982	1983
New work: total	6 933	6 009	6 375	6 874	7 182	8 927	10 024	10 110	10 722	11 443	13 518
New housing: total	2 509	2 009	2 663	2 880	2 627	3 231	3 321	2 702	2 685	3 912	5 063
From public sector	850	1 093	1 481	1 465	1 173	1 271	1 056	758	672	984	985
From private sector	1 659	916	1 181	1 416	1 455	1 960	2 265	1 944	2 013	2 928	4 078
Other new work: total	4 424	4 000	3 712	3 994	4 555	5 696	6 703	7 408	8 037	7 531	8 455
From public sector: total	2 188	1 958	2 248	2 135	2 188	2 618	2 920	3 243	3 689	3 432	4 175
Gas, electricity, coalmining	99	190	253	182	220	247	291	390	431	280	287
Railways and air transport	58	51	85	75	121	120	78	173	275	82	136
Schools	343	281	318	281	251	231	305	292	239	219	326
Universities	43	19	23	27	24	26	26	38	42	32	34
Health	218	164	210	189	202	261	287	320	478	467	444
Offices, factories, etc.	246	222	294	312	327	585	582	589	519	584	691
Roads	460	389	390	368	392	424	466	562	781	770	799
Harbours	40	74	84	53	98	108	111	97	95	95	122
Water	66	74	95	118	96	78	82	67	129	110	128
Sewerage	287	148	201	189	142	184	196	227	211	221	304
Miscellaneous	328	346	295	341	316	354	497	487	489	574	905
From private sector: total[2]	2 236	2 042	1 464	1 859	2 367	3 078	3 783	4 165	4 348	4 099	4 280
Industrial: total	1 053	1 029	684	879	1 188	1 447	1 864	1 803	1 554	1 327	1 543
Commercial: total	1 182	1 013	780	980	1 179	1 631	1 919	2 362	2 794	2 772	2 737
Offices	547	509	304	469	524	678	821	1 045	1 451	1 414	1 209
Shops	272	189	184	210	270	380	414	536	531	521	549
Entertainment	165	130	92	133	161	248	308	342	388	382	363
Garages	42	32	22	34	55	99	114	125	98	134	166
Schools and colleges	18	15	9	12	29	35	60	44	48	48	67
Miscellaneous	138	137	169	121	140	191	202	270	278	273	384

1. Classified to construction in the *Standard Industrial Classification. Revised 1980.*
2. Figures for private sector include work to be carried out by contractors on their own initiative for sale.

Source Department of the Environment

8.33 Metal goods, engineering and vehicles industries
Estimated total sales of UK manufactured goods[1,2]
Standard Industrial Classification 1980

£ millions

	Activity heading	1978	1979	1980	1981	1982	1983
Division 3							
Manufacture of metal goods not elsewhere specified[3]							
Class 31							
Total		5 375	6 016	5 881	5 968	6 515	7 217
Forging, pressing and stamping	3120	962	1 073	1 005	890	946	1 026
Bolts, nuts, washers, rivets, springs and non-precision chains	3137	474	472	440	405	419	463
Heat and surface treatment of metals, (including sintering)	3138	305	331	288	318	400	434
Metal doors, windows, etc.	3142	273	346	474	495	525	599
Hand tools and implements	3161	167	178	173	193	192	214
Cutlery, spoons, forks and similar tableware; razors	3162	74	74	79	82	83	92
Metal storage vessels (mainly non-industrial)	3163	60	66	64	68	72	82
Packaging products of metal	3164	1 083	1 210	1 126	1 107	1 200	1 299
Domestic heating and cooking appliances (non-electrical)	3165	199	222	224	239	241	259
Metal furniture and safes	3166	289	358	365	348	362	401
Domestic utensils of metal	3167	207	214	213	172	180	179
Miscellaneous finished metal products	3169	1 282	1 474	1 430	1 651	1 895	2 169
Mechanical engineering[4]							
Class 32							
Total		13 126	14 470	15 330	14 721	15 900	15 882
Fabricated constructional steelwork	3204	773	957	886	1 004	1 234	1 151
Boilers and process plant fabrications	3205	914	1 053	1 103	1 222	1 530	1 557
Agricultural machinery	3211	297	308	282	246	261	301
Wheeled tractors	3212	806	973	908	915	881	903
Metal-working machine tools	3221	601	664	726	542	558	502
Engineers' small tools	3222	545	617	727	609	595	594
Textile machinery	3230	282	294	278	256	240	232
Food, drink and tobacco processing machinery; packaging and bottling machinery	3244	391	429	457	445	506	520
Chemical industry machinery; furnaces and kilns; gas, water and waste treatment plant	3245	351	380	386	347	377	370
Mining machinery	3251	501	599	675	603	724	639
Construction and earth moving equipment	3254	869	954	965	1 019	936	821
Mechanical lifting and handling equipment	3255	1 044	1 163	1 205	1 014	1 111	1 177
Precision chains and other mechanical power transmission equipment	3261	420	449	513	439	425	405
Ball, needle and roller bearings	3262	195	214	248	209	205	190
Machinery for working wood, rubber, plastics, leather and making paper, glass, bricks and similar materials; laundry and dry cleaning machinery	3275	321	349	364	331	338	317
Printing, bookbinding and paper goods machinery	3276	297	346	376	355	387	407
Industrial (including marine) engines	3281	751	663	781	861	872	750
Compressors and fluid power equipment	3283	538	549	592	531	580	582
Refrigerating, space-heating, ventilating and air-conditioning equipment	3284	771	867	913	865	986	1 094
Scales, weighing machinery and portable power tools	3285	181	230	246	224	227	234
Miscellaneous industrial and commercial machinery	3286	458	515	550	525	559	616
Pumps	3287	335	352	395	390	407	375
Industrial valves	3288	290	332	397	400	426	414
Miscellaneous mechanical marine and precision engineering	3289	632	680	782	769	793	881
Ordnance, small arms and ammunition	3290	563	533	575	600	742	850
Manufacture of office machinery and data processing equipment							
Class 33							
Total		853	1 076	1 141	1 122	1 208	1 579
Office machinery	3301	115	122	120	111	111	115
Electronic data processing equipment	3302	738	954	1 021	1 011	1 097	1 464

See footnotes on page 173.

Source Department of Trade and Industry

8.33
(continued)

Metal goods, engineering and vehicles industries
Estimated total sales of UK manufactured goods[1, 2]
Standard Industrial Classification 1980

£ million

	Activity heading	1978	1979	1980	1981	1982	1983
Electrical and electronic engineering[5] Class 34							
Total		8 528	9 495	10 632	10 898	11 881	13 062
Insulated wires and cables	3410	654	781	861	893	948	1 029
Basic electrical equipment	3420	1 750	1 791	2 030	1 938	2 174	2 124
Batteries and accumulators	3432	294	320	334	300	326	289
Alarms and signalling equipment	3433	137	169	189	187	203	242
Electrical equipment for motor vehicles, cycles and aircraft	3434	441	472	456	398	433	484
Miscellaneous electrical equipment for industrial use	3435	201	228	233	218	243	231
Telegraph and telephone apparatus and equipment	3441	588	690	939	1 124	1 284	1 434
Electrical instruments and control systems	3442	501	580	641	708	800	912
Radio and electronic capital goods	3443	983	1 168	1 474	1 752	1 933	2 127
Components other than active components, mainly for electronic equipment	3444	498	604	731	650	749	851
Gramophone records and pre-recorded tapes	3452	143	154	134	127	124	141
Active components and electronic sub-assemblies	3453	603	665	699	643	665	850
Electronic consumer goods and miscellaneous equipment	3454	544	550	522	544	585	734
Domestic-type electric appliances	3460	782	871	916	922	902	1 055
Electric lamps and other electric lighting equipment	3470	409	452	473	494	512	559
Manufacture of motor vehicles and parts thereof Class 35							
Total		7 964	8 597	8 349	7 787	8 296	8 626
Motor vehicles and their engines	3510	4 425	4 761	4 603	4 396	4 843	4 778
Motor vehicle bodies and vehicle parts	3521 and 3530	3 107	3 353	3 338	3 058	3 111	3 424
Trailers, semi-trailers and caravans	3522/3	432	483	408	334	342	424
Manufacture of other transport equipment[6] Class 36							
Total		2 575	3 014	4 225	4 702	5 234	5 243
Railway and tramway vehicles	3620	216	308	341	355	344	276
Cycles and motor cycles	3633/4	137	130	134	92	102	121
Aerospace equipment manufacturing, repairing and modification	3640	2 182	2 528	3 701	4 209	4 738	4 789
Baby carriages and wheelchairs	3650	41	49	48	45	50	56
Instrument engineering Class 37							
Total		1 277	1 430	1 575	1 526	1 728	1 892
Measuring, checking and precision instruments and apparatus	3710	611	707	810	785	877	994
Medical and surgical equipment and orthopaedic appliances	3720	165	198	218	251	308	331
Spectacles and unmounted lenses	3731	68	77	91	100	98	123
Optical precision instruments	3732	65	69	82	89	107	135
Photographic and cinematographic equipment	3733	233	265	273	215	221	207
Clocks, watches and other timing devices	3740	136	115	100	86	120	102

Note More detailed information can be found in the PQ series of
Business Monitors for the activities listed above.

1. These figures represent the total sales of principal products of each
activity excluding waste products and work done. Estimates of the
sales of principal products of establishments falling below the
employment threshold of the Quarterly Sales Inquiries are included.
2. The total may differ from the sum of its constituent parts due to
rounding.

3. Excluding ferrous and non-ferrous metal foundries AH 3111/2.
4. Excluding process engineering contractors AH 3246.
5. Excluding electrical equipment installation AH 3480.
6. Excluding shipbuilding and repairing AH 3610.

Source Department of Trade and Industry

8.34 Volume index numbers of sales and orders for the engineering industries

	Total			Home			Export		
	Orders on hand end of period	Net orders[1]	Sales	Orders on hand end of period	Net orders[1]	Sales	Orders on hand end of period	Net orders[1]	Sales
	1980 Average = 100	1980 Average monthly sales = 100		1980 Average = 100	1980 Average monthly sales = 100		1980 Average = 100	1980 Average monthly sales = 100	
Engineering industries combined SIC 1980 Class 32, 33, 34, 37									
1978	106	112	105	105	112	105	110	110	105
1979	106	106	106	107	108	106	104	100	103
1980	93	93	100	91	92	100	97	95	100
1981	104	96	90	102	94	89	111	99	91
1982	101	89	92	102	90	92	99	85	91
1983	97	93	94	96	93	96	101	91	89
Percentage change 1983 on 1982[2]	−4.0	+4.5	+2.0	−6.0	+3.0	+4.0	+2.0	+7.0	−2.0
Mechanical engineering SIC 1980 Class 32									
1978	114	115	110	114	118	112	113	108	105
1979	114	109	109	115	110	110	112	106	106
1980	89	89	100	84	87	100	95	92	100
1981	103	93	86	100	91	85	109	96	89
1982	92	82	87	94	85	87	88	76	85
1983	84	78	81	80	78	85	92	77	76
Percentage change 1983 on 1982[2]	−8.5	−5.0	−7.0	−15.0	−8.0	−2.5	+4.5	+1.5	−10.5
Electrical engineering SIC 1980 Class 33, 34									
1978	99	107	99	96	105	97	108	114	107
1979	100	102	102	100	104	101	99	95	102
1980	98	99	100	97	98	100	101	102	100
1981	107	98	92	104	97	92	113	103	94
1982	108	99	97	108	99	97	109	96	100
1983	110	111	110	110	112	110	109	110	109
Percentage change 1983 on 1982[2]	+2.0	+12.0	+13.0	+2.0	+13.0	+13.5	−	+14.5	+9.0
Instrument engineering SIC 1980 Class 37									
1978	116	108	103	114	110	107	120	104	96
1979	110	100	102	112	103	104	108	96	99
1980	91	96	100	91	95	100	90	96	100
1981	104	103	100	116	103	97	85	101	102
1982	97	91	92	98	83	87	95	103	101
1983	94	93	93	96	89	90	91	98	99
Percentage change 1983 on 1982[2]	−3.0	+2.0	+1.0	−2.0	+7.0	+3.5	−4.0	−5.0	−2.0

1. Net of cancellations.
2. The percentage changes have been rounded to the nearest half percentage point.

Source Department of Trade and Industry

8.35 Merchant shipbuilding[1]: vessels of 100 gross tons and over

	1973	1974	1975	1976	1977	1978	1979	1980	1981	1982	1983
Completions											
Value (£ million): total	230	228	270	375	363	404	412	363	194	408	390
For export[2]	61	62	98	144	134	134	122	168	57	57	200
Number of vessels: total	137	134	144	140	104	96	95	88	51	67	68
Tankers of 300 gross tons and over	9	10	12	14	8	11	10	10	2	8	4
Cargo and passenger[3]	50	35	38	44	40	45	45	42	23	23	25
Other (excluding non-propelled)[4]	67	85	81	76	52	36	40	25	26	36	39
Non-propelled	11	4	13	6	4	4	–	11	–	–	–
For export[2]	26	31	41	43	25	27	27	33	10	12	22
Thousand gross tons[5]: total	1 069	1 189	1 203	1 460	1 007	1 135	707	431	217	453	540
Tankers of 300 gross tons and over	221	457	592	720	426	649	331	87	3	134	212
Cargo and passenger[3]	804	673	573	691	540	474	353	320	186	280	297
Other (excluding non-propelled)[4]	40	56	34	42	36	11	22	20	28	39	30
Non-propelled	4	3	5	7	6	1	–	2	–	–	–
For export[2]	327	235	365	589	410	396	243	232	101	104	276
Net new orders[5]											
Value (£ million): total	989	364	59	104	271	234	252	283	383	313	279
For export[2, 6]	90	285	– 15	145	39	151	4	31	251	151	82
Number of vessels: total	292	140	22	87	90	64	46	58	72	57	45
Tankers of 300 gross tons and over[6]	58	2	– 1	– 12	5	4	5	7	3	1	–
Other	234	138	23	99	85	60	41	51	69	56	45
For export[2]	63	52	3	38	7	34	–	10	26	21	12
Thousand gross tons[5, 6]: total	4 357	90	– 76	– 523	111	273	315	506	484	355	114
Tankers of 300 gross tons and over[6]	3 233	– 535	– 125	– 919	– 101	9	147	170	12	2	–
Other[6]	1 124	625	49	397	211	265	168	336	472	353	114
For export[2, 6]	– 30	723	– 118	192	200	173	15	97	386	123	92
Orders on hand (at end of year)											
Value (£ million): total	1 402	1 538	1 327	1 057	1 011	854	670	601	783	720	563
For export[2]	251	474	363	364	314	310	194	57	251	339	194
Not yet laid down											
Number of vessels: total	217	210	114	85	76	40	23	20	36	22	13
Tankers of 300 gross tons and over	54	42	31	7	7	4	5	2	1	–	–
Other	163	168	83	78	69	36	18	18	35	22	13
For export[2]	56	72	38	35	20	19	2	1	19	13	6
Thousand gross tons[5]: total	5 384	4 256	3 002	1 190	561	247	264	300	350	229	65
Tankers of 300 gross tons and over	3 982	2 841	2 147	470	178	43	164	142	6	–	–
Other	1 402	1 414	855	720	383	204	100	158	344	229	65
For export[2]	781	1 075	576	460	149	158	23	16	317	135	41
Under construction											
Number of vessels: total	158	171	145	119	113	117	85	58	63	66	50
Tankers of 300 gross tons and over	23	27	25	23	20	16	10	10	12	6	2
Other	135	144	120	96	93	101	75	48	51	60	48
For export[2]	32	38	34	33	31	40	31	9	7	22	18
Thousand gross tons[5]: total	1 881	1 951	1 945	1 754	1 477	917	508	555	766	761	497
Tankers of 300 gross tons and over	1 029	1 202	1 189	1 216	970	453	151	259	405	280	67
Other	852	749	755	538	506	464	356	295	361	481	430
For export[2]	313	507	521	348	564	302	213	86	69	250	154

1. Includes naval vessels, registered as merchant ships.
2. Vessels recorded for export if they are for other than United Kingdom registration.
3. Includes bulk carriers, container ships, coasters (300 gross tons and over), colliers, tramps, passenger liners and passenger/cargo liners.
4. Ferries, trawlers, tugs, dredgers and other miscellaneous self-propelled vessels.

5. The total tonnage specified on ordering vessels differs slightly from the total actual measured tonnage at completion. Figures with a minus sign show the effects of cancellations, alterations of tonnage and changes of registration of ships already on order.
6. Modifications and cancellations exceed new orders for the types and periods, indicated by a minus sign.

Source Department of Trade and Industry

8.36 Motor vehicle production

Number

	1973	1974	1975	1976	1977	1978	1979	1980	1981	1982	1983
Motor vehicles											
SIC 1980, Group 351											
Passenger cars: Total[1]	1 747 321	1 534 119	1 267 696	1 333 449	1 315 972	1 222 949	1 070 452	923 744	954 650	887 679	1 044 597
1 000 c.c. and under	234 014	205 106	165 164	134 748	146 900	145 271	127 157	156 735	229 189	197 153	194 064
Over 1 000 c.c. but not over											
1 600 c.c.	907 965	784 379	649 062	736 020	725 463	696 658	616 105	521 933	526 498	547 676	723 289
Over 1 600 c.c. but not over											
2 800 c.c.	523 174	467 106	403 921	404 712	379 603	314 138	277 199	209 635	153 957	97 536	77 504
Over 2 800 c.c.	82 168	77 528	49 549	57 969	64 006	66 882	49 991	35 441	45 006	45 314	49 740
Commercial vehicles											
Total	416 623	402 566	380 705	372 057	398 268	384 518	408 440	389 170	229 555	268 798	244 514
Of which:											
Light commercial vehicles						243 756	261 974	261 143	157 744	189 094	175 338
Trucks:	373 811	356 439	335 592	329 448	358 670						
Under 7.5 tonnes						23 336	32 970	24 199	14 294	16 367	12 792
Over 7.5 tonnes						82 532	77 807	74 890	41 152	43 469	34 850
Motive units for articulated											
vehicles	12 376	12 460	9 470	9 433	11 965	11 852	9 778	7 366	3 921	6 761	5 918
Buses and coaches:											
Single deck buses	28 689	31 776	33 202	30 761	25 830	20 583	23 407	19 007	9 903	11 518	13 870
Double deck buses	1 747	1 891	2 441	2 415	1 803	2 459	2 504	2 565	2 541	1 589	1 746

TIME SERIES. Figures for motor vehicles relate to periods of 52 weeks (53 weeks in 1976 and 1983).

1. From 1981, certain models previously recorded under assembly were re-categorised under production. Further details are in Business Monitor *PM3510.*

Source   Department of Trade and Industry

8.37 Alcoholic drink

	Unit	1973	1974	1975	1976	1977	1978	1979	1980	1981	1982	1983
Spirits[1]	Thousand											
Production	hectolitres of alcohol	5 119	5 252	4 446	3 994	4 322	5 211	5 207	4 907	3 251	3 021	2 898
Released for home consumption												
Total[2]	,,	781	863	821	925	794	957	1 055	996	945	891	916
Imported:												
Rum	,,	88	95	86	86	76	90	99	86	80	73	73
Brandy	,,	73	67	60	66	57	69	77	71	64	66	69
Other	,,	35	40	38	43	41	52	62	57	58	59	66
Home produced:												
Whisky (mature)[3]	,,	398	451	424	484	403	488	525	502	477	448	445
Gin	,,	133	142	137	152	124	141	158	144	130	124	137
Other	,,	54	68	75	93	92	117	133	136	136	122	127
Beer[4]	Thousand											
Production	hectolitres	60 567	63 042	64 568	65 636	65 239	66 418	67 419	64 830	61 721	59 786	60 324
Released for home consumption												
Total	,,	62 637	63 988	65 627	66 531	65 891	67 802	68 248	65 490	62 317	60 920	62 232
Home produced	,,	59 061	61 228	62 842	63 663	63 531	65 416	65 688	63 188	60 024	58 668	59 586
Imported	,,	3 576	2 761	2 785	2 867	2 360	2 386	2 558	2 302	2 293	2 252	2 646
Imported wine/wine of fresh grapes												
Released for home consumption												
Total	,,	2 897	2 988	2 913	3 156	3 021	3 620	3 962	4 022	4 328	4 399	4 810
Heavy	,,	831	839	797	1 254	1 140	1 364	1 356	1 257	1 191	1 074	1 079
Light	,,	1 915	2 024	1 995	1 767	1 744	2 095	2 428	2 581	2 941	3 132	3 512
Sparkling	,,	150	127	121	136	138	161	179	183	196	193	218
British wine/made-wine												
Released for home consumption	,,	673	778	593	541	534	566	572	515	539	509	549
Cider and perry												
Released for home consumption	,,					2 215	2 222	2 324	2 255	2 409	2 899	3 258

1. Potable spirits distilled including spirits produced from molasses.
2. Includes a small amount of spirits unclassified by origin and/or tariff code number.
3. Before April 1983, the figures represent quantities of all mature home produced spirits.
4. From January 1976 the figures take account of brewing at high gravity with the addition of some brewing liquor after fermentation.

Source HM Customs and Excise

8.38 Tobacco products[1]

	Unit	1977	1978	1979	1980	1981	1982	1983
Released for home consumption								
Cigarettes: total	Thousand million	124.9	125.7	124.5	122.0	109.8	102.3	102.6
Home produced	,,	124.4	124.2	122.7	120.0	108.3	100.6	100.6
Imported	,,	0.5	1.4	1.9	2.0	1.5	1.8	2.0
Cigars: total	Million kg.	3.4	3.1	3.3	3.2	2.9	2.7	2.7
Home produced	,,	2.7	2.4	2.5	2.5	2.2	2.3	2.4
Imported	,,	0.7	0.7	0.8	0.7	0.7	0.4	0.2
Hand-rolling tobacco: total	,,	7.2	6.1	5.7	5.8	6.2	6.3	5.9
Home produced	,,	7.2	6.1	5.7	5.8	6.2	6.2	5.9
Imported	,,	–	–	–	–	–	–	–
Other smoking and chewing tobacco: total	,,	5.5	4.3	4.0	3.7	3.6	3.3	3.1
Home produced	,,	5.5	4.2	3.8	3.6	3.5	3.3	3.1
Imported	,,	–	0.1	0.2	0.1	–	–	–

1. Figures before 1977 are not available.

Source HM Customs and Excise

9 Agriculture, fisheries and food

Agricultural censuses and surveys (Tables 9.3 – 9.5)

The data in these tables vary between the different countries of the United Kingdom as follows:

The coverage from 1973 to 1979 includes all holdings in the United Kingdom with 40 standard man days or more (a standard man day (smd) represents 8 hours productive work by an adult male worker under average conditions). All holdings with less than 40 smd in Scotland are excluded but in England and Wales and Northern Ireland holdings with less than 40 smd are excluded only if they have less than 4 hectares of crops and grass and no regular whole-time worker.

From 1977 (table 9.4 from 1980) figures for England and Wales relate to all known agricultural holdings including minor holdings. Data on minor holdings in Scotland and Northern Ireland are excluded but see footnote 2 to table 9.4.

From 1981 the figures included for Northern Ireland relate to all holdings with one European Size Unit (ESU) or more; or 6 hectares or more of total area; or one or more whole-time workers (excluding the owner). This revised threshold resulted in the deletion of 7 000 holdings.

The estimated yields of sugar beet and hops (table 9.4) are obtained from production figures supplied by British Sugar plc, Producers' Association and the Hops Marketing Board Ltd. In Great Britain potato yields are estimated in consultation with the Potato Marketing Board.

This information relates also to table 6.5.

Average weekly earnings of agricultural workers (Table 9.7)

Data on the earnings of agricultural workers have been collected since 1945 through a series of investigations known as the Wages and Employment Enquiry. Appointed officers of the Ministry of Agriculture, Fisheries and Food, the Department of Agriculture and Fisheries for Scotland and the Welsh Office Agricultural Department undertake this series of investigations in the course of their duties as Wages Inspectors. Under the Agricultural Wages Act 1948, these officers monitor minimum wages determined by the Agricultural Wages Board. They visit a random sample of farms each year (approximately 4 000 in 1983) and collect information on workers' earnings, hours, overtime, bonuses, perquisites, etc.; the analysed results of which are published in quarterly press notices and annual reports. Summary tables of earnings and hours are also published by the Department of Employment, the Welsh Office Agricultural Department and the Department of Agriculture and Fisheries for Scotland. The enquiry also provides data used by the Agricultural Wages Board when considering wage claims and by the Ministry in estimating the cost of labour in agriculture for the Annual Review and similar purposes.

Fisheries (Tables 9.12 – 9.14)

Data relating to the weight and value of landings of fish in Great Britain (Table 9.12) is generally obtained from sales notes completed at fish market auctions.

Fishing fleet information (Tables 9.13 and 9.14) is obtained from vessel registers maintained by the Ministry of Agriculture, Fisheries and Food in England and Wales and the Department of Agriculture and Fisheries for Scotland.

Estimated household food consumption by all households in Great Britain—National Food Survey (Table 9.17)

The Sample

In the course of a year the National Food Survey investigates the food budgets of about 7 500 households in 44 parliamentary constituencies, selected so as to be representative of Great Britain as a whole. A full description of the sampling methods of the National Food Survey is given in the Annual Report for 1981, *Household Food Consumption and Expenditure: 1981* (HMSO 1983).

Household

A group of persons living in the same dwelling and sharing common catering arrangements. The size of household is defined in terms of the number of persons who spend at least four nights in the household during the week of the Survey *and* also have at least one meal a day from the household food supply on at least four days. The head of the household and the housewife are regarded as persons in *all* cases.

Adult—A person aged 18 years or over.

Child—A person under 18 years of age.

Food purchased

Quantities of all foods purchased during the week for consumption in the home (but including *purchases* of milk at school). The Survey excludes food eaten outside the home (except packed meals prepared at home), chocolate and sugar confectionery, soft drinks, alcoholic drinks, vitamin preparations, and food obtained specifically for consumption by domestic pets. For a few minor miscellaneous items, expenditure is recorded, but not the quantity (e.g. artificial sweeteners, flavourings, colourings, etc.).

Free food

Quantity of food entering the household without payment, for consumption during the Survey week. Milk supplied under the Milk in Schools Scheme is included although it does not actually enter the household. Food grown or produced by the household and stored in bulk is recorded only when it is withdrawn from store.

Consumption

Averaged over a sufficiently large number of households and a sufficiently long period, the average quantity of food purchased *plus* the quantity of 'free' food will equal the average consumption if there is no general change in the level of larder stocks.

9.1 Agricultural output, input and income at current prices[1]
Calendar years

£ million

	1973	1974	1975	1976	1977	1978	1979	1980	1981	1982	1983[2]
Output											
1. Farm crops[3]: total	726	890	1 115	1 464	1 387	1 525	1 895	2 126	2 463	3 054	3 008
Wheat	226	283	296	318	366	449	605	786	855	1 165	1 136
Barley	248	319	329	379	414	550	557	651	811	899	839
Oats	15	16	14	18	20	19	19	24	25	29	27
Potatoes	127	150	328	585	376	260	385	312	392	452	504
Sugar beet	69	59	85	97	133	159	206	195	192	252	213
Hops	9	9	9	11	11	13	17	23	25	28	25
Beans for stockfeed	6	8	9	5	6	9	16	15	21	17	19
Oilseed rape	2	9	8	15	23	28	43	69	87	157	182
Other[4]	22	37	37	34	39	38	47	52	55	54	63
2. Horticulture: total	416	506	570	641	768	753	858	902	968	1 016	1 126
Vegetables (including mushrooms)	246	312	376	412	497	469	548	559	590	599	681
Fruit	88	105	95	116	145	153	158	170	187	212	230
Other[5]	81	90	98	114	126	131	153	173	191	205	216
3. Livestock: total	1 385	1 543	1 918	2 202	2 476	2 754	3 043	3 287	3 529	3 805	4 015
Fat cattle and calves	564	617	897	995	1 060	1 258	1 420	1 500	1 600	1 668	1 831
Fat sheep and lambs	156	164	187	240	267	300	319	405	465	517	562
Fat pigs	421	468	494	557	642	689	744	790	862	925	911
Poultry	211	256	296	360	445	444	488	508	515	603	617
Other[6]	34	38	43	50	61	63	71	85	87	91	93
4. Livestock products: total	1 022	1 184	1 388	1 692	1 941	2 065	2 276	2 500	2 679	2 964	3 047
Milk and milk products	694	833	1 063	1 292	1 484	1 620	1 764	1 960	2 101	2 383	2 486
Eggs for food	304	326	294	362	412	400	462	489	522	526	501
Clip wool	16	17	20	24	30	33	35	36	35	34	36
Other[7]	7	8	11	14	14	12	16	16	21	20	23
5. Own account capital formation: total[8]	60	7	− 7	27	16	65	24	47	94	136	123
6. Total output i.e. items 1 to 5	3 608	4 130	4 984	6 025	6 588	7 161	8 096	8 862	9 732	10 974	11 319
7. Compensation payments and sundry receipts: total	24	36	40	36	23	31	29	33	60	62	106
Deficiency payments on retained cereal	5	–	–	–	–	–	–				
PMB compensation payments	–	4	–	–	–	8	2	6	4	–	0.6
CAP support	3	2	3	3	2	3	4	5	6	8	5
Brucellosis eradication incentive	3	5	7	3	2	2	2	2	3	1	2
Animal disease compensation	6	18	21	19	6	5	7	8	2	2	13
Other[9]	7	8	10	12	13	13	14	14	17	18	19
8. Production grants: total	97	93	152	115	101	91	84	130	141	150	139
Fertilisers and lime	19	13	4	5	–	–	–	–	–	–	–
Other[10]	78	80	147	110	101	90	84	130	141	150	139
9. Total receipts i.e. items 6 to 8	3 729	4 259	5 176	6 177	6 712	7 283	8 209	9 024	9 933	11 186	11 564
10. Work-in-progress and output stocks Value of physical change: total	46	20	− 163	− 44	178	15	− 29	− 28	− 89	44	32
Work-in-progress[11]	61	− 9	− 53	− 23	16	1	− 23	− 42	− 15	47	3
Output stocks[12]	− 15	29	− 110	− 21	162	15	− 6	14	− 74	− 2	29
11. Gross output i.e. item 9 *plus* 10	3 775	4 278	5 013	6 133	6 890	7 298	8 180	8 996	9 843	11 230	11 595
12. Intermediate output[13]: total	293	358	354	437	480	481	643	689	687	859	972
Feed[14]	254	308	291	336	364	393	539	586	564	725	840
Seed	39	50	64	101	116	88	104	102	123	134	132
13. Final output i.e. item 11 *minus* 12	3 481	3 921	4 658	5 696	6 411	6 817	7 537	8 308	9 157	10 371	10 623

See footnotes on page 178.

Source Agricultural Departments

9.1
Agriculture output, input and income at current prices[1]
Calendar years

(*continued*)

£ million

	1973	1974	1975	1976	1977	1978	1979	1980	1981	1982	1983[2]
Input											
14. Expenditure: total[15]	1 909	2 329	2 578	3 189	3 717	3 859	4 461	4 842	5 256	5 880	6 260
Feedingstuffs	977	1 157	1 180	1 567	1 827	1 774	2 089	2 188	2 282	2 612	2 832
Seeds	84	103	124	188	216	197	220	218	257	282	285
Livestock (imported and interfarm expenses)	94	103	127	109	145	175	137	151	154	167	171
Fertilisers and lime (before subsidy)	213	296	325	376	426	491	548	651	787	816	826
Machinery: total	224	278	330	380	453	493	593	668	737	825	901
Repairs	114	131	159	180	209	244	274	307	330	362	387
Fuel and oil	85	122	139	163	200	202	265	299	337	388	436
Other expenses	25	25	32	37	44	47	54	62	70	76	79
Farm maintenance: total	71	83	103	122	133	144	165	183	193	218	233
by occupier	55	67	84	101	109	117	134	147	152	172	183
by landlord	16	17	19	21	24	27	31	36	41	46	50
Miscellaneous expenditure[16]	247	309	389	448	517	584	709	784	845	961	1 011
15. Input stocks: Value of physical usage of stocks[17]	−7	−15	8	−10	7	22	−24	23	−56	−22	28
16. Gross input i.e. item 14 *plus* 15	1 902	2 314	2 585	3 179	3 724	3 881	4 437	4 865	5 200	5 859	6 288
17. Net input i.e. item 16 *minus* 12	1 609	1 956	2 231	2 742	3 244	3 400	3 794	4 177	4 514	5 000	5 315
18. Gross product i.e. item 11 *minus* 16, or item 13 *minus* 17	1 873	1 965	2 427	2 954	3 166	3 417	3 743	4 131	4 643	5 371	5 308
19. Depreciation: total	298	402	518	607	722	820	957	1 133	1 205	1 270	1 332
Plant machinery and vehicles	200	261	350	422	511	581	658	726	753	821	869
Building and works	98	141	168	185	211	239	300	407	452	450	463
20. Net product i.e. item 18 *minus* 19 Comprising:	1 575	1 563	1 910	2 347	2 445	2 597	2 786	2 998	3 439	4 101	3 976
Labour[18] – hired	358	431	529	623	705	796	910	1 023	1 100	1 180	1 265
– family and partners	152	185	229	259	276	304	347	422	472	515	562
Interest[19]	88	124	124	139	153	190	323	467	466	500	492
Net rent[20]	25	20	24	32	42	55	65	69	83	105	121
21. Farming income[21]	952	803	1 005	1 293	1 269	1 252	1 141	1 018	1 318	1 802	1 536

1. Output values include subsidies on products sold. Output is net of VAT collected on the sale of inedible products, which is repaid by HM Customs and Excise.
2. Forecast prepared in November 1983.
3. Includes receipts from crops sold off farms and subsequently bought back for feed and seed; excludes deficiency payments on retained cereals and compensation payments on unsold potatoes which are included under Sundry receipts.
4. Maize, mixed corn, rye, hay and dried grass, grass and clover seed and other farm crops.
5. Flowers, bulbs, nursery stock, etc.
6. Horses, breeding animals exported, poultry for export, rabbits and game, knacker animals and other minor livestock.
7. Honey, goat's milk, exports of eggs for hatching and other minor livestock products.
8. That part of investment in buildings and works which is physically undertaken by the farmer or farm labour and the value of the physical increase in breeding livestock (breeding livestock capital formation).
9. Dividends from agricultural co-ops, non-agricultural horses grazing and includes from 1981 annual payments made under the sheep meat régime.
10. Hill livestock compensatory allowances, aid to less favoured areas and other non-capital production grants.

11. Livestock except breeding livestock.
12. Stocks of cereals, potatoes and fruit.
13. Sales included in output but subsequently repurchased and so reappearing as input.
14. Cereals, potatoes, beans, hay and dried grass.
15. Expenditure is net of VAT reclaimed in the normal way, but each heading includes VAT paid without recovery by, for example unregistered producers.
16. Electricity, veterinary expenses, pesticides, rates, insurances and miscellaneous costs.
17. Input stocks comprise fertilisers and purchased feed.
18. Includes employers' national insurance contributions. The estimate in respect of family workers (except spouses) and partners is calculated on the basis of the earnings of hired labour.
19. On commercial debt for current farming purposes (i.e. excluding interest on land purchases but including interest on purchases of buildings and works).
20. Landlords' expenses are included within farm maintenance, miscellaneous expenditure and depreciation on buildings and works. Net rent is rent paid on tenanted land *less* these landlords' expenses and the benefit value of dwellings on that land.
21. The income of farmers and their spouses after providing for depreciation and payment of interest and excluding stock appreciation.

Source Agricultural Departments

9.2 Agricultural output, input and net product at constant prices[1]
1980 prices
Calendar years

£ million

	1973	1974	1975	1976	1977	1978	1979	1980	1981	1982	1983[2]
Output											
1. Farm crops[3]: total	1 659	1 545	1 604	1 387	1 489	1 810	1 892	2 126	2 255	2 601	2 305
Wheat	490	470	528	438	436	521	626	786	780	1 014	901
Barley	543	516	533	488	496	652	579	651	749	769	668
Oats	36	28	26	27	26	25	21	24	25	28	24
Potatoes	315	321	296	217	255	309	326	312	333	313	311
Sugar beet	179	106	119	123	170	184	202	195	187	249	184
Hops	25	24	20	19	17	22	24	23	22	24	20
Beans for stockfeed	16	17	20	7	8	11	17	15	20	14	14
Oilseed rape	7	12	15	26	33	35	46	69	78	133	135
Other[4]	50	51	47	43	48	51	51	52	62	56	48
2. Horticulture: total	925	951	886	818	879	938	925	902	892	921	925
Vegetables (including mushrooms)	559	577	547	486	564	600	565	559	554	572	572
Fruit	186	197	163	162	145	166	185	170	148	163	169
Other[5]	180	177	176	170	170	172	176	173	190	185	184
3. Livestock: total	2 902	3 182	3 241	3 087	3 081	3 101	3 223	3 287	3 183	3 181	3 306
Fat cattle and calves	1 220	1 494	1 680	1 484	1 433	1 456	1 496	1 500	1 422	1 343	1 426
Fat sheep and lambs	332	355	365	348	323	335	350	405	378	386	412
Fat pigs	825	826	688	712	763	742	791	790	794	820	849
Poultry	442	429	427	461	476	484	502	508	503	549	538
Other[6]	82	78	82	82	86	85	84	85	85	83	81
4. Livestock products: total	2 309	2 251	2 236	2 317	2 418	2 518	2 523	2 500	2 478	2 589	2 647
Milk and milk products	1 749	1 703	1 704	1 764	1 863	1 949	1 952	1 960	1 946	2 058	2 114
Eggs for food	513	501	484	502	508	523	524	489	478	482	478
Clip wool	32	32	32	31	30	32	32	36	36	35	37
Other[7]	16	15	17	20	17	13	15	16	18	15	18
5. Own account capital formation: total[8]	182	34	− 15	48	30	89	30	47	85	114	93
6. Total output i.e. items 1 to 5	7 977	7 962	7 951	7 657	7 896	8 457	8 594	8 862	8 892	9 405	9 275
7. Compensation payments and sundry receipts: total	54	67	64	46	27	37	30	33	54	53	87
Deficiency payments on retained cereal	11	−	−	−	−	−	−	−	−	−	−
PMB compensation payments	−	5	−	−	−	9	2	6	4	−	1
CAP support	7	3	5	4	3	4	4	5	5	6	4
Brucellosis eradication incentive	7	10	11	4	3	3	2	2	3	1	1
Animal disease compensation	14	35	33	23	7	6	7	8	2	2	11
Other[9]	15	15	15	15	15	16	15	14	41	44	70
8. Production grants: total	213	179	241	146	121	107	89	130	129	128	114
Fertilisers and lime	42	24	7	7	−	−	−	−	−	−	−
Other[10]	172	155	234	139	121	107	89	130	129	128	114
9. Total receipts i.e. items 6 to 8	8 243	8 208	8 257	7 849	8 045	8 600	8 714	9 024	9 076	9 586	9 476
10. Work-in-progress and output stocks Value of physical change: total	129	52	− 264	− 74	231	15	− 33	− 28	− 77	36	34
Work-in-progress[11]	166	− 8	− 101	− 39	24	1	− 26	− 42	− 14	40	2
Output in stocks[12]	− 38	60	− 163	− 35	207	14	− 6	14	− 64	− 4	32
11. Gross output i.e. item 9 plus 10	8 372	8 259	7 992	7 775	8 276	8 615	8 681	8 996	8 999	9 622	9 510
12. Intermediate output[13]: total	660	591	584	529	532	565	659	688	646	751	777
Feed[14]	578	511	501	457	444	475	560	586	522	630	670
Seed	82	80	83	72	88	90	99	102	124	121	107
13. Final output i.e. item 11 minus 12	7 712	7 668	7 408	7 246	7 744	8 050	8 022	8 308	8 353	8 872	8 733

See footnotes page 180.

Source Agricultural Departments

9.2

(continued)

Agricultural output, input and net product at constant prices[1]
1980 prices
Calendar years

£ million

	1973	1974	1975	1976	1977	1978	1979	1980	1981	1982	1983[2]
Input											
14. Expenditure: total[15]	4 994	4 780	4 729	4 852	4 883	4 853	5 000	4 842	4 796	5 014	5 065
Feedingstuffs	2 201	2 058	2 049	2 204	2 189	2 139	2 250	2 188	2 134	2 314	2 387
Seeds	211	207	214	211	218	227	238	218	238	235	213
Livestock (imported and interfarm expenses)	204	215	234	170	188	197	138	151	130	132	128
Fertilisers and lime (before subsidy)	590	594	536	595	618	605	646	651	716	716	712
Machinery: total	837	747	756	739	749	752	735	668	651	653	656
Repairs	353	342	337	332	329	333	323	307	307	307	307
Fuel and oil	424	346	357	345	357	357	350	299	280	281	284
Other expenses	59	59	62	62	63	62	62	62	65	65	65
Farm maintenance: total	207	205	213	213	199	196	194	183	175	179	180
by occupier	168	166	174	175	161	159	158	147	139	144	145
by landlord	39	39	39	39	38	37	36	36	36	35	35
Miscellaneous expenditure[16]	744	753	727	721	721	738	798	784	752	784	788
15. Input Stocks: Value of physical usage of stocks[17]	−7	−42	13	−13	8	28	−30	23	−51	−18	22
16. Gross input i.e. item 14 *plus* 15	4 988	4 738	4 742	4 839	4 891	4 881	4 969	4 865	4 745	4 996	5 086
17. Net input i.e. item 16 *minus* 12	4 328	4 147	4 158	4 310	4 359	4 316	4 310	4 177	4 099	4 245	4 310
18. Gross product i.e. item 11 *minus* 16 or 13 *minus* 17	3 384	3 521	3 251	2 936	3 385	3 734	3 712	4 131	4 254	4 627	4 423
19. Depreciation: total	1 052	1 058	1 094	1 089	1 079	1 094	1 109	1 133	1 148	1 168	1 183
Plant machinery and vehicles	734	723	745	728	708	712	715	726	730	737	740
Building and works	318	335	349	361	371	382	394	407	419	430	443
20. Net product i.e. item 18 *minus* 19	2 332	2 463	2 157	1 847	2 305	2 640	2 602	2 998	3 106	3 459	3 240
Index of net product 1980 = 100	78	82	72	62	77	88	87	100	104	115	108

1. Output values include subsidies on products sold. Output is net of VAT collected on the sale of inedible products, which is repaid by HM Customs and Excise.
2. Forecast prepared in November 1983.
3. Includes receipts from crops sold off farms and subsequently bought back for feed and seed; excludes deficiency payments on retained cereals and compensation payments on unsold potatoes which are included under Sundry receipts.
4. Maize, mixed corn, rye, hay and dried grass, grass and clover seed and other farm crops.
5. Flowers, bulbs, nursery stock, etc.
6. Horses, breeding animals exported, poultry for export, rabbits and game, knacker animals and other minor livestock.
7. Honey, goat's milk, exports of eggs for hatching and other minor livestock products.
8. That part of investment in buildings and works which is physically undertaken by the farmer of farm labour and the value of the physical increase in breeding livestock (breeding livestock capital formation).

9. Dividends from agricultural co-ops, non-agricultural horses grazing and includes from 1981 annual payments made under the sheep meat régime.
10. Hill livestock compensatory allowances, aid to less favoured areas and other non-capital production grants.
11. Livestock except breeding livestock.
12. Stocks of cereals, potatoes and fruit.
13. Sales included in output but subsequently repurchased and so reappearing as input.
14. Cereals, potatoes, beans, hay and dried grass.
15. Expenditure is net of VAT reclaimed in the normal way, but each heading includes VAT paid without recovery by, for example unregistered producers.
16. Electricity, veterinary expenses, pesticides, rates, insurances and miscellaneous costs.
17. Input stocks comprise fertilisers and purchased feed.

Source Agricultural Departments

9.3 Agriculture—land use
Area at the June census[1]

Thousand hectares

	1973	1974	1975	1976	1977	1978	1979	1980	1981	1982	1983
Cereals											
Wheat	1 146	1 233	1 034	1 231	1 078	1 258	1 372	1 441	1 491	1 663	1 695
Barley	2 267	2 214	2 345	2 182	2 404	2 352	2 347	2 330	2 327	2 222	2 143
Oats	281	253	232	235	195	180	136	148	144	129	108
Mixed corn for threshing	51	42	35	28	24	17	16	13	11	10	8
Rye for threshing	5	4	6	8	10	9	7	6	6	6	7
Potatoes											
Early crop	26	26	24	27	30	29	26	27	24	25	24
Main crop	198	190	180	195	203	185	178	179	167	167	171
Fodder crops											
Beans for stockfeeding	60	66	40	44	37	38	42	48	45	40	34
Turnips and swedes	98	102	107	103	97	91	87	84	79	71	66
Fodder beet and mangolds[2]	7	7	7	6	7	6	6	6	5	5	5
Maize for threshing or stockfeeding	8	17	27	29	35	26	25	22	18	16	15
Kale, cabbage, savoys, kohl rabi	62	63	64	59 ⎫	78	70	61	54	49	43	40
Rape for stockfeeding	27	24	25	23 ⎭							
Peas harvested dry for stockfeeding	..	..	..	..	..	..	..	..	..	..	29
Other crops for stockfeeding	18	19	26	25	24	30	25	29	26	31	25
Horticultural crops											
Orchards and small fruit	75	73	71	68	66	65	67	65	62	60	58
Vegetables grown in the open:											
Brussels sprouts	16	15	15	15	15	15	14	14	13	13	11
Cabbage (all kinds), kale, cauliflower and broccoli[3]	30	29	29	29	31	29	29	26	26	27	25
Carrots	14	13	15	16 ⎫	23	21	18	16	17	14 ⎧	13
Parsnips	2	2	2	3 ⎭						3 ⎩	2
Turnips and swedes[4]	3	3	4	4	5	4	4	4	3	3	–
Beetroot	3	2	3	3	3	3	2	2	2	2	2
Onions	7	7	7	8	10	9	7	8	8	9	8
Beans (broad, runner and French)	17	17	16	18	18	18	18	13	11	12	11
Green peas	58	63	64	61	63	59	60	59	55	56	47
Peas, for harvesting dry	22	27	30	31	37	36	36	34	28	27	18
Celery	2	1	1	1	1	1	1	1	1	1	1
Lettuce	5	5	4	4	4	4	4	4	4	4	4
Sweet corn	..	..	..	..	..	..	..	..	..	..	1
Other vegetables	8	8	8	10	12	12	10	10	10	9	10
Hardy nursery stock bulbs and other flowers grown in the open:											
Hardy nursery stock	7	7	7	7	7	7	7	7	7	7	7
Bulbs	7	7	6	5	5	4	5	4	5	5	4
Other flowers	1	1	1	1	1	1	1	1	1	1	1
Area under glass	2	2	2	2	2	2	2	2	2	2	2
Other crops											
Sugar beet	194	195	198	206	203	210	214	213	210	204	199
Rape grown for oilseed	14	25	39	48	55	64	74	92	125	174	222
Hops	7	7	7	6	6	6	6	6	6	6	6
Other crops not for stockfeeding	7	7	9	11	13	11	8	7	7	6	7
Bare fallow	61	61	129	65	70	68	73	59	76	55	97
Total tillage	4 818	4 838	4 816	4 821	4 873	4 943	4 986	5 031	5 071	5 127	5 124
All grasses under five years old[5]	2 346	2 316	2 138	2 154	2 126	2 071	1 922	1 965	1 911	1 859	1 846
Total arable	7 164	7 154	6 954	6 975	7 000	7 014	6 909	6 996	6 982	6 986	6 970
All grasses five years old and over[6]	4 914	4 920	5 074	5 081	5 067	5 065	5 191	5 140	5 103	5 097	5 107
Total crops and grass	12 079	12 074	12 028	12 055	12 066	12 079	12 100	12 136	12 085	12 083	12 078
Rough grazings											
Sole rights	5 480	5 437	5 429	5 386	5 214	5 193	5 140	5 119	5 021	4 984	4 927
Common (estimated)	1 125	1 127	1 126	1 126	1 209	1 206	1 212	1 214	1 214	1 214	1 212
Woodland on agricultural holdings[7]	164	212	225	239	250	260	264	271	277	285	292
All other land on agricultural holdings[8]	141	141	171	180	208	214	221	214	211	217	227
Total area of agricultural land	18 988	19 010	18 978	18 987	18 948	18 953	18 936	18 953	18 808	18 783	18 735
Total area of the United Kingdom	24 093	24 100	24 105	24 102	24 104	24 100	24 098	24 088	24 089	24 088	24 088

1. Figures from 1977 onwards include estimates for minor holdings not surveyed at the June census in England and Wales. See notes on page 176.
2. See footnote 5 to table 9.4.
3. Excludes kale in 1983 which is included with 'Other vegetables'.
4. From 1983 included with 'Other vegetables.'
5. Before June 1975 collected in Scotland as 'Grass under seven years old' and in Northern Ireland as 'Grass under four years old'.

6. Before 1975 collected as; in England and Wales—permanent grass; in Scotland—grass seven years old and over; in Northern Ireland—grass four years old and over.
7. Before June 1974 in England and Wales and June 1976 in Scotland collected as 'Woodland ancillary to farming.'
8. Before June 1974 in England and Wales collected as 'Other land used for agriculture' and in Scotland as 'Area of yards, roads and buildings.'

Source Agricultural Departments

9.4 Estimated quantity of crops and grass harvested[1,2]

Thousand tonnes

	1973	1974	1975	1976	1977	1978	1979	1980	1981	1982	1983[3]
Cereals											
Wheat	5 002	6 130	4 490	4 740	5 275	6 615	7 170	8 470	8 710	10 310	10 880
Barley	9 007	9 133	8 510	7 650	10 530	9 850	9 525	10 325	10 230	10 960	10 080
Oats	1 080	955	795	765	790	705	540	600	620	575	465
Mixed corn for threshing	192	147	120	90	95	65	60	60	44	39	35
Rye for threshing	16	14	19	20	35	30	25	24	25	25	24
Maize for threshing[4]	6	3	3	3	2	2	..	..	..	..	..
Potatoes											
Early crop	470	458	350	371	406	422	367	453	375	430	305[11]
Main crop	6 338	6 333	4 201	4 418	6 215	6 909	6 119	6 656	5 840	6 445	4 475[11]
Fodder crops											
Beans for stockfeeding	187	200	95	70	112	130	128	149	123	122	105
Turnips, swedes[5]	5 631	6 217	6 035	4 816	5 869	5 565	5 370	5 065	4 795	4 575	3 655
Fodder beet and mangolds[5]	507	477	411	360	457	425	385	370	320	370	295
Maize for threshing or stock-feeding[4]	330	606	884	836	1 196	1 015	895	785	635	635	550
Rape for stockfeeding	568	504	618	601	578	625	1 825	2 115	2 195	1 985	1 660
Kale, cabbage, savoys and kohl rabi	2 747	2 750	2 607	1 633	2 450	2 205					
Other crops											
Sugar beet	7 427	4 588	4 864	6 325	6 382	7 081	7 659	7 380	7 395	10 005	7 494
Rape grown for oilseed	31	55	61	111	142	155	198	300	325	581	563
Hops	10	10	8	8	7	9	10	10	9	10	9
Hay[6]											
From all grasses under five years old[7,8]	4 640	4 149	3 757	4 413	4 530	8 109	8 028	6 945	6 780	6 580	4 580[12]
From all grasses five years old and over[9]	4 251	3 674	3 120	3 892	4 104						
Straw											
Wheat[10]	1 121	1 431	2 134	2 073	1 420	1 460	1 680	1 665	1 585	1 660	..
Barley[10]	2 975	2 990	3 521	3 792	3 800	3 280	3 590	3 595	3 390	3 440	..
Oats[10]	368	365	383	433	305	305	240	265	260	260	..
Horticultural crops											
Vegetables grown in the open											
Brussels sprouts	204	200	162	135	226	223	224	228	197	223	159
Cabbage (including savoys and spring greens)	542	623	571	496	789	610	606	587	571	613	516
Cauliflowers	340	324	293	244	348	367	348	367	325	353	312
Carrots	606	495	573	494	854	753	684	553	711	723	543
Parsnips	53	46	45	52	66	65	56	54	53	55	54
Turnips and swedes	131	147	150	135	223	196	170	163	109	144	119
Beetroot	120	116	103	96	110	109	98	109	97	105	96
Onions, Dry Bulb	195	219	221	170	306	231	214	224	232	232	179
Onions, Salad	28	27	25	29	23	28	28	26	25	27	27
Leeks	26	25	24	27	42	35	38	36	40	43	41
Broad beans	39	15	18	17	21	28	28	18	17	19	17
Runner beans including French	125	133	92	94	112	100	109	62	69	92	66
Peas, Green for market	38	37	34	19	38	34	38	18	25	28	21
Peas, Green for processing	258	296	263	170	267	210	229	223	277	238	192
Celery	71	64	69	60	70	66	64	54	50	51	41
Lettuce	171	164	123	103	145	133	127	135	134	161	151
Rhubarb	46	43	40	34	40	45	47	43	41	39	36
Protected crops											
Tomatoes	120	122	123	130	126	129	143	129	125	118	120
Cucumbers	32	43	47	52	52	58	53	57	54	55	60
Lettuce	30	31	32	30	36	36	35	36	37	45	49
Orchard fruit and soft fruit	687	582	532	546	431	568	600	565	405	555	542

1. UK gross production in calendar years; for horticultural crops it is in crop years.
2. Figures from 1980 onwards include estimates for minor holdings not surveyed at the June census in England and Wales and from 1981 for barley, oats, early and main crop potatoes in Northern Ireland. See notes on page 176.
3. Provisional figures only.
4. From 1979 maize for threshing is included with maize for threshing or stock feeding.
5. Before 1977 fodder beet was included with turnips and swedes for stock-feeding. In 1977, as a result of changes in the census categories, fodder beet was included with mangolds in England and Wales but continued to be included with turnips and swedes for stockfeeding in Scotland and Northern Ireland.

6. The production of hay in England and Wales is calculated from the area cut for hay and actually harvested and does not include the area mown for silage, drying or seed: the production of hay in Scotland and Northern Ireland is calculated from the area cut for hay only and does not include grass mown for silage or drying.
7. Before 1975 collected in England and Wales as clover, sainfoin and temporary grasses; in Scotland as grass under seven years old; in Northern Ireland as grass under four years old.
8. Includes hay from lucerne in England and Wales, and from all grassland in Scotland.
9. Before 1975 collected as: in England and Wales—permanent grass; in Scotland—grass seven years old and over; in Northern Ireland—grass four years old and over.
10. The estimates of production and yield for straw in 1975 are calculated on the actual area harvested and not on the total area used for growing wheat, barley and oats, as in previous years.
11. Excludes Scotland.
12. England and Wales only.

Source Agricultural Departments

9.5 Cattle, sheep, pigs and poultry on agricultural holdings
At June in each year[1]

Thousands

	1973	1974	1975	1976	1977	1978	1979	1980	1981	1982	1983
Cattle and calves: total	14 445	15 203	14 717	14 069	13 899	13 670	13 589	13 426	13 138	13 244	13 290
Dairy herd	3 436	3 394	3 242	3 228	3 269	3 274	3 292	3 228	3 191	3 250	3 333
Beef herd	1 678	1 887	1 899	1 764	1 688	1 588	1 543	1 478	1 420	1 389	1 358
Heifers in calf (first calf)	988	1 041	903	939	824	859	864	838	863	851	847
Bulls for service	115	103	97	93	93	92	90	86	84	84	83
Other cattle:											
Two years old and over	898	958	987	981	1 015	1 029	1 033	1 005	963	937	904
One year old and under two	3 104	3 389	3 559	3 287	3 235	3 251	3 123	3 153	3 041	3 057	3 059
Six months old and under one year	} 4 227	{ 2 226	2 062	1 840	1 926	1 766	1 839	1 866	1 876	1 890	1 924
Under six months old		2 205	1 968	1 938	1 849	1 812	1 804	1 770	1 699	1 786	1 783
Sheep and lambs: total	27 943	28 498	28 270	28 265	28 190	29 772	29 946	31 446	32 097	33 067	34 069
Breeding ewes	10 921	11 192	11 279	11 298	11 247	11 475	11 709	12 178	12 528	12 909	13 310
Rams for service	314	322	326	320	320	333	342	353	358	366	383
Other sheep	3 643	3 620	3 442	3 198	3 362	3 681	3 843	3 672	3 584	3 748	3 764
Lambs under one year old	13 066	13 364	13 222	13 449	13 260	14 282	14 051	15 243	15 628	16 044	16 612
Pigs: total	8 979	8 544	7 532	7 947	7 756	7 728	7 864	7 815	7 828	8 023	8 174
Breeding herd	1 015	889	814	884	832	845	851	831	836	864	856
Boars for service	48	44	40	43	41	42	43	42	43	45	45
Gilts not yet in pig	..	80	87	101	76	90	82	84	87	89	82
Barren sows for fattening	18	24	14	12	17	12	14	12	11	12	15
Other pigs:[2]											
110 Kg and over		107	79	116	114	105	112	102	90	117	100
80 Kg and under 110 Kg		704	611	708	647	671	695	657	638	630	605
50 Kg and under 80 Kg	7 899	1 908	1 697	1 784	1 762	1 777	1 770	1 772	1 776	1 824	1 868
20 Kg and under 50 Kg		2 607	2 255	2 271	2 268	2 221	2 258	2 240	2 227	2 281	2 362
Under 20 Kg		2 181	1 935	2 028	1 999	1 965	2 040	2 074	2 119	2 163	2 241
Poultry: total	144 079	139 672	136 572	142 222	134 931	137 973	135 345	135 105	132 286	135 363	128 260
Fowls: total	135 929	132 038	130 259	134 917	128 453	131 116	127 433	127 063	122 639	126 091	118 496
Growing pullets	18 808	18 958	18 195	18 383	16 411	17 343	15 504	14 457	14 219	14 766	12 079
Laying flock	51 766	49 924	49 359	49 085	49 616	50 985	48 120	46 012	44 473	44 792	41 518
Breeding flock	6 989	6 455	5 997	6 125	6 252	6 447	6 657	6 678	6 117	6 457	6 012
Table birds	58 366	56 701	56 708	61 325	56 174	56 340	57 153	59 917	57 830	60 075	58 887
Ducks[3]	1 489	1 313	1 201	1 272	1 229	1 343	} 1 552	{ 1 390	1 333	1 443	} 1 566
Geese[3]	148	128	112	127	136	139		133	148	157	
Turkeys	6 513	6 192	5 000	5 905	5 113	5 376	6 359	6 519	8 167	7 672	8 198

1. Figures from 1977 onwards include estimates for minor holdings not surveyed at the June census in England and Wales. See notes on page 176.
2. Prior to 1974 collected by age and in 1974 and 1975 by equivalent imperial weight bands.
3. Excludes Scotland except for years 1979 and 1983.

Source Agricultural Departments

9.6 Forest area
End of period

Thousand hectares

	1973/ 1974	1974/ 1975	1975/ 1976	1976/ 1977	1977/ 1978	1978/ 1979	1979/ 1980	1980/ 1981	1981/ 1982	1982/ 1983	1983/ 1984
	Years ending 31 March										
Forest area[1]											
United Kingdom	1 981	2 018	2 043	2 057	2 061	2 079	2 102	2 121	2 142	2 233	2 257[6]
Great Britain	1 920	1 956	1 980	1 994	1 997	2 014	2 036	2 054	2 075	2 165	2 188[6]
Northern Ireland[2]	61	62	63	63	64	65	66	67	67	68	69
Forestry Commission (Great Britain)											
Total estates	1 206	1 212	1 231	1 251	1 253	1 256	1 263	1 264	1 259	1 251	1 209
Lands under plantation	789	809	826	841	856	868	884	896	905	909	902
Plantable land acquired during year[3]	6.6	8.0	18.6	17.7	6.9	5.7	7.6	1.8	4.5	3.6	2.8
Total area planted during year[4]	21.7	23.2	20.5	18.7	17.2	15.4	21.5	16.6	16.5	14.8	15.3
Area lost by fire during year	0.5	0.5	0.3	2.2	0.5	0.8	0.4	1.3	0.3	0.6	0.1
	Years ending 30 September			1976[2]	1977	1978	1979	1980	1981/82[2]	1982/83	1983/84
State afforestation in Northern Ireland											
Total estates	65.0	66.0	67.0	67.3	69.1	69.5	70.5	71.5	71.9	72.5	73.2
Land under plantation	46.8	48.0	49.2	49.2	51.2	52.2	53.0	53.9	54.4	55.2	56.3
Plantable land acquired during year	1.0	1.0	1.1	1.1	0.7	2.6	1.0	0.8	0.3	0.6	0.4
Total area planted during year[5]	1.6	1.1	1.2	1.2	1.0	1.0	1.0	1.1	1.1	1.2	1.1
Area lost by fire during year	0.2	0.2	0.1	0.1	0.5	0.2	0.02	0.8	0.01	0.14	0.06

1. Includes unproductive woodland. Since 1974 40 000 hectares of unproductive forest land consisting of old felled woodland have been excluded from the figures as it is considered that this area is more properly regarded as agricultural land. Similarly a reduction to unproductive land was made in 1978 to adjust for a reclassification of this land to meet the figure of 'Retained Scrub' pubilshed in the *Forestry Commission Annual Report*.
2. The figures for Northern Ireland refer to year ending 30 September up to and including 1975/76, to year ending 31 December up to and including 1980, and thereafter to year ending 31 March.

3. Gross area acquired.
4. Including replanting after felling and change by fire.
5. Including areas replanted.
6. Provisional.

Sources Forestry Commission; Department of Agriculture (Northern Ireland)

9.7 Average weekly earnings of agricultural workers[1]
Great Britain

£

	1973	1974	1975	1976	1977	1978	1979	1980	1981	1982	1983
Adult males[2]	27.50	34.20	43.04	50.45	54.77	61.99	72.04	86.26	96.52	105.87	117.02
Youth[3]	17.90	22.87	29.49	34.07	37.10	42.04	47.25	56.66	62.15	69.40	76.02
Women and girls	17.94	22.95	29.58	40.20	43.54	49.19	54.87	65.53	70.35	80.35	87.70

1. Total earnings of hired regular whole-time workers, including payments in kind valued, where applicable, in accordance with Agricultural Wages Orders.
2. Twenty years and over.
3. Under twenty years.

Source Agricultural Departments

9.8 Sales for food of agricultural produce and livestock

	Unit	1973	1974	1975	1976	1977	1978	1979	1980	1981	1982	1983
Cereals:												
Wheat[1]	Thousand tonnes	2 215	2 376	2 471	2 360	2 170	2 234	2 867	2 628	3 222	3 196	3 398
Barley	,,	2 043	2 070	2 767	1 994	2 213	4 123	2 903	3 530	5 142	4 316	4 399
Oats[2]	,,	121	131	124	109	111	128	102	121	139	136	116
Potatoes[3]	,,	5 314	5 385	4 933	3 335	4 004	4 853	5 072	5 119	5 225	4 974	
Milk: total	Million litres	13 468	13 098	13 133	13 618	14 406	15 094	15 116	15 182	15 084	15 943	16 441
For consumption as liquid milk	,,	7 524	7 698	7 862	7 760	7 484	7 381	7 305	7 196	7 082	6 979	6 942
For manufacture[4]	,,	5 945	5 399	5 270	5 858	6 921	7 713	7 811	7 986	7 992	8 951	9 485
Eggs in shell	Million dozens	1 170	1 151	1 113	1 153	1 160	1 192	1 184	1 104	1 073	1 079	1 043
Animals slaughtered:												
Cattle and calves: total	Thousands	3 436	4 597	5 358	4 481	4 111	4 030	4 057	4 255	4 049	3 629	3 928
Cattle	,,	3 294	4 182	4 828	4 186	3 847	3 876	3 913	4 110	3 929	3 536	3 811
Calves	,,	142	415	531	295	264	155	145	145	120	94	117
Sheep and lambs	,,	11 759	12 947	13 133	12 670	11 356	11 591	11 884	14 316	13 978	13 894	15 068
Pigs: total	,,	15 083	15 274	12 766	13 499	14 194	13 787	14 717	14 624	14 865	15 055	15 989
For bacon:												
Used wholly	,,	2 873	2 726	2 259	2 487	2 449	2 124	2 056	2 042	1 811	1 786	1 866
Used in part	,,	4 063	4 146	3 695	3 850	3 628	3 998	4 052	4 046	4 053	3 686	3 966
Other uses	,,	7 734	7 933	6 482	6 816	7 726	7 311	8 244	8 208	8 673	9 230	9 717
Sows and boars	,,	414	470	331	346	391	354	365	328	329	353	440
Poultry	Millions	400	395	394	418	431	432	445	441	442	470	454

TIME SERIES. The figures for cereals and for animals slaughtered relate to periods of 52 weeks (53 weeks in 1976 and 1981)

1. Flour millers' receipts of home-grown wheat.
2. Oatmeal millers' receipts of home-grown oats.
3. Including consumption on farms and seed sold for food but excluding imported potatoes.
4. The method of calculating liquid milk has been revised from April 1981 to include a measurement adjustment. Therefore the total of liquid and manufactured milk do not add up to the total.

Source Ministry of Agriculture, Fisheries and Food

9.9 Stocks of food and feedingstuffs[1]
At end-December in each year

Thousand tonnes

	1973	1974	1975	1976	1977	1978	1979	1980	1981	1982	1983
Wheat and flour (as wheat)	986	933	1 115	1 174	1 238	1 148	1 246	1 164	927	813	909
Barley	725	1 032	912	991	1 112	1 144	1 237	1 151	1 157	1 181	1 158
Maize	162	228	159	250	261	209	256	202	145	142	128
Oilcake and meal[2]	141	127	74	90	94	95	133	119	83	170	158
Oilseeds and nuts (crude oil equivalent)	13	9	15	21	24	22	19	23	23	27	29
Vegetable oil (as crude oil)	82	63	48	61	58	64	70	81	64	79	63
Marine oil (as crude oil)	47	28	17	27	40	47	25	48	40	54	44
Butter[3]	61	67	83	107	127	129	94	64	43	52	149
Imported meat and offal[3]	82	99	76	87	70	75	61	50	34	60	106
Raw coffee[4]	36	27	15	15	9	8	10	6	9	8	5
Tea[5]	84	92	88	82	109	94	89	92	72	74	62
Sugar	873	559	898	796	881	932	931	1 114	1 010	1 013	787
Jam and marmalade	20.7	16.9	23.5	21.6	22.1	23.3	36.5	33.2	32.9	..	..
Chocolate and sugar confectionery[6]	46.9	57.3	57.1	56.2	62.1	74.8	78.4	70.4	68.5	67.8	70.6

1. Recorded stocks, including stocks in bond or held by the main processors.
2. Excluding castor meal, cocoa cake and meal.
3. Stocks held in public cold stores at all temperatures. The coverage of the cold store survey was improved during 1983 and the closing stocks for 1983 are on the new basis. For meat and offals, from 1983 the figure represents imported and home-produced stocks.
4. Including manufacturers' stocks and additional public warehouses.
5. Including stocks held by primary wholesalers.
6. Manufacturers' stocks only.

Source Ministry of Agriculture, Fisheries and Food

9.10 Processed food and animal feedingstuffs: production

Thousand tonnes

	1973	1974	1975	1976	1977	1978	1979	1980	1981	1982	1983
Flour milling:											
Wheat milling: total	5 082	5 075	5 213	5 268	5 150	5 159	5 053	4 958	4 781	4 616	4 477
Home produced	2 175	2 337	2 428	2 300	2 140	2 116	2 775	2 842	3 210	3 172	3 255
Imported	2 907	2 739	2 785	2 968	3 010	3 043	2 278	2 116	1 571	1 444	1 222
Flour produced	3 765	3 751	3 887	3 949	3 896	3 848	3 785	3 702	3 596	3 504	3 426
Offals produced	1 316	1 310	1 312	1 302	1 266	1 307	1 259	1 231	1 174	1 121	1 050
Oat milling:											
Oats milled by oatmeal millers	135	143	128	148	147	147	144	142	147	137	140
Products of oat milling	77	81	80	83	85	85	84	83	85	82	81
Seed crushing:											
Oilseeds and nuts processed	1 054	1 045	1 091	1 452	1 527	1 658	1 597	1 829	1 724	1 706	1 342
Crude oil produced, including production of maize oil	263	270	247	360	391	408	432	479	449	431	398
Oilcake and meal produced, excluding castor meal, cocoa cake and meal	746	759	722	1 057	1 111	1 221	1 139	1 337	1 241	1 240	945
Production of home-killed meat: total including meat subsequently canned	1 906	2 173	2 215	2 069	2 018	2 034	2 125	2 226	2 188	2 107	2 264
Beef	848	1 061	1 200	1 065	993	1 022	1 042	1 097	1 053	961	1 046
Veal	6	12	16	9	9	6	5	6	5	5	6
Mutton and lamb	234	252	259	248	223	228	231	277	263	264	287
Pork	682	690	569	593	647	630	694	684	710	728	763
Offal	136	159	168	154	146	148	152	162	157	149	162
Production of poultry meat	664	652	652	695	717	727	751	754	745	807	796
Production of bacon and ham, including meat subsequently canned	252	243	212	229	221	217	212	210	203	197	212
Production of milk products:											
Butter	97	54	48	89	134	164	161	170	172	216	241
Cheese (including farmhouse)	182	218	235	204	206	216	234	238	242	244	245
Condensed milk excluding skim concentrate and condensed milk used in manufacture of chocolate crumb	164	155	140	142	157	159	145	129	124	118	110
Milk powder: excluding buttermilk and whey powder											
Full cream	22	27	19	16	19	20	20	27	29	34	35
Skimmed	156	105	105	170	246	272	233	237	251	296	302
Cream, fresh and sterilised; including farm cream	82	85	84	81	82	84	87	85	77	75	74
Sugar: production from home-grown sugar-beet (as refined sugar)	836	770	666	605	900	984	1 137	1 239	1 061	1 213	1 275
Production of compound fats:											
Margarine	341	299	298	342	379	368	359	383	398	399	387
Compound fat	161	144	127	128	111	131	131	130	153	157	153
Production of other processed foods:											
Jam and marmalade	184	178	165	176	193	169	168	155	173	171	164
Syrup and treacle	69	73	70	67	73	71	71	61	60	52	52
Canned vegetables[1]	787	852	871	895	896	850	821	778	753	810	811
Canned and bottled fruit[1]	75	91	68	60	51	59	56	30	29	39	42
Soups, canned and powdered	299	341	313	299	315	297	295	282	261	286	269
Canned meat	153	137	122	141	124	115	135	115	94	87	96
Canned fish	7	7	11	10	13	13	12	9	6	6	3
Biscuits, total disposals of home produced	624	643	603	631	652	645	626	629	632	622	698
Breakfast cereals, other than oatmeal and oatmeal flakes	213	210	207	229	226	229	208	229	219	229	233
Chocolate confectionery	415	415	353	391	391	424	425	407	409	451	464
Sugar confectionery, excluding medicated confectionery	372	383	344	395	391	404	362	325	317	311	298
Cocoa powder and drinking chocolate, based on total manufacturers' despatches	20	23	20	21	21	19	16	16	20	20	..
Glucose	411	441	442	491	506	540	492	473	434	446	449
Production of soft drinks (million litres):											
Concentrated	382	431	493	517	466	446	509	544	497	532	553
Unconcentrated	1 618	1 706	1 890	2 096	2 057	2 051	2 262	2 095	1 974	1 920	2 188
Compound feedingstuffs: total	11 044	10 222	10 137	11 351	10 790	10 973	11 645	11 108	10 943	11 855	12 234
Cattle food	3 864	3 590	4 076	4 743	4 451	4 516	4 936	4 556	4 538	5 012	5 456
Calf food	442	380	357	410	396	423	455	428	478	504	
Pig food	2 749	2 575	2 162	2 456	2 317	2 303	2 380	2 267	2 169	2 317	2 292
Poultry food	3 760	3 455	3 320	3 473	3 350	3 432	3 483	3 492	3 445	3 640	3 532
Other compounds	229	222	222	269	276	299	391	365	355	408	450

TIME SERIES. The figures relate to periods of 52 weeks (53 weeks in 1976 and 1981) with the following exceptions which are on a calendar year basis: butter, cheese, cream, canned meat, soft drinks, condensed milk and milk powder, canned vegetables, canned and bottled fruit, jam and marmalade and soups.

1. From 1981 the method of collecting these figures has changed. They are therefore not comparable with previous years.

Source Ministry of Agriculture, Fisheries and Food

9.11 Food and animal feedingstuffs: disposals

Thousand tonnes

	1973	1974	1975	1976	1977	1978	1979	1980	1981	1982	1983
Flour	3 781	3 693	3 842	3 952	3 899	3 854	3 777	3 706	3 041	3 547	3 492
Sugar (as refined sugar): total disposals	3 006	3 246	2 553	2 707	2 600	2 545	2 495	2 396	2 375	2 426	2 607
For food in the United Kingdom [1]	2 657	2 944	2 199	2 445	2 436	2 459	2 425	2 302	2 255	2 276	2 287
Syrup and treacle	69	73	70	67	73	71	71	61	60	52	52
Meat and fish:											
Fresh and frozen meat and offal, including usage for canning:											
Beef and veal	1 109	1 301	1 424	1 282	1 258	1 310	1 329	1 328	1 263	1 141	1 226
Mutton and lamb	500	466	509	472	445	444	444	469	432	457	462
Pork	697	696	583	603	664	668	732	724	746	756	788
Offal	235	239	272	256	269	271	270	277	275	270	274
Poultry-meat	664	658	669	694	712	757	775	778	785	833	846
Bacon and ham, including usage for canning	573	542	500	498	507	520	519	512	505	482	483
Fresh, frozen and cured fish (landed weight, excluding shellfish, including usage for canning):											
total disposals	1 075	1 088	991	1 023	1 007	1 275	1 126	1 104	1 034	1 063	1 015
For food in the United Kingdom	746	772	751	785	695	706	640	715	703	706	667
Dairy products:											
Butter	437	490	515	460	426	458	435	398	400	382	367
Cheese	331	341	358	351	319	341	365	353	366	372	374
Condensed milk [2]	176	166	153	154	164	160	151	142	119	126	116
Milk powder, excluding buttermilk and whey powder:											
Full cream	37	39	27	21	22	27	25	30	30	35	38
Skimmed	198	125	159	215	177	305	258	227	262	298	333
Eggs in shell	838	822	796	813	817	839	847	798	773	762	747
Oils (as crude oil):											
Vegetable oil	851	773	660	837	844	873	931	891	882	936	990
Marine oil for the manufacture of margarine and compound fat	190	167	175	170	152	182	206	212	217	203	182
Jam and marmalade	195	194	159	178	192	172	161	156	153	..	..
Potatoes: total disposals [3]	5 590	5 641	5 331	3 984	4 627	5 527	5 813	5 671	6 056	5 682	..
For food in the United Kingdom	5 421	5 566	5 287	3 962	4 584	5 172	5 442	5 518	5 635	5 560	..
Other foods:											
Chocolate and sugar confectionery, excluding medicated confectionery	814	804	709	797	803	896	797	764	764	801	803
Tea excluding re-exports	192	200	198	208	180	163	176	184	178	187	167
Raw coffee	119	102	103	97	85	79	94	76	89	91	98
Cocoa beans excluding re-exports	107	93	72	83	75	72	67	66	86	88	77
Barley:											
For brewing and distilling and for food	2 231	1 953	2 928	2 067	2 368	4 078	2 893	3 706	5 056	4 279	4 435
Maize (including maize meal): total disposals	3 460	3 208	3 097	3 676	4 112	3 394	3 101	2 868	2 315	2 123	1 819
Animal feed	1 828	1 587	1 632	2 181	2 521	1 647	1 310	1 083	815	592	357
Oilcake and meal	1 543	1 417	1 405	1 798	1 779	1 990	2 189	2 380	2 505	2 837	2 889
Wheat milling offals	1 370	1 332	1 342	1 338	1 298	1 351	1 316	1 298	1 258	1 270	1 194
Fish and meat meal for animal feed, figures relate to sales	293	317	326	327	330	296	311	365	275	255	291

TIME SERIES. The figures relate to periods of 52 weeks (53 weeks in 1976 and 1981) with the following exceptions which are on a calendar year basis: fish and potatoes; condensed milk; milk powder; and butter.

1. Including sugar used in the manufacture of other foods subsequently exported. Excluding sugar in imported manufactured foods.
2. Excluding skim concentrate and condensed milk used in manufacture of chocolate crumb.
3. Disposals (excluding seed and chats) of home grown and imported potatoes for human consumption, processing, export and sales for stockfeed through schemes for implementing the Agricultural Act, 1947.

Sources Ministry of Agriculture, Fisheries and Food; Business Statistics Office

9.12 Landings of fish of British taking: landed weight and value
Great Britain

	Landed weight (Thousand tonnes)						Value (£ thousand)					
	1978	1979	1980	1981	1982	1983[4]	1978	1979	1980	1981	1982	1983[4]
Total all fish	945.1	826.6	747.6	727.5	749.4	726.1	249 905	247 550	217 092	222 557	251 793	271 868
Total wet fish	880.7	764.1	679.0	664.6	689.4	659.2	219 418	211 957	184 847	188 152	213 108	224 625
Demersal: total	429.0	363.2	376.2	398.8	431.6	413.4	176 521	170 576	156 338	161 869	186 424	197 893
Catfish	1.7	1.2	1.1	0.9	1.1	1.3	588	440	358	308	398	498
Cod	125.3	107.6	102.1	112.9	111.1	110.0	67 003	62 852	57 429	59 806	70 122	71 717
Dogfish	17.3	14.7	12.2	10.9	9.7	10.0	4 253	4 261	3 361	3 110	3 045	3 091
Haddock	82.4	72.7	84.7	100.0	129.0	123.0	39 351	35 910	34 069	38 117	50 299	57 220
Hake	1.6	1.5	2.1	3.8	2.9	2.0	1 359	1 408	1 831	4 302	3 740	2 159
Halibut	0.3	0.3	0.2	0.1	0.1	0.1	488	564	389	256	363	350
Lemon sole	4.7	4.8	5.4	4.5	5.0	5.9	3 517	4 005	4 839	4 857	5 060	5 493
Plaice	31.8	31.9	26.1	25.1	24.2	20.9	15 930	17 071	12 931	12 760	13 768	13 706
Redfish	3.5	1.8	1.4	0.5	0.4	0.3	804	433	266	100	96	74
Saithe (Coalfish)	30.8	18.6	14.5	13.7	15.8	12.2	8 496	5 938	4 540	3 781	4 627	3 386
Skate and ray	6.5	6.1	6.1	5.7	6.0	6.2	2 571	2 587	2 618	2 631	2 718	2 818
Sole	1.6	1.9	1.8	1.7	2.1	2.2	3 632	4 714	4 820	5 258	5 498	5 821
Turbot	0.9	1.0	0.7	0.6	0.5	0.5	1 808	1 745	1 402	1 350	1 294	1 418
Whiting	54.9	58.2	52.5	42.9	40.7	51.8	15 983	18 535	15 774	12 621	11 562	16 450
Livers[1]	1.2	0.9	0.1	0.2	0.1	..	105	82	4	5	4	..
Roes	0.8	0.5	0.5	0.5	0.5	..	329	311	324	286	329	..
Other demersal	63.7	39.5	64.7	74.8	82.4	67.0	10 253	9 712	11 383	12 321	13 501	13 692
Pelagic: total	451.7	400.9	302.8	265.8	257.8	245.8	42 898	41 381	28 509	26 282	26 684	26 732
Herring	14.7	2.8	3.1	34.5	45.7	52.2	5 806	1 428	1 195	4 545	5 504	6 694
Mackerel[2]	320.9	353.4	253.0	197.2	184.0	174.5	30 998	36 962	24 068	19 434	19 170	18 532
Other pelagic	116.1	44.7	46.7	34.1	28.1	19.1	6 172	2 990	3 246	2 303	2 010	1 506
Total shell fish	64.4	62.5	68.6	62.9	60.0	66.9	30 486	35 593	32 245	34 405	38 685	47 243
Cockles	11.6	10.4	15.2	10.4	8.3	5.9	329	504	807	592	458	327
Crab	9.6	10.4	9.7	9.7	8.6	11.3	3 241	3 903	3 967	4 257	4 245	6 395
Lobster	0.8	0.8	0.7	0.8	0.8	1.0	4 298	4 059	3 295	3 806	4 181	5 695
Mussels	7.2	5.5	9.1	2.5	4.4	5.9	268	271	460	229	461	468
Nephrop (Norway lobster)	13.3	14.5	12.1	14.4	15.4	17.1	13 003	18 042	13 094	14 112	17 798	20 225
Oysters[3]	0.5	0.7	0.6	0.6	0.4	0.3	695	1 009	1 001	1 116	925	636
Shrimps	3.2	1.4	1.2	1.4	1.6	3.0	2 096	979	998	1 097	1 147	2 556
Whelks	3.3	1.8	1.2	1.5	1.6	1.3	405	261	259	351	380	226
Other shell fish	14.9	17.0	18.8	21.6	18.9	21.1	6 150	6 549	8 364	8 845	9 090	10 715

1. Including the raw equivalent of any liver oils landed.
2. Includes transhipments of mackerel i.e. caught by British vessels but not
   actually landed at British ports. These quantities are transhipped to foreign
   vessels and are later recorded as exports.
3. The weight of oysters is calculated on the basis of one tonne being equal to
   15 748 oysters in England and Wales.
4. Contains some provisional information.

Sources Ministry of Agriculture, Fisheries and Food; Department of Agriculture
and Fisheries for Scotland

9.13 Fishing fleet[1]
England and Wales
At 31 December in each year

Number

	1973	1974	1975	1976	1977	1978	1979	1980	1981	1982	1983[5]
Total fishing vessels	3 612	3 872	3 721	3 832	4 080	4 146	4 409	4 047	4 637	4 228	4 662
Trawlers[2]: total	1 457	1 555	1 489	1 477	1 592	1 560	1 741	1 573	1 750	1 755	1 750
Steam[3]	49	42	19	–	–	–	–	–	–	–	–
Motor: 40 ft. and over	821	850	859	832	787	751	746	756	758	747	700
Under 40 ft.	587	663	611	645	805	809	995	817	992	1 008	1 050
Drifters: total	73	67	87	92	106	90	95	87	133	88	129
Motor: 40 ft. and over	3	3	2	2	2	2	2	2	–	2	1
Under 40 ft.	70	64	85	90	104	88	89	81	129	83	125
Other than motor[4]	–	–	–	–	–	–	4	4	4	3	3
Liners: total	498	583	610	610	647	678	723	697	794	469	678
Motor: 40 ft. and over	70	71	74	80	77	73	69	75	75	67	52
Under 40 ft.	428	512	536	530	570	605	654	622	719	402	626
Seiners: total	195	208	224	212	210	219	240	236	231	219	193
Motor: 40 ft. and over	188	201	209	204	202	211	232	225	219	206	187
Under 40 ft.	7	7	15	8	8	8	8	11	12	13	6
Others: total	1 389	1 459	1 311	1 441	1 525	1 599	1 610	1 454	1 729	1 697	1 912
Motor: 40 ft. and over	71	77	75	67	64	65	68	72	81	80	81
Under 40 ft.	1 305	1 375	1 227	1 362	1 452	1 524	1 532	1 372	1 637	1 603	1 824
Other than motor[4]	13	7	9	12	9	10	10	10	11	14	7

1. Figures exclude vessels (all under 40 ft.) which are not used at all for
commercial fishing.
2. Including drifter/trawlers.
3. All 40 ft. and over.
4. All under 40 ft.
5. Contains some provisional data.

Source Ministry of Agriculture, Fisheries and Food

9.14 Fishing fleet
Scotland
At 31 December in each year

Number

	1973	1974	1975	1976	1977	1978	1979	1980	1981	1982	1983
Total fishing vessels[1]	2 689	2 754	2 678	2 616	2 580	2 616	2 517	2 514	2 370	2 233	2 214
Trawlers: total	736	781	768	741	730	744	772	755	769	746	740
80 ft. and over	118	107	96	78	68	59	46	34	32	18	18
Under 80 ft.	618	674	672	663	662	685	726	721	737	728	722
Liners	380	377	359	319	315	322	296	235	208	147	112
Seiners	439	431	407	365	342	336	316	320	308	296	302
Drifters	4	4	4	3	4	4	1	2	1	1	1
Ringers	25	16	10	8	7	1	–	–	–	–	–
Creel fishing	1 008	1 041	1 022	1 038	1 070	1 094	1 011	1 055	929	877	878
Purse seine	18	21	23	26	26	32	40	46	43	45	42
Other	79	83	85	116	86	83	81	101	112	121	139

1. All motor vessels.

Source Department of Agriculture and Fisheries for Scotland

9.15 Estimated food and drink supplies per head of population

Kg per head per year

	1973	1974	1975	1976	1977	1978	1979	1980	1981	1982	1983[6]
Cereal products and sugar:											
Flour	63.6	61.6	64.5	66.2	65.3	63.7	63.1	61.4	59.4	59.4	..
Rice	1.6	1.5	1.5	2.1	2.1	1.9	1.8	2.2	2.2	2.3	..
Oat products	1.4	1.4	1.4	1.4	1.4	1.4	1.5	1.4	1.4	1.4	..
Other cereal products	3.9	3.9	3.7	4.1	4.1	4.1	3.8	3.9	3.7	4.3	..
Starch and other farinaceous foods	1.4	1.7	1.2	1.3	1.3	1.9	1.1	0.9	0.9	0.7	..
Sugar[1]	47.0	47.9	42.8	42.9	42.6	42.9	42.3	39.9	39.3	40.2	..
Meat and fish:											
Beef-bone in	14.8	19.7	21.4	18.7	18.7	19.5	19.9	20.6	19.8	18.3	..
Beef-bone out (expressed as bone in equivalent)	4.5	2.7	2.2	2.4	2.4	2.5	2.6				..
Mutton and lamb	8.3	7.7	8.3	7.6	7.0	7.0	7.1	7.5	6.7	7.3	..
Pork	12.1	12.0	10.3	10.2	11.5	11.7	12.7	12.5	12.7	13.0	..
Offal[2]	3.4	3.4	4.0	3.7	3.9	3.9	3.9	2.3	2.2	2.2	..
Imported meat products	3.5	3.1	3.2	3.9	3.9	3.9	4.1	3.6	3.8	3.3	..
Bacon and ham	10.1	9.5	8.7	8.5	9.0	9.2	9.3	9.1	8.8	8.4	..
Poultry	11.7	11.6	11.4	12.1	12.1	12.9	13.3	13.3	13.6	14.4	..
Fresh, frozen and cured fish	6.2	6.4	6.1	6.5	5.7	5.1	5.0	5.4	4.9	5.0	..
Imported canned fish	1.3	1.0	1.2	1.2	1.2	1.0	1.2	1.4	1.5	1.3	..
Dairy products:											
Liquid milk (litres)	136.5	139.5	142.3	140.4	135.3	133.4	131.9	128.9	126.8	124.9	..
Cream (40 per cent fat content)	1.6	1.6	1.6	1.5	1.5	1.6	1.6	1.6	1.5	1.5	..
Cheese	5.8	5.9	6.3	6.1	5.5	5.8	6.2	6.0	5.8	6.2	..
Condensed milk	3.6	3.1	2.9	2.7	2.5	2.7	2.5	1.7	1.8	2.1	..
Milk powder	1.7	1.6	1.7	1.2	1.6	1.2	1.7	1.1	1.7	1.3	..
Eggs in shell (number)	244	240	232	237	236	239	238	227	219	216	..
Egg products (equivalent number of eggs)	18	16	14	11	12	12	11	10	10	11	..
Fats:											
Butter	7.6	8.3	8.4	8.3	7.8	7.5	6.8	6.3	6.0	5.8	..
Margarine	5.8	4.9	5.0	5.8	6.5	6.3	6.5	6.9	7.1	7.3	..
Lard and compound cooking fat	5.5	6.1	5.9	5.5	6.2	5.9	5.8	5.4	5.4	5.4	..
Other edible oils and fats	6.4	6.0	5.5	5.7	5.5	5.7	6.6	6.0	6.5	7.6	..
Fruit and vegetables:											
Fresh citrus fruit	10.5	9.4	9.3	9.2	8.8	9.5	8.9	10.2	9.7	9.2	..
Other fresh fruit	22.2	23.3	22.3	24.3	22.3	23.8	26.6	27.7	27.3	26.2	..
Canned and bottled fruit	8.6	7.1	6.8	6.6	6.0	5.6	5.3	5.3	5.2	4.7	..
Imported dried fruit	2.4	2.2	2.1	2.3	2.2	2.2	2.2	1.9	2.0	2.0	..
Potatoes (including products)	99.0	99.5	101.9	85.0	95.8	101.6	105.8	105.0	103.4	105.6	..
Fresh tomatoes	5.8	5.7	5.9	6.0	5.7	5.6	5.9	5.8	6.0	6.0	..
Other fresh vegetables	47.8	48.8	44.6	47.8	51.6	52.0	49.7	50.7	49.7	48.6	..
Imported canned tomatoes (including juice and puree)	4.1	4.4	2.9	4.0	4.4	3.2	4.5	4.0	4.5	4.5	..
Other canned vegetables	5.0	4.6	4.7	4.9	4.0	4.2	4.7	3.6	4.3	4.3	..
Pulses[3]	3.4	2.9	3.1	3.2	3.0	2.9	3.5	3.1	2.6	3.0	..
Other foods:											
Tea	3.4	3.5	3.5	3.6	3.2	2.9	3.1	3.2	3.2	3.3	..
Coffee	2.7	2.1	2.2	2.1	1.7	1.9	2.5	2.1	2.5	2.4	..
Cocoa powder	0.6	0.4	0.3	0.3	0.2	0.1	0.1	0.1	0.2	0.3	..
Alcoholic drink:											
Spirits (proof litres)	2.4	2.7	2.6	2.9	2.5	3.0	3.3	3.1	3.0	2.8	..
Beer (litres)	111.9	114.3	117.3	118.9	117.8	121.4	122.0	116.4	109.6	108.2	..
Wine (litres)	6.3	6.7	6.3	6.7	6.4	7.5	8.1	8.1	8.6	9.0	..
Cider and perry (litres)	3.2	3.2	3.6	4.2	3.9	4.0	4.1	4.0	4.3	5.2	..
Nutritional value of supplies per head per day:[4]											
Protein (grammes)	84.2	83.5	84.2	83.1	82.9	82.6	85.1	82.0	81.2	80.5	..
Fat (grammes)	141	132	130	130	131	130	134	125	126	128	..
Carbohydrate[5] (grammes)	384	383	376	378	378	379	375	364	359	364	..
Energy (kilojoules): from food	12 730	12 390	12 210	12 210	12 260	12 210	12 340	11 700	11 600	11 800	..
from alcohol	656	681	686	713	688	735	756	670	650	640	..

1. Total supplies for home use, including sugar content of imported manufactured foods.
2. Figures for 1980 onwards are not comparable with those for earlier years because of a revised method of estimating offal for human consumption.
3. Includes dried beans and dried peas for canning.
4. Estimates for 1980–82 are based on updated factors and also include in the nutrient totals the contribution from alcoholic drink. An indication of the net effect of these changes is provided by the following figures for 1980 which are on the old basis: 81.7, 128, 363, 11 920, 727.
5. Available carbohydrate expressed as monosaccharides.

6. Estimates for 1983 were not ready at the time of going to press. They will be published, as soon as they are available, in the *Food Facts* series of MAFF press notices, available from: Ministry of Agriculture, Fisheries and Food, Press Office, Whitehall Place, London SW1A 2HH.

Source Ministry of Agriculture, Fisheries and Food

9.16 Self-sufficiency in food and the cost of food processing and distribution in the United Kingdom

	Unit	1973	1974	1975	1976	1977	1978	1979	1980	1981	1982	1983
At current prices												
Home production adjusted for trade in agricultural inputs (i.e. feed, live-stock and seeds)	£ million	2 551	2 823	3 656	4 327	4 694	5 313	5 990	6 719	7 467	8 079	8 394
Home production for home consumption	,,	2 733	3 122	3 687	4 538	4 888	5 067	5 812	6 206	6 648	7 091	7 235
Imports for home consumption	,,	2 388	2 981	3 432	3 911	4 872	4 918	5 508	5 132	5 529	5 995	6 290
All foods consumed in the United Kingdom [1]	,,	5 121	6 103	7 119	8 449	9 760	9 985	11 320	11 338	12 177	13 086	13 525
Indigenous-type imports for home consumption	,,	1 371	1 751	2 083	2 187	2 627	2 770	3 066	2 892	3 129	3 430	3 515
All indigenous-type food consumed in the United Kingdom	,,	4 104	4 872	5 771	6 725	7 515	7 837	8 878	9 098	9 778	10 520	10 750
Adjusted home production as a percentage of all food consumed in the United Kingdom	percentage	49.8	46.3	51.4	51.2	48.1	53.2	52.9	59.3	61.3	61.7	62.1
Adjusted home production as a percentage of all indigenous-type food consumed in the United Kingdom	,,	62.2	57.9	63.4	64.3	62.5	67.8	67.5	73.9	76.4	76.8	78.1
Total final expenditure on food [2]	£ million	9 867	11 597	14 275	16 433	18 602	20 499	23 273	25 977	27 391	28 884	30 797
Cost of processing and distributing all food in the United Kingdom [3]	,,	4 746	5 494	7 156	7 984	8 842	10 514	11 953	14 639	15 214	15 798	17 272
Cost of processing and distributing all food in the United Kingdom as a percentage of total expenditure	percentage	48.1	47.4	50.1	48.6	47.5	51.3	51.4	56.4	55.5	54.7	56.1
At constant (1980) prices												
Home production adjusted for trade in agricultural inputs (i.e. feed, live-stock and seeds)	£ million	5 866	6 054	6 117	5 811	6 048	6 385	6 358	6 719	6 850	6 947	7 187
Home production for home consumption	,,	6 058	6 274	5 999	5 855	6 073	5 936	6 169	6 206	6 117	6 180	6 123
Imports for home consumption	,,	5 948	5 617	5 597	5 703	5 464	5 398	5 611	5 132	5 042	5 605	5 700
All foods consumed in the United Kingdom	,,	12 006	11 890	11 596	11 558	11 537	11 335	11 780	11 338	11 160	11 786	11 822
Indigenous-type imports for home consumption	,,	3 493	3 528	3 534	3 408	3 451	3 289	3 241	2 892	2 546	2 954	2 954
All indigenous-type food consumed in the United Kingdom	,,	9 551	9 801	9 534	9 263	9 524	9 226	9 410	9 098	8 663	9 134	9 077
Adjusted home production as a percentage of all food consumed in the United Kingdom	percentage	48.9	50.9	52.8	50.3	52.4	56.3	54.0	59.3	61.4	58.9	60.8
Adjusted home production as a percentage of all indigenous-type food consumed in the United Kingdom	,,	61.4	61.8	64.2	62.7	63.5	69.2	67.6	73.9	79.1	76.1	79.2
Total final expenditure on food [2]	£ million	25 476	25 166	24 947	25 082	24 774	25 463	26 046	25 977	25 728	25 509	25 931
Cost of processing and distributing all foods in the United Kingdom [3]	,,	13 470	13 276	13 351	13 524	13 237	14 128	14 266	14 639	14 568	13 723	14 109
Cost of processing and distributing all food in the United Kingdom as a percentage of total expenditure	percentage	52.9	52.8	53.5	53.9	53.4	55.5	54.8	56.4	56.6	53.8	54.4

1. At farmgate or landed value.
2. Taxes on food have been deducted and the value of subsidies added.
3. Derived as the difference between 'Total final expenditure on food' and 'All food consumed in the United Kingdom'. The latter is based on supplies data adjusted for known changes in stocks. These, however, are known to be incomplete (retailers' stocks are a particular omission); hence when stocks are increasing, 'Cost of processing and distribution' will tend to be understated, when they are being run down (e.g. in 1980) it will tend to be overstated.

Source Ministry of Agriculture, Fisheries and Food

9.17 Estimated household food consumption by all households in Great Britain

Ounces per person per week

	1973	1974	1975	1976	1977	1978	1979	1980	1981	1982	1983
Liquid milk (pints)	4.75	4.74	4.76	4.71	4.54	4.44	4.31	4.16	4.01	3.95	3.80
Other milk (pints or equivalent pints)	0.38	0.35	0.33	0.34	0.35	0.35	0.41	0.40	0.42	0.43	0.49
Cheese	3.75	3.74	3.79	3.79	3.80	3.72	3.84	3.89	3.89	3.80	4.01
Butter	5.24	5.61	5.63	5.16	4.70	4.55	4.45	4.05	3.69	3.17	3.27
Margarine	3.03	2.60	2.60	3.06	3.48	3.54	3.63	3.83	4.11	4.33	4.08
Lard and compound cooking fat	1.83	1.82	1.97	1.86	1.88	1.91	1.86	1.81	1.80	1.76	1.70
Eggs (number)	4.23	4.09	4.14	4.08	4.00	3.96	3.88	3.69	3.68	3.51	3.53
Preserves	2.51	2.47	2.43	2.30	2.36	2.15	2.17	2.05	2.08	1.99	2.05
Sugar	13.69	13.03	11.29	12.20	12.09	11.89	11.55	11.17	11.08	10.31	9.84
Beef and veal	6.31	7.41	8.32	7.62	8.25	8.27	8.27	8.13	6.96	7.06	6.57
Mutton and lamb	4.44	4.11	4.25	4.20	3.97	3.92	4.28	4.51	4.25	3.59	3.87
Pork	3.00	3.20	2.73	2.89	3.32	3.34	3.63	4.13	3.82	4.02	3.53
Bacon and ham, uncooked	4.41	4.18	3.99	4.03	4.34	4.31	4.35	4.20	4.14	3.95	4.02
Bacon and ham, cooked (including canned)	0.93	0.93	1.00	0.99	1.03	1.08	1.11	1.07	1.13	1.15	1.09
Poultry and cooked chicken	6.09	5.18	5.73	6.00	6.17	6.15	6.82	6.67	7.30	6.85	6.99
Other cooked and canned meats	3.03	2.71	2.80	2.83	2.55	2.66	2.64	2.40	2.42	2.51	2.65
Offals	1.17	1.05	1.15	1.16	1.21	1.11	1.04	1.03	1.04	0.97	0.84
Sausages, uncooked	3.41	3.50	3.22	3.29	3.47	3.54	3.49	3.25	3.41	3.33	3.33
Other meat products	3.72	3.61	3.85	3.97	4.23	4.46	4.57	4.70	4.81	5.19	5.18
Fish, fresh and processed	2.97	2.76	2.76	2.67	2.41	2.56	2.74	2.78	2.81	2.75	2.81
Canned fish	0.68	0.60	0.66	0.65	0.56	0.51	0.54	0.64	0.69	0.63	0.77
Fish and fish products, frozen	1.06	0.96	1.05	1.26	1.20	1.18	1.26	1.40	1.42	1.65	1.55
Potatoes (excluding processed)	45.93	45.66	43.90	35.30	40.79	44.05	43.59	40.95	41.87	41.11	39.88
Fresh green vegetables	12.48	12.70	11.58	11.40	12.15	13.45	10.88	12.42	11.98	11.24	10.78
Tomatoes, fresh	3.82	3.74	3.87	3.94	3.75	3.67	3.85	3.79	3.92	3.98	3.84
Other fresh vegetables and frozen vegetables	12.89	12.85	13.18	13.81	14.61	15.72	15.76	16.66	11.83	16.92	16.79
Canned tomatoes	0.91	0.94	0.98	1.06	1.17	1.16	1.27	1.43	1.52	1.38	1.44
Canned peas	2.76	2.76	2.76	2.84	2.54	2.46	2.67	2.25	2.36	2.53	2.30
Canned beans	3.78	3.58	3.83	3.99	3.97	3.92	4.09	4.00	4.12	4.16	4.45
Apples	6.66	7.08	6.77	7.44	6.46	7.02	7.88	7.85	7.28	7.02	7.08
Oranges	3.51	3.21	3.43	3.20	3.15	2.93	3.14	3.23	3.05	2.70	2.82
Other citrus fruit	1.73	1.37	1.49	1.53	1.75	1.84	1.87	2.04	1.92	1.72	1.97
All other fresh fruit	6.00	6.14	5.82	6.14	6.16	6.37	6.75	7.70	7.72	7.31	7.76
Canned fruit	4.49	3.70	3.75	3.56	3.19	3.05	2.84	2.79	2.61	2.65	2.42
Dried fruit, nuts and fruit and nut products	1.19	1.20	1.27	1.42	1.33	1.32	1.28	1.31	1.25	1.21	1.43
Flour	5.25	5.30	5.16	6.02	6.46	5.96	5.75	5.67	5.96	5.28	4.97
Bread	33.42	33.50	33.67	33.17	32.73	32.13	31.38	31.12	31.23	31.03	30.74
Buns, scones and teacakes	1.07	0.94	1.12	1.11	1.07	1.10	1.15	0.96	0.96	1.02	0.97
Cakes and pastries	3.74	3.51	3.12	2.85	2.80	2.67	2.86	2.77	2.81	2.74	2.62
Biscuits	5.82	5.63	5.59	5.62	5.62	5.45	5.54	5.40	5.39	5.66	5.47
Breakfast cereals	2.95	2.88	3.05	3.25	3.30	3.45	3.38	3.50	3.53	3.54	3.83
Oatmeal and oat products	0.46	0.53	0.50	0.49	0.51	0.47	0.45	0.42	0.46	0.37	0.45
Tea	2.16	2.24	2.18	2.21	2.07	1.99	2.11	2.05	1.98	2.02	2.04
Instant coffee	0.47	0.51	0.50	0.51	0.36	0.44	0.51	0.54	0.52	0.51	0.53
Canned soups	3.58	3.46	2.98	3.19	2.80	2.76	2.98	2.77	2.81	2.66	2.69
Pickles and sauces	1.57	1.55	1.71	1.66	1.66	1.74	1.83	1.81	2.01	1.97	2.15

Note: Page 176 contains a description of National Food Survey   *Source*   Ministry of Agriculture, Fisheries and Food (National Food Survey)

10 Transport and Communications

10.1 Goods transport in Great Britain

	1973	1974	1975	1976	1977	1978	1979	1980[1]	1981	1982	1983
Total tonne kilometres (thousand millions)	142.5	141.6	139.6	144.2	154.8	161.9	172.8	165.4	165.8	170.0	172.0
Road[2]	90.4	89.9	91.8	95.6	98.0	99.1	104.6	95.9	97.1	100.0	100.4
Rail[3]	22.7	21.6	20.8	20.4	20.1	20.0	19.9	17.6	17.5	15.9	17.1
Water: seagoing[4]	24.2	24.4	20.7	22.1	27.5	32.6	37.6	41.4	41.5	44.4	44.2[7]
Water: internal[5]	0.4	0.4	0.4	0.4	0.4	0.4	0.4	0.4	0.4	0.4	0.4[7]
Pipelines[6]	4.8	5.3	5.9	5.7	8.8	9.8	10.3	10.1	9.3	9.5	9.9
Total (million tonnes)	1 962	1 820	1 879	1 799	1 726	1 811	1 827	1 725	1 635	1 679	1 698
Road[2]	1 660	1 537	1 602	1 516	1 422	1 494	1 504	1 418	1 339	1 390	1 402
Rail[3]	196	176	175	176	171	171	169	154	154	142	145
Water: seagoing[4]	44	44	38	41	46	51	56	58	57	60	60[7]
Water: internal[5]	11	10	11	11	11	11	11	11	9	9	9[7]
Pipelines[6]	50	50	52	53	75	83	85	83	75	78	82

1. Estimates for 1980 do not include figures for road vehicles under 1½ tons unladen weight.
2. See footnotes to Table 10.5.
3. British Rail only. During 1982, traffics were affected by industrial action which took place on 34 days.

4. Movements between seaports in Great Britain, including Scottish islands. Excludes one-port traffic and traffic with Northern Ireland, Isle of Man and Channel Islands. Tonne-kilometre estimates include movement on inland waterways.
5. Non-seagoing traffic on inland waterways and estuaries.
6. Excluding movements of gases by pipelines.
7. Water figures are provisional.

Source Department of Transport

10.2 Passenger transport in Great Britain: estimated passenger kilometres

Thousand million passenger kilometres

	1973	1974	1975	1976	1977	1978	1979	1980	1981	1982	1983
Total	458.5	446.4	448.6	459.7	470.0	494.9	498.7	511.4	504.3	531.6	498.7
Air[1]	2.4	2.3	2.2	2.3	2.1	2.4	2.8	2.8	2.6	2.8	2.8
Rail[2]	35.1	36.1	35.1	32.9	33.6	35.2	36.5	36.0	34.9	31.3	34.8
Road:											
Public service vehicles[3]	53	54	55	53	51	50	48	45	42	41	42
Cars and taxis[4,5]	307	297	294	309	323	342	347	374	377	397	407
Motorcycles[4,5]	3	3	4	5	5	5	5	6	7	8	7
Pedal cycles[5]	3.2	3.2	3.8	4.2	5.1	4.3	3.9	4.3	4.6	5.2	5.1

1. Domestic scheduled services, including Northern Ireland, Isle of Man and Channel Islands.
2. Including British Rail, London Transport and Passenger Transport Executive railway systems. The basis of calculating London Transport railways' passenger kilometres has been revised from passenger kilometres paid for to passenger kilometres travelled. During 1982, British Rail traffics were affected by industrial action which took place on 34 days.

3. Calculated from operators' returns of numbers of passengers carried, using estimates for average length of journey.
4. Based on statistics of vehicle mileage derived from the traffic counts and estimates of average numbers of persons per vehicle, derived from the National Travel surveys.
5. Revised.

Sources Department of Transport; Civil Aviation Authority

10.3 Length of public roads in Great Britain
At 1 April in each year[1]

Kilometres

	1973	1974	1975	1976	1977	1978	1979	1980	1981	1982	1983
Total	327 135	328 995	329 959	332 884	334 699	336 231	337 844	339 446	341 704	343 292	344 978
Motorway[2]	1 731	1 869	1 970	2 162	2 245	2 385	2 451	2 555	2 621	2 652	2 709
Trunk	13 351	13 343	13 365	13 449	13 092	12 544	12 465	12 393	12 369	12 319	12 321
Principal	32 755	32 765	32 835	33 145	33 507	34 095	34 325	34 201	34 458	34 510	34 587
Other[3]	279 297	281 019	281 789	284 128	285 855	287 206	288 603	290 296	292 256	293 811	295 361

1. In Scotland as at 16 May up to and including 1975.
2. Including local authority motorways, the percentage of which is small.
3. Excluding unsurfaced roads and green lanes.

Sources Department of Transport; Scottish Development Department; Welsh Office

10.4 Estimated traffic on all roads in Great Britain[1]

Thousand million vehicle kilometres

	1973	1974	1975	1976	1977	1978	1979	1980	1981	1982	1983
All motor vehicles	212.31	208.09	209.84	220.35	225.18	234.30	236.48	252.87	255.15	266.63	271.22
Cars and taxis[2]	167.86	163.90	165.39	173.38	178.23	185.92	187.66	202.10	203.55	214.77	220.00
Two wheeled motor vehicles	3.01	3.22	3.84	4.74	4.76	4.74	5.00	6.03	6.72	7.06	6.20
Buses and coaches	3.13	2.95	2.90	2.97	2.86	2.91	2.95	3.07	3.21	3.30	3.29
Total goods vehicles	38.31	38.03	37.71	39.27	39.33	40.72	40.86	41.67	41.67	41.50	41.72
Light vans[3]	18.69	19.01	18.88	19.41	19.77	20.34	20.22	21.08	21.37	21.77	21.91
Other goods vehicles	19.61	19.02	18.84	19.85	19.56	20.39	20.65	20.59	20.30	19.73	19.81
Pedal cycles	3.24	3.24	3.77	4.21	5.11	4.25	3.87	4.32	4.61	5.21	5.14

1. Figures from 1973 have been revised.
2. This category includes three-wheeled cars; excluding all vans whether licensed for private or for commercial use.
3. Not exceeding 30 cwt. unladen weight.

Source Department of Transport

10.5 Vehicles with licences current[1, 2, 3]
Great Britain

Thousands

	1972	1973	1974	1975	1976	1978	1979	1980	1981	1982	1983
Total	16 117	17 014	17 252	17 501	17 832	17 772	18 625	19 210	19 355	19 770	20 216
Private and light goods[4]	13 699	14 540	14 724	14 854	15 156	15 166	15 722	16 233	16 421	16 816	17 158
Private cars[4]	12 466	13 231	13 399	13 517	13 792	13 801	14 307	14 772	14 943	15 303	15 543
Other vehicles[4]	1 233	1 309	1 325	1 337	1 364	1 365	1 415	1 461	1 478	1 513	1 615
Motor cycles, etc: total	982	1 006	1 042	1 161	1 220	1 194	1 292	1 372	1 371	1 370	1 290
Bicycles:											
Up to 50 c.c.	454	487	509	546	538	458	466	473	472	489	474
Other	528	519	533	615	682	736	826	899	899	881	816
Public road passenger vehicles: total	105	106	107	112	113	110	111	110	110	111	113
Buses, coaches, taxis, etc.											
Not over 8 passengers	28	29	28	32	34	37	37	39	40	43	46
Over 8 passengers	77	77	79	80	79	73	74	71	70	68	67
Goods[5, 6]	663	679	677	668	647	606	624	575	558	549	565
Agricultural tractors, etc.[7]	419	421	429	414	403	394	402	397	365	372	376
Other licensed vehicles[8]	106	109	108	115	120	111	106	100	95	91	86
Exempt from licence duty: total[9, 10]	143	153	166	177	173	191	368	423	435	462	628
Crown vehicles	20	21	32	35	36	36	35	38	37	38	38
All other exempt vehicles	123	132	134	142	137	155	333	385	398	424	590

1. The figures are based on a sample count during the third quarter for the years 1972–74. From 1974 the census method underlying the count of the stock of licensed vehicles has been changing as vehicle records have gradually been transferred from Local Taxation Offices to the Driver and Vehicle Licensing Centre in Swansea. Consequently stock figures from 1974 to 1978 are not strictly comparable. No census results are available for 1977. Since 1978, censuses have been taken annually on 31 December, and are obtained from a full count of licensing records held at the Driver and Vehicle Licensing Centre. Vehicles operating under the Crown Vehicles Scheme are included. Those operating under defence permits are excluded.
2. The methodology underlying the census is different from 1978 onwards, compared to previous years.
3. Excludes vehicles officially registered by the armed forces.
4. Includes taxis also used privately.

5. As a result of changes in the taxation system since October 1982, about 970,000 vans and light goods vehicles previously licensed as Goods vehicles, have now been regrouped, together with 14,000 newly licensed goods vehicles under the heading private and light goods; which has replaced the old private category. Figures for previous years have been estimated to provide a continuous series of data.
6. Includes agricultural vans and lorries, showmen's goods vehicles licensed to draw trailers.
7. Includes combine harvesters, mowing machines, digging machines, mobile cranes and works trucks.
8. Includes three wheelers, pedestrian controlled vehicles and showmen's haulage.
9. From 1979 includes exempt tax classes 61 and 62 not previously included.
10. From 1980 includes electric vehicles which are now exempt from licence duty.

Source Department of Transport

10.6 New vehicle registrations by taxation class
Great Britain

Number

	1973	1974	1975	1976	1977	1978	1979	1980	1981	1982	1983
Total[1]	2 230 183	1 750 352	1 749 883	1 837 871	1 861 979	2 151 438	2 369 865	2 155 789	2 030 335	2 103 885	2 307 495
Private and light goods[2]: total				1 401 711	1 445 039	1 745 826	1 891 542	1 679 555	1 627 221	1 727 955	1 971 163
Private Cars	} 1 851 251	1 399 641	1 317 195 {	1 221 557	1 253 925	1 519 898	1 625 427	1 436 823	1 434 784	1 526 992	1 773 331
Other vehicles				180 154	191 114	225 928	266 115	242 732	192 437	200 963	197 832
Motor cycles, etc.: total	193 612	189 768	264 814	270 590	251 290	225 289	285 863	312 667	271 878	231 552	174 454
Bicycles:											
Up to 50 c.c.	98 304	94 623	106 795	94 672	84 688	56 226	86 468	96 399	94 775	94 038	67 405
Other	95 308	95 145	158 019	175 918	166 602	169 063	199 395	216 268	177 103	137 514	107 049
Public road passenger vehicles: total	9 957	7 835	7 842	8 738	8 799	9 142	9 107	8 764	7 500	7 062	7 271
Buses, coaches, taxis, etc.											
Not over 8 seats	2 780	2 615	2 361	2 822	2 885	3 064	2 816	2 511	2 647	2 806	2 975
Over 8 seats	7 177	5 220	5 481	5 916	5 914	6 078	6 291	6 253	4 853	4 256	4 296
Heavy general goods[2] and farmers[3] goods vehicles: by weight	82 691	67 935	67 005	63 846	68 802	79 834	91 264	74 693	56 305	58 809	64 611
Privately owned agricultural tractors and engines[4]	49 718	45 623	48 467	51 783	48 279	49 982	47 672	36 657	32 640	38 891	42 118
Other licensed vehicles[5]	12 008	12 364	12 665	9 914	7 404	6 780	6 025	4 931	3 393	3 883	3 771
Exempt from license duty: total	30 946	27 186	31 895	31 289	32 366	34 585	38 392	38 522	31 398	35 733	44 107
Crown vehicles	2 897	2 811	3 871	4 239	4 215	4 668	4 371	5 938	4 617	4 609	5 010
All other exempt vehicles[1,6]	28 049	24 375	28 024	27 050	28 151	29 921	34 021	32 584	26 781	31 124	39 097

1. Including personal and direct export vehicles.
2. Estimates of the total of vehicles within the Private and Light Goods taxation class, and within the Other Goods class were estimated by assuming that all goods vehicles less than 1.5 tons unladen weight would have been registered in the Private and Light Goods class if it had existed prior to October 1982 when it first became effective.

3. Owned by a farmer and available for hauling produce and requisites for his farm.
4. Agricultural tractors are excluded unless driven on public roads.
5. Includes three wheelers, pedestrian controlled vehicles, general haulage and showmen's tractors.
6. From 1980 includes electric vehicles which are now exempt from licence duty.

Source Department of Transport

10.7 Driving tests
Great Britain
Applications and results

Thousands

	1973	1974	1975	1976	1977	1978	1979	1980	1981	1982	1983
Applications received	1 862.2	1 612.1	1 693.8	2 044.1	1 646.7	1 908.9	1 786.4	1 800.5	1 837.3	1 891.6	1 917.0
Tests conducted	1 533.8	1 677.8	1 825.0	1 882.7	1 767.8	1 632.2	1 569.6	1 962.0	2 031.3	2 005.3	1 892.3
Tests passed	705.7	764.6	828.9	849.2	810.8	757.5	742.1	927.8	966.8	965.0	921.0
Percentage of passes	*46.0*	*45.6*	*45.4*	*45.1*	*45.9*	*46.4*	*47.3*	*47.3*	*47.6*	*48.1*	*48.7*

Source Department of Transport

10.8 Vehicles with licences current[1]
Northern Ireland

Number

	1972[2]	1974[2]	1975	1976	1977	1978	1979[3]	1980	1981	1982	1983
Total	380 513	379 273	383 654	403 219	416 057	428 956	438 949	442 348	436 695	462 560	481 854
Private, cars, etc.	304 144	309 237	313 665	325 766	337 890	347 091	358 010	364 590	365 000	388 030	411 780
Cycles and tricycles	10 957	11 211	12 346	15 252	16 826	17 006	14 860	14 720	14 550	15 500	14 790
Public road passenger vehicles: total	2 267	2 072	1 902	2 317	2 224	1 888	2 110	2 270	2 510	2 210	2 200
Taxis	748	717	706	867	771	386	410	710	840	720	940
Buses, coaches, etc.	1 519	1 355	1 196	1 450	1 453	1 502	1 700	1 560	1 670	1 490	1 260
Goods vehicles: total	41 168	38 846	38 357	40 306	39 190	39 708	41 810	38 900	33 760	34 060	29 450
General haulage vehicles: total	38 620	33 368	35 748	36 647	35 067	36 426	37 950	34 170	29 840	32 880	27 960
Unladen weight:											
Not over 1½ tons	21 736	17 680	19 017	18 426	18 123	17 936	18 820	16 720	13 190	15 490	10 530
Over 1½ and not over 3 tons	6 116	5 164	6 513	7 164	6 149	6 971	6 780	6 710	6 140	5 730	9 690
Over 3 tons	10 768	10 524	10 218	11 057	10 795	11 519	12 350	10 740	10 510	11 660	7 740
Agricultural vans and lorries[4]	2 256	5 360	2 540	3 641	4 054	3 222	3 710	4 620	3 770	1 090	1 440
Tractors for general haulage	279	108	49	7	59	50	130	80	130	70	50
Tower wagons	13	10	20	9	10	10	20	30	20	20	–
Agricultural tractors and engines, etc[5]	17 102	12 360	11 151	11 535	11 329	13 980	11 040	9 580	7 660	9 150	9 870
Vehicles exempt from duty: total	4 767	5 547	6 233	8 043	8 598	9 283	11 119	12 288	13 215	13 610	13 764
Owned by government authorities	2 156	3 430	3 736	5 645	6 534	7 088	7 756	7 978	9 395	9 390	9 604
Other:											
Ambulances	64	98	118	19	–	10	50	70	10	290	342
Fire engines	167	118	108	49	49	59	–	60	110	140	40
Other	2 380	1 901	2 271	2 330	2 015	2 126	3 313	4 180	3 700	3 790	3 778

1. Licences current at any time during the September quarter.
2. No census was taken in 1973.
3. Licences current at any time during the quarter ended December.

4. Owned by a farmer and available for hauling produce and requisites for his farm.
5. Agricultural tractors are excluded unless driven on public roads.

Source Department of the Environment for Northern Ireland

10.9 New vehicles registrations
Northern Ireland

Number

	1973	1974	1975	1976	1977	1978	1979	1980	1981	1982	1983
Total	54 277	50 241	57 736	66 783	66 033	71 191	70 165	59 656	54 899	65 996	76 667
Private cars, etc.	42 767	39 797	44 824	51 989	50 287	56 728	56 053	47 228	44 427	54 793	64 493
Cycles and tricycles	2 763	2 698	4 348	5 174	4 813	4 133	3 471	3 543	3 533	3 111	2 814
Public road passenger vehicles: total	164	220	182	163	209	140	151	171	150	141	273
Taxis	57	50	57	33	35	21	27	26	32	38	153
Buses, coaches, etc.	107	170	125	130	174	119	124	145	118	103	120
Goods vehicles: total	6 479	5 136	5 573	6 002	6 522	6 705	7 226	5 917	4 631	5 482	5 961
General haulage vehicles: total	6 343	5 037	5 346	5 616	6 079	6 287	6 843	5 617	4 288	5 136	5 701
Unladen weight:											
Not over 1½ tons	4 372	3 301	3 371	3 492	3 529	3 839	4 324	3 590	2 561	3 225	3 466
Over 1½ and not over 3 tons	723	628	722	823	837	853	755	815	722	638	1 061
Over 3 tons	1 248	1 108	1 253	1 301	1 713	1 595	1 764	1 212	1 005	1 273	1 174
Agricultural vans and lorries[1]	117	94	223	382	439	407	370	282	339	343	249
Tractors for general haulage	19	5	4	4	4	11	13	18	4	3	11
Agricultural tractors and engines, etc.[2]	1 666	1 602	1 879	2 558	3 230	2 626	2 222	1 489	1 158	1 324	1 894
Vehicles exempt from duty: total	438	788	930	897	972	859	1 042	1 308	1 000	1 145	1 232
Ambulances	8	18	31	37	6	3	5	1	34	10	13
Fire engines	1	34	2	7	–	10	16	2	7	8	1
Road construction vehicles	27	41	62	20	32	14	25	10	24	38	24
Other	402	695	835	833	934	832	996	1 295	935	1 089	1 194

1. Owned by a farmer and available for hauling produce and requisites for his farm.
2. Agricultural tractors are excluded unless driven on public roads.

Source Department of the Environment for Northern Ireland

10.10 Buses and Coaches[1]
Great Britain

	1973	1974	1975	1976	1977	1978	1979	1980	1981	1982	1983
Number of vehicles (end of year)	74 402	76 874	76 898	75 510	73 531	73 792	72 942	69 136	69 919	70 710	70 191
Buses and coaches	74 306	76 774	76 797	75 416	73 437	73 699	72 850	69 061	69 837	70 631	70 112
Single deck	45 160	47 298	48 022	47 553	46 400	47 024	47 015	43 534	44 657	44 787	44 786
Double deck	29 146	29 476	28 775	27 863	27 037	26 675	25 835	25 527	25 180	25 844	25 326
Tramcars	96	100	101	94	94	93	92	75	82	79	79
London Transport	6 201	6 387	6 405	6 364	6 328	6 322	6 157	6 185	5 909	6 203	5 638
Passenger transport executives	11 604	11 618	11 533	11 186	10 923	10 950	10 669	10 287	10 062	9 898	9 612
Municipal operators	6 195	6 154	6 160	6 124	5 993	5 905	5 853	5 677	5 490	5 331	5 271
National Bus Company[2]	20 532	20 831	20 387	19 371	18 786	18 162	17 826	15 981	15 301	15 027	14 614
Scottish Bus Group	4 540	4 607	4 301	4 134	4 087	3 879	3 823	3 631	3 416	3 274	3 117
Other operators	25 330	27 277	28 112	28 331	27 414	28 574	28 614	27 375	29 741	30 977	31 939
Vehicle kilometres (millions)	3 426	3 462	3 550	3 511	3 451	3 404	3 338	3 280	3 227	3 231	3 311
London Transport	292	281	285	293	289	278	265	279	282	265	264
Passenger transport executives	556	546	554	545	524	517	505	510	487	485	482
Municipal operators	257	259	261	259	250	246	242	241	233	232	231
National Bus Company[2]	1 191	1 188	1 191	1 142	1 110	1 075	1 045	1 026	973	972	969
Scottish Bus Group	245	221	240	231	216	212	208	203	206	200	202
Other operators	886	967	1 019	1 041	1 062	1 077	1 073	1 020	1 048	1 077	1 162
Passenger journeys (millions)	8 455	8 312	8 168	7 797	7 505	7 305	7 100	6 783	6 269	6 083	6 185
London Transport	1 439	1 473	1 455	1 423	1 374	1 302	1 234	1 183	1 081	1 043	1 089
Passenger transport executives	2 336	2 310	2 313	2 187	2 091	2 012	1 993	1 973	1 805	1 736	1 751
Municipal operators	1 217	1 207	1 180	1 115	1 077	1 052	1 019	952	886	854	854
National Bus Company[2]	2 366	2 235	2 113	1 923	1 858	1 825	1 795	1 669	1 529	1 479	1 460
Scottish Bus Group	456	395	392	379	358	351	350	339	322	314	319
Other operators	639	691	716	770	746	764	709	666	647	657	712
Passenger receipts (£ million)	580.7	655.8	859.4	1 037.1	1 146.5	1 268.8	1 409.7	1 644.1	1 753.8	1 929.2	2 060.1
London Transport	73.7	74.9	92.6	127.1	146.8	156.8	162.7	206.9	208.6	255.5	267.1
Passenger transport executives	127.0	136.3	177.6	213.7	236.7	258.5	287.7	334.7	342.7	374.7	398.6
Municipal operators	51.6	58.5	80.5	96.5	112.7	127.1	136.9	160.4	172.8	181.1	196.3
National Bus Company[2]	189.1	219.0	291.9	339.0	363.3	396.3	429.9	491.4	519.9	543.0	572.8
Scottish Bus Group	41.7	43.3	59.7	71.1	74.3	82.1	92.5	108.8	116.8	127.4	134.1
Other operators	97.7	123.8	157.1	189.7	212.8	248.0	300.0	341.8	393.1	447.4	491.3

1. The first four passenger transport executives were formed in 1969/70, three further PTEs have been formed, in Glasgow during 1973, and in South and West Yorkshire in 1974, and the other PTEs were enlarged to cover the other metropolitan counties. Figures prior to 1976 have been revised to take into account all changes between the various parts of the public sector and between the private and public sectors.
2. Includes the operations of the York-West Yorkshire Joint Committee.

Source Department of Transport

10.11 Indices of stage bus service fares
Index 31 December 1973 = 100
Great Britain

	1973	1974	1975	1976	1977	1978	1979	1980	1981	1982	1983[1]
London Transport	100.0	100.0	149.2	190.8	223.3	245.3	299.5	428.1	283.8	554.1	454.2
Passenger transport executives	100.0	108.5	170.3	182.2	214.7	241.6	280.6	359.4	333.7	396.1	390.6
Municipal operators	100.0	124.0	182.7	216.8	242.2	264.0	302.1	387.0	436.6	477.8	514.7
Municipal operators and Passenger transport executives	100.0	115.3	173.7	192.0	222.3	247.6	286.4	366.9	365.1	421.4	429.2
Other operators	100.0	124.5	183.6	208.7	233.0	265.1	308.7	374.5	423.6	476.2	506.1
All operators except London Transport	100.0	119.2	178.9	200.8	227.9	257.0	298.5	371.3	395.8	450.6	469.7
All operators	100.0	116.2	174.6	200.0	228.2	256.3	300.0	381.3	380.8	474.6	476.4

Source Department of Transport

10.12 Road accidents, vehicles involved and casualties
Great Britain

Number

	1973	1974	1975	1976	1977	1978	1979	1980	1981	1982	1983
Road accidents[1]	262 413	244 042	246 286	258 639	265 861	264 769	254 967	250 958	248 276	255 980	242 876
Vehicles involved:											
Pedal cycles	20 701	19 528	21 728	24 067	24 383	23 113	24 792	25 884	26 496	29 428	31 824
Motor vehicles	396 908	369 926	373 822	396 731	411 558	414 573	397 595	391 870	390 736	401 460	377 289
Mopeds	8 218	9 684	12 250	15 550	15 589	13 491	11 781	11 703	11 478	13 081	13 203
Motor scooters	6 174	4 239	3 390	2 513	1 821	1 488	1 414	2 195	2 319	2 813	2 990
Motor cycles	32 031	34 914	42 484	51 380	56 266	56 403	55 978	59 156	57 152	57 139	49 769
Cars and taxis	269 729	249 265	245 025	257 667	268 813	275 098	265 327	262 979	265 531	275 507	261 714
Light goods vehicles[2]	32 287	28 481	26 931	26 987	26 340	25 798	24 715	22 319	22 106	21 704	19 853
Heavy goods vehicles[3]	23 163	19 347	18 415	17 996	18 508	18 795	18 194	15 343	14 554	14 688	13 504
Buses and coaches	17 751	16 666	16 953	16 039	15 548	15 443	14 808	13 814	13 083	12 911	12 763
Other motor vehicles	7 555	7 330	8 374	8 599	8 673	8 057	5 378	4 361	4 513	3 617	3 493
Vehicles involved per hundred million kilometres travelled[4]											
Pedal cycles	639	602	577	572	477	543	641	599	575	565	619
All two-wheeled motor vehicles	1 544	1 518	1 513	1 466	1 548	1 505	1 383	1 212	1 056	1 034	1 063
Cars and taxis	161	152	148	149	151	148	141	130	130	128	119
Light goods vehicles[2]	173	150	143	139	133	127	122	106	103	100	91
Heavy goods vehicles[3]	118	102	98	91	95	92	88	75	72	74	68
Total casualties	353 780	324 918	324 950	339 673	348 061	349 795	334 513	326 732	324 840	334 296	308 584
Killed[5]:											
Total	7 406	6 876	6 366	6 570	6 614	6 831	6 352	5 953	5 846	5 934	5 445
Pedestrians	2 806	2 642	2 344	2 335	2 313	2 427	2 118	1 941	1 874	1 869	1 914
Pedal cycles	336	282	278	300	301	316	320	302	310	294	323
All two wheeled motor vehicles	750	797	838	990	1 182	1 163	1 160	1 163	1 131	1 090	963
Cars and taxis	3 048	2 709	2 444	2 520	2 441	2 569	2 429	2 278	2 287	2 443	2 019
Others	466	446	462	425	377	356	325	269	244	238	226
Killed and seriously injured[6]:											
By age group[7]											
0–4	2 832	2 365	2 138	1 894	1 777	1 552	1 464	1 351	1 286	1 345	1 403
5–9	6 774	5 897	5 150	5 006	5 209	4 906	4 576	4 203	3 909	3 717	3 586
10–14	5 632	5 288	5 098	5 068	5 494	5 366	5 151	5 255	5 162	5 474	5 450
15–19	17 950	17 621	18 292	20 623	21 330	21 609	20 859	21 501	21 848	21 413	18 456
20–24	14 759	12 834	11 856	12 343	12 854	13 433	13 555	13 243	13 682	14 522	12 575
25–29	8 912	7 820	7 423	7 322	7 167	7 206	7 270	6 741	6 466	6 964	6 072
30–39	10 076	9 478	8 614	8 734	9 018	9 518	9 437	9 045	8 973	9 366	8 102
40–49	8 051	7 446	6 745	6 597	6 557	6 752	6 608	6 236	6 161	6 250	5 441
50–59	8 109	7 335	6 516	6 532	6 697	6 738	6 569	6 027	5 771	5 784	4 980
60 and over	13 749	12 780	11 630	11 490	11 723	11 801	10 870	10 806	10 399	10 464	10 003
By type of road user:											
Child pedestrians[8]	10 522	9 337	8 181	7 866	8 303	7 925	7 359	6 893	6 547	6 695	6 640
Adult pedestrians	15 141	14 325	12 631	12 635	13 052	13 309	12 969	12 004	11 817	12 169	12 139
Child pedal cyclists[8]	2 041	1 879	2 052	2 124	2 124	1 875	2 085	2 135	2 096	2 058	2 287
Adult pedal cyclists	2 716	2 565	2 511	2 786	2 889	2 854	3 135	3 386	3 393	3 893	4 109
Moped riders	2 092	2 492	2 900	3 707	3 697	3 347	2 908	2 933	2 903	3 109	3 294
Motor scooter riders	1 446	997	842	614	475	402	356	500	515	608	742
Motor scooter passengers	227	112	105	73	62	43	36	51	62	106	647
Motor cycle riders	9 499	9 949	11 317	13 580	15 166	15 510	15 797	16 926	16 398	16 296	16 281
Motor cycle passengers	1 242	1 110	1 379	1 797	2 028	2 142	2 133	2 246	2 400	2 514	2 021
Car and taxi drivers	23 850	21 438	19 213	19 229	19 363	20 441	19 970	18 932	19 149	19 460	15 472
Car and taxi passengers	20 173	17 753	15 969	15 650	15 315	15 950	14 993	14 309	14 476	14 525	11 574
Users of buses and coaches	1 653	1 616	1 655	1 365	1 333	1 200	1 071	952	961	962	969
Users of goods vehicles	5 611	4 757	4 198	3 937	3 762	3 744	3 530	3 093	2 891	2 797	2 283
Users of other vehicles	617	507	449	503	504	405	367	305	308	312	278
All severities											
Total	353 780	324 918	324 950	339 673	348 061	349 795	334 513	326 732	324 840	334 296	308 584
Pedestrians	80 060	74 585	69 322	68 509	71 276	70 295	66 714	63 299	60 750	61 419	61 674
Vehicle users	273 720	250 333	255 628	271 164	276 785	279 500	267 799	263 433	264 090	272 877	246 910

1. Accidents on public roads, involving injury, which are reported to the police.
2. 1½ tons unladen weight and under.
3. Over 1½ tons unladen weight.
4. Traffic figures have been revised.
5. Died within 30 days of accident.

6. Hospital inpatients plus casualties with any fracture, internal injury, concussion, crushing, severe general shock, etc, plus deaths after 30 days.
7. These figures may not add up to total fatal and serious figures, due to the exclusion of road users whose age was not reported.
8. Age 0 – 14.

Sources Department of Transport; Scottish Development Department; Welsh Office

10.13 Casualties in road accidents, pedestrian crossings, seat belt wearing, breath tests and related casualties
Great Britain

Number/*percentage*

	1973	1974	1975	1976	1977	1978	1979	1980	1981	1982	1983
Pedestrian casualties											
on crossings	6 694	6 339	5 841	5 657	5 891	5 772	5 366	5 247	4 745	4 974	4 916
crossing within 50 metres[1] of											
crossings	4 121	4 180	3 977	4 299	4 884	5 222	5 541	5 146	4 863	4 806	5 931
elsewhere	67 705	64 014	59 504	58 553	60 501	59 301	55 807	52 906	40 558	51 639	50 837
Percentage wearing of seat belts among front seat car and van occupants											
all[2]	*32*	*32*	*32*	*33*	*31*	*32*	*33*	*30*	*. .*	*38*	*95*
casualties[3]: killed	*13*	*12*	*11*	*15*	*14*	*14*	*15*	*14*	*15*	*18*	*79*
seriously injured	*16*	*15*	*15*	*17*	*17*	*18*	*18*	*18*	*20*	*24*	*89*
slightly injured	*20*	*20*	*21*	*25*	*24*	*24*	*25*	*25*	*28*	*34*	*93*
Breath tests on car drivers involved in accidents											
all drivers	269 729	249 019	245 025	257 667	268 813	275 098	265 327	262 979	265 531	275 507	261 714
tested	27 862	27 612	28 291	28 949	29 485	31 531	32 447	32 735	32 640	34 472	33 769
failed test[4]	10 856	11 903	11 788	9 878	9 549	10 543	11 329	10 777	10 121	11 145	10 200

1. 50 yards before 1978.
2. At one survey during the year, in daytime (8.30am – 6.30 pm) 1972 – 80, no survey in 1981. Continuous monitoring (8.30am – 9.50 pm), from February 1982.
3. In vehicles with seat belt fitted, includes an apportionment of not knowns.
4. Positive result, or refused to provide a specimen.

Sources Department of Transport; Scottish Development Department; Welsh Office

10.14 Road goods transport: analysis by mode of working
Great Britain

	1973	1974	1975	1976	1977	1978[1]	1979	1980	1981	1982[3]	1983[3]
Estimated tonne kilometres[2] (Thousand million)											
Total	87.6	87.1	89.0	92.9	95.4	96.3	101.9	93.2	94.4	97.0	97.5
Own account	31.2	31.3	32.5	34.5	32.2	37.2	39.9	36.1	35.9	36.9	35.4
Public haulage	56.4	55.8	56.5	58.4	63.2	59.1	62.0	57.1	58.5	60.1	62.1
Estimated tonnes carried[2] (Millions)											
Total	1 570	1 451	1 439	1 434	1 353	1 420	1 436	1 349	1 270	1 321	1 335
Own account	727	666	675	678	619	720	724	672	615	640	624
Public haulage	843	785	764	756	734	700	712	677	655	681	711

1. From 1978 onwards includes the small amount of work performed in Northern Ireland by British registered goods vehicles.
2. Excludes work done by small goods vehicles under 3.5 tonnes gross vehicle weight.
3. Provisional estimates.

Source Department of Transport

10.15 British Rail: assets and privately-owned freight vehicles operated
Great Britain

	Unit	1973	1974	1975	1976	1977	1978	1979	1980	1981	1982	1983
Rolling stock												
Tractive units: total[1]	Number	8 712	8 665	8 568	8 439	8 397	8 413	8 506	8 358	7 947	7 690	7 374
Locomotives: total[1]	,,	3 972	3 971	3 860	3 689	3 610	3 580	3 571	3 379	3 131	3 016	2 850
Diesel[2]	,,	3 639	3 619	3 508	3 338	3 290	3 268	3 261	3 078	2 864	2 750	2 603
Electric	,,	333	352	352	351	320	312	310	301	267	266	247
Power cars: total	,,	4 730	4 694	4 708	4 750	4 787	4 833	4 935	4 979	4 816	4 674	4 524
Advanced passenger train	,,	–	–	–	–	–	2	5	6	6	6	6
High speed train	,,	–	–	2	42	76	109	136	142	181	197	197
Diesel[3]	,,	2 060	2 047	2 042	2 018	1 979	1 981	1 962	1 955	1 836	1 734	1 641
Electric[4]	,,	2 670	2 647	2 664	2 690	2 732	2 741	2 832	2 876	2 793	2 737	2 680
Coaching vehicles: total	,,	23 344	23 238	22 902	22 415	21 958	21 569	21 652	21 216	19 149	17 831	17 166
Passenger carriages: total[5]	,,	17 793	17 737	17 461	17 111	17 044	17 028	17 175	17 042	16 166	15 400	14 807
Locomotive-hauled	,,	7 152	7 154	6 826	6 365	6 086	5 967	5 885	5 567	5 070	4 468	4 059
Advanced passenger train	,,	–	–	–	–	–	6	15	30	30	30	30
High speed train	,,	–	–	8	151	302	421	533	630	664	709	709
Diesel multiple unit[6]	,,	3 468	3 427	3 402	3 367	3 313	3 293	3 284	3 257	3 096	2 917	2 703
Electric multiple unit[7]	,,	7 173	7 156	7 225	7 228	7 343	7 341	7 458	7 558	7 306	7 276	7 306
Non passenger-carrying vehicles[8]	,,	5 551	5 501	5 441	5 304	4 914	4 541	4 477	4 174	2 983	2 431	2 359
Seats or berths in passenger carriages	Thousands	1 108	1 106	1 099	1 082	1 073	1 080	1 091	1 090	1 044	1 003	971
Freight wagons operated: total	Thousands											
Wagons owned by British Rail: total	,,	246.6	239.3	214.3	184.9	164.8	148.2	136.3	117.8	86.2	69.4	52.4
Air-braked wagons	,,	9.3	9.9	11.2	12.9	14.2	15.9	17.5	18.8	20.0	20.1	19.8
Vacuum-braked wagons	,,	102.7	102.4	92.2	86.0	76.3	70.7	66.3	59.8	50.1	40.2	28.3
Unbraked wagons	,,	134.6	127.0	110.9	86.0	74.3	61.6	52.5	39.2	16.1	9.1	4.3
Wagons owned by Freightliners Ltd	,,	2.0	2.0	2.1	2.1	2.1	2.1	2.1	2.1	2.1	2.1	2.1
Wagons owned by customers of British Rail	,,	18.0	18.4	18.6	18.4	18.5	18.4	18.7	18.8	17.2	16.4	15.9
Permanent way[9] and stations												
Route open for traffic: total	Kilometres	18 227	18 168	18 118	18 007	17 973	17 901	17 735	17 645	17 431	17 229	16 964
Electrified	,,	3 462	3 647	3 655	3 735	3 767	3 716	3 718	3 718	3 729	3 753	3 750
Non-electrified	,,	14 765	14 521	14 463	14 272	14 206	14 185	14 017	13 927	13 702	13 476	13 214
route open for passenger traffic	,,	14 375	14 373	14 431	14 407	14 413	14 396	14 412	14 394	14 394	14 371	14 375
Track open for traffic: total	,,	47 294	47 102	46 465	46 188	45 988	45 578	44 405	43 883	42 760	42 012	41 302
Running lines	,,	36 308	36 191	36 051	35 887	35 768	35 628	35 307	35 101	34 705	34 289	33 778
Sidings	,,	10 985	10 911	10 414	10 301	10 221	9 951	9 098	8 782	8 055	7 723	7 524
Stations: total[10]	Number	2 735	2 790	2 873	2 865	2 848	2 837	2 821	2 787	2 742	2 711	2 619
Passenger and freight	,,	178	93	–	–	–	–	–	–	–	–	–
Passenger	,,	2 177	2 262	2 358	2 361	2 358	2 364	2 365	2 366	2 361	2 369	2 363
Parcel	,,	16	17	18	17	15	15	14	12	3	3	3
Freight	,,	364	418	497	487	475	458	442	409	378	339	253

1. Excludes three narrow gauge steam locomotives.
2. Includes shunting locomotives (681 in 1983).
3. Diesel multiple unit power cars except for small number of non-passenger carrying power cars (five in 1983).
4. Electric multiple unit power cars except for small number of non-passenger carrying power cars (17 in 1983).
5. Excludes 16 narrow gauge passenger carriages.
6. Includes Diesel multiple unit power cars (1 636 in 1983, also included under Tractive units—Power cars—Diesel).

7. Includes Electric multiple unit power cars (2 663 in 1983, also included under Tractive units—Power cars—Electric).
8. Excludes one narrow gauge non-passeger carrying vehicle. Includes Advanced Passenger Train and High Speed Train power cars; also includes non-passenger carrying power cars (5 diesel, 17 electric in 1983 which are also shown under Tractive units, Power cars); also includes brake vans (902 in 1983).
9. Excluding narrow gauge route open to traffic (19 kilometres in 1983).
10. Combined passenger and freight stations have been reclassified as single purpose stations over the period.

Source Department of Transport

10.16 British Rail: passenger and freight receipts and traffic
Great Britain

	Unit	1973	1974	1975	1976	1977	1978	1979	1980	1981	1982[1]	1983
Traffic receipts: total[2]	£ million	581.5	621.5	774.2	924.6	1 066.9	1 219.7	1 383.1	1 564.5	1 664.8	1 513.4	1 793.6
Passenger: total[2, 3]	£ million	297.3	328.8	428.8	505.1	593.4	701.8	799.7	954.0	1 022.7	924.0	1 137.5
Full fares	,,	139.7	144.0	195.4	219.4	250.9	292.0	336.4	394.5	419.1	358.0	464.0
Reduced fares	,,	96.9	119.9	143.8	168.7	204.1	250.4	284.9	339.6	347.7	335.4	385.8
Season tickets	,,	60.7	65.0	89.7	117.0	138.4	159.4	178.4	219.9	255.9	230.6	287.6
Freight: total	,,	272.3	280.8	332.5	405.2	457.8	503.8	562.9	592.5	623.4	570.5	633.3
Coal and coke	,,	86.6	90.9	119.8	152.0	177.7	192.0	218.0	248.0	274.1	270.6	280.4
Iron and steel	,,	39.1	39.4	40.8	57.3	56.4	59.4	67.5	46.3	65.0	51.9	57.5
Other	,,	72.8	75.2	84.2	97.6	114.0	133.0	146.6	157.0	164.6	155.8	180.4
Merchandise by coaching train	,,	47.0	46.0	53.4	64.9	73.7	82.6	89.9	91.4	119.4	92.2	115.0
Postal parcels and letter mails by coaching train	,,	26.8	29.2	34.3	33.3	35.9	36.8	40.9	49.8			
Miscellaneous receipts[4]	,,	11.9	11.9	12.8	14.4	15.7	14.1	20.4	18.0	18.9	18.9	22.8
Traffic												
Passenger journeys: total[3]	Million	728.3	732.8	729.5	701.5	702.1	723.8	748.2	760.2	718.5	630.1	695.2
Full fares	,,	234.8	227.5	223.5	200.1	195.9	203.2	211.1	201.5	184.4	159.0	174.2
Reduced fares	,,	193.1	209.0	209.0	203.8	211.6	227.0	227.8	227.5	211.5	202.9	212.2
Season tickets[5]	,,	300.4	296.3	297.0	297.6	294.6	293.6	309.3	331.2	322.5	268.2	308.9
Passenger kilometres: (estimated) total[3]	,,	29 800	30 900	30 300	28 400	29 200	30 700	32 000	31 700	30 700	27 400	30 100
Full fares	,,	9 700	9 300	10 300	9 300	9 300	9 800	10 600	10 800	10 500	8 500	10 000
Reduced fares	,,	11 700	13 400	11 600	10 900	11 700	12 700	13 000	12 400	11 700	11 900	12 400
Season tickets[5]	,,	8 400	8 200	8 400	8 200	8 200	8 200	8 400	8 500	8 500	7 000	7 700
Freight traffic originating: total[6]	Million tonnes	197.9	177.4	176.3	177.9	172.1	171.8	170.5	154.7	155.1	142.6	146.0
Coal and coke	,,	101.0	88.0	97.2	97.0	93.8	94.0	93.5	94.1	95.2	88.4	87.9
Iron and steel	,,	35.5	31.0	25.7	29.5	26.0	24.7	25.1	12.9	18.2	14.3	16.0
Other	,,	59.5	56.6	51.7	50.0	50.9	51.8	50.7	46.5	40.8	39.2	41.2
Merchandise by coaching train	,,	1.1	1.0	1.0	0.9	0.9	0.9	0.8	0.8	0.9	0.7	0.9
Postal parcels and letter mails by coaching train	,,	0.8	0.8	0.7	0.5	0.5	0.4	0.4	0.4			
Tonne kilometres: (estimated) total[6, 7]	Millions	22 800	21 700	20 900	20 600	20 300	19 982	19 893	17 640	17 505	15 880	17 144
Coal and coke	,,	7 300	6 600	7 300	6 900	6 900	6 832	6 788	6 455	6 544	5 741	5 875
All other freight train traffic	,,	15 500	15 100	13 600	13 700	13 400	13 150	13 105	11 185	10 961	10 139	11 269

1. During 1982, traffics were affected by industrial action which took place on 34 days.
2. Grants received by British Rail in respect of certain subsidised passenger services are not included in passenger receipts.
3. The receipts and passenger kilometres include an appropriate proportion in respect of through bookings with the railways of London Transport and other administrations. Passenger journeys in respect of such through bookings are included. In 1983, 688 million journeys originated on British Rail only. From 1979 season ticket journeys include those in respect of West Midlands travel cards.
4. Miscellaneous receipts include charges for platform tickets, seat reservations, demurrage, provision of shunting services, etc.

5. For the period prior to 1975 all season ticket journeys and passenger kilometres were calculated on the basis of 540 journeys per annum. From 1975 these calculations are based on a rate of 480 journeys per year per annual season ticket and 540 journeys for shorter period tickets. Return tickets have been counted as two journeys.
6. Excluding free-hauled traffic on freight trains.
7. Excluding freight carried by coaching trains. In 1978 the method of estimating tonne-kilometres was changed to reflect the changing pattern in the operational working of freight trains. Pre-1978 figures have been re-estimated to bring them approximately onto the same basis as 1978 and subsequent years and rounded to the nearest 100 million.

Source Department of Transport

10.17 British Rail: operations
Great Britain

	Unit	1973	1974	1975	1976	1977	1978	1979	1980	1981	1982[1]	1983
Loaded train kilometres												
Coaching: total[2]	Millions	313.1	319.0	328.8	325.7	330.9	335.3	333.4	344.3	336.2	298.1	325.4
High speed trains	,,	–	–	–	0.8	6.1	9.7	16.4	21.0	23.3	26.2	32.3
Diesel: locomotives	,,	89.9	85.2	85.7	84.5	83.4	80.9	74.9	73.0	69.0	57.9	62.0
multiple units	,,	89.2	90.0	90.9	91.9	88.9	88.4	87.2	88.5	86.7	74.5	78.4
Electric: locomotives	,,	20.9	29.2	33.0	31.8	31.3	31.2	32.1	32.5	30.9	26.4	27.2
multiple units	,,	113.0	114.6	119.3	117.5	121.2	125.2	122.8	129.3	126.3	113.0	125.5
of which, Non-passenger[3]	,,	*20.5*	*20.3*	*20.3*	*20.7*	*20.2*	*19.7*	*18.1*	*17.5*	*13.7*	*11.6*	*14.5*
Freight: total[4]	,,	86.7	82.3	76.0	69.7	65.1	60.4	58.0	52.3	49.0	43.4	45.4
Diesel locomotives	,,	78.8	73.0	66.3	61.2	56.3	51.9	49.6	44.2	41.6	37.0	38.5
Electric locomotives	,,	8.0	9.4	9.7	8.6	8.5	8.5	8.4	8.1	7.3	6.4	6.9

1. During 1982, operations were affected by industrial action which took place on 34 days.
2. Train kilometres worked by British Rail trains over all lines including certain London Transport lines.
3. Non-passenger trains consist of vehicles for the conveyance of freight at coaching train rates.

4. Excludes free-hauled traffic on freight trains. From 1978, figures have been revised to reflect a change in the calculation of loaded train kilometres for 'Merry-Go-Round' coal traffic to power stations.

Source Department of Transport

10.18 London Transport railways: receipts, operations and assets

	Unit	1973	1974	1975	1976	1977	1978	1979	1980	1981	1982	1983
Receipts[1]												
Passenger: total	£ million	78.2	77.7	94.6	121.8	144.8	177.2	204.4	253.7	251.3	276.5	285.4
Ordinary	,,	50.4	50.4	60.3	71.5	84.4	104.5	123.1	145.8	137.5	161.5	158.0
Reduced rate	,,	4.3	4.3	5.6	9.3	12.2	16.4	19.6	25.5	28.8	31.2	27.4
Season tickets	,,	23.5	23.0	28.7	41.1	48.2	56.4	61.6	82.4	85.1	83.8	100.0
Traffic[1]												
Passenger journeys: total	Million	644	636	601	546	545	568	594	559	541	498	563
Ordinary	,,	398	396	361	307	318	340	353	318	296	289	273
Reduced rate	,,	25	26	27	34	37	45	51	52	63	49	77
Season tickets[2]	,,	221	213	213	205	191	184	190	189	182	159	212
Passenger kilometres (estimated)	,,	5 220	5 170	4 780	4 360	4 340	4 510	4 460	4 250	4 090	3 650	4 350
Operations[3]												
Loaded train kilometres	Million	47	43	47	48	48	47	46	47	49	46	46
Place kilometres[4]	,,	39 675	36 487	39 989	40 605	40 990	41 042	39 578	40 928	41 638	39 479	39 685
Rolling stock												
Railway cars	Number	4 379	4 318	4 409	4 519	4 323	4 223	4 228	4 353	4 267	4 069	3 885
Seating capacity	thousand	175.3	176.0	173.2	176.8	174.1	172.0	170.0	174.0	165.7	169.0	165.0
Permanent way and stations												
Route kilometres open for traffic	Kilometres	383	383	381	381	383	383	388	388	388	388	388
Stations	Number	249	249	248	248	249	249	248	248	247	247	247

1. The receipts and passenger kilometres include an appropriate proportion in respect of through bookings from British Rail. Passenger journeys in respect of such through bookings are included.
2. Season ticket journeys and passenger kilometres are calculated on the basis of 600 journeys per annum.
3. Train and place kilometres exclude kilometres run by London Transport trains over British Rail lines but include kilometres run by British Rail trains over London Transport lines.

4. Assuming full loads with standing passengers travelling in reasonable comfort; under crush load conditions the trains carry up to 50 per cent more passengers for short distances.

Source Department of Transport

10.19 Accidents on railways
Great Britain

Number

	1973	1974	1975	1976	1977	1978	1979	1980	1981	1982	1983[1]
Train accidents											
Number of accidents: total	1 274	1 334	1 310	1 122	1 056	1 044	1 035	930	1 014	998	1 255
Collisions	327	341	335	327	306	283	256	290	280	250	315
Derailments	252	238	221	192	182	176	183	138	148	173	220
Running into level-crossing gates and other obstructions	444	500	443	331	345	336	323	286	353	284	363
Fires	150	140	202	168	153	166	186	151	165	163	165
Miscellaneous	101	115	109	104	70	83	87	65	68	128	192
Persons killed	18	6	57	18	12	22	20	7	7	11	10
Passengers	14	1	47	–	–	13	8	–	4	–	2
Railway staff	3	4	7	8	3	3	8	4	1	8	1
Others	1	1	3	10	9	6	4	3	2	3	7
Persons injured	523	311	446	290	308	233	422	447	195	264	218
Passengers	430	238	364	210	230	176	354	387	127	150	88
Railway staff	66	57	65	64	50	48	60	45	34	92	93
Others	27	16	17	16	28	9	8	15	34	22	37
Other accidents through movement of railway vehicles											
Persons killed	64	64	58	65	61	76	74	52	58	40	53
Passengers	28	24	22	29	27	32	42	25	31	18	25
Railway staff	28	31	27	30	28	33	24	20	21	17	24
Others	8	9	9	6	6	11	8	7	6	5	4
Persons injured	2 339	2 521	2 365	2 277	2 184	2 352	2 221	2 265	2 450	1 946	2 459
Passengers	1 913	2 048	1 879	1 872	1 778	1 959	1 887	1 945	2 218	1 822	2 341
Railway staff	418	456	469	397	395	383	325	309	219	121	97
Others	8	17	17	8	11	10	9	11	13	3	21
Other accidents on railway premises											
Persons killed	15	8	12	14	11	16	13	10	11	6	6
Passengers	–	1	–	1	3	2	2	1	4	2	2
Railway staff	11	3	12	8	3	9	11	8	5	2	3
Others	4	4	–	5	5	5	–	1	2	2	1
Persons injured	9 628	8 292	7 966	7 754	7 472	8 942	8 878	8 138	7 379	6 490	6 590
Passengers	3 217	3 064	2 592	2 409	2 514	2 842	2 805	2 977	2 657	2 571	3 381
Railway staff	6 149	5 041	5 201	5 128	4 797	5 726	5 737	4 848	4 530	3 740	2 981
Others	262	187	173	217	161	374	336	313	192	179	228
Trespassers and suicides											
Persons killed	220	286	301	299	320	345	314	360	369	296	356
Persons injured	123	130	149	105	134	121	136	141	127	141	154

1. Provisional.

Source Department of Transport

203

10.20 Railways: permanent way and rolling stock
Northern Ireland
At end of year

Number

	1973	1974	1975	1976	1977	1978	1979	1980	1981	1982	1983
Length of road open for traffic[1] (Miles)	203	203	203	204	206	206	206	206	206	206	206
Length of track open for traffic (Miles)											
Total	355	355	355	355	357	357	357	357	357	357	357
Running lines	320	320	320	322	324	324	324	324	324	324	324
Sidings (as single track)	35	35	35	33	33	33	33	33	33	33	33
Locomotives											
Diesel-electric, petrol and oil	6	6	6	6	6	6	6	8	8	8	8
Passenger carrying vehicles											
Total	163	168	151	138	134	116	107	113	114	115	105
Rail motor vehicles:											
Steam, oil, diesel-electric, etc.	81	82	70	63	56	39	36	35	35	35	30
Trailer carriages:											
Total locomotive hauled	22	21	23	23	23	23	21	33	33	33	32
Ordinary coaches	21	20	22	22	22	22	20	32	32	32	30
Restaurant cars	1	1	1	1	1	1	1	1	1	1	2
Rail car trailers	60	65	58	52	55	54	50	45	46	47	43
Non-passenger carrying vehicles											
Post Office and luggage vans, etc.	25	27	29	29	29	27	27	27	27	27	20
Trucks and wagons owned											
Total	116	146	149	149	144	144	144	139	123	119	111
Merchandise wagons:											
Open	90	87	84	84	82	82	82	82	82	78	74
Covered	6	6	6	6	6	6	6	6	6	6	6
Rail and timber trucks	3	3	3	3	2	2	2	2	2	2	2
Brake vans	2	2	2	2	1	1	1	1	1	1	–
Special wagons	15	48	54	54	53	53	53	48	32	32	29
Containers	10	10	10	10	10	10	10	10	10	10	10
Rolling stock for maintenance and repair	158	155	153	..	149	151	151	162	170	158	115

1. The total length of railroad open for traffic irrespective of the number of tracks comprising the road.

Source   Department of the Environment for Northern Ireland

10.21 Operating statistics of railways
Northern Ireland

	Unit	1973	1974	1975	1976	1977	1978	1979	1980	1981	1982	1983
Maintenance of way and works												
Material used:												
Ballast	Thousand cu. yds.	55.0	26.3	36.0	35.4	33.0	38.0	32.0	37.2	33.7	25.9	19.7
Rails	Thousand tons	4.5	1.5	–	–	1.2	2.3	3.6	1.01	1.36	1.68	1.05
Sleepers	Thousands	68.0	24.5	4.8	–	20.6	28.5	69.0	13.3	16.5	21.1	13.68
Track renewed	Miles	26.0	25.5	7.0	1.3	10.0	13.5	30.0	5.6	7.75	10.0	6.0
Engine miles												
Total[1]	Thousand miles	3 556	3 219	2 755	2 969	2 631	2 195	2 257	2 318	2 307	2 289	2 224
Train miles:												
Total	,,	1 954	1 891	1 870	1 887	1 792	1 886	1 945	1 989	1 930	1 928	2 108
Coaching	,,	1 792	1 755	1 748	1 796	1 711	1 798	1 865	1 905	1 865	1 918	2 096
Freight	,,	162	136	122	91	81	88	80	84	65	10[2]	12

1. Including shunting, assisting, light, departmental, maintenance and repair.
2. The reduction in mileage from 1982 is a result of changes in C.I.E./N.I.R. freight contract.

Source   Department of the Environment for Northern Ireland

10.22 Main output[1] of UK airlines

	1973	1974	1975	1976	1977	1978	1979	1980	1981	1982	1983
All services: total	9 003	8 283	8 924	9 727	10 505	11 970	12 751	13 212	13 087	11 848	12 011
Percentage growth on previous year	*9.1*	*−8.0*	*7.7*	*9.0*	*8.0*	*13.9*	*6.5*	*3.6*	*−0.9*	*−9.5*	*1.4*
Scheduled services: total	5 953	5 745	5 981	6 602	6 834	8 095	8 841	9 829	9 936	9 068	8 989
Percentage growth on previous year	*10.3*	*−3.5*	*4.1*	*10.3*	*3.5*	*18.5*	*9.2*	*11.2*	*1.1*	*−8.7*	*−0.9*
Non-scheduled services: total	3 051	2 538	2 943	3 125	3 671	3 875	3 910	3 383	3 151	2 780	3 022
Percentage growth on previous year	*7.0*	*−16.8*	*16.0*	*6.2*	*17.5*	*5.6*	*0.9*	*−13.5*	*−6.9*	*−11.8*	*8.7*

Mean rates of growth

Percentage

	1946 to 50	1951 to 55	1956 to 60	1961 to 65	1966 to 70	1971 to 75	1976 to 80	Last 20 years	Last 10 years	Last 5 years
All services	..	..	..	13.8	10.8	5.1	8.4	8.5	4.7	−2.3
Scheduled services	27.1	11.9	16.2	13.9	8.5	6.1	11.1	8.1	6.4	−0.5
Non-scheduled services	..	..	..	13.5	17.5	3.1	2.3	9.9	0.6	−6.9

1. Available million tonne-kilometres.

Source Civil Aviation Authority

10.23 Air traffic between the United Kingdom and abroad[1]
Aircraft flights and passengers carried

Thousands

	1973	1974	1975	1976	1977	1978	1979[2]	1980	1981	1982	1983
Flights											
Total	421.3	402.8	403.7	401.3	436.7	459.3	479.6	506.9	495.8	511.4	518.5
Aircraft registered in the United Kingdom:											
Scheduled services	252.8	135.6	136.0	118.3	144.3	165.9	172.9	166.1	149.7	143.5	141.9
Non-scheduled services		148.6	111.2	113.4	121.6	115.1	121.8	153.9	162.2	176.3	184.9
Aircraft registered abroad[3]											
Scheduled services	168.5	100.7	146.0	145.7	145.6	150.7	155.8	157.8	152.0	154.3	155.2
Non-scheduled services		17.9	10.7	23.9	25.0	27.7	29.2	29.1	31.9	37.3	36.5
Passengers carried											
Total	31 065.8	28 350.6	30 278.1	32 881.4	34 648.2	38 912.1	41 603.8	42 644.6	43 732.0	44 131.9	46 284.9
Aircraft registered in the United Kingdom:											
Scheduled services	19 160.2	8 894.3	9 339.2	9 841.5	10 435.1	12 620.6	13 634.6	13 901.0	13 559.0	12 214.7	12 140.0
Non-scheduled services		7 761.9	8 500.2	8 902.2	8 776.5	9 340.1	9 997.9	11 195.3	12 128.9	13 216.6	14 661.9
Aircraft registered abroad:											
Scheduled services	11 905.6	10 125.0	10 791.5	11 961.7	13 042.0	14 284.3	15 113.0	14 900.9	15 398.8	15 520.5	16 065.6
Non-scheduled services		1 569.5	1 647.1	2 176.0	2 394.6	2 667.1	2 858.3	2 647.4	2 645.4	3 180.1	3 417.4

1. Excluding Transport command operations and travel to and from the Channel Islands.
2. 1979 figures do not include Sumburgh.
3. Including aircraft registered in the Irish Republic operating the services between the United Kingdom and Ireland, and aircraft of Commonwealth companies operating in pool with British Airways.

Source Civil Aviation Authority

10.24 UK airways[1]
Operations and traffic on scheduled services: revenue traffic

	Unit	1974	1975	1976	1977	1978	1979	1980	1981	1982	1983
All services											
Aircraft stage flights											
Number	Number	380 176	350 943	364 772	363 182	411 314	441 653	440 651	410 115	414 167	431 615
Average length	Kilometres	816	816	825	826	843	845	872	878	801	752
Aircraft-kilometres											
flown	Thousands	310 270	286 404	301 032	300 306	346 649	373 357	384 373	359 911	331 729	324 581
Passengers uplifted	,,	16 396	16 322	17 470	17 147	20 336	22 311	22 164	21 374	20 609	20 389
Seat-kilometres used	Millions	25 396.9	27 543.9	31 078.1	31 871.1	40 441.6	47 084.8	50 163.8	52 209.6	46 404.3	43 887.4
Cargo and Mail											
uplifted: total	Tonnes	305 864	245 750	247 686	256 658	278 016	294 380	294 692	294 866	263 798	294 247
Tonne-kilometres											
used: total	Thousands	3 165 491	3 315 034	3 725 661	3 928 058	4 871 960	5 549 854	5 894 807	6 188 432	5 593 180	5 521 755
Passenger	,,	2 261 012	2 458 161	2 805 967	2 907 959	3 710 290	4 300 894	4 503 200	4 674 458	4 223 655	4 003 952
Cargo	,,	785 950	724 790	774 931	861 107	988 516	1 070 303	1 214 801	1 343 499	1 200 417	1 338 085
Mail	,,	118 529	132 083	144 763	158 992	173 154	178 657	176 806	170 465	169 107	179 719
Domestic services											
Aircraft stage flights:											
Number	Number	156 027	145 113	155 884	151 900	176 628	199 101	201 227	188 534	201 887	221 560
Average length	Kilometres	300	296	299	286	283	279	287	282	279	274
Aircraft-kilometres											
flown	Thousands	46 810	42 973	46 654	43 549	49 954	55 483	57 666	53 110	56 229	60 680
Passengers uplifted	,,	6 062	5 755	6 147	5 484	6 429	7 240	7 199	6 613	7 068	7 169
Seat-kilometres used	Millions	2 256.1	2 151.0	2 326.5	2 081.1	2 444.6	2 763.9	2 770.3	2 600.7	2 752.7	2 791.4
Cargo and Mail											
uplifted: total	Tonnes	68 279	46 744	46 078	41 413	44 608	39 339	31 005	35 212	37 993	39 739
Tonne-kilometres											
used: total	Thousands	213 674	198 341	212 218	189 751	220 783	248 657	242 627	229 743	237 313	240 667
Passenger	,,	188 566	181 327	195 876	175 928	206 459	235 198	231 748	218 142	224 713	227 047
Cargo	,,	22 069	14 199	13 671	11 214	11 415	10 218	7 122	7 306	7 454	7 724
Mail	,,	3 039	2 814	2 671	2 610	2 909	3 241	3 757	4 292	5 145	5 896
International services											
Aircraft stage flights:											
Number	Number	224 149	205 830	208 888	211 282	234 686	242 552	239 424	221 581	212 280	210 055
Average length	Kilometres	1 175	1 183	1 218	1 215	1 264	1 310	1 365	1 385	1 298	1 256
Aircraft-kilometres											
flown	Thousands	263 460	243 432	254 379	256 757	296 695	317 873	326 708	306 802	275 500	263 901
Passengers uplifted	,,	10 333	10 567	11 323	11 663	13 907	15 072	14 964	14 761	13 541	13 220
Seat-kilometres used	Millions	23 140.8	25 392.9	28 751.6	29 790.0	37 997.0	44 320.9	47 393.5	49 608.9	43 651.6	41 096.1
Cargo and Mail											
uplifted: total	Tonnes	237 585	199 006	201 608	215 246	233 407	255 039	263 687	259 654	225 806	254 507
Tonne-kilometres											
used: total	Thousands	2 951 817	3 116 696	3 513 441	3 738 310	4 651 176	5 301 198	5 652 180	5 958 689	5 355 869	5 281 088
Passenger	,,	2 072 446	2 276 835	2 610 090	2 732 030	3 503 831	4 065 697	4 271 452	4 456 317	3 998 944	3 776 905
Cargo	,,	763 881	710 591	761 259	849 892	977 101	1 060 085	1 207 679	1 336 192	1 192 962	1 330 361
Mail	,,	115 490	129 270	142 092	156 388	170 244	175 416	173 049	166 172	163 961	173 823

1. Includes services of British Airways Board and private companies (including
operations performed by Cathay Pacific Airways on their Scheduled Service
London—Hong Kong from May, 1981).

Source Civil Aviation Authority

10.25 Non-scheduled services by UK air lines[1]

	Unit	1973	1974	1975	1976	1977	1978	1979	1980	1981	1982	1983
All non-scheduled services[2] Total	Tonne km available (millions)	3 051.2	2 538.3	2 943.0	3 125.3	3 670.9	3 875.2	3 909.8	3 383.4	3 151.3	2 780.0	3 022.2
Percentage of all UK services		*33.9*	*30.7*	*33.0*	*32.1*	*34.9*	*32.4*	*30.7*	*25.6*	*24.1*	*23.5*	*25.2*
Inclusive tours[3] Total	Tonne km available (millions)	1 338.0	1 029.2	1 030.9	1 145.6	1 119.9	1 234.7	1 546.4	1 813.2	1 950.1	2 180.1	2 371.8
Percentage of all UK services		*14.9*	*12.4*	*11.6*	*11.8*	*10.7*	*10.3*	*12.1*	*13.7*	*14.9*	*18.4*	*19.7*
Other separate fare and advance booking charters[3] Total	Tonne km available (millions)	628.6	532.0	577.5	631.4	793.2	616.1	352.3	344.9	335.9	184.5	240.4
Percentage of all UK services		*7.0*	*6.4*	*6.5*	*6.5*	*7.5*	*5.1*	*2.8*	*2.6*	*2.6*	*1.6*	*2.0*
Other charters Total	Tonne km available (millions)	1 084.6	977.1	1 334.6	1 348.3	1 757.9	2 024.4	2 011.1	1 225.3	864.8	415.4	410.0
Percentage of all UK services		*12.0*	*11.8*	*15.0*	*13.9*	*16.7*	*16.9*	*15.8*	*9.3*	*6.6*	*3.5*	*3.4*
Load factors and distances												
Inclusive tours[3] Seat-kilometres available (A)	Millions	15 573	11 820	11 773	13 050	12 819	14 229	17 635	20 344.8	21 709.9	24 560.8	26 479.9
Seat-kilometres used (B)	,,	12 493	9 399	10 132	10 732	10 796	12 571	14 921	17 117.0	18 515.8	20 775.4	22 731.0
(B) as a percentage of (A)		*80.2*	*79.5*	*86.1*	*82.2*	*84.2*	*88.3*	*84.6*	*84.1*	*85.3*	*84.6*	*85.8*
Passengers uplifted	Millions	8.405	6.233	6.700	6.783	6.825	7.673	8.750	9.663	10.156	11.902	13.038
Stage flights	Number	83 081	61 515	61 902	64 942	64 678	68 608	80 441	86 298	87 689	104 700	108 173
Aircraft-kilometres flown	Millions	119.3	89.2	91.0	99.1	97.4	107.8	130.8	147.1	154.3	178.5	181.9
Average distance per stage flight	Kilometres	1 436	1 451	1 470	1 527	1 507	1 571	1 626	1 705	1 760	1 705	1 682
Average distance per passenger	Kilometres	1 486	1 508	1 512	1 582	1 582	1 638	1 705	1 771	1 823	1 746	1 743
Other separate fare and advance booking charters[3] Seat-kilometres available (C)	Millions	6 082	5 241	5 672	6 467	8 190	6 312	3 732	3 729	3 715	2 104	2 526
Seat-kilometres used (D)	,,	4 899	4 238	4 458	5 199	6 786	5 068	2 872	2 943	3 071	1 759	2 189
(D) as a percentage of (C)		*80.6*	*80.9*	*78.6*	*80.7*	*82.9*	*80.3*	*77.0*	*78.9*	*82.7*	*83.6*	*86.6*
Passengers uplifted	Millions	1.231	1.259	1.349	1.467	1.731	1.535	1.069	1.161	1.457	0.685	0.677
Stage flights	Number	19 807	18 285	18 895	19 552	17 616	15 143	10 933	12 655	13 058	6 353	5 914
Aircraft-kilometres flown	Millions	33.9	29.7	31.3	34.6	41.6	33.2	20.8	21.8	22.8	12.1	13.9
Average distance per stage flight	Kilometres	1 713	1 624	1 657	1 772	2 358	2 193	1 903	1 724	1 746	1 905	2 344
Average distance per passenger	Kilometres	3 981	3 366	3 305	3 545	3 920	3 303	2 687	2 534	2 108	2 568	3 232

1. Includes services of the British Airways Board and private companies.
2. Excludes Air Taxi operations.
3. From 1974 Inclusive Tours performed under Class 4 licences are included with
   Other separate fare and advance booking charters.

Source Civil Aviation Authority

10.26 UK private companies[1]
Operations and traffic on scheduled services: revenue traffic

	Unit	1974	1975	1976	1977	1978	1979	1980	1981	1982	1983
All services											
Aircraft stage flights:											
Number	Number	133 967	129 852	145 731	159 903	187 373	210 415	226 301	218 965	231 447	258 046
Average length	Kilometres	410	343	357	368	419	415	479	552	456	435
Aircraft-kilometres flown	Thousands	54 927	44 552	51 833	58 856	78 519	87 209	108 419	119 846	105 585	112 278
Passengers uplifted	,,	3 152	2 972	3 271	3 757	4 331	5 044	6 002	6 024	5 619	6 160
Seat-kilometres used	Millions	2 467.6	1 928.7	2 100.2	3 005.7	5 081.2	6 125.2	10 163.1	13 321.3	8 975.7	9 448.4
Cargo and Mail uplifted	Tonnes	63 908	54 747	54 815	49 964	58 260	60 922	68 806	94 118	88 544	96 962
Tonne-kilometres used: total	Thousands	293 703	227 711	244 918	340 117	561 012	680 858	1 109 795	1 585 338	1 233 909	1 319 358
Passenger	,,	216 528	170 870	185 630	270 138	445 869	531 669	866 112	1 153 572	822 643	861 140
Cargo	,,	72 130	50 544	53 088	62 617	106 947	139 657	233 497	415 997	390 312	432 895
Mail	,,	5 045	6 295	6 201	7 363	8 196	9 530	10 186	15 768	20 953	25 323
Domestic services											
Aircraft stage flights:											
Number	Number	65 543	62 405	72 338	78 680	94 519	117 742	132 955	130 330	142 613	165 850
Average length	Kilometres	267	251	252	238	221	219	239	237	236	240
Aircraft-kilometres flown	Thousands	17 528	15 687	18 203	18 688	20 935	25 751	31 839	30 934	33 695	39 742
Passengers uplifted	,,	1 668	1 513	1 658	1 794	1 949	2 500	3 115	2 867	3 126	3 586
Seat-kilometres used	Millions	584.5	506.5	550.9	615.0	616.0	784.7	1 009.1	951.6	1 019.6	1 244.9
Cargo and Mail uplifted	Tonnes	22 045	22 102	24 766	22 404	25 008	21 696	18 989	23 820	27 363	27 574
Tonne-kilometres used: total	Thousands	55 530	49 604	53 589	57 659	57 889	71 498	88 021	84 444	90 962	108 713
Passenger	,,	48 138	42 385	45 873	51 303	51 561	65 465	81 948	77 541	82 695	100 137
Cargo	,,	6 348	5 445	6 033	4 589	4 376	3 811	3 695	4 596	5 129	5 205
Mail	,,	1 044	1 773	1 681	1 766	1 951	2 221	2 378	2 306	3 137	3 370
International services											
Aircraft stage flights:											
Number	Number	68 424	67 447	73 393	81 223	92 854	92 673	93 346	88 635	88 834	92 196
Average length	Kilometres	547	428	458	494	620	663	820	1 003	809	787
Aircraft-kilometres flown	Thousands	37 401	28 865	33 631	40 166	57 584	61 457	76 581	88 914	71 889	72 536
Passengers uplifted	,,	1 484	1 459	1 613	1 962	2 382	2 544	2 887	3 156	2 494	2 574
Seat-kilometres used	Millions	1 883.1	1 422.2	1 549.3	2 390.7	4 465.2	5 340.4	9 154 .1	12 369.8	7 956.2	8 203.4
Cargo and Mail uplifted	Tonnes	41 865	32 645	30 050	27 561	33 252	39 224	49 817	70 298	61 180	69 387
Tonne-kilometres used: total	Thousands	238 168	178 108	191 329	282 458	503 123	609 360	1 021 774	1 500 894	1 142 949	1 210 645
Passenger	,,	168 390	128 487	139 756	218 834	394 308	466 205	784 164	1 076 033	739 949	761 003
Cargo	,,	65 777	45 100	47 053	58 026	102 571	135 846	229 802	411 400	385 183	427 690
Mail	,,	4 000	4 522	4 520	5 597	6 244	7 309	7 808	13 460	17 816	21 953

1. These operations are included in Table 10.24.

Source Civil Aviation Authority

10.27 United Kingdom airlines[1]
Accidents on scheduled fixed wing passenger-carrying services[2]

	Number of fatal accidents	Passenger casualties		Crew casualties		Thousand aircraft stage flights per fatal accident	Million aircraft-Kms. flown per fatal accident	Thousand passengers carried per passenger killed	Million passenger Kms. flown per passenger killed	Fatal accidents		Passengers killed per hundred million passenger-Kms.
		Killed	Seriously injured	Killed	Seriously injured					per 100,000 aircraft stage flights	per hundred million aircraft-Kms.	
1950–54	7	194	9	28	4	107.4	61.8	46.1	50.0	0.93	1.62	1.99
1955–59	7	123	28	29	8	158.3	92.1	155.2	158.5	0.63	1.09	0.63
1960–64	5	104	35	21	6	303.7	182.3	373.4	390.6	0.33	0.55	0.25
1965–69	6	273	2	32	2	282.7	194.9	222.2	255.2	0.35	0.52	0.39
1970–74	2	167	5	14	2	897.4	737.6	466.3	657.7	0.11	0.14	0.15
1975–79	1	54	6	9	–	1 797.2	1 481.6	1 697.0	3 240.0	0.06	0.07	0.03
1978	–	–	1	–	–							
1979	–	–	1	–	–							
1980	–	–	–	–	–	–	–	–	–	–	–	–
1981	–	–	–	–	–							
1982	–	–	–	–	–							
1983	–	–	4	–	–							

1. Including services of UK Airways Corporations (reconstituted as the British Airways Board in 1973) and private companies.
2. Excluding accidents involving the deaths of third parties only.

Source Civil Aviation Authority

10.28 Activity at civil aerodromes

	1973	1974	1975	1976	1977	1978	1979	1980	1981	1982	1983
Movement of civil aircraft (thousands)	1 892	1 849	1 911	1 896	1 912	1 981	2 170	2 181	2 103	2 113	2 238
Commercial: total	803	792	781	821	846	905	987	1 046	1 028	1 072	1 243
Transport	719	710	701	740	759	827	903	954	927	974	1 019
Other[1]	85	82	80	81	87	78	84	92	101	98	224
Non-commercial[2]	1 089	1 057	1 130	1 075	1 066	1 076	1 183	1 135	1 075	1 041	995
Passengers handled (thousands): total	44 389	41 220	43 006	45 864	47 078	53 369	57 848	58 942	58 979	60 033	62 301
Terminal	43 125	40 082	41 846	44 666	45 927	52 160	56 615	57 823	57 771	58 778	61 099
Transit	1 265	1 137	1 160	1 198	1 151	1 208	1 233	1 119	1 208	1 255	1 202
Commercial freight handled[3] (tonnes): total	699 402	720 704	637 701	659 357	704 849	746 103	795 315	744 244	723 709	692 693	725 897
Set down	330 036	323 947	277 401	276 515	286 921	325 531	364 662	352 133	341 932	320 604	332 162
Picked up	369 366	396 757	360 300	382 842	417 928	420 572	430 653	392 111	381 777	372 088	393 737
Mail handled (tonnes): total	57 875	57 708	59 423	62 536	66 812	71 109	86 097	98 336	106 497	118 406	124 080
Set down	25 096	24 316	24 870	25 974	27 412	29 404	36 675	44 978	50 063	55 200	56 943
Picked up	32 779	33 391	34 554	36 562	39 400	41 705	49 422	53 358	56 434	63 206	67 138

1. Local pleasure flights and non-transport charter flights for reward (for example: aerial survey work, crop dusting and delivery of empty aircraft).
2. Test and training flights, scheduled service positioning flights, private, aero-club and official flights, etc.
3. Figures include weight of vehicles carried on vehicle ferry services.

Source Civil Aviation Authority

10.29 United Kingdom merchant vessels of 500 gross tons and over[1]
Summary of tonnage by type
End of year

	1973	1974	1975	1976	1977	1978	1979	1980	1981	1982	1983
Number											
All vessels	1 776	1 767	1 682	1 573	1 545	1 421	1 305	1 275	1 118	985	866
Passenger[2]	122	119	116	104	107	102	101	102	94	87	89
Cargo liners	570	556	514	487	453	404	346	304	248	212	186
Tramps	326	324	307	293	301	283	262	252	226	191	178
Bulk carriers[3]	269	267	267	266	271	234	203	190	174	146	109
Tankers	489	501	478	423	413	398	393	427	376	349	304
Thousand gross tons											
All vessels	29 106	30 795	31 489	29 839	30 061	28 078	25 232	25 769	22 117	19 233	15 894
Passenger[2]	920	855	748	661	654	614	606	617	604	582	602
Cargo liners	5 095	5 021	4 692	4 497	4 547	4 374	3 899	3 592	3 189	2 920	2 642
Tramps	1 060	1 027	958	910	882	743	613	554	470	409	372
Bulk carriers[3]	7 366	7 694	8 022	8 030	8 181	7 174	6 555	6 428	5 985	5 101	3 911
Tankers	14 665	16 199	17 069	15 742	15 797	15 173	13 558	14 578	11 870	10 221	8 367
Thousand deadweight tons											
All vessels	46 778	50 155	51 916	49 313	49 706	46 327	41 221	42 308	35 625	30 399	24 467
Passenger[2]	349	299	254	205	207	186	174	179	171	164	165
Cargo liners	6 084	5 982	5 557	5 325	5 309	5 133	4 561	4 122	3 535	3 189	2 850
Tramps	1 556	1 528	1 435	1 371	1 340	1 143	951	858	737	636	579
Bulk carriers[3]	12 483	13 133	13 761	13 767	14 025	12 323	11 299	11 128	10 322	8 804	6 743
Tankers	26 307	29 213	30 909	28 645	28 827	27 542	24 236	26 021	20 861	17 607	14 131

1. Steam and motor vessels only, excluding miscellaneous craft.
2. All vessels with passenger certificates.
3. Bulk carriers of 10 000 deadweight tons and over or approximately 6 000
   gross tons and over including combination—ore/oil and ore/bulk/oil—carriers.

Source   Department of Transport

10.30 United Kingdom merchant vessels of 500 gross tons and over[1]
Analysis by age and type
End of year

	1973 Total	Passenger[2]	Cargo liners	Tramps	Bulk carriers[3]	Tankers	1983 Total	Passenger[2]	Cargo liners	Tramps	Bulk carriers[3]	Tankers
Number												
All vessels	1 776	122	570	326	269	489	866	89	186	178	109	304
Under 5 years	598	25	168	77	156	172	178	10	46	40	27	55
5 and under 10 years	358	19	101	66	62	110	244	22	47	48	41	86
10 and under 15 years	402	18	138	75	39	132	260	25	76	35	35	89
15 and under 20 years	257	22	89	73	9	64	113	19	11	30	2	51
20 and under 25 years	99	15	49	30	–	5	48	7	5	18	3	15
25 years and over	62	23	25	5	3	6	23	6	1	7	1	8
Thousand gross tons												
All vessels	29 106	920	5 095	1 060	7 366	14 665	15 894	602	2 642	372	3 911	8 367
Under 5 years	15 660	133	2 049	230	5 095	8 153	2 629	75	541	93	879	1 042
5 and under 10 years	5 730	133	769	263	1 533	3 031	6 904	100	655	90	1 522	4 538
10 and under 15 years	4 728	209	1 058	323	576	2 562	4 609	141	1 334	59	1 330	1 745
15 and under 20 years	1 957	198	618	173	137	832	1 215	158	70	90	114	784
20 and under 25 years	623	146	404	56	–	17	418	102	35	29	59	194
25 years and over	409	101	196	16	25	70	119	26	8	12	8	65
Thousand deadweight ton												
All vessels	46 778	349	6 084	1 556	12 483	26 307	24 467	165	2 850	579	6 743	14 131
Under 5 years	26 744	29	2 221	361	8 804	15 329	3 854	18	663	131	1 474	1 570
5 and under 10 years	9 363	36	949	396	2 588	5 393	11 530	40	716	158	2 651	7 966
10 and under 15 years	6 863	65	1 355	465	850	4 128	6 621	31	1 340	98	2 315	2 837
15 and under 20 years	2 671	99	811	238	209	1 315	1 804	38	77	136	213	1 340
20 and under 25 years	651	50	503	74	–	25	510	29	43	41	80	317
25 years and over	487	71	245	22	32	117	148	10	10	15	11	101

1. Steam and motor vessels only excluding miscellaneous craft.
2. All vessels with passenger certificates.
3. Bulk carriers of 10 000 deadweight tons and over or approximately 6 000 gross
   tons and over including combination—ore/oil and ore/bulk/oil—carriers.

Source   Department of Transport

10.31 United Kingdom merchant vessels of 500 gross tons and over[1]
End of year
Analysis by deadweight tonnage, size and type

	1973			1978			1983		
	Number	Thousand deadweight tons	Thousand gross tons	Number	Thousand deadweight tons	Thousand gross tons	Number	Thousand deadweight tons	Thousand gross tons
All vessels									
Total	1 776	46 778	29 106	1 421	46 327	28 078	866	24 467	15 894
Under 10 000 deadweight tons	756	2 673	2 445	649	2 130	1 893	444	1 230	1 239
10 000 and under 20 000 deadweight tons	501	7 099	5 411	281	4 033	3 096	116	1 739	1 441
20 000 and under 50 000 deadweight tons	324	9 465	6 586	293	8 402	6 233	190	5 773	4 586
50 000 and under 100 000 deadweight tons	78	5 195	3 012	66	4 213	2 490	50	3 295	2 036
100 000 and under 250 000 deadweight tons	97	16 808	8 868	84	13 641	7 267	45	6 229	3 419
250 000 deadweight tons and over	20	5 538	2 784	48	13 908	7 099	21	6 202	3 174
Passenger[2]									
Total	122	349	920	102	186	614	89	165	602
Under 10 000 deadweight tons	111	205	596	100	157	505	87	136	494
10 000 deadweight tons and over	11	144	324	2	29	109	2	29	108
Cargo liners									
Total	570	6 084	5 095	404	5 133	4 374	186	2 850	2 642
Under 10 000 deadweight tons	251	1 427	1 129	159	879	674	66	297	235
10 000 and under 20 000 deadweight tons	286	3 616	2 843	197	2 701	2 096	76	1 123	912
20 000 deadweight tons and over	33	1 041	1 123	48	1 553	1 604	44	1 430	1 495
Tramps									
Total	326	1 556	1 060	283	1 143	743	178	579	372
Under 10 000 deadweight tons	271	778	541	257	776	501	172	500	318
10 000 deadweight tons and over	55	778	520	26	367	242	6	79	54
Bulk carriers[3]									
Total	269	12 483	7 366	234	12 323	7 174	109	6 743	3 911
10 000 and under 20 000 deadweight tons	51	821	566	20	303	210	13	189	136
20 000 and under 50 000 deadweight tons	153	4 290	2 696	133	3 722	2 340	50	1 521	958
50 000 and under 100 000 deadweight tons	25	1 615	934	38	2 411	1 394	18	1 154	675
100 000 and under 250 000 deadweight tons	38	5 231	2 882	42	5 626	3 086	28	3 879	2 142
250 000 deadweight tons and over	2	525	288	1	260	144	–	–	–
Tankers									
Total	489	26 307	14 665	398	27 542	15 173	304	14 131	8 367
Under 10 000 deadweight tons	123	263	180	133	317	213	119	297	192
10 000 and under 20 000 deadweight tons	98	1 741	1 159	36	634	439	19	319	231
20 000 and under 50 000 deadweight tons	138	4 134	2 767	113	3 178	2 320	96	2 821	2 133
50 000 and under 100 000 deadweight tons	53	3 579	2 079	27	1 750	1 066	32	2 141	1 361
100 000 and under 250 000 deadweight tons	59	11 577	5 985	42	8 015	4 181	17	2 350	1 277
250 000 deadweight tons and over	18	5 013	2 496	47	13 648	6 955	21	6 202	3 174

1. Steam and motor vessels only, excluding miscellaneous craft.
2. All vessels with passenger certificates.
3. Bulk carriers of 10 000 deadweight tons and over or approximately 6 000 gross tons and over including combination—ore/oil and ore/bulk/oil—carriers.

Source Department of Transport

10.32 International seaborne trade of the United Kingdom
Total and proportion carried by UK registered vessels

	Total seaborne trade							Percentage carried by UK registered vessels						
	1977	1978	1979	1980	1981	1982	1983	1977	1978	1979	1980	1981	1982	1983
Exports by sea[1]														
Weight (million tonnes)														
All cargo	70.5	80.9	95.6	100.3	122.0	121.6	129.7	40	37	33	37	28	27	24
Dry cargo	40.3	43.7	42.8	46.1	55.8	47.2	45.9	44	43	44	43	30	32	29
Tanker cargo	30.2	37.1	52.8	54.2	66.2	74.4	83.8	35	29	24	32	26	24	20
Tonne-miles (Thousand million)														
All cargo	135.6	146.6	138.3	138.4	191.4	195.6	195.8	35	29	27	27	20	18	17
Dry cargo	99.6	101.9	84.0	79.4	97.3	87.6	88.7	36	34	33	31	23	25	22
Tanker cargo	36.0	44.7	54.3	59.0	94.1	108.0	107.1	29	18	20	23	18	12	12
Value (£ hundred million)														
All cargo	249.5	278.4	317.2	371.0	408.2	443.1	477.2	46	45	43	42	36	34	33
Dry cargo	229.8	256.3	275.8	309.8	317.2	335.5	349.9	47	46	45	44	39	37	37
Tanker cargo	19.7	22.1	41.4	61.2	91.0	107.6	127.3	37	31	27	33	27	24	21
Imports by sea														
Weight (million tonnes)														
All cargo	158.6	154.3	155.7	131.5	120.6	120.7	117.2	33	29	27	31	29	29	25
Dry cargo	76.4	75.5	84.3	73.2	74.0	75.2	78.6	34	30	28	32	31	33	29
Tanker cargo	82.2	78.8	71.4	58.3	46.6	45.5	38.6	32	29	25	30	25	23	18
Tonne-miles (thousand million)														
All cargo	720.1	721.8	711.5	617.6	489.2	415.6	354.9	32	29	24	28	25	30	25
Dry cargo	224.1	232.9	256.3	221.2	206.1	208.1	219.4	34	30	29	33	29	32	29
Tanker cargo	495.9	488.9	455.2	396.4	283.1	207.5	135.5	31	28	22	25	22	28	19
Value (£ hundred million)														
All cargo	293.3	316.0	378.2	380.5	403.6	455.8	516.5	42	41	39	39	36	35	36
Dry cargo	242.5	270.0	325.7	319.3	341.8	392.4	460.2	44	43	41	41	38	37	38
Tanker cargo	50.8	46.0	52.5	61.2	61.8	63.4	56.3	32	29	26	30	25	24	19
Exports[1] *plus* **Imports by sea**														
Weight (million tonnes)														
All cargo	229.1	235.2	251.3	231.8	242.6	242.3	246.9	35	32	29	34	28	28	24
Dry cargo	116.7	119.2	127.1	119.3	129.8	122.5	124.5	37	35	33	36	31	32	29
Tanker cargo	112.4	115.9	124.2	112.5	112.8	119.8	122.4	33	29	25	31	26	24	20
Tonne-miles (thousand million)														
All cargo	855.7	868.4	849.8	756.0	680.6	611.2	550.7	32	29	25	28	23	26	22
Dry cargo	323.7	334.8	340.3	300.6	303.4	295.7	308.1	35	31	30	32	27	30	27
Tanker cargo	531.9	533.6	509.5	455.4	377.2	315.5	242.6	31	28	22	25	21	23	16
Value (£ hundred million)														
All cargo	542.8	594.4	695.4	751.5	811.8	898.9	993.7	44	43	41	40	36	35	35
Dry cargo	472.3	526.3	601.5	629.1	659.0	727.9	810.1	45	45	43	42	39	37	38
Tanker cargo	70.5	68.1	93.9	122.4	152.8	171.0	183.6	33	30	27	32	26	24	20

1. Including re-exports.

Sources Department of Transport; HM Customs and Excise

10.33 International seaborne trade of the United Kingdom
Weight of cargo: analysis by area of consignment and proportion carried by UK registered vessels

	1982						1983					
	All cargo		Dry cargo		Tanker cargo		All cargo		Dry cargo		Tanker cargo	
	Total	UK flag	Total	UK flag	Total	UK flag	Total	UK flag	Total	UK flag	Total	UK flag
	Th. tonnes	Per cent	Th. tonnes	Per cent	Th. tonnes	Per cent	Th. tonnes	Per cent	Th. tonnes	Per cent	Th. tonnes	Per cent
Exports[1]												
Total—all trades	121 582	27	47 235	32	74 347	24	129 711	24	45 911	29	83 800	20
Near and short sea trades	87 974	33	37 268	34	50 706	32	99 197	27	36 174	32	63 023	25
of which:												
European Community[2]	66 476	36	24 932	45	41 544	32	74 140	31	22 379	43	51 761	25
Scandinavia and Baltic[3]	13 617	27	5 943	10	7 674	39	15 025	21	6 021	13	9 004	27
Iberia and Mediterranean	7 881	15	6 393	17	1 488	6	10 032	12	7 774	15	2 258	4
Deep sea trades	33 608	12	9 967	24	23 641	6	30 514	11	9 737	21	20 777	6
of which:												
Central and West Africa	1 511	27	1 350	26	162	30	1 177	30	1 107	29	70	39
South and East Africa	924	18	901	18	23	12	790	7	769	7	21	1
Persian Gulf and Indian Ocean	3 013	19	2 916	19	94	15	3 111	16	2 912	16	199	19
Far East	1 381	24	1 320	24	61	7	2 057	27	1 815	22	242	64
Australasia	609	56	601	56	8	40	502	47	495	47	7	61
North America	24 694	7	1 740	26	22 954	6	21 742	6	2 006	23	19 736	4
Central and South America	504	21	471	21	33	13	396	22	364	15	32	98
West Indies	972	16	666	20	306	7	739	49	269	25	470	63
Imports												
Total—all trades	120 710	29	75 233	33	45 476	23	117 209	25	78 551	29	38 658	18
Near and short sea trades[4]	69 116	27	43 844	32	25 272	19	71 039	25	47 343	29	23 696	18
of which:												
European Community[2]	37 766	37	26 850	39	10 916	34	38 098	36	27 880	38	10 218	30
Scandinavia and Baltic[3]	17 616	15	11 429	22	6 188	3	21 924	13	13 129	16	8 795	8
Iberia and Mediterranean	13 734	15	5 565	20	8 168	10	11 017	14	6 334	17	4 683	9
Deep sea trades	51 594	32	31 389	34	20 204	29	46 170	26	31 208	29	14 962	19
of which:												
Central and West Africa	3 348	24	1 306	21	2 042	26	4 563	14	1 343	38	3 220	4
South and East Africa	3 463	35	3 219	37	244	13	2 296	21	2 099	21	197	23
Persian Gulf and Indian Ocean	14 121	32	772	10	13 349	33	7 675	22	766	7	6 909	23
Far East	3 033	25	2 592	23	441	31	3 592	17	2 873	19	719	6
Australasia	3 975	40	3 877	40	98	47	5 604	41	5 487	42	117	10
North America	15 745	36	14 881	37	863	4	14 030	29	13 707	30	323	7
Central and South America	5 684	28	3 639	28	2 046	27	6 205	24	3 820	25	2 385	24
West Indies	2 225	22	1 103	30	1 121	15	2 205	25	1 113	17	1 092	34

1. Including re-exports.
2. Figures for European Community relate to the nine member countries, i.e. Belgium, Denmark, France, Germany (Federal Republic), Irish Republic, Italy, Luxembourg, Netherlands and Greece.
3. Excluding Denmark.
4. Total near and short sea imports for tanker cargo includes imports from the Continental Shelf (Foreign) not separately identified.

Sources Department of Transport; HM Customs and Excise

Seaport traffic of Great Britain (*Table 10.35*)
'Mode of Appearance' Classification
The mode of appearance classification was introduced by the Department of Transport and the British Ports Association from 1982 onwards and corresponds with similar classifications used in other countries including the Statistical Office of the European Communities. It refers to the way cargoes are presented for loading/unloading at ports. Primarily, it distinguishes between bulk and break-bulk cargoes but the latter are further sub-divided into categories which are more meaningful to ports, shipping and inland transport from an operational point of view. Further details of this new classification are provided in *Port Statistics 1982* available from the British Ports Association, London.

10.34 International seaborne trade of the United Kingdom
Proportion of trade carried by the principal flags

Percentage

	1982						1983					
	All cargo		Dry cargo		Tanker cargo		All cargo		Dry cargo		Tanker cargo	
	Weight	Value	Weight	Value	Weight	Value	Weight	Value	Weight	Value	Weight	Value
Exports[1]												
United Kingdom	27.1	34.2	32.4	37.3	23.8	24.4	23.5	32.8	29.5	37.1	20.3	20.8
Germany (Federal Republic)	10.0	10.8	14.4	11.9	7.2	7.2	10.0	11.1	14.7	12.4	7.4	7.5
Norway	6.8	4.1	3.4	2.5	8.9	8.9	6.9	4.4	3.3	2.7	8.9	9.0
Netherlands	5.4	5.7	8.8	6.5	3.2	3.2	6.1	5.4	8.7	5.7	4.7	4.6
Liberia	11.1	5.0	1.1	1.0	17.4	17.2	8.2	3.9	1.1	0.9	12.1	11.9
Denmark	1.2	2.5	2.0	3.1	0.8	0.9	1.2	2.3	2.1	2.8	0.8	0.8
Other European Community flags	14.7	15.1	13.1	15.1	15.8	15.4	13.0	14.5	12.6	15.1	13.2	12.8
All other flags	23.7	22.6	24.8	22.6	22.9	22.8	31.1	25.6	28.0	23.3	32.6	32.6
Imports												
United Kingdom	29.2	34.9	32.7	36.6	23.5	24.1	25.4	36.3	29.0	38.3	18.2	19.4
Liberia	9.6	3.7	4.7	1.5	17.7	17.2	7.6	2.7	3.4	1.1	16.2	15.1
Norway	7.2	3.3	5.2	2.1	10.4	10.6	8.2	3.5	5.6	2.2	13.5	13.8
Greece	5.2	2.0	4.0	1.3	7.3	5.9	4.5	1.3	3.3	0.8	6.9	5.9
Germany (Federal Republic)	8.9	11.6	12.9	13.0	2.2	2.8	10.1	12.6	13.5	13.6	3.3	4.3
Netherlands	4.8	5.7	6.0	6.1	2.8	3.5	4.8	4.9	6.2	5.2	1.9	2.3
Other European Community flags	10.8	16.6	11.2	17.8	10.4	10.3	10.4	16.7	10.8	17.6	9.5	9.5
All other flags	24.3	22.2	23.3	21.6	25.7	25.6	29.0	22.0	28.2	21.2	30.5	29.7

1. Including re-exports.

Sources: Department of Transport; HM Customs and Excise

10.35 Seaport traffic of Great Britain
Analysis of all foreign and domestic[1] traffic by mode of appearance[2]

Thousand gross[3] tonnes

	1965	1970	1975	1976	1977	1978	1979	1980	1981	1982	1983
Inwards traffic											
Bulk fuel traffic	131 551	167 696	143 647	140 156	131 704	134 809	140 513	126 980	111 774	114 550	110 781
Other bulk traffic	53 164	56 715	52 319	57 355	54 572	51 710	55 620	44 239	47 302	47 129	50 890
Container and roll-on traffic	2 194	8 426	15 449	16 972	18 249	20 414	22 514	22 336	23 826	25 466	28 966
Semi-bulk traffic	13 517	14 689	12 293	14 551	13 641	14 111	14 802	13 369	12 361	13 587	13 898
Conventional traffic	14 187	9 641	6 123	6 429	5 852	5 655	5 866	5 272	4 091	3 636	3 490
All inwards foreign and domestic traffic	214 614	257 166	229 831	235 463	224 018	226 699	239 315	212 196	199 353	204 369	208 025
Outwards traffic											
Bulk fuel traffic	70 119	73 217	62 657	76 131	92 472	107 802	131 162	141 329	147 148	154 815	157 837
Other bulk traffic	18 093	20 977	23 538	23 594	25 982	28 295	28 257	30 711	31 173	30 224	31 561
Container and roll-on traffic	2 330	8 468	13 633	15 697	17 253	18 885	19 264	19 412	19 162	19 887	21 973
Semi-bulk traffic	4 768	4 573	3 421	3 746	4 352	4 033	3 814	2 907	3 859	3 088	3 552
Conventional traffic	9 287	5 624	7 157	5 695	6 108	6 721	4 969	5 233	4 821	4 979	4 074
All outwards foreign and domestic traffic	104 598	112 859	110 406	124 863	146 167	165 736	187 466	199 591	206 163	212 994	218 996
Total foreign and domestic traffic	319 212	370 025	340 237	360 326	370 185	392 436	426 782	411 787	405 516	417 362	427 021

1. Domestic traffic refers to traffic, through the ports of Great Britain only, to all
   parts of the United Kingdom, Isle of Man and the Channel Islands. Traffic to
   and from offshore installations, landing of sea dredged aggregates and
   material shipped for dumping at sea are included.
2. Page 213 contains a brief explanation of this new classification.
3. Including crates and immediate packaging.

Sources: HM Customs and Excise; Department of Transport

10.36 United Kingdom inward passenger movement by sea and air[1]
Analysis by countries of embarkation

Thousands

	1973	1974	1975	1976	1977	1978	1979	1980	1981	1982	1983
All passengers: total	21 891	20 930	22 984	24 460	26 329	29 345	31 347	33 048	33 980	35 129	36 490
By sea[2]	6 439	6 871	7 939	8 283	9 145	9 969	10 658	11 801	12 573	13 167	13 383
By air[3]	15 452	14 059	15 045	16 177	17 184	19 376	20 689	21 247	21 407	21 962	23 107
Irish Republic: total	1 668	1 643	1 663	1 644	1 834	2 121	2 174	2 178	2 103	2 170	2 198
By sea	814	820	826	780	967	1 152	1 171	1 248	1 205	1 312	1 374
By air	854	823	837	864	867	969	1 003	930	898	858	824
European continent and Mediterranean Sea area[4]											
By sea: total	5 404	5 828	6 944	7 367	8 046	8 714	9 380	10 438	11 268	11 801	11 929
Belgium	1 332	1 519	1 819	1 988	2 196	2 224	2 214	2 619	2 368	2 351	2 210
France[5]	3 082	3 268	3 865	3 907	4 282	4 882	5 535	6 268	7 315	7 833	8 064
Netherlands	558	594	751	920	1 007	1 048	1 044	980	984	995	1 106
Other European Community[6]	197	226	282	293	310	332	342	343	357	372	312
Other countries	234	220	227	259	251	228	244	228	244	250	237
By air: total	11 287	9 934	10 553	11 056	11 592	12 998	13 803	14 022	14 235	15 302	16 215
Belgium	464	438	401	433	436	445	438	405	375	371	416
Denmark	246	245	248	287	316	313	314	279	255	244	276
Germany	1 268	1 130	1 140	1 218	1 303	1 440	1 542	1 571	1 514	1 483	1 573
France	1 463	1 336	1 372	1 461	1 473	1 540	1 564	1 550	1 567	1 610	1 656
Italy	1 032	895	937	968	1 015	1 136	1 272	1 343	1 163	1 184	1 244
Netherlands	860	800	819	917	972	999	980	960	899	918	915
Norway	137	136	173	258	296	282	269	277	271	289	306
Portugal	295	218	158	149	203	241	297	348	425	481	533
Sweden	140	141	168	213	263	260	246	219	225	214	225
Switzerland	604	525	555	598	656	697	713	732	739	794	866
Greece	379	278	346	439	440	582	778	914	1 042	1 058	1 001
Spain	2 991	2 426	2 651	2 332	2 310	2 779	2 835	2 801	3 167	3 811	4 142
Yugoslavia	199	161	204	207	143	215	255	207	247	239	240
Soviet Union and E. Europe	220	221	253	263	172	212	269	269	229	179	204
Middle East countries	352	408	512	635	808	908	838	906	1 093	917	907
Other countries	637	576	617	679	786	949	1 195	1 239	1 024	1 510	1 711
Rest of world											
By sea: total	80.5	66.5	56.7	43.5	41.3	27.0	20.6	25.1	19.5	10.9	20.3
United States of America	22.0	19.0	16.6	12.1	16.1	16.8	13.5	17.6	15.2	8.2	16.1
Canada	2.2	1.2	0.8	1.1	2.3	1.9	1.4	1.3	1.0	0.7	1.0
Australia	19.4	14.9	11.0	9.3	8.7	4.7	3.3	2.8	1.2	0.9	1.2
New Zealand	6.4	4.9	4.0	2.7	2.2	0.7	0.5	0.5	0.2	0.1	0.2
South Africa	18.1	16.1	16.6	13.7	8.3	0.1	0.2	1.4	0.4	0.2	0.7
West Africa	2.0	1.6	0.2	0.2	0.1	0.1	0.2	0.2	0.2	0.1	0.2
British West Indies and Bermuda	1.4	1.1	0.7	0.4	0.4	0.3	0.2	0.1	–	–	0.1
Other countries[7]	8.9	7.8	6.8	3.9	3.2	2.5	1.2	1.3	1.1	0.8	0.7
By air: total	3 310.5	3 239.2	3 562.5	4 132.7	4 728.8	5 243.5	5 735.1	6 006.9	6 273.6	5 802.4	6 068.1
United States of America	1 657.4	1 446.7	1 476.6	1 768.7	2 049.1	2 552.0	2 665.6	2 913.5	3 024.9	2 650.0	2 891.1
Canada	630.0	636.8	681.9	712.0	749.4	751.6	810.7	738.6	713.0	674.8	679.8
Australia and New Zealand	86.9	109.6	152.9	206.0	191.7	223.0	316.0	297.0	253.8	256.6	255.7
South Africa	78.1	95.0	124.4	169.6	159.1	166.8	185.0	199.4	206.5	217.5	210.0
East Africa	80.8	70.7	79.9	86.5	103.5	114.5	127.7	131.0	123.5	111.8	109.4
West Africa	55.6	63.7	73.2	95.5	133.6	147.6	159.3	194.2	234.7	241.2	256.5
British West Indies and Bermuda	126.7	130.2	133.7	145.1	143.1	152.5	177.3	185.0	189.0	174.6	175.3
India, Pakistan[8] and Sri Lanka	114.0	141.6	183.6	210.0	230.4	240.8	284.5	305.8	320.6	322.7	307.5
Japan	58.3	64.8	90.6	85.3	101.1	106.3	128.5	123.2	132.8	138.2	136.6
Other countries	422.7	480.1	565.8	654.0	867.9	788.3	880.4	919.2	1 074.8	1 015.0	1 046.2
Pleasure cruises ending at United Kingdom seaports: total	141	157	113	92	91	76	86	90	81	43	59

1. Excluding movement by land across the frontier between the Irish Republic and Northern Ireland, passengers travelling between the Channel Islands and Great Britain, passengers carried in aircraft chartered by British government departments and, as far as possible, passengers travelling by sea on day trips and HM and other armed forces travelling in the course of their duties.
2. Including passengers on pleasure cruises beginning and/or ending at United Kingdom seaports.
3. From 1974 figures for oil rigs are included in the total.
4. Passengers to and from North Africa and Middle East Mediterranean countries have been attributed to the European continent and Mediterranean Sea area.
5. Includes hovercraft passengers.
6. Consists of Denmark, Germany (Federal Republic), Greece and Italy.
7. Figures for Other countries cover mainly passengers to or from the Canary Islands, Madeira and the Azores.
8. Figures for Pakistan include East Pakistan, now Bangladesh.

Sources Department of Transport; Civil Aviation Authority.

10.37 United Kingdom outward passenger movement by sea and air[1]
Analysis by countries of landing

Thousands

	1973	1974	1975	1976	1977	1978	1979	1980	1981	1982	1983
All passengers: total	21 820	20 983	22 982	24 478	26 382	29 398	31 421	33 218	34 256	35 361	36 562
By sea[2]	6 378	6 889	7 955	8 348	9 150	9 958	10 631	11 820	12 649	13 192	13 394
By air[3]	15 442	14 094	15 027	16 130	17 232	19 440	20 790	21 398	21 607	22 169	23 168
Irish Republic: total	1 671	1 659	1 673	1 652	1 836	2 129	2 182	2 186	2 115	2 168	2 209
By sea	815	841	838	796	976	1 164	1 171	1 254	1 217	1 309	1 387
By air	856	818	835	856	860	965	1 011	932	898	859	822
European continent and Mediterranean Sea area[4]											
By sea: total	5 338	5 814	6 949	7 417	8 042	8 686	9 352	10 454	11 335	11 828	11 927
Belgium	1 274	1 510	1 823	1 986	2 195	2 204	2 207	2 572	2 346	2 327	2 205
France[5]	3 069	3 266	3 873	3 954	4 320	4 923	5 577	6 353	7 418	7 914	8 076
Netherlands	565	573	745	921	970	1 008	999	960	974	973	1 105
Other European Community[6]	197	232	285	294	307	329	332	340	347	357	311
Other countries	232	233	222	262	250	223	237	228	249	257	231
By air: total	11 173	9 841	10 453	11 051	11 560	12 941	13 807	14 017	14 256	15 353	16 241
Belgium	470	421	387	416	418	425	429	403	372	371	416
Denmark	228	234	238	280	311	307	312	279	255	246	272
Germany	1 257	1 117	1 137	1 252	1 316	1 441	1 537	1 565	1 526	1 514	1 592
France	1 465	1 342	1 368	1 439	1 431	1 485	1 538	1 520	1 530	1 573	1 619
Italy	1 000	876	923	973	1 023	1 143	1 278	1 348	1 172	1 194	1 250
Netherlands	874	819	815	919	962	991	979	943	890	909	909
Norway	141	140	178	264	295	282	271	280	272	295	310
Portugal	283	211	151	147	196	234	295	352	424	483	535
Sweden	135	140	168	210	262	264	253	229	225	218	229
Switzerland	577	507	537	582	633	675	700	712	728	774	846
Greece	368	265	345	444	444	579	784	925	1 052	1 065	1 006
Spain	2 983	2 416	2 647	2 332	2 308	2 775	2 815	2 791	3 164	3 802	4 151
Yugoslavia	195	162	206	207	143	212	254	206	245	237	239
Soviet Union and E. Europe	209	216	252	252	167	206	265	262	225	182	206
Middle East countries	337	393	488	654	862	967	890	970	1 162	967	952
Others	651	582	614	680	790	954	1 206	1 231	1 014	1 523	1 709
Rest of world											
By sea: total	87.3	78.3	56.7	42.7	39.8	25.0	19.7	20.8	15.8	11.6	15.1
United States of America	21.1	16.3	15.7	12.6	17.1	17.1	13.5	15.8	12.2	8.8	12.5
Canada	2.8	2.8	3.2	2.2	1.7	1.4	1.0	1.2	1.0	0.7	0.7
Australia	23.2	21.6	9.5	9.4	10.3	2.9	2.4	1.3	0.8	0.8	0.1
New Zealand	9.5	8.1	2.9	2.7	2.5	0.8	0.8	0.2	0.3	0.3	–
South Africa	13.9	17.1	17.6	11.1	4.7	0.1	0.2	0.6	0.2	0.1	0.7
West Africa	3.9	2.5	0.4	0.4	0.3	0.1	0.2	0.4	0.2	0.2	0.1
British West Indies and Bermuda	3.5	2.6	0.9	0.6	0.5	0.3	0.2	0.1	–	–	–
Other countries[7]	9.4	7.5	6.4	3.8	2.7	2.2	1.3	1.1	1.2	0.7	0.9
By air: total	3 413.2	3 373.9	3 646.8	4 097.0	4 812.3	5 365.8	5 822.7	6 160.1	6 453.0	5 957.0	6 104.2
United States of America	1 662.7	1 479.0	1 462.4	1 749.1	2 042.0	2 576.5	2 722.6	3 000.1	3 118.0	2 683.6	2 892.6
Canada	658.8	666.1	725.0	736.3	761.1	753.4	826.2	757.9	739.2	694.0	686.3
Australia and New Zealand	120.2	147.4	175.5	167.9	193.1	206.4	301.8	298.6	255.5	281.7	244.0
South Africa	103.2	136.9	164.8	160.3	165.3	176.7	186.5	210.5	233.0	241.5	210.4
East Africa	72.2	66.8	70.5	75.7	96.6	109.4	111.9	118.4	113.5	102.6	102.3
West Africa	61.7	71.5	83.9	110.9	206.2	222.4	206.4	246.3	283.3	307.8	318.6
British West Indies and Bermuda	119.1	128.4	142.3	151.7	139.4	150.3	176.0	181.6	192.6	181.6	179.8
India, Pakistan[8] and Sri Lanka	112.6	136.2	162.9	178.1	201.5	239.3	268.4	298.5	306.9	320.7	302.0
Japan	55.8	61.7	90.0	85.8	98.5	109.7	128.7	111.5	119.6	126.4	127.3
Other countries	446.9	479.9	569.4	681.1	908.8	821.8	894.3	936.7	1 091.4	1 017.1	1 040.9
Pleasure cruises beginning at United Kingdom seaports: total	138	156	112	92	93	82	89	90	81	43	65

1. Excluding movement by land across the frontier between the Irish Republic and Northern Ireland, passengers travelling between the Channel Islands and Great Britain, passengers carried in aircraft chartered by British government departments and, as far as possible, passengers travelling by sea on day trips and HM and other armed forces travelling in the course of their duties.
2. Including passengers on pleasure cruises beginning and/or ending at United Kingdom seaports.
3. From 1974 figures for oil rigs are included in the total.

4. Passengers to and from North Africa and Middle East Mediterranean countries have been attributed to the European continent and Mediterranean Sea area.
5. Includes hovercraft passengers.
6. Consists of Denmark, Germany (Federal Republic), Greece and Italy.
7. Figures for Other countries cover mainly passengers to or from the Canary Islands, Madeira and the Azores.
8. Figures for Pakistan include East Pakistan, now Bangladesh.

Sources Department of Transport; Civil Aviation Authority.

10.38 Postal, telegraph and telephone services
Years ended 31 March[1]

	Unit	1974	1975	1976	1977	1978	1979	1980	1981	1982	1983	1984
Letters and parcel post												
Letters, etc. posted[2]	Millions	11 010	10 878	9 903	9 383	9 485	9 965	10 207	10 071	9 985	10 255	10 665
of which:												
Registered and insured	,,	*43.8*	*43.8*	*38.4*	*39.1*	*37.4*	*37.1*	*36.7*	*36.6*	*33.5*	*33.5*	*32.5*
Airmail (Commonwealth and foreign)[3]	,,	467	492	479	529	511	503	493.4	436.8	393.0	378.0	379.3
Business reply and freepost items	,,	128.1	140.1	180.0	206.4	215.7	225.3	305.1	309.2	308.2	336.2	356.9
Parcels posted[4]	,,	191.0	196.8	165.9	159.1	156.6	168.3	176.8	168.8	179.6	189.6	194.9
of which:												
Registered and insured[5]	,,	*5.1*	*5.5*	*4.6*	*4.6*	*5.0*	*5.3*	*4.7*	*4.2*	*3.8*	*3.6*	*3.8*
Inward and transit parcels handled	,,	3.9	3.7	3.9	3.4	3.3	3.2	3.4	3.6	3.4	3.2	3.1
Money orders												
Total handled[6]	Thousands	5 443	3 402	2 653	1 998	1 789	1 424	1 035	[11]			
Inland	,,	3 255	1 446	1 148	879	842	831	1 037				
Commonwealth and foreign	,,	2 188	1 956	1 505	1 119	947	593	398				
Postal orders												
Total issued[7]	,,	360 631	303 756	224 752	192 231	180 308	169 989	153 947	121 636	87 154	68 605	63 511
Telegrams and telephones												
Telegrams: total	Thousands	27 525	25 532	21 053	18 676	17 312	16 601	15 546	13 662	11 521	7 694[12]	5 710
Inland	,,	7 252	6 200	4 230	3 440	3 259	3 347	3 372	2 963	2 276	901[12]	
Foreign (via Post Office system)[8]	,,	20 273	19 332	16 823	15 236	14 053	13 254	12 174	10 699	9 245	6 793	5 710
Telex connections	Number	48 995	54 256	59 142	64 804	71 586	79 503	85 752	89 930	92 378	92 622	95 115
Telephone calls (Inland): total	Millions	13 238	14 313	15 156	15 956	17 303	19 122	19 857	20 175	20 806	21 403	22 686
Local	,,	11 100	12 000	12 800	13 500	14 600	16 100	16 600	16 840	17 360	17 800	18 750
Trunk	,,	2 138	2 313	2 356	2 456	2 703	3 022	3 257	3 335	3 446	3 603	3 936
Telephone calls (International): total	Thousands	29 178	36 252	44 326	54 603	70 537	86 930	106 427	116 533	132 255	148 478	172 746
Continental	,,	23 904	29 577	34 974	42 364	52 689	62 998	75 287	79 467	86 352	93 109	104 065
Intercontinental	,,	5 217	6 608	9 284	12 166	17 767	23 850	31 045	36 971	45 806	55 265	68 574
Maritime	,,	57	67	68	73	81	82	95	95	97	104	107
Telephone stations[9]: total	Thousands	18 955	20 191	20 884	21 516	23 016	24 760	26 807	27 870	28 450	28 882	29 336
Public call offices	,,	77	77	77	77	77	77	77	77	77	77	77
Private stations	,,	18 878	20 114	20 807	21 439	22 939	24 683	26 730	27 793	28 373	28 805	29 259
Telephone exchanges[10]: total	Number	6 245	6 255	6 263	6 260	6 231	6 231	6 300	6 338	6 318	6 296	
Automatic	,,	6 215	6 242	6 260	6 260	6 231	6 231	6 300	6 338	6 318	6 296	
Manual	,,	30	13	3								
Television licences												
in force on 31 March	Thousands	17 325	17 701	17 788	18 056	18 149	18 381	18 285	18 667	18 554	18 494	18 632
of which:												
Colour	,,	*5 558*	*7 580*	*8 639*	*9 958*	*11 049*	*12 131*	*12 902*	*13 780*	*14 261*	*14 699*	*15 370*

1. Years ended 31 March for letter and parcel post, money and postal orders, telegrams sent and telephone calls made in the United Kingdom. For all other items figures relate to 31 March in each year.
2. Including printed papers, newspapers, postcards and sample packets.
3. Including letters without special charge for air transport.
4. Includes Irish Republic inward traffic.
5. Includes compensation fee parcels.
6. Irish Republic money orders are included in the Inland figures.
7. Excluding those issued on HM ships, in many British possessions and in other places abroad. For 1980 and 1981 includes Overseas and Army.
8. Excluding those sent abroad via the private cable companies system.
9. A station is a telephone provided for the use of a customer or renter.
10. Excluding auto-manual and trunk exchanges.
11. Service ceased in 1980.
12. Inland telegram service ceased from 1 October 1982, 1983 figures are therefore not comparable with earlier years.

Sources Home Office, Post Office, British Telecommunications plc

Films (*Table 10.39*)

Films showing to the public in cinemas must be registered with, and cinema exhibitors and film distributors must be licensed by the Department of Trade and Industry.

The Film Levy Finance Act 1981 imposes a levy on the prices of admission to cinemas exhibiting 35mm and 70mm films to the public and the proceeds are paid into the British Film Fund for the benefit of the makers of eligible British films. There is no element of subsidy from public funds in the levy arrangements.

The obligation on cinema exhibitors of 35mm films to show a specified proportion of British and Community (national films of another member state) films each year was suspended from 1 January 1983 under The Films (Suspension of Quota Requirements) Order 1982.

Cinemas and films

10.39 Films registered in Great Britain[1]
Years ended 31 March

	1973/74	1974/75	1975/76	1976/77	1977/78	1978/79	1979/80	1980/81	1981/82	1982/83	1983/84
Cinematograph films registered:[2, 3]											
Total	695	662	518	545	456	444	429	373	333	321	329
Long	442	453	379	374	324	307	320	282	256	254	257
Short	149	116	87	118	80	85	100	91	77	67	72
Newsreels	104	93	52	53	52	52	9	–	–	–	–
British films:											
Long	99	88	81	80	50	54	61	52	38	34	31
Short	75	72	63	82	59	71	85	74	64	50	40
Newsreels	104	93	52	53	52	52	9	–	–	–	–
Community films:[3]											
Long	124	118	72	87	82	66	43	34	28	19	16
Short	2	4	1	2	3	3	2	1	–	1	–
Foreign films:											
Long	219	247	226	207	192	187	216	196	190	201	210
Short	72	40	23	34	18	11	13	16	13	16	32

See note on page 217
1. Registered under the Films Acts, 1960 to 1970 as amended with effect from 1 January 1973 by the European Communities Act 1972.
2. Long films are $33\frac{1}{3}$ minutes playing time and over.

3. Community films, which are also quota films, are national films of the member states of the European Community and the figures for 1973/74, and 1974/75 are inflated by the inclusion of films which had previously been registered as foreign.

Source Department of Trade and Industry

10.40 Cinemas: admissions and distribution of takings[1]
Great Britain

	1973	1974	1975	1976	1977	1978	1979	1980	1981	1982	1983
Number of cinemas reporting[2]	1 530	1 535	1 530	1 525	1 510	1 519	1 564	1 562	1 514	1 432	1 293
Number of admissions (millions)	134	138	116	104	103	126	112	96	84	60	63
	£ million										
Gross box office takings: total[3]	58.0	69.3	71.2	75.8	85.5	118.2	126.8	135.7	135.8	106.8	119.7
Payment to the British Film Production Fund	3.7	4.4	4.9	4.8	5.4	7.2	7.0	5.8	5.7	4.0	5.0
Payment for film hire	16.4	20.3	21.4	24.3	26.8	41.3	41.0	42.2	41.1	30.4	36.2
Exhibitors' share	37.9	44.6	44.9	46.7	53.4	69.7	78.7	87.7	89.0	72.5	78.5
	pence										
Average price of admission	43.2	50.1	61.2	73.0	82.6	93.7	113.4	141.3	162.4	177.4	189.8

Regional analysis

	Number of cinemas		Admissions (thousands)		Gross box office takings (£ thousand)		Seating capacity of cinemas (thousands)		Percentage of capacity filled[4]		Average price of admission (pence)	
	1982	1983	1982	1983	1982	1983	1982	1983	1982	1983	1982	1983
Great Britain	1 432	1 293	60 170	63 058	106 806	119 715	568.4	504.8	16.4	17.6	177.4	189.8
North	81	64	2 334	2 248	3 744	3 693	29.8	23.5	12.6	17.7	160.4	164.3
Yorkshire and Humberside	111	103	4 108	4 495	6 950	7 814	41.2	39.8	14.3	16.1	169.2	173.8
East Midlands	76	73	2 862	3 022	4 807	5 367	27.5	25.2	15.3	17.3	168.0	177.6
East Anglia	46	44	2 282	2 404	3 945	4 259	20.5	19.2	18.4	18.7	172.9	177.2
South East:												
Greater London Council Area	242	231	13 880	15 836	30 800	38 143	97.5	95.0	17.3	17.2	221.9	240.9
Outer Metropolitan Area	116	105	5 616	5 866	9 723	10 629	48.6	41.9	17.4	18.7	173.1	181.2
Remainder	126	115	5 408	5 848	9 412	10 629	54.1	48.2	16.1	18.2	174.1	181.8
South West	121	114	4 171	4 381	6 850	7 495	45.1	41.4	17.9	19.4	164.2	171.1
West Midlands	102	90	4 230	4 093	6 953	6 919	43.8	34.1	15.4	16.4	164.4	169.0
North West	192	159	6 110	6 134	9 919	10 297	67.4	56.9	15.5	17.1	162.3	167.9
Wales	89	78	2 892	2 580	3 737	3 682	34.3	27.6	19.3	19.7	129.2	142.7
Scotland	130	117	6 278	6 148	9 966	10 788	58.8	52.0	17.2	17.0	158.8	175.5

1. The figures in this table are derived from returns made by cinemas to the annual inquiry into the Film Exhibition Industry. Cinemas showing only 16 mm film are excluded throughout.
2. Number of licensed cinemas open at end of year and also those open for 26 weeks or more during the year but temporarily closed at the end of the year.

3. Including VAT from April 1973.
4. Based on the number of complete performances during one week in November.

Source Department of Trade and Industry

11 Distributive Trades, Research and Development

Annual retailing inquiries *(Table 11.1)*

These inquiries are based on a sample from the register of businesses compiled by the Business Statistics Office (BSO) from information on the name and address, trade classification and turnover of traders registered for Value Added Tax (VAT). They cover those businesses whose VAT trade code shows them to be registered for VAT purposes to the retail trade headings in trade group 24 of the VAT Trade Classification (other than VAT trade code 8228 covering opticians). Also included are those businesses with other VAT trade codes which are believed, on the basis of previous inquiries, to undertake a significant amount of retailing activity.

The results of the 1980 and 1982 inquiries are presented using a 'kind of business' classification which is consistent with the Standard Industrial Classification 1980. The 1982 figures were compiled using a revised method of grossing, known as 'hybrid' grossing. The 1980 figures have been reworked using this method. Full details of the inquiry are given in Business Monitor *SDO 25 Retailing* (HMSO).

'Full' inquiries such as those for 1980 and 1982 collecting a broad range of information from a sample of 20 000 retail businesses now alternate with 'Slimline' inquiries addressed to 10 000 businesses. The slimline inquiries collect only summary information on turnover, stocks and capital expenditure. The first of these inquiries related to 1981. No kind of business or form of organisation breakdown is available.

Retail trade: index numbers of value and volume *(Table 11.3)*

The index numbers are based on the retailing inquiry for 1980 with 1980 = 100. The rebasing was completed at the beginning of 1984.

The retail sales index is based on monthly returns provided voluntarily by a panel of contributors. The retail sales index has been adjusted to take account of the results of the 1982 retailing inquiry. An article in *British business* (HMSO) 2 March 1984 gives more details.

The index numbers for 1973 to 1979 in the tables have been prepared on an approximate basis and no separate estimates are available for large and small businesses.

Motor Trades and Catering inquiries *(Tables 11.2 and 11.4)*

These inquiries are taken as sample surveys from the Business Statistics Office (BSO) VAT based register of legal units. The results relate to all businesses registered for Value Added Tax, whatever their turnover, whose VAT trade code shows them, for VAT purposes, to be registered to an inquiry trade heading.

Research and Development

Research and experimental development (R & D) in the United Kingdom is financed and carried out mainly by the Government, industry, universities and further education institutions, and various non-profit-making bodies. In 1981 £6 billion was spent on R & D. Full-scale inquiries covering industrial R & D were held every third year until 1981; these have been superseded by a four-year cycle, with an intervening sample survey. The first of these sample inquiries has been made to examine spending in 1983, and results are expected to appear in early 1985. There is an annual survey of government expenditure and employment on R & D.

In line with international recommendations, research and experimental development is defined for statistical purposes as 'creative work undertaken on a systematic basis in order to increase the stock of knowledge, including knowledge of man, culture and society, and the use of this stock of knowledge to devise new applications'.

Definitions of the sectors surveyed and notes on the survey procedures employed are given in an article which appeared in *Economic Trends* (HMSO) August 1984.

For the 1981 inquiry, industrial firms were asked to provide figures relating to the calendar year 1981, or the business year ending on a date between 6 April 1981 and 5 April 1982. The corresponding returns from government departments relate to financial years ended 31 March.

Further details of all sectors' expenditure on R & D up to 1981, government figures up to 1986/87, numbers of persons engaged on research work in the government and industry sectors, and a commentary on recent trends in R & D expenditure, are given in the issue of *Economic Trends* referred to above.

Table 11.5

This table covers R & D in the natural and medical sciences and engineering, and excludes research in the social sciences and humanities.

The totals of both sections of the table are the amounts of R & D performed in the United Kingdom and exclude R & D performed abroad which is financed from within this country. No surveys of R & D performed by local authorities have been carried out since 1972, but estimates of local authorities' expenditure in these years have been included in the all-sector figures.

The figures of government financing of R & D as returned by the government and as returned by the sectors carrying out the work vary, largely because of differences in timing (see **Introduction** above).

Tables 11.6 and 11.7

Central government expenditure on R & D, including that of research councils, is surveyed annually and covers R & D in the social sciences as well as R & D in the natural sciences. The distinction between social science and other R & D has been retained in the accompanying tables, though it has been found difficult to make in practice. The borderline between research and other related activities, such as information services and general purpose data collection, is also difficult to define, especially for the social sciences. The figures for social science research are therefore considered to be less reliable than those for government R & D as a whole. The series which appeared in earlier editions of this publication has been amended by taking into account recently developed estimates for government expenditure on R & D in universities. These now include payments through the Treasury Grant for the research costs of postgraduate students, and also expenditure on research in the fields of the social services and humanities.

Table 11.6, as distinct from Table 11.7, includes money spent by the government to finance R & D work performed overseas. It shows the gross expenditure of government on R & D: 'gross' in that any receipts used to finance the expenditure are not deducted. Money spent on R & D work done by government itself (intra-mural expenditure) is distinguished from money passed to other sectors to fund R & D work (extra-mural expenditure). Table 11.6 shows natural and social science R & D separately, the former being analysed by functional groups of expenditure.

Table 11.7 relates to net government expenditure on R & D (budgeted expenditure), that is, gross expenditure *less* receipts allocated directly towards financing the expenditure. The table shows total expenditure broken down according to the Statistical Office of the European Communities' revised objectives classification of budgeted expenditure on R & D. It is not possible to provide any analysis for years earlier than 1981/82 on this new basis. However, estimates are made for the forward years of the Public Expenditure Survey, when government R & D expenditure data are collected. These forward estimates are included in this table.

Table 11.8

The trend in the 'volume' of R & D performed can be shown by means of estimates of expenditure at constant prices, using the most appropriate price indices which can be prepared to revalue the current price figures. Work on constructing price indices specifically for R & D expenditure has been undertaken by the Department of Trade and Industry and by international organisations only in recent years. Table 11.8 shows figures for each of the industrial survey years from 1964 to

Continued on page 221

11.1 Retail trades by form of organisation and kind of business
Standard Industrial Classification 1980
Great Britain

	1980				1982			
	Businesses[1]	Outlets	Persons engaged	Total turnover (inclusive of VAT)	Businesses[1]	Outlets	Persons engaged	Total turnover (inclusive of VAT)
	Number		Thousand	£ million	Number		Thousand	£ million
Total retail trade[2]	239 646	362 494	2 419	59 455	232 948	349 659	2 264	69 784
Single outlet retailers[3]	208 185	208 185	896	18 797	203 157	203 157	828	21 093
Small multiple retailers[3]	30 177	80 141	390	8 702	28 657	76 346	355	9 609
Large multiple retailers[3]	1 284	74 168	1 133	31 957	1 135	70 153	1 081	39 082
of which								
Co-operative societies								
accounted for	*191*	*8 556*	*139*	*3 869*	*148*	*6 945*	*116*	*4 061*
Food retailers	85 996	122 852	878	22 888	82 625	114 774	818	27 211
Large grocery retailers	116	12 218	387	13 206	113	10 892	379	16 703
Other grocery retailers	40 945	46 644	189	4 165	38 277	43 342	164	4 368
Dairymen	6 720	8 602	54	1 481	6 985	8 350	53	1 718
Butchers	15 658	21 972	91	2 211	14 954	20 997	84	2 405
Fishmongers, poulterers	2 334	2 815	9	174	2 543	3 278	11	197
Greengrocers, fruiterers	13 041	16 424	64	844	13 262	16 360	59	1 009
Bread and flour confectioners	7 183	14 177	84	807	6 490	11 556	68	810
Drink, confectionery and tobacco retailers	41 341	57 080	256	6 160	40 862	57 195	264	7 641
Retailers of confectionery, tobacco and								
newsagents	38 277	48 042	223	4 697	37 525	47 919	230	5 888
Off-licences	3 064	9 038	33	1 463	3 338	9 276	34	1 753
Clothing, footwear and leather goods retailers	31 656	59 424	300	5 413	28 923	55 649	269	5 911
Men's and boys' wear retailers	4 571	10 936	53	1 192	3 965	9 930	44	1 231
Women's, girls', children's and								
infants' wear retailers	17 291	26 929	119	1 925	15 105	23 592	99	2 020
General clothing businesses	5 119	7 938	47	964	5 150	8 141	44	1 079
Footwear retailers	3 642	11 989	75	1 249	3 422	12 075	77	1 467
Leather and travel goods retailers	1 032	1 632	5	82	1 280	1 912	6	115
Household goods retailers	40 947	60 816	289	8 201	39 112	58 230	269	9 358
Household textiles retailers	3 430	4 873	20	376	3 070	4 600	18	418
Carpet retailers	3 047	4 543	22	705	3 425	4 870	21	772
Furniture retailers	10 554	13 839	72	2 272	9 533	12 909	64	2 505
Electrical and music goods retailers	7 709	13 749	73	2 443	8 044	14 607	74	2 959
Hardware, china and fancy goods retailers	11 102	15 618	62	1 368	9 816	13 528	53	1 408
Do-it-yourself retailers	5 105	8 195	39	1 037	5 224	7 717	39	1 296
Other non-food retailers	33 527	46 352	227	4 749	33 759	46 363	216	5 788
Chemists	7 924	11 252	66	1 547	7 910	11 627	66	2 074
Booksellers, stationers and newsagents	4 525	6 197	37	724	4 817	6 626	36	907
Photographic goods retailers	603	1 264	7	299	758	1 590	8	365
Cycle and perambulator retailers	1 424	1 726	6	114	1 486	1 689	5	130
Jewellers	4 682	7 590	41	832	4 999	7 647	37	955
Toys, hobby and sports goods retailers	6 386	8 109	31	654	5 449	6 935	26	644
Florists, nurserymen and seedsmen	4 037	5 238	24	334	4 093	4 964	22	392
Non-food retailers (nes)	3 948	4 975	16	244	4 246	5 284	16	321
Mixed retail businesses	3 525	9 754	421	11 100	5 205	10 963	383	12 770
Large mixed businesses	49	4 527	325	8 069	40	4 247	298	9 551
Other mixed businesses	3 437	5 135	43	696	5 144	6 651	41	799
General mail order houses	40	93	53	2 335	21	65	44	2 421
Hire and repair businesses	2 653	6 215	48	945	2 462	6 484	43	1 105
Television hire businesses	1 381	4 268	39	846	1 281	4 399	36	998
Other hire or repair	1 272	1 947	9	99	1 181	2 085	7	106

1. These figures relate, as does all the other retailing data, to businesses with registered turnover at or above the VAT registration threshold each year.
2. The results include figures for businesses registered to other VAT trade codes which are believed to undertake retail activity.
3. The terms 'single outlet retailers', 'small multiple retailers' and 'large multiple retailers' are used in the table to denote retail businesses with 1, 2–9 and 10 or more retail outlets respectively.

Source Business Statistics Office

11.2 Motor trades
Great Britain

£m exclusive of VAT

6148, 6510, 6520 and 6710 SIC 1980		No of businesses	Turnover	Stocks		Capital expenditure				
				Beginning of year	End of year	New build-ing work	Vehicles[1]	Plant and machinery	Net capital expenditure	Land and exist-ing buildings
1979	Total motor trades	..	30 781[1]	2 912	3 775	92	193	129	414	53
1980	,, ,, ,,	65 707	32 658[1]	3 627	3 764	110	82	114	304	64
1981	,, ,, ,,	67 166	33 096[1]	3 701	3 431	88	72	88	248	35
1982	,, ,, ,,	67 289	33 084[2]	3 337	3 524	88	101	93	281	27
1979	Distribution, repair and servicing	..	27 647[1]	2 807	3 633	85	183	114	382	50
1980	of motor vehicles (including	57 319	28 522[1]	3 481	3 587	99	69	102	270	61
1981	caravans, tyres, motor accessories	58 819	28 091[1]	3 533	3 237	81	66	79	226	31
1982	and spares)	59 198	28 144[2]	3 149	3 337	75	91	77	242	20
1979	Petrol filling stations	..	3 134[1]	105	142	7	10	15	32	3
1980	,, ,, ,,	8 387	4 136[1]	146	177	10	12	11	33	2
1981	,, ,, ,,	8 348	5 005[1]	167	195	6	7	9	22	4
1982	,, ,, ,,	8 090	4 940[2]	187	186	13	10	16	39	7

1. Inclusive of VAT

Motor trades: commodity analysis[2] of 1982 sales
Great Britain

£m exclusive of VAT

	Turnover	of which Motor trades turnover	Retail sales		Sales to other dealers		Used motor vehicles and motor cycles	Petrol and oil	Other sales and receipts
			New cars	Other new motor vehicles and motor cycles	New cars	Other new motor vehicles and motor cycles			
Total motor trades	33 084	32 767	6 497	1 386	3 306	633	5 691	6 951	8 303
Distribution repair and servicing of motor vehicles (including caravans, tyres, motor accessories and spares)	28 144	27 898	6 362	1 376	3 298	632	5 556	2 740	7 934
Petrol filling stations	4 940	4 869	135	11	9	1	135	4 210	369

2. Up to 1981 commodity analysis of motor trades' turnover was requested on a VAT-inclusive basis but in 1982 it was collected on a VAT-exclusive basis in order to facilitate the provision of information by motor trades. VAT-inclusive data for earlier years was published in previous editions of the *Annual Abstract of Statistics*.

Source Business Statistics Office.

continued from page 219
1981 at constant (1975) prices for total R & D in the natural sciences performed in the United Kingdom and the amounts performed by the government and industry, the latter being analysed by major product group. An article giving broad details of the method used in producing figures of R & D expenditure at constant prices was published in *Trade and Industry* (HMSO) on 6 April 1979.

Table 11.9

The table gives details of the 1981 survey of industrial R & D, and uses the Standard Industrial Classification rebased on 1980.

Firms covered in the survey were asked to provide figures for each product group in which they had incurred research and development expenditure. Product groups generally correspond quite closely to industry groups, since manufacturing industries are defined in terms of the products they make and a high proportion of the output of a particular product usually comes from a single industry group. Fuller details are given in Business Monitor *MO14 Industrial Research and Development Expenditure and Employment 1981* (HMSO). Results for the 1975 and 1978 surveys are published in earlier Business Monitors with the same number and name apart from the reference year. The 1968 Standard Industrial Classification was used for these earlier inquiries.

11.3 Retail trade: Index numbers of value and volume of sales[1,2]

	Weekly average 1980 = 100							Sales in 1980 £ million	Weekly average 1980 = 100		
	1973	1974	1975	1976	1977	1978	1979		1981	1982	1983
Value											
All kinds of business: all retailers total	36.8	42.7	50.8	58.2	66.5	76.1	88.8	57 406	108.2	116.9	127.7
Small retailers	..	..	..	..	..	..	..	21 042	105	111	116
Large retailers	..	..	..	..	..	..	..	36 364	110	121	135
Food retailers: total	37.5	43.6	51.8	59.8	68.2	74.1	85.5	22 556	110.0	119.4	128.9
Small retailers	..	..	..	..	..	..	..	7 168	106	109	109
Large retailers	..	..	..	..	..	..	..	15 388	112	124	138
Grocery retailers including co-operative societies	35	42	51	59	67	73	84	17 172	111	122	134
of which co-operative societies	38	44	56	64	71	79	89	3 701	105	108	112
Dairymen	35	34	46	61	72	74	90	1 458	111	119	125
Butchers	47	53	58	64	71	80	90	2 165	105	110	108
Greengrocers, fruiterers, fishmongers and poulterers	52	57	65	71	74	79	85	978	105	110	114
Bread and flour confectioners	48	54	57	57	70	70	87	783	106	111	112
Non food retailers: total	37.6	42.8	50.5	57.4	65.2	77.4	90.6	23 937	107.5	115.7	127.6
Clothing and footwear retailers: total	43	49	55	60	65	79	92	5 281	102	108	120
Small retailers	..	..	..	..	..	..	..	2 441	98	102	109
Large retailers	..	..	..	..	..	..	..	2 840	105	114	131
Men's and boys' wear retailers	53	60	67	72	74	84	93	1 157	99	104	117
Women's and girls' wear retailers	42	48	53	59	63	79	92	2 803	102	108	119
Footwear, and leather and travel goods retailers	35	41	47	54	60	74	92	1 321	103	113	126
Household goods retailers: total	38	41	49	55	64	76	91	8 923	107	114	130
Small retailers	..	..	..	..	..	..	..	4 629	104	106	118
Large retailers	..	..	..	..	..	..	..	4 294	110	123	143
Furniture, carpets and household textiles retailers	37	41	49	57	64	76	92	3 245	104	109	125
Electrical and music goods retailers	42	45	51	56	62	74	93	2 036	107	118	134
Electricity showrooms	51	45	51	57	64	81	92	352	102	111	131
Televisions and other hire and repair business	46	53	62	70	76	84	87	936	111	120	135
DIY hardware, china and fancy goods retailers	29	34	39	44	57	72	88	2 114	110	116	131
Gas showrooms	35	40	50	56	68	86	96	240	105	112	119
Other non food retailers: total	35	41	50	58	67	78	89	9 733	111	121	130
Small retailers	..	..	..	..	..	..	..	6 440	110	119	125
Large retailers	..	..	..	..	..	..	..	3 293	115	126	138
Retailers of confectionery, tobacco and newspapers	33	39	49	57	68	82	88	4 545	114	124	130
Off licences	35	42	53	64	72	76	91	1 427	117	129	135
Booksellers, stationers and newsagents	36	39	44	47	57	70	84	704	109	119	132
Chemists[2,3]	} 37	44	51	58	66	{ 86	94	647	111	121	131
Jewellers[3]						78	96	814	100	102	111
All other non food retailers[3,4]						68	87	1 596	107	117	131
Mixed retail businesses: total[5]	33.8	40.5	49.2	56.8	65.9	77.6	91.7	10 913	105.9	114.5	125.6
Mixed businesses with turnover exceeding £8 million in 1980	} 34	41	50	58	66	{ 78	91	7 899	108	118	131
Other mixed businesses						74	82	692	100	108	117
General mail order houses	34	40	47	54	65	77	95	2 322	99	104	110

See footnotes on page 223.

Source Business Statistics Office

11.3
(continued)

Retail Trade: Index numbers of value and volume of sales[1]

	Weekly average 1980 = 100							Sales in 1980 £ million	Weekly average 1980 = 100		
	1973[3]	1974[3]	1975[3]	1976[3]	1977[3]	1978	1979		1981	1982	1983
Volume											
All retailers	96.6	95.6	93.5	93.1	91.5	96.4	100.6	57 406	100.4	102.5	107.9
Food retailers	100.3	99.6	96.0	93.1	91.2	92.3	95.9	22 556	100.7	101.6	105.9
Mixed retail businesses	86.2	86.9	89.2	91.3	90.9	98.6	103.3	10 913	100.9	104.5	110.2
Non food retailers	97.7	95.8	93.1	93.8	92.0	99.3	103.7	23 937	100.0	102.4	108.7
Clothing and footwear retailers	43	49	55	60	65	79	92	5 281	102	108	120
Household goods retailers	38	41	49	55	64	76	91	8 923	107	114	130
Other non food retailers	35	41	50	58	67	78	89	9 733	111	121	130

1. A description of the series was published in *British business* 2 March 1984.
2. Excluding receipts under the National Health Service.
3. Series up to 1977 were supplied on a different kind of business classification. These are available on request from the Business Statistics Office.

4. Includes photographic goods, cycle and perambulator retailers and toys, hobby and sports goods retailers.
5. Including general mail order houses.

Source Business Statistics Office

11.4
Catering and allied trades 1979 – 1982
Great Britain

£m exclusive of VAT

	Year	No of businesses	Turnover (inclusive of VAT)	Stocks		Capital expenditure					
				Beginning of year	End of year	New building work	Vehicles	Plant and machinery	Net capital expenditure	Land and existing buildings	
Total catering	1979	..	10 895	358	426	285	71	222	578	74	
	1980	109 471	12 424	423	467	343	63	238	645	88	
	1981	111 532	13 627	447	490	316	68	266	651	118	
	1982	113 333	14 926	487	501	337	43	262	642	74	
Hotels and other residential establishments	1979	..	2 152	51	62	91	13	52	156	54	
	1980	14 281	2 483	63	71	146	9	63	218	6	
	1981	13 929	2 752	71	74	91	11	62	165	33	
	1982	13 385	2 880	72	74	83	9	61	153	31	
Holiday camps, camping and holiday caravan sites	1979	..	341	12	14	22	3	17	43	8	
	1980	1 587	405	17	19	22	2	18	43	6	
	1981	1 565	421	16	18	19	3	13	35	6	
	1982	1 542	390	15	14	21	2	11	35	2	
Restaurants, cafes, snack bars, etc. selling food for consumption on the premises only	1979	..	1 229	34	43	26	10	25	60	− 1	
	1980	11 512	1 431	44	50	22	5	26	53	28	
	1981	11 735	1 529	43	47	37	8	25	70	5	
	1982	11 817	1 639	48	50	27	4	31	62	3	
Fish and chip shops, sandwich and snack bars and other establishments selling food partly or wholly for consumption off the premises	1979	..	1 025	14	18	7	18	23	49	14	
	1980	22 715	1 103	19	20	17	18	19	56	10	
	1981	24 980	1 284	22	24	24	7	29	60	10	
	1982	26 256	1 497	24	26	34	4	36	73	5	
Public houses[1]	1979	..	4 297	177	206	65	22	78	165	− 4	
	1980	40 608	4 857	196	214	84	24	88	196	20	
	1981	40 145	5 273	203	228	104	23	104	231	40	
	1982	41 457	6 002	229	238	134	18	102	254	15	
Clubs (excluding sports clubs and gaming clubs)	1979	..	1 413	62	73	73	2	22	97	3	
	1980	17 571	1 570	75	84	51	2	19	72	17	
	1981	17 873	1 718	81	88	40	12	28	80	21	
	1982	17 568	1 776	89	89	34	4	13	51	16	
Catering contractors	1979	..	438	8	10	1	3	5	8	1	
	1980	1 196	575	9	9	−	3	5	8	1	
	1981	1 304	650	11	11	1	4	5	10	3	
	1982	1 308	743	10	10	3	3	8	14	1	

1. The figures for 1980 and subsequent years include, besides those businesses registered as Public houses, brewers known to operate Public houses. These businesses account for about one-third of the total activity of Public houses. The figures for 1979 have been adjusted to incorporate estimates for these businesses.

Source Business Statistics Office

11.5 Cost of research and development[1]: analysis by sector

Work performed within each sector

	1969 £ million	1969 Per cent	1972 £ million	1972 Per cent	1975 £ million	1975 Per cent	1978 £ million	1978 Per cent	1981 £ million	1981 Per cent
Sector carrying out the work										
Central government										
Defence	104.8	10.0	133.0	10.1	252.3	11.7	331.0	9.4	557.7	9.4
Civil:										
Research councils	46.9	4.5	64.2	4.9	108.2	5.0	152.3	4.3	250.2	4.2
Other	110.2	10.5	138.2	10.5	203.7	9.5	271.8	7.7	526.5	8.9
Local government[2]	0.8	0.1	1.3	0.1	2.1	0.1	3.0	0.1	5.0	0.1
Total	262.7	25.1	336.7	25.6	566.3	26.3	758.1	21.6	1 339.4	22.6
Universities and further education establishments	80.4	7.7	115.6	8.8	179.2	8.3	317.3	9.0	629.6	10.6
Public corporations	44.9	4.3	69.2	5.3	124.0	5.8	212.5	6.1	384.8	6.5
Research associations	16.5	1.6	18.8	1.4	31.1	1.4	50.8	1.4	88.1	1.5
Private industry	619.0	59.2	742.5	56.6	1 185.1	55.1	2 061.0	58.7	3 319.5	56.1
Other	21.9	2.1	30.6	2.3	65.6	3.1	110.6	3.2	159.6	2.7
Total cost of research and development performed	1 045.4	100.0	1 313.4	100.0	2 151.3	100.0	3 510.3	100.0	5 921.1	100.0

Finance provided by each sector

	1969 £ million	1969 Per cent	1972 £ million	1972 Per cent	1975 £ million	1975 Per cent	1978 £ million	1978 Per cent	1981 £ million	1981 Per cent
Sector providing the funds										
Central government[3]										
Defence	220.6	21.2	327.3	22.1	611.2	25.3	949.8	25.4	1 666.7	24.8
Civil:										
Research councils	72.5	7.0	106.1	7.2	131.1	5.4	186.2	4.9	363.5	5.4
Other	230.2	22.1	283.6	19.1	499.9	20.8	610.9	16.4	1 161.3	17.3
Local government[2]	3.6	0.3	4.9	0.3	9.0	0.4	10.0	0.3	20.0	0.3
Total as returned by Government	526.9	50.6	721.9	48.7	1 251.2	51.9	1 756.9	47.0	3 211.5	47.7
Total as returned by sectors carrying out work	529.4	50.6	640.0	48.7	1 117.4	51.9	1 651.4	47.0	2 825.9	47.7
Universities	10.0	1.0	13.2	1.0	15.5	0.7	28.4	0.8	58.0	1.0
Public corporations	51.7	5.0	76.1	5.8	137.1	6.4	259.7	7.4	449.2	7.6
Private industry[4]	397.4	38.0	495.1	37.7	739.5	34.4	1 292.4	36.8	2 080.1	35.1
Overseas	40.2	3.8	72.6	5.5	107.8	5.0	222.6	6.3	411.4	6.9
Other	16.7	1.6	16.4	1.3	34.0	1.6	55.8	1.6	96.6	1.6
Total	1 045.4	100.0	1 313.4	100.0	2 151.3	100.0	3 510.3	100.0	5 921.1	100.0

1. Excluding social science research.
2. Estimated for years after 1972.
3. The percentages applying to the government sector have been calculated using the figures returned by the sectors carrying out the work and these percentages have been apportioned *pro rata* over those subdivisions of the government sector shown here.
4. Including research associations.

Source Department of Trade and Industry

11.6 Gross central government expenditure on research and development

£ million

	1979/80[1]		1980/81[1]		1981/82		1982/83	
	Intra-mural	Extra-mural	Intra-mural	Extra-mural	Intra-mural	Extra-mural	Intra-mural	Extra-mural
R & D in the natural sciences:								
Defence	398.8	963.9	447.4	1 256.6	557.7	1 275.0	642.8	1 152.3
Civil:								
Aerospace	0.3	165.4	–	158.5	0.5	200.4	0.6	173.7
Energy	206.1	30.7	256.6	43.4	317.4	54.7	335.0	48.4
Research councils	179.8	167.4	219.5	200.7	250.2	246.8	267.9	262.6
Universities	–	290.0	–	350.0	–	400.0	–	440.0
Other programmes	129.1	105.7	171.4	136.2	208.6	150.6	215.9	182.8
Total	914.1	1 723.2	1 094.8	2 145.3	1 334.4	2 327.5	1 462.1	2 259.7
Social science R & D	9.8	132.9	11.8	165.0	14.0	178.6	14.3	200.2
Total expenditure on R & D	923.8	1 856.0	1 106.7	2 310.3	1 348.4	2 506.1	1 476.3	2 459.9
	2 779.9		3 416.9		3 854.5		3 936.3	

1. Revised

Source Department of Trade and Industry

11.7 Net central government expenditure on research and development, using revised European Community objectives for R&D expenditure

£ million

	1981/82	1982/83	1983/84	1984/85	1985/86	1986/87
Exploration and exploitation of the earth	63.9	67.7	70.8	74.5	76.8	78.5
Infrastructure and general planning of land-use	59.6	61.1	57.6	67.1	68.4	70.4
Control of environmental pollution	42.4	49.0	42.4	54.7	59.9	62.8
Protection and promotion of human health	132.9	141.7	149.9	154.7	156.3	160.0
Production, distribution and rational utilization of energy	226.7	224.2	214.1	211.4	209.0	207.8
Agricultural production and technology	190.9	202.0	209.9	218.2	222.8	227.9
Industrial production and technology	224.4	218.1	284.0	375.7	399.2	407.0
Social structures and relationships	27.2	25.9	27.2	29.2	30.5	30.6
Exploration and exploitation of space	69.0	73.2	74.7	98.3	101.8	89.3
Research financed from General University Funds	540.0	600.0	620.0	640.0	660.0	670.0
Non-oriented research	194.0	210.6	216.6	223.4	230.3	233.6
Other civil research	53.1	58.0	67.3	78.6	81.6	83.7
Defence	1 739.4	1 758.2	1 965.3	..	..	..
Total	3 563.6	3 689.8	3 999.8	..	..	..

Source Department of Trade and Industry

11.8 Intra-mural expenditure on research and development at 1975 prices

£ million

	1964	1966	1967	1968	1969	1972	1975	1978	1981
Total, all sectors	2 200	2 302	2 327	2 325	2 325	2 242	2 151	2 365	2 603
Government performed	608	594	598	588	584	572	574	528	600
Industry performed	1 400	1 504	1 514	1 506	1 513	1 418	1 340	1 566	1 661
of which Total manufacturing	1 365	1 478	1 488	1 485	1 491	1 376	1 293	1 512	1 555
Chemical and allied industries	196	218	216	223	236	231	245	284	277
Mechanical engineering	115	155	154	148	133	94	103	118	124
Electronics	222	288	285	297	308	302	279	442	511
Other electrical engineering	82	93	92	91	85	68	73	69	53
Motor vehicles	100	120	113	106	112	97	88	88	80
Aerospace	390	331	356	354	351	366	292	285	337
Other manufacturing	260	274	272	265	266	219	213	226	173

Source Department of Trade and Industry

11.9 Expenditure on research and development in industry
Work performed within industry by sector and product group
1981

£ million

Product group	Research and development carried out within the following industrial sectors			
	Total industry	Private industry	Public corporations	Research associations
Total	3 792.5	3 319.5	384.8	88.1
Extractive industries	62.6	57.6	4.9	0.1
Mineral oil refining	9.4	9.4	–	–
Other treatment of petroleum products (excluding petrochemical manufacture)	27.8	27.6	–	0.2
Products of manufacturing industry				
Total	3 511.7	3 205.2	244.1	62.4
Metal manufacture				
Iron and steel	31.7	4.8	23.4	3.5
Non-ferrous metals	21.6	17.2	1.2	3.2
Non-metallic mineral products				
Bricks, cement, building materials, etc	12.9	12.3	–	0.6
Pottery, china and glass	20.2	18.7	–	1.4
Chemical industry: total	617.4	609.9	1.3	6.2
Synthetic resins and plastic materials	42.4	39.8	0.2	2.3
Paint	13.3	12.4	–	0.8
Pharmaceutical products	296.1	295.8	0.2	0.1
Other chemical products	265.7	261.9	1.0	2.8
Metal goods	22.7	19.2	2.9	0.6
Mechanical engineering: total	234.0	198.0	28.2	7.8
Industrial plant and steelwork	15.0	12.3	0.8	1.9
Metal-working machine tools	13.0	11.2	–	1.9
Construction and earth moving equipment, etc	34.2	19.2	13.5	1.6
Other machinery and equipment	171.8	155.4	13.9	2.5
Office machinery	41.9	41.9	–	–
Electronic data processing equipment	160.8	159.5	0.5	0.8
Electrical and electronic engineering: total	1 181.1	1 008.7	168.1	4.3
Insulated wires and cables	16.3	15.9	–	0.5
Basic electrical equipment	55.6	55.0	0.2	0.4
Telegraph and telephone apparatus	279.9	127.3	152.1	0.4
Electrical instruments and control systems	67.9	61.0	6.5	0.4
Radio and electronic capital goods	610.4	600.7	8.9	0.8
Components other than active components	26.3	25.9	–	0.4
Active components and electronic sub-assemblies	55.2	54.7	–	0.4
Electronic consumer goods	20.8	20.1	0.3	0.4
Other electrical goods	48.8	48.1	0.2	0.4
Motor vehicles and parts	180.4	171.9	4.8	3.7
Shipbuilding and repairs	9.5	4.9	0.2	4.3
Aerospace equipment manufacturing and repairing	762.9	758.4	0.2	4.3
Instrument engineering	32.7	19.6	10.5	2.6
Food, drink and tobacco	91.5	84.8	0.2	6.6
Textiles, other than man-made fibres	9.7	6.9	–	2.8
Leather, footwear and clothing	4.7	2.5	–	2.2
Timber and wooden furniture	3.6	1.0	–	2.6
Paper and paper products: printing and publishing	18.3	16.2	–	2.2
Processing of rubber and plastics	30.0	27.9	–	2.1
Other manufactured products	24.1	20.9	2.5	0.6
Construction[1]	15.3	6.5	0.1	8.7
Utilities and services[2]	165.6	13.2	135.7	16.8

1. The figures for this product group do not include the sums for the appreciable development work undertaken in civil engineering.
2. Gas, electricity, water, railway, road, sea and air transport systems, industrial health and safety, etc.

Source Department of Trade and Industry

12 External Trade

The tables covering external trade have been compiled from information published in the *Annual Statement of Overseas Trade of the United Kingdom* (discontinued after 1975) and from the annual and monthly *Overseas Trade Statistics of the United Kingdom* from 1976. United Kingdom is defined as Great Britain, Northern Ireland, the Isle of Man, the Channel Islands and the Continental Shelf (United Kingdom part). The grouping of the commodities, previously shown in the sections and divisions of the Standard International Trade Classification (Revised), is currently based on those of the SITC (Revision 2) or SITC (R2) which was introduced into the *Overseas Trade Statistics* from January 1978. The statistics in Table 12.1 are on a balance of payments basis; all other statistics in this section are on an *Overseas Trade Statistics* basis. For more detailed figures, notes and definitions relating to external trade, reference should be made to these volumes and also to the annual publication *United Kingdom Balance of Payments* (the Pink Book) and *Supplement of Definitions and Explanatory Notes* to the *Monthly Digest of Statistics*.

Changes in the coverage of the overseas trade statistics are made from time to time but as far as possible figures in these tables have been adjusted to the current basis. For further data on unit value indices and volume indices reference should be made to the *Monthly Review of External Trade Statistics*.

The value of UK trade with selected areas, analysed by commodity divisions, is obtainable from the annual edition of the *Overseas Trade Statistics of the United Kingdom*.

Import penetration and export sales ratios *(Table 12.2)*

The ratios were first introduced in the August 1977 edition of *Economic Trends* in an article 'The Home and Export Performance of United Kingdom Industries' . The article described the conceptual and methodological problems involved in measuring such variables as import penetration. The industries are currently grouped according to the 1980 Standard Industrial Classification. The latest ratios for the full detail within manufacturing (over 200 activity headings) are shown in Business Monitor MQ12, '*Import Penetration and Export Sales Ratios for Manufacturing Industry*'.

12.1 Visible trade of the United Kingdom
On a balance of payments basis[1]

	1973	1974	1975	1976	1977	1978	1979	1980	1981	1982	1983
Value (£ million)											
Exports (fob)	11 937	16 395	19 330	25 191	31 728	35 063	40 686	47 422	50 977	55 565	60 625
Imports (fob)	14 523	21 745	22 663	29 121	34 012	36 605	44 135	45 909	47 325	53 181	61 341
Visible balance	− 2 586	− 5 351	− 3 333	− 3 930	− 2 284	− 1 542	− 3 449	+ 1 513	+ 3 652	+ 2 384	− 716
Unit value index numbers											
1980 = 100											
Exports (fob)	32.6	41.5	50.9	60.8	72.0	79.1	87.6	100.0	108.8	116.7	126.6
Imports (fob)	34.8	50.9	58.0	70.9	82.1	85.2	90.9	100.0	108.1	117.9	129.1
Terms of trade[2]	93.5	81.5	87.6	85.7	87.7	92.7	96.4	100.0	100.7	99.0	98.0
Volume index numbers											
1980 = 100											
Exports	75.6	81.0	77.8	85.4	92.1	94.5	99.1	100.0	99.2	101.5	102.3
Imports	91.9	92.7	84.7	89.7	91.3	95.5	105.7	100.0	96.1	100.7	107.6

1. Statistics of visible trade on a balance of payments basis are obtained by making certain adjustments in respect of valuation and coverage to the statistics recorded in the *Overseas Trade Statistics*. These adjustments are described in detail in *United Kingdom Balance of Payments 1984 Edition* (HMSO).
2. Export unit value index as a percentage of the import unit value index.

Source Department of Trade and Industry

12.2 Import penetration and export sales ratios for products of manufacturing industry

	1980 SIC Class	1975	1976	1977	1978	1979	1980	1981	1982	1983
Ratio 1 Imports/Home demand										
Div 2–4 Manufacturing industries	21–49	22.8	24.4	25.1	26.0	26.9	26.2	27.8	29.2	31.4
Class:										
Metals	21–22	32	33	32	31	32	33	30	34	36
Other minerals and mineral products	23–24	11	12	12	12	13	12	12	11	13
Chemicals and man-made fibres	25–26	23	25	27	28	30	29	31	34	33
Metal goods n.e.s.	31	8	9	9	10	10	11	11	12	13
Mechanical engineering	32	26	31	30	32	29	29	32	32	33
Office machinery and data processing equipment	33	71	79	84	92	92	96	96	107	109
Electrical and electronic engineering	34	25	28	30	31	31	31	36	40	43
Motor vehicles and their parts	35	26	29	35	35	41	39	42	46	51
Other transport equipment	36	49	37	45	41	38	38	41	39	42
Instrument engineering	37	47	49	51	52	53	52	58	56	56
Food, drink and tobacco	41–42	18	17	17	18	18	16	16	16	17
Textile industry	43	23	26	27	31	33	34	39	39	41
Leather and leather goods	44	27	30	32	34	40	40	42	42	44
Clothing and footwear	45	21	25	25	26	29	29	33	33	34
Timber and wooden furniture	46	24	29	28	27	29	27	29	28	31
Paper, printing and publishing	47	20	21	21	19	19	19	20	20	20
Rubber and plastics processing	48	14	16	17	18	18	18	21	22	24
Other manufacturing industries	49	27	31	34	35	36	41	48	46	49
Ratio 2 Imports/Home demand and Exports										
Div 2–4 Manufacturing industries	21–49	18.4	19.6	19.9	20.6	21.6	20.7	21.8	23.0	25.0
Class:										
Metals	21–22	27	28	27	26	27	29	26	28	30
Other minerals and mineral products	23–24	10	10	10	10	11	10	10	10	11
Chemicals and man-made fibres	25–26	17	18	19	20	21	20	22	23	25
Metal goods n.e.s.	31	7	8	8	9	9	10	10	11	12
Mechanical engineering	32	16	19	19	21	19	19	20	20	22
Office machinery and data processing equipment	33	44	50	51	54	53	52	57	62	63
Electrical and electronic engineering	34	19	20	21	22	23	23	27	29	32
Motor vehicles and their parts	35	17	19	23	25	31	28	30	35	40
Other transport equipment	36	33	26	30	27	26	26	25	24	25
Instrument engineering	37	31	33	34	35	35	33	36	36	38
Food, drink and tobacco	41–42	17	16	16	16	16	14	15	15	16
Textile industry	43	19	21	21	25	26	26	30	31	34
Leather and leather goods	44	22	24	25	27	32	31	34	33	34
Clothing and footwear	45	19	22	21	22	25	25	28	29	29
Timber and wooden furniture	46	23	28	26	26	27	26	27	27	30
Paper, printing and publishing	47	18	19	19	17	18	17	18	18	19
Rubber and plastics processing	48	12	13	14	14	15	14	17	18	20
Other manufacturing industries	49	20	23	25	25	27	31	36	35	37

1. Certain sectors are excluded since they are inappropriate for this analysis.
   They are the following activity headings: 2396 (pt) unworked precious stones,
   2436 ready-mixed concrete, 3138 heat and surface treatment of metals, 3246
   process engineering contractors, 3480 electrical equipment installation, 4121
   slaughterhouses, 4370 textile finishing, 4560 fur goods, 4672 shop and office
   fitting, 4820 retreading and specialist repairing of rubber tyres, 4910 jewellery
   and coins, 4930 photographic and cinematographic processing laboratories.

Source Department of Trade and Industry

12.2

Import penetration and export sales ratios for products of manufacturing industry

(*continued*)

	1980 SIC Class	1975	1976	1977	1978	1979	1980	1981	1982	1983
Ratio 3 Exports/Manufacturers' sales										
Div 2–4 Manufacturing industries	21–49	23.6	24.7	25.7	26.1	25.1	26.5	27.3	27.4	27.0
Class:										
Metals	21–22	21	21	22	22	23	21	23	24	25
Other minerals and mineral products	23–24	14	15	17	16	15	16	15	13	12
Chemicals and man-made fibres	25–26	32	33	35	36	36	38	39	40	42
Metal goods n.e.s.	31	12	13	14	13	12	14	14	14	12
Mechanical engineering	32	43	46	44	44	42	45	47	46	41
Office machinery and data processing equipment	33	69	74	80	90	90	96	94	111	114
Electrical and electronic engineering	34	33	36	37	37	33	34	36	38	38
Motor vehicles and their parts	35	43	41	42	38	36	38	41	38	37
Other transport equipment	36	49	42	47	45	43	42	50	52	55
Instrument engineering	37	48	48	50	51	53	55	59	57	52
Food, drink and tobacco	41–42	8	8	9	11	10	10	10	11	11
Textile industry	43	22	25	27	27	27	30	30	29	28
Leather and leather goods	44	25	27	27	26	29	32	30	33	33
Clothing and footwear	45	11	15	19	18	18	19	20	18	18
Timber and wooden furniture	46	5	6	7	7	6	7	6	6	5
Paper, printing and publishing	47	9	10	11	11	10	10	10	10	10
Rubber and plastics processing	48	21	22	22	21	20	23	24	23	22
Other manufacturing industries	49	32	35	37	38	36	36	38	36	37
Ratio 4 Exports/Manufacturers' sales and Imports										
Div 2–4 Manufacturing industries	21–49	19.2	19.9	20.6	20.7	19.7	21.0	21.4	21.1	20.2
Class:										
Metals	21–22	16	15	16	16	17	15	17	17	18
Other minerals and mineral products	23–24	13	14	15	15	14	14	13	11	11
Chemicals and man-made fibres	25–26	27	27	29	29	28	31	31	31	32
Metal goods n.e.s.	31	11	12	13	12	11	13	12	12	11
Mechanical engineering	32	36	37	36	35	33	36	38	36	32
Office machinery and data processing equipment	33	39	38	39	42	42	45	40	43	42
Electrical and electronic engineering	34	27	29	29	28	26	27	27	27	26
Motor vehicles and their parts	35	36	33	32	28	25	28	29	25	22
Other transport equipment	36	33	31	33	33	32	31	38	40	41
Instrument engineering	37	33	33	33	33	34	37	38	37	32
Food, drink and tobacco	41–42	7	7	7	9	9	9	9	9	9
Textile industry	43	18	20	21	20	20	22	21	20	19
Leather and leather goods	44	20	21	20	19	20	22	20	22	22
Clothing and footwear	45	9	12	15	14	14	14	14	13	13
Timber and wooden furniture	46	4	4	5	5	4	5	4	5	4
Paper, printing and publishing	47	7	8	9	9	8	9	8	8	8
Rubber and plastics processing	48	18	19	19	18	17	19	20	18	18
Other manufacturing industries	49	26	27	28	28	26	25	25	23	23

1. Certain sectors are excluded since they are inappropriate for this analysis. They are the following activity headings: 2396 (pt) unworked precious stones, 2436 ready-mixed concrete, 3138 heat and surface treatment of metals, 3246 process engineering contractors, 3480 electrical equipment installation, 4121 slaughterhouses, 4370 textile finishing, 4560 fur goods, 4672 shop and office fitting, 4820 retreading and specialist repairing of rubber tyres, 4910 jewellery and coins, 4930 photographic and cinematographic processing laboratories.

Source Department of Trade and Industry

12.3 Value of United Kingdom exports (fob)[1]
Analysis by sections and divisions

£ million

	1973	1974	1975	1976	1977	1978	1979	1980	1981	1982	1983
Total UK exports	12 087.0	16 309.2	19 606.9	25 276.6	31 990.1	35 380.3	40 637.0	47 357.1	50 998.1	55 557.8	60 533.7
0. Food and live animals chiefly for food	512.1	610.4	884.1	1 034.2	1 417.5	1 827.2	1 745.2	2 050.8	2 338.5	2 508.3	2 748.6
00. Live animals chiefly for food	58.8	45.4	53.4	62.4	109.3	130.7	170.9	139.9	175.6	179.1	187.4
01. Meat and meat preparations	79.9	80.0	139.9	182.0	250.3	282.3	275.4	327.2	328.9	347.5	496.2
02. Dairy products and birds' eggs	44.4	41.1	51.7	115.0	98.0	221.8	226.2	298.4	307.2	325.6	305.9
03. Fish, crustaceans and molluscs, and preparations thereof	43.1	51.7	57.8	81.2	107.3	144.0	146.3	145.6	150.2	162.3	203.6
04. Cereals and cereal preparations	54.5	76.7	169.1	134.3	210.7	364.8	264.4	455.7	697.8	773.9	736.7
05. Vegetables and fruit	43.3	52.7	67.4	84.1	110.3	132.8	148.5	152.5	152.2	154.0	163.2
06. Sugar, sugar preparations and honey	61.5	94.8	162.0	128.7	111.9	106.9	103.6	112.2	116.4	121.1	144.9
07. Coffee, tea, cocoa, spices, and manufactures thereof	61.4	91.7	101.0	142.2	278.5	292.9	268.2	261.1	245.2	252.2	291.3
08. Feeding stuff for animals (not including unmilled cereals)	29.6	29.0	32.2	45.1	60.4	58.4	56.9	63.6	60.9	69.0	78.7
09. Miscellaneous edible products and preparations	35.5	47.3	49.6	59.1	80.9	92.7	85.0	94.6	104.0	123.8	140.7
1. Beverages and tobacco	363.5	452.9	543.5	658.3	798.9	1 084.3	1 195.3	1 205.9	1 311.7	1 451.5	1 486.2
11. Beverages	305.4	384.0	437.1	524.5	629.2	805.1	854.3	897.9	951.6	1 060.1	1 051.2
12. Tobacco and tobacco manufactures	58.1	68.9	106.3	133.8	169.7	279.1	341.0	308.0	360.1	391.4	435.0
2. Crude materials, inedible, except fuels	379.8	521.0	503.1	728.6	845.0	940.8	1 215.3	1 378.5	1 247.6	1 293.7	1 527.3
21. Hides, skins and furskins, raw	80.7	91.6	102.3	157.8	160.8	161.0	221.5	189.9	173.9	180.5	200.2
22. Oil seeds and oleaginous fruit	3.2	4.0	2.4	3.6	5.0	5.7	3.1	2.9	4.5	7.9	37.8
23. Crude rubber (including synthetic and reclaimed)	37.9	53.6	41.8	61.5	76.6	69.9	79.2	75.6	108.1	122.8	141.7
24. Cork and wood	4.4	6.2	5.6	8.7	12.3	11.2	13.5	16.0	27.2	28.6	24.1
25. Pulp and waste paper	3.6	11.7	8.6	9.2	8.5	7.7	13.8	22.8	13.9	11.6	15.8
26. Textile fibres (other than wool tops) and their wastes (not manufactured into yarn or fabric)	134.0	175.6	156.0	225.9	268.6	282.2	315.7	312.9	298.3	314.2	374.7
27. Crude fertilisers and crude minerals (excluding coal, petroleum and precious stones)	60.2	79.5	80.0	107.0	128.7	139.2	217.7	235.3	227.0	224.2	223.9
28. Metalliferous ores and metal scrap	37.6	74.8	83.8	123.1	145.8	222.4	307.0	474.4	347.8	346.6	444.2
29. Crude animal and vegetable materials	18.3	23.9	22.7	31.8	38.9	41.6	43.8	48.6	46.9	57.3	64.9
3. Mineral fuels, lubricants and related materials	374.0	781.6	826.6	1 264.7	2 092.0	2 374.6	4 323.6	6 428.8	9 616.5	11 237.1	13 126.5
33. Petroleum, petroleum products and related materials	344.5	710.6	733.9	1 171.6	1 979.0	2 235.0	4 157.5	6 133.2	9 107.5	10 685.7	12 525.0
32, 34 and 35. Coal, coke, gas and electric current	29.5	71.1	92.8	93.0	113.0	139.6	166.0	295.6	508.9	551.4	601.6
4. Animal and vegetable oils, fats and waxes	17.1	31.5	27.0	36.2	57.1	56.6	65.7	71.0	65.1	46.5	59.1
5. Chemicals and related products	1 256.6	2 113.0	2 144.6	3 006.8	3 817.1	4 198.9	4 910.9	5 286.2	5 550.1	6 119.3	6 929.3
51. Organic chemicals	249.1	549.9	453.9	704.2	830.8	913.3	1 237.3	1 297.6	1 496.3	1 592.3	1 927.3
52. Inorganic chemicals	113.7	177.6	197.3	337.8	523.1	560.9	681.8	619.9	586.5	694.9	699.8
53. Dyeing, tanning and colouring materials	140.5	213.8	201.4	282.1	351.8	347.7	392.0	432.5	433.6	464.1	568.7
54. Medicinal and pharmaceutical products	221.2	301.2	373.0	451.9	554.5	654.1	638.8	744.8	851.9	978.0	1 074.2
55. Essential oils and perfume materials; toilet, polishing and cleansing materials	96.8	145.5	169.3	235.7	325.6	382.2	408.2	464.7	483.3	525.1	574.3
56. Fertilisers, manufactured	14.8	46.4	53.4	51.1	60.6	57.9	58.2	52.3	62.3	48.8	69.7
57. Explosives and pyrotechnic products	9.2	15.8	18.1	21.2	27.0	31.1	31.1	36.6	39.4	36.8	40.1
58. Artificial resins and plastic materials, and cellulose esters and ethers	218.2	356.8	344.2	516.7	618.3	648.3	777.0	874.4	810.7	875.3	980.1
59. Chemical materials and products, not elsewhere specified	193.1	305.9	334.0	406.0	525.4	603.5	686.4	763.4	786.2	904.1	995.0

Note: The statistics are on an overseas trade statistics basis (see footnote 1 to Table 12.1).

1. The numbers of the left hand side of the table refer to the Section and Division code numbers of the *Standard International Trade Classification (Revision 2).*

Source Department of Trade and Industry

12.3

Value of United Kingdom exports (fob)[1]
Analysis by sections and divisions

(*continued*)

£ million

	1973	1974	1975	1976	1977	1978	1979	1980	1981	1982	1983
6. Manufactured goods classified chiefly by material	2 859.5	3 609.5	3 852.0	5 132.8	6 416.3	6 840.4	7 761.7	8 754.0	7 719.3	7 940.5	8 862.2
61. Leather, leather manufactures, nes, and dressed furskins	83.8	94.4	98.8	148.3	176.7	187.9	223.6	212.2	207.2	202.1	232.9
62. Rubber manufactures, nes	121.2	166.5	221.0	299.6	328.7	340.2	363.4	447.1	464.6	417.9	451.8
63. Cork and wood manufactures (excluding furniture)	15.5	25.3	28.5	53.3	72.7	76.6	76.0	84.4	86.4	83.2	85.2
64. Paper, paperboard, and articles of paper pulp, of paper or of paperboard	128.8	199.2	205.8	278.2	354.6	390.6	435.6	475.0	461.5	503.1	543.1
65. Textile yarn, fabrics, made-up articles, nes, and related products	629.3	773.7	729.2	972.0	1 193.4	1 237.8	1 339.4	1 363.0	1 202.7	1 192.0	1 284.6
66. Non-metallic mineral manufactures, nes	567.4	632.2	720.0	1 018.9	1 412.9	1 494.7	1 713.7	2 110.2	1 538.2	1 609.9	1 995.0
67. Iron and steel	433.2	552.5	681.9	823.8	1 016.9	1 105.8	1 277.6	983.4	1 239.4	1 291.8	1 330.9
68. Non-ferrous metals	534.8	677.4	525.7	711.0	816.3	834.7	1 140.4	1 770.6	1 244.1	1 244.7	1 614.5
69. Manufactures of metal, nes	345.5	488.3	641.1	827.7	1 044.1	1 172.0	1 192.1	1 308.0	1 275.2	1 395.6	1 324.0
7. Machinery and transport equipment	4 853.1	6 149.2	8 298.0	10 178.8	12 456.2	13 407.5	14 235.5	16 267.3	16 784.1	18 100.9	18 313.7
71. Power generating machinery and equipment	637.5	769.2	1 110.1	1 307.4	1 525.8	1 769.0	1 789.2	2 230.8	2 642.2	2 809.1	2 472.5
72. Machinery specialised for particular industries	844.5	1 101.6	1 533.3	1 818.8	2 036.2	2 169.4	2 312.7	2 573.6	2 557.9	2 601.3	2 336.3
73. Metalworking machinery	143.2	176.4	264.4	291.1	325.1	385.7	383.9	486.4	510.8	522.4	416.2
74. General industrial machinery and equipment, nes, and machine parts, nes	595.0	793.3	1 110.8	1 327.4	1 641.1	1 837.6	1 960.3	2 316.8	2 305.7	2 411.8	2 333.2
75. Office machines and automatic data processing equipment	362.8	440.2	515.3	618.8	760.0	918.6	1 163.7	1 345.5	1 291.8	1 599.5	2 049.2
76. Telecommunications, sound recording and reproducing apparatus and equipment	237.7	321.7	427.6	627.0	712.0	742.1	734.4	712.5	820.5	897.2	991.7
77. Electrical machinery, apparatus and appliances, nes, and electrical parts thereof (including non-electrical counterparts, nes, of electrical household type equipment)	449.0	653.5	820.5	1 003.0	1 331.9	1 398.6	1 457.4	1 798.6	1 758.7	2 117.0	2 289.5
78. Road vehicles (including air cushion vehicles)	1 168.7	1 397.6	1 854.0	2 376.9	2 871.9	3 070.3	3 148.1	3 158.0	3 170.5	3 109.0	3 084.1
79. Other transport equipment	414.7	495.8	661.9	808.6	1 252.1	1 116.2	1 285.8	1 645.1	1 726.2	2 033.5	2 341.1
8. Miscellaneous manufactured articles	1 098.2	1 434.8	1 768.5	2 382.3	3 134.0	3 581.8	3 961.4	4 503.7	4 844.6	5 151.8	5 814.1
81. Sanitary, plumbing, heating and lighting fixtures and fittings, nes	26.0	38.6	51.0	55.6	82.5	93.7	89.9	109.0	113.0	107.0	108.3
82. Furniture and parts thereof	44.2	69.4	98.4	142.3	210.8	234.6	231.2	239.2	222.1	240.9	257.8
83. Travel goods, handbags and similar containers	4.6	5.8	6.9	9.6	13.1	14.4	16.7	19.5	20.1	19.1	19.3
84. Articles of apparel and clothing accessories	178.9	228.3	266.3	412.5	598.8	669.6	751.2	807.5	846.6	840.0	865.4
85. Footwear	35.6	47.2	52.9	68.2	102.4	98.1	113.3	130.4	121.2	114.9	123.4
87. Professional, scientific and controlling instruments and apparatus, nes	220.2	278.9	370.6	475.6	589.1	691.0	785.3	948.3	1 107.5	1 255.4	1 472.4
88. Photographic apparatus, equipment and supplies and optical goods, nes, watches and clocks	133.7	177.8	219.0	273.5	335.8	409.7	437.0	519.5	504.6	551.9	573.6
89. Miscellaneous manufactured articles, nes	455.0	588.7	703.3	945.0	1 201.6	1 370.7	1 536.9	1 730.4	1 909.4	2 022.7	2 393.8
5 – 8. Manufactured goods	10 067.3	13 306.4	16 063.0	20 700.7	25 823.6	28 028.6	30 869.5	34 811.2	34 898.0	37 312.6	39 919.1
9. Commodities and transactions not classified elsewhere	373.3	605.3	759.5	853.9	956.0	1 068.3	1 222.4	1 411.0	1 520.7	1 708.2	1 666.9

Note: The statistics are on an overseas trade statistics basis (see footnote 1 to Table 12.1).

1. The numbers on the left hand side of the table refer to the Section and Division code numbers of the *Standard International Trade Classification (Revision 2)*.

Source Department of Trade and Industry

12.4 Value of United Kingdom imports (cif)[1]
Analysis by sections and divisions

£ million

	1973	1974	1975	1976	1977	1978	1979	1980	1981	1982	1983
Total UK imports	15 723.6	23 138.9	24 046.4	31 084.1	36 219.1	39 533.0	46 924.9	49 772.9	51 168.6	56 978.2	65 993.1
0. Food and live animals chiefly for food	2 710.3	3 355.6	3 920.7	4 495.4	5 375.1	5 327.9	5 688.5	5 477.8	5 785.2	6 414.1	6 891.3
00. Live animals chiefly for food	80.2	76.9	108.0	84.0	98.5	136.9	88.3	102.1	109.5	133.1	170.3
01. Meat and meat preparations	715.8	681.3	701.9	838.5	974.3	1 139.0	1 258.0	1 225.5	1 260.0	1 370.9	1 313.5
02. Dairy products and birds' eggs	225.1	332.8	522.6	504.6	460.3	510.0	534.4	493.7	592.2	567.9	629.2
03. Fish, crustaceans and molluscs, and preparations thereof	132.1	122.0	136.5	191.2	210.0	260.6	323.7	348.8	403.5	404.2	505.6
04. Cereals and cereal preparations	369.8	590.9	612.0	747.5	820.4	674.6	668.4	603.2	565.9	549.9	595.3
05. Vegetables and fruit	561.3	655.0	690.8	941.5	1 107.9	1 041.3	1 174.6	1 238.9	1 389.4	1 608.3	1 718.9
06. Sugar, sugar preparations and honey	174.6	367.0	631.6	428.8	427.5	450.7	402.4	391.7	393.8	429.5	424.4
07. Coffee, tea, cocoa, spices and manufactures thereof	248.8	322.4	322.0	493.9	923.4	758.5	790.8	676.6	579.5	722.4	800.0
08. Feeding stuff for animals (not including unmilled cereals)	153.6	127.0	110.5	172.8	209.8	212.3	276.8	248.9	328.7	446.6	523.6
09. Miscellaneous edible products and preparations	49.0	80.3	84.7	92.8	143.1	143.9	171.3	148.4	162.8	181.1	210.4
1. Beverages and tobacco	383.5	406.8	414.1	487.9	561.9	813.4	828.4	674.8	752.1	836.7	962.1
11. Beverages	229.8	221.3	222.1	251.3	305.7	359.4	477.5	439.8	482.7	517.5	617.3
12. Tobacco and tobacco manufactures	153.7	185.4	192.0	236.6	256.1	454.0	350.9	235.0	269.5	319.2	344.7
2. Crude materials, inedible, except fuels	1 861.5	2 373.7	2 081.8	3 192.1	3 538.7	3 316.2	3 865.3	3 788.5	3 736.8	3 612.9	4 364.5
21. Hides, skins and furskins, raw	112.5	106.3	106.7	171.6	210.4	196.0	224.6	227.6	192.5	189.5	184.9
22. Oil seeds and oleaginous fruit	104.0	141.9	127.7	205.6	298.6	253.8	260.4	264.8	305.3	259.6	216.9
23. Crude rubber (including synthetic and reclaimed)	74.8	100.3	92.8	140.5	166.5	160.8	185.2	182.8	171.5	182.9	197.4
24. Cork and wood	458.3	587.2	362.3	585.2	632.6	599.6	743.0	683.1	603.7	673.8	938.0
25. Pulp and waste paper	201.0	329.8	357.8	463.3	439.6	348.7	388.8	398.7	438.5	412.0	428.0
26. Textile fibres (other than wool tops) and their wastes (not manufactured into yarn or fabric)	316.8	305.4	258.6	434.7	461.3	480.0	475.5	376.1	376.0	410.8	475.6
27. Crude fertilisers and crude minerals (excluding coal, petroleum and precious stones)	80.9	140.1	155.7	195.3	207.6	197.3	312.3	302.8	255.9	263.5	285.7
28. Metalliferous ores and metal scrap	422.2	552.8	515.6	861.4	964.1	905.7	1 077.5	1 168.6	1 185.0	977.5	1 358.1
29. Crude animal and vegetable materials	91.0	109.9	104.6	134.4	158.1	174.4	198.0	183.9	208.4	243.3	279.9
3. Mineral fuels, lubricants and related materials	1 732.9	4 643.9	4 316.3	5 668.7	5 254.8	4 805.2	5 782.2	6 875.4	7 166.4	7 408.6	7 067.1
33. Petroleum, petroleum products and related materials	1 687.5	4 550.4	4 175.2	5 535.4	5 088.7	4 503.7	5 228.2	6 072.7	6 235.6	6 276.9	5 738.0
32, 34 and 35. Coal, coke, gas and electric current	45.4	93.6	141.1	133.3	166.1	301.6	554.0	802.7	930.8	1 131.6	1 329.0
4. Animal and vegetable oils, fats and waxes	129.4	216.2	164.7	200.8	281.3	278.4	314.6	260.9	263.3	317.0	358.8
5. Chemicals and related products	861.6	1 523.0	1 349.6	1 924.3	2 360.9	2 756.7	3 402.2	3 146.9	3 596.6	4 179.1	5 119.5
51. Organic chemicals	238.3	508.4	402.0	576.8	701.1	791.0	1 020.1	897.4	1 062.4	1 171.9	1 456.3
52. Inorganic chemicals	102.3	175.9	234.0	258.9	328.8	431.6	452.7	432.9	454.4	539.3	561.3
53. Dyeing, tanning and colouring materials	60.3	78.2	62.2	104.7	125.6	148.0	167.9	145.7	170.7	198.0	235.1
54. Medicinal and pharmaceutical products	67.0	92.3	97.0	139.1	173.6	201.1	229.3	222.6	298.3	374.6	470.1
55. Essential oils and perfume materials; toilet, polishing and cleansing materials	51.5	76.2	68.7	97.0	125.9	139.5	177.1	174.7	203.6	242.2	305.3
56. Fertilisers, manufactured	35.1	57.0	55.1	60.5	69.5	75.9	96.6	89.9	104.9	127.1	172.5
57. Explosives and pyrotechnic products	1.4	3.6	4.3	7.3	6.6	5.6	6.9	7.5	7.7	10.9	14.1
58. Artificial resins and plastic materials, and cellulose esters and ethers	199.6	352.6	256.8	453.2	544.1	630.1	828.1	763.2	862.9	1 017.7	1 323.4
59. Chemical materials and products, not elsewhere specified	106.1	178.9	169.5	226.6	285.8	333.8	423.5	413.1	431.7	497.4	581.3

1. See *Note* and footnote on page 236.

Source Department of Trade and Industry

12.4
Value of United Kingdom imports (cif)[1]
Analysis by sections and divisions
(*continued*)

£ million

	1973	1974	1975	1976	1977	1978	1979	1980	1981	1982	1983
6. Manufactured goods classified chiefly by material	3 170.9	4 568.4	4 486.8	5 696.6	6 860.9	7 652.8	9 291.9	10 333.8	8 936.3	9 852.5	11 840.1
61. Leather, leather manufactures, nes, and dressed furskins	67.4	60.6	68.9	107.5	134.2	133.0	196.8	137.1	140.7	154.6	184.0
62. Rubber manufactures, nes	57.1	87.7	97.2	130.5	201.9	215.2	259.2	263.5	281.0	326.2	419.6
63. Cork and wood manufactures (excluding furniture)	244.3	232.2	217.5	290.1	310.9	382.7	464.9	368.9	443.0	436.3	578.8
64. Paper, paperboard, and articles of paper pulp, of paper or of paperboard	401.9	725.1	621.8	826.1	971.8	1 054.9	1 240.3	1 286.7	1 536.9	1 675.1	1 906.3
65. Textile yarn, fabrics, made-up articles, nes, and related products	523.0	695.3	690.2	920.1	1 129.7	1 453.9	1 691.1	1 543.7	1 761.6	1 927.6	2 320.1
66. Non-metallic mineral manufactures, nes	630.4	739.9	799.4	984.7	1 463.1	1 569.5	1 889.4	1 938.0	1 443.4	1 520.3	2 085.5
67. Iron and steel	373.3	716.3	826.4	967.5	984.9	1 056.4	1 215.2	1 448.0	1 089.5	1 367.3	1 260.7
68. Non-ferrous metals	658.2	1 002.0	808.9	1 026.5	1 131.1	1 144.0	1 564.4	2 487.4	1 425.3	1 495.7	1 976.3
69. Manufactures of metal, nes	215.3	309.3	356.5	443.6	533.4	643.2	770.7	860.5	815.1	949.5	1 108.9
7. Machinery and transport equipment	3 374.1	3 993.5	4 905.4	6 486.3	8 466.1	10 198.8	12 226.4	12 565.6	13 399.2	16 464.2	20 230.7
71. Power generating machinery and equipment	288.6	382.0	455.2	571.9	694.5	811.2	853.6	961.1	1 272.8	1 482.7	1 569.2
72. Machinery specialised for particular industries	431.3	539.8	563.0	742.3	880.8	1 083.0	1 271.1	1 205.2	1 183.3	1 485.9	1 731.8
73. Metalworking machinery	101.6	148.0	195.3	215.7	223.2	320.6	412.8	408.4	346.4	380.6	342.4
74. General industrial machinery and equipment, nes, and machine parts, nes	394.6	525.1	670.5	803.3	990.7	1 186.7	1 351.6	1 414.7	1 394.9	1 634.4	1 845.6
75. Office machines and automatic data processing equipment	383.8	496.8	542.7	749.9	911.9	1 103.0	1 330.4	1 393.4	1 631.7	2 121.9	3 019.9
76. Telecommunications and sound recording and reproducing apparatus and equipment	355.9	341.6	333.0	442.5	544.0	617.3	796.5	823.6	1 291.4	1 586.2	1 916.4
77. Electrical machinery, apparatus and appliances, nes, and electrical parts thereof (including non-electrical counterparts, nes, of electrical household type equipment)	458.6	568.3	578.2	779.2	1 049.6	1 210.6	1 410.5	1 518.5	1 759.6	2 179.1	2 807.3
78. Road vehicles (including air cushion vehicles)	668.1	668.7	909.8	1 431.6	2 133.5	2 796.9	3 943.2	3 351.6	3 408.1	4 489.6	5 753.7
79. Other transport equipment	291.5	323.2	657.7	749.9	1 037.8	1 069.7	856.6	1 488.9	1 111.1	1 103.8	1 244.4
8. Miscellaneous manufactured articles	1 291.1	1 608.3	1 863.9	2 470.5	3 014.7	3 813.2	4 768.1	5 130.7	6 061.1	6 618.4	7 714.7
81. Sanitary, plumbing, heating and lighting fixtures and fittings, nes	22.7	25.6	25.5	29.2	37.6	54.9	81.1	78.1	81.8	103.5	126.7
82. Furniture and parts thereof	62.9	70.0	92.0	122.5	139.3	194.5	253.8	283.2	349.2	400.1	490.5
83. Travel goods, handbags and similar containers	14.9	19.2	25.5	37.8	45.0	65.1	92.3	94.9	117.7	108.6	131.1
84. Articles of apparel and clothing accessories	332.8	402.2	505.7	684.1	767.2	920.5	1 194.1	1 230.7	1 438.4	1 500.0	1 601.5
85. Footwear	84.3	109.1	123.3	165.5	214.3	252.2	352.5	354.0	415.6	468.3	542.0
87. Professional, scientific and controlling instruments and apparatus, nes	160.9	218.8	274.0	352.6	418.4	555.4	634.4	743.5	865.6	1 052.1	1 303.7
88. Photographic apparatus, equipment and supplies and optical goods, nes, watches and clocks	152.2	196.2	246.7	329.2	421.2	538.3	608.9	655.0	749.0	761.0	862.3
89. Miscellaneous manufactured articles, nes	460.4	567.2	571.3	749.6	971.7	1 232.3	1 551.0	1 691.3	2 043.8	2 224.9	2 657.0
5–8. Manufactured goods	8 697.7	11 693.2	12 605.7	16 577.7	20 702.5	24 421.4	29 688.7	31 177.0	31 993.2	37 114.2	44 905.0
9. Commodities and transactions not classified elsewhere	208.2	449.4	543.2	461.5	504.8	570.4	757.2	1 518.5	1 471.6	1 274.8	1 444.3

Note The statistics are on an overseas trade statistics basis (see footnote 1 to Table 12.1).

1. The numbers on the left hand side of the table refer to the Section and Division code numbers of the *Standard International Trade Classification (Revision 2)*.

Source Department of Trade and Industry

12.5 Value of United Kingdom exports (fob)
Analysis by destination

£ million

	1973	1974	1975	1976	1977	1978	1979	1980	1981	1982	1983
Total trade	12 087.0	16 309.2	19 606.9	25 276.6	31 990.1	35 380.3	40 637.0	47 357.1	50 998.1	55 557.8	60 533.7
European Community											
Total	3 926.5	5 467.2	6 390.5	9 101.0	11 848.6	13 620.8	17 479.4	20 542.6	21 119.1	23 123.6	26 516.3
France	679.2	916.7	1 166.3	1 748.8	2 164.8	2 495.6	3 026.6	3 594.5	3 625.9	4 491.8	5 651.5
Belgium and Luxembourg	424.8	671.9	771.0	1 107.7	1 386.6	1 605.1	1 890.6	2 258.9	2 092.0	2 309.6	2 572.7
Netherlands	603.8	989.2	1 121.0	1 511.5	2 153.3	2 251.3	3 061.3	3 838.7	4 019.4	4 642.8	5 440.7
Germany, Federal Republic	791.6	1 033.1	1 309.6	1 856.4	2 513.6	3 086.5	4 217.6	5 067.4	5 516.0	5 412.5	6 064.0
Italy	386.3	511.2	564.5	830.8	982.4	1 121.8	1 463.1	1 896.9	1 742.5	2 024.3	2 292.8
Irish Republic	612.3	810.7	895.2	1 235.9	1 619.3	2 024.1	2 544.9	2 639.0	2 813.0	2 889.4	3 055.3
Denmark	329.3	428.7	445.1	660.1	802.3	830.6	1 015.3	1 024.6	1 056.1	1 098.2	1 159.2
Greece	99.3	105.5	117.7	149.8	226.4	205.7	260.1	222.5	254.2	255.1	280.2
Rest of Western Europe											
Total	1 943.8	2 624.4	3 003.1	3 774.1	4 734.1	4 424.7	5 559.1	6 749.8	6 341.3	6 680.9	7 516.5
Norway	240.9	335.4	392.5	476.3	776.9	637.8	773.2	790.6	877.0	933.9	828.6
Sweden	514.7	725.3	827.7	1 049.3	1 198.0	1 169.7	1 536.9	1 624.7	1 601.2	1 935.6	2 397.5
Finland	167.9	229.7	265.4	290.1	346.6	349.0	410.6	525.6	525.0	513.3	539.7
Switzerland	338.1	441.1	545.4	635.5	806.1	870.8	1 249.2	1 953.2	1 458.6	1 195.7	1 385.9
Austria	136.7	153.9	165.8	213.6	252.1	237.5	257.3	278.8	246.9	250.8	273.7
Portugal	150.2	186.6	157.5	224.4	300.3	284.1	305.4	390.0	368.1	428.5	397.0
Spain	199.3	261.0	296.4	368.5	466.6	470.6	567.3	700.4	740.7	871.4	1 128.4
Yugoslavia	56.3	83.5	94.2	128.5	175.0	158.8	173.8	176.3	194.8	158.8	148.6
Turkey	81.8	104.8	143.6	211.9	210.2	110.5	135.6	147.1	159.6	218.1	244.0
Other countries	57.9	103.1	114.6	176.0	202.3	135.9	149.8	163.1	169.4	174.8	173.1
North America											
Total	1 937.9	2 290.6	2 368.5	3 104.8	3 790.5	4 249.3	4 791.4	5 329.2	7 130.9	8 353.3	9 341.6
Canada	414.5	494.9	543.8	629.9	702.3	736.6	767.2	751.8	845.0	852.1	968.3
United States	1 516.1	1 785.3	1 810.2	2 454.1	3 064.6	3 485.0	4 003.1	4 553.6	6 258.2	7 474.8	8 337.0
Other Countries[1]	7.3	10.4	14.5	20.8	23.6	27.7	21.1	23.8	27.7	26.4	36.3
Other developed countries											
Total	1 212.6	1 705.9	1 875.1	1 951.1	2 088.8	2 323.0	2 474.8	2 661.8	2 939.2	3 235.4	3 133.2
South Africa	366.0	519.9	669.2	632.3	564.7	659.1	715.7	998.4	1 220.0	1 190.7	1 109.0
Japan	273.8	320.6	310.7	361.7	470.9	541.8	606.2	596.5	620.3	680.9	797.8
Australia	405.6	606.7	638.7	700.9	763.3	854.2	840.8	815.8	863.6	1 041.5	940.3
New Zealand	167.3	259.0	256.6	256.2	289.9	267.8	312.1	251.1	235.4	322.3	286.1
Oil exporting countries											
Total	800.9	1 220.6	2 284.5	3 162.2	4 323.5	4 664.9	3 648.1	4 777.0	5 931.6	6 445.1	6 122.0
Algeria	37.9	54.8	78.8	102.0	99.0	121.4	108.9	140.4	173.0	199.2	233.4
Libya	61.1	62.6	107.5	134.9	173.9	214.2	248.7	288.4	530.4	261.0	274.2
Nigeria	172.6	223.0	512.7	776.0	1 074.1	1 121.1	627.2	1 191.5	1 428.0	1 225.8	798.3
Gabon	2.8	3.6	2.9	4.2	5.6	6.2	6.5	9.2	12.1	14.2	18.8
Saudi Arabia	58.5	119.7	200.1	400.8	584.8	729.7	808.3	945.2	1 133.9	1 361.5	1 478.6
Kuwait	36.1	60.1	100.2	146.6	247.4	307.8	224.8	250.8	281.2	333.1	333.3
Bahrain	24.3	34.9	61.2	90.0	114.1	116.7	110.8	95.1	102.3	152.0	150.3
Qatar	19.4	22.1	55.9	87.0	117.5	91.8	101.7	102.0	135.7	245.4	216.4
Abu Dhabi	24.9	43.6	91.7	126.0	133.7	124.9	154.9	214.6	246.7	272.9	219.2
Dubai	24.7	53.9	105.2	190.0	264.9	272.5	303.2	268.5	230.4	253.9	312.9
Sharjah, etc.	–	0.5	2.5	9.0	56.3	37.1	23.5	17.5	15.0	32.1	35.6
Oman	22.2	44.3	98.2	106.2	184.2	121.2	122.3	121.0	170.8	265.2	448.9
Iraq	27.0	61.8	137.3	152.0	167.4	216.7	201.2	322.1	623.9	873.7	400.3
Iran	169.8	279.6	495.3	515.5	658.4	751.2	231.8	392.7	402.8	333.6	630.0
Brunei	2.6	5.1	9.7	14.7	17.4	16.3	22.8	23.1	24.2	41.8	106.5
Indonesia	33.2	48.7	62.2	80.8	86.7	83.6	75.8	112.2	139.2	212.1	193.6
Trinidad and Tobago	32.9	37.6	52.7	74.5	97.4	110.7	104.6	120.4	121.5	158.4	148.8
Venezuela	39.2	51.0	91.7	128.5	180.7	188.9	137.7	131.5	126.3	148.6	87.9
Ecuador	11.8	13.9	18.8	23.3	59.5	33.0	33.5	30.9	34.1	60.8	35.0

1. Greenland, Puerto Rico and St. Pierre and Miqelon.

Source Department of Trade and Industry

12.5
(continued)

Value of United Kingdom exports (fob)
Analysis by destination

£ million

	1973	1974	1975	1976	1977	1978	1979	1980	1981	1982	1983
Other developing countries											
Total	1 809.6	2 420.6	2 956.4	3 397.2	4 201.4	4 927.4	5 353.8	5 847.5	6 279.8	6 607.8	6 660.9
Egypt	27.1	52.7	107.8	172.3	190.6	205.1	253.1	324.0	325.1	338.8	370.5
Ghana	30.4	55.1	51.2	81.3	100.1	115.1	87.8	88.2	87.8	66.7	82.2
Kenya	60.8	82.2	87.1	99.2	118.6	192.8	170.3	257.0	173.7	153.7	111.2
Tanzania	21.8	29.4	42.0	44.2	72.3	112.2	121.4	110.9	83.0	71.9	62.1
Zambia	41.0	66.1	81.7	66.6	86.2	68.4	85.5	96.3	68.2	61.2	55.5
Cyprus	42.4	41.0	28.0	54.3	89.2	90.3	97.6	108.4	115.6	111.8	127.8
Lebanon	42.0	61.1	70.7	10.0	48.8	57.9	65.7	70.7	61.9	67.6	81.4
Israel	187.2	220.3	237.8	250.2	276.0	243.4	270.8	230.6	212.0	264.1	354.9
Pakistan[2]	34.3	46.0	77.6	93.0	121.1	112.0	139.9	139.8	149.4	199.1	191.6
India	133.4	128.8	165.6	208.4	277.9	348.4	455.8	529.2	638.9	805.0	804.8
Thailand	36.3	57.0	56.0	59.5	82.5	86.4	94.4	97.0	91.5	104.8	131.8
Malaysia	78.3	114.2	115.5	119.4	147.9	186.4	187.5	223.3	196.2	210.6	248.2
Singapore	105.2	154.6	164.6	172.2	201.5	255.7	270.9	327.6	355.0	406.0	469.2
Taiwan	25.5	39.2	33.9	54.1	63.1	92.5	103.1	92.4	120.0	125.2	128.5
Hong Kong	128.3	160.1	160.7	207.7	271.5	361.7	439.5	559.2	618.5	730.7	726.7
South Korea	21.4	36.1	52.5	63.2	76.0	129.1	145.2	101.4	155.8	167.7	168.9
Philippines	29.1	51.4	58.6	86.9	94.6	111.9	104.3	86.2	85.7	97.7	102.9
Jamaica	43.5	51.0	62.2	52.0	39.9	48.6	44.7	33.3	42.9	55.9	116.2
Mexico	39.7	60.1	111.9	119.9	79.0	108.6	134.8	188.1	209.6	162.9	95.7
Chile	17.4	38.9	36.2	36.4	39.5	37.5	43.1	55.8	62.2	56.9	43.5
Brazil	115.3	147.1	161.0	174.6	255.7	221.0	285.8	220.2	174.4	158.8	157.8
Argentina	43.0	50.3	68.0	63.8	130.3	114.6	128.4	172.9	161.2	37.3	4.5
Other countries	506.2	677.9	925.8	1 107.8	1 339.1	1 627.8	1 624.2	1 734.9	2 091.2	2 153.4	2 025.0
Centrally planned economies											
Total	411.1	519.6	669.8	730.7	906.6	1 070.0	1 185.6	1 308.3	1 130.4	974.2	1 112.2
Soviet Union	97.4	110.4	211.4	241.5	347.1	422.9	416.2	449.2	408.3	356.1	445.0
German Democratic Republic	13.7	39.2	32.6	45.1	54.5	47.4	57.0	93.0	83.0	63.7	61.0
Poland	111.2	141.2	183.4	191.7	200.6	266.0	260.1	296.2	175.7	133.2	151.7
Czechoslovakia	27.2	45.0	51.4	60.3	65.2	73.2	73.8	81.0	70.7	70.1	69.5
Romania	34.2	33.9	39.8	48.9	83.5	74.9	70.3	99.1	150.3	115.2	82.2
Other countries[2]	127.4	149.9	151.2	143.2	155.7	185.6	308.2	289.8	242.4	235.9	302.8
Low value trade[3]	44.5	60.3	58.9	55.5	96.5	100.1	144.9	140.9	125.8	137.5	131.0

2. Hungary, Albania, Bulgaria, China, North Korea, Vietnam and Mongolia.
3. Items valued at less than £50 (raised to £100 with effect from 1 September 1973; to £150 from 1 January 1977 and to £200 from 1 January 1979) have not been allocated to specific countries and areas.

Source Department of Trade and Industry

12.6 Value of United Kingdom imports (cif)
Analysis by source

£ million

	1973	1974	1975	1976	1977	1978	1979	1980	1981	1982	1983
Total trade	15 723.5	23 138.9	24 046.4	31 084.1	36 219.1	39 533.0	46 924.9	49.772.9	51 168.6	56 978.2	65 993.1
European Community											
Total	5 261.7	7 799.6	8 871.8	11 503.5	14 160.4	16 547.1	20 887.6	20 574.2	21 718.0	25 269.0	30 098.1
France	979.3	1 346.1	1 623.6	2 092.9	2 672.4	3 198.1	4 015.8	3 848.7	3 978.6	4 266.9	5 043.1
Belgium and Luxembourg	458.7	730.2	952.0	1 287.8	1 664.8	1 757.2	2 272.9	2 380.7	2 448.6	2 857.5	3 133.9
Netherlands	911.8	1 640.3	1 872.8	2 432.2	2 494.6	2 518.4	3 442.8	3 397.9	3 895.5	4 512.0	5 097.8
Germany, Federal Republic	1 352.5	1 908.7	2 007.7	2 772.8	3 591.4	4 498.3	5 778.1	5 654.1	5 941.1	7 405.9	9 667.4
Italy	507.4	723.0	808.0	1 108.7	1 536.2	1 926.8	2 478.8	2 291.2	2 330.4	2 736.6	3 188.2
Irish Republic	528.0	808.1	920.9	1 037.1	1 291.7	1 601.3	1 681.4	1 769.4	1 782.1	2 003.4	2 290.1
Denmark	477.3	574.9	621.6	707.0	813.4	954.5	1 079.6	1 100.6	1 179.1	1 335.3	1 512.6
Greece	46.9	68.2	65.2	65.0	95.9	92.5	138.0	131.5	162.6	151.3	164.9
Rest of Western Europe											
Total	2 595.8	3 329.5	3 407.9	4 346.3	5 083.2	5 998.3	7 192.0	7 265.0	7 798.8	8 390.4	10 444.3
Norway	326.3	410.4	606.1	623.4	848.8	1 438.2	1 316.9	1 439.5	1 943.2	2 019.2	2 820.8
Sweden	739.7	925.1	885.3	1 188.1	1 262.6	1 337.5	1 600.2	1 466.3	1 533.6	1 672.9	2 051.9
Finland	331.2	493.7	399.1	562.3	594.4	637.0	792.2	793.4	844.4	921.8	996.0
Switzerland	537.2	693.7	632.2	787.8	961.2	1 304.6	1 835.1	1 893.8	1 708.1	1 664.5	2 154.1
Austria	178.2	204.9	204.1	232.6	268.6	322.9	345.2	307.0	348.0	402.4	438.4
Portugal	190.5	236.4	201.0	199.5	230.6	254.3	338.1	334.4	333.4	379.9	475.9
Spain	203.7	263.0	278.9	359.9	437.0	496.3	706.4	795.2	788.6	941.0	1 110.0
Yugoslavia	24.6	30.8	24.4	33.6	40.4	37.7	51.3	48.2	42.4	52.1	84.0
Turkey	33.9	34.9	34.6	60.4	57.7	62.6	65.8	49.3	128.2	207.8	185.0
Other countries	30.5	36.6	142.2	298.7	381.9	107.2	140.8	137.9	128.9	128.8	128.2
North America											
Total	2 393.9	3 272.7	3 248.2	4 275.9	4 983.8	5 313.7	6 197.2	7 464.2	7 587.8	8 095.0	9 027.4
Canada	740.6	940.2	863.9	1 169.3	1 217.0	1 134.0	1 272.2	1 411.7	1 508.8	1 436.2	1 522.2
United States	1 641.5	2 270.0	2 362.1	3 091.8	3 728.3	4 149.0	4 883.6	6 019.2	6 048.3	6 624.1	7 442.7
Other countries[1]	11.8	62.5	22.2	14.8	38.5	30.7	41.4	33.3	30.7	34.7	62.5
Other developed countries											
Total	1 471.4	1 686.4	1 918.1	2 255.6	2 846.3	2 997.9	3 042.7	3 367.5	3 678.1	4 436.1	5 159.3
South Africa	406.5	558.4	632.6	713.8	1 015.2	911.2	648.9	752.4	649.2	745.7	764.9
Japan	446.1	572.2	674.1	797.6	1 060.7	1 283.0	1 488.2	1 707.2	2 206.4	2 658.8	3 355.5
Australia	342.6	312.9	289.6	413.4	386.6	369.6	489.7	498.8	395.4	492.7	552.6
New Zealand	276.2	242.8	321.7	330.8	383.8	434.1	415.9	409.0	427.2	538.9	486.3
Oil exporting countries											
Total	1 499.7	3 803.8	3 280.2	4 209.9	3 703.9	3 326.2	3 212.7	4 253.1	3 666.9	3 453.4	2 824.3
Algeria	46.6	36.2	87.5	80.8	50.1	37.9	83.4	113.8	159.5	176.3	157.6
Libya	169.0	385.9	128.1	166.6	141.3	96.5	58.4	46.2	74.8	342.5	224.1
Nigeria	207.2	367.8	313.4	319.2	223.8	275.8	176.3	144.3	95.1	356.8	388.0
Gabon	12.1	28.4	3.7	9.2	3.2	2.9	10.9	10.6	36.7	27.6	66.1
Saudi Arabia	319.9	1 186.1	857.5	977.9	1 100.5	798.0	1 000.6	1 874.3	1 892.6	1 447.8	897.7
Kuwait	236.1	568.3	418.2	587.2	543.3	589.7	736.9	646.8	477.3	104.7	67.3
Bahrain	15.8	20.9	17.9	30.2	16.4	30.1	9.3	13.1	16.7	35.5	37.5
Qatar	47.7	169.1	159.6	248.7	100.8	29.8	40.5	44.7	10.7	34.0	10.1
Abu Dhabi	33.4	165.0	98.7	77.8	137.1	121.9	90.3	246.3	274.7	184.3	59.0
Dubai	37.0	58.7	60.3	122.0	121.8	148.3	141.7	235.2	116.0	57.5	202.2
Sharjah, etc.	–	–	–	0.2	0.7	0.8	1.1	0.8	2.7	25.2	48.6
Oman	15.9	27.6	114.9	73.2	15.6	30.4	26.0	19.2	40.5	46.4	91.2
Iraq	30.7	105.6	102.6	279.4	331.6	496.6	393.5	532.3	72.6	79.6	30.3
Iran	236.3	511.6	701.0	1 046.7	787.0	526.8	242.7	107.2	154.4	225.9	100.5
Brunei	0.2	1.9	0.6	0.3	0.5	0.4	0.4	0.8	2.7	2.4	27.2
Indonesia	14.5	15.5	15.1	22.5	28.8	33.4	56.1	57.0	73.8	90.7	169.5
Trinidad and Tobago	16.3	15.4	34.7	48.3	29.7	31.6	41.2	35.0	37.2	65.1	52.7
Venezuela	58.7	137.7	164.3	117.6	66.7	71.3	97.3	116.9	124.0	141.9	183.7
Ecuador	2.2	2.1	2.1	2.6	5.0	4.1	6.2	8.6	5.1	9.3	11.0

1. Greenland, Puerto Rico and St. Pierre and Miqelon.

Source Department of Trade and Industry

12.6

Value of United Kingdom imports (cif)
Analysis by source

(continued)

£ million

	1973	1974	1975	1976	1977	1978	1979	1980	1981	1982	1983
Other developing countries											
Total	2 046.7	2 642.9	2 700.4	3 536.5	4 258.6	4 186.8	5 104.4	5 679.9	5 599.9	5 895.8	6 786.3
Egypt	23.7	37.3	41.2	67.5	88.5	99.0	237.7	333.9	414.6	412.8	79.8
Ghana	48.6	73.5	58.0	82.8	127.0	110.7	89.9	100.0	61.2	78.4	58.2
Kenya	38.9	37.1	39.4	61.6	155.2	111.1	115.4	103.1	95.2	104.3	128.5
Tanzania	30.3	32.0	32.2	34.1	43.6	41.5	40.4	34.6	25.3	19.5	46.5
Zambia	80.1	134.9	93.0	73.3	95.4	67.9	101.4	88.9	41.4	40.0	50.2
Cyprus	28.6	30.7	30.6	63.9	88.8	75.7	87.3	97.7	80.6	89.9	87.4
Lebanon	23.2	49.9	9.2	6.0	8.4	8.1	9.4	9.1	7.5	24.2	11.5
Israel	69.7	78.9	91.2	125.8	159.7	176.4	219.3	232.7	255.9	276.1	314.1
Pakistan[2]	31.0	40.0	38.0	40.6	48.3	54.9	68.0	58.3	63.2	81.5	80.3
India	148.3	202.5	235.5	355.8	384.1	322.1	365.5	318.0	294.3	378.7	366.9
Thailand	11.7	18.5	13.6	25.6	34.9	37.3	49.9	51.0	56.3	76.5	87.8
Malaysia	95.1	128.5	116.7	157.1	223.7	200.1	221.7	186.9	188.3	185.2	222.7
Singapore	85.6	75.6	64.6	94.6	103.0	116.8	185.3	535.5	207.0	245.5	404.1
Taiwan	52.0	68.3	73.1	97.1	149.8	147.0	213.5	230.5	321.1	335.3	458.3
Hong Kong	263.4	293.3	309.8	440.6	456.9	528.1	689.3	849.8	896.6	870.8	1 178.3
South Korea	27.1	51.0	74.5	135.7	178.8	214.5	263.6	242.5	325.5	321.6	440.4
Philippines	18.0	27.8	53.2	42.5	53.0	57.1	81.3	99.4	105.5	127.0	160.7
Jamaica	44.3	46.8	81.1	63.1	78.2	100.1	82.1	99.0	114.2	92.8	94.0
Mexico	10.2	17.9	10.9	23.4	40.8	41.3	35.5	111.6	108.8	106.1	161.0
Chile	57.5	86.3	62.2	80.5	73.9	82.2	131.2	128.6	87.9	111.2	107.6
Brazil	158.9	195.5	174.9	239.8	303.2	282.2	399.3	296.4	369.9	443.9	560.3
Argentina	106.1	93.3	53.5	92.5	120.6	153.2	144.2	116.2	136.9	58.3	0.2
Other countries	594.4	823.2	944.0	1 132.6	1 242.8	1 159.5	1 273.2	1 355.9	1 342.7	1 416.2	1 687.5
Centrally planned economies											
Total	430.4	580.0	582.3	924.7	1 125.4	1 099.7	1 196.0	1 069.7	1 014.6	1 327.2	1 533.5
Soviet Union	163.8	225.4	235.8	460.1	545.1	488.8	491.6	422.0	426.7	645.4	728.5
German Democratic Republic	26.4	44.1	38.8	60.4	95.3	88.4	109.7	88.2	93.6	133.9	167.6
Poland	94.9	111.6	114.6	154.4	178.6	211.9	227.4	193.7	133.6	151.9	177.1
Czechoslovakia	39.1	55.3	59.4	70.3	86.3	85.8	96.8	87.8	70.5	82.0	101.3
Romania	31.7	34.1	35.9	49.4	52.5	51.7	65.9	64.8	46.5	51.5	58.9
Other countries[2]	74.5	109.5	97.8	130.1	167.6	173.1	204.6	213.1	243.7	262.5	300.1
Low value trade[3]	23.9	24.0	37.5	31.4	57.5	63.3	92.3	99.3	104.7	111.3	119.9

2. Hungary, Albania, Bulgaria, China, North Korea, Vietnam and Mongolia.
3. Items valued at less than £50 (raised to £100 with effect from 1 September 1973; to £150 from 1 Janury 1977 and to £200 from January 1979) have not been allocated to specific countries and areas.

Source Department of Trade and Industry

13 Balance of Payments

Tables 13.1, 13.2 and 13.3 in this section are derived from *United Kingdom Balance of Payments 1984 Edition*—the CSO Pink Book and Tables 13.4 and 13.5 are based on the annual publication *British Aid Statistics,* the latest edition of which covers the period 1978 to 1982.

The following general notes and footnotes to the tables provide brief definitions and explanations of the figures and terms used. Further notes are included in the publications named above. As far as possible transactions have been included in the balance of payments at the rate of exchange at which the transactions took place.

CURRENT ACCOUNT

In principle, transactions are recorded when the ownership of goods or assets changes and when services are rendered.

Visible trade

The *Overseas Trade Statistics of the United Kingdom* are the basis of the balance of payments figures, with certain adjustments in respect of valuation and coverage.

Invisibles: Services

General government covers all UK government current expenditure and receipts not appropriate to other items in the current account.

Transport—sea transport covers both dry and wet cargo transactions of UK operators with overseas residents, and of overseas operators with UK residents. The figures relate to freight, charter hire, port disbursements and passage money.

Transport—civil aviation covers overseas transactions of British Airways and the British independent airlines, and the transactions of overseas airlines with UK residents. Figures relate to passenger fares, freight, charter hire and airport disbursements.

Travel covers personal expenditure by overseas residents in the United Kingdom and by UK residents in overseas countries.

Financial services comprises the earnings, net of expenses, of financial and allied institutions for services.

Other services includes all services transactions not included elsewhere.

Invisibles: Interest, profits and dividends

Includes all interest, profits and dividends accruing to UK residents from non-residents or payable overseas by UK residents (after deduction of local taxes and depreciation) and includes profits retained for re-investment.

Invisibles: Transfers

General government transfers includes principally grants to overseas countries and contributions and subscriptions to international organisations.

Private transfers. Value of private assets passing from non-resident to resident ownership or *vice versa* without a *quid pro quo* including transfers of assets by migrants other than their personal or household belongings.

CAPITAL TRANSFERS

Payments made by the central government in implementation of the guarantee clauses of the Sterling Agreements of 1968, as renewed subsequently.

INVESTMENT AND OTHER CAPITAL TRANSACTIONS

Inward and outward investment

Direct investment comprises net investment by overseas companies in their United Kingdom affiliates, including the re-investment of retained profits, and by United Kingdom companies in their overseas branches, subsidiaries and associates. Government departments and oil companies are excluded. Outward investment of a number of public corporations is included.

Investment by oil companies is measured on a basis generally comparable to the estimates of direct investment except that unrelated trade credit is also included in the estimates of investment overseas. Further details are given in the Pink Book notes.

Portfolio investment

Overseas investment in the United Kingdom comprises investment in: UK company securities, representing the changes in the holdings by overseas residents of United Kingdom company securities, including securities issued abroad;

British government stocks, consisting of net transactions by overseas residents (other than by overseas monetary authorities);

British government foreign currency bonds; Local authorities' securities and public sector net issues abroad other than under the exchange cover scheme.

United Kingdom portfolio investment overseas consists mainly of net purchases and sales of overseas government, municipal and company securities.

Miscellaneous investment. Inward investment consists mainly of identified transactions in real estate. Outward investment includes transactions in real estate, non-bank financial institutions loans and mortgages and Commonwealth Development Finance Company investments.

Official long-term capital

Inter-government loans cover drawings and repayments of loans between the UK government and overseas governments.

Other official long-term capital includes mainly the UK capital subscriptions to international lending bodies, other than the IMF and net loans and investment by the Commonwealth Development Corporation.

Import credit

This item consists of the change in trade credit received by UK businesses from overseas businesses other than affiliates and parent companies, *less* advance and progress payments made by UK businesses. From 1983 only ships, commercial aircraft and North Sea installations are covered.

Export credit

The entries consist of the net changes in credit extended by banks in the United Kingdom and trade credit extended by UK businesses to overseas businesses other than affiliates and parent companies, *less* advance and progress payments. Net credit extended by UK merchants on third-country trade is included. From 1983 only bank credit under ECGD schemes and certain public corporations transactions are covered.

Foreign currency borrowing or lending abroad by UK banks

This item consists of changes in deposits of foreign currencies made with UK resident banks and certain other UK institutions by non-residents and loans by the banks in those currencies to non-residents.

It covers the financing of UK banks' net foreign currency business with UK residents (subject to certain exclusions listed below) *plus* any switching by the banks between foreign currencies and sterling. It excludes borrowing to finance lending to Her Majesty's Government; to local authorities and public bodies under the exchange cover scheme; and export credit in foreign currencies under ECGD schemes.

There are certain other exclusions described in detail in the Pink Book.

Exchange reserves in sterling

Changes in sterling reserves of overseas countries and international organisations, other than the International Monetary Fund, as reported by UK banks, etc.

Balance of payments (*contd.*)

Other external banking and money market liabilities in sterling

Transactions by overseas holders other than overseas monetary authorities in Treasury bills, and sterling deposits with UK banks, other financial institutions and local authorities.

External sterling lending by UK banks

This series consists of sterling advances and overdrafts (net of repayments) provided to overseas residents (including banks abroad) by UK banks and certain other UK financial institutions; and sterling commercial bills discounted and acceptances, other than bills connected with UK export credit.

Other external borrowing or lending

These items comprise borrowing or lending abroad, net of repayments, by UK residents other than UK banks.

Other transactions

Consists of changes in the following: official assets and liabilities (n.e.i.): other commercial short-term transactions (net); expenditure and receipts in sterling for IMF gold restitution.

Balancing item

Represents the net total of errors and omissions in other items.

Official financing liabilities and official reserves
(Table 13.3)

The official reserves and official financing liabilities are valued in dollars, but for the purposes of this table the end-year US dollar totals have been converted to sterling at the relevant end-period US dollar/sterling middle market closing rates. Their valuation in terms of dollars is described in detail in the Pink Book (page 67, 1984 edition).

Official financing liabilities
These constitute the short and medium-term foreign currency borrowing by the authorities recorded as official financing liabilities in the balance of payments accounts. Drawings from the IMF are net of repayments by the United Kingdom and drawings of sterling from the IMF by other countries. They exclude interest, charges in sterling, and transactions which affect the UK reserve position in the IMF. During 1976 several drawings, totalling $1 545 million, were made under the $5.3 billion short-term credit facility arranged in June 1976 with the Group of Ten countries and Switzerland, together with the Bank for International Settlements. This borrowing does not appear in the table as it was repaid before the end of 1976, but end-month levels during 1976 can be found in the March 1977 *Bank of England Quarterly Bulletin*, Table 24.

Foreign currency borrowing by HM Government represents (a) Drawings and repayments on two euro-dollar facilities arranged by the Bank of England with UK clearing banks and their associates on behalf of HM Government to borrow US$2 500 million and US$1 500 million. The transactions are allocated to the debtor (HM Government) rather than the transactor (the clearing banks). (b) An issue of US$350 million of HM Government seven and fifteen year bonds made in New York in 1978.

Foreign currency borrowing by UK public bodies under the exchange cover scheme includes all such borrowing in the form of issues abroad or borrowing from banks, etc. overseas or through UK

banks. It includes loans from the European Investment Bank to the Northern Ireland Government and British Nuclear Fuels Limited (a private sector body).

Official reserves
These comprise gold, convertible currencies and special drawing rights held in the Exchange Equalisation Account together with the United Kingdom's reserve position in the International Monetary Fund (IMF). A reserve position represents an automatic drawing right on the Fund and equals the amount by which the UK quota exceeds holdings of sterling by the IMF. Apart from UK drawings/repurchases, it will rise or fall as other countries draw sterling from, or repay sterling to, the IMF.

OVERSEAS AID
(Tables 13.4 and 13.5)

The UK aid programme is administered by the Overseas Development Administration (ODA) to promote the economic development of developing countries. It is managed within financial years, the money being voted annually by Parliament. However the statistics relating to the programme are published for the calendar year as this basis is used both for international aid comparisons and for national purposes such as the balance of payments. Fluctuations may thus occur in the calendar year figures which are not reflected in the financial year figures. This has been particularly true in the case of India, the largest bilateral recipient, whose aid receipts in 1976, 1979 and 1981 were abnormally high, while its receipts in 1980 and 1982 were abnormally low.

Aid flows can be measured before (gross) or after (net) deduction of repayments of principal on past loans. These tables show only the gross figures.

Aid is provided in two main ways: *bilateral,* that is directly to governments of developing countries or to institutions in the UK for work on behalf of such countries, or *multilateral,* that is to international institutions for their economic development programmes. Table 13.4 shows the three main groups of multilateral agencies, the International Development Association being the largest in the World Bank Group.

Bilateral aid takes various forms. *Project aid* is finance for the establishment of new, or expansion of existing, production and infrastructure facilities. The bulk is provided by the ODA, either from country programmes or from the Aid and Trade Provision (a special allocation to soften the terms of credits to developing countries by mixing aid funds with private export credits). The Commonwealth Development Corporation invests in productive public or private sector projects in developing countries. *Non-project aid* includes programme aid (for import finance not related to specific projects), debt relief, budgetary aid, food aid and disaster relief. *Technical Co-operation* is used to provide experts to work overseas, training for developing country nationals, consultancies, small items of equipment, to fund research and development in the UK of benefit to developing countries and support to voluntary organisations. Most of the aid not allocable by country in Table 13.5 is for technical co-operation provided through organisations in the UK.

Fuller statistics of Britain's aid effort are published annually in *British Aid Statistics* (obtainable from the Library, ODA). International comparisons are available in the OECD's annual *Development Co-operation: Efforts and Policies of the Members of the Development Assistance Committee* (available from HMSO).

13.1 Balance of payments of the United Kingdom

£ million

	1973	1974	1975	1976	1977	1978	1979	1980	1981	1982	1983
Current account											
Visible trade											
Exports (fob)	11 937	16 394	19 330	25 191	31 728	35 063	40 687	47 422	50 977	55 565	60 625
Imports (fob)	14 523	21 745	22 663	29 120	34 012	36 605	44 136	45 909	47 325	53 181	61 341
Visible balance	−2 586	−5 351	−3 333	−3 929	−2 284	−1 542	−3 449	+1 513	+3 652	+2 384	−716
Invisibles											
Credits	8 506	10 503	11 447	15 029	16 846	19 134	23 861	25 934	29 644	31 307	34 975
Debits	6 899	8 430	9 637	11 946	14 509	16 430	20 937	23 818	26 075	28 485	31 343
Invisible balance	+1 607	+2 073	+1 810	+3 083	+2 337	+2 704	+2 924	+2 116	+3 569	+2 822	+3 632
of which:											
Services balance	*+786*	*+1 075*	*+1 515*	*+2 503*	*+3 356*	*+3 858*	*+4 155*	*+4 356*	*+4 458*	*+3 706*	*+3 902*
Interest, profits and dividends balance	*+1 257*	*+1 415*	*+763*	*+1 355*	*+97*	*+623*	*+1 034*	*−161*	*+1 056*	*+1 165*	*+1 948*
Transfers balance	*−436*	*−417*	*−468*	*−775*	*−1 116*	*−1 777*	*−2 265*	*−2 079*	*−1 945*	*−2 049*	*−2 218*
CURRENT BALANCE	−979	−3 278	−1 523	−846	+53	+1 162	−525	+3 629	+7 221	+5 206	+2 916
Capital transfers	−59	−75	−	−	−	−	−	−	−	−	−
Investment and other capital transactions[1]											
Overseas investment in United Kingdom											
Direct	+734	+854	+615	+799	+1 326	+1 261	+1 740	+2 541	+998	+1 085	+2 457
Oil companies	+382	+924	+883	+819	+1 131	+666	+1 215	+1 714	+1 882	+1 770	+1 263
Portfolio	+386	+323	−4	+438	+1 853	−85	+1 253	+851	+508	+450	+1 640
of which: British government stocks	*+42*	*+105*	*−13*	*+116*	*+979*	*−3*	*+929*	*+571*	*+201*	*+495*	*+709*
Miscellaneous investment	−5	+103	+20	+35	+89	+35	+75	+100	+70	+120	+85
Total overseas investment in United Kingdom	+1 497	+2 204	+1 514	+2 091	+4 399	+1 877	+4 283	+5 206	+3 458	+3 425	+5 445
United Kingdom private investment overseas											
Direct	−1 621	−1 575	−1 171	−2 145	−1 885	−2 710	−3 035	−3 317	−5 152	−2 530	−2 609
Oil and miscellaneous investment	−415	−298	−137	−214	−461	−821	−2 858	−1 566	−1 418	−1 984	−1 841
Portfolio	+276	+725	−59	+90	+12	−1 073	−909	−3 150	−4 090	−6 210	−6 110
Total	−1 760	−1 148	−1 367	−2 269	−2 334	−4 604	−6 802	−8 033	−10 660	−10 724	−10 560
Official long-term capital	−255	−287	−291	−161	−303	−336	−401	−91	−336	−337	−389
Import credit	+349	+88	+59	+111	+280	+292	+64	−254	+130	−220	−33
Export credit	−552	−810	−577	−1 103	−635	−922	−856	−902	−969	−1 165	−1 484
Foreign currency borrowing or lending abroad	+535	−295	+253	−108	+367	−434	+1 622	+2 054	+1 462	+4 271	+1 167
Exchange reserves in sterling:											
British government stocks	+74	−124	+7	+12	+6	−113	+247	+945	+267	−52	+194
Banking and money market liabilities, etc.	+87	+1 534	−622	−1 413	−16		+509	+317	−118	+438	+714
Other external banking and money market liabilities in sterling	−7	+148	+549	+256	+1 481	+293	+2 580	+2 558	+2 607	+4 134	+3 225
External sterling lending by UK banks[2]	+35	+53	+96	−350	+58	−504	+205	−2 500	−2 954	−3 299	−1 386
Other external borrowing or lending											
United Kingdom public sector[3]	+19	+72	+56	+27	+750	+22	−7	−166	−18	−105	−87
United Kingdom private sector	+320	+279	+260	+94	+63	+84	+456	−341	−323	+194	+10
Other transactions	−164	−112	+217	−164	+53	+81	−66	−243	+101	+253	−464
Total investment and other capital transactions	+178	+1 602	+154	−2 977	+4 169	−4 264	+1 834	−1 450	−7 353	−3 187	−3 648
Allocation of SDRs	−	−	−	−	−	−	+195	+180	+158	−	−
Official financing											
Net transactions with overseas monetary authorities	−	−	−	+984	+1 113	−1 016	−596	−140	−145	−163	−36
Foreign currency borrowing (net)	+999	+1 751	+810	+1 792	+1 114	−187	−250	−941	−1 587	+26	+249
(Drawings on (+)/additions to (−) official reserves	−228	−105	+655	+853	−9 588	+2 329	−1 059	−291	+2 419	+1 421	+603
Total official financing	+771	+1 646	+1 465	+3 629	−7 361	+1 126	−1 905	−1 372	+687	+1 284	+816
Balancing item	+89	+105	−96	+194	+3 139	+1 976	+401	−987	−713	−3 303	−84

1. Assets: increase −/decrease +. Liabilities: increase +/decrease −.
2. Excluding credit for United Kingdom exports.
3. Excluding official financing.

Source Central Statistical Office

13.2 Current account

£ million

	1973	1974	1975	1976	1977	1978	1979	1980	1981	1982	1983
Credits											
Exports (fob)	11 937	16 394	19 330	25 191	31 728	35 063	40 687	47 422	50 977	55 565	60 625
Services:											
General government	104	110	139	215	241	254	267	317	407	406	470
Private sector and public corporations											
Sea transport	2 055	2 665	2 651	3 233	3 433	3 149	3 804	3 816	3 784	3 267	3 023
Civil aviation	480	625	780	1 049	1 203	1 455	1 755	2 210	2 359	2 471	2 665
Travel	726	898	1 218	1 768	2 352	2 507	2 797	2 961	2 970	3 168	3 655
Financial services	601	785	1 025	1 303	1 409	1 575	1 649	1 693	2 100	2 326	2 745
Other services	1 330	1 645	2 044	2 710	3 283	3 824	4 289	4 879	5 445	5 906	6 585
Interest, profits and dividends											
General government	176	237	266	253	384	691	816	943	948	816	616
Private sector and public corporations	2 647	3 049	2 565	3 708	3 629	4 466	7 133	7 337	9 030	9 760	11 857
Transfers											
General government	67	132	366	253	298	439	550	958	1 658	2 157	2 221
Private sector	320	357	393	537	614	774	801	820	943	1 030	1 138
Total invisibles	8 506	10 503	11 447	15 029	16 846	19 134	23 861	25 934	29 644	31 307	34 975
Total credits	20 443	26 897	30 777	40 220	48 574	54 197	64 548	73 356	80 621	86 872	95 600
Debits											
Imports (fob)	14 523	21 745	22 663	29 120	34 012	36 605	44 136	45 909	47 325	53 181	61 341
Services:											
General government	513	629	709	867	940	986	1 073	1 014	965	1 238	1 302
Private sector and public corporations											
Sea transport	2 160	2 776	2 562	3 155	3 345	3 162	3 677	3 675	3 944	3 797	4 099
Civil aviation	415	540	675	840	984	1 176	1 467	1 815	1 922	2 080	2 237
Travel	695	703	917	1 068	1 186	1 549	2 109	2 738	3 271	3 640	4 054
Other services	727	1 005	1 479	1 845	2 110	2 033	2 080	2 278	2 505	3 083	3 549
Interest, profits and dividends											
General government	375	589	780	901	1 105	1 285	1 356	1 548	1 616	1 616	1 768
Private sector and public corporations	1 191	1 282	1 288	1 705	2 811	3 249	5 559	6 893	7 306	7 795	8 757
Transfers											
General government	425	452	724	1 056	1 414	2 142	2 608	2 781	3 344	4 001	4 228
Private sector	398	454	503	509	614	848	1 008	1 076	1 202	1 235	1 349
Total invisibles	6 899	8 430	9 637	11 946	14 509	16 430	20 937	23 818	26 075	28 485	31 343
Total debits	21 422	30 175	32 300	41 066	48 521	53 035	65 073	69 727	73 400	81 666	92 684
Balances											
Visible balance	− 2 586	− 5 351	− 3 333	− 3 929	− 2 284	− 1 542	− 3 449	1 513	3 652	2 384	− 716
Services:											
General government	− 409	− 519	− 570	− 652	− 699	− 732	− 806	− 697	− 558	− 832	− 832
Private sector and public corporations											
Sea transport	− 105	− 111	89	78	88	− 13	127	141	− 160	− 530	− 1 076
Civil aviation	65	85	105	209	219	279	288	395	437	391	428
Travel	31	195	301	700	1 166	958	688	223	− 301	− 472	− 399
Financial services	601	785	1 025	1 303	1 409	1 575	1 649	1 693	2 100	2 326	2 745
Other services	603	640	565	865	1 173	1 791	2 209	2 601	2 940	2 823	3 036
Interest, profits and dividends											
General government	− 199	− 352	− 514	− 648	− 721	− 594	− 540	− 605	− 668	− 800	− 1 152
Private sector and public corporations	1 456	1 767	1 277	2 003	818	1 217	1 574	444	1 724	1 965	3 100
Transfers											
General government	− 358	− 320	− 358	− 803	− 1 116	− 1 703	− 2 058	− 1 823	− 1 686	− 1 844	− 2 007
Private sector	− 78	− 97	− 110	28	−	− 74	− 207	− 256	− 259	− 205	− 211
Invisible balance	1 607	2 073	1 810	3 083	2 337	2 704	2 924	2 116	3 569	2 822	3 632
of which: private sector and public corporations: services and interest, profits and dividends	*2 651*	*3 361*	*3 362*	*5 158*	*4 873*	*5 807*	*6 535*	*5 497*	*6 740*	*6 503*	*7 834*
Current balance	− 979	− 3 278	− 1 523	− 846	53	1 162	− 525	3 629	7 221	5 206	2 916

Source Central Statistical Office

13.3 Official financing liabilities and official reserves
End of period

£ million

	1973	1974	1975	1976	1977	1978	1979	1980	1981	1982	1983
IMF	–	–	–	1 205	2 100	1 055	471	294	200	36	–
Other foreign currency borrowing by:											
HM Government	–	638	1 235	1 469	2 085	2 131	1 955	1 191	183	216	241
Public bodies under exchange cover scheme	1 283	2 380	3 174	5 646	5 219	4 579	4 129	3 525	3 998	4 612	5 397
Total official financing liabilities	1 283	3 018	4 409	8 320	9 404	7 765	6 555	5 010	4 381	4 864	5 638
Official reserves	2 787	2 890	2 683	2 426	10 715	7 689	10 129	11 487	12 217	10 508	12 271

Sources   HM Treasury, Bank of England

13.4 United Kingdom public expenditure on overseas aid
Gross aid—analysis by major components[1]

£ million

	1973	1974	1975	1976	1977	1978	1979	1980	1981	1982	1983
Total public expenditure on overseas aid	300.3	366.8	454.3	549.8	611.7	752.1	939.4	966.5	1151.1	1 085.3	1 169.7
Bilateral: total	234.7	277.8	320.2	408.7	405.8	564.2	682.6	702.6	804.8	673.9	692.8
Project aid: total	105.2	109.3	119.9	131.0	137.3	188.7	270.0	288.8	425.5	308.0	325.6
Overseas Development Administration	84.3	74.5	92.6	105.1	101.4	155.3	189.3	219.7	323.9	194.2	236.9
Aid and Trade Provision	–	–	–	–	–	1.3	36.8	24.0	33.3	62.6	32.7
Commonwealth Development Corporation	20.9	34.7	27.3	25.9	35.9	32.2	44.0	45.1	68.3	51.1	56.0
Non project aid	47.8	81.1	89.0	134.4	124.9	202.3	202.9	160.4	130.9	121.5	102.6
Technical co-operation	72.6	76.4	96.3	127.4	126.6	153.2	185.7	223.3	216.4	211.4	231.6
Administrative costs	9.0	11.0	15.0	16.0	17.0	20.0	24.0	30.0	32.0	33.0	33.0
Multilateral: total	65.7	89.0	134.1	141.1	205.9	187.8	256.8	263.9	346.3	411.4	476.8
European Community	4.4	13.7	19.0	26.2	55.2	44.5	117.8	120.4	158.1	173.9	184.6
World Bank Group	31.5	49.2	66.0	69.4	88.9	64.5	43.9	73.4	115.5	153.7	205.5
UN Agencies	24.2	19.8	39.7	28.9	42.8	53.8	68.9	48.0	47.7	55.9	54.3
Other multilateral	5.6	6.4	9.4	16.6	18.9	25.1	26.1	22.1	25.0	28.0	32.5

1. See introductory notes on page 239.

Source   Overseas Development Administration

13.5 United Kingdom public expenditure on overseas aid
Gross bilateral aid-analysis by main recipient countries[1]

£ million

	1973	1974	1975	1976	1977	1978	1979	1980	1981	1982	1983
Total bilateral aid	234.7	277.8	320.2	408.7	405.8	564.2	682.6	702.6	804.8	673.9	692.8
Africa: total	68.4	74.7	79.2	107.3	116.5	176.7	230.7	257.0	267.1	247.2	235.7
Botswana	4.0	4.0	4.8	6.6	5.7	5.6	8.0	11.5	10.2	7.6	13.3
Egypt	1.6	2.2	2.9	2.6	3.6	3.7	17.8	12.3	8.1	7.5	10.6
Ghana	1.8	1.1	1.4	3.1	2.8	4.5	11.2	15.6	7.5	7.0	6.7
Kenya	11.7	16.4	9.5	21.0	16.4	31.3	33.1	31.7	39.7	37.5	31.9
Lesotho	1.9	2.5	3.9	2.1	2.2	5.8	6.6	4.6	6.4	4.2	4.7
Malawi	6.9	8.1	10.7	16.0	16.5	16.0	24.9	16.5	16.3	17.0	14.6
Morocco	–	–	–	–	–	–	–	0.1	12.4	3.8	0.1
Mozambique	–	–	–	–	2.9	5.8	6.4	4.6	5.4	1.9	1.8
Nigeria	7.8	6.0	5.8	5.5	8.3	9.8	5.1	4.9	4.2	4.9	5.5
St. Helena and Dependencies	0.7	1.1	1.3	1.6	2.4	3.7	3.9	3.8	4.1	5.8	6.5
Seychelles	3.4	3.7	3.3	3.9	5.1	4.9	4.8	4.9	3.9	3.5	3.2
Sudan	1.1	1.5	3.0	7.7	5.0	7.1	13.9	22.6	32.7	39.4	32.2
Swaziland	3.4	3.5	3.4	2.5	10.0	8.7	8.4	6.5	4.1	6.4	5.7
Tanzania	1.5	1.5	4.1	5.7	6.7	10.4	24.1	32.1	30.0	27.3	30.4
Zambia	10.1	8.4	9.9	11.4	12.6	33.3	29.2	20.7	24.1	14.2	14.5
Zimbabwe	0.2	0.3	1.1	2.3	2.6	3.5	5.1	36.4	17.1	21.5	19.6
Other Countries	12.3	14.4	14.1	15.3	13.7	22.6	28.2	28.2	40.9	37.7	34.4
America: total	25.4	30.2	40.2	41.7	32.9	53.4	42.4	36.5	49.0	92.2	67.9
Barbados	1.2	0.5	0.2	0.3	0.2	0.3	0.7	0.6	3.6	2.5	0.4
Belize	1.6	1.9	2.3	3.9	2.5	3.9	7.5	4.5	4.8	2.9	6.1
Brazil	0.5	1.9	3.3	2.3	1.2	0.7	1.0	1.0	0.6	10.0	5.6
Chile	0.6	0.5	0.3	0.9	2.1	1.1	2.1	2.0	1.5	0.7	0.4
Dominica	1.4	0.9	1.5	1.9	1.4	2.6	2.9	2.5	1.6	1.9	1.7
Falkland Islands	0.2	1.2	1.4	1.5	1.1	2.1	0.9	1.0	1.1	4.0	9.1
Guyana	0.8	1.5	1.7	1.4	0.9	6.4	2.6	2.4	2.5	1.7	1.6
Honduras	0.1	0.1	0.3	0.2	0.6	0.3	0.2	0.3	5.0	2.3	6.7
Jamaica	3.3	4.8	2.3	0.9	0.9	19.6	6.4	4.8	8.0	8.9	8.9
Mexico	0.3	0.4	0.7	0.6	0.8	0.8	1.2	1.6	1.5	34.3	2.8
Montserrat	0.9	0.8	1.6	1.2	1.6	0.5	0.5	1.2	1.1	1.8	1.0
St. Lucia	1.5	1.9	2.8	3.0	0.6	0.6	0.8	1.2	2.2	1.6	2.6
St. Vincent	1.3	1.2	1.9	1.4	1.1	1.8	2.5	0.8	1.3	1.2	0.7
Turks and Caicos Islands	1.2	1.0	1.4	2.0	2.0	1.4	1.0	1.3	3.4	5.7	4.2
Other countries	10.5	11.6	18.5	20.2	15.9	11.3	12.1	11.3	10.8	12.7	16.1
Asia: total	89.9	120.1	124.7	170.2	168.5	218.7	292.3	264.0	317.4	182.2	245.1
Bangladesh	2.7	6.4	14.3	14.0	22.0	44.0	33.8	66.2	33.4	23.5	24.7
Burma	0.3	0.7	0.5	0.8	2.5	1.4	2.2	6.5	5.3	3.4	1.8
India	49.4	75.4	68.1	108.8	79.8	118.9	153.3	86.1	168.6	54.2	127.6
Indonesia	8.1	8.9	6.8	4.7	5.6	6.5	13.1	11.2	15.4	17.2	12.4
Jordan	2.4	1.0	6.9	3.9	3.3	3.1	13.6	4.7	7.1	3.3	2.7
Malaysia	4.8	5.4	7.0	4.5	10.1	1.5	1.6	10.5	10.1	6.4	3.9
Nepal	2.3	3.2	2.3	1.7	4.3	4.4	11.3	6.8	8.0	9.6	7.4
Pakistan	4.4	3.6	6.6	19.8	25.8	18.2	27.7	22.3	24.6	18.7	16.6
Philippines	0.1	0.2	0.2	0.2	0.2	0.2	0.8	3.2	3.3	1.2	3.7
Sri Lanka	2.1	1.6	2.7	5.5	4.0	8.3	14.1	32.9	26.3	33.3	29.5
Thailand	1.2	2.6	2.5	0.6	1.4	1.3	5.0	4.7	7.8	4.0	5.6
Yemen North (YAR)	0.1	0.3	0.6	0.9	0.9	1.3	1.8	2.7	2.5	2.8	3.8
Yemen South (PDRY)	0.6	1.3	1.0	1.2	2.7	1.6	1.7	1.3	1.8	0.9	0.8
Other countries	11.4	9.5	5.2	3.6	5.9	8.0	11.7	4.9	3.2	3.7	4.6
Europe: total	9.8	7.7	7.4	6.5	10.0	17.1	8.6	14.2	37.3	19.6	8.8
Gibraltar	2.6	2.8	1.4	1.7	2.6	1.9	3.2	4.9	4.0	1.9	2.4
Malta	4.4	3.5	3.5	3.6	3.6	3.8	0.3	0.2	0.2	0.2	0.2
Turkey	2.5	0.9	1.5	0.3	3.3	0.6	4.3	8.0	32.1	16.9	5.4
Other countries	0.3	0.5	1.0	0.9	0.5	10.8	0.8	1.1	1.0	0.6	0.8
Oceania: total	13.8	14.1	19.4	25.5	24.2	30.4	28.6	36.3	33.0	31.6	24.7
Fiji	3.6	3.9	3.9	5.5	6.0	5.1	6.9	5.3	7.0	8.7	4.0
Kiribati and Tuvalu	2.2	2.1	2.4	3.6	3.8	4.5	3.7	7.1	6.0	7.3	7.4
Papua New Guinea	–	–	–	0.4	0.8	2.4	3.1	3.7	7.0	3.8	0.1
Solomon Islands	4.6	4.8	8.8	9.4	7.9	10.4	7.4	10.0	7.3	6.3	6.8
Vanuatu	2.8	2.8	3.8	5.5	5.1	7.6	6.7	8.7	4.6	4.3	5.9
Other countries	0.6	0.5	0.5	1.1	0.6	0.4	0.8	1.5	1.1	1.2	0.5
Unallocated: total	18.3	20.3	34.3	41.4	36.9	48.0	56.0	64.6	68.9	68.1	77.7
Administrative costs	9.0	11.0	15.0	16.0	17.0	20.0	24.0	30.0	32.0	33.0	33.0

1. See introductory notes on page 239.

Source Overseas Development Administration

14 National Income and Expenditure

The tables which follow are taken from those in *United Kingdom National Accounts 1984 Edition,* published by Her Majesty's Stationery Office (September 1984). Some of the figures are provisional and may have to be revised later; this applies particularly to the figures for 1982 and 1983. The 1983 and earlier editions were called *National Income and Expenditure.*

A general description of the statistics, together with a detailed description of the sources, methods and definitions used in making the estimates, is given in *National Accounts Statistics: Sources and Methods* (HMSO 1968) and is brought up to date in *United Kingdom National Accounts 1984 Edition.* Further information on the structure and inter-relationships of the tables in the national accounts is given in *The National Accounts—A short guide* (HMSO 1981).

In the tables in this section the analyses by industry are based, as far as possible, on the Standard Industrial Classification 1980.

The first aggregate measured in these tables is the **gross domestic product.** This is an estimate of the value of the goods and services produced by UK residents. Adding net property income from abroad to this aggregate produces the gross national product. The gross national product is not identical with the **national income.** The latter is defined as equal to the total of goods and services becoming available after deducting what is required to maintain real capital intact (the gross national product *less* capital consumption).

Gross national product (*Table 14.1*). The upper half of this table shows the various money flows which generate the gross domestic product and the gross national product. These include expenditure by UK final buyers—that is, expenditure on goods and services other than for use in current production and resale—and expenditure on British exports by overseas purchasers. The sum of these two items overstates the amount of income generated in the United Kingdom by the value of imports of goods and services; this item is therefore subtracted to produce gross domestic product at market prices. Deducting taxes on expenditure and adding subsidies produces the expenditure-based measure of the gross domestic product at factor cost, which is equivalent to the sum of the incomes of the factors of production before deduction of depreciation (capital consumption).

The lower half of the table shows the contribution to the gross national product of the different factors of production. The profit items in the table—income from self-employment, trading profits of companies, trading surpluses of public corporations and of other public enterprises—are shown before any deduction for depreciation and before providing for stock appreciation. (Stock appreciation is the change in value of stocks due to the change, if any, in the prices at which stocks are valued in the reckoning of profits.) This element of stock appreciation is deducted in reckoning the total of the gross national product.

Personal income and expenditure (*Table 14.2*). 'Persons' are here defined as including unincorporated businesses and private non-profit-making bodies serving persons. Income is shown gross before providing for depreciation or stock appreciation. Employers' national insurance contributions (but not the surcharge) are treated as employee income taxed at source and therefore appear under both income and expenditure. Personal income also includes employers' contributions to pension funds. Personal saving before providing for depreciation or stock appreciation is estimated as a residual and is subject to a wide margin of error.

Corporate income appropriation account (*Table 14.3*). Trading profits earned in the United Kingdom are shown both before and after providing for stock appreciation but before deduction of depreciation allowances. Profits from operations outside the United Kingdom are included under income earned abroad. Dividends paid by one company to another are excluded both from dividends and from non-trading income.

Current account of general government (*Table 14.4*). This table is a consolidation of central government and local authorities' transactions on current account.

Summary capital account (*Table 14.5*). This table brings together the saving and investment of the several sectors of the economy and shows the total investment at home and overseas.

The index of output of the production industries, (*Table 14.6*) (i.e.'index of production'), which accounts for 36 per cent of the output measure of gross domestic product shown in the same table, provides a general measure of changes in the volume of industrial production in the United Kingdom. Production industries comprise Division 1, energy and water supply (coal mining, oil and gas extraction, production of other fuels and water) and Divisions 2 to 4, manufacturing. The index of output of the production and construction industries, which comprises production industries and construction, accounts for 42 per cent of gross domestic product. These indices are prepared by the Central Statistical Office in collaboration with the statistics divisions of government departments. The index of output of the production industries is published monthly approximately six weeks after the end of the month to which it applies but the index of output of the production and construction industries is published only quarterly and in arrears of the latest index data, when definitive construction output estimates have been made available by the Department of the Environment. These indices are calculated currently with 1980 as the base year, with the volume of production in other periods expressed as a percentage of either the average monthly production in 1980 for the index of output of the production industries or the average quarterly production in 1980 for the index of output of the production and construction industries. Annual series for the major aggregates from 1948, and quarterly series from 1952, were published in *Economic Trends,* No 360 October 1983 (HMSO). The monthly index of output of the production industries series and the quarterly index of output of the production and construction industries are published in the *Monthly Digest of Statistics* (HMSO).

The index of output of the production and construction industries is a weighted arithmetic average of 329 indicators, each representing the 'value added' by an individual industry or part of an industry as its contribution to total output of the United Kingdom. The weight given to each industry is proportional to its contribution to gross domestic product at factor cost in 1980; that is to say, the value the industry adds to its purchased materials, fuels and services. This is equal to the sum of income from employment *plus* profits after the deduction of stock appreciation. The weights are derived from the Annual Census of Production for that year, constrained to the aggregates shown in Table 3.1 of *National Income and Expenditure 1983 Edition* (HMSO). The weights shown in the table are those used in the compilation of the index from 1978 onwards. The 1980-based data were linked to the figures for earlier years on the basis of the annual figures for 1978 (see notes on rebasing below).

The gross output (that is, the total production) of an industry is the most frequently used proxy indicator for assessing change in value added, since the latter is difficult to measure in the short-term. In some cases the volume of production can be measured and such indicators make up about two-fifths of the index of production. About three-fifths of the index of production is derived from the volume of sales or deliveries or their value deflated by the relevant producer prices indices: however, since compilation of the 1980-based index of production, adjustments for changes to stocks and work done in the industries represented by these indicators are made at a more aggregate level. A very small proportion of the index of production is derived from work done or input of labour or materials indicators. For further notes on the general method of constructing the index see Industry Statistics: Occasional Paper No 18 *Series and weights used in the index of output of the production industries – 1980 base* (CSO 1983), which is obtainable from the Central Statistical Office, OSS Branch, Room 73/3, Great George Street, London SW1P 3AQ, price £2.50 (cash with order).

The index of production with the national accounts is rebased at approximately five-yearly intervals. Regular rebasing is required because the rate of growth in relative prices of net output of the various sectors may vary over time. In addition, the relative importance of each sector may change because of advances of technology, or variations in the pattern of demand for its goods. Index numbers for all years from 1978 were recalculated when the index was rebased on

1980 in Summer 1983. The index numbers from 1973 to 1978 (available on a 1975 = 100 basis and a different industrial classification, i.e. Standard Industrial Classification Revised 1968) were linked to the later figures by a simple rescaling of series approximating as closely as possible to series based on *Standard Industrial Classification Revised 1980,* using the two sets of index numbers for 1978. An article describing the effect of rebasing appeared in *Economic Trends* No 360 October 1983.

Industrial classification. The industrial analysis of the index of production is in conformity with the *Standard Industrial Classification Revised 1980* (HMSO) to which reference should be made for the details of the composition of each industrial group.

Market sector classification. These groupings combine the output of industries which meet broadly similar categories of demand: consumer goods, investment goods and intermediate goods (materials and fuels). Because the index of production measures the output of an industry and not of commodities, each market sector group will include some output from the other sector. The industrial composition of the market sectors is set out in Industry Statistics: Occasional Paper No 21 *Supplementary analyses of series used in the index of output of the production industries 1980 base* (CSO 1983) which is obtainable from the Central Statistical Office, price £2.50 (address shown in penultimate paragraph of previous page).

Gross domestic product by industry (*Table 14.7*). This table shows the contribution of each industry to the gross domestic product, measured as the sum of incomes, before providing for depreciation, arising in the industry. This is also equal to the 'value added' by the industry, that is, the excess of the value of its current output over the value of goods and services purchased from outside the industry and used in production.

Expenditure and output at constant prices (*Tables 14.6, 14.8 and 14.9*). These tables contain two virtually independent estimates of the gross domestic product of the United Kingdom at 1980 prices. The estimates in Table 14.6 are based on the index of industrial production and other statistics relating to the volume of output; those in Table 14.8 have been derived by revaluing estimates of final expenditure on goods and services at average 1980 prices. With full and accurate information the two methods would in theory lead to the same result. In practice, because there are numerous imperfections and gaps in the data, the two methods produce different results. Notes on the rebasing of constant price estimates on 1980 are given in *United Kingdom National Accounts 1984 Edition.* For a general account of the methods of compiling the output index numbers, see *The measurement of changes in production,* Studies in Official Statistics No 25 (HMSO 1976), which describes the compilation of the index numbers on the basis 1970 = 100. See *Series and weights used in estimating the gross domestic product at constant factor cost,* 1980 = 100 Industry Statistics: Occasional Paper No 20 (CSO 1984) for a list of series and weights currently used in compiling the index numbers, which is obtainable from the Central Statistical Office, price £2.50 (address shown in penultimate paragraph of previous page).
In Table 14.9 each of the components of expenditure shown in Table 14.8 is expressed in index form, taking 1980 = 100.

Consumers' expenditure at current and constant prices (*Table 14.10*). Consumers' expenditure is a major component of final expenditure contributing to gross domestic product calculated by the expenditure method, at current prices (*Table 14.1*) and at constant prices (*Table 14.8*).

Consumers' expenditure consists of personal expenditure on goods and services for current use. It is now classified in two ways, first in certain commodity groups which are also available on a quarterly basis in the *Monthly Digest of Statistics* and secondly (in more detail) according to purpose. It includes the value of income-in-kind; imputed rent of owner-occupied dwellings; and final expenditure by private non-profit-making bodies serving perions. It excludes business expenditure allowed as deductions in computing income for tax purposes of both employed and self-employed persons.

It includes expenditure on durable goods, for instance motor cars, which from the point of view of the individual might more appropriately be treated as capital expenditure. The only exceptions are the purchase of land and dwellings and costs incurred in connection with the transfer of their ownership and expenditure on major improvements by occupiers, which are treated as personal capital expenditure.

The estimates of consumers' expenditure include purchases of second-hand as well as new goods, *less* the proceeds of sales of used goods.

Index numbers of gross domestic product and gross national disposable income (*Table 14.13*). This table brings together the various estimates of gross domestic product and the average estimate of gross national disposable income at constant market prices. They are shown in index number form with the base year for the constant price estimates as 1980 = 100. The average estimates relate to the unweighted arithmetic average of the three estimates based on expenditure, income and output data.

Value of physical increase in stocks and work in progress (*Table 14.14*). This table gives a broad analysis by industry, and, for manufacturing industry, by asset, of the physical increase in stocks and work in progress. The physical increase at current prices equals the change in the book value of stocks *less* stock appreciation.

Gross domestic fixed capital formation (*Table 14.15*). Fixed capital formation comprises expenditure on the replacement of, and additions to, the stock of fixed capital assets located in the United Kingdom, including all ships and aircraft of UK ownership.

Gross capital stock (*Table 14.16*). The table shows estimates of the value of the reproducible capital assets (buildings, plant and machinery, vehicles, ships and aircraft) owned by various industry groups, without allowance for depreciation during the expended proportions of asset lives. The estimates are expressed at 1980 replacement cost. Leased assets are mainly included under 'distributive trades and other service industries' on the basis of ownership. No analysis of these assets by use is available, and they still constitute only a small proportion of total gross capital stock. Gross capital stock is a relevant measure of capital as a factor of production because the productive potential of most assets remains little impaired through the greater part of their lives.

14.1 Gross national product by category of expenditure

£ million

	1973	1974	1975	1976	1977	1978	1979	1980	1981	1982	1983
Expenditure at market prices											
Consumers' expenditure	46 004	53 072	65 216	75 712	86 537	99 486	117 912	136 789	152 125	166 477	182 427
General government final consumption	13 429	16 701	23 085	27 005	29 420	33 334	38 775	48 810	55 322	60 202	65 859
of which: Central government	*7 872*	*10 106*	*13 493*	*16 140*	*17 787*	*20 069*	*23 351*	*29 851*	*33 826*	*36 950*	*40 623*
Local authorities	*5 557*	*6 595*	*9 592*	*10 865*	*11 633*	*13 265*	*15 424*	*18 959*	*21 496*	*23 252*	*25 236*
Gross domestic fixed capital formation	14 835	17 308	21 312	24 718	27 021	31 137	36 882	41 628	41 794	45 993	49 559
Value of physical increase in stocks and work in progress	1 529	1 290	−1 531	789	1 804	1 690	2 123	−2 899	−3 148	−1 428	267
Total domestic expenditure	75 797	88 371	108 082	128 224	144 782	165 647	195 692	224 328	246 093	271 244	298 112
Exports of goods and services	17 233	23 122	27 187	35 469	43 649	47 827	55 248	63 298	68 042	73 109	79 768
Total final expenditure	93 030	111 493	135 269	163 693	188 431	213 474	250 940	287 626	314 135	344 353	377 880
less Imports of goods and services[1]	−19 033	−27 398	−29 005	−36 895	−42 577	−45 511	−54 542	−57 429	−59 932	−67 019	−76 582
Gross domestic product at market prices[2]	73 997	84 095	106 264	126 798	145 854	167 963	196 398	230 197	254 203	277 334	301 298
less Taxes on expenditure	−10 124	−11 452	−14 131	−16 458	−20 026	−22 958	−29 884	−36 197	−42 087	−46 991	−49 865
plus Subsidies	1 437	2 998	3 679	3 459	3 301	3 663	4 451	5 317	5 904	5 416	6 056
Gross domestic product at factor cost[2]	65 310	75 641	95 812	113 799	129 129	148 668	170 965	199 317	218 020	235 759	257 489
Factor incomes											
Income from employment	43 919	52 480	68 656	78 205	86 743	99 088	115 734	136 933	148 154	158 183	170 072
Income from self-employment[3]	7 598	8 282	9 388	11 175	12 400	14 106	16 442	17 585	19 237	21 527	23 123
Gross trading profits of companies[3, 4]	10 389	11 429	11 741	14 693	19 967	22 599	28 942	29 008	29 957	33 886	41 530
Gross trading surplus of public corporations[3]	2 064	2 561	3 095	4 505	5 095	5 391	5 587	6 149	7 750	9 175	9 661
Gross trading surplus of general government enterprises[3]	123	100	79	89	122	143	102	69	85	29	−109
Rent[5]	4 137	5 286	6 375	7 537	8 350	9 523	11 483	13 493	15 306	16 579	17 424
Imputed charge for consumption of non-trading capital	589	714	909	1 080	1 221	1 383	1 639	2 044	2 292	2 376	2 456
Total domestic income[3]	68 819	80 852	100 243	117 284	133 898	152 233	179 929	205 281	222 781	241 755	264 157
less Stock appreciation	−2 806	−5 751	−5 240	−6 440	−4 931	−4 174	−8 664	−6 451	−5 816	−3 758	−4 326
Gross domestic product (income-based)	66 013	75 101	95 003	110 844	128 967	148 059	171 265	198 830	216 965	237 997	259 831
Residual error	−703	540	809	2 955	162	609	−300	487	1 055	−2 238	−2 342
Net property income from abroad	1 257	1 415	763	1 355	97	623	1 034	−161	1 056	1 165	1 948
Gross national product at factor cost	66 567	77 056	96 575	115 154	129 226	149 291	171 999	199 156	219 076	236 924	259 437
less Capital consumption	−7 365	−9 201	−11 734	−14 172	−16 955	−19 857	−23 666	−28 546	−32 133	−34 415	−36 490
National income—(i.e. net national product)	59 202	67 855	84 841	100 982	112 271	129 434	148 333	170 610	186 943	202 509	222 947

1. Excluding taxes on expenditure levied on imports.
2. Including taxes on expenditure levied on imports.
3. Before providing for depreciation and stock appreciation.
4. Including financial institutions.
5. Before providing for depreciation.

Source Central Statistical Office

14.2 Personal income and expenditure

£ million

	1973	1974	1975	1976	1977	1978	1979	1980	1981	1982	1983
Income before tax											
Income from employment:											
Wages and salaries	38 531	45 636	59 182	66 414	73 573	84 236	98 466	116 305	124 803	133 527	143 348
Pay in cash and kind of HM Forces	925	1 071	1 283	1 474	1 506	1 645	2 020	2 436	2 689	2 905	3 121
Total	39 456	46 707	60 465	67 888	75 079	85 881	100 486	118 741	127 492	136 432	146 469
Employers' contributions:											
National insurance, etc.	2 054	2 791	4 079	5 075	5 702	6 084	6 947	8 330	8 940	9 525	10 632
Other	2 409	2 982	4 112	5 242	5 962	7 123	8 301	9 862	11 722	12 226	12 971
Total income from employment	43 919	52 480	68 656	78 205	86 743	99 088	115 734	136 933	148 154	158 183	170 072
Income from self-employment:											
After deducting stock appreciation	7 204	7 616	8 806	10 505	11 835	13 667	15 689	16 835	18 676	21 240	22 674
Stock appreciation	394	666	582	670	565	439	753	750	561	287	449
Total[1]	7 598	8 282	9 388	11 175	12 400	14 106	16 442	17 585	19 237	21 527	23 123
Rent, dividends and net interest:											
Receipts by life assurance and superannuation schemes	1 993	2 334	2 688	3 199	4 012	4 766	6 406	7 790	8 758	10 116	11 313
Imputed rent of owner-occupied dwellings	2 121	2 795	3 456	4 140	4 669	5 367	6 525	7 827	9 103	10 106	10 895
Other receipts, net	1 798	2 229	2 595	2 727	2 457	2 695	4 261	5 194	4 161	4 184	3 034
Total	5 912	7 358	8 739	10 066	11 138	12 828	17 192	20 811	22 022	24 406	25 242
Current transfers to charities from companies	42	42	42	42	43	45	51	52	62	66	74
National insurance benefits and other current grants from general government	6 420	7 873	10 278	12 752	15 070	17 872	20 960	25 468	31 137	36 375	39 528
Imputed charge for capital consumption of private non-profit making bodies	85	107	136	161	179	199	226	269	300	311	321
Total personal income[1]	63 976	76 142	97 239	112 401	125 573	144 138	170 605	201 118	220 912	240 868	258 360
Deductions from income											
UK taxes on income	7 726	10 421	15 040	17 421	18 149	19 459	21 570	25 554	28 802	31 436	32 822
National insurance, etc. contributions	3 937	5 000	6 848	8 426	9 508	10 107	11 531	13 944	15 923	18 141	20 643
Transfers abroad (net)	78	97	110	− 28	−	74	207	256	259	205	211
Personal disposable income[2]	52 235	60 624	75 241	86 582	97 916	114 498	137 297	161 364	175 928	191 086	204 684
Expenditure											
Consumers' expenditure	46 004	53 072	65 216	75 712	86 537	99 486	117 912	136 789	152 125	166 477	182 427
Balance saving[2]	6 231	7 552	10 025	10 870	11 379	15 012	19 385	24 575	23 803	24 609	22 257
Total	52 235	60 624	75 241	86 582	97 916	114 498	137 297	161 364	175 928	191 086	204 684
Memorandum items											
Saving ratio (per cent)[3]	11.9	12.5	13.3	12.6	11.6	13.1	14.1	15.2	13.5	12.9	10.9
Real personal disposable income[4]:											
At 1980 prices	144 697	143 507	143 924	143 146	140 943	151 197	159 821	161 364	158 106	158 554	161 578
1980 = 100	89.7	88.9	89.2	88.7	87.3	93.7	99.0	100.0	98.0	98.3	100.1

1. Before providing for depreciation and stock appreciation.
2. Before providing for depreciation stock appreciation and additions to tax reserves.
3. Saving as a percentage of personal disposable income.
4. Personal disposable income revalued by the implied consumers' expenditure deflator (1980 = 100).

Source Central Statistical Office

14.3 Corporate income appropriation account

£ million

	1973	1974	1975	1976	1977	1978	1979	1980	1981	1982	1983
Income											
Income arising in the United Kingdom:											
Gross trading profits of companies and trading surplus of public corporations:											
After deducting stock appreciation	10 041	8 905	10 178	13 428	20 696	24 255	26 618	29 456	32 452	39 590	47 314
Stock appreciation	2 412	5 085	4 658	5 770	4 366	3 735	7 911	5 701	5 255	3 471	3 877
Total[1]	12 453	13 990	14 836	19 198	25 062	27 990	34 529	35 157	37 707	43 061	51 191
Rent and non-trading income	4 485	5 619	5 956	7 328	8 329	8 670	11 806	15 467	17 586	19 677	19 852
Total	16 938	19 609	20 792	26 526	33 391	36 660	46 335	50 624	55 293	62 738	71 043
Income from abroad[2]	2 511	2 885	2 400	3 497	3 420	4 229	6 802	6 883	8 457	8 817	10 661
Total income	19 449	22 494	23 192	30 023	36 811	40 889	53 137	57 507	63 750	71 555	81 704
Allocation of income											
Dividends and interest payments	5 991	7 352	8 038	9 180	9 849	10 309	14 949	19 251	19 910	23 100	22 448
Current transfers to charities from companies	42	42	42	42	43	45	51	52	62	66	74
Profits due abroad, net of UK tax	744	649	602	964	1 997	2 229	4 017	4 838	4 740	4 765	5 681
UK taxes on income[3]	1 853	2 858	2 383	2 274	3 202	4 025	5 018	6 621	8 579	10 440	11 978
Royalties and licence fees on oil and gas production	15	18	23	76	234	286	531	1 156	1 362	1 600	1 886
Balance: undistributed income after taxation[4]	10 804	11 575	12 104	17 487	21 486	23 995	28 571	25 589	29 097	31 584	39 637
Total	19 449	22 494	23 192	30 023	36 811	40 889	53 137	57 507	63 750	71 555	81 704

1. Before providing for depreciation and stock appreciation.
2. After deducting depreciation allowances but before providing for stock appreciation.
3. From April 1973 figures reflect change to imputation system of corporation tax.
4. Before providing for depreciation, stock appreciation and additions to tax reserve.

Source Central Statistical Office

14.4 General government current account

£ million

	1973	1974	1975	1976	1977	1978	1979	1980	1981	1982	1983
Receipts											
Taxes on income	9 236	12 694	16 740	18 928	20 419	22 549	25 177	30 806	35 937	40 453	43 129
Taxes on expenditure	10 124	11 452	14 131	16 458	20 026	22 958	29 884	36 197	42 087	46 991	49 865
National insurance, etc. contributions	3 937	5 000	6 848	8 426	9 508	10 107	11 531	13 944	15 923	18 141	20 643
Gross trading surplus[1]	123	100	79	89	122	143	102	69	85	29	− 109
Rent, dividends and interest, etc	2 317	3 050	3 600	4 381	4 962	5 385	6 577	8 148	9 045	10 206	9 961
Imputed charge for consumption of non-trading capital	504	607	773	919	1 042	1 184	1 413	1 775	1 992	2 065	2 135
Total	26 241	32 903	42 171	49 201	56 079	62 326	74 684	90 939	105 069	117 885	125 624
Expenditure											
Final consumption	13 429	16 701	23 085	27 005	29 420	33 334	38 775	48 810	55 322	60 202	65 859
Subsidies	1 437	2 998	3 679	3 459	3 301	3 663	4 451	5 317	5 904	5 416	6 056
National insurance benefits	3 927	4 922	6 376	7 918	9 225	10 534	11 897	14 405	17 170	18 679	20 001
Other current grants to personal sector	2 493	2 951	3 902	4 834	5 845	7 338	9 063	11 063	13 967	17 696	19 527
Current grants paid abroad	358	320	358	803	1 116	1 703	2 058	1 823	1 686	1 844	2 007
Debt interest	2 738	3 607	4 211	5 393	6 390	7 207	8 952	11 363	13 292	14 474	14 658
Total current expenditure	24 382	31 499	41 611	49 412	55 297	63 779	75 196	92 781	107 341	118 311	128 108
Balance: current surplus[1]	1 859	1 404	560	− 211	782	− 1 453	− 512	− 1 842	− 2 272	− 426	− 2 484
Total	26 241	32 903	42 171	49 201	56 079	62 326	74 684	90 939	105 069	117 885	125 624

1. Before providing for depreciation.

Source Central Statistical Office

14.5 Summary capital account

£ million

	1973	1974	1975	1976	1977	1978	1979	1980	1981	1982	1983
Receipts											
Saving[1]											
Personal sector	6 231	7 552	10 025	10 870	11 379	15 012	19 385	24 575	23 803	24 609	22 257
Industrial and commercial companies	8 245	8 953	9 194	12 783	15 479	17 660	21 108	17 502	19 533	20 560	26 651
Financial companies[2]	1 308	1 237	1 246	1 844	2 670	2 588	3 803	3 945	4 087	4 737	5 689
Public corporations	1 251	1 385	1 664	2 860	3 337	3 747	3 660	4 142	5 477	6 287	7 297
Central government	1 071	827	−718	−2 337	−1 009	−3 076	−2 016	−3 063	−5 048	−3 830	−5 073
Local authorities	788	577	1 278	2 126	1 791	1 623	1 504	1 221	2 776	3 404	2 589
Total	18 894	20 531	22 689	28 146	33 647	37 554	47 444	48 322	50 628	55 767	59 410
Capital transfers (net):											
Personal sector	−325	−324	−305	−57	82	287	160	275	202	507	1 137
Industrial and commercial companies	355	341	412	367	264	394	349	416	629	603	475
Financial companies[2]	−63	−90	9	−65	−73	8	−103	−128	−399	−252	−182
Public corporations	150	213	289	377	425	516	436	500	568	514	667
Central government	−258	−235	−448	−616	−682	−1 254	−970	−1 182	−1 098	−1 302	−1 514
Local authorities	82	20	43	−6	−16	49	128	119	98	−70	−583
Residual error	−703	540	809	2 955	162	609	−300	487	1 055	−2 238	−2 342
Total	18 132	20 996	23 498	31 101	33 809	38 163	47 144	48 809	51 683	53 529	57 068
Expenditure											
Gross domestic fixed capital formation:											
Personal sector	2 842	2 623	4 088	4 597	5 483	6 301	8 062	9 046	9 920	12 642	14 977
Industrial and commercial companies	4 853	5 797	6 790	8 037	9 775	12 077	14 090	15 192	15 028	15 634	15 919
Financial companies[2]	1 394	1 640	1 512	1 962	2 157	3 165	3 900	5 151	5 352	5 872	5 215
Public corporations	2 073	2 858	3 920	4 693	4 781	4 944	5 621	6 643	6 802	7 163	8 017
Central government	785	970	1 261	1 408	1 294	1 290	1 563	1 758	1 851	2 169	2 484
Local authorities	2 888	3 420	3 741	4 021	3 531	3 360	3 646	3 838	2 841	2 513	2 947
Total	14 835	17 308	21 312	24 718	27 021	31 137	36 882	41 628	41 794	45 993	49 559
Increase in book value of stocks and work in progress:											
Personal sector	618	694	317	756	918	740	1 139	435	333	336	446
Industrial and commercial companies	3 633	6 056	2 551	5 671	5 483	4 821	9 089	2 460	1 995	1 108	3 335
Financial companies[2]	−58	−13	9	34	−15	−10	−17	6	9	4	38
Public corporations	121	289	841	766	299	282	611	599	473	876	452
Central government	21	15	−9	2	50	31	−35	52	−142	6	322
Total	4 335	7 041	3 709	7 229	6 735	5 864	10 787	3 552	2 668	2 330	4 593
Net investment abroad	−1 038	−3 353	−1 523	−846	53	1 162	−525	3 629	7 221	5 206	2 916
Total	18 132	20 996	23 498	31 101	33 809	38 163	47 144	48 809	51 683	53 529	57 068
Financial surplus/deficit:											
Personal sector	2 446	3 911	5 315	5 460	5 060	8 258	10 344	15 369	13 752	12 138	7 971
Industrial and commercial companies	114	−2 559	265	−558	485	1 156	−1 722	266	3 139	4 421	7 872
Financial companies[2]	−91	−480	−266	−217	455	−559	−183	−1 340	−1 673	−1 391	254
Public corporations	−793	−1 549	−2 808	−2 222	−1 318	−963	−2 136	−2 600	−1 230	−1 238	−505
Central government	7	−393	−2 418	−4 363	−3 035	−5 651	−4 514	−6 055	−7 855	−7 307	−9 393
Local authorities	−2 018	−2 823	−2 420	−1 901	−1 756	−1 688	−2 014	−2 498	33	821	−941

1. Saving before providing for depreciation and stock appreciation, but after providing for additions to reserves.
2. Including financial institutions.

Source Central Statistical Office

14.6 Index numbers of output at constant factor cost

1980 = 100

	Weight per 1 000	1973	1974	1975	1976	1977	1978	1979	1980	1981	1982	1983
Agriculture, forestry and fishing	22	87.8	88.8	81.9	75.3	85.1	91.5	90.6	100.0	103.1	111.9	107.2
Production:												
Energy and water supply:												
Coal and coke	15	114.0	94.5	109.9	102.3	99.1	97.6	97.6	100.0	97.3	93.2	89.5
Extraction of mineral oil and natural gas	44	2.2	0.1	0.3	16.2	47.4	68.9	98.7	100.0	110.3	125.6	137.6
Mineral oil processing	5	126.9	124.4	103.9	110.9	108.8	109.6	113.7	100.0	92.9	92.7	95.2
Other energy and water supply	31	87.1	87.6	89.2	90.8	94.5	97.9	102.2	100.0	99.6	98.6	101.2
Total	95	55.8	52.2	54.5	60.9	74.8	85.0	100.5	100.0	103.8	110.0	116.0
Manufacturing (revised definition):												
Metals	9	154.8	142.1	122.9	131.2	129.2	126.8	132.1	100.0	106.2	103.8	104.2
Other minerals and mineral products	15	128.0	121.7	112.2	112.3	111.4	114.2	111.8	100.0	89.7	94.9	94.3
Chemicals	24	96.4	101.6	91.0	102.8	106.3	107.5	110.5	100.0	100.2	100.8	107.0
Man-made fibres	1	175.6	151.0	136.1	149.6	133.4	143.1	137.0	100.0	84.9	68.1	78.1
Metal goods nes	16	141.8	136.8	123.8	125.0	128.7	123.8	121.6	100.0	92.6	94.3	97.0
Mechanical engineering	38	115.1	122.6	120.4	115.6	114.9	112.0	108.3	100.0	88.0	89.0	85.7
Electrical and instrument engineering	34	95.0	99.3	93.9	92.5	96.6	101.3	101.0	100.0	92.9	97.4	106.7
Motor vehicles and parts	15	137.8	127.0	115.2	116.3	125.5	118.9	115.7	100.0	83.0	79.8	84.0
Other transport equipment	14	101.5	104.1	99.5	95.0	90.9	95.8	92.4	100.0	103.5	100.5	97.1
Food	24	99.0	97.2	93.3	96.2	98.4	99.1	100.5	100.0	99.1	102.5	103.4
Drink and tobacco	12	89.8	91.6	91.7	94.3	94.0	99.8	101.9	100.0	95.2	91.7	94.5
Textiles	9	149.3	136.6	125.7	129.7	130.7	126.2	121.0	100.0	91.3	87.7	89.5
Clothing, footwear and leather	10	111.3	108.8	109.0	106.3	112.1	113.5	115.2	100.0	92.2	89.0	91.2
Paper, printing and publishing	24	109.6	109.4	94.6	97.5	101.8	103.8	108.0	100.0	94.9	91.4	91.7
All other manufacturing (including timber, furniture, rubber and plastics)	21	120.3	110.0	103.0	110.4	112.1	115.4	116.0	100.0	91.2	88.1	91.9
Total	266	114.1	112.6	104.9	106.8	108.9	109.6	109.3	100.0	93.7	93.7	95.9
Total production	361	99.4	97.5	92.2	95.2	100.1	103.1	107.0	100.0	96.4	98.1	101.2
Construction	63	118.0	105.8	100.2	98.8	98.4	105.1	105.8	100.0	90.0	91.7	95.3
Total production and construction	424	102.6	98.8	93.5	95.8	99.8	103.4	106.9	100.0	95.4	97.1	100.4
Distribution, hotels and catering; repairs	128	106.5	102.3	98.6	99.6	99.0	104.8	107.9	100.0	98.3	100.2	104.0
Transport and communication:												
Transport	46	101.0	100.3	98.7	98.3	100.4	100.6	104.0	100.0	97.6	95.5	98.2
Communication	26	81.8	83.6	83.1	82.3	85.8	91.3	97.4	100.0	101.2	105.1	109.8
Total	72	93.7	94.0	92.8	92.3	94.9	97.3	101.6	100.0	98.9	99.0	102.4
Banking, finance, insurance, business services and leasing	116	74	77	79	82	85	90	96	100	105	113	121
Ownership of dwellings	62	87	89	91	94	96	98	99	100	101	102	103
Public administration, national defence and compulsory social security	69	99	98	100	101	100	99	99	100	99	98	97
Education and health services	87	80	85	90	93	94	96	98	100	101	103	104
Other services	61	78	78	80	84	87	91	94	100	99	100	103
Adjustment for financial services	– 41	75	80	80	82	83	89	95	100	105	112	120
Gross Domestic product	1000	95.2	93.8	92.0	93.9	96.5	99.9	103.0	100.0	98.3	100.3	103.2

Source Central Statistical Office

14.6 Index numbers of output at constant factor cost
(continued)

1980 = 100

	Weight per 1 000	1973	1974	1975	1976	1977	1978	1979	1980	1981	1982	1983
Consumer goods industries:												
Cars, etc.	4	191.8	166.5	133.4	141.0	144.4	140.4	120.7	100.0	95.1	86.1	98.7
Other durables	13	127.9	124.7	117.7	116.1	117.3	120.7	116.8	100.0	92.8	91.8	93.7
Clothing and footwear, etc.	14	110.4	108.6	107.5	106.1	111.6	112.2	113.7	100.0	93.2	90.1	91.7
Food, drink and tobacco[1]	33	96.8	96.5	93.7	95.7	97.2	99.4	101.2	100.0	97.8	98.4	100.1
Other	24	100.8	102.2	93.0	98.2	103.3	106.4	108.2	100.0	97.1	95.1	98.2
Total	88	109.4	107.6	100.9	103.0	106.3	108.5	108.4	100.0	96.0	94.6	97.2
Investment goods industries:												
Electrical	21	83.2	88.4	85.1	85.2	90.5	96.3	96.6	100.0	91.8	97.5	107.5
Transport	27	110.2	109.8	107.0	104.4	107.4	105.1	104.1	100.0	91.5	89.8	88.6
Other	40	115.7	123.4	119.6	114.1	113.3	110.8	108.2	100.0	89.4	89.3	86.6
Total	88	105.0	109.5	106.1	103.2	105.5	105.7	104.3	100.0	90.6	91.4	92.1
Intermediate goods industries:												
Energy	91	53.2	49.1	51.6	58.5	73.4	84.2	100.5	100.0	104.0	110.1	116.5
Materials	94	126.3	120.1	107.9	113.8	114.3	114.0	115.0	100.0	94.6	95.5	98.7
Total	185	91.6	86.4	81.1	87.4	94.5	99.3	107.9	100.0	99.3	102.7	107.5

1. This does not include grain milling, starch, compound animal feeds, and processing organic oils and fats, which are classified to intermediate goods industries: materials.

Source Central Statistical Office

14.7 Gross domestic product by industry[1]

£ million

	1973	1974	1975	1976	1977	1978	1979	1980	1981	1982	1983
Agriculture, forestry and fishing	2 006	2 099	2 573	3 131	3 370	3 588	3 910	4 268	4 775	5 536	5 535
Extraction of mineral oil and natural gas	58	24	9	602	2 100	2 777	5 705	8 809	11 994	13 898	16 193
All other energy and water	2 960	3 317	4 796	5 859	6 691	7 653	7 803	10 117	10 763	11 881	13 452
Manufacturing (revised definition)	20 919	22 829	27 615	31 757	38 142	43 722	48 298	52 490	53 883	58 282	62 258
Construction	4 995	5 604	6 750	7 611	8 321	9 574	11 204	12 687	13 611	14 289	15 319
Distribution; hotels and catering; repairs	8 982	9 943	12 139	13 955	16 870	19 843	22 834	25 504	27 941	31 134	35 002
Transport	3 248	3 717	4 874	5 742	6 513	7 556	8 526	8 968	9 707	10 439	11 543
Communication	1 608	2 121	2 721	3 369	3 484	3 938	4 403	5 184	6 053	6 939	7 092
Banking, finance, insurance, business services and leasing	7 365	8 199	9 652	11 451	13 650	15 436	18 999	22 283	24 522	27 955	31 067
Ownership of dwellings	3 525	4 596	5 636	6 776	7 575	8 601	10 384	12 227	13 920	15 050	15 761
Public administration, national defence and compulsory social security	4 220	5 199	6 946	8 097	8 569	9 494	10 918	13 761	15 496	16 707	18 027
Education and health services	5 276	6 562	9 152	10 605	11 290	12 516	14 252	18 095	20 931	21 970	24 021
Other services	3 507	4 360	5 528	6 338	7 517	8 829	10 202	11 852	13 171	14 623	16 415
Total	68 669	78 570	98 391	115 293	134 092	153 527	177 438	206 245	226 767	248 703	271 685
Adjustment for financial services	− 2 656	− 3 469	− 3 388	− 4 449	− 5 125	− 5 468	− 6 173	− 7 415	− 9 802	− 10 706	− 11 854
Residual error	− 703	540	809	2 955	162	609	− 300	487	1 055	− 2 238	− 2 342
Gross domestic product at factor cost	65 310	75 641	95 812	113 799	129 129	148 668	170 965	199 317	218 020	235 759	257 489

1. The contribution of each industry to the gross domestic product before providing for depreciation but after providing for stock appreciation.

Source Central Statistical Office

14.8 Expenditure and output at 1980 prices[1]

£ million

	1973	1974	1975	1976	1977	1978	1979	1980	1981	1982	1983
At 1980 market prices											
Consumers' expenditure	127 436	125 630	124 748	125 175	124 564	131 373	137 256	136 789	136 714	138 135	144 008
General government final consumption	43 206	43 870	46 278	46 861	46 085	47 125	48 107	48 810	48 811	49 224	50 523
of which: Central government	*25 548*	*26 452*	*27 939*	*28 533*	*28 252*	*28 579*	*29 097*	*29 851*	*30 058*	*30 286*	*30 910*
Local authorities	*17 608*	*17 406*	*18 329*	*18 336*	*17 857*	*18 546*	*19 010*	*18 959*	*18 753*	*18 938*	*19 613*
Gross domestic fixed capital formation	43 535	41 734	41 808	42 434	41 323	42 938	43 925	41 628	38 075	40 645	42 348
Value of physical increase in stocks and work in progress	5 023	2 837	−2 969	1 035	2 566	2 054	2 474	−2 899	−2 739	−1 247	207
Total domestic expenditure	219 264	214 103	209 797	215 425	214 489	223 490	231 762	224 328	220 861	226 757	237 086
Exports of goods and services	49 451	53 072	51 657	56 282	59 939	61 067	63 367	63 298	62 140	62 729	63 329
of which: Goods	*35 835*	*38 419*	*36 874*	*40 510*	*43 660*	*44 802*	*46 988*	*47 422*	*47 054*	*48 126*	*48 505*
Services	*13 609*	*14 644*	*14 767*	*15 759*	*16 274*	*16 265*	*16 379*	*15 876*	*15 086*	*14 603*	*14 824*
Total final expenditure	268 538	267 083	261 358	271 663	274 451	284 557	295 129	287 626	283 001	289 486	300 415
less Imports of goods and services[2]	−57 693	−53 350	−49 576	−51 641	−52 251	−54 267	−59 908	−57 429	−55 446	−57 591	−60 789
of which: Goods	*−42 421*	*−42 831*	*−39 119*	*−41 392*	*−42 150*	*−44 117*	*−48 819*	*−45 909*	*−44 132*	*−46 217*	*−49 412*
Services	*−10 251*	*−10 490*	*−10 397*	*−10 218*	*−10 084*	*−10 150*	*−11 089*	*−11 520*	*−11 314*	*−11 374*	*−11 377*
Gross domestic product at market prices[3]	215 599	213 332	211 827	220 050	222 215	230 290	235 221	230 197	227 555	231 895	239 626
Net property income from abroad	3 480	2 755	1 304	1 897	119	743	1 136	−161	977	1 001	1 546
Gross national product at market prices[3]	219 540	216 430	213 234	222 144	222 235	231 033	236 357	230 036	228 532	232 896	241 172
At 1980 factor cost											
Gross domestic product at market prices[3]	215 599	213 332	211 827	220 050	222 215	230 290	235 221	230 197	227 555	231 895	239 626
Adjustment to factor cost[4]	−28 421	−27 529	−27 178	−28 200	−28 190	−30 935	−32 168	−30 880	−30 078	−31 556	−32 454
Gross domestic product at factor cost	187 037	185 509	184 317	191 496	193 593	199 355	203 053	199 317	197 477	200 339	207 172
Net property income from abroad	3 480	2 755	1 304	1 897	119	743	1 136	−161	977	1 001	1 546
Gross national product at factor cost	190 865	188 523	185 698	193 541	193 637	200 098	204 189	199 156	198 454	201 340	208 718
less Capital consumption	−21 718	−22 421	−23 446	−24 406	−25 624	−26 863	−27 826	−28 546	−29 257	−30 167	−30 941
Net national product at factor cost	168 978	165 977	162 188	169 068	167 997	173 235	176 363	170 610	169 197	171 173	177 777

1. For the years before 1978, totals differ from the sum of their components: see notes on page 113 of *United Kingdom National Accounts 1984 Edition.*
2. Excluding taxes on expenditure levied on imports.
3. Including taxes on expenditure levied on imports.
4. This represents taxes on expenditure *less* subsidies valued at constant rates.

Source Central Statistical Office

14.9 Index numbers of expenditure at 1980 prices

1980 = 100

	1973	1974	1975	1976	1977	1978	1979	1980	1981	1982	1983
At 1980 market prices											
Consumers' expenditure	93.2	91.8	91.2	91.5	91.1	96.0	100.3	100.0	99.9	101.0	105.3
General government final consumption	88.5	89.9	94.8	96.0	94.4	96.5	98.6	100.0	100.0	100.8	103.5
Gross domestic fixed capital formation	104.6	100.3	100.4	101.9	99.3	103.1	105.5	100.0	91.5	97.6	101.7
Total domestic expenditure	97.7	95.4	93.5	96.0	95.6	99.6	103.3	100.0	98.5	101.1	105.7
Exports of goods and services	78.1	83.8	81.6	88.9	94.7	96.5	100.1	100.0	98.2	99.1	100.0
Total final expenditure	93.4	92.9	90.9	94.5	95.4	98.9	102.6	100.0	98.4	100.6	104.4
Imports of goods and services	91.8	92.9	86.3	89.9	91.0	94.5	104.3	100.0	96.5	100.3	105.9
Gross domestic product at market prices	93.7	92.7	92.0	95.6	96.5	100.0	102.2	100.0	98.9	100.7	104.1
Gross national product at market prices	95.4	94.1	92.7	96.6	96.6	100.4	102.7	100.0	99.3	101.2	104.8
At 1980 factor cost											
Gross domestic product at factor cost[1]	93.8	93.1	92.5	96.1	97.1	100.0	101.9	100.0	99.1	100.5	103.9
Gross national product at factor cost	95.8	94.7	93.2	97.2	97.2	100.5	102.5	100.0	99.6	101.1	104.8
Capital consumption	76.1	78.5	82.1	85.5	89.8	94.1	97.5	100.0	102.5	105.7	108.4
Net national product at factor cost	99.0	97.3	95.1	99.1	98.5	101.5	103.4	100.0	99.2	100.3	104.2

1. Alternative estimates of the gross domestic product are given in tables 14.7 and 14.11.

Source Central Statistical Office

14.10 Consumers' expenditure at current prices classified by function

£ million

	1973	1974	1975	1976	1977	1978	1979	1980	1981	1982	1983
Food (household expenditure): total	8 471	9 759	11 961	13 941	16 047	17 927	20 364	22 873	24 170	25 590	27 148
Bread and cereals	1 064	1 341	1 589	1 746	2 061	2 345	2 641	3 056	3 311	3 497	3 649
Meat and bacon	2 512	2 846	3 330	3 855	4 390	5 043	5 789	6 471	6 715	7 215	7 346
Fish	273	304	363	423	485	550	624	731	768	806	907
Milk, cheese and eggs	1 341	1 347	1 632	2 042	2 386	2 662	3 016	3 423	3 658	3 874	3 975
Oils and fats	328	399	504	595	718	793	875	920	933	941	951
Fruit	521	588	682	753	905	1 001	1 076	1 273	1 318	1 362	1 564
Potatoes	294	349	546	806	681	569	745	789	904	1 059	1 191
Vegetables	630	741	914	1 020	1 153	1 216	1 432	1 621	1 747	1 786	2 032
Sugar	115	146	260	247	253	269	293	322	350	357	368
Preserves and confectionery	628	797	981	1 080	1 351	1 577	1 764	1 959	2 135	2 313	2 447
Coffee, tea and cocoa	240	282	311	397	637	704	701	746	725	739	884
Soft drinks	228	275	430	498	524	603	758	856	843	856	968
Other manufactured food	297	344	419	479	503	595	650	706	763	785	866
Alcoholic drink: total	3 423	3 915	4 848	5 714	6 545	7 281	8 664	9 954	11 153	12 007	13 372
Beer	1 807	2 071	2 672	3 237	3 649	3 974	4 570	5 320	5 970	6 453	7 140
Spirits	1 004	1 125	1 342	1 491	1 769	1 998	2 454	2 720	2 909	3 003	3 289
Wine, cider and perry	612	719	834	986	1 127	1 309	1 640	1 914	2 274	2 551	2 943
Tobacco	1 938	2 229	2 735	3 092	3 628	3 885	4 233	4 822	5 515	5 882	6 208
Clothing and footwear: total	3 860	4 498	5 206	5 797	6 630	7 837	9 176	9 863	10 259	10 921	12 114
Clothing other than footwear	3 232	3 773	4 365	4 834	5 520	6 488	7 555	8 103	8 406	8 854	9 804
Footwear	628	725	841	963	1 110	1 349	1 621	1 760	1 853	2 067	2 310
Housing: total	5 863	7 093	8 735	10 158	11 596	13 135	15 612	18 827	22 554	25 863	27 326
Rents, rates and water charges	4 996	6 039	7 436	8 729	9 978	11 330	13 350	16 044	19 465	22 372	23 361
Maintenance, etc. by occupiers	867	1 054	1 299	1 429	1 618	1 805	2 262	2 783	3 089	3 491	3 965
Fuel and power: total	1 880	2 249	2 887	3 557	4 219	4 613	5 291	6 353	7 728	8 696	9 395
Electricity	896	1 085	1 514	1 860	2 159	2 396	2 703	3 370	3 973	4 264	4 449
Gas	534	611	764	993	1 204	1 359	1 566	1 851	2 458	3 063	3 530
Coal and coke	313	362	394	433	518	521	617	677	789	829	839
Other	137	191	215	271	338	337	405	455	508	540	577
Household goods and services: total	3 727	4 211	5 006	5 728	6 340	7 541	9 029	9 937	10 433	11 119	12 274
Furniture and floor coverings	1 282	1 440	1 772	2 072	2 250	2 610	3 265	3 429	3 513	3 698	4 150
Major appliances	712	770	907	1 038	1 168	1 437	1 795	1 997	2 065	2 257	2 514
Other household goods	1 178	1 373	1 591	1 830	2 083	2 533	2 837	3 123	3 331	3 521	3 862
Household and domestic services	555	628	736	788	839	961	1 132	1 388	1 524	1 643	1 748
Transport and communication: total	6 437	7 146	9 342	11 217	12 638	15 180	18 998	22 462	25 141	27 460	31 475
Cars, motorcycles and other vehicles	1 879	1 669	2 255	2 782	3 101	4 550	6 137	6 307	6 511	7 064	9 142
Petrol and oil	1 249	1 717	2 232	2 500	2 676	2 597	3 528	4 604	5 639	6 258	6 817
Vehicle excise duty	275	273	390	447	530	590	601	726	839	1 021	1 184
Other running costs of vehicles	1 010	1 197	1 471	1 811	2 283	2 710	3 159	3 768	4 128	4 477	4 886
Rail travel	324	355	456	548	658	787	898	1 088	1 134	1 075	1 290
Buses and coaches	567	628	802	951	1 049	1 157	1 291	1 498	1 588	1 713	1 890
Air travel	355	394	514	615	702	865	1 119	1 510	1 716	1 932	2 142
Other travel	225	261	295	341	395	454	576	715	793	812	918
Communications	553	652	927	1 222	1 244	1 470	1 689	2 246	2 793	3 108	3 206
Recreation, entertainment and education: total	4 191	4 938	5 960	6 918	8 033	9 335	10 897	12 621	14 019	15 451	16 541
Radio, television and other durable goods	665	727	867	1 006	1 137	1 313	1 553	1 587	1 796	2 146	2 504
TV and video rental, licence fees, etc.	570	664	817	953	1 054	1 179	1 346	1 578	1 669	1 942	2 047
Recreational goods not elsewhere specified	1 093	1 378	1 626	1 859	2 120	2 508	3 037	3 538	3 761	3 981	4 310
Recreational and entertainment services	1 001	1 142	1 345	1 552	1 847	2 176	2 539	2 970	3 321	3 522	3 751
Books, newspapers and magazines	619	751	931	1 042	1 225	1 376	1 539	1 856	2 137	2 414	2 528
Education	243	276	374	506	650	783	883	1 092	1 335	1 446	1 401
Other goods and services: total	5 473	6 315	7 696	8 954	10 655	12 180	14 668	17 248	18 558	20 476	23 356
Pharmaceutical products and medical goods	208	235	276	313	349	403	484	575	645	710	775
NHS payments and other medical expenses	200	225	261	318	383	423	516	684	859	1 055	1 237
Toilet articles; perfumery	537	611	712	790	894	1 007	1 190	1 337	1 499	1 670	1 819
Hairdressing and beauty care	262	302	355	413	487	560	669	783	849	943	1 027
Jewellery, etc. and other goods	642	807	971	1 136	1 396	1 713	2 080	2 349	2 433	2 582	2 786
Catering (meals and accommodation)	2 463	2 845	3 446	4 087	4 882	5 523	6 665	7 853	8 112	8 683	9 967
Life assurance, etc. costs and other services	1 161	1 290	1 675	1 897	2 264	2 551	3 064	3 667	4 161	4 833	5 745
Total household and tourist expenditure in the United Kingdom	45 263	52 353	64 376	75 076	86 331	98 914	116 932	134 960	149 530	163 465	179 209
less Expenditure by foreign tourists, etc. in the United Kingdom	− 863	− 1 067	− 1 442	− 2 046	− 2 712	− 2 907	− 3 246	− 3 505	− 3 617	− 3 799	− 4 277
Household expenditure abroad	758	772	1 009	1 125	1 219	1 591	2 083	2 653	3 131	3 483	3 834
Total household expenditure on goods and services	45 158	52 058	63 943	74 155	84 838	97 598	115 769	134 108	149 044	163 149	178 766
Final expenditure by private non-profit making bodies	846	1 014	1 273	1 557	1 699	1 888	2 143	2 681	3 081	3 328	3 661
Total consumers' expenditure	46 004	53 072	65 216	75 712	86 537	99 486	117 912	136 789	152 125	166 477	182 427

Source Central Statistical Office

14.10

(continued)

Consumers' expenditure at 1980 prices classified by function[1]

£ million

	1973	1974	1975	1976	1977	1978	1979	1980	1981	1982	1983
Food (household expenditure): total	22 442	22 122	22 001	22 159	21 883	22 501	22 893	22 873	22 676	22 587	22 858
Bread and cereals	3 121	3 053	3 017	3 044	3 034	3 034	3 055	3 056	3 086	3 105	3 117
Meat and bacon	5 761	5 809	5 976	5 971	6 116	6 272	6 475	6 471	6 275	6 228	6 093
Fish	703	625	688	690	635	648	668	731	750	752	778
Milk, cheese and eggs	3 657	3 606	3 613	3 617	3 480	3 520	3 480	3 423	3 341	3 303	3 329
Oils and fats	939	939	952	937	927	950	931	920	894	861	849
Fruit	1 208	1 173	1 133	1 203	1 105	1 148	1 193	1 273	1 248	1 185	1 255
Potatoes	786	786	730	644	675	750	779	789	823	843	898
Vegetables	1 476	1 432	1 456	1 449	1 452	1 540	1 563	1 621	1 659	1 618	1 669
Sugar	391	375	325	353	348	345	332	322	320	298	284
Preserves and confectionery	2 237	2 158	1 949	2 013	2 026	2 098	2 054	1 959	2 032	2 141	2 181
Coffee, tea and cocoa	740	787	760	770	665	694	733	746	734	732	819
Soft drinks	618	637	701	763	735	776	874	856	815	843	873
Other manufactured food	855	800	772	791	719	726	756	706	699	678	713
Alcoholic drink: total	9 211	9 435	9 350	9 448	9 487	9 930	10 382	9 954	9 612	9 383	9 730
Beer	5 394	5 396	5 567	5 623	5 467	5 548	5 588	5 320	5 000	4 838	4 914
Spirits	2 334	2 495	2 378	2 325	2 428	2 616	2 890	2 720	2 561	2 428	2 494
Wine, cider and perry	1 522	1 564	1 459	1 554	1 618	1 766	1 904	1 914	2 051	2 117	2 322
Tobacco	5 309	5 247	4 995	4 821	4 602	4 982	4 960	4 822	4 470	4 128	4 082
Clothing and footwear: total	8 346	8 244	8 354	8 406	8 529	9 333	9 996	9 863	10 170	10 734	11 683
Clothing other than footwear	6 860	6 750	6 828	6 838	6 961	7 596	8 149	8 103	8 334	8 676	9 405
Footwear	1 476	1 487	1 522	1 569	1 565	1 737	1 847	1 760	1 836	2 058	2 278
Housing: total	16 961	17 152	17 191	17 346	17 626	17 979	18 483	18 827	19 041	19 388	19 814
Rents, rates and water charges	14 121	14 387	14 655	14 941	15 232	15 516	15 790	16 044	16 279	16 530	16 764
Maintenance, etc. by occupiers	2 835	2 761	2 534	2 406	2 394	2 463	2 693	2 783	2 762	2 858	3 050
Fuel and power: total	6 145	6 253	6 107	6 050	6 202	6 314	6 622	6 353	6 335	6 211	6 220
Electricity	3 399	3 407	3 308	3 239	3 275	3 303	3 425	3 370	3 314	3 237	3 245
Gas	1 143	1 244	1 343	1 425	1 496	1 627	1 816	1 851	1 942	1 946	1 986
Coal and coke	1 085	1 138	959	851	865	790	797	677	667	654	626
Other	672	592	571	582	603	594	584	455	412	374	363
Household goods and services: total	10 286	9 816	9 512	9 615	9 117	9 787	10 354	9 937	9 791	10 001	10 629
Furniture and floor coverings	3 403	3 151	3 278	3 417	3 155	3 322	3 696	3 429	3 354	3 424	3 724
Major appliances	1 869	1 807	1 625	1 685	1 597	1 784	2 018	1 997	1 950	2 056	2 225
Other household goods	3 288	3 218	3 086	3 100	3 061	3 355	3 291	3 123	3 126	3 164	3 330
Household and domestic services	1 760	1 673	1 551	1 422	1 313	1 326	1 349	1 388	1 361	1 357	1 350
Transport and communication: total	20 470	18 948	19 062	19 598	19 374	21 022	22 499	22 462	22 628	22 923	24 861
Cars, motorcycles and other vehicles	6 365	4 855	5 152	5 325	4 725	5 804	6 668	6 307	6 366	6 510	7 900
Petrol and oil	4 256	4 125	4 044	4 294	4 333	4 445	4 492	4 604	4 657	4 827	4 909
Vehicle excise duty	622	619	631	637	638	670	682	726	701	755	811
Other running costs of vehicles	3 223	3 274	3 276	3 399	3 541	3 719	3 768	3 768	3 820	3 892	4 009
Rail travel	1 075	1 072	1 034	961	1 023	1 073	1 102	1 088	1 041	919	1 035
Buses and coaches	2 012	1 988	1 921	1 823	1 756	1 655	1 633	1 498	1 407	1 344	1 407
Air travel	982	894	956	971	980	1 121	1 332	1 510	1 639	1 700	1 670
Other travel	670	650	608	598	604	621	671	715	719	688	723
Communications	1 488	1 542	1 534	1 633	1 733	1 914	2 151	2 246	2 278	2 288	2 388
Recreation, entertainment and education: total	10 468	10 825	10 733	11 075	11 333	11 989	12 478	12 621	12 772	13 132	13 615
Radio, television and other durable goods	1 037	1 078	1 076	1 203	1 243	1 374	1 581	1 587	1 816	2 203	2 601
TV and video rental, licence fees, etc.	1 019	1 163	1 252	1 386	1 419	1 482	1 547	1 578	1 626	1 706	1 828
Recreational goods not elsewhere specified	2 820	3 076	3 080	3 055	3 016	3 189	3 401	3 538	3 575	3 640	3 799
Recreational and entertainment services	2 994	2 930	2 814	2 825	2 902	3 032	3 015	2 970	2 805	2 722	2 711
Books, newspapers and magazines	2 044	1 999	1 892	1 831	1 822	1 840	1 856	1 856	1 805	1 744	1 671
Education	761	740	736	810	964	1 072	1 078	1 092	1 145	1 117	1 005
Other goods and services: total	16 455	16 549	16 545	16 500	16 872	17 234	17 709	17 248	16 867	17 184	18 078
Pharmaceutical products and medical goods	556	560	531	528	506	536	559	575	564	562	574
NHS payments and other medical expenses	619	611	542	559	588	594	632	684	754	839	921
Toilet articles; perfumery	1 469	1 484	1 389	1 341	1 302	1 359	1 419	1 337	1 398	1 439	1 493
Hairdressing and beauty care	873	852	815	792	797	799	804	783	757	763	773
Jewellery, etc. and other goods	2 335	2 485	2 433	2 528	2 686	2 893	2 802	2 349	2 368	2 431	2 325
Catering (meals and accommodation)	7 773	7 569	7 643	7 649	7 778	7 736	7 964	7 853	7 269	7 146	7 644
Life assurance, etc. costs and other services	2 814	2 962	3 149	3 085	3 211	3 317	3 529	3 667	3 757	4 004	4 348
Total household and tourist expenditure in the United Kingdom	125 970	124 511	123 771	124 947	124 919	131 071	136 376	134 960	134 362	135 671	141 570
less Expenditure by foreign tourists, etc. in the United Kingdom	- 2 446	- 2 655	- 3 010	- 3 694	- 4 208	- 3 949	- 3 836	- 3 505	- 3 202	- 3 082	- 3 271
Household expenditure abroad	1 654	1 452	1 564	1 400	1 355	1 679	2 119	2 653	2 823	2 801	2 833
Total household expenditure on goods and services	125 074	123 183	122 260	122 600	122 046	128 801	134 659	134 108	133 983	135 390	141 132
Final expenditure by private non-profit making bodies	2 358	2 446	2 489	2 577	2 520	2 572	2 597	2 681	2 731	2 745	2 876
Total consumers' expenditure	127 436	125 630	124 748	125 175	124 564	131 373	137 256	136 789	136 714	138 135	144 008

1. For the years before 1978, totals differ from the sum of their components due to the method of rebasing used. See notes on page 113 of *United Kingdom National Accounts 1984 Edition*. (HMSO)

Source Central Statistical Office

14.11 Consumers' expenditure at current prices classified by commodity

£ million

	1973	1974	1975	1976	1977	1978	1979	1980	1981	1982	1983
Durable goods:											
Cars, motorcycles and other vehicles	1 879	1 669	2 255	2 782	3 101	4 550	6 137	6 307	6 511	7 064	9 142
Furniture and floor coverings	1 282	1 440	1 772	2 072	2 250	2 610	3 265	3 429	3 513	3 698	4 150
Other durable goods	1 377	1 497	1 774	2 044	2 305	2 750	3 348	3 584	3 861	4 403	5 018
Total	4 538	4 606	5 801	6 898	7 656	9 910	12 750	13 320	13 885	15 165	18 310
Other goods:											
Food (household expenditure)	8 471	9 759	11 961	13 941	16 047	17 927	20 364	22 873	24 170	25 590	27 148
Beer	1 807	2 071	2 672	3 237	3 649	3 974	4 570	5 320	5 970	6 453	7 140
Other alcoholic drink	1 616	1 844	2 176	2 477	2 896	3 307	4 094	4 634	5 183	5 554	6 232
Tobacco	1 938	2 229	2 735	3 092	3 628	3 885	4 233	4 822	5 515	5 882	6 208
Clothing other than footwear	3 232	3 773	4 365	4 834	5 520	6 488	7 555	8 103	8 406	8 854	9 804
Footwear	628	725	841	963	1 110	1 349	1 621	1 760	1 853	2 067	2 310
Energy products	3 129	3 966	5 119	6 057	6 895	7 210	8 819	10 957	13 367	14 954	16 212
Other goods	4 725	5 698	6 757	7 700	8 930	10 614	12 473	14 369	15 538	16 810	18 238
Services:											
Rents, rates and water charges	4 996	6 039	7 436	8 729	9 978	11 330	13 350	16 044	19 465	22 372	23 361
Other services[1]	10 924	12 362	15 353	17 784	20 228	23 492	28 083	34 587	38 773	42 776	47 464
Total consumers' expenditure	46 004	53 072	65 216	75 712	86 537	99 486	117 912	136 789	152 125	166 477	182 427

1. Including the adjustments for international travel, etc. and final expenditure
   by private non-profit-making bodies serving persons.

Source Central Statistical Office

14.12 Consumers' expenditure at 1980 prices classified by commodity[1]

£ million at 1980 prices

	1973	1974	1975	1976	1977	1978	1979	1980	1981	1982	1983
Durable goods:											
Cars, motorcycles and other vehicles	6 365	4 855	5 152	5 325	4 725	5 804	6 668	6 307	6 366	6 510	7 909
Furniture and floor coverings	3 403	3 151	3 278	3 417	3 155	3 322	3 696	3 429	3 354	3 424	3 724
Other durable goods	2 821	2 819	2 665	2 867	2 842	3 158	3 599	3 584	3 766	4 259	4 826
Total	12 408	10 886	11 067	11 613	10 809	12 284	13 963	13 320	13 486	14 193	16 459
Other goods:											
Food (household expenditure)	22 442	22 122	22 001	22 159	21 883	22 501	22 893	22 873	22 676	22 587	22 858
Beer	5 394	5 396	5 567	5 623	5 467	5 548	5 588	5 320	5 000	4 838	4 914
Other alcoholic drink	3 855	4 058	3 836	3 878	4 046	4 382	4 794	4 634	4 612	4 545	4 816
Tobacco	5 309	5 247	4 995	4 821	4 602	4 982	4 960	4 822	4 470	4 128	4 082
Clothing other than footwear	6 860	6 750	6 828	6 838	6 961	7 596	8 149	8 103	8 334	8 676	9 405
Footwear	1 476	1 487	1 522	1 569	1 565	1 737	1 847	1 760	1 836	2 058	2 278
Energy products	10 394	10 353	10 127	10 347	10 533	10 759	11 114	10 957	10 992	11 038	11 129
Other goods	13 895	14 203	13 603	13 573	13 629	14 603	14 872	14 369	14 420	14 626	14 934
Services:											
Rents, rates and water charges	14 121	14 387	14 655	14 941	15 232	15 516	15 790	16 044	16 279	16 530	16 764
Other services[2]	31 388	30 874	30 673	29 917	29 927	31 465	33 286	34 587	34 609	34 916	36 369
Total consumers' expenditure	127 436	125 630	124 748	125 175	124 564	131 373	137 256	136 789	136 714	138 135	144 008

1. For the years before 1978, totals differ from the sum of their components;
   see notes on page 113 of *United Kingdom National Accounts 1984 Edition*.
   (HMSO).

2. Including the adjustments for international travel, etc. and final expenditure
   by private non-profit-making bodies serving persons.

# 14.13 Index numbers of gross domestic product and gross national disposable income
1980 = 100

	1973	1974	1975	1976	1977	1978	1979	1980	1981	1982	1983
Gross domestic product at current factor cost											
Based on expenditure data	32.8	38.0	48.1	57.1	64.8	74.6	85.8	100.0	109.4	118.3	129.2
Based on income data	33.2	37.8	47.8	55.7	64.9	74.5	86.1	100.0	109.1	119.7	130.7
Gross domestic product at constant factor cost											
Based on expenditure data	93.8	93.1	92.5	96.1	97.1	100.0	101.9	100.0	99.1	100.5	103.9
Based on income data	95.1	92.6	91.9	93.8	97.2	99.9	102.3	100.0	98.8	101.7	105.1
Based on output data	95.2	93.8	92.0	93.9	96.5	99.9	103.0	100.0	98.3	100.3	103.2
Average estimate	94.7	93.2	92.1	94.6	97.0	99.9	102.4	100.0	98.7	100.8	104.1
Gross domestic product at current market prices											
Average estimate	32.4	36.6	46.0	54.3	63.3	72.9	85.7	100.0	110.1	120.8	131.1
Gross domestic product at constant market prices											
Average estimate	94.4	92.8	91.7	94.3	96.4	99.9	102.6	100.0	98.5	101.0	104.2
Gross national disposable income at constant market prices											
Average estimate	95.4	90.6	90.2	92.5	93.9	98.5	101.8	100.0	99.5	101.7	105.1

Source Central Statistical Office

14.14 Value of physical increase in stocks and work in progress

£ million

	1973	1974	1975	1976	1977	1978	1979	1980	1981	1982	1983
All current prices[1]											
Manufacturing[2]	679	963	− 1 002	349	992	348	228	− 2 321	− 1 581	− 1 325	− 325
Materials and fuel	497	310	− 853	68	266	137	16	− 1 251	− 1 036	− 574	− 277
Work in progress	231	217	− 190	261	306	124	− 260	− 714	− 54	− 519	129
Finished products	− 49	436	41	20	420	87	472	− 356	− 491	− 233	− 177
Retail distribution	306	− 200	− 100	340	281	660	774	− 619	− 82	− 26	− 69
Wholesale distribution	337	299	− 240	224	676	671	1 162	− 575	− 583	− 96	83
Other industries	207	228	− 189	− 124	− 145	11	− 41	616	− 902	19	578
Total	1 529	1 290	− 1 531	789	1 804	1 690	2 123	− 2 899	− 3 148	− 1 428	267
Revalued at 1980 prices											
Manufacturing[2]	2 018	2 124	− 1 825	437	1 354	476	275	− 2 321	− 1 529	− 1 138	− 256
Materials and fuel	1 408	691	− 1 580	−	357	174	15	− 1 251	− 996	− 514	− 234
Work in progress	722	455	− 315	408	398	176	− 261	− 714	− 59	− 431	109
Finished products	− 112	978	70	29	599	126	521	− 356	− 475	− 193	− 131
Retail distribution	1 287	− 451	− 211	530	378	819	874	− 619	− 69	− 5	− 29
Wholesale distribution	903	633	− 459	319	937	834	1 398	− 575	− 519	− 39	5
Other industries	764	554	− 453	− 345	− 213	− 75	− 73	616	− 622	− 65	487
Total	5 023	2 837	− 2 969	1 035	2 566	2 054	2 474	− 2 899	− 2 739	− 1 247	207

1. It is estimated that a fall in the book value of stocks of £280 million took place in 1973 on the introduction of VAT as a result of the change in treatment of tax in the valuation of stocks. The fall has been allocated as follows:

	£ million
Manufacturers	34
of which:	
Materials and fuel	4
Work in progress	8
Finished products	22
Wholesalers	36
Retailers	181
Other industries	29

This allocation is approximate particularly in relation to the asset analysis of manufacturers' stocks. The 1980 price figures are not affected.

2. Differences between totals and the sum of constituent parts of manufacturing at 1980 prices for 1978 onwards and for all current prices are due to rounding. Differences between totals and components at 1980 prices before 1978 arise from the method of rebasing these years on to 1980 prices.

Sources Central Statistical Office; Department of Industry

14.15 Gross domestic fixed capital formation
At current prices

£ million

	1973	1974	1975	1976	1977	1978	1979	1980	1981	1982	1983
By type of asset											
Buses and coaches	60	59	85	120	127	158	183	181	175	146	175
Other road vehicles	823	1 010	1 100	1 484	2 217	2 972	3 720	3 183	2 955	3 737	3 949
Railway rolling stock	39	47	59	57	79	98	127	164	138	124	97
Ships	626	580	638	433	528	529	309	355	305	372	238
Aircraft	79	90	104	192	213	261	359	688	372	–	312
Plant and machinery	4 915	5 701	6 722	8 333	9 670	11 412	13 500	15 065	15 241	16 718	18 176
Dwellings	3 153	3 599	4 964	5 671	5 682	6 384	7 541	8 419	8 244	9 521	10 947
Other new buildings and works	4 575	5 727	7 015	7 712	7 673	8 220	9 669	11 899	12 449	13 217	13 099
By industry group											
Agriculture, forestry and fishing	509	540	586	677	798	959	966	1 033	950	1 191	1 312
Extraction of mineral oil and natural gas	213	592	1 374	2 070	2 108	2 152	2 057	2 399	2 882	3 081	2 736
All other energy and water supply	889	1 131	1 553	1 761	1 789	2 113	2 506	3 241	3 667	3 807	4 189
Manufacturing (revised definition)	2 358	3 062	3 458	3 910	4 731	5 626	6 515	6 471	5 302	5 456	5 662
Construction	254	295	349	360	407	484	587	467	440	538	531
Distribution, hotels and catering; repairs	1 085	1 256	1 244	1 369	1 904	2 326	3 025	3 223	3 201	3 522	3 963
Transport	1 137	1 224	1 407	1 454	1 866	2 153	2 337	2 414	1 931	1 794	2 149
Communication	732	731	774	899	876	965	1 141	1 456	1 466	1 490	1 675
Banking, finance, insurance business services and leasing											
Leased assets	} 1 361	} 1 605	{ 320	434	633	1 146	1 733	2 157	2 240	2 699	2 483
Other assets			{ 1 380	1 672	1 933	2 183	2 765	3 596	4 290	4 685	4 960
Other services	2 579	2 778	3 278	3 725	3 462	3 543	4 234	5 078	5 266	6 051	6 386
Dwellings	3 153	3 599	4 964	5 671	5 682	6 384	7 541	8 419	8 244	9 521	10 947
Transfer costs of land and buildings	565	495	625	716	832	1 103	1 475	1 674	1 915	2 158	2 566
Total	14 835	17 308	21 312	24 718	27 021	31 137	36 882	41 628	41 794	45 993	49 559

Revalued at 1980 prices[1]

£ million

	1973	1974	1975	1976	1977	1978	1979	1980	1981	1982	1983
By type of asset											
Buses and coaches	221	193	197	230	200	207	211	181	159	126	147
Other road vehicles	2 924	3 059	2 471	2 792	3 402	3 911	4 375	3 183	2 733	3 165	3 271
Railway rolling stock, ships and aircraft	1 856	1 553	1 513	1 103	1 105	1 090	874	1 207	722	423	507
Plant and machinery	12 593	12 908	12 230	12 758	12 913	13 904	14 966	15 065	14 064	14 408	14 909
Dwellings	9 476	8 497	9 681	9 831	8 990	9 209	9 295	8 419	7 294	8 147	8 937
Other new buildings and works	14 933	14 214	14 163	14 171	13 145	12 815	12 479	11 899	11 318	12 336	12 370
By industry group											
Agriculture, forestry and fishing	1 635	1 411	1 247	1 238	1 234	1 312	1 159	1 033	894	1 090	1 172
Extraction of mineral oil and natural gas	640	1 357	2 687	3 607	3 321	3 089	2 525	2 399	2 692	2 815	2 437
All other energy and water supply	2 688	2 788	3 047	2 996	2 711	2 896	3 004	3 241	3 315	3 307	3 492
Manufacturing (revised definition)	6 787	7 431	6 688	6 470	6 773	7 235	7 497	6 471	4 853	4 684	4 619
Construction	772	765	711	615	588	614	671	467	409	459	447
Distribution, hotels and catering; repairs	3 205	3 094	2 508	2 416	2 909	3 150	3 582	3 223	2 947	3 124	3 438
Transport	3 222	2 952	2 807	2 491	2 749	2 829	2 729	2 414	1 740	1 567	1 803
Communication	2 109	1 842	1 554	1 492	1 301	1 287	1 331	1 456	1 327	1 264	1 380
Banking, finance, insurance, business services and leasing[2]											
Leased assets	} 3 614	} 3 501	{ 522	622	795	1 396	1 926	2 157	2 073	2 344	2 087
Other assets			{ 2 542	2 807	2 859	2 981	3 257	3 596	4 007	4 376	4 639
Other services	8 028	6 964	6 382	6 419	5 552	5 138	5 224	5 078	4 739	5 428	5 690
Dwellings	9 476	8 497	9 681	9 831	8 990	9 209	9 295	8 419	7 294	8 147	8 937
Transfer costs of land and buildings	1 584	1 284	1 552	1 572	1 641	1 802	1 725	1 674	1 785	2 040	2 207
Total	43 535	41 734	41 808	42 434	41 323	42 938	43 925	41 628	38 075	40 645	42 348

1. For the years before 1978, totals differ from the sum of their components due to the method of rebasing used. See notes on page 113 of *United Kingdom National Accounts,* 1984 edition (HMSO).
2. Leased assets are classified, on the basis of ownership rather than use, to the finance industry.

Source Central Statistical Office

14.16 Gross capital stock at 1980 replacement cost by industry[1]

£ thousand million at 1980 prices

	1973	1974	1975	1976	1977	1978	1979	1980	1981	1982	1983
Agriculture	17.4	18.0	18.4	18.8	19.2	19.7	20.0	20.2	20.2	20.3	20.7
Forestry and fishing	3.9	3.9	4.0	4.1	4.1	4.1	4.2	4.2	4.2	4.2	4.3
Coal and coke	8.0	7.8	7.8	7.9	8.0	8.3	8.7	9.2	9.6	10.0	10.4
Extraction of mineral oil and natural gas	2.1	3.5	6.2	9.8	13.1	16.0	18.1	19.8	21.4	23.0	24.4
Mineral oil processing	6.6	6.7	6.9	7.0	7.1	7.3	7.5	7.8	8.1	8.2	8.3
Electricity, etc.	50.1	50.8	51.5	51.9	52.1	52.1	52.0	51.8	51.7	51.8	51.9
Gas supply	12.3	12.6	13.1	13.4	13.7	13.9	14.1	14.5	14.8	15.1	15.4
Water supply	15.9	16.1	16.2	16.3	16.4	16.6	16.8	16.9	16.9	17.1	17.2
Manufacturing (revised definition)[2]:											
Metals	20.3	20.9	21.7	22.4	23.0	23.2	23.3	23.3	23.1	22.9	22.5
Other minerals and mineral products	9.5	9.9	10.1	10.3	10.5	10.7	10.9	11.2	11.2	11.2	11.2
Chemicals and man-made fibres	25.6	26.2	26.9	27.6	28.4	29.3	30.2	30.8	31.1	31.3	31.6
Metal goods nes	9.5	9.8	10.0	10.1	10.2	10.4	10.6	10.6	10.6	10.5	10.4
Mechanical engineering	13.9	14.3	14.7	15.1	15.4	15.9	16.3	16.6	16.7	16.7	16.7
Electrical and instrument engineering	10.7	11.1	11.4	11.7	12.0	12.4	12.8	13.2	13.4	13.7	14.0
Motor vehicles and parts	11.3	11.5	11.6	11.7	11.9	12.3	12.8	13.2	13.4	13.6	13.7
Other transport equipment	8.8	8.8	8.8	8.8	8.8	8.7	8.7	8.7	8.6	8.6	8.5
Food	13.4	13.8	14.2	14.5	14.8	15.2	15.6	15.9	16.1	16.4	16.5
Drink and tobacco	7.0	7.4	7.7	7.9	8.1	8.4	8.7	8.9	9.0	9.1	9.3
Textiles	11.1	11.4	11.4	11.4	11.4	11.3	11.3	11.1	11.0	10.8	10.6
Clothing, footwear and leather	3.7	3.7	3.8	3.7	3.7	3.8	3.8	3.7	3.7	3.7	3.6
Timber and wooden furniture	3.0	3.2	3.3	3.3	3.4	3.5	3.6	3.7	3.7	3.7	3.7
Paper, printing and publishing	11.1	11.5	11.8	11.9	12.2	12.5	12.9	13.2	13.4	13.6	13.7
Rubber and plastics	5.8	6.0	6.2	6.3	6.5	6.7	6.9	7.1	7.1	7.1	7.1
Other manufacturing	2.1	2.1	2.2	2.2	2.2	2.2	2.2	2.3	2.2	2.2	2.2
Total	166.9	171.6	175.5	179.1	182.7	186.6	190.7	193.5	194.4	195.0	195.3
Construction	10.1	10.6	11.0	11.3	11.6	11.9	12.2	12.3	12.3	12.4	12.4
Distribution, hotels and catering; repairs	43.6	46.1	48.0	49.8	52.1	54.7	57.7	60.3	62.6	65.0	67.6
Railways	35.0	34.6	34.3	34.0	33.7	33.4	33.0	32.4	31.8	31.2	30.5
Other inland transport	9.8	10.1	10.2	10.5	10.8	11.4	11.9	12.2	12.2	12.3	12.5
Sea transport	9.7	10.2	10.3	9.9	10.0	9.3	8.4	8.4	7.3	6.4	5.3
Air transport	3.2	3.3	3.3	3.4	3.5	3.5	3.6	3.8	3.6	3.1	3.0
Other transport	9.8	10.0	10.1	10.1	10.3	10.4	10.6	10.7	10.8	10.9	11.0
Communication	19.6	21.0	22.0	23.0	23.8	24.6	25.3	26.3	27.1	27.7	28.4
Banking, finance, insurance, business services and leasing											
Leased assets	1.8	2.4	2.9	3.5	4.3	5.6	7.4	9.4	11.3	13.4	15.2
Other assets	39.5	42.1	44.5	47.2	50.0	52.7	55.8	59.1	62.9	66.9	71.1
Other services[4]	131.0	136.9	142.2	147.6	152.1	156.2	160.4	164.3	167.9	172.2	176.7
Dwellings	279.1	286.9	295.8	304.8	313.0	321.4	329.8	337.3	343.6	350.7	358.4
Total[2]	875.3	904.9	934.3	963.6	991.6	1 019.5	1 048.0	1 074.4	1 094.8	1 116.9	1 139.9

1. For an account of the principles of valuation, see *National Accounts Statistics: Sources and Methods*, pages 383–7 (HMSO 1968) and *Economic Trends*, October 1975 (HMSO). Figures relate to end of year. Assets are classified to industry on the basis of ownership, not use.

2. Differences between totals and the sums of constituent parts of manufacturing and of all industries are due to rounding.

Source Central Statistical Office

15 Personal Income, Expenditure and Wealth

Family Expenditure Survey *(Tables 15.3 – 15.5)*

The Family Expenditure Survey, introduced in 1957, covers all types of private households in the United Kingdom. It is a continuing enquiry in which a sample of about 11 000 addresses is selected annually, from which an effective sample of some 10 400 households is obtained, of which about 70 per cent co-operate. The main purpose of the survey is to provide a source of the weighting pattern of the Index of Retail Prices and so it is primarily concerned with household expenditure on a wide range of goods and services.

The income information the survey collects is basically to enable households to be classified into income groups and although most of the income information obtained is on a current basis, income from investment, self-employment and some other sources relate to a previous twelve-month period. As income and expenditure figures relate to different periods, the difference between expenditure and income as measured in the survey should not be regarded as savings or dis-savings.

Although the survey is primarily concerned with the expenditure of private households, much additional information is collected about the characteristics of each co-operating household. Consequently the survey provides a unique fund of important economic and social data.

Like all surveys based on a sample of the population, its results are subject to sampling error, and to some bias due to non-response. The sampling error is smallest in relation to the average expenditure of large groups of households or items purchased frequently when expenditure does not vary greatly between households. Conversely, it is largest in relation to small groups of households, and for items purchased infrequently for which expenditure varies considerably between households. However, comparison of the survey results over successive years justifies confidence in their reliability.

The results of the survey are published in an annual report, the latest being *Family Expenditure Survey 1983* (HMSO). This includes a list of the definitions used in the survey, items on which information is collected and a brief account of the field work procedure.

15.1 Average incomes of households before and after taxes and benefits[1,2]

£ per year

	1972	1973	1974	1975	1976	1977	1978	1979	1980	1981	1982
1 adult—non-pensioner											
Original income	1 055	1 149	1 419	1 724	1 943	2 235	2 479	2 870	3 341	4 082	4 191
Disposable income	1 049	1 157	1 404	1 699	1 908	2 221	2 504	2 892	3 467	4 175	4 289
Income after all taxes and benefits	916	1 051	1 301	1 594	1 782	2 032	2 313	2 593	3 154	3 729	3 815
1 adult—pensioner[3]											
Original income	32	32	40	52	61	66	84	93	103	143	166
Disposable income	477	521	660	846	980	1 139	1 298	1 444	1 714	2 067	2 278
Income after all taxes and benefits	496	596	748	982	1 154	1 312	1 502	1 673	2 133	2 501	2 708
2 adults—non-pensioner											
Original income	2 007	2 366	2 831	3 594	3 935	4 417	5 123	5 836	7 317	8 237	8 339
Disposable income	1 846	2 149	2 534	3 096	3 448	3 941	4 658	5 380	6 654	7 546	7 761
Income after all taxes and benefits	1 583	1 891	2 246	2 783	3 097	3 508	4 163	4 670	5 748	6 554	6 678
2 adults—pensioner[3]											
Original income	68	80	103	133	174	180	193	249	297	328	344
Disposable income	719	837	1 041	1 314	1 546	1 744	2 004	2 276	2 722	3 150	3 459
Income after all taxes and benefits	742	918	1 159	1 543	1 809	2 056	2 320	2 570	3 222	3 720	3 939
2 adults, 1 child											
Original income	2 223	2 673	3 097	3 880	4 328	4 838	5 418	6 163	7 707	8 757	9 724
Disposable income	1 939	2 319	2 614	3 176	3 603	4 125	4 746	5 537	6 845	7 686	8 511
Income after all taxes and benefits	1 775	2 124	2 464	3 041	3 483	3 860	4 428	5 136	6 255	7 115	7 768
2 adults, 2 children											
Original income	2 388	2 755	3 293	4 039	4 540	5 160	6 070	7 027	8 499	8 993	9 778
Disposable income	2 128	2 409	2 834	3 345	3 815	4 401	5 289	6 304	7 457	8 003	8 560
Income after all taxes and benefits	2 041	2 339	2 865	3 461	3 915	4 479	5 349	6 231	7 410	8 093	8 503
2 adults, 3 children											
Original income	2 387	2 890	3 385	4 266	4 726	5 637	5 436	6 538	8 091	8 599	8 948
Disposable income	2 227	2 587	3 006	3 539	4 039	4 876	5 165	6 157	7 442	8 199	8 784
Income after all taxes and benefits	2 319	2 742	3 297	4 105	4 574	5 402	5 882	6 768	8 149	9 180	9 758
3 adults											
Original income	2 781	3 366	3 914	4 896	5 705	6 153	7 122	8 357	9 625	11 011	11 337
Disposable income	2 509	3 011	3 425	4 132	4 849	5 321	6 316	7 434	8 618	9 777	10 246
Income after all taxes and benefits	2 230	2 703	3 064	3 765	4 345	4 805	5 623	6 622	7 580	8 576	8 919
3 adults, 1 child											
Original income	2 991	3 506	4 216	5 186	5 972	6 507	8 013	8 558	10 507	11 152	12 206
Disposable income	2 655	3 122	3 673	4 316	4 928	5 640	6 900	7 535	9 150	9 782	10 748
Income after all taxes and benefits	2 547	3 051	3 688	4 391	4 932	5 676	6 774	7 276	8 813	9 490	10 509
4 adults											
Original income	3 866	4 520	5 342	6 989	8 105	8 416	10 037	11 475	13 443	16 140	15 397
Disposable income	3 334	3 873	4 625	5 625	6 514	6 990	8 475	9 655	11 352	13 335	13 238
Income after all taxes and benefits	3 047	3 632	4 330	5 107	6 033	6 399	7 777	8 690	10 180	11 908	11 853
1 adult with child(ren)[4]											
Original income	..	..	..	..	1 626	1 571	2 024	2 416	2 854	3 610	2 388
Disposable income	..	..	..	..	2 178	2 316	2 947	3 303	3 826	4 983	4 203
Income after all taxes and benefits	..	..	..	..	2 822	2 975	3 672	4 042	4 674	6 046	5 289
Other households											
Original income	..	..	..	..	6 241	6 705	7 682	8 960	11 030	11 881	13 035
Disposable income	..	..	..	..	5 561	6 193	7 206	8 352	10 157	11 227	12 564
Income after all taxes and benefits	..	..	..	..	6 185	6 843	7 761	8 805	10 764	11 757	13 238
All households in the sample											
Original income	1 997	2 309	2 719	3 386	3 781	4 234	4 826	5 451	6 706	7 587	7 872
Disposable income	1 884	2 156	2 509	3 016	3 413	3 906	4 548	5 206	6 332	7 212	7 566
Income after all taxes and benefits	1 764	2 046	2 453	3 000	3 361	3 808	4 405	4 953	6 016	6 867	7 148

1. Original income is the total income in cash and kind of the household before the deduction of taxes or the addition of state benefits. The addition of cash benefits (retirement pensions, child benefit, etc.) and the deduction of income tax and employees' national insurance contributions give disposable income. By further allowing for taxes paid on goods and services purchased (such as VAT) and benefits in kind received from public expenditure (housing subsidies, education, health, etc.) an estimate of 'final' income is derived.

2. These income figures are derived from estimates made by the Central Statistical Office, based largely on information from the Family Expenditure Survey, and published each year in Economic Trends. As a result of changes in the coverage of taxes and benefits and the method of allocating them to households, these figures are not exactly comparable from year to year. In order to produce figures on as consistent a basis as possible adjustments have been made to the data published in Economic Trends.

3. A pensioner household is one in which the head is over state retirement pension age and when more than three quarters of the household's income consists of national insurance retirement and similar state pensions, or related supplementary benefit.

4. Due to the smaller sample size of this household type, the figures may be subject to greater than average year to year variation.

Source Central Statistical Office

15.2 Distribution of total incomes before and after tax
Years ended 5 April

1978/79 Annual Survey

Lower limit of range of income	Thousands	£ million		
	Number of incomes	Total income before tax	Tax	Total income after tax
All incomes[1,2]	22 600	105 000	20 200	84 500
Income before tax £				
1 000	1 540	1 920	61	1 860
1 500	1 870	3 270	237	3 030
2 000	2 140	4 820	538	4 280
2 500	1 890	5 200	715	4 490
3 000	1 850	5 990	941	5 050
3 500	1 920	7 170	1 220	5 950
4 000	1 630	6 930	1 220	5 710
4 500	1 640	7 800	1 410	6 390
5 000	2 680	14 600	2 660	12 000
6 000	1 920	12 400	2 370	10 100
7 000	1 280	9 520	1 920	7 600
8 000	1 210	10 700	2 320	8 380
10 000	447	4 850	1 170	3 690
12 000	277	3 670	1 000	2 660
15 000	148	2 520	819	1 700
20 000	100	2 680	1 200	1 470
50 000	6	384	256	128
100 000 and over	1	156	116	41
Income after tax £				
1 000	1 920	2 540	115	2 420
1 500	2 610	5 130	542	4 590
2 000	2 710	7 080	1 000	6 080
2 500	2 450	8 040	1 330	6 710
3 000	2 320	9 100	1 570	7 530
3 500	2 120	9 710	1 750	7 970
4 000	1 760	9 100	1 640	7 450
4 500	1 550	8 980	1 620	7 360
5 000	2 330	15 700	2 980	12 700
6 000	1 280	10 400	2 150	8 260
7 000	638	6 150	1 390	4 760
8 000	521	6 270	1 670	4 600
10 000	178	2 830	904	1 930
12 000	91	1 920	721	1 200
15 000	36	1 090	486	609
20 000 and over	11	587	312	274

1979/80 Annual Survey

Lower limit of range of income	Thousands	£ million		
	Number of incomes	Total income before tax	Tax	Total income after tax
All incomes[1,2]	23 000	123 000	22 300	101 000
Income before tax £				
1 000 / 1 500	2 770	4 280	174	4 110
2 000	1 720	3 860	335	3 520
2 500	1 810	4 950	573	4 380
3 000	1 800	5 820	802	5 020
3 500	1 610	6 040	914	5 130
4 000	1 570	6 650	1 070	5 580
4 500	1 560	7 400	1 240	6 160
5 000	2 660	14 200	2 470	11 800
6 000	2 180	14 200	2 480	11 800
7 000	1 700	12 700	2 280	10 400
8 000	1 930	17 100	3 270	13 800
10 000	832	9 070	1 860	7 210
12 000	502	6 650	1 500	5 150
15 000	274	4 640	1 210	3 430
20 000	174	4 720	1 640	3 080
50 000	10	628	303	325
100 000 and over	2	314	166	148
Income after tax £				
1 000 / 1 500	3 440	5 700	329	5 370
2 000	2 400	6 130	720	5 410
2 500	2 320	7 400	1 040	6 360
3 000	2 120	8 150	1 290	6 860
3 500	1 990	8 960	1 490	7 470
4 000	1 820	9 270	1 570	7 700
4 500	1 500	8 610	1 480	7 130
5 000	2 600	17 300	3 020	14 300
6 000	1 890	14 900	2 670	12 200
7 000	1 150	10 600	2 030	8 610
8 000	1 050	11 600	2 400	9 230
10 000	409	5 780	1 360	4 420
12 000	220	3 990	1 090	2 900
15 000	100	2 510	812	1 700
20 000 and over	50	2 350	983	1 360

1. The distributions cover only incomes as computed for tax purposes and above a level which for each year corresponds approximately to the single person's allowance. Incomes below these levels are not shown because the information about them is incomplete.
2. All figures have been independently rounded.

Source Board of Inland Revenue

15.2
(continued)

Distribution of total incomes before and after tax
Years ended 5 April

Lower limit of range of income	1980/81 Annual Survey				Lower limit of range of income	1981/82 Annual Survey			
	Thousands	£ million				Thousands	£ million		
	Number of incomes	Total income before tax	Tax	Total income after tax		Number of incomes	Total income before tax	Tax	Total income after tax
All incomes [1,2]	22 200	141 000	26 600	114 000	All incomes [1,2]	21 900	152 000	30 300	121 000
Income before tax £					**Income before tax £**				
1 350	300	427	3	424	1 350	273	389	3	386
1 500	1 290	2 250	92	2 160	1 500	1 050	1 840	64	1 770
2 000	1 300	2 920	218	2 700	2 000	1 130	2 540	190	2 350
2 500	1 550	4 260	424	3 830	2 500	1 290	3 550	363	3 190
3 000	1 500	4 870	612	4 260	3 000	1 350	4 380	546	3 840
3 500	1 530	5 710	825	4 880	3 500	1 380	5 170	731	4 440
4 000	1 420	6 020	938	5 090	4 000	1 280	5 450	861	4 580
4 500	1 290	6 100	994	5 110	4 500	1 370	6 490	1 090	5 400
5 000	2 530	13 900	2 380	11 500	5 000	2 460	13 490	2 410	11 080
6 000	2 150	13 900	2 450	11 400	6 000	2 010	13 000	2 430	10 600
7 000	1 930	14 400	2 630	11 800	7 000	1 800	13 500	2 540	11 000
8 000	2 440	21 700	4 040	17 700	8 000	2 540	22 700	4 370	18 300
10 000	1 300	14 200	2 840	11 400	10 000	1 560	17 000	3 410	13 600
12 000	874	11 600	2 460	9 160	12 000	1 170	15 600	3 350	12 300
15 000	530	9 010	2 190	6 820	15 000	714	12 100	2 920	9 220
20 000	296	7 970	2 580	5 390	20 000	443	11 780	3 750	8 030
50 000	19	1 190	578	612	50 000	29	1 860	856	999
100 000 and over	4	621	320	301	100 000 and over	5	793	440	353
Income after tax £					**Income after tax £**				
1 350	409	594	8	586	1 350	328	475	7	468
1 500	1 640	3 060	182	2 880	1 500	1 320	2 440	125	2 310
2 000	1 810	4 580	478	4 100	2 000	1 590	4 000	413	3 580
2 500	2 060	6 550	865	5 680	2 500	1 790	5 680	754	4 930
3 000	1 960	7 490	1 140	6 350	3 000	1 840	7 060	1 080	5 990
3 500	1 800	8 030	1 290	6 740	3 500	1 770	7 990	1 340	6 650
4 000	1 580	8 080	1 360	6 710	4 000	1 740	8 950	1 580	7 370
4 500	1 620	9 310	1 630	7 680	4 500	1 470	8 540	1 540	7 000
5 000	2 650	17 700	3 100	14 600	5 000	2 490	16 730	3 110	13 620
6 000	2 140	16 900	3 050	13 800	6 000	1 980	15 900	2 990	12 900
7 000	1 460	13 500	2 500	11 000	7 000	1 540	14 200	2 710	11 500
8 000	1 630	18 000	3 560	14 400	8 000	1 950	21 600	4 340	17 300
10 000	735	10 200	2 230	8 000	10 000	971	13 600	2 970	10 600
12 000	453	7 990	1 980	6 010	12 000	613	10 800	2 640	8 120
15 000	198	4 780	1 420	3 360	15 000	309	7 370	2 150	5 220
20 000 and over	95	4 360	1 770	2 590	20 000 and over	137	6 330	2 560	3 780

1. The distributions cover only incomes as computed for tax purposes and above a level which for each year corresponds approximately to the single person's allowance. Incomes below these levels are not shown because the information about them is incomplete.
2. All figures have been independently rounded.

Source Board of Inland Revenue

15.3 Sources of household income[1]

	1972	1973	1974	1975	1976	1977	1978	1979	1980	1981	1982
Number of households supplying data[2]	7 017	7 126	6 695	7 203	7 203	7 198	7 001	6 777	6 944	7 525	7 428
Average weekly household income by source (£)											
Wages and salaries	32.36	36.33	42.25	54.51	60.23	66.92	76.10	86.27	104.78	114.22	118.50
Self-employment	2.57	3.34	4.38	4.03	4.38	5.47	5.29	5.63	8.16	10.24	10.59
Investments	1.28	1.70	1.97	2.57	2.51	2.81	2.95	3.28	4.49	6.35	6.94
Annuities and pensions (other than social security benefits)	0.99	1.24	1.43	1.70	2.15	2.29	3.03	3.14	3.79	5.20	5.26
Social security benefits	3.92	4.45	5.45	7.00	8.68	10.57	12.50	14.88	17.60	21.87	24.58
Imputed income from owner/rent-free occupancy[3]	1.34	1.92	2.24	2.44	3.46	3.93	4.93	5.65	6.75	7.79	8.57
Other sources[4]	0.39	0.42	0.60	0.64	0.89	0.99	1.33	1.59	1.61	1.93	2.24
Total	42.85	49.41	58.33	72.87	82.30	92.98	106.13	120.45	147.18	167.60	176.67
Sources of household income as a percentage of total household income (per cent)											
Wages and salaries	75.5	73.5	72.4	74.8	73.2	72.0	71.7	71.6	71.2	68.1	67.1
Self-employment	6.0	6.8	7.5	5.5	5.3	5.9	5.0	4.7	5.5	6.1	6.0
Investments	3.0	3.4	3.4	3.5	3.1	3.0	2.8	2.7	3.0	3.8	3.9
Annuities and pensions (other than social security benefits)	2.3	2.5	2.5	2.3	2.6	2.5	2.9	2.6	2.6	3.1	3.0
Social security benefits	9.2	9.0	9.4	9.6	10.5	11.4	11.8	12.4	12.0	13.1	13.9
Imputed income from owner/rent-free occupancy[3]	3.1	3.9	3.8	3.4	4.2	4.2	4.6	4.7	4.6	4.6	4.8
Other sources[4]	0.9	0.9	1.0	0.9	1.1	1.0	1.2	1.3	1.1	1.2	1.3
Total	100.0	100.0	100.0	100.0	100.0	100.0	100.0	100.0	100.0	100.0	100.0

1. Information derived from the Family Expenditure Survey.
2. In 1974 and 1979 data were not collected for a few weeks at the time of the General Elections.
3. Imputed income is the weekly equivalent of the rateable value: this is adjusted to allow for general increases in rents since date of valuation, and is also included in income of households living rent-free. From 1976 the method of calculating this adjustment is changed.
4. From 1982 'other sources' includes very small amounts of income previously classified under self employment.

Source Department of Employment

15.4 Availability in households of certain durable goods[1]

	1972	1973	1974	1975	1976	1977	1978	1979	1980	1981	1982
Number of households supplying data[2]	7 017	7 126	6 695	7 203	7 203	7 198	7 001	6 777	6 944	7 525	7 428
	Percentage										
Car	53.3	53.9	55.7	57.0	55.2	57.2	57.6	57.9	60.3	61.8	61.4
One	45.3	45.1	45.3	46.4	44.5	46.2	45.2	44.3	45.0	46.3	46.6
Two	7.4	8.0	9.3	9.6	9.6	9.7	10.9	11.7	13.1	13.4	12.7
Three or more	0.6	0.8	1.1	1.0	1.1	1.3	1.5	1.9	2.2	2.1	2.0
Central heating, full or partial	37.4	38.5	43.0	46.7	47.1	50.8	53.8	55.0	59.1	60.5	62.8
Washing machine	65.5	66.6	68.9	71.9	72.3	74.6	75.0	76.6	78.7	80.7	81.1
Refrigerator	74.2	77.6	81.8	85.3	88.1	89.9	91.6	92.9	94.8	96.1	96.4
Television	93.2	93.4	94.0	94.8	95.6	96.0	95.6	95.8	96.9	96.6	96.8
Telephone	42.1	43.4	49.5	51.9	52.6	56.8	62.0	67.2	71.6	75.8	75.7

1. Information derived from Family Expenditure Survey.
2. In 1974 and 1979 data were not collected for a few weeks at the time of the General Elections.

Source Department of Employment

15.5 Households and their expenditure[1]

	1972	1973	1974	1975	1976	1977	1978	1979	1980	1981	1982
Number of households supplying data[2]	7 017	7 126	6 695	7 203	7 203	7 198	7 001	6 777	6 944	7 525	7 428
Total number of persons	20 472	20 121	18 974	20 254	19 793	19 885	19 019	18 314	18 844	20 535	20 022
Total number of adults[3]	14 574	14 058	13 134	14 094	13 978	14 072	13 581	13 021	13 408	14 685	14 386
Household percentage distribution by tenure											
Rented unfurnished	46.1	45.0	44.0	42.7	43.0	44.1	41.9	41.2	40.9	41.6	39.0
Rented furnished	3.5	3.7	3.8	4.3	4.4	2.9	3.5	2.7	2.6	2.5	2.7
Rent-free	3.1	2.6	2.5	2.8	2.6	2.2	2.8	2.6	2.2	2.2	2.0
Owner-occupied	47.3	48.7	49.7	50.2	50.0	50.8	51.8	53.5	54.3	53.7	56.3
Average number of persons per household											
All persons	2.917	2.824	2.834	2.812	2.748	2.763	2.717	2.702	2.714	2.729	2.695
Males	1.421	1.379	1.369	1.370	1.346	1.338	1.314	1.300	1.307	1.329	1.317
Females	1.497	1.445	1.465	1.442	1.402	1.425	1.403	1.403	1.407	1.400	1.378
Adults[3]	2.077	1.973	1.962	1.957	1.941	1.955	1.940	1.921	1.931	1.951	1.937
Persons 16 and under 65	1.745	..	..	..	..	..	..	..	..	..	..
Persons under 65	..	1.611	1.598	1.603	1.570	1.592	1.579	1.550	1.563	1.585	1.584
Persons 65 and over	0.332	0.362	0.364	0.353	0.370	0.363	0.361	0.371	0.368	0.366	0.353
Children[3]	0.841	0.851	0.872	0.855	0.807	0.808	0.777	0.781	0.783	0.777	0.759
Children under 2	0.104	0.091	0.085	0.080	0.073	0.075	0.073	0.086	0.076	0.078	0.081
Children 2 and under 5	0.161	0.152	0.152	0.147	0.127	0.128	0.117	0.118	0.116	0.109	0.119
Children 5 and under 16	0.576	..	..	..	..	..	..	..	..	..	..
Children 5 and under 18	..	0.608	0.635	0.628	0.607	0.604	0.587	0.577	0.591	0.591	0.559
Persons working[4]	1.397	1.357	1.350	1.351	1.338	1.352	1.348	1.334	1.357	1.363	1.221
Persons not working[4]	1.520	1.466	1.484	1.461	1.410	1.410	1.369	1.369	1.356	1.366	1.474
Men 65 and over, women 60 and over[5]	0.180	0.377	0.372	0.377	0.387	0.388	0.377	0.386	0.386	0.396	0.383
Others	1.340	1.090	1.112	1.084	1.023	1.022	0.992	0.983	0.971	0.970	1.092
Average weekly household expenditure on commodities and services (£)											
Housing[6]	4.42	5.31	6.36	7.16	9.21	10.31	11.87	13.72	16.56	19.76	22.29
Fuel, light and power	2.06	2.17	2.42	2.99	3.53	4.38	4.76	5.25	6.15	7.46	8.35
Food	8.72	9.63	11.29	13.52	15.36	17.74	19.31	21.83	25.15	27.20	28.19
Alcoholic drink	1.65	1.85	2.21	2.81	3.11	3.51	3.92	4.56	5.34	6.06	6.13
Tobacco	1.39	1.47	1.66	1.95	2.29	2.60	2.72	2.85	3.32	3.74	3.85
Clothing and footwear	3.14	3.48	4.19	4.75	4.99	5.78	6.78	7.79	8.99	9.23	9.69
Durable household goods	2.60	3.09	3.62	4.03	4.06	4.99	5.66	7.05	7.70	9.40	9.65
Other goods	2.53	2.85	3.53	4.14	4.49	5.33	5.99	7.28	8.75	9.45	10.06
Transport and vehicles	4.97	5.37	6.19	7.54	8.14	9.71	10.90	13.13	16.15	18.70	19.79
Services	3.45	4.02	4.44	5.39	6.19	6.93	7.66	9.74	11.96	13.84	15.37
Miscellaneous[7]	0.13	0.20	0.22	0.31	0.32	0.56	0.69	0.97	0.53	0.58	0.53
Total	35.06	39.43	46.13	54.58	61.70	71.84	80.26	94.17	110.60	125.41	133.92
Expenditure on commodity or service as a percentage of total expenditure (per cent)											
Housing[6]	12.6	13.5	13.8	13.1	14.9	14.4	14.8	14.6	15.0	15.8	16.6
Fuel, light and power	5.9	5.5	5.2	5.5	5.7	6.1	5.9	5.6	5.6	5.9	6.2
Food	24.9	24.4	24.5	24.8	24.9	24.7	24.1	23.2	22.7	21.7	21.1
Alcoholic drink	4.7	4.7	4.8	5.1	5.1	4.9	4.9	4.8	4.8	4.8	4.6
Tobacco	3.9	3.7	3.6	3.6	3.7	3.6	3.4	3.0	3.0	3.0	2.9
Clothing and footwear	9.0	8.8	9.1	8.7	8.1	8.0	8.4	8.3	8.1	7.4	7.2
Durable household goods	7.4	7.9	7.8	7.4	6.6	6.9	7.0	7.5	7.0	7.5	7.2
Other goods	7.2	7.2	7.7	7.6	7.3	7.4	7.5	7.7	7.9	7.5	7.5
Transport and vehicles	14.2	13.6	13.4	13.8	13.2	13.5	13.6	13.9	14.6	14.9	14.8
Services	9.8	10.2	9.6	9.9	10.0	9.7	9.5	10.4	10.8	11.0	11.5
Miscellaneous[7]	0.4	0.5	0.5	0.5	0.5	0.8	0.9	1.0	0.5	0.5	0.4
Total	100.0	100.0	100.0	100.0	100.0	100.0	100.0	100.0	100.0	100.0	100.0

1. Information derived from the Family Expenditure Survey.
2. In 1974 and 1979 data were not collected for a few weeks at the time of the General Elections.
3. Adults and children are:

    | 1972 | Adults = all persons 16 and over |
    | | Children = all persons under 16 |
    | 1973 to 1982 | Adults = all persons 18 and over and married persons under 18 |
    | | Children = all unmarried persons under 18. |

4. From 1982, figures for persons working (and persons not working) are on a revised basis: see *Family Expenditure Survey Report* for 1982 for details.

5. In 1972 this group included only those retired from work.
6. Excludes mortgage payments but includes imputed expenditure from owner-occupancy and from rent-free occupancy. Imputed expenditure is the weekly equivalent of the rateable value which is adjusted to allow for general increase in rents since date of valuation. From 1976 the method of calculating this adjustment is changed.
7. Miscellaneous expenditure was greater before 1980 when changes in classifying credit card expenditure were introduced.

Source Department of Employment

16 Home Finance

Public sector

In Table 16.1 the term public sector describes the consolidation of central government, local authorities and public corporations. The table sets out the relationship between the public sector financial deficit and the public sector borrowing requirement, (PSBR). A financial deficit (or surplus) represents the extent to which a sector's gross savings—that is, the balance of receipts and expenditure on current transactions—*plus* net capital transfers are insufficient (or more than sufficient) to finance the sector's expenditure on physical assets.

In recent years the public sector has been in deficit and has had to borrow. The deficit is not a complete indication of the borrowing requirement because it does not take into account lending to the private sector and overseas other non-borrowing financial transactions. The borrowing requirement equals the financial deficit *plus* the net increase in these financial assets. Net increase in bank deposits and other liquid assets, however, is counted as an offset to borrowing.

Details of public sector borrowing and the contributions to the PSBR are given in Table 16.2. Generally net acquisition of public sector debt and lending within the public sector is counted as an offset to borrowing so that the PSBR represents the net requirement for finance from the private sector and overseas. But the central government borrowing requirement is counted as covering direct on-lending by central government to local authorities and public corporations. Their additional 'contributions' to the PSBR are therefore equal to their borrowing requirements *less* their direct borrowing from central government.

The borrowing requirements are measured from the financing items rather than as the difference between receipts and payments because financing information is available sooner and, for local authorities and public corporations, is probably more reliable.

Central government

The central government embraces all bodies for whose activities a Minister of the Crown, or other responsible person, is accountable to Parliament. It includes, in addition to the ordinary government depart-ments, a number of bodies administering public policy but without the substantial degree of financial independence which characterises the public corporations; it also includes certain extra-budgetary funds and accounts controlled by departments.

The government's financial transactions are handled through a number of statutory funds, or accounts. The most important of these is the Consolidated Fund which is the government's main account with the Bank of England. Up to 31 March 1968 the Consolidated Fund was virtually synonymous with the term 'Exchequer' which was then the Government's central cash account. From 1 April 1968 the National Loans Fund, with a separate account at the Bank of England, was set up by the National Loans Act, 1968. The general effect of this Act was to remove from the Consolidated Fund most of the Government's domestic lending and the whole of the Government's borrowing transactions and to provide for them to be brought to account in the National Loans Fund.

Revenue from taxation and miscellaneous receipts, including interest and dividends on loans made from Votes, continue to be paid into the Consolidated Fund. After meeting the ordinary expenditure on Supply Services and the Consolidated Fund Standing Services, the surplus or deficit on the Consolidated Fund (Table 16.4), is payable into or met by the National Loans Fund.

Table 16.4 also provides a summary of the transactions of the National Loans Fund. The service of the National Debt, previously borne on the Consolidated Fund, is now met from the National Loans Fund which receives (a) interest payable on loans to the nationalised industries, local authorities and other bodies, whether the loans were made before or after 1 April 1968 and (b) the profits of the Issue Department of the Bank of England, mainly derived from interest on government securities, which were formerly paid into the Exchange Equalisation Account. The net cost of servicing the National Debt after applying these interest receipts and similar items is a charge on the Consolidated Fund as part of the standing services. Details of National Loans Fund loans outstanding are shown in Table 16.7.

Details of borrowing and repayments of debt, other than loans from the National Loans Fund, are shown in Table 16.6.

16.1 Public sector financial account

£ million

	1973/74	1974/75	1975/76	1976/77	1977/78	1978/79	1979/80	1980/81	1981/82	1982/83	1983/84
Financial surplus or deficit											
Public sector total	−3 510	−6 018	−8 186	−7 474	−6 545	−8 528	−8 294	−12 232	−6 612	−8 761	−11 514
Transactions in financial Liabilities											
Total	5 002	8 780	10 386	9 356	6 662	10 757	12 995	14 729	8 860	10 737	12 307
Public sector borrowing requirement: total	4 351	7 976	10 303	8 346	5 386	9 252	10 018	12 682	8 629	8 863	9 669
Contributions by											
Central government	2 106	5 108	8 723	5 856	4 522	7 910	8 262	12 744	7 614	12 732	12 284
Local authorities	1 528	2 199	1 237	1 387	391	1 017	2 174	842	971	−2 629	−2 197
Public corporations	717	669	343	1 103	473	325	−418	−904	44	−1 241	−418
Other financial liabilities	651	804	83	1 010	1 276	1 505	2 977	2 047	231	1 874	2 638
Transactions in financial assets											
Total	1 975	2 918	1 981	2 389	585	2 630	3 832	2 433	3 183	1 668	694
Net lending, etc to private sector and overseas											
Central government	411	964	1 013	729	−779	330	−694	983	−40	51	−931
Local authorities	361	708	419	57	−35	59	408	290	485	253	−241
Public corporations	113	188	339	420	500	365	472	−797	598	490	170
Other financial assets	1 090	1 058	210	1 183	899	1 876	3 646	1 957	2 140	874	1 696
Total financial transactions	−3 027	−5 862	−8 405	−6 967	−6 077	−8 127	−9 163	−12 296	−5 677	−9 069	−11 613
Balancing item	−483	−156	219	−507	−468	−401	869	64	−935	308	99

Source Central Statistical Office

16.2 Public sector borrowing and contributions to the public sector borrowing requirement

£ million

	1973/74	1974/75	1975/76	1976/77	1977/78	1978/79	1979/80	1980/81	1981/82	1982/83	1983/84
Central government borowing requirement	2 106	5 108	8 723	5 856	4 522	7 910	8 262	12 744	7 614	12 733	12 284
of which: own account	*604*	*2 529*	*5 493*	*4 156*	*2 749*	*5 792*	*4 293*	*9 066*	*6 356*	*7 256*	*8 185*
Local authorities:											
Direct borrowing from central government[1]	1 000	1 135	1 178	627	1 063	337	817	1 301	−1 172	2 757	3 430
Net borrowing from other sources	1 525	2 194	1 207	1 372	357	1 005	2 116	852	1 099	−2 798	−2 220
less Transactions in other public sector debt[2]:											
Central government	−3	−10	4	3	0	7	9	7	11	5	23
Public corporations	−	5	−34	−18	−34	−19	−67	3	117	−174	−46
Borrowing requirement	2 528	3 334	2 415	2 014	1 454	1 354	2 991	2 143	−201	128	1 233
General government borrowing requirement[3]	3 634	7 307	9 960	7 243	4 913	8 927	10 436	13 586	8 585	10 104	10 087
Public corporations:											
Direct borrowing from central government[1]	502	1 444	2 052	1 073	710	1 781	3 152	2 377	2 430	2 720	669
Net borrowing from other sources	689	702	368	1 442	576	239	−458	−756	336	−966	126
less Transactions in other public sector debt:											
Central government	−17	−1	18	8	136	36	96	−3	329	228	468
Local authorities	−11	34	7	331	−33	−122	−136	151	−37	47	76
Borrowing requirement	1 219	2 113	2 395	2 176	1 183	2 106	2 734	1 473	2 474	1 479	251
Public sector borrowing requirement[3]	4 351	7 976	10 303	8 346	5 386	9 252	10 018	12 682	8 629	8 863	9 669

1. Excluding market transactions of central government in public sector debt; these transactions are included in Borrowing from other sources.
2. Including direct lending to public corporations.

3. General government borrowing requirement is the sum of the borrowing requirements of central government and local authorities *less* direct borrowing by local authorities from central government. The public sector borrowing requirement is the general government borrowing requirement *plus* public corporations borrowing requirement *less* public corporations direct borrowing from central government.

Source Central Statistical Office

16.3 Debt of the public sector: nominal amount outstanding[1]
At 31 March in each year

£ million

	1973	1974	1975	1976	1977	1978	1979	1980	1981	1982	1983
Central government											
National debt[2]											
Sterling debt	35 269	38 582	43 587	53 135	62 796	74 550	82 597	91 366	109 953	116 030	125 326
Foreign currency debt[3]	1 889	1 875	2 817	3 451	4 370	4 630	4 288	3 949	3 083	2 360	2 601
less Official holdings [4,5]	10 194	11 805	12 802	13 644	14 418	18 363	17 741	18 161	18 277	14 506	14 100
equals Market holdings	26 964	28 652	33 602	42 942	52 748	60 817	69 144	77 154	94 759	103 884	113 827
Other liabilities:											
Net indebtedness of the central government to the Bank of England banking department	1 098	1 801	1 255	1 554	1 397	2 193	653	599	650	725	652
Deposits with:											
National Savings Bank: ordinary accounts	1 518	1 534	1 540	1 581	1 550	1 722	1 849	1 821	1 740	1 702	1 734
Trustee savings banks: ordinary department[6]	1 330	1 423	1 592	1 737	1 626	1 735	1 665				
Fund for banks for savings' liability to Trustee Savings Banks[6]								1 266	1 116	937	745
Accrued interest, etc. on national savings[7]	544	532	547	569	653	844	1 087	1 430	1 954	2 493	3 000
Notes and coin in circulation[8]	4 626	5 073	5 994	6 613	7 346	8 628	9 658	10 666	11 203	11 386	12 592
Market holdings of Northern Ireland Government debt	110	116	134	92	116	121	170	168	201	238	250
Other stocks issued by government funds[9]	139	73	71	71	70	58	58	57	56	55	55
Consolidated fund liability to Post Office Superannuation Fund[10]	1 278	1 218	1 121	1 019	901	792	662	530	370	168	
Total central government liabilities	37 607	40 422	45 856	56 148	66 407	76 910	84 946	93 691	112 049	121 588	132 855
Government guaranteed stocks of nationalised industries[11]	1 257	908	908	908	808	808	794	254	224	224	224
Total held by other sectors	38 864	41 330	46 764	57 056	67 215	77 718	85 740	93 945	112 273	121 812	133 079
of which:											
Local authorities	39	32	20	21	31	32	50	51	56	61	74
Public corporations	68	45	32	33	35	109	159	353	464	619	791
Domestic private sector[12]	32 011	34 502	38 963	48 523	57 689	66 953	76 179	83 096	99 652	108 842	119 722
Overseas	6 746	6 751	7 749	8 479	9 460	10 624	9 352	10 445	12 101	12 290	12 492
Local authorities											
Sterling debt	19 063	21 329	24 281	26 888	28 624	30 083	31 326	34 551	36 842	36 932	37 239
less debt held by other local authorities	356	462	541	592	747	715	717	671	652	794	874
equals debt held outside local authority sector	18 707	20 867	23 740	26 296	27 877	29 368	30 609	33 880	36 190	36 138	36 365
Foreign currency debt[3]	51	380	579	699	779	759	572	233	192	222	359
Total held by other sectors	18 758	21 247	24 319	26 995	28 656	30 127	31 181	34 113	36 382	36 360	36 724
of which:											
Central government	8 627	9 741	10 762	12 155	12 950	13 948	14 456	15 577	16 711	15 804	18 260
Public corporations	90	79	113	120	334	219	202	231	262	279	326
Domestic private sector[12]	9 616	10 773	12 897	14 169	14 816	15 386	15 940	17 883	18 966	19 784	17 494
Overseas	425	654	547	551	556	574	583	422	443	493	644

See footnotes on page 267.

Source Central Statistical Office

16.3 Debt of the public sector: nominal amount outstanding
At 31 March in each year
(continued)

£ million

	1973	1974	1975	1976	1977	1978	1979	1980	1981	1982	1983
Public corporations											
Sterling debt	13 425	13 912	15 413	17 452	18 499	19 668	20 927	24 689	26 599	26 399	27 499
Foreign currency debt[3]	296	1 381	2 157	3 395	5 392	5 794	5 225	4 526	4 224	4 841	5 445
Total held by other sectors	13 721	15 293	17 570	20 847	23 891	25 462	26 152	29 215	30 823	31 240	32 944
of which:											
Central government	*12 904*	*13 380*	*14 865*	*16 908*	*17 924*	*18 941*	*20 093*	*23 444*	*25 538*	*24 703*	*26 314*
Domestic private sector[12]	*582*	*1 499*	*1 623*	*1 799*	*2 287*	*2 052*	*1 739*	*1 667*	*1 511*	*2 505*	*2 358*
Overseas	*235*	*414*	*1 082*	*2 140*	*3 680*	*4 469*	*4 320*	*4 104*	*3 774*	*4 032*	*4 272*
Public sector debt held outside the public sector											
Total	49 615	54 593	62 861	75 661	88 488	100 058	108 113	117 617	136 447	147 946	156 982
Sterling debt held by:											
Domestic private sector	42 118	45 602	50 984	61 436	70 458	80 338	90 562	100 094	118 301	130 052	138 187
Overseas	5 261	5 355	6 324	6 680	7 489	8 537	7 466	8 815	10 647	10 471	10 390
Foreign currency debt held by:											
Domestic private sector	91	1 172	2 499	3 055	4 334	4 053	3 296	2 552	1 828	1 079	1 387
Overseas	2 145	2 464	3 054	4 490	6 207	7 130	6 789	6 156	5 671	6 344	7 018
Contingent liabilities of central government[13]											
Export credit guarantees	6 269	7 657	9 978	12 242	16 380	19 046	21 058	24 337	25 585	30 838	50 901
Assistance to industry, guaranteed loans[14]				1 316	1 223	1 201	1 552	1 492	1 652	2 116	1 917
Overseas Development and Co-operation Act, 1980, guaranteed loans	51	47	40	43	39	29	30	25	54	53	61
Other identified	6	10	7	7	7	13	13	13	13	14	14
Total	6 326	7 714	10 025	13 608	17 649	20 289	22 653	25 867	27 304	33 021	52 893
Public sector debt ratios											
Percentage of total debt held outside public sector	*69.5*	*70.1*	*70.9*	*72.1*	*73.9*	*75.1*	*75.6*	*74.8*	*76.0*	*78.1*	*77.4*
Debt held outside sector as a percentage of GDP (at current market prices)	*74.5*	*73.4*	*70.8*	*68.0*	*68.3*	*66.6*	*63.3*	*57.6*	*58.2*	*57.8*	*55.6*
Debt held overseas as a percentage of debt held outside public sector	*14.9*	*14.3*	*14.9*	*14.8*	*15.5*	*15.7*	*13.2*	*12.7*	*12.0*	*11.4*	*11.1*
Debt held overseas as a percentage of GDP (at current market prices)	*11.1*	*10.5*	*10.6*	*10.0*	*10.6*	*10.4*	*8.3*	*7.3*	*7.0*	*6.6*	*6.2*
Foreign currency debt as a percentage of debt held outside public sector	*4.5*	*6.7*	*8.8*	*10.0*	*11.9*	*11.2*	*9.3*	*7.4*	*5.5*	*5.0*	*5.4*

1. An article describing these statistics was published in *Economic Trends* No. 283, May 1977.
2. Comprises the total liabilities of the National Loans Fund, full details of which are given in Section 3 of *Consolidated Fund and National Loans Fund; Supplementary Statements* each year.
3. Total foreign currency debt for each sub-sector is valued at middle closing spot exchange rates on the last working day of March of each year. Much of the foreign currency debt of local authorities and public corporations has been contracted through the exchange cover scheme under which the Treasury guarantees the debt against depreciation of sterling *vis-a-vis* the currency in which the debt is denominated. Thus the market exchange rate valuation used will overstate the liability of these authorities when sterling depreciates, but not the liability of the public sector as a whole.
4. Including sterling stocks of nationalised industries guaranteed by the British government.
5. Official holdings at 31 March 1983 were made up as follows: Treasury bills—£684 million, marketable securities—£8 739 million, ways and means advances—£4 566 million, other (longstanding) debt to the Bank of England Issue Department—£11 million, and non-marketable stocks issued to the National Debt Commissioners—£100 million.
6. From November 1979 Trustee savings banks' ordinary department and new department were amalgamated. The deposit liabilities of the former are now shown as a diminishing claim on the fund for banks for savings.

7. Includes accrued interest, index-linking and bonus as applicable on national savings certificates and SAYE contracts and, from 1981, National Savings Bank investment accounts.
8. Excluding notes and coin held by the Bank of England.
9. For details see Section 4 of *Consolidated Fund and National Loans Fund: Supplementary Statements* for each year.
10. The nominal amount outstanding. The Consolidated Fund's actual liability to the Post Office Superannuation Fund has been up to 1982 to make quarterly payments partly to meet interest at $2\frac{1}{2}$ per cent on the nominal debt and partly to reduce it in the form of a holding of consols. The amount of this nominal reduction therefore depends upon the price of consols at the time of payment.
11. These stocks are liabilities of public corporations but cannot be distinguished from British government securities in the sector analysis of holdings.
12. Holdings by the domestic private sector are obtained as a residual and may contain some unidentified holdings by public sector bodies.
13. Where data are readily available and other than guarantees of loans to the public sector. Further details are given in *Consolidated Fund and National Loans Fund Accounts: Supplementary Statements* for each year.
14. Data are not readily available before 1976.

Source Central Statistical Office

16.4 Consolidated Fund: revenue and expenditure
Years ended 31 March

£ million

	1973/74	1974/75	1975/76	1976/77	1977/78	1978/79	1979/80	1980/81	1981/82	1982/83	1983/84
Revenue											
Inland Revenue	10 633.3	14 191.1	18 159.4	20 710.0	21 917.0	24 080.1	28 153.4	32 981.8	40 318.3	43 793.7	45 926.0
Customs and Excise	6 219.6	7 406.5	9 176.4	10 900.1	12 284.1	13 835.0	18 031.9	22 095.2	25 247.8	27 895.5	31 434.3
Motor vehicle duties	533.5	532.2	780.7	845.9	1 071.7	1 113.0	1 148.9	1 418.7	1 640.2	1 823.4	2 036.1
Selective employment tax and national insurance surcharge[1]	45.0	2.0	–	–	1 162.7	1 914.4	2 987.0	3 541.9	3 596.3	2 831.3	1 670.5
Miscellaneous receipts	795.0	1 438.3	1 300.6	1 322.1	2 337.7	2 145.4	4 010.3	6 175.9	5 952.4	6 927.5	7 297.0
Total revenue	18 226.4	23 570.1	29 417.1	33 778.1	38 773.2	43 087.9	54 331.5	66 213.5	76 755.0	83 271.4	88 363.9
Expenditure											
Supply services	18 624.2	25 605.3	34 072.1	37 066.2	40 043.0	45 762.4	53 774.0	67 997.4	74 090.8	80 456.4	86 749.3
Debt interest[2]	676.7	576.3	964.0	1 133.5	2 220.2	3 222.4	4 143.2	5 043.8	6 503.5	5 392.7	6 485.1
Payments to Northern Ireland	349.5	420.7	576.2	637.7	688.9	765.2	986.8	1 236.5	1 475.2	1 607.1	1 603.0
Payments to the European Community, etc.	219.3	242.9	381.7	548.7	977.4	1 669.2	2 007.5	1 905.6	2 642.0	2 804.6	2 618.4
Other expenditure[3]	95.6	– 42.7	53.0	– 13.8	59.5	50.2	95.9	– 13.2	73.9	210.0	– 4.8
Total expenditure	19 965.3	26 802.5	36 047.0	39 372.3	43 989.0	51 469.4	61 007.4	76 170.1	84 785.5	90 470.8	97 451.0
Deficit met from the National Loans Fund	1 738.9	3 232.4	6 629.9	5 594.2	5 215.8	8 381.5	6 675.9	9 956.6	8 030.5	7 199.4	9 087.1

National Loans Fund: summary of receipts and payments

£ million

	1973/74	1974/75	1975/76	1976/77	1977/78	1978/79	1979/80	1980/81	1981/82	1982/83	1983/84
Receipts											
Interest on loans, and profits of Issue Department of the Bank of England	1 663.8	2 281.9	2 595.9	3 400.8	2 972.2	3 235.9	4 256.4	4 810.0	4 702.1	5 430.9	5 347.4
Service of the national debt-balance met from the Consolidated Fund	676.7	576.3	964.0	1 133.5	2 220.2	3 222.4	4 143.2	5 043.8	6 503.5	5 392.7	6 485.1
	2 340.5	2 858.2	3 559.9	4 534.3	5 192.4	6 458.3	8 399.6	9 853.8	11 205.6	10 823.6	11 832.5
Exchange Equalisation Account—sterling capital[4]	–	– 200.0	600.0	– 2 100.0	– 6 150.0	1 850.0	200.0	1 400.0	3 600.0	2 800.0	600.0
Net borrowing[5]	3 188.7	5 772.0	8 979.0	8 944.1	12 595.5	6 796.4	8 530.9	12 617.8	4 833.6	7 906.9	13 372.7
International Monetary Fund—maintenance of sterling holdings	–	–	–	–	–	35.1	228.5	152.2	44.4	–	–
Reduction of National Debt Commissioners Liability in respect of the National Savings Bank Investment Account	–	–	–	–	–	–	–	179.2	315.5	1 215.9	46.9
Change in balances and other items[6]	10.5	11.4	12.7	0.5	– 0.2	– 0.1	–	–	–	2.0	– 8.1
	5 539.7	8 441.6	13 151.6	11 378.9	11 637.7	15 139.7	17 359.0	24 203.0	19 999.1	22 748.4	25 844.0
Payments											
Service of the national debt:											
Interest	2 284.3	2 789.5	3 482.1	4 449.3	5 100.9	6 369.4	8 290.5	9 732.7	11 075.5	10 687.3	11 692.2
Management and expenses	56.2	68.7	77.9	85.0	91.5	88.9	109.1	121.1	130.1	136.3	140.3
	2 340.5	2 858.2	3 560.0	4 534.3	5 192.4	6 458.3	8 399.6	9 853.8	11 205.6	10 823.6	11 832.5
Consolidated Fund deficit met from the National Loans Fund	1 738.9	3 232.4	6 629.9	5 594.2	5 215.8	8 381.5	6 675.9	9 956.6	8 030.5	7 199.4	9 087.1
Net lending	1 403.2	2 351.0	2 736.3	940.4	943.8	216.2	2 283.5	3 557.0	763.0	4 463.8	3 413.3
International Monetary Fund—maintenance of value of sterling holding	57.1	–	225.4	310.0	285.7	–	–	–	–	261.6	188.5
International Monetary Fund—additional subscription	–	–	–	–	–	83.7	–	835.6	–	–	1 322.6
	5 539.7	8 441.6	13 151.6	11 378.9	11 637.7	15 139.7	17 359.0	24 203.0	19 999.1	22 748.4	25 844.0

1. Actual receipts in the year are shown gross, and payments of refunds and premiums are included in expenditure on supply services, national insurance surcharge from April 1977 and selective employment tax before 1st quarter 1975.
2. Payment to National Loans Fund representing its payments for the service of the national debt *less* its receipts of interest on loans outstanding, etc.
3. Includes net issues to Contingences Fund.
4. Minus sign indicates a net issue.
5. See Table 16.6.
6. Includes transfer of surplus on the death duties surrendered securities account.

Source: HM Treasury

16.5 Central government borrowing requirement (net balance)[1]
Years ended 31 March

£ million

	1973/74	1974/75	1975/76	1976/77	1977/78	1978/79	1979/80	1980/81	1981/82	1982/83	1983/84
National Loans Fund:											
Net lending	1 403	2 351	2 736	940	944	216	2 283	3 557	746	4 464	3 412
less Surplus from Consolidated Fund[2]	1 739	3 232	6 630	5 594	5 216	8 381	6 676	9 957	8 049	7 200	9 086
Other items	− 10	− 12	− 13	−	−	−	−	−	−	−	−
Borrowing required	3 132	5 571	9 353	6 534	6 160	8 597	8 959	13 514	8 794	11 664	12 498
Surplus of National Insurance Funds[2]	− 271	− 605	− 294	− 957	− 612	− 341	− 381	25	604	216	− 520
Departmental balances and miscellaneous	− 768	111	− 308	259	− 1 024	− 409	− 318	− 828	− 1 801	820	272
Northern Ireland central government debt	13	31	− 28	20	− 2	63	2	33	17	33	34
Central government borrowing requirement (net balance)	2 106	5 108	8 723	5 856	4 522	7 910	8 262	12 744	7 614	12 733	12 284
Borrowing requirement analysed by type of asset											
Net indebtedness to Bank of England, Banking Department	704	− 544	292	− 138	800	− 1 568	− 26	50	55	− 69	− 143
Notes and coin	454	921	619	733	1 282	1 030	1 008	552	189	1 206	323
Non-marketable debt:											
National savings	− 7	128	500	888	1 197	1 604	985	2 140	4 321	3 028	3 258
Tax instruments[3]	− 139	− 51	− 4	− 7	436	1 119	− 953	490	558	1 035	− 235
Other	5	12	17	− 1	53	− 9	− 16	− 68	− 99	− 177	299
Market Treasury bills[4]	− 347	1 597	2 169	− 1 175	− 592	− 840	56	− 1 025	− 111	195	126
British government securities	1 651	2 177	4 159	6 290	6 684	6 256	8 977	13 107	5 959	5 140	11 677
Government guaranteed stock (redemptions)	349	−	−	94	6	14	540	30	−	−	−
Public sector debt and commercial bills[5]	− 313	109	31	− 296	− 7	− 104	− 1 102	− 1 697	− 4 505	658	− 2 934
Northern Ireland central government debt[6]	13	31	− 28	20	− 2	48	2	28	17	33	34
Bank deposits	− 56	26	− 102	− 16	− 32	− 142	51	− 107	− 81	79	30
Exchange cover scheme: payment of claims	− 2	− 2	− 45	− 19	− 3	− 160	− 118	59	21	− 94	− 79
Direct borrowing net from overseas governments and institutions[7]	− 83	− 83	− 84	− 21	327	144	51	100	− 75	− 202	− 100
Overseas official financing:											
Net change in official reserves (increase −)	− 123	− 280	619	− 2 166	− 6 345	1 328	− 561	− 153	2 749	2 062	28
Other	−	1 067	580	1 670	718	− 810	− 632	− 762	− 1 384	− 161	−

1. This is equal to National Loans Fund borrowing and special transactions (net) less receipts from other central government funds, etc.
2. A negative item represents a surplus, a positive item a deficit.
3. Includes tax reserve certificates, tax deposit accounts, and certificates of tax deposit from October 1975.
4. Excluding bills held as the sterling counterpart of assistance from overseas central banks, which are part of Overseas official financing.
5. Market transactions by the Issue department, Bank of England and by the National Debt Commissioners.
6. Excluding foreign currency borrowed under the exchange cover scheme which is included in Overseas official financing—other.
7. Excluding net drawings from the IMF and the sterling equivalent of foreign currency deposits by overseas central banks which are part of Overseas official financing.

Sources HM Treasury; Central Statistical Office

16.6 Borrowing and repayment of debt
Years ended 31 March

£ million

	1973/74	1974/75	1975/76	1976/77	1977/78	1978/79	1979/80	1980/81	1981/82	1982/83	1983/84
Borrowing											
Marketable securities: new issues	1 614.4	4 382.8	6 509.1	8 623.0	12 914.6	7 845.1	14 925.3	16 083.7	10 997.6	10 704.6	15 888.4
National savings securities:											
National savings certificates	218.6	310.6	580.6	1 106.3	840.1	1 507.0	1 458.5	2 081.9	4 116.2	2 077.8	1 631.4
Income bonds	–	–	–	–	–	–	–	–	–	878.1	1 115.4
Deposit bonds	–	–	–	–	–	–	–	–	–	–	106.3
National development bonds	–	–	–	0.2	–	–	–	–	–	–	–
British savings bonds	214.9	114.8	116.1	71.7	132.7	94.6	24.0	–	–	–	–
Premium savings bonds	115.7	117.7	136.0	144.1	160.3	193.0	121.2	167.3	144.5	179.8	186.9
Save As You Earn	51.9	45.4	62.9	90.0	98.2	109.6	120.6	128.7	136.7	138.0	123.9
National savings stamps and gift tokens	123.5	89.6	104.3	80.9	0.4	1.8	1.3	1.2	1.2	1.2	1.2
National Savings Bank Deposits	–	–	–	–	–	–	–	486.7	1 096.7	1 413.8	1 506.5
Tax deposit accounts	14.6	8.0	–	–	–	–	–	–	–	–	–
Certificate of tax deposit	–	–	15.0	13.4	886.5	2 408.2	893.7	1 921.6	2 777.5	2 499.9	2 359.9
Tax reserve certificates	11.5	–	–	–	–	–	–	–	–	–	–
Nationalised industries' etc. temporary deposits	–	–	–	–	–	–	–	–	–	–	2 894.0
British Gas Corporation deposits	–	–	–	–	–	–	200.0	100.0	–	–	–
Treasury bills (net receipt)	2 411.7	2 011.0	3 331.8	342.5	–	–	–	–	–	8.2	160.2
Ways and means (net receipt)	195.8	147.2	168.1	–	4 202.4	1 951.8	–	1 178.6	–	658.7	–
Other debt: payable in sterling:											
Interest free notes	65.7	–	971.6	1 370.2	717.9	97.1	13.0	624.6	–	–	1 312.1
Other debt: payable in external currencies	–	1 066.9	–	583.6	682.3	696.9	242.3	–	–	261.5	–
Total receipts	5 038.3	8 294.0	11 995.5	12 425.9	20 635.4	14 905.1	17 999.9	22 774.3	19 270.4	18 821.6	27 286.2
Repayment of debt											
Marketable securites: redemptions	687.1	1 499.0	2 120.1	2 652.8	3 200.2	2 102.3	2 859.4	3 645.5	6 119.3	6 266.0	4 600.1
Statutory sinking funds	21.7	21.7	14.1	5.5	5.1	4.8	4.5	4.2	4.0	3.8	3.6
Terminable annuities:											
National Debt Commissioners	55.5	53.5	47.9	14.7	9.2	9.4	2.6	–	–	–	–
National savings securities:											
National savings certificates	382.8	350.1	399.0	419.2	258.9	275.8	591.6	756.7	922.1	1 331.6	1 144.3
Income bonds	–	–	–	–	–	–	–	–	–	1.8	60.1
Defence bonds	0.1	0.1	–	–	–	–	–	–	–	–	–
National development bonds	2.3	0.4	0.1	0.2	–	–	–	–	–	–	–
British savings bonds	239.1	195.0	102.5	111.2	92.2	138.1	176.3	191.9	153.4	90.3	99.2
Premium savings bonds	80.1	74.5	69.7	76.3	75.3	74.1	119.0	110.1	102.3	100.0	102.6
Save As You Earn	6.5	25.3	20.8	41.9	31.8	69.6	70.5	83.9	67.7	184.2	110.0
National savings stamps and gift tokens	117.0	102.0	95.9	104.4	13.9	3.7	9.6	1.2	1.2	1.2	1.2
National Savings Bank deposits (repayments)	–	–	–	–	–	–	–	102.0	722.0	874.3	1 127.8
Tax deposit accounts	8.9	9.7	2.5	1.6	–	–	–	–	–	–	–
Certificates of tax deposit	–	–	1.8	14.0	449.7	1 288.1	1 846.6	1 431.4	2 219.7	1 465.0	2 595.2
Tax reserve certificates	156.7	49.0	15.2	3.6	2.3	0.9	0.3	0.2	0.1	0.2	0.1
Nationalised industries' etc. temporary deposits	–	–	–	–	–	–	–	–	–	–	2 489.0
Treasury bills (net repayment)	–	–	–	–	3 831.6	2 503.7	250.4	2 550.2	80.8	–	–
Ways and means (net repayment)	–	–	–	15.4	–	–	2 148.1	–	2 393.7	–	1 394.5
Other debt: payable in sterling:											
Interest free notes	0.5	56.1	43.4	0.3	1.5	1 066.7	1 031.7	593.1	341.8	394.8	89.0
Other	2.3	1.6	0.5	0.1	0.2	0.2	0.1	0.1	0.1	–	0.1
Other debt: payable in external currencies	89.0	84.0	83.0	20.6	68.0	571.4	358.3	686.0	1 308.6	201.5	96.7
Total payments	1 849.6	2 522.0	3 016.5	3 481.8	8 039.9	8 108.8	9 469.0	10 156.5	14 436.8	10 914.7	13 913.5
Net borrowing	3 188.7	5 772.0	8 979.0	8 944.1	12 595.5	6 796.3	8 530.9	12 617.8	4 833.6	7 906.9	13 372.7

Source HM Treasury

16.7 Consolidated Fund and National Loans Fund: assets and liabilities
At 31 March in each year

£ million

	1973	1974	1975	1976	1977	1978	1979	1980	1981	1982	1983
Consolidated Fund											
Total estimated assets	2 755.7	3 010.8	4 565.1	5 749.5	6 812.0	7 229.3	8 659.0	10 786.9	9 853.8	7 562.3	7 239.1
Subscriptions and contributions to international financial organisations	275.1	318.1	369.4	486.5	574.6	702.1	760.2	815.4	881.4	1 063.4	1 248.3
International Bank for Reconstruction and Development	108.3	108.3	106.4	116.3	118.4	116.8	114.9	114.1	113.5	117.7	119.8
International Finance Corporation	6.0	6.0	5.0	7.5	8.4	7.7	18.3	17.5	16.9	21.3	25.6
International Development Association	147.4	179.3	215.0	285.6	349.9	449.8	484.6	512.8	562.7	713.4	871.1
African Development Fund	–	0.1	0.1	0.1	0.1	1.0	2.5	3.1	6.0	7.8	9.8
Asian Development Bank	4.9	8.1	11.3	16.2	24.0	26.2	30.6	35.2	37.9	40.9	45.4
Caribbean Development Bank	1.0	1.3	1.6	3.2	6.3	6.2	8.5	11.2	12.0	12.1	12.3
European Investment Bank	7.5	15.0	30.0	57.6	62.9	68.6	85.8	100.5	104.1	115.2	120.6
Inter-American Development Bank	–	–	–	–	4.6	7.8	13.2	19.2	25.7	30.1	36.1
International Fund for Agricultural Development	–	–	–	–	–	18.0	1.8	1.8	2.6	4.8	7.6
Amounts due from overseas governments	99.2	101.4	103.6	110.1	113.0	115.2	117.0	118.3	118.3	98.7	84.1
War of 1939–45	79.5	79.5	79.5	83.3	83.4	83.5	83.7	83.8	84.0	64.3	64.5
Other	19.7	21.9	24.1	26.8	29.6	31.7	33.3	34.5	34.3	34.4	19.6
Loans from Votes	1 602.4	1 750.0	3 110.0	3 642.4	4 105.8	3 818.1	4 017.4	3 589.4	3 007.7	2 558.6	2 050.0
Issues of public dividend capital:	625.0	636.3	796.3	1 234.3	1 796.7	2 327.8	3 557.0	5 704.1	5 576.4	3 513.5	3 369.2
British Airways Board	125.0	136.3	216.3	280.0	290.0	300.0	310.0	320.0	170.0	180.0	180.0
British Steel Corporation	500.0	500.0	545.0	889.5	1 379.5	1 824.0	2 674.0	3 579.0	4 812.0	2 618.0	2 361.0
Royal ordnance factories	–	–	35.0	35.0	35.0	35.0	35.0	35.0	35.0	35.0	35.0
National Enterprise Board	–	–	–	9.2	69.3	110.4	470.7	1 432.3	179.7	187.7	224.2
Royal Mint	–	–	–	7.0	7.0	7.0	7.0	7.0	7.0	7.0	7.0
Post Office	–	–	–	13.0	13.0	13.0	17.0	17.0	17.0	22.0	22.0
Scottish Development Agency	–	–	–	0.6	2.9	9.6	11.5	12.1	6.8	6.8	11.4
Welsh Development Agency	–	–	–	–	–	1.8	4.8	5.7	2.9	4.0	5.6
British Aerospace	–	–	–	–	–	27.0	27.0	60.0	–	–	–
British Shipbuilders	–	–	–	–	–	–	–	236.0	346.0	453.0	523.0
Contingencies Fund—capital	50.0	113.0	45.0	81.0	51.0	94.0	126.0	176.0	138.0	186.0	346.0
Balance on revenue accounts	104.0	92.0	140.6	195.2	170.9	172.0	81.4	383.7	132.0	142.2	141.6
Total liabilities	14 937.2	16 596.5	19 946.0	28 242.2	34 635.0	39 737.3	48 208.0	55 723.4	70 213.0	78 512.9	86 580.4
Liability to balance National Loans Fund	14 261.1	16 067.6	19 433.9	27 733.6	34 108.1	39 113.4	47 396.1	54 836.6	69 147.4	77 187.7	84 742.1
Payment from Votes:	179.6	137.5	97.5	78.0	75.9	75.2	74.8	74.1	73.2	72.8	72.4
Purchases of United States military aircraft	81.8	44.9	12.7	–	–	–	–	–	–	–	–
Married quarters for armed forces	85.1	83.9	80.3	77.3	75.9	75.2	74.8	74.1	73.2	72.8	72.4
Town and country planning compensation	12.7	8.7	4.5	0.7	–	–	–	–	–	–	–
Liability to Post Office Superannuation Fund	311.6	207.8	200.4	183.3	182.4	173.2	152.6	103.3	75.8	33.3	–
Post-war credits outstanding and interest due-estimated	51.0	33.0	29.0	68.0	67.0	66.0	64.0	62.0	62.0	62.0	62.0
Revenue paid over in advance of collection	–	2.4	–	–	–	5.5	6.9	–	63.5	11.8	29.8
Broadcast receiving licences	–	2.4	3.8	–	–	5.4	5.5	–	0.7	3.5	4.8
Vehicle Excise Duty	–	–	–	–	–	–	–	–	–	7.9	–
National insurance surcharge—Great Britain	–	–	–	–	–	–	–	–	62.8	–	24.3
National insurance surcharge—Northern Ireland	–	–	–	–	–	0.1	1.4	–	–	0.4	0.7

Source HM Treasury

16.7
(continued)

Consolidated Fund and National Loans Fund: assets and liabilities
At 31 March in each year

£ million

	1973	1974	1975	1976	1977	1978	1979	1980	1981	1982	1983
Consolidated Fund (*continued*)											
Promissory notes issued by Minister of Overseas Development	133.9	148.2	181.4	179.3	201.6	304.0	513.6	803.9	791.1	1 145.3	1 674.1
International Development Association	101.3	121.0	159.6	161.6	173.8	245.4	377.6	510.4	552.9	680.9	709.3
African Development Fund	–	0.7	1.5	2.5	2.5	1.6	10.0	9.4	18.8	23.2	29.3
Asian Development Bank	2.1	3.2	4.4	4.2	3.7	3.2	3.0	2.7	3.5	3.5	3.5
Asian Development Fund	–	–	7.6	9.8	12.3	17.4	21.0	33.0	45.6	57.5	67.8
Caribbean Development Bank	0.5	0.8	0.8	1.2	–	–	–	–	0.1	0.3	0.5
European Community/International Development Association Special Action Account	–	–	–	–	–	–	63.0	61.0	37.0	24.5	7.2
European Investment Bank	30.0	22.5	7.5	–	–	–	–	47.3	31.8	87.9	86.1
Inter-American Development Bank	–	–	–	–	9.3	18.4	22.7	1.2	2.6	3.8	6.7
Fund for special operations	–	–	–	–	–	–	–	13.5	22.9	32.6	47.8
International Fund for Agricultural Development	–	–	–	–	–	18.0	16.2	16.2	15.4	13.2	14.7
Other contributions and instalments due in respect of international subscriptions, etc.	–	–	–	–	–	–	–	109.2	60.5	217.9	701.2
National Loans Fund											
Total assets	36 884.6	40 124.5	45 925.5	56 571.6	67 165.8	79 179.9	86 884.9	95 314.2	113 036.0	118 390.4	127 927.3
Total National Loans Fund loans outstanding	20 628.3	22 001.2	24 228.3	26 951.7	27 898.7	29 348.2	29 511.4	31 399.1	34 799.7	35 023.4	39 411.0
Loans to nationalised industries:											
Post Office	2 752.4	3 019.0	3 382.3	3 382.7	3 344.1	3 305.5	3 323.6	3 139.1	3 148.4	190.6	178.6
National Coal Board	418.8	437.4	437.1	534.5	527.9	622.6	845.3	1 084.3	1 656.8	2 588.9	2 989.1
Electricity Council	3 569.5	3 413.4	3 620.6	3 715.9	3 396.1	3 286.5	3 279.8	4 116.7	4 413.0	3 963.7	3 988.3
North of Scotland Hydro-Electric Board	205.1	214.2	240.6	225.8	208.4	247.4	279.6	293.1	440.1	369.6	419.1
South of Scotland Electricity Board	458.7	489.8	490.4	491.2	461.7	474.4	436.4	503.3	457.6	670.5	739.7
British Gas Corporation	1 621.3	1 583.4	1 651.4	1 574.5	1 438.5	882.6	217.0	97.0	–	–	40.0
British Steel Corporation	502.4	499.4	421.3	552.2	712.6	929.0	767.5	558.9	509.3	–	–
British Airways Board	151.9	116.0	80.1	108.2	83.6	60.6	46.2	40.2	34.3	41.3	42.4
British Airways Authority	57.8	57.5	57.2	64.8	64.2	63.5	62.8	62.2	61.5	62.3	57.6
British Railways Board	404.0	438.7	251.3	339.6	330.9	332.2	348.1	374.1	457.9	471.4	449.2
British Transport Docks Board	123.4	123.4	123.4	123.4	117.1	110.6	89.5	89.5	81.3	81.3	–
British Waterways Board	8.1	8.1	9.0	9.9	10.5	11.0	10.5	13.2	17.3	19.6	21.3
National Freight Corporation	124.3	124.3	139.3	153.1	153.1	153.1	100.0	100.0	–	–	–
National Bus Company	99.6	99.6	109.6	128.6	133.0	133.0	138.0	150.0	163.0	161.0	151.2
Scottish Transport Group	19.9	19.9	19.9	18.8	16.8	14.8	14.8	16.8	14.8	12.8	10.8
British National Oil Corporation	–	–	–	178.6	340.4	–	–	–	–	–	1.7
British Aerospace	–	–	–	–	–	17.1	15.3	35.5	32.6	28.6	–
British Shipbuilders	–	–	–	–	–	–	55.0	–	–	–	–
British Telecommunications	–	–	–	–	–	–	–	–	–	3 056.1	2 943.7
Loans to other public corporations:											
New Towns—Development Corporations and Commission	1 026.9	1 156.0	1 363.3	1 683.9	2 034.0	2 369.7	2 713.3	3 144.1	3 612.2	3 940.9	4 271.5
Scottish Special Housing Association	179.1	190.3	212.2	246.9	277.7	311.9	343.6	380.5	424.7	451.3	476.7
Housing Corporation	91.3	137.8	261.5	368.0	435.5	444.0	481.7	568.6	892.1	1 104.0	1 620.8
Covent Garden Market Authority	18.7	24.4	28.1	32.6	36.9	25.8	25.1	23.2	23.1	23.1	21.1
Sugar Board	7.8	25.0	21.0	–	–	–	–	–	–	–	–
Civil Aviation Authority	–	32.6	49.1	49.8	50.8	63.7	76.0	80.8	82.9	73.8	73.8
Maplin Development Authority	–	0.2	0.7	2.4	–	–	–	–	–	–	–
Regional water authorities	–	1.6	267.0	688.9	702.3	792.4	1 060.7	1 424.4	1 859.8	2 224.5	2 680.4
National Enterprise Board	–	–	–	3.0	100.6	931.4	624.9	84.5	34.2	3.3	1.4
Land Authority for Wales	–	–	–	–	2.1	4.8	5.5	6.4	7.2	7.5	8.6
Scottish Development Agency	–	–	–	–	0.4	2.0	4.5	9.4	7.6	6.5	8.7
Welsh Development Agency	–	–	–	–	0.3	3.2	4.7	6.3	5.2	5.7	5.1
Development Board for Rural Wales	–	–	–	–	–	3.3	7.5	12.2	16.5	20.7	25.2
Royal Mint	–	–	–	10.4	9.9	7.1	6.7	6.3	5.5	4.6	3.7
Royal Ordnance factories	–	–	57.4	48.3	44.1	39.9	28.6	21.8	15.2	10.5	6.3
Property Services Agency	–	–	–	–	1.0	18.1	16.5	25.5	22.5	16.5	15.7
Crown Agents	–	–	–	–	–	–	–	30.0	30.0	20.8	20.3
Her Majesty's Stationery Office	–	–	–	–	–	–	–	–	75.1	75.9	69.8
Urban Development Corporations	–	–	–	–	–	–	–	–	–	0.7	1.0
Harbour authorities	125.7	121.5	125.3	148.2	155.7	162.6	171.1	172.7	175.9	167.0	158.9

Source HM Treasury

16.7
(continued)

Consolidated Fund and National Loans Fund: assets and liabilities
At 31 March in each year

£ million

	1973	1974	1975	1976	1977	1978	1979	1980	1981	1982	1983
National Loans Fund *(continued)*											
Loans to local authorities	8 035.3	9 028.9	10 155.0	11 328.8	11 924.0	12 950.7	13 254.8	14 015.3	15 272.4	14 126.6	16 866.6
Loans to private sector:											
Shipbuilding Industry Board	18.4	18.1	17.4	9.4	8.5	3.5	3.5	3.5	3.5	3.5	2.2
Shipowners (Ship credit scheme)	8.0	4.7	1.6	0.6	–	–	–	–	–	–	–
Housing associations	24.1	24.1	24.1	24.0	23.9	23.8	23.7	23.7	23.5	23.3	21.2
Building societies	33.2	30.9	27.4	19.8	17.4	11.5	8.2	4.6	2.2	–	–
British Nuclear Fuels Ltd	–	–	–	–	9.5	8.9	8.9	8.5	8.1	7.6	7.1
British Aerospace plc	–	–	–	–	–	–	–	–	–	–	24.6
Loans within central government:											
Northern Ireland Exchequer	359.2	423.5	486.2	603.1	649.3	450.8	537.7	598.8	639.2	653.8	707.7
Purchases of United States military aircraft	81.8	44.9	12.7	–	–	–	–	–	–	–	–
Married quarters for armed forces	85.1	83.9	80.3	77.3	75.9	75.2	74.8	74.1	73.2	72.8	72.4
Town and country planning compensation	12.7	8.7	4.5	0.7	–	–	–	–	–	–	–
Redundancy Fund	3.8	–	–	3.8	–	–	–	–	–	260.8	207.5
Other assets:											
Exchange Equalisation Account—capital	800.0	800.0	1 000.0	400.0	2 500.0	8 650.0	6 800.0	6 600.0	5 200.0	1 600.0	–
Subscriptions and contributions to international financial organisations:											
International Monetary Fund	1 166.7	1 223.8	1 223.8	1 449.2	1 759.2	2 044.9	2 128.6	2 128.6	2 964.3	2 539.1	2 800.7
Victory bonds sinking fund—balance	7.2	7.5	7.8	0.4	–	–	–	–	–	–	–
Borrowing included in national debt but not brought to account by 31 March	19.4	22.5	29.6	34.7	897.9	21.4	1 046.6	347.9	2 022.6	755.2	893.1
National Debt Commissioners' liability in respect of the National Savings Banks Investment Fund	–	–	–	–	–	–	–	–	1 611.9	1 285.6	80.5
Other	1.9	1.9	2.1	2.0	1.9	2.0	2.1	2.0	2.0	2.0	–
Consolidated Fund liability	14 261.1	16 067.6	19 439.9	27 733.6	34 108.1	39 113.4	47 396.1	54 836.6	66 435.5	77 185.1	84 742.1
Total liabilities											
National Loans Fund—national debt outstanding	36 884.6	40 457.0	46 403.7	56 585.2	67 165.8	79 179.9	86 884.9	95 314.2	113 036.0	118 390.4	127 927.3

Source HM Treasury

16.8

British government and government guaranteed marketable securities[1]
Nominal values of official and other holdings by maturity[2]
At 31 March in each year

£ million

	1973	1974	1975	1976	1977	1978	1979	1980	1981	1982	1983
Total holdings	27 069	27 656	30 725	35 580	42 503	52 112	59 340	70 985	86 475	91 150	96 414
Up to 5 years	6 923	7 347	11 499	13 753	15 664	19 209	21 574	24 233	25 484	25 470	27 635
Over 5 and up to 15 years	6 590	7 828	6 476	6 500	6 644	9 022	12 473	16 772	27 574	34 297	36 490
Over 15 years (including undated)	13 556	12 481	12 750	15 327	20 195	23 881	25 293	29 980	33 417	31 383	32 289
Official holdings:											
Total	7 676	6 388	6 871	6 432	5 690	8 616	7 815	10 688	10 939	9 616	8 739
Up to 5 years	1 675	1 534	2 491	2 864	2 536	4 091	4 033	5 796	4 528	3 106	3 520
Over 5 and up to 15 years	2 776	2 289	1 841	1 590	1 554	2 121	2 290	2 878	4 953	5 235	3 695
Over 15 years (including undated)	3 225	2 565	2 539	1 978	1 600	2 404	1 492	2 014	1 458	1 275	1 524
Other holdings:											
Total	19 393	21 268	23 854	29 148	36 813	43 496	51 525	60 297	75 536	81 534	87 675
Up to 5 years	5 248	5 813	9 008	10 889	13 128	15 118	17 541	18 437	20 956	22 364	24 115
Over 5 and up to 15 years	3 814	5 539	4 635	4 910	5 090	6 901	10 183	13 894	22 621	29 062	32 795
Over 15 years (including undated)	10 331	9 916	10 211	13 349	18 595	21 477	23 801	27 966	31 959	30 108	30 765

1. The government guaranteed securities of nationalised industries only. A relatively small amount of other government guaranteed securities is excluded.
2. Securities with optional redemption dates are classified according to the final redemption date.

Source Bank of England

16.9 National savings
Years ended 31 March

£ million

	1973/74	1974/75	1975/76	1976/77	1977/78	1978/79	1979/80	1980/81	1981/82	1982/83	1983/84
Receipts											
Total	4 233.1	4 687.1	5 799.4	6 434.4	5 453.4	5 731.8	2 800.5	3 913.3	5 898.6	5 211.8	5 290.1
National savings certificates	218.0	311.7	588.8	1 259.6	686.2	1 488.1	1 431.0	2 247.9	4 045.3	2 019.2	1 632.9
Save As You Earn:											
Department for National Savings	29.6	26.7	42.6	74.0	90.2	103.7	116.3	127.7	136.0	135.3	124.5
Trustee savings banks	22.8	21.8	18.3	13.4	7.5	4.6	2.7	–	–	–	–
National Savings Bank:											
Ordinary accounts	552.8	535.6	546.9	544.3	675.2	670.6	661.7	569.7	576.2	639.8	670.2
Investment accounts	103.8	91.8	110.1	109.2	930.4	398.9	440.2	803.1	992.5	1 346.3	1 436.5
Trustee savings banks:											
Ordinary departments	2 976.3	3 466.7	4 234.6	4 217.8	2 775.6	2 781.4	[2]				
Premium savings bonds	115.0	117.9	140.5	145.6	156.0	191.1	124.5	164.9	148.6	178.1	182.3
Income bonds										893.1	1 134.3
British savings bonds[1]	214.8	114.9	117.6	70.5	132.3	93.4	24.1	–	–	–	
Deposit bonds											109.4
Repayments											
Total	4 484.0	4 815.1	5 570.9	5 786.1	4 008.1	4 982.5	2 262.4	2 520.7	3 026.9	3 698.2	3 785.6
National savings certificates:											
Principal	380.4	353.2	402.8	429.2	246.4	283.4	580.3	744.1	930.7	1 335.0	1 144.5
Accrued interest	129.0	120.8	127.4	146.8	83.7	101.0	200.2	299.6	394.2	477.6	418.5
Save As You Earn:											
Department for National Savings											
Principal	3.8	15.7	12.6	22.9	20.8	41.4	39.5	67.3	59.6	159.2	119.2
Accrued interest/index increase	0.2	2.4	2.1	6.6	5.9	17.7	16.2	27.6	22.0	87.7	54.5
Trustee savings banks											
Principal	2.5	9.6	8.2	17.5	11.9	28.1	32.0	11.5	10.1	–	–
Accrued interest	–	1.5	1.4	4.9	3.5	12.3	13.8	4.7	4.6	–	–
Defence bonds:											
On maturity	0.3	–	–	–	–	–	–	–	–	–	–
National Savings Bank:											
Ordinary accounts	593.7	587.7	593.6	608.5	578.8	627.0	776.5	733.6	695.6	678.2	717.5
Investment accounts	123.8	110.1	108.6	130.6	171.2	749.2	312.5	334.2	670.8	770.3	1 072.2
Trustee savings banks:											
Ordinary departments	2 929.7	3 346.6	4 143.3	4 234.3	2 723.6	2 911.5	[2]				
Premium savings bonds	80.3	74.1	70.5	75.9	74.1	76.5	119.0	108.7	103.9	98.6	102.2
National development bonds:											
On maturity	2.2	0.2	0.4	–	–	–	–	–	–	–	–
British savings bonds:											
Before maturity	219.9	169.8	64.1	74.2	40.7	87.2	124.6	79.8	32.9	16.0	6.4
On maturity	18.2	23.4	35.9	34.7	47.5	47.2	47.8	109.6	102.5	73.8	89.9
Income bonds										1.8	60.7
Deposit Bonds										–	0.1

1. Excluding conversions of Defence bonds and National development bonds to British savings bonds (£3.0 million in 1973/74).
2. From 21 November 1976 Trustee savings banks' Current accounts formerly included in the Ordinary departments' totals and the Special investment department were amalgamated to form the New department. From 21 November 1979 the Ordinary and New departments of the Trustee savings banks amalgamated and will no longer be part of National Savings.

Sources Department for National Savings; National Investment and Loans Office

16.9
(continued)

National savings
Years ended 31 March

£ million

	1973/74	1974/75	1975/76	1976/77	1977/78	1978/79	1979/80	1980/81	1981/82	1982/83	1983/84
Interest accruing											
On national savings certificates (estimated)	113.3	126.1	144.5	219.7	259.4	335.4	542.4	699.6	885.1	980.2	1 173.8
Save As You Earn:											
Department for National Savings	2.0	8.9	5.2	15.8	16.5	24.0	25.9	83.2	43.9	93.8	53.9
Trustee savings banks	1.4	4.6	3.8	6.2	8.1	15.2	4.4	0.1	1.8	–	–
Credited to accounts in:											
National Savings Bank:											
Ordinary accounts	57.4	57.8	57.9	62.6	76.1	83.2	87.0	83.0	81.3	70.5	78.8
Investment accounts	42.7	48.0	51.0	58.0	104.4	119.6	174.5	246.0	353.1	380.2	435.8
Trustee savings banks:											
Ordinary departments	46.3	49.0	53.6	55.2	57.1	59.7	[2]				
Deposit Bonds											1.6
Amounts remaining invested (at end of period)											
Total[3]	8 475.2	8 747.1	9 376.0	10 369.5	12 304.0	13 758.6	13 457.2	16 010.8	20 322.4	23 328.8	26 582.7
National savings certificates:											
Principal	1 980.9	1 939.4	2 125.4	2 955.8	3 395.6	4 600.3	5 451.0	6 954.8	10 069.4	10 753.5	11 241.9
Accrued interest (estimated)	525.3	530.6	547.7	620.6	796.3	1 030.7	1 372.9	1 772.9	2 263.8	2 766.4	3 521.7
Save As You Earn:											
Department for National Savings											
Principal	90.3	101.3	131.3	182.4	251.8	314.1	390.9	451.3	527.7	503.8	509.1
Accrued interest/index increase	3.9	10.4	13.5	22.7	33.3	39.6	49.3	104.9	126.8	132.9	132.3
Trustee savings banks											
Principal	62.7	74.9	85.0	80.9	76.5	53.0	23.7	12.2	2.1	–	–
Accrued interest	2.7	5.8	8.2	9.5	14.1	17.0	7.6	3.0	0.2	–	–
Other securities on the National Savings register[4]	360.4	474.6	550.8	662.7	638.4	708.1	706.0	755.1	842.1	812.5	818.0
National Savings Bank[5]											
Ordinary accounts	1 534.2	1 539.9	1 551.1	1 549.5	1 722.0	1 848.8	1 821.0	1 740.1	1 702.0	1 734.1	1 765.6
Investment accounts	551.5	581.2	633.7	670.3	1 533.9	1 303.2	1 605.4	2 320.3	2 995.1	3 951.3	4 751.4
Trustee savings banks[5]											
Ordinary departments[6]	1 422.6	1 591.7	1 736.6	1 626.1	1 735.2	1 665.8	[2]				
Premium savings bonds	1 019.8	1 063.6	1 133.6	1 203.3	1 285.2	1 399.8	1 405.3	1 461.5	1 506.2	1 585.7	1 665.8
National developments bonds	0.6	0.4	–	–	–	–	–	–	–	–	–
British savings bonds	867.2	788.9	806.5	768.1	812.2	771.2	622.9	433.5	285.8	196.0	99.8
National savings stamps and gift tokens[7]	53.1	44.4	52.6	17.6	9.5	8.0	1.2	1.2	1.2	1.3	1.3
Income bonds										891.3	1 964.9
Deposit bonds											
Principal											109.3
Accrued interest											1.6

2. From 21 November 1976 Trustee savings banks' Current accounts formerly included in the Ordinary departments' totals and the Special investment department were amalgamated to form the New department. From 21 November 1979 the Ordinary and New departments of the Trustee savings banks amalgamated and will no longer be part of National Savings.
3. Including National savings stamps and gift tokens and securities on the National Savings register, which (except for Defence bonds, National development bonds and British savings bonds) do not appear in the first part of the table.
4. Nominal value held in National Savings section, and also (until November 1979) in Trustee Savings banks' section.
5. Including accrued interest to date.
6. In 1976/77 includes £1.0 million transferred from Greenock Provident TSB and £2.8 million transferred from Birmingham Municipal TSB.
7. From September 1979 excludes £7.7m deemed to be outstanding National savings stamps written off on 15 August 1979.

Sources Department for National Savings; National Investment and Loans Office

16.10 Income tax: allowances and reliefs

Personal allowances	1974/75	1975/76	1976/77	1977/78	1978/79	1979/80	1980/81	1981/82	1982/83	1983/84[1]	1984/85
Married man's allowance[1]	£865	£955	£1 085	£1 455	£1 535	£1 815	£2 145	£2 145	£2 445	£2 795	£3 155
Single person's allowance	£625	£675	£735	£945	£985	£1 165	£1 375	£1 375	£1 565	£1 785	£2 055
Wife's earned income allowance[2]	£625	£675	£735	£945	£985	£1 165	£1 375	£1 375	£1 565	£1 785	£2 055
Age allowance[3]:											
Married	–	£1 425	£1 555	£1 975	£2 075	£2 455	£2 895	£2 895	£3 295	£3 755	£3 955
Single	–	£950	£1 010	£1 250	£1 300	£1 540	£1 820	£1 820	£2 070	£2 360	£2 490
Income limit	–	£3 000	£3 250	£3 500	£4 000	£5 000	£5 900	£5 900	£6 700	£7 600	£8 100
Marginal fraction	–	2/3	2/3	2/3	2/3	2/3	2/3	2/3	2/3	2/3	2/3
Child allowance[4]:											
Aged under 11	£240	£240	£300	£170	£100	–	–		–	–	–
Aged 11–15	£275	£275	£335	£205	£135	–	–		–	–	–
Aged 16 and over	£305	£305	£365	£235	£165	–	–		–	–	–
Limits of child's income:	£115	£115	£350	£350	£500	–	–		–	–	–
Family allowance deduction[5]	£52	£52	£52	–	–	–	–		–	–	–
Additional personal allowance[6]	£180	£280	£350	£510	£550	£650	£770	£770	£880	£1 010	£1 150
Widow's bereavement allowance[7]	–	–	–	–	–	–	£770	£770	£880	£1 010	£1 150
Dependent relative allowance[8]:											
Maintained by single woman	£145	£145	£145	£145	£145	£145	£145	£145	£145	£145	£145
Other cases	£100	£100	£100	£100	£100	£100	£100	£100	£100	£100	£100
Limit of relative's income	£486	£637	£731	£839	£950	£1 090	£1 284	£1 458	£1 601	£1 708	£1 804
Daughter's or son's services allowance[9]	£55	£55	£55	£55	£55	£55	£55	£55	£55	£55	£55
Housekeeper allowance[10]	£100	£100	£100	£100	£100	£100	£100	£100	£100	£100	£100
Blind person's allowance[11]:											
Single or married (one spouse blind)	£180	£180	£180	£180	£180	£180	£180	£360	£360	£360	£360
Married (both spouses blind)	£360	£360	£360	£360	£360	£360	£360	£720	£720	£720	£720
Age exemption[12]:											
Income limit – single	£810	–	–	–	–	–	–	–	–	–	–
– married	£1 170	–	–	–	–	–	–	–	–	–	–

Life insurance relief[13]

1974/75 to 1978/79

Total allowable premiums	Amount of premiums upon which tax relief at basic rate allowed
Not over £10	All
Over £10 but not over £20	£10
Over £20	1/2

Life assurance relief[14]

(Percentage of gross premium)	1979/80	1980/81	1981/82	1982/83	1983/84	1984/85
	17.5	17.5	15.0	15.0	15.0	15.0 or NIL

1. The married man's allowance is that for a full year. In the year of marriage the allowance is reduced by one twelfth of the difference between the married and single personal allowances for each complete month (beginning on the sixth day of each calendar month) prior to the date of marriage.
2. The wife's earned income allowance has as its maximum value the amount shown. Where the earned income is less, the allowance is reduced to the actual amount of earned income.
3. The age allowance is due where the taxpayer or his wife is aged 65 or over during the tax year. It replaces the single or married allowances, provided the taxpayer's income is below the limit shown. For incomes in excess of the limit, the allowance is reduced by £2 for each additional £3 of income until the ordinary single or married allowance is reached.
4. The child allowance depends upon the age of the child at the start of the tax year (6 April). Where the child's income exceeds the limit shown, the child allowance is reduced by the excess. For unmarried children under 18, there is a further limit of £115 investment income. From 1978–79, special rules apply in respect of certain students and certain children resident overseas. All child allowances were discontinued from 1982–83.
5. The family allowance deduction was a reduction in personal allowances for each child for whom a family allowance was received. Where the family allowance was payable for only part of the year, the family allowance deduction was reduced accordingly.
6. The additional personal allowance may be claimed by a single parent (or by a married man if his wife is totally incapacitated) who maintains a resident child at his or her own expense.
7. Widow's bereavement allowance is due to a widow in the year of her husband's death. For deaths occurring after 5 April, 1982 it has been due in the following year provided the widow has not remarried before the beginning of that year.

8. The dependent relative allowance is due to a taxpayer who maintains, wholly or partially, either (a) an aged or infirm relative, or (b) his or his wife's separated, divorced or widowed mother. The relative's income must be below the limits shown in order for the full allowance to be given (the limit is equal to the basic National Insurance Retirement Pension). The allowance is reduced by the excess of the relative's income over the income limit.
9. The daughter's or son's services allowance may be claimed by an aged or infirm taxpayer who maintains a daughter or son (before 1978–79 a daughter only) on whose services the taxpayer or his wife are dependent.
10. The housekeeper allowance may be claimed by a widow or widower who has a resident housekeeper (before 1978–79 a female housekeeper only). For 1978–79 and earlier years this allowance could also have been claimed by an unmarried person who maintained a resident relative (before 1978–79 a female relative only) to look after a brother or sister for whom child allowance was given.
11. The blind person's allowance is due to a registered blind taxpayer and up to 1980/81 was reduced by the amount of any tax-free blindness disability pension which was receivable.
12. From 1975/76 replaced by age allowance.
13. From 1979–80 relief on life assurance premiums is given by deduction from the premium payable.
14. From 1984–85 life insurance relief is confined to policies starting before 14 March, 1984.

Source Board of Inland Revenue

16.11 Rates of income tax

	1975/76		1976/77		1977/78		1978/79		1979/80	
	Slice of taxable income	Rate per cent	Slice of taxable income	Rate per cent	Slice of taxable income	Rate per cent	Slice of taxable income	Rate per cent	Slice of taxable income	Rate per cent
	£		£		£		£		£	
Lower rate[1]							1–750	25	1–750	25
Basic rate	1–4 500	35	1–5 000	35	1–6 000	34	751–8 000	33	751–10 000	30
Higher rates	4 501–5 000	40	5 001–5 500	40	6 001–7 000	40	8 001–9 000	40	10 001–12 000	40
	5 001–6 000	45	5 501–6 500	45	7 001–8 000	45	9 001–10 000	45	12 001–15 000	45
	6 001–7 000	50	6 501–7 500	50	8 001–9 000	50	10 001–11 000	50	15 001–20 000	50
	7 001–8 000	55	7 501–8 500	55	9 001–10 000	55	11 001–12 500	55	20 001–25 000	55
	8 001–10 000	60	8 501–10 000	60	10 001–12 000	60	12 501–14 000	60	over 25 000	60
	10 001–12 000	65	10 001–12 000	65	12 001–14 000	65	14 001–16 000	65		
	12 001–15 000	70	12 001–15 000	70	14 001–16 000	70	16 001–18 500	70		
	15 001–20 000	75	15 001–20 000	75	16 001–21 000	75	18 501–24 000	75		
	over 20 000	83	over 20 000	83	over 21 000	83	over 24 000	83		
Investment Income surcharge[2]	Slice of net investment income	Rate per cent	Slice of net investment income	Rate per cent	Slice of net investment income	Rate per cent	Slice of net investment income	Rate per cent	Slice of net investment income	Rate per cent
	£		£		£		£		£	
Non-aged persons Exempt slice	1–1 000	–	1–1 000	–	1–1 500	–	1–1 700	–	1–5 000	–
	1 001–2 000	10	1 001–2 000	10	1 501–2 000	10	1 701–2 250	10	over 5 000	15
	over 2 000	10	over 2 000	15	over 2 000	15	over 2 250	15		
Aged persons Exempt slice	1–1 000	–	1–1 000	–	1–2 000	–	1–2 500	–	1–5 000	–
	1 001–1 500	–	1 001–1 500	–	2 001–2 500	10	2 501–3 000	10	over 5 000	15
	1 501–2 000	10	1 501–2 000	10	over 2 500	15	over 3 000	15		
	over 2 000	15	over 2 000	15						

	1980/81		1981/82		1982/83		1983/84		1984/85	
	Slice of taxable income	Rate per cent	Slice of taxable income	Rate per cent	Slice of taxable income	Rate per cent	Slice of taxable income	Rate per cent	Slice of taxable income	Rate per cent
	£		£		£		£		£	
Lower rate[1]	–	–	–	–	–	–	–		–	–
Basic rate	1–11 250	30	1–11 250	30	1–12 800	30	1–14 600	30	1–15 400	30
Higher rates	11 251–13 250	40	11 251–13 250	40	12 801–15 100	40	14 601–17 200	40	15 401–18 200	40
	13 251–16 750	45	13 251–16 750	45	15 101–19 100	45	17 201–21 800	45	18 201–23 100	45
	16 751–22 250	50	16 751–22 250	50	19 101–25 300	50	21 801–28 900	50	23 101–30 600	50
	22 251–27 750	55	22 251–27 750	55	25 301–31 500	55	28 901–36 000	55	30 601–38 100	55
	over 27 750	60	over 27 750	60	over 31 500	60	over 36 000	60	over 38 100	60
Investment Income surcharge[2]	Slice of net investment income	Rate per cent	Slice of net investment income	Rate per cent	Slice of net investment income	Rate per cent	Slice of net investment income	Rate per cent	Slice of net investment income	Rate per cent
	£		£		£		£		£	
Non-aged persons Exempt slice	1–5 500	–	1–5 500	–	1–6 250	–	1–7 100	–	–	–
	over 5 500	15	over 5 500	15	over 6 250	15	over 7 100	15	–	–
Aged persons Exempt slice	1–5 500	–	1–5 500	–	1–6 250	–	1–7 100	–	–	–
	over 5 500	15	over 5 500	15	over 6 250	15	over 7 100	15	–	–

1. The lower rate slice applies additionally to wife's earned income, but any increase is deducted from the slice of total income chargeable at the basic rate.
2. Chargeable in addition to any basic or higher rates of tax where an individual's investment income exceeds the limits shown.

Source Board of Inland Revenue

16.12 Rateable values
Rateable values
England and Wales
At April in each year

	1973[1]	1974	1975	1976	1977	1978	1979	1980	1981	1982	1983
Number of properties (Thousands)											
Total—all classes	20 431.4	20 492.2	20 727.9	21 076.5	21 371.8	21 634.9	21 876.3	22 102.5	22 291.1	22 463.1	22 621.6
Domestic: total	16 940.5	17 004.1	17 204.3	17 513.5	17 761.4	17 984.9	18 199.0	18 405.5	18 578.4	18 736.7	18 873.8
Houses and flats with rateable values:											
Not over £75	1 283.7	1 592.6	1 541.8	1 572.8	1 523.5	1 459.5	1 408.2	1 366.2	1 323.5	1 291.5	1 267.8
Over £75 but not over £100	1 220.6	1 295.3	1 290.0	1 291.3	1 291.7	1 290.1	1 288.4	1 287.0	1 286.2	1 285.5	1 288.3
Over £100	14 069.0	13 752.0	14 006.0	14 279.1	14 578.5	14 873.8	15 143.3	15 396.6	15 618.1	15 814.3	15 976.6
Agricultural dwelling-houses, etc.	367.3	364.3	366.5	370.3	367.7	361.6	359.1	355.7	350.6	345.3	341.2
Commercial: total	2 893.3	2 895.9	2 927.9	2 962.9	3 007.0	3 039.2	3 062.5	3 079.7	3 092.3	3 102.9	3 120.7
Shops and cafes	623.5	616.3	608.9	600.1	592.2	585.3	580.2	574.9	570.1	567.2	566.2
Offices	171.4	169.8	171.1	171.3	171.8	172.5	174.0	175.3	177.3	179.7	182.9
Other	2 098.4	2 109.8	2 147.9	2 191.5	2 243.0	2 281.4	2 308.3	2 329.5	2 344.9	2 355.9	2 371.7
On-licensed premises: total	56.4	56.3	55.9	55.6	55.4	55.3	55.1	55.0	54.9	54.8	54.8
Entertainment and recreational: total	71.6	71.0	71.3	71.7	72.2	72.9	73.6	74.1	74.7	75.3	76.1
Cinemas	1.4	1.3	1.3	1.3	1.3	1.2	1.2	1.1	1.1	1.0	1.0
Theatres and music-halls	0.4	0.4	0.4	0.4	0.4	0.4	0.4	0.4	0.4	0.4	0.4
Other	69.8	69.3	69.6	70.0	70.5	71.3	72.0	72.6	73.2	73.9	74.7
Public utility: total	42.0	39.0	39.1	39.1	39.2	39.0	39.0	39.0	38.8	38.5	38.6
Educational and cultural: total	41.3	41.3	41.7	41.9	42.1	42.3	42.3	42.3	42.2	42.1	41.8
Miscellaneous: total	281.6	280.1	282.9	287.2	290.2	297.2	300.4	301.7	302.9	304.9	306.6
Industrial: total	104.7	104.4	104.8	104.6	104.3	104.1	104.4	105.2	106.9	107.9	109.1
Value of assessments (£ million)											
Total—all classes	6 583.0	6 660.1	6 742.2	6 809.2	6 934.7	7 058.0	7 181.9	7 317.8	7 441.5	7 552.6	7 641.4
Domestic: total	3 234.1	3 204.1	3 260.6	3 325.7	3 393.4	3 459.2	3 519.7	3 578.5	3 630.7	3 678.2	3 719.2
Houses and flats with rateable values:											
Not over £75	72.4	90.0	87.4	88.0	85.4	82.4	79.8	77.6	75.4	73.8	72.7
Over £75 but not over £100	108.2	114.6	114.1	114.2	114.2	114.1	114.0	114.0	113.7	113.8	114.0
Over £100	2 995.9	2 928.3	2 987.0	3 049.9	3 119.1	3 187.8	3 251.2	3 312.4	3 367.5	3 417.4	3 459.7
Agricultural dwelling-houses, etc.	57.7	71.2	72.1	73.6	74.6	74.8	74.7	74.5	74.1	73.3	72.8
Commercial: total	1 626.7	1 616.3	1 621.5	1 619.4	1 627.2	1 654.8	1 698.8	1 746.6	1 792.8	1 847.6	1 897.3
Shops and cafes	599.7	597.0	595.2	590.8	588.9	590.5	594.4	600.8	607.4	615.2	621.1
Offices	576.0	567.2	565.5	559.6	558.0	570.9	595.2	618.7	637.2	660.3	681.7
Other	450.9	452.2	460.8	469.1	480.3	493.4	509.2	527.1	548.2	572.1	594.5
On-licensed premises: total	65.9	65.4	65.0	64.3	63.8	63.5	63.6	64.0	65.1	65.8	65.5
Entertainment and recreational: total	67.5	67.4	68.9	70.3	71.4	72.8	74.1	75.7	77.3	79.4	81.3
Cinemas	5.5	5.4	5.3	5.1	4.6	4.3	4.1	4.0	3.9	3.8	3.8
Theatres and music-halls	1.6	1.6	1.7	1.6	1.6	1.6	1.7	1.7	1.8	1.9	1.9
Other	60.3	60.3	61.9	63.6	65.1	66.9	68.3	70.0	71.6	73.7	75.6
Public utility: total	319.3	326.9	334.6	334.1	379.2	391.0	392.8	398.3	407.7	406.1	406.7
Educational and cultural: total	211.5	211.2	215.6	221.0	226.2	233.3	238.9	242.2	244.3	244.6	243.9
Miscellaneous: total	240.3	356.4	366.2	378.2	387.6	402.8	413.6	428.6	436.4	444.2	450.0
Industrial: total	817.8	812.4	809.9	796.2	786.1	780.6	780.4	784.0	787.2	786.8	777.5

1. From 1 April 1973 all properties were revalued.

Source Board of Inland Revenue

16.13 Local authorities: gross loan debt outstanding[1]
At 31 March in each year[2]

£ million

	1973	1974	1975	1976	1977	1978	1979	1980	1981	1982	1983
United Kingdom											
Total debt[3]	19 797	22 247	23 145	26 569	29 787	31 831	33 586	36 715	38 810	41 607	44 392
Public Works Loan Board	8 031	9 025	10 104	11 267	11 893	12 931	13 214	13 994	15 259	14 111	16 846
Northern Ireland Government Loans Fund	266	268	260	252	244	238	229	238	238	225	215
Other debt	11 500	12 955	12 781	15 050	17 650	18 662	20 143	22 483	23 313	27 271	27 331
England and Wales											
Total debt	17 063	19 407	19 939	23 134	25 839	27 694	29 112	31 802	33 796	35 862	38 116
of which Public Works Loan Board	*7 039*	*7 919*	*8 859*	*9 881*	*10 409*	*11 285*	*11 434*	*12 100*	*13 124*	*12 129*	*14 331*
Scotland											
Total debt[3]	2 521	2 810	3 175	3 398	3 908	4 096	4 430	4 864	4 956	5 679	6 209
of which Public Works Loan Board	*992*	*1 106*	*1 245*	*1 384*	*1 484*	*1 646*	*1 780*	*1 894*	*2 135*	*1 982*	*2 515*
Northern Ireland											
Total debt[4, 5]	213	30	32	37	40	41	44	49	58	66	67

1. The sums shown exclude inter-authority loans and debt transfers, and temporary loans and overdrafts obtained for the purpose of providing for current expenses. No deduction has been made in respect of sums held in sinking funds for the repayment of debt.
2. At 15 May for Scotland up to 1975.

3. Figures for 1983 are provisional.
4. During the year 1972/73 the main housing functions were transferred to the Northern Ireland Housing Executive.
5. Exclusive of certain loan debt recoupable from certain government departments and other bodies in respect of services transferred on 1 October 1973.

Sources Department of the Environment; Scottish Office, Central Statistics Unit; Public Works Loan Board; Department of the Environment for Northern Ireland; Welsh Office

16.14 Expenditure and income of local authorities: summary
Years ended 31 March[1]

£ million

	1972/73	1973/74	1974/75	1975/76	1976/77	1977/78	1978/79	1979/80	1980/81	1981/82	1982/83[2]
United Kingdom[2]											
Total expenditure: On capital works	3 140.3	4 166.0	4 578.2	4 842.5	4 881.8	4 552.0	4 787.4	5 517.4	5 861.0	5 637.1	6 911.0
Other	9 029.1	10 830.4	13 112.3	16 570.7	19 146.8	20 948.9	23 917.4	28 332.4	34 109.8	37 633.8	40 715.6
Total income[3]	12 444.7	15 146.2	17 761.7	21 848.2	24 328.5	25 841.7	28 747.5	33 524.1	40 121.4	44 189.6	4 745.0
England and Wales[2]											
Total expenditure: On capital works	2 794.8	3 739.3	4 075.7	4 351.3	4 337.9	4 039.3	4 229.8	4 837.6	5 176.0	4 903.3	6 111.8
Other	8 004.2	9 732.6	11 734.3	14 961.5	17 132.6	18 768.2	21 409.8	25 264.9	30 337.5	36 124.3
Total income[3]	11 058.9	13 602.0	15 920.7	19 801.0	21 804.5	23 155.2	25 734.8	29 979.7	35 915.8	39 311.2	42 236.1
Scotland[2]											
Total expenditure: On capital works	303.7	397.2	493.4	477.8	532.0	499.3	542.4	658.5	660.9	708.7	775.1
Other	841.6	1 001.4	1 344.1	1 566.1	1 963.5	2 123.2	2 442.3	2 985.9	3 675.5	4 082.2	4 469.4
Total income[3]	1 163.5	1 429.0	1 802.3	1 986.5	2 455.1	2 617.0	2 934.4	3 449.8	4 085.5	4 742.2	5 087.8
Northern Ireland[4, 5]											
Total expenditure: On capital works	41.8	29.5	9.1	13.4	11.9	13.4	15.2	21.3	24.1	25.1	24.1
Other	183.3	96.4	33.9	43.1	50.6	57.4	65.3	81.6	96.8	110.6	121.9
Total income[3]	222.3	115.2	38.7	60.7	68.9	69.5	78.3	94.6	120.1	136.2	151.1

1. Years ended 15 May for Scotland up to 1974/75.
2. Figures for 1982/83 are provisional.
3. Including government grants.
4. During the year 1972/73 the main housing functions were transferred to the Northern Ireland Housing Executive.

5. On reorganisation of local government on 1 October 1973 the following services were transferred to central government and other bodies—education, local health and welfare authority services, water and sewerage, highways and bridges, electricity and passenger transport. See Table 16.23, 16.24 and 16.25.

Sources Department of the Environment; Scottish Office, Central Statistics Unit; Department of the Environment for Northern Ireland; Welsh Office

16.15 Revenue account expenditure of local authorities[1]
England and Wales
Years ended 31 March

£ thousand

	1973/74	1974/75	1975/76	1976/77	1977/78	1978/79	1979/80	1980/81	1981/82	1982/83
Total	9 732 625	11 734 287	14 961 456	17 132 576	18 768 136	21 409 787	25 264 875	30 337 528	33 441 014	36 124 321
Education	3 356 654	4 404 395	5 639 961	6 434 482	7 031 701	7 965 754	9 117 703	10 959 016	12 067 947	12 694 348
Libraries, museums and art galleries	105 811	139 405	178 034	204 550	225 313	253 864	292 225	348 875	383 711	418 829
Local health authority services including port health[2]	193 574	1 317	1 923	2 104	2 342	2 541	2 995	3 359	3 752	3 950
Personal social services	522 434	753 103	963 376	1 131 220	1 267 077	1 441 032	1 755 420	2 155 468	2 387 807	2 609 425
Sheltered employment and workshops	8 379	10 870	13 895	18 175	20 593	23 678	27 153	27 590	30 077	34 498
Police including school crossing patrols	534 838	660 850	869 040	1 033 059	1 129 410	1 272 409	1 639 616	1 979 491	2 343 472	2 600 177
Fire service	122 782	165 242	216 172	247 865	252 334	305 880	378 473	451 336	515 080	573 469
Administration of justice	55 501	72 384	99 615	116 075	129 583	146 351	179 827	233 629	269 498	295 782
Sewerage and sewage disposal[3]	242 118									
Refuse collection and disposal	166 889	229 691	290 488	328 598	373 342	428 142	532 309	632 169	667 880	704 935
Baths and laundries[4]	49 333									
Agriculture and fisheries[5]	45 988	38 992	53 161	60 643	70 980	77 758	90 209	100 023	123 398	132 687
Local transport	559 915	761 620	1 104 573	1 216 863	1 300 338	1 472 100	1 708 626	2 086 930	2 353 479	2 574 827
Parks and open spaces[4]	134 018	263 567	360 915	414 387	458 355	527 278	648 079	770 001	832 813	935 228
Environmental health[4]	71 071	104 075	143 156	168 148	185 159	213 404	270 513	332 638	353 124	383 218
Town and country planning	115 746	171 527	230 327	250 902	271 980	301 549	383 700	494 567	537 104	573 639
Housing to which the Housing Revenue Account relates	1 208 448	1 621 155	1 975 205	2 356 243	2 589 771	3 048 656	3 787 707	4 564 027	4 840 523	5 087 065
Other housing	282 707	412 093	564 616	680 684	699 287	761 268	836 368	933 627	904 599	908 526
Trading services:										
Water supply[6]	208 173									
Passenger transport	90 319	74 165	90 577	90 539	99 916	108 910	135 402	162 365	172 819	182 556
Cemeteries and crematoria	20 248	25 463	32 528	35 284	38 310	42 835	51 791	62 435	67 662	73 292
Harbours, docks and piers	14 264	23 504	24 031	25 457	29 783	36 498	43 360	47 390	51 788	51 888
Other trading services	137 933	194 994	251 971	284 435	303 698	436 894	410 288	503 706	570 818	658 182
Other rate fund services[7]	510 097	300 701	366 474	407 327	460 688	507 726	591 058	679 419	816 105	900 665
Expenditure on general administration and all other expenditure and transfers[8]	975 385	1 305 174	1 491 418	1 625 537	1 828 176	2 035 260	2 382 053	2 809 467	3 147 558	3 727 135
Total loan charges included in expenditure above	2 083 399	2 290 368	2 617 338	3 116 053	3 209 299	3 643 648	4 428 819	5 132 094	5 360 460	5 281 623
Allocated to:										
Rate fund services	906 343	992 916	1 238 056	1 462 403	1 460 936	1 611 855	1 873 994	2 132 841	2 257 041	2 178 073
Housing revenue	826 353	1 104 649	1 315 111	1 576 828	1 663 204	1 940 889	2 448 960	2 876 539	2 953 678	2 911 281
Trading services	110 712	57 743	64 171	76 822	85 159	90 904	105 865	122 714	149 741	192 269
Debt repayments included in table 16.16	239 991	135 060	207 005	326 544	367 661	413 756	346 961	425 926	587 906	669 533

1. Expenditure of superannuation and statutory special funds is not included for 1974/75 and later.
2. From 1974/75 local authority services were transferred to regional health authorities.
3. From 1974/75 sewerage and sewage disposal were transferred to regional water authorities.
4. From 1974/75 baths and laundries are included with parks and open spaces, and from 1978/79 swimming baths are included with parks and open spaces; and other public baths and public laundries are included with environmental health.
5. Before 1974/75 excluded land drainage, small-holdings, etc.
6. From 1974/75 water supply was transferred to regional water authorities.
7. For 1973/74 and earlier years, rate fund contributions to the Housing Revenue Account are included.
8. For all years, expenditure on general administration and rate fund contributions to trading services and statutory special funds are included. For 1973/74 and earlier years, expenditure of special funds and superannuation funds are included. For 1974/75 and later years, rate fund contributions to the Housing Revenue Account are included.

Footnotes to table 16.16
1. Expenditure met out of loans, government grants for capital works, sales of property, etc. and sums repaid to lenders or transferred to sinking funds out of unexpected balances of loans and other capital receipts.
2. From 1974/75 local authorities services were transferred to regional health authorities.

3. From 1974/75 sewerage and sewage disposal and water supply were transferred to regional water authorities.
4. From 1974/75 baths and laundries are included with parks and open spaces and from 1978/79 swimming baths are included with parks and open spaces; and other public baths and public laundries are included with environmental health.
5. Before 1974/75 excluded land drainage, small-holdings, etc.
6. From 1972/73 transactions relate to municipally owned undertakings only.

Footnotes to table 16.17
1. Up to and including 1980/81 revenue expenditure comprises all running costs, interest, depreciation and (where charged to service revenue accounts) supplementary depreciation. The method of accounting was changed at the start of 1981/82; supplementary depreciation was omitted and interest was shown as a separate expenditure head rather than apportioned to the other heads. Thus caution is needed when comparing expenditure by expenditure head.
2. In 1982/83 capital expenditure by water authorities on behalf of other bodies on assets not in the ownership of water authorities has been excluded. This affects mainly land drainage and flood protection where an additional £46 million have been spent on assets not owned by water authorities.

Source Department of the Environment; Welsh Office

16.16 Capital account expenditure of local authorities[1]
England and Wales
Years ended 31 March

£ thousand

	1973/74	1974/75	1975/76	1976/77	1977/78	1978/79	1979/80	1980/81	1981/82	1982/83
Total	3 739 330	4 075 657	4 351 260	4 337 929	4 039 338	4 229 785	4 837 638	5 176 038	4 903 289	6 111 775
Education	457 430	415 007	450 574	428 156	364 741	332 811	367 542	477 762	431 177	474 214
Libraries, museums and art galleries	17 615	20 925	19 265	14 217	10 644	11 991	15 122	24 743	20 504	29 248
Local health authority services including port health[2]	21 515	–	–	52	–	80	3	62	16	17
Personal social services	74 306	72 261	79 732	68 334	51 232	61 598	77 801	101 437	99 751	104 002
Sheltered employment and workshops	254	486	618	910	870	1 046	1 304	1 136	1 362	2 685
Police including school crossing patrols	45 551	35 048	49 467	53 627	43 077	44 204	42 120	36 267	58 877	80 519
Fire service	9 127	8 089	10 140	9 579	10 349	10 321	11 736	17 493	21 426	32 238
Administration of justice	10 044	12 101	14 983	16 062	13 859	8 901	8 926	11 365	9 126	9 928
Sewerage and sewage disposal[3]	283 775									
Refuse collection and disposal	18 351	21 529	33 358	34 448	27 973	28 869	40 890	60 082	55 240	64 192
Baths and laundries[4]	21 043									
Agriculture and fisheries[5]	31 270	17 447	34 412	47 761	44 618	61 850	96 113	90 983	116 209	112 083
Local transport	296 322	359 689	422 996	399 759	352 973	368 846	459 415	610 937	606 653	700 783
Parks and open spaces[4]	52 612	89 930	95 171	83 148	70 300	82 868	116 370	169 385	140 858	202 835
Environmental health[4]	6 789	6 124	7 276	6 935	6 614	8 521	13 283	16 227	10 912	18 499
Town and country planning	120 671	105 099	118 184	134 900	120 265	132 392	178 258	236 453	199 936	297 993
Housing to which the Housing Revenue Account relates	1 106 659	1 620 498	1 886 106	1 974 909	1 866 667	1 890 746	2 055 639	1 868 996	1 707 558	2 106 908
Other housing	773 792	1 066 251	870 189	838 556	823 024	897 721	999 972	976 741	942 139	1 201 398
Trading services:										
Water supply[3]	153 142									
Passenger transport	18 487	6 134	9 591	9 004	12 220	13 512	13 345	16 437	15 377	11 963
Cemeteries and crematoria	1 593	1 653	1 694	1 493	1 529	2 016	2 765	3 629	3 490	6 464
Harbours, docks and piers	10 308	10 266	12 314	11 772	6 169	6 626	9 697	16 125	12 313	12 012
Other trading services	106 877	102 846	106 666	83 025	88 316	97 907	144 895	221 860	225 339	268 211
Other rate fund services	52 415	27 849	42 397	44 607	56 970	86 698	94 602	86 352	89 122	126 339
General administration	49 382	76 425	86 127	76 675	66 928	80 261	87 840	131 566	135 904	249 244

See footnote on page 280

Source Department of the Environment; Welsh Office

16.17 Water authority expenditure
England and Wales

£ million (current prices)

	1974/75	1975/76	1976/77	1977/78	1978/79	1979/80	1980/81	1981/82	1982/83
Revenue expenditure[1]									
Water resources	8.5	17.8	27.0	34.4	40.2	78.9	101.9	57.3	58.5
Water supply	260.0	325.9	377.0	447.2	514.4	595.6	698.5	559.6	600.5
Sewerage }	319.2	417.6	481.0	249.8	285.7	331.9	388.3	176.1	193.9
Sewage treatment and disposal }				318.4	361.8	430.0	498.0	367.0	390.9
Water quality regulation }			7.6	9.0	10.5	12.7	14.9	17.0	16.3
Pollution alleviation and Specific environmental improvement }	4.7	6.7	1.2	1.5	1.6	2.3	3.0	2.9	3.8
Recreation and amenity	2.0	3.1	2.1	3.0	4.1	5.1	6.2	6.3	6.0
Navigation	0.3	0.7	2.0	2.3	2.8	3.3	3.9	3.9	4.1
Fisheries	1.8	2.5	3.2	3.8	4.6	5.5	6.6	7.1	7.3
Land drainage and flood protection	23.5	30.2	34.9	40.4	47.3	57.0	63.5	60.2	64.2
Interest								513.2	526.6
Other	–	–	–	0.1	0.2	–	–	–	–
Total Revenue expenditure	620.1	804.6	936.1	1 109.9	1 273.0	1 522.3	1 784.8	1 770.5	1 872.1
Capital expenditure[2]									
Water resources	19.4	30.1	38.4	55.6	56.3	49.2	55.9	41.3	38.7
Water supply	100.1	128.8	150.2	136.4	148.8	164.1	177.5	193.9	212.8
Sewerage }	278.0	307.8	296.8	261.2	274.1	298.3	204.5	191.5	216.4
Sewage treatment and disposal }							143.1	148.5	153.8
Water quality regulation }			0.5	0.5		0.5	0.4	0.6	0.6
Pollution alleviation and Specific environmental improvement }	0.3	0.5	0.3	0.3	1.2	1.6	1.8	1.8	0.7
Recreation and amenity	0.1	0.9	0.7	1.2	1.3	1.4	1.9	1.8	1.3
Navigation			0.5	0.5	0.3	1.0	0.6	0.4	1.3
Fisheries	0.1	0.2	0.4	0.4	0.4	0.4	0.4	0.3	0.2
General	7.1	9.6	11.5	17.3	16.9	15.7	25.7	32.0	46.0
Land drainage	17.0	27.0	31.4	40.8	52.5	72.5	81.0	84.4	19.5
Gross Total Capital expenditure	422.1	505.0	530.8	514.2	551.9	604.6	692.7	696.4	691.3
Grants and contributions				51.1	68.0	84.6	104.3	94.5	68.8
Total Net expenditure				463.0	483.8	520.0	588.4	599.9	622.5

See footnotes on page 280

Source: National Water Council

16.18 Income of local authorities: classified according to source[1]
England and Wales
Years ended 31 March

£ thousand

	1972/73	1973/74	1974/75	1975/76	1976/77	1977/78	1978/79	1979/80	1980/81	1981/82	1982/83
Total income	11 058 882	13 601 957	15 920 675	19 800 964	21 804 105	23 155 238	25 734 853	29 979 696	35 915 804	39 311 213	42 617 618
Capital income: total	2 844 045	3 771 740	4 078 948	4 338 383	4 374 681	4 132 824	4 341 816	5 001 245	5 555 754	5 488 790	7 306 638
Loans	2 150 861	2 960 484	3 407 642	3 457 725	3 254 021	2 815 850	2 751 052	3 135 903	3 050 494	2 668 918	3 572 576
Government grants	130 230	155 162	139 696	192 472	269 434	213 975	380 089	412 140	524 812	508 922	456 845
Sales and other sources	562 954	656 094	531 610	688 186	851 226	1 102 999	1 210 675	1 453 202	1 980 448	2 310 950	3 277 217
Revenue income: total	8 214 837	9 830 217	11 841 727	15 462 581	17 429 424	19 022 414	21 393 037	24 978 451	30 360 050	33 822 423	35 310 980
Rates	2 179 584	2 414 631	2 927 262	3 795 654	4 151 034	4 686 733	5 166 634	6 122 518	7 845 479	9 450 945	10 693 917
Government grants	3 135 048	3 897 294	5 651 767	7 666 082	8 639 836	9 138 334	10 103 779	11 684 364	13 784 425	13 998 687	14 246 491
Miscellaneous income including rents, tolls, fees and interest	2 900 205	3 518 292	3 262 698	4 000 845	4 638 554	5 197 347	6 122 624	7 171 569	8 730 146	10 372 791	10 370 572

1. Expenditure of superannuation and statutory special funds is not included for 1974/75 and later.

Source Department of the Environment; Welsh Office

16.19 Income of local authorities from government grants including grants for capital works
England and Wales
Years ended 31 March

£ thousand

	1972/73	1973/74	1974/75	1975/76	1976/77	1977/78	1978/79	1979/80	1980/81	1981/82	1982/83
Total	3 265 278	4 052 456	5 791 463	7 858 554	8 909 270	9 352 309	10 483 868	12 096 504	14 309 237	14 507 609	14 703 336
Allocated to specific services:											
Education	9 281	12 056	127 278	198 367	260 431	395 356	459 663	534 881	665 279	769 811	694 028
Libraries, museums and art galleries	101	116	160	327	596	730	1 190	1 643	1 914	2 689	2 878
Local health authority services including port health[1]	957	1 103	–	–	–	–	–	–	–	–	–
Personal social services	6 670	4 172	5 505	8 342	11 822	13 790	16 236	21 682	27 417	29 187	33 791
Sheltered employment and workshops	1 698	1 916	2 202	3 201	5 419	4 508	5 872	6 015	6 847	7 672	9 342
Police including school crossing patrols	204 766	233 466	288 877	389 912	454 759	503 483	554 951	717 714	859 959	1 033 595	1 130 067
Fire service	20	9	4	28	21	3	9	9	42	55	128
Administration of justice	25 907	37 660	51 246	72 135	85 343	93 068	105 098	129 161	172 863	196 957	216 088
Sewerage and sewage disposal[2]	6 949	8 628	–	–	–	–	–	–	–	–	–
Refuse collection and disposal	63	87	175	382	97	958	1 130	602	621	797	550
Agriculture and fisheries[3]	12 914	13 753	7 110	18 138	29 990	25 238	44 377	58 986	65 026	73 576	66 113
Local transport	112 155	130 303	128 630	271 499	292 958	300 921	292 045	369 527	458 834	436 285	515 440
Parks and open spaces[4]	3 093	5 975	5 004	7 059	8 978	7 741	13 545	17 461	22 162	23 968	27 128
Environmental health[4]	2 831	2 914	2 048	2 134	1 950	1 562	2 530	3 870	4 313	2 817	3 255
Town and country planning	9 630	17 445	10 833	15 023	20 138	22 755	33 553	35 332	43 344	43 436	68 831
Housing to which the Housing Revenue Account relates[5]	186 331	237 683	639 548	798 931	1 048 523	1 141 639	1 322 009	1 637 489	1 867 979	1 273 442	1 058 408
Other housing	99 025	212 159	118 475	159 159	258 335	215 232	377 591	390 355	483 535	461 646	520 486
Trading services:											
Water supply[2]	2 663	2 760	–	–	–	–	–	–	–	–	–
Passenger transport	6 407	6 489	5 942	6 770	4 966	5 769	7 331	7 714	8 341	7 369	4 146
Cemeteries and crematoria	9	16	1	50	101	12	53	59	75	47	96
Harbours, docks and piers	55	19	29	49	255	606	964	862	837	291	245
Other trading services	2 625	2 738	2 568	5 016	3 529	4 718	9 835	13 177	16 735	24 331	37 088
Other services	13 293	16 010	5 854	10 116	12 324	18 775	17 285	27 092	31 067	39 907	48 478
Not allocated to specific services:											
Local Government Acts grants	2 556 617	3 103 555	4 389 630	5 891 640	6 408 452	6 595 196	7 218 301	8 122 377	9 571 553	10 079 109	10 265 908
Local taxation licence duties	1 218	1 424	344	276	284	249	300	496	494	622	842

1. From 1974/75 local authorities services were transferred to regional health authorities.
2. From 1974/75 sewerage and sewage disposal and water supply were transferred to regional water authorities.
3. Before 1974/75 excluded land drainage, smallholdings, etc.
4. From 1974/75 baths and laundries are included with parks and open spaces and from 1978/79 swimming baths are included with parks and open spaces, and other public baths and public laundries are included with environmental health. Nil figures for 1972/73 and 1973/74.
5. From 1974/75 includes the rent rebate subsidy.

Source Department of the Environment; Welsh Office.

16.20 Expenditure of local authorities
Scotland
Year ended 31 March
Out of revenue[1]

£ thousand

	1975/76	1976/77	1977/78	1978/79	1979/80	1980/81	1981/82	1982/83[2]
Total	1 566 110	1 963 566	2 123 248	2 442 348	2 985 930	3 657 541	4 082 220	4 469 440
Rate Fund Services	1 188 234	1 467 035	1 593 182	1 860 261	2 276 196	2 799 715	3 131 773	3 447 271
Education	546 044	674 604	721 565	830 182	975 555	1 190 993	1 331 560	1 423 957
Libraries, museums and galleries	15 575	19 448	21 563	26 603	32 282	40 263	45 639	49 423
Social work	93 297	119 799	129 846	156 542	196 210	249 554	277 681	299 723
Law, order and protective services	105 547	134 434	141 053	166 171	213 441	254 434	294 266	325 742
Roads[3]	103 368	124 448	153 237	180 185	229 117	299 278	320 862	359 373
Environmental services[4]	93 271	112 995	125 292	153 591	189 645	228 933	237 974	275 552
Planning	26 073	35 504	36 112	39 617	49 851	58 948	60 008	64 592
Leisure and recreation	51 651	67 373	74 193	91 371	114 378	133 956	146 218	157 598
Central administration	57 737	71 748	74 359	92 127	114 370	143 483	163 741	161 538
Other services[4]	33 465	35 256	41 832	50 999	56 782	79 123	103 451	159 441
Other rate fund expenditure[5]	62 206	71 426	74 130	72 873	104 565	120 750	150 373	170 332
Housing	309 198	404 299	431 536	469 851	578 271	689 972	745 431	816 859
Trading Services	68 678	92 232	98 530	112 236	131 463	167 854	205 016	205 310
Water supply	45 867	57 628	59 111	65 817	79 243	101 395	117 672	118 887
Passenger transport	16 513	20 912	23 034	28 917	30 249	36 682	36 836	39 703
Ferries	513	745	812	898	1 504	2 090	2 283	2 485
Harbours, docks and piers	641	1 099	1 436	8 602	11 497	14 822	33 297	30 010
Airports	100	131	170	323	404	1 216	1 364	1 432
Road bridges	2 017	2 338	3 187	2 621	2 936	3 275	5 672	4 321
Slaughterhouses	1 926	2 382	2 538	3 001	3 492	4 152	3 937	2 338
Markets	727	833	937	975	1 107	1 213	1 630	1 813
Other trading services[4]	374	6 164	7 305	1 082	1 031	3 009	2 325	4 321
Loan Charges (included above): total	371 822	496 778	514 770	577 199	713 930	846 434	898 174	959 089
Allocated to: Rate fund services	143 698	195 914	204 572	233 458	293 982	349 889	365 594	416 589
Housing	207 650	272 872	281 667	308 015	379 867	445 701	467 086	477 775
Trading services	20 474	27 992	28 531	35 726	40 081	50 844	65 494	64 725

On capital works[6]

	1975/76	1976/77	1977/78	1978/79	1979/80	1980/81	1981/82	1982/83[2]
Total	477 834	532 022	499 287	542 109	658 485	660 868	708 742	775 063
Rate Fund Services	230 798	263 721	228 699	243 955	299 614	293 966	320 396	347 649
Education	66 774	88 294	75 789	58 241	56 761	58 857	66 545	60 897[7]
Libraries, museums and galleries	2 429	3 854	4 617	6 007	7 602	8 927	10 513	8 449
Social work	7 437	10 971	8 119	8 724	11 688	12 244	13 314	14 992
Law, order and protective services	9 480	10 253	9 973	10 308	11 908	12 795	10 541	13 215
Roads	45 512	52 108	46 487	58 123	77 724	78 479	96 348	107 364
Environmental services[4]	49 220	43 084	40 331	48 374	64 347	61 024	61 329	58 878
Planning	24 781	25 827	20 553	24 910	28 578	23 761	21 718	32 695
Leisure and recreation	17 611	15 946	12 201	13 810	20 663	19 766	19 237	22 516
Central administration	4 880	11 455	8 386	6 830	12 633	10 539	10 111	18 053
Other services[4]	2 674	1 929	2 243	8 628	7 710	7 574	10 740	10 590
Housing	218 664	234 734	229 413	243 956	293 763	311 010	329 276	370 628
Trading Services	28 372	33 567	41 175	54 198	65 108	55 892	59 070	56 786
Water supply	16 890	20 500	21 317	27 803	37 968	35 757	39 101	38 493
Passenger transport	2 563	3 495	1 990	3 658	3 238	4 700	5 264	5 575
Ferries	455	36	71	221	881	843	1 925	879
Harbours, docks and piers	6 582	5 842	14 768	21 140	20 373	8 646	7 730	5 604
Airports	33	253	215	64	294	268	123	161
Road bridges	86	425	727	21	121	371	1 929	398
Slaughterhouses	1 465	1 941	1 165	860	1 979	3 725	2 587	42
Markets	264	447	326	31	21	7	—	30
Other trading services[4]	34	628	596	400	233	1 575	411	5 604

1. Gross expenditure *less* inter-authority and inter-account transfers.
2. Provisional.
3. Including rate fund support for transport (LA and non-LA).
4. Burial grounds and Crematoria were treated as trading services for 1976/77 and 1977/78, and were included amongst 'Other trading services'. In 1975/76, 1978/79, 1979/80 and 1980/81 they were included amongst 'Environmental services'. From 1981/82 they were included amongst 'Other services'.
5. Rate fund contributions to Housing and Trading Services (excluding transport) and public water requisitions.
6. Expenditure out of loans, government grants and other capital receipts.

Source Scottish Office, Central Statistics Unit

16.21 Income of local authorities: classified according to source
Scotland
Year ended 31 March

£ thousand

	1975/76	1976/77	1977/78	1978/79	1979/80	1980/81	1981/82	1982/83[2]
Total income	1 986 520	2 455 125	2 617 020	2 934 460	3 449 800	4 085 530	4 742 171	5 087 849
Revenue account								
Rates[1]	408 354	470 905	544 656	616 555	716 966	938 618	1 322 432	1 398 412
Government grants								
RSG: Needs element	520 730	665 600	705 900	822 400	946 400	1 256 300	1 376 300	1 416 600
Resources element	130 180	167 800	177 300	204 900	234 900	180 900	152 900	202 400
Domestic element	32 340	42 200	49 700	13 400	13 500	13 800	14 100	14 100
Rate rebate grant	15 690	18 480	21 548	19 063	24 511	28 786	52 200	56 437
Specific grants and subsidies	174 955	238 738	242 017	265 572	345 136	412 348	389 334	410 590
Sales	10 401	21 840	31 125	25 968	33 027	35 491	46 531	42 135
Fees and charges	68 578	85 898	98 895	125 306	146 217	182 892	217 039	242 317
Other income	146 562	210 846	246 089	298 161	329 379	372 407	458 736	557 019
Capital account								
Sale of fixed assets	2 662	6 016	8 416	21 936	22 616	38 022	75 050	125 200
Loans	444 989	489 460	453 664	481 862	583 444	566 914	575 269	537 448
Government grants	9 727	8 773	12 941	10 837	18 673	31 628	33 630	31 434
Revenue contributions to capital	6 317	8 888	8 392	10 678	16 217	12 392	11 635	12 958
Transfers from special funds	1 265	761	1 932	1 343	1 234	709	1 094	1 393
Other receipts	13 770	18 920	14 445	16 479	17 580	14 323	15 921	39 406

1. Excluding Government grants towards rate rebates and domestic element of
   rate support grant (RSG) but including payments in lieu of rates under Part V
   of The Local Government Act 1948 for years to 1977/78. Including domestic
   water rate receipts.
2. Provisional.

Source Scottish Office, Central Statistics Unit

16.22 Income of local authorities from government grants[1]
Scotland
Year ended 31 March

£ thousand

	1975/76	1976/77	1977/78	1978/79	1979/80	1980/81	1981/82	1982/3[3]
Total	883 621	1 141 585	1 209 406	1 336 171	1 583 465	1 923 742	2 018 510	2 131 561
Rate fund services	51 436	63 840	72 833	82 411	107 875	135 668	164 065	206 294
Education	477	134	696	3 174	1 776	2 247	3 067	3 850
Libraries, museums and galleries	–	3	35	200	905	2 371	3 147	2 180
Social work	702	902	680	934	797	1 169	1 697	2 521
Law, order and protective services	38 182	47 704	51 225	59 708	75 173	90 443	105 858	117 292
Roads and transport	4 643	3 346	4 781	2 902	7 871	13 727	10 675	17 259
Environmental services	741	987	2 889	2 550	5 235	6 030	9 578	6 374
Planning	4 786	6 287	6 377	6 331	7 139	7 167	7 714	7 747
Leisure and recreation	923	1 685	1 391	1 767	1 584	1 220	2 216	3 017
Central administration	2	3	7	57	13	20	96	68
Other rate fund services	980	2 789	4 752	4 788	7 382	11 274	20 017	45 986
Housing	130 393	178 853	176 626	188 085	248 184	299 990	248 456	226 692
Trading services	2 852	4 812	5 499	5 912	8 095	8 298	10 489	9 038
Water supply	1 715	2 802	3 951	3 700	6 321	6 352	7 448	5 602
Ferries	14	–	60	257	243	250	450	10
Other trading services	1 123	2 010	1 488	1 955	1 531	1 696	2 591	3 426
Grants not allocated to specific services[2]	698 940	894 080	954 448	1 059 763	1 219 311	1 479 786	1 595 500	1 689 537

1. Including grants for capital works.
2. Rate support grant and rate rebates grant.
3. Provisional.

Source Scottish Office, Central Statistics Unit

16.23 Expenditure of local authorities
Northern Ireland
Years end 31 March

Out of revenue and special funds

£ thousand

	1972/73	1973/74[1]	1974/75	1975/76	1976/77	1977/78	1978/79	1979/80	1980/81	1981/82	1982/83
Total	183 306	96 427	33 880	43 094	50 593	57 366	65 267	81 599	96 828	110 557	121 856
Education	52 198	26 139	–	–	–	–	–	–	–	–	–
Libraries, museums and art galleries	1 834	1 094	2	6	22	28	44	50	113	218	271
Local health authority services	6 608	3 583	–	–	–	–	–	–	–	–	–
Environmental health services:											
Sewerage services	3 161	1 934	–	–	–	–	–	–	–	–	–
Refuse collection and disposal	2 670	3 547	4 810	6 473	7 618	9 086	10 295	12 337	14 932	15 871	17 986
Public baths	721	920	1 336	1 977	2 410	3 006	3 114	3 191	3 762	3 957	4 630
Parks, recreation grounds, etc.	1 640	2 418	3 782	5 650	8 072	10 390	12 928	16 739	20 834	25 274	30 338
Other sanitary services	2 065	2 916	5 139	5 966	6 319	6 741	7 352	8 593	10 467	11 619	12 980
Welfare services	7 638	4 532	–	–	–	–	–	–	–	–	–
Housing (grants and small dwellings acquisition)[2]	3 319	1 921	1 143	1 147	1 111	1 122	1 094	1 241	1 466	1 369	1 345
Highways and bridges	17 101	9 569	–	–	–	–	–	–	–	–	–
Public lighting	1 185	494	–	–	–	–	–	–	–	–	–
Trading services:											
Water supply	7 862	5 359	–	–	–	–	–	–	–	–	–
Gas supply	5 675	7 026	10 540	12 486	13 313	13 835	16 363	21 789	23 061	25 337	25 773
Electricity supply	23 679	–	–	–	–	–	–	–	–	–	–
Passenger transport	4 356	–	–	–	–	–	–	–	–	–	–
Cemeteries	416	478	620	897	1 072	1 231	1 348	1 640	2 065	2 418	2 508
Other trading services (including markets, fairs and harbours)	200	576	1 106	1 635	1 852	2 056	1 990	2 495	3 681	4 047	4 313
Miscellaneous	40 978	23 921	5 402	6 857	8 804	9 871	10 739	13 524	16 447	20 447	21 712
Total loan charges	22 226	10 131	4 072	4 564	5 292	5 526	5 757	7 018	9 068	10 236	11 538
Loan charges included in terms of expenditure above:											
Allocated to rate fund services	10 864	5 965	1 586	1 928	2 513	2 865	3 216	3 793	4 963	6 113	7 071
Allocated to trading services	8 375	3 707	1 948	2 104	2 239	2 137	2 024	2 643	3 401	3 437	3 717
Not allocated	1 005	459	538	532	540	524	517	582	704	686	750
Loan charges included below	1 982	–	–	–	–	–	–	–	–	–	–

On capital works[2]

	1972/73	1973/74[1]	1974/75	1975/76	1976/77	1977/78	1978/79	1979/80	1980/81	1981/82	1982/83
Total[3]	41 767	29 483	9 069	13 371	11 879	13 377	15 163	21 318	24 079	25 078	24 073
Education	7 870	3 838	–	–	–	–	–	–	–	–	–
Libraries, museums and art galleries	113	15	4	10	6	17	1	–	94	120	65
Local health authority services	744	529	–	–	–	–	–	–	–	–	–
Environmental health services:											
Sewerage services	5 301	3 262	–	–	–	–	–	–	–	–	–
Refuse collection and disposal	214	177	704	621	1 611	892	737	1 233	1 337	1 964	2 170
Public baths	339	660	619	856	744	450	354	787	1 205	811	454
Parks, recreation grounds, etc.	1 506	2 600	3 609	6 164	5 051	6 824	8 080	9 957	11 675	11 395	11 985
Other sanitary services	45	128	166	368	343	275	642	689	554	742	719
Welfare services	841	560	–	–	–	–	–	–	–	–	–
Housing (including small dwellings acquisition)[2]	6 387	2 030	1 477	1 301	1 004	850	1 100	1 815	965	639	211
Highways and bridges	6 386	4 025	–	–	–	–	–	–	–	–	–
Public lighting	420	227	–	–	–	–	–	–	–	–	–
Trading services:											
Water supply	5 105	6 457	–	–	–	–	–	–	–	–	–
Gas supply	1 303	1 019	846	1 250	782	528	757	419	421	282	648
Electricity supply	2 040	–	–	–	–	–	–	–	–	–	–
Passenger transport	287	–	–	–	–	–	–	–	–	–	–
Cemeteries	21	27	39	33	78	61	58	28	139	280	103
Other trading services (including markets, fairs and harbours)	390	116	177	195	319	563	1 149	2 983	3 215	3 113	2 679
Miscellaneous	2 457	3 813	1 428	2 573	1 941	2 917	2 285	3 407	4 474	5 732	5 041

1. On reorganisation of local government on 1 October 1973 the following services were transferred to central government and other bodies—education, local health and welfare authority services, water and sewerage, highways and bridges, electricity and passenger transport.

2. Expenditure met out of loans, government grants for capital works, sales of property and other capital receipts.
3. During the year 1972/73 the main housing functions were transferred to the Northern Ireland Housing Executive.

Source Department of the Environment for Northern Ireland

Home finance

16.24 Income of local authorities: classified according to source
Northern Ireland
Years ended 31 March

£ thousand

	1972/73	1973/74[1]	1974/75	1975/76	1976/77	1977/78	1978/79	1979/80	1980/81	1981/82	1982/83
Total income	222 268	115 212	38 682	60 671	68 907	69 565	78 285	94 584	120 114	136 219	151 064
Capital receipts: total	37 933	24 821	8 098	12 442	11 441	11 428	12 631	15 214	19 420	21 676	23 502
Loans	19 706	14 724	3 259	5 117	3 970	3 279	3 871	5 831	9 616	9 533	8 296
Government grants	12 876	7 782	3 645	5 029	4 712	5 049	6 192	6 824	6 778	7 604	9 878
Other sources	5 351	2 315	1 194	2 296	2 759	3 100	2 568	2 559	3 026	4 539	5 328
Other income: total	184 335	90 391	30 584	31 952	39 634	37 947	41 675	48 826	61 513	73 019	83 684
Rates	36 925	26 770	12 971	20 388	25 397	27 130	30 376	35 532	45 579	54 261	60 924
Government grants	84 759	40 471	6 005	8 009	9 292	10 267	10 754	12 695	15 196	18 045	17 844
Housing [2,3]											
Rents, etc.	3 593										
Grants and small dwellings acquisition		601	561	593	596	550	545	599	738	713	729
Miscellaneous income	22 234	14 045	3 464	2 962	4 349	4 671	5 304	7 147	7 963	9 415	11 306
Trading services [4]											
Total (capital and revenue)				16 277	17 832	15 519	18 675	23 397	31 218	32 109	32 572
Gas: total	5 740	5 707	7 583	14 210	15 423	12 601	15 118	18 275	24 342	24 666	26 056
Loans				1 217	616	701	451	174	272	308	392
Government grants				2 764	2 404	494	3 374	5 774	9 712	8 887	10 916
Miscellaneous				10 229	12 403	11 406	11 293	12 327	14 358	15 471	14 748
Cemeteries: total				190	297	298	317	359	507	830	637
Loans				14	59	38	28	10	78	170	20
Government grants				–	3	–	–	–	–	4	15
Miscellaneous				176	235	260	289	349	429	656	602
Other trading: total				1 877	2 112	2 620	3 240	4 763	6 369	6 613	5 879
Loans				102	155	436	888	2 153	1 700	1 522	824
Government grants				146	140	52	556	307	1 346	1 551	1 453
Miscellaneous				1 629	1 817	2 132	1 796	2 303	3 323	3 540	3 602
Water supply	3 334	2 088									
Electricity supply	23 074										
Passenger transport	3 389										

1. On reorganisation of local government on 1 October 1973 the following services were transferred to central government and other bodies—education, local health and welfare authority services, water and sewerage, highways and bridges, electricity and passenger transport.
2. Including annuity repayments made by borrowers under the Small Dwellings Acquisition scheme.
3. During the year 1972/73 the main housing functions were transferred to the Northern Ireland Housing Executive.
4. Reclassified in 1975/76.

Source Department of the Environment for Northern Ireland

16.25 Income of local authorities from government grants[1]: classified according to services
Northern Ireland
Years ended 31 March

£ thousand

	1972/73	1973/74[2]	1974/75	1975/76	1976/77	1977/78	1978/79	1979/80	1980/81	1981/82	1982/83
Total	97 635	48 253	9 650	15 948	16 551	15 862	20 586	25 600	33 032	36 091	44 293
Allocated to specific services:											
Education	28 820	11 484									
Local health authority services	2 778	1 513									
Environmental health services	6 261	4 452	4 724	6 635	5 873	6 602	7 353	8 027	8 118	8 951	12 190
Welfare services	3 402	1 951									
Housing [3]	1 660	984	1 085	842	672	560	546	539	438	318	16
Highways and bridges	15 237	5 445									
Other services	15 003	1 370	664	3 372	2 871	1 135	4 529	7 136	12 329	12 420	14 072
Not allocated to specific services [4]	24 474	21 054	3 177	5 099	7 135	7 565	8 158	9 898	12 147	14 402	18 015

1. Including grants for capital works.
2. On reorganisation of local government on 1 October 1973 the following services were transferred to central government and other bodies—education, local health and welfare authority services, water and sewerage, highways and bridges, electricity and passenger transport.
3. During the year 1972/73 the main housing functions were transferred to the Northern Ireland Housing Executive.
4. Assistance to local authorities under various Local Government Acts.

Source Department of the Environment for Northern Ireland

286

17 Banking, Insurance, etc.

17.1 Bank of England

	1973 Dec 12	1974 Dec 11	1975 Dec 10	1976 Dec 8	1977 Dec 14	1978 Dec 13	1979 Dec 12	1980 Dec 10	1981 Dec 9	1982 Dec 8	1983 Dec 14
Issue Department											
Liabilities:											
Notes in circulation	4 788	5 520	6 138	6 858	8 019	9 122	10 089	10 611	11 001	11 271	12 152
Notes in Banking Department	12	5	12	17	6	28	11	14	24	4	8
Assets:											
Government securities[1]	4 027	5 284	5 430	5 952	7 095	8 085	8 635	8 430	6 329	3 217	4 699
Other securities	773	241	720	923	930	1 065	1 465	2 195	4 696	8 058	7 461
Banking Department											
Liabilities:											
Total[2]	1 982	1 595	1 766	2 647	2 237	2 250	1 999	1 162	2 039	2 754	2 356
Public deposits[3]	23	18	21	17	23	25	20	33	40	41	44
Special deposits[4]	1 439	928	989	1 806	1 185	1 099	805	–	–	–	–
Bankers' deposits[5]	194	300	322	326	428	423	462	487	482	647	650
Reserves and other accounts	311	334	420	484	586	689	697	627	1 503	2 051	1 647
Assets:											
Total	1 982	1 595	1 766	2 647	2 237	2 251	2 000	1 162	2 039	2 754	2 356
Government securities	1 675	1 248	1 405	1 905	1 591	1 848	1 462	447	433	456	382
Advances and other accounts	32	189	264	640	486	206	161	175	1 026	1 283	947
Premises, equipment and other securities	263	153	84	85	153	169	365	526	556	1 011	1 018
Notes and coin	12	5	13	18	6	28	12	15	24	4	8

1. Including the historic liability of the Treasury of £11 million.
2. The only liability not shown separately is the Bank's capital (held by the Treasury) which has been constant at £14.6 million.
3. Excluding local authorities' and public corporations' deposits, which are included under Reserves and other accounts:
4. Deposits called from institutions are not at their free disposal. Until 19 August 1981, all banks and finance houses which observed the common reserve ratio were liable for calls to lodge special deposits. With effect from 20 August 1981 only reporting institutions with eligible liabilities of £10 million or more are liable for special deposit calls. This item also includes deposits under the supplementary special deposits scheme which was in force on three occasions before 1980.
5. Up to 19 August 1981 these constituted the current accounts held at the Bank by the banks and discount houses. From the introduction of new arrangements for monetary control on 20 August, they consist of operational deposits held mainly by the clearing banks and non-operational cash ratio deposits for which recognised banks and licensed deposit takers are liable.

Source Bank of England

17.2 Bank clearing[1]

	1973	1974	1975	1976	1977	1978	1979	1980	1981	1982	1983
Credit clearing											
Total	16 255	18 580	22 089	26 946	31 607	36 887	43 497	51 808	61 480	62 563	67 978
Debit clearing											
Total	1 457 238	1 641 088	1 795 833	2 205 286	2 599 495	2 847 030	3 616 555	4 458 326	4 835 414	5 771 350	6 800 818
Bankers' Clearing House											
Total	1 456 420	1 640 190	1 794 767	2 204 091	2 598 298	2 845 901	3 615 313	4 456 893	4 835 414	5 771 350	6 800 818
Town	1 310 885	1 479 238	1 605 547	1 980 730	2 336 486	2 544 254	3 258 830	4 051 203	4 403 794	5 291 926	6 257 551
General	145 535	160 952	189 220	223 361	261 812	301 647	356 483	405 690	431 620	479 424	543 267
Provincial clearing houses											
Total	818	898	1 066	1 195	1 197	1 129	1 242	1 433	2	2	2

1. Figures are not strictly comparable throughout owing to changes in the composition of the clearings. This table includes only inter-bank clearings.
2. Data no longer collected.

Source Bankers' Clearing House

17.3 UK monetary sector: liabilities and assets outstanding[1]
End-year

£ million

	1973[2]	1974	1975[2]	1976	1977	1978	1979	1980	1981[3]	1982	1983
Liabilities											
Total	74 693	88 153	107 682	136 274	144 849	167 407	199 590	233 392	331 705	407 531	477 930
Public sector deposits											
Sterling	725	656	924	1 019	1 423	1 312	1 257	1 595	1 729	2 185	2 296
Other currencies [4]	..	..	39	73	124	102	117	154	202	282	308
Private sector deposits											
Sterling	26 944	29 559	30 767	33 525	36 313	41 846	47 719	57 571	73 826	80 895	89 916
Other currencies [4]	1 432	2 398	2 939	3 896	4 151	4 799	5 202	6 189	9 849	12 621	16 293
Overseas sector deposits											
Sterling	2 959	3 686	3 824	3 966	5 615	5 476	8 475	11 477	14 412	18 889	23 234
Other currencies	38 460	46 999	63 196	86 801	89 558	105 046	127 347	145 684	217 904	276 514	326 603
Non-deposit liabilities (net)	4 173	4 855	5 993	6 994	7 665	8 826	9 473	10 722	13 783	16 145	19 280
Assets											
Total	74 693	88 153	107 682	136 274	144 849	167 407	199 590	233 392	331 705	407 531	477 930
Lending to public sector											
Sterling	9 277	8 907	11 907	11 801	13 633	13 478	14 980	17 325	22 650	20 375	18 357
Other currencies	909	1 980	2 637	3 529	3 751	3 151	2 325	1 485	1 000	1 170	1 443
Lending to private sector											
Sterling	22 937	26 671	25 384	28 422	31 917	36 756	45 278	54 870	67 420	80 340	94 394
Other currencies	3 436	4 373	5 615	6 993	7 422	8 088	8 326	8 852	15 616	20 032	24 658
Lending to overseas sector											
Sterling	1 967	2 256	3 185	3 831	4 236	5 096	5 074	7 879	11 764	15 883	18 752
Other currencies	36 167	43 966	58 954	81 698	83 890	100 838	123 607	142 981	213 255	269 731	320 326

1. At end-1981, in the quarterly series, the old banking sector was replaced by the new monetary sector. The UK monetary sector comprises the UK offices of institutions either recognised as banks or licensed to take deposits under the Banking Act 1979, together with the National Girobank, the trustee savings banks, the Banking Department of the Bank of England, and those institutions (including branches of mainland banks) in the Channel Islands and the Isle of Man which have opted to participate in the new monetary control arrangements introduced in August 1981. Inter-bank items are excluded and adjustments made to allow for transit items. Figures for other currencies are affected by changes in exchange rates.

2. During 1973 further new contributors added £70 million; to total assets and liabilities, during 1975 changes in statistical reporting and the number of contributors added about £400 million.
3. The introduction of the new monetary sector at end-1981 added about £9,850 to total assets and liabilities.
4. Before the introduction of new statistical returns during 1975 all UK residents' deposits in foreign currency were allocated to the private sector.

Source Bank of England

17.4 Banks: summary of monthly reporting institutions
As at second Wednesday in December

£ million

	1977	1978	1979	1980		1981[1]	1982	1983
Liabilities					**Liabilities**			
Notes outstanding	406	460	498	554	Notes outstanding	625	716	836
Sterling deposits: total	56 568	62 755	76 915	90 354	Sterling deposits: total	109 906	134 649	156 792
Sight deposits					Sight deposits			
UK banking sector	1 520	1 987	3 710	2 299	UK monetary sector	3 458	5 887	7 637
UK Public sector	526	625	750	659	UK Public sector	823	992	1 118
UK Private sector	15 615	17 907	19 477	21 000	UK Private sector	23 023	26 662	32 532
Overseas	2 241	2 116	2 698	2 946	Overseas	3 137	3 748	4 699
Time deposits					Time deposits			
UK banking sector	9 977	11 437	15 607	15 377	UK monetary sector	20 728	28 542	28 358
UK Public sector	393	286	163	303	UK Public sector	460	1 119	1 245
UK Private sector	19 061	21 773	25 839	34 108	UK Private sector	41 124	44 796	53 843
Overseas	2 594	2 814	4 838	7 936	Overseas	10 458	14 377	17 570
Certificates of deposit	4 641	3 809	3 833	5 727	Certificates of deposit	6 695	8 525	9 792
Other currency deposits total	121 594	141 192	169 497	193 374	Other currency deposits: total	288 379	376 259	439 302
Sight and time deposits					Sight and time deposits			
UK banking sector	24 410	27 977	36 737	42 727	UK monetary sector	64 614	84 886	87 442
Other United Kingdom	3 875	4 538	4 968	5 574	Other United Kingdom	9 663	12 081	15 430
Overseas	80 854	94 546	108 017	124 125	Overseas	173 678	221 993	265 972
Certificates of deposit	12 455	14 132	19 775	20 947	Certificates of deposit	40 424	57 299	70 457

1. From 1981 this table relates to the business of the United Kingdom offices of those members of the monetary sector which report on a monthly basis, other than members of the London Discount Market Association (LDMA), the trustee savings banks and the Banking Department of the Bank of England. For a description of the background of these changes see the December 1981 *Bank of England Quarterly Bulletin*, page 531.

2. From 1983, the trustee savings bank and the Banking Department of the Bank of England are included.
3. From 1983, market loans to UK public corporations and the UK private sector are included as advances.

Source Bank of England

17.4

Banks: summary of monthly reporting institutions
As at second Wednesday in December

(continued)

£ million

	1977	1978	1979	1980		1981[1]	1982	1983
Sterling and other currencies					**Sterling and other currencies**			
Items in suspense and transmission	3 045	3 081	3 592	3 966	Items in suspense and transmission	6 140	6 106	7 198
Capital and other funds	10 029	11 441	13 341	15 032	Capital and other funds	19 056	22 343	27 423
Total liabilities/assets	191 644	218 929	263 842	303 279	Total liabilities/assets	424 105	540 074	631 551
of which Sterling Liabilities	*69 025*	*76 213*	*92 666*	*108 043*	*of which Sterling Liabilities*	*131 270*	*158 561*	*185 573*
Sterling Assets	*68 569*	*75 453*	*92 423*	*108 022*	*Sterling Assets*	*131 257*	*159 595*	*185 669*
Sterling assets					**Sterling assets**			
Notes and coin	1 334	1 423	1 489	1 591	Notes and coin	1 612	1 586	1 938
Reserve assets: total	6 061	6 132	6 861	9 084	Balances with Bank of England:			
					Cash ratio deposits	321	434	497
Balances with Bank of England	425	420	449	485	Special deposits	–	–	–
Money at call					Other	159	209	147
Discount market	2 567	3 002	3 399	4 601	Market loans[3]			
Other	214	220	230	295	LDMA—secured	4 317	4 685	5 764
UK and Northern Ireland Treasury					LDMA—unsecured	21	20	37
bills	1 549	838	1 118	1 168	Other UK monetary sector	21 658	30 695	32 830
Other bills					UK monetary sector CDs	4 094	4 573	4 980
Local authority	164	148	152	502	Building Society CDs			
Commercial	710	804	947	1 251	and time deposits	–	–	365
British government stocks up to 1					UK local authorities	5 386	5 172	5 085
year	432	700	565	782	UK public corporations	320	61	–
					UK private sector	1 129	1 160	–
Special and supplementary deposits	1 177	1 087	797	–	Overseas	4 060	4 441	4 634
Market loans (other than reserve					Bills:			
assets): total	18 282	19 702	27 433	28 908	Treasury bills	707	313	333
					Eligible local authority	278	226	351
Banks in United Kingdom	11 027	13 093	19 305	17 403				
Loans to discount market	263	422	766	206				
Certificates of deposit	2 912	2 344	2 982	3 510				
UK local authorities	2 697	2 699	2 922	3 939				
UK public corporations	241	104	166	229				
UK private sector	470	528	649	804				
Overseas	671	513	644	2 817	Eligible bank bills	1 389	1 335	2 286
					Other	278	253	258
Bills (other than reserve assets)	699	361	471	435				
Advances: total	30 283	35 203	42 743	52 939	Advances: total	66 772	83 905	100 067
UK public sector	569	845	1 370	1 885	UK public sector	3 053	3 033	2 613
UK private sector	26 620	30 509	37 329	46 469	UK private sector	58 266	73 126	87 475
Overseas	3 094	3 849	4 044	4 586	Overseas	5 453	7 746	9 979
					Banking Dept lending to central			
					government (net)	–	–	387
Investments					**Investments**			
British government stocks					British government stocks			
Over 1 year and up to 1½ years	416	388	210	198	Up to 1 year	505	567 ⎫	
Over 1½ years and up to 5 years	1 682	1 706	1 369	1 890	Over 1 year and up to 5	2 355	2 469 ⎬	6 618
Over 5 years and undated	282	187	593	1 152	Over 5 years and undated	1 287	1 196 ⎭	
Other					Other			
Public sector	269	318	390	470	Public sector	520	361	366
Other	1 486	1 857	1 957	2 291	Other	3 229	3 797	5 264
Sterling					**Sterling**			
Miscellaneous assets					**Miscellaneous assets**			
Items in suspense and collections	4 218	4 436	5 150	5 705	Items in suspense and collections	6 143	7 023	7 373
Assets leased	130	253	336	396	Assets leased	1 292	1 076	1 195
Other	2 250	2 399	2 626	2 963	Other	3 424	4 038	4 896
Other currency					**Other currency**			
Items in suspense and collections	135	196	266	314	Items in suspense and collections	1 829	1 782	2 172
Assets leased	15	17	15	13	Assets leased	12	20	17
Other	379	438	673	1 291	Other	1 405	3 265	2 613
Other currency assets					**Other currency assets**			
Market loans and advances: total	120 759	140 618	167 690	189 871	Market loans and advances: total	283 400	365 773	426 195
of which Advances	*33 058*	*37 692*	*39 677*	*45 833*	*of which Advances*	*68 849*	*90 062*	*109 133*
Banks in United Kingdom and					UK monetary sector			
discount market	24 544	27 989	35 826	41 484	UK monetary sector CDs	61 325	80 013	83 767
Certificates of deposit	1 866	2 043	2 283	3 931	Certificates of deposit	5 407	7 200	10 615
UK public sector	3 881	3 255	2 398	1 523	UK public sector	902	1 028	1,376
UK private sector	7 480	8 302	8 069	8 675	UK private sector	15 287	19 946	24 134
Overseas	82 987	99 029	119 113	134 259	Overseas	200 480	257 585	306 304
Bills	454	440	415	592	Bills	822	1 070	1 242
Investments: total	1 333	1 768	2 361	3 176	Investments: total	5 380	8 570	13 642
United Kingdom	70	105	120	154	United Kingdom	315	308	436
Overseas	1 264	1 662	2 241	3 022	Overseas	5 065	8 262	13 205
Acceptances					**Acceptances**			
Sterling	2 227	3 426	5 670	5 106	Sterling	7 921	12 198	13 386
Other currencies	369	413	594	454	Other currencies	827	1 261	1 524

See footnote on page 288.

Source Bank of England

17.5

Analysis of bank lending to UK residents[1]
Amounts outstanding
As at third Wednesday in November

£ million

	1983
Total to UK residents	122 732
Loans and advances	113 711
of which in sterling	*89 642*
Acceptances	9 021
of which in sterling	*8 662*
Agriculture, Forestry and Fishing	
Total	5 184
of which in sterling	*5 160*
Energy and water supply	
Total	4 821
of which in sterling	*2 538*
Oil and extraction of natural gas	3 542
Other energy industries	1 261
Water supply	18
Manufacturing industry	
Total	22 209
of which in sterling	*17 405*
Extraction of minerals and ores	784
Metal manufacturing	1 372
Mineral products	757
Chemical industry	1 855
Mechanical engineering	1 572
Electrical engineering	2 197
Motor vehicles	1 021
Other transport equipment	1 622
Other engineering and metal goods	1 918
Food, drink and tobacco	3 414
Textiles, leather, clothing and footwear	1 337
Other manufacturing	4 359
Construction	
Total	3 968
of which in sterling	*3 697*
Garages, distribution, hotels and catering	
Total	17 140
of which in sterling	*13 276*
Retail motor trades	1 918
Other retail distribution	5 180
Wholesale distribution	7 488
Hotels and catering	2 554
Transport	
Total	3 387
of which in sterling	*2 029*
Air transport	872
Other transport	2 515
Postal services and telecommunications	
Total	234
of which in sterling	*109*
Financial	
Total	22 206
of which in sterling	*12 139*
Building societies	843
Investment and unit trusts	2 093
Insurance companies and pension funds	1 381
Leasing companies	4 070
Other financial	13 819
Business and other services	
Total	14 601
of which sterling	*13 068*
Central and local government	2 202
Property companies	4 448
Hiring of movables	545
Other services	7 406
Persons	
Total (loans and advances only)	28 983
of which sterling	*28 880*
Bridging finance for house purchase	919
Other house purchase	13 062
Other advances to persons	15 002

1. This is a new series of statistics based on the Standard Industrial
   Classification 1980 and comprises loans, advances and acceptances by all
   monthly reporting institutions other than members of the London Discount
   Markets Association (LDMA). The table includes lending under the DTI
   special scheme for domestic shipbuilding, secured money placed with money
   brokers and gilt-edged jobbers and sterling time deposits and holdings of
   sterling certificates of deposit issued by building societies. The series based
   on Standard Industrial Classification 1968 was last published in *Annual
   Abstract of Statistics 1984 No. 120*

Source Bank of England

17.6 Discount market[1]
Mid-December

£ million

	1973	1974	1975[2]	1976	1977	1978	1979	1980	1981	1982	1983
Assets											
Total	2 517	2 821	2 814	2 869	3 934	4 308	4 909	5 305	5 086	5 461	6 953
Treasury bills	269	535	819	563	1 052	845	709	556	99	70	31
Other bills[3]:											
Sterling	628	1 352	980	1 019	1 213	2 038	2 638	2 484	2 892	2 394	3 577
Other currencies	10	8	14	15	30	16	12	22	34	24	13
British government securities[4]	25	13	96	261	557	454	754	957	742	555	364
UK monetary sector CDs:											
Sterling	923	401	303	403	509	333	84	613	642	1 468	2 044
Other currencies	110	84	129	175	115	75	109	50	198	149	70
Building Society CDs and time deposits	–	–	–	–	–	–	–	–	–	–	280
Local authority securities	387	346	315	280	267	282	373	377	243	216	154
Other assets[5]:											
Sterling	155	81	157	151	189	262	220	234	214	576	410
Other currencies	10	1	1	2	2	3	10	12	22	9	10
Borrowed funds[6]											
Total	2 456	2 708	2 679	2 735	3 752	4 111	4 705	5 140	4 926	5 286	6 738
Bank of England, Banking Dept.	–	–	–	361	246	–	–	–	20	–	55
Other UK monetary sector:											
Sterling	2 133	2 393	2 262	1 934	2 963	3 425	4 228	4 804	4 360	4 733	5 838
Other currencies	85	68	84	155	73	41	85	16	157	136	49
Other sources:											
Sterling	195	222	274	251	401	597	341	296	327	391	774
Other currencies	43	25	59	34	69	48	51	24	62	26	22

1. Before 1975 this group comprised the members of the London Discount Market Association. Between 1975 and November 1981 figures for two discount brokers (who became members of the LDMA in 1980) and for the money trading departments of five banks carrying on an essentially similar type of business are included. Since November 1981 this group has again comprised members of the LDMA.
2. In 1975 new statistical forms were introduced; this may have caused some inconsistencies with earlier figures. From this date, securities, etc., are generally reported at the value standing in the reporting institution's books.
3. Including local authority and public corporation bills.
4. Before 1975 this item is shown at nominal values.
5. Including funds lent to the United Kingdom monetary sector and in the local authority market.
6. Excluding capital and reserves.

Source Bank of England

17.7 Public sector borrowing requirement and other counterparts to changes in money stock during the year

£ million

	1973	1974	1975	1976	1977	1978	1979	1980	1981	1982	1983
Public sector borrowing requirement (surplus−)	+4 100	+6 439	+10 439	+9 031	+5 479	+8 414	+12 669	+11 809	+10 580	+4 947	+11 571
Sales (−) of public sector debt to UK private sector (other than banks)	−2 295	−3 168	−5 573	−5 721	−8 440	−6 007	−10 914	−9 426	−11 255	−10 529	−10 775
Sterling lending to the private sector[1]	+5 972	+3 435	−365	+3 407	+3 188	+4 698	+8 585	+10 025	+11 405	+17 557	+12 806
Domestic counterparts	+7 777	+6 706	+4 501	+6 717	+227	+7 105	+10 340	+12 400	+10 730	+11 975	+13 602
External and foreign currency counterparts[2]	−690	−2 700	−1 318	−2 129	+3 936	+663	−3 116	−422	+309	−2 294	−495
Net non-deposit liabilities (increase−)	−485	−682	−882	−1 055	−395	−1 065	−573	−1 391	−1 743	−2 157	−3 601
Money stock (£ M3)	+6 602	+3 324	+2 084	+3 532	+3 769	+6 703	+6 651	+10 595	+9 296	+7 524	+9 506

1. Bank lending, *plus* holdings of commercial bills by the Issue Department of the Bank of England.
2. Including sterling lending to overseas sector.

Source Bank of England

17.8 Money stock and liquidity

£ million

	1973[1]	1974	1975[2]	1976	1977	1978	1979	1980	1981[3]	1982	1983
Amounts outstanding at end-year											
Notes and coin in circulation with the public[4]	4 377	5 085	5 808	6 582	7 563	8 733	9 511	10 239	10 767	11 228	11 906
UK private sector sterling sight deposits[5,6]	8 926	9 654	11 579	12 753	15 960	18 631	20 345	20 805	25 766	29 436	33 322
Money stock (M1)	13 303	14 739	17 387	19 335	23 523	27 364	29 856	31 044	36 533	40 664	45 228
UK private sector sterling time deposits[5,7]	18 018	19 905	19 188	20 772	20 353	23 215	27 374	36 766	48 060	51 459	56 632
Money stock (£M3)	31 321	34 644	36 575	40 107	43 876	50 579	57 230	67 810	84 593	92 123	101 860
UK private sector deposits in other currencies[5,7,8,10]	1 432	2 398	2 939	3 896	4 151	4 799	5 202	6 189	9 849	12 621	16 263
Money stock (M3)[10]	32 753	37 042	39 514	44 003	48 027	55 378	62 432	73 999	94 442	104 744	118 123
Private Sector Liquidity (PSL 1)	33 872	38 342	39 956	43 600	47 194	54 414	63 227	73 339	88 210	95 605	105 504
Private Sector Liquidity (PSL 2)	56 001	61 467	67 247	74 380	82 962	95 300	108 240	122 741	137 478	149 206	169 089
Changes during year[9]											
Notes and coin in circulation with the public[4]	+305	+709	+830	+774	+981	+1 170	+778	+743	+585	+461	+700
UK private sector sterling sight deposits[5,6]	+348	+728	+1 202	+1 174	+3 207	+2 671	+1 714	+460	+2 823	+3 668	+3 858
Money stock (M1)	+653	+1 437	+2 032	+1 948	+4 188	+3 841	+2 492	+1 203	+3 408	+4 129	+4 558
UK private sector sterling time deposits[5,7]	+5 949	+1 887	+52	+1 584	−419	+2 862	+4 159	+9 392	+5 888	+3 395	+4 948
Money stock (£M3)	+6 602	+3 324	+2 084	+3 532	+3 769	+6 703	+6 651	+10 595	+9 296	+7 524	+9 506
UK private sector deposits in other currencies[5,7,8,10]	+530	+966	+572	+957	+255	+648	+403	+987	+3 668	+2 772	+3 378
Money stock (M3)[10]	+7 132	+4 290	+2 656	+4 489	+4 024	+7 351	+7 054	+11 582	+12 964	+10 296	+12 884
Private Sector Liquidity (PSL 1)	+7 318	+4 471	+2 060	+3 644	+3 593	+7 227	+8 813	+10 272	+8 553	+7 452	+9 660
Private Sector Liquidity (PSL 2)	+9 263	+5 465	+6 225	+7 009	+8 581	+12 400	+12 948	+14 660	+14 140	+11 785	+18 766

1. There were changes in the number of contributors to the banking statistics during 1973 (see also footnote 9).
2. The figures at end-year are affected by the introduction of new statistical returns (see also footnote 9).
3. The stock figures for end-1981 are on the basis of the new monetary sector; changes during the years, up to and including 1981, are on the basis of the old banking sector.
4. The estimates of levels of coin in circulation include allowance for wastage, hoarding, etc.

5. Deposits are confined to those with institutions included in the United Kingdom monetary sector (see Table 17.3).
6. After deducting 60 per cent of transit items.
7. Including UK residents' holdings of certificates of deposit.
8. The figures include changes in the sterling value of the deposits caused by changes in exchange rates.
9. As far as possible the changes exclude the effect of changes in the number of contributors to the series, and also of the introduction of new statistical returns in 1975.
10. Includes public sector deposits in other currencies for 1973 and 1974 (amounts outstanding) and for 1973, 1974 and 1975 (changes during year).

Source Bank of England

17.9 Money and bill rates
London clearing banks' base rates[1]
Percentage rates operative between dates shown

Rate

Date	Percent	Date	Percent	Date	Percent	Date	Percent	Date	Percent	Date	Percent
1974		1976		May 3	8½	1979		1982		1984	
Apr. 11	12½	Jan. 5	10½-11	Aug. 9	8	Feb. 14	13½	Jan. 22	14	Mar. 7	8¾-9
May 13	12-12½	Jan. 13	10½	Sept. 13	7	Mar. 6	13	Feb. 25	13½	Mar. 15	8½-8¾
May 23 and 24	12	Feb. 2	10	Oct. 17	6	Apr. 6	12	Mar. 12	13	May 10	9-9¼
		Feb. 9	9½	Nov. 29	6-7½	June 15	14	June 8	12½	June 27	9¼
1975		May 25	10½-11	Dec. 5	6¾-7½	Nov. 16	17	July 13	12	July 9	10
Jan. 20 and 21	11½	June 14	10½					Aug. 2	11½	July 12	12
Mar. 4 and 6	10¾-11	Sept. 13	12	1978		1980		Aug. 18	11	Aug. 9	11½
Mar. 20, 21 and 25	10¼-10½	Oct. 8	13½	Jan. 10	6½	July 4	16	Aug. 31	10½	Aug. 10	11
Apr. 21, 22 and 23	9½	Oct. 21	14	Apr. 20	7½	Nov. 24	14	Oct. 7	10	Aug. 20	10½
Aug. 5 and 6	10			May 10	9			Oct. 14	9½	Nov. 7	10
Oct. 6 and 7	11	1977		June 12	10	1981		Nov. 4	9		
		Jan. 26	13	Nov. 6	11½	Mar. 11	12	Nov. 26	10-10¼		
		Feb. 4	12½	Nov. 15	12½	Sept. 16	14				
		Feb. 18	11½			Oct. 1	16	1983			
		Mar. 14	10½			Oct. 14	15½	Jan. 12	11		
		Mar. 31	9½			Nov. 9	15	Mar. 15	10½		
		Apr. 26	9			Dec. 3	14½	Apr. 15	10		
								June 15	9½		
								Oct. 4	9		

1. See footnote on page 293.

17.9 Money and bill rates

(*continued*)

Rate per cent

	1972	1973	1974	1975	1976	1977	1978	1979	1980	1981	1982	1983	1984
Treasury bills: [2]													
January	4.368	8.233	12.092	10.626	9.922	12.733	5.814	11.859	15.793	12.851	14.062	10.593	8.869
February	4.368	8.083	11.920	9.906	8.748	11.023	5.958	12.624	16.144	12.088	13.564	10.740	8.854
March	4.337	8.075	11.955	9.500	8.461	9.837	5.939	11.348	16.181	11.535	12.490	10.466	8.433
April	4.298	7.696	11.515	9.257	9.182	8.306	6.771	11.316	16.166	11.327	12.835	9.841	8.376
May	4.269	7.884	11.346	9.467	10.431	7.400	8.401	11.349	16.091	11.348	12.633	9.697	8.816
June	5.209	7.040	11.229	9.430	10.958	7.452	9.147	12.566	15.800	12.088	12.227	9.471	8.863
July	5.603	8.822	11.204	9.713	10.870	7.432	9.220	13.323	14.548	13.282	11.581	9.367	10.975
August	5.792	10.938	11.237	10.428	10.878	6.542	8.896	13.317	14.865	13.416	10.336	9.343	10.213
September	6.503	10.974	11.105	10.364	12.034	5.686	8.999	13.382	14.405	13.962	9.909	9.158	10.021
October	6.736	10.773	10.922	11.430	14.018	4.519	9.921	13.380	14.295	15.549	9.140	8.841	
November	6.889	11.615	10.983	11.107	14.162	4.890	11.507	15.330	13.946	14.075	8.938	8.843	
December	7.816	12.472	10.991	10.838	13.795	6.368	11.566	15.897	13.070	14.511	9.897	8.870	
Three months' bank bills: [3]													
January	4.43	8.75	13.72	11.91	10.04	13.02	6.01	12.34	16.63	13.38	14.35	10.69	8.93
February	4.85	9.35	13.63	11.42	8.94	11.33	6.42	12.93	17.36	12.34	13.66	10.84	8.88
March	4.79	9.77	14.40	10.37	8.56	10.00	6.45	11.68	17.57	11.71	12.66	10.50	8.49
April	4.62	8.72	13.93	9.53	9.04	8.34	7.40	11.54	17.13	11.53	12.92	9.82	8.39
May	4.62	8.46	13.34	10.10	10.28	7.58	8.86	11.55	15.74	11.56	12.67	9.82	8.98
June	5.72	8.07	12.60	9.68	11.09	7.71	9.63	12.83	16.24	12.08	12.36	9.54	8.99
July	6.80	8.74	13.22	9.92	10.98	7.61	9.83	13.74	15.18	13.11	11.68	9.48	10.90
August	7.08	12.55	12.81	10.52	10.97	6.74	9.39	13.87	15.58	13.52	10.53	9.44	10.47
September	7.13	12.59	12.09	10.46	11.98	5.87	9.23	14.10	15.15	14.04	10.09	9.23	10.13
October	7.34	11.98	11.95	11.40	14.25	4.83	10.29	14.10	15.04	15.54	9.31	8.88	10.05
November	7.84	12.40	12.09	11.19	14.30	5.14	11.86	15.93	15.05	14.30	8.89	8.88	
December	8.09	13.76	12.93	10.92	13.90	6.58	12.06	16.65	13.90	14.50	10.09	8.90	
Three months' inter-bank deposits: [4, 5]													
January	4.61	9.41	15.94	11.85	10.17	13.65	6.26	12.70	17.17	14.28	15.13	11.22	9.47
February	5.13	10.52	15.25	11.30	9.08	11.69	6.87	13.32	17.78	13.04	14.48	11.35	9.39
March	4.89	10.86	15.44	10.45	8.65	10.41	6.82	12.06	18.11	12.65	13.57	10.98	8.95
April	4.62	9.35	13.86	9.58	9.13	8.62	7.62	11.69	17.64	12.33	13.77	10.27	8.90
May	4.81	9.33	13.24	10.16	10.36	7.71	9.30	11.82	17.06	12.41	13.35	10.27	9.39
June	6.11	8.84	12.72	9.69	11.20	7.85	10.04	13.12	16.77	12.67	13.00	9.95	9.45
July	8.17	9.33	13.37	9.93	11.22	7.83	10.18	13.98	15.88	13.79	12.37	9.91	11.48
August	7.70	13.66	12.80	10.60	11.04	6.97	9.45	14.12	16.53	14.18	11.11	9.89	11.06
September	7.44	13.45	11.93	10.48	12.17	6.08	9.37	14.17	16.00	14.78	10.89	9.70	10.83
October	7.58	12.93	11.66	11.52	14.53	5.10	10.57	14.22	15.99	16.33	9.79	9.39	10.66
November	8.07	14.10	12.02	11.35	14.75	5.22	12.07	16.24	15.84	15.06	9.39	9.31	
December	8.58	15.92	12.93	11.09	14.41	6.83	12.36	16.82	14.73	15.44	10.16	9.43	
Three months' local authority deposits: [4, 6]													
January	4.52	9.12	15.75	12.17	10.27	13.95	6.22	12.66	17.26	14.32	15.15	11.13	9.41
February	4.99	10.32	15.51	11.47	9.19	11.89	6.71	13.46	17.93	13.14	14.43	11.23	9.36
March	4.88	10.85	15.72	10.86	8.83	10.59	6.74	12.24	18.50	12.70	13.54	10.94	8.94
April	4.62	9.38	14.06	9.70	9.19	8.80	7.42	11.81	17.93	12.37	13.75	10.26	8.91
May	4.78	9.34	13.39	10.23	10.31	7.66	8.97	11.90	17.19	12.42	13.33	10.23	9.36
June	5.91	8.84	12.77	9.75	11.19	7.82	9.79	13.15	16.81	12.68	12.99	9.88	9.43
July	7.79	9.03	13.30	9.86	11.18	7.81	10.02	13.99	15.96	13.70	12.40	9.81	11.46
August	7.67	13.09	12.89	10.54	11.11	7.05	9.43	14.16	16.52	14.22	11.11	9.81	11.07
September	7.44	13.37	12.17	10.50	12.13	6.08	9.28	14.23	15.98	14.73	10.83	9.62	10.85
October	7.50	13.01	11.81	11.54	14.47	5.14	10.38	14.26	15.97	16.30	9.82	9.36	10.64
November	7.82	13.85	12.09	11.47	14.92	5.22	11.99	16.12	15.88	15.14	9.32	9.26	
December	8.93	15.73	13.17	11.21	14.87	6.79	12.31	16.96	14.74	15.42	10.54	9.37	

1. Each bank has a single base rate, which may sometimes differ from those of other banks. The rates of interest charged by the London clearing banks for their advances to customers and their discounting of trade bills are, in general, linked to their own individually declared base rates. The rates charged for advances depend on the nature and status of the customer; most lending is between 1 per cent and 5 per cent higher than base rate. Some lending is related to market rates instead of base rates.
At the beginning of 1973 and until September 1973 the rate paid on ordinary deposit account was generally 1¾ per cent below base rate. Between 11 September 1973 and 28 February 1975 the banks were not allowed to pay more than 9½ per cent on deposits under £10 000.
Since February 1975 the margin between base rate and that on deposit accounts has fluctuated between 2 per cent and 4½ per cent.

2. Weighted averages of discount rates at the weekly allotments of 91 day bills.
3. The mean of the discount market's buying rates (discount rates per cent per annum). Averages of working days.
4. Figures are averages of working days.
5. The mean of the lowest bid and highest offer rates over the day. The yield on a three-month sterling certificate of deposit is usually close to that for a three-months' inter-bank deposit.
6. For a minimum term of three months and thereafter at seven days' notice. The mean of the daily range. From June 1982 the rates are for 10.30 a.m.

Source Bank of England

17.10 Security yields and prices

	1973	1974	1975	1976	1977	1978	1979	1980	1981	1982	1983	1984
British government securities												
Short-dated[1]:												
(5 years)	10.45	12.51	11.48	12.06	10.08	11.32	12.64	13.84	14.65	12.79	11.19	
Medium-dated[1]:												
(10 years)	10.65	14.21	13.18	13.61	12.02	12.12	12.93	13.91	14.88	13.08	11.27	
Long-dated[1]:												
(20 years)	10.78	14.77	14.39	14.43	12.73	12.47	12.99	13.79	14.74	12.88	10.80	
2½ per cent Consols[2]:												
Average net price	23.2	16.8	17.1	17.6	20.43	21.0	22.1	21.1	19.3	21.4	24.5	
Average flat yield	10.85	14.95	14.66	14.25	12.31	11.93	11.39	11.88	13.01	11.90	10.24	
January	9.79	12.79	16.03	13.78	13.67	10.67	12.51	11.41	12.12	13.72	10.73	9.83
February	9.89	13.49	14.94	13.54	13.47	11.21	12.63	11.76	12.05	13.01	10.87	9.93
March	10.16	13.84	13.92	13.95	12.85	11.18	11.36	12.62	12.02	12.41	10.34	9.83
April	10.23	14.61	14.58	13.97	12.55	11.65	10.68	12.35	12.11	12.92	10.09	9.93
May	10.34	14.11	15.22	13.72	12.41	12.07	11.02	12.18	12.70	12.66	10.19	10.29
June	10.38	14.73	14.70	14.01	12.85	12.31	11.39	11.98	12.96	12.48	9.83	10.48
July	10.84	15.13	14.06	13.95	13.11	12.20	10.88	11.55	13.44	12.22	10.24	10.88
August	11.37	15.65	14.12	14.11	12.56	12.15	10.54	11.80	13.46	11.64	10.42	10.33
September	11.60	15.14	14.08	14.47	11.52	12.17	10.75	11.64	13.72	10.87	10.18	10.42
October	11.31	15.93	14.90	15.43	10.84	12.42	11.07	11.55	14.16	10.29	10.09	10.27
November	11.89	16.89	14.79	15.22	11.04	12.63	11.86	11.54	13.53	9.92	9.97	10.17
December	12.38	17.10	14.86	14.82	10.90	12.38	11.85	11.94	13.63	10.65	9.90	
Industrial securities[3]												
Debentures[4]:												
Price index	65.5	45.3	46.3	48.7	55.6	58.3	56.27	52.42	77.33	92.25	103.37	
Average yield	11.40	16.44	15.95	15.19	13.41	12.75	13.23	14.16	15.44	13.95	12.14	
Preference shares:												
Price index	71.5	54.6	62.0	65.5	71.7	72.7	69.48	64.60	63.93	69.41	79.04	
Average dividend yield	10.97	15.00	15.26	14.48	12.81	12.68	13.21	13.91	15.28	14.46	12.50	
Ordinary shares[5]:												
Price index	185.3	108.8	136.0	162.9	208.8	235.3	267.31	285.68	322.16	373.31	471.23	
Average dividend yield	4.10	8.00	6.70	6.16	5.50	5.48	5.78	6.59	5.96	5.47	4.60	
January	3.50	5.29	10.84	5.38	6.14	5.39	5.66	6.86	6.46	5.80	4.90	4.30
February	3.82	5.41	7.34	5.34	5.88	5.73	5.70	6.46	6.22	5.63	4.78	4.33
March	3.93	5.85	6.71	5.37	5.72	5.78	5.08	6.83	6.06	5.75	4.72	4.20
April	3.85	6.10	6.49	5.37	5.81	5.68	4.85	7.07	5.64	5.71	4.50	4.24
May	3.87	6.32	6.09	5.41	5.39	5.42	4.90	7.07	5.61	5.56	4.61	4.35
June	3.79	7.14	6.05	5.87	5.53	5.49	5.17	6.85	5.74	5.67	4.40	4.59
July	4.06	7.58	6.52	5.93	5.61	5.50	5.71	6.49	5.87	5.74	4.52	4.88
August	4.20	8.72	6.76	6.31	5.33	5.15	5.93	6.49	5.56	5.61	4.41	4.66
September	4.48	9.73	6.17	6.77	4.96	5.14	6.14	6.38	6.00	5.25	4.56	
October	4.15	10.24	6.00	7.74	4.96	5.34	6.20	6.27	6.43	5.03	4.71	
November	4.40	11.16	5.66	7.49	5.33	5.62	6.94	6.04	6.01	4.87	4.59	
December	5.28	12.48	5.75	6.91	5.35	5.56	7.02	6.25	5.91	4.99	4.54	

1. Gross redemption yields derived from yield-maturity curves fitted mathematically. The figures are averages of Wednesday yields until 1979. From 1980 the average is of all observations (usually 3 per week); from January 1982 figures are the average of working days. The method of calculation is described in the *Bank of England Quarterly Bulletin,* December 1972, September 1973, June 1976 and June 1982.

2. Averages of working days, based, up to and including March 1982, on the mean of the middle opening and middle closing prices each day; thereafter the figures are based on closing prices only. Gross accrued interest is excluded; tax is ignored.

3. The series are arithmetic averages of daily figures from the *Financial Times—Actuaries* share indices. Price indices (using weighted arithmetic averages) are based on 10 April 1962 = 100.

4. Up to and including 1980, series are based on 15 redeemable debentures, weighted to give average term to maturity of 20 years. The yields used are redemption yields. The *Financial Times* published a new rebased series of debenture and preference share indices from 17 March 1981. The series from 1981 relate to the price index and redemption yield on 25 year stocks.

5. Based on 500 shares.

Sources Bank of England; *Financial Times*; Institute of Actuaries; Faculty of Actuaries

17.11 Securities quoted on The Stock Exchange[1]
At last working day in March

£ million

	1974	1975	1976	1977	1978	1979	1980	1981	1982	1983	1984
Total of all securities at market values	176 899	210 269	273 849	293 228	302 586	328 331	280 793	375 931	455 995	688 493	832 098
British government and government guaranteed stocks[2]											
Nominal values	27 717	30 854	36 530	42 090	52 151	59 256	70 959	85 384	91 106	96 039	107 932
Market values	17 294	22 111	26 758	36 548	46 917	54 850	57 766	76 079	81 087	97 001	111 060
Other securities at market values:											
Irish government stocks	590	553	990	1 658	3 001	3 095	3 015	2 690	2 457	4 732	5 013
Corporation stocks, public boards, etc.	1 819	2 167	2 564	2 775	3 143	2 967	2 678	2 609	2 425	2 364	2 237
Dominion and foreign government and corporation stocks	2 626	2 061	3 240	4 005	5 843	6 151	6 067	10 062	20 071	35 976	42 802
Company securities											
Total	154 570	183 377	240 297	248 242	243 682	261 268	211 267	284 491	349 955	548 420	670 986
Loan capital	4 415	4 238	4 381	4 764	5 026	4 750	3 803	4 144	4 905	6 320	8 256
Preference and preferred capital	687	673	779	813	1 095	1 596	1 836	1 916	1 860	3 070	6 416
Ordinary and deferred capital[3]	142 803	170 929	225 614	233 514	229 327 ⎫	254 922	205 628	278 431	343 190	539 030	656 314
Shares of no par value[3]	6 665	7 537	9 523	9 152	8 234 ⎭						

1. At the end of March 1973 the stock exchanges of the United Kingdom and the Republic of Ireland united to form one exchange (The Stock Exchange). Figures prior to 1974 relate to the London Stock Exchange only and are available in earlier editions of the *Annual Abstract of Statistics*.
2. Excluding marketable unlisted securities; including all outstanding amounts of 4 per cent Victory Bonds and 4 per cent Funding Loan, 1960–90 (that is, amounts for death duties and held by the National Debt Commissioners are included).
3. From 1978 shares of no par value are no longer distinguished separately.

Source   Council of The Stock Exchange

Footnotes to table 17.12 on page 296.

1. The estimates relate to new money raised on the main stock market by issues of ordinary, preference and loan capital (public issues, offers for sale, issues by tender, placings, and issues to shareholders and employees) by listed public companies and local authorities in the United Kingdom; and by overseas borrowers split between central government, state and local governments and companies. The estimates include UK local authority negotiable bonds (of not less than one year) issues to or through the agency of banks, discount houses, issuing houses or brokers. Mortgages, bank advances and any other loans redeemable in less than twelve months are excluded; so also are loans from UK government funds (including the former Industrial Reorganisation Corporation and the National Enterprise Board) but not government subscriptions to company issues made *pari passu* with the market. Issues to shareholders are included only if the sole or principal share register is maintained in the United Kingdom. Estimates of issues are based on the prices at which securities are offered to the market. Subscriptions are recorded under the periods in which they are due to be paid. Redemptions relate to fixed interest securities of the kinds included as issues; conversion issues in lieu of cash repayment are included in the gross figures of both issues and redemptions. These figures include issues of debentures and loan stock carrying the right of conversion into, or subscription to, equity capital. Estimates for these issues *less* redemptions are: 1977 −5; 1978 −21; 1979 23; 1980 178; 1981 194; 1982 8; 1983 47.

The division between United Kingdom and overseas company borrowers is determined by the location of the registered office. The industrial classification of companies is according to the primary occupation of the borrowing company or group and is based up to 1982 on the former Standard Industrial Classification 1968 and from 1983 on the Revised Standard Industrial Classification 1980. Figures prior to 1977 are available in the *Annual Abstract of Statistics* No. 118, 1982 Edition.
2. The estimates exclude issues on the unlisted securities market which was launched by the Stock Exchange in November 1980. These issues are mainly of ordinary shares by industrial and commercial companies. Estimates of new money raised are 1980–88; 1981–54; 1982–87; 1983–163.
3. The figures for 1978 and 1979 include £449 mn and £149 mn respectively for rights issues by BL Ltd. Over 99 per cent of both issues was taken up by the National Enterprise Board. However, the figures for 1980 exclude £375 mn issued by BL Ltd to the Government via the National Enterprise Board.
4. Overseas companies including public corporations.
5. Prior to the introduction of the Monetary Sector in November 1981 statistics relate to issues by the banking sector.
6. 'Other' includes special finance agencies (listed public companies engaged in the provision of medium and long-term finance to industry e.g. ICFC) and those finance houses and other consumer credit grantors not covered by the Monetary sector.

Source   Bank of England

17.12 Capital issues and redemptions in the United Kingdom[1,2]

£ million

	1977	1978[3]	1979[3]	1980[3]	1981	1982		1983
Total issues and redemptions								
Gross issues	2 226	1 983	1 743	2 083	3 311	2 907		4 675
Gross redemptions	1 300	1 163	1 005	1 310	1 341	1 351		1 347
Issues *less* redemptions: total	926	820	738	773	1 970	1 556		3 328
Loan capital	121	− 127	− 276	− 209	67	582		980
Preference shares	16	22	54	29	68	9		59
Ordinary shares	789	925	960	953	1 835	965		2 289
United Kingdom borrowers: total	969	882	762	767	1 675	993		2 746
Local authorities	239	48	− 170	− 166	− 157	− 174		− 66
Listed public companies: total	730	834	932	933	1 832	1 167		2 812
Overseas borrowers: total	− 43	− 62	− 24	6	295	563		582
Central government	− 40	− 59	− 23	9	124	201		246
State, local government	− 1	−	−	− 1	6	85		− 13
Companies[4]	− 2	− 3	− 1	− 2	165	277		349
United Kingdom listed public companies								
All companies: total	730	834	932	933	1 832	1 167		2 812
Loan capital	− 75	− 113	− 82	− 50	− 72	195		565
Preference shares	16	22	54	30	68	8		59
Ordinary shares	789	925	960	953	1 836	964		2 188
Financial companies: total	104	109	75	− 7	123	296		684
Loan capital	28	− 22	− 6	− 62	− 83	278		219
Preference shares	− 3	3	−	− 6	− 8	−		−
Ordinary shares	79	128	81	61	214	18		465
Other companies: total	626	725	857	940	1 709	871		2 128
Loan capital	− 103	− 91	− 76	12	11	− 83		346
Preference shares	19	19	54	36	76	8		59
Ordinary shares	710	797	879	892	1 622	946		1 723
United Kingdom listed public companies								
Financial companies: total	104	109	75	− 7	123	296		684
Monetary sector[5]	− 13	98	79	− 34	−	298		549
Insurance companies	75	32	−	− 2	198	2		5
Investment trust companies	− 23	− 22	7	33	9	18		92
Other[6]	65	1	− 11	− 4	− 84	− 22		38

	1977	1978[3]	1979[3]	1980[3]	1981	1982		1983
Other companies: total	626	725	857	940	1 709	871		2 128
Manufacturing industries: total	400	648	446	211	632	407		1 386
Food, drink and tobacco	58	24	− 8	39	50	102	Minerals and Metal Manufacture	253
Chemicals and allied industries	37	84	17	6	85	111	Chemicals and allied industries	314
Metal manufacture	56	2	−	− 6	− 1	1	Metal goods, engineering and vehicles	157
Engineering, shipbuilding and electrical goods	48	20	32	23	302	194	Electrical and electronic engineering	200
Vehicles	2	452	154	− 4	97	− 2	Food, Drink and Tobacco	200
Textiles	19	33	11	−	1	4	Other manufacturing	262
Clothing and footwear	3	1	1	−	1	− 5	Energy	192
Paper, printing and publishing	33	− 3	16	6	4	−	Water	30
Other	144	35	223	147	93	2	Construction	53
Public utilities, transport and communication	14	21	17	38	83	6	Distribution, hotels and repairs	172
Distributive trades	129	21	111	89	50	15	Transport and communications	9
Property companies	− 12	− 2	79	147	97	258	Property companies	78
Rest	95	37	204	455	847	185	Services, Agriculture, Forestry and Fishing	208

See footnotes 1 – 6 on page 295.

Source Bank of England

17.13

Building societies[1]
Great Britain

Number and balance sheets

	1973	1974	1975	1976	1977	1978	1979	1980	1981	1982	1983
Societies on register (Number)	447	416	382	364	339	316	287	273	253	227	206
Share Investors (Thousands)	14 385	15 856	17 916	19 991	22 536	24 999	27 878	30 636	33 388	36 607	37 711
Depositors (Thousands)	672	641	677	712	760	781	797	915	995	1 094	1 200
Borrowers (Thousands)	4 204	4 250	4 397	4 609	4 836	5 108	5 251	5 383	5 490	5 645	5 928
Liabilities and provisions (£ million):											
total	16 911.0	19 369.8	23 392.9	27 203.9	32 996.0	38 039.4	44 119.5	51 860.1	59 486.5	70 167.4	82 326.5
Shares	16 021.5	18 021.4	22 134.1	25 760.3	31 109.7	36 185.9	42 023.1	48 914.6	55 463.4	64 968.0	75 197.3
Deposits	596.3	632.8	761.9	847.6	1 224.1	1 254.0	1 281.2	1 742.0	2 538.7	3 455.4	5 585.1
HM Government advances[2]	32.2	339.2	28.6	18.5	14.2	10.1	6.5	2.9	0.4	–	–
Other[3]	261.1	376.4	468.3	577.5	648.0	589.4	808.6	1 200.6	1 484.0	1 744.0	1 544.1
Reserves and unappropriated surplus (£ million):	634.5	723.7	810.8	998.5	1 292.4	1 498.8	1 669.6	1 932.7	2 328.1	2 865.1	3 542.3
Assets (£ million): total	17 545.5	20 093.5	24 203.7	28 202.4	34 288.4	39 538.4	45 789.1	53 792.9	61 814.6	73 032.5	85 868.8
Mortgages	14 532.4	16 029.6	18 801.9	22 564.5	26 426.5	31 598.3	36 800.5	42 437.0	48 874.8	56 695.7	67 473.5
Investments[4]	2 164.6	2 924.0	4 141.7	4 339.2	5 945.6	6 064.0	7 146.7	8 403.8	10 106.4	12 430.4	13 641.1
Cash[5]	622.5	859.0	921.8	907.7	1 463.9	1 350.8	1 218.2	2 202.3	1 949.9	2 925.2	3 676.3
Other	225.9	280.9	338.4	391.1	452.4	525.2	623.8	749.8	883.6	981.2	1 077.9

Current transactions

£ million

	1973	1974	1975	1976	1977	1978	1979	1980	1981	1982	1983
Shares:											
Subscribed	5 804.1	6 126.7	8 784.6	10 146.2	13 549.3	15 684.6	18 849.4	21 916.5	26 126.9	32 434.8	39 310.3
Interest thereon	971.0	1 248.2	1 446.9	1 681.6	1 985.2	2 172.9	3 297.7	4 699.4	4 795.7	5 298.6	4 951.1
Withdrawn (including interest)	4 574.2	5 375.8	6 119.0	8 200.8	10 183.9	12 769.4	16 313.6	19 726.1	24 373.0	28 218.0	34 093.8
Deposits:											
Received	255.8	254.1	369.8	407.9	783.4	670.1	678.4	1 091.2	1 571.5	2 029.3	4 777.6
Interest thereon	35.9	42.3	47.0	53.2	63.5	70.7	97.2	147.6	186.4	273.2	324.2
Withdrawn (including interest)	287.8	259.6	287.7	375.3	470.3	710.1	749.0	780.9	961.5	1 388.8	2 982.2
Advances on mortgage:											
Advances	3 512.7	2 945.1	4 908.0	6 183.3	6 745.1	8 807.8	9 002.3	9 503.4	12 005.3	15 036.4	18 903.7
Repayments of principal	1 526.0	1 447.3	2 134.2	2 422.9	2 882.2	3 614.8	3 805.4	3 867.9	5 566.9	7 214.0	8 124.1
Interest[6]	1 282.9	1 688.5	1 929.3	2 287.7	2 706.1	2 770.1	4 082.5	5 912.9	6 398.1	7 030.7	6 516.9
Management expenses	118.9	145.2	196.6	237.4	296.8	363.5	449.3	589.6	731.6	874.6	800.9
Percentage rate of interest[7]											
Paid on shares	6.51	7.33	7.21	7.02	6.98	6.46	8.43	10.34	9.19	8.80	7.06
Paid on deposits	6.04	6.88	6.74	6.61	6.13	5.65	7.67	9.77	8.71	9.12	7.17
Received on mortgage advances	9.59	11.05	11.08	11.06	11.05	9.19	11.94	14.92	13.60	12.88	10.50

1. The figures for each year relate to accounting years ending on any date between 1 February of that year and 31 January of the following year.
2. Includes HM Government advances under the 1959 Act, and loans by HM Government under the 1974 Scheme.
3. The 1983 figures contain bank loans of £16.3 million.
4. For 1981 and 1983 includes sterling certificates of deposit.
5. From 1973 until 1980 includes sterling certificates of deposit.
6. Includes amounts recoverable from HM Government under Option Mortgage Scheme.
7. Based on the mean of the amounts outstanding at the end of the previous and the current year.

Source Registry of Friendly Societies

17.14 Total consumer credit grantors' business[1]
Great Britain

£ million

	1976	1977	1978	1979	1980	1981	1982	1983
Total new credit extended[2]	3 480	4 778	6 167	7 351	7 819	7 854	9 109	10 524
By retailers[3]	1 945	2 306	2 698	3 020	3 259	3 204	3 470	3 685
By finance houses and other specialist consumer credit grantors[4, 5]	1 535	2 472	3 469	4 331	4 560	4 650	5 639	6 839
Change in amounts outstanding[2]		888	1 315	1 402	943	637	1 212	2 528
Total amount outstanding at end of period[2, 6]	3 296	4 184	5 499	6 901	7 844	8 481	9 693	12 221
Owing directly to[2, 6]:								
Finance houses and other specialist consumer credit grantors[4]	2 410	3 198	4 350	5 558	6 419	7 007	8 099	10 506
Clothing retailers	70	44	52	60	71	80	81	83
Household goods retailers	274	304	370	423	435	427	479	546
Mixed retail businesses	171	200	214	201	218	235	263	280
General mail order houses	371	438	513	659	701	732	771	806

1. Finance houses, other specialist consumer credit grantors (check traders, money lenders, finance houses specialising in personal loan or second mortgage business), clothing retailers, household goods retailers, mixed retail businesses and general mail order houses.
2. Excludes charges for credit.
3. Credit advanced on all types of credit sale including those on budget and other running-account agreements. Excludes sales on Access, Barclaycard and other bank credit cards.

4. Direct business only, i.e. excludes agreements block discounted with finance houses by retailers. Includes lending to companies.
5. Includes all types of credit agreement where the total amount of credit advanced is known at the outset of the agreement. It includes credit advanced in a hire purchase, conditional sale or credit sale agreement as well as trading checks, vouchers and cash loans of a fixed amount.
6. Includes amounts outstanding on running-account credit agreements.

Source Department of Trade and Industry

17.15 Non-bank consumer credit companies in Great Britain
Assets and liabilities outstanding
End-year

£ million

	1976	1977	1978	1979	1980	1981	1981[1] New coverage	1982	1983
Assets									
Total	2 606	3 058	4 004	5 309	5 807	6 295	2 234	2 620	3 435
Cash in hand and balances with UK monetary sector[2]	137	136	153	152	157	204	49	30	43
Amounts outstanding on loans and advances:									
on agreements block discounted by retailers and financial institutions	22	23	28	37	42	38	3	3	3
on other loans and advances[3]:									
to individuals (including unincorporated businesses)	1 187	1 411	1 834	2 441	2 767	3 039	1 145	1 278	1 790
to UK financial institutions outside the monetary sector	120	125	190	286	238	262	–	–	–
to UK industrial and commercial companies	613	764	996	1 296	1 487	1 537	502	636	914
to overseas residents	–	11	6	10	–	–	–	–	–
Other current assets:									
Certificates of deposit	19	15	11	26	11	17	7	8	6
Other	58	63	72	103	101	81	48	83	115
Real assets	259	294	495	659	777	896	420	537	521
Company and government securities	125	127	140	201	131	104	30	25	25
Other assets	66	89	79	98	96	117	30	20	18
Liabilities									
Total	2 606	3 058	4 004	5 309	5 807	6 295	2 234	2 620	3 435
Borrowing (including deposits by and borrowing from other group companies):									
Commercial bills	166	228	451	756	693	944	339	452	557
Short term borrowing from UK monetary sector (excl. deposits)	212	294	413	547	450	415	739	771	895
Deposits and medium and long term borrowing from UK monetary sector	545	676	764	917	1 429	1 465	385	503	901
Borrowing from other UK financial institutions	411	563	729	993	827	888	33	25	28
Other borrowing:									
UK	500	525	643	853	931	890	99	113	150
Overseas	97	94	116	135	146	165	21	22	21
Other current liabilities	151	124	152	202	249	295	135	132	174
Issued capital	189	198	234	258	320	585	111	106	106
Reserves and provisions	335	356	502	648	762	648	372	496	603

1. Many companies included in these statistics became part of the new monetary sector at end-1981. This now shows the position immediately after they transferred.
2. Data up to end-1981 was collected on a different return and data are estimated in some cases.
3. Net of unearned credit charges.

Source Department of Trade and Industry

17.16 End-year assets and liabilities of investment trust companies, unit trusts and property unit trusts[1,2]

£ million

	1973	1974	1975	1976	1977	1978	1979	1980	1981	1982	1983
Investment trust companies											
Short-term assets and liabilities (net):	479	611	323	322	223	314	202	230	283	249	154
Cash and UK bank deposits	214	294	181	180	159	210	163	187	210	186	273
Other short-term assets	388	376	215	217	146	176	213	216	221	269	244
Short-term liabilities	−123	−59	−73	−75	−82	−72	−174	−173	−148	−206	−363
Medium and long-term liabilities and capital:	..	..	..	..	..	..	−7 194	−8 546	−9 188	−10 241	−13 419
Issued share and loan capital	..	..	..	..	..	..	−1 951	−2 013	−2 211	−2 087	−2 258
Foreign currency borrowing	..	..	..	..	..	..	−342	−280	−228	−361	−538
Other borrowing	..	..	..	..	..	..	−12	−24	−69	−88	−100
Reserves and provisions, etc.	..	..	..	..	..	..	−4 889	−6 229	−6 680	−7 705	−10 523
Investments:	5 337	3 132	5 381	5 745	6 341	6 460	6 996	8 352	8 904	10 051	13 371
British government securities	66	82	161	164	321	232	320	266	183	199	310
UK company securities:											
Loan capital and preference shares	194	116	155	156	177	172	134	132	136	129	172
Ordinary and deferred shares	2 864	1 320	2 808	2 711	3 729	3 734	4 160	4 620	4 673	4 604	5 306
Overseas company securities:											
Loan capital and preference shares	72	62	82	112	82	87	75	98	203	344	396
Ordinary and deferred shares	2 023	1 385	2 039	2 459	1 891	2 067	2 139	3 042	3 514	4 256	6 570
Other investments	118	167	136	143	141	168	168	194	195	519	617
Unit trusts											
Short-term assets and liabilities:	332	397	256	362	324	400	209	179	254	348	569
Cash and UK bank deposits	245	285	249	323	293	427	178	126	210	189	475
Other short-term assets	136	151	65	101	93	100	89	90	90	204	205
Short-term liabilities	−49	−39	−58	−62	−62	−127	−58	−37	−46	−45	−111
Foreign currency borrowing	..	..	..	..	..	..	−35	−12	−3	−58	−123
Investments:	1 765	1 010	2 299	2 271	3 109	3 474	3 600	4 629	5 369	7 309	10 843
British government securities	8	22	22	32	32	32	52	72	175	322	415
UK company securities:											
Loan capital and preference shares	63	35	57	63	78	102	76	64	106	154	225
Ordinary and deferred shares	1 389	704	1 816	1 705	2 572	2 732	2 758	3 357	3 566	4 457	5 954
Overseas company securities:											
Loan capital and preference shares	6	6	6	5	12	10	6	14	31	49	58
Ordinary and deferred shares	299	237	393	463	411	594	688	1 081	1 454	2 229	4 091
Other assets	−	6	5	3	4	4	20	41	37	98	100
Property unit trusts											
Short-term assets and liabilities (net)	..	..	..	..	..	..	135	152	158	143	152
Property	..	..	..	..	..	..	757	951	1 271	1 282	1 224
Other assets	..	..	..	..	..	..	49	166	259	214	330
Long-term borrowing	..	..	..	..	..	..	−60	−50	−69	−67	−77

Note: Assets are shown as being positive: liabilities as being negative.

1. Investments are at market value.
2. From end-1979 revised reporting forms for investment trust companies and for unit trusts, giving additional information, were introduced and their reported figures have been grossed up to cover non-contributors to the series. Also from end-1979 annual balance sheet returns were introduced for property unit trusts.

Source Bank of England

17.17 Market value of superannuation funds assets

£ million, end year

	1973	1974	1975	1976	1977	1978	1979	1980	1981	1982	1983
Local authorities											
Total	1 748	1 372	2 134	2 652	3 849	4 303	4 942	6 891	8 167	11 365	14 274
Short-term assets (net):											
Cash and balances with UK monetary sector institutions[1,2]	..	80	46	57	32	64	89	84	100	102	191
United Kingdom local authority temporary debt	79	141	105	62	51	79	117	92	125	99	120
Other short-term assets	75	40	30	44	55	61	73	87	79	105	135
Short-term liabilities[2,3]	..	−13	−23	−22	−35	−30	−21	−39	−31	−47	−66
British government securities	320	262	485	717	1 169	1 227	1 411	1 845	1 977	2 925	3 249
United Kingdom local authority long-term debt	227	226	196	167	118	102	94	85	66	66	68
Overseas government securities	4	1	1	1	1	1	1	2	5	22	28
Company securities:											
Debentures and preference shares	117	58	78	71	79	75	42	92	97	125	168
Ordinary shares	739	464	1 033	1 336	2 042	2 299	2 562	3 917	4 803	6 833	9 094
Local authorities mutual investment trust	130	66	80	83	85	74	104	116	141	79	89
Land, property and ground rents	20	15	57	90	140	210	287	387	493	613	692
Property unit trusts	20	25	41	43	106	123	160	172	258	363	400
Other assets	17	7	5	3	6	18	23	51	54	80	106
Other public sector[4,5]											
Total	2 813	2 521	4 104	5 516	8 005	9 701	12 261	15 501	18 348	23 964	29 436
Short-term assets (net):											
Cash and balances with UK monetary sector institutions[1]	154	217	115	144	170	220	199	255	255	424	777
United Kingdom local authority temporary debt	24	97	127	97	45	61	67	40	59	113	121
Other short-term assets	27	95	124	207	270	281	486	461	439	366	611
Short-term liabilities[3]	−34	−18	−72	−118	−159	−85	−145	−194	−138	−113	−361
Long-term borrowing	−83	−57	−103	−110	−112	−217	−133	−140	−139	−158	−183
British government securities	212	201	513	931	1 432	1 646	2 194	2 518	2 957	4 590	5 611
United Kingdom local authority long-term debt	26	20	46	63	46	12	24	15	14	30	23
Overseas government securities	2	2	10	1	−	8	5	44	49	157	173
Company securities:											
Debentures and preference shares	190	133	174	171	169	128	102	167	208	300	387
Ordinary shares	1 469	781	1 995	2 692	3 982	4 790	6 032	8 030	9 373	12 163	15 909
Loans and mortgages	223	217	177	137	95	300	294	182	193	191	200
Land, property and ground rents	549	765	921	1 159	1 866	2 259	2 634	3 447	4 074	4 676	4 737
Property unit trusts	52	66	70	102	141	184	246	289	340	337	276
Other assets	2	2	7	40	60	114	256	387	664	888	1 155
Private sector[6]											
Total	7 489	6 307	9 642	11 847	16 983	20 253	23 622	31 543	36 921	48 869	62 532
Short-term assets (net):											
Cash and balances with UK monetary sector institutions[1]	265	490	381	435	648	654	722	645	751	895	1 519
United Kingdom local authority temporary debt	105	266	177	101	170	180	278	236	200	209	283
Other short-term assets	292	297	179	358	415	391	548	585	563	741	983
Short-term liabilities[3]	−118	−69	−107	−52	−40	−182	−167	−201	−189	−273	−410
Long-term borrowing	..	..	..	−88	−123	−181	−239	−221	−247	−222	−234
British government securities	837	872	1 528	2 512	4 000	4 755	5 530	7 157	7 547	10 734	12 897
United Kingdom local authority long-term debt	123	128	113	105	128	124	111	87	67	56	55
Overseas government securities	22	16	31	15	15	60	38	57	89	250	306
Company securities:											
Debentures and preference shares	906	678	778	793	899	820	759	828	865	1 065	1 167
Ordinary shares	3 878	2 443	5 118	5 791	8 265	10 161	11 437	16 319	19 843	27 039	36 543
Loans and mortgages	94	71	73	62	41	194	174	119	113	125	126
Land, property and ground rent[7]	822	892	1 081	1 459	2 064	2 394	3 248	4 374	5 093	5 244	5 588
Property unit trusts	263	223	290	356	501	594	772	916	994	1 270	1 357
Other assets[7]	..	..	..	..	..	289	411	643	1 232	1 735	2 352

1. Before 1982 the figures are for cash and balances with UK banks.
2. In 1973 included in Other short-term assets.
3. Liabilities are shown negative.
4. These are funded schemes only and therefore exclude the main superannuation arrangements with central government sector.
5. Prior to 1978 no adjustment has been made for funds representing some 42 per cent (other public sector) of total assets which have an accounting year other than end-December (usually end-March).

6. All figures are based on information relating to the population of funds at 31 December 1978. Including the assets of funds which are not included in the sample or which have not responded to the questionnaire in full.
7. Other assets are included with Land, property and ground rent prior to 1978.

Source Department of Trade and Industry

17.18 Market value of insurance companies assets

£ million, end year

	1974[1]	1975[1]	1976	1977	1978	1979	1980	1981	1982	1983
Long-term funds										
Total	20 718	23 342	24 487	34 256	38 371	42 677	53 746	61 084	79 869	95 913
Current assets (gross):										
Cash and balances with UK										
monetary sector institutions[2]	484	409	426	678	824	867	903	1 372	1 777	2 050
UK local authority temporary debt	365	238	271	166	205	202	220	175	169	212
Other short-term assets[3]	351	303	232	231	582	745	765	977	1 156	1 273
Agents' balances[4]	405	455	472	561	536	542	607	714	768	909
British government securities	4 465	5 606	4 917	8 834	9 620	11 340	14 632	15 249	22 782	25 794
UK local authority long-term debt	518	559	425	601	558	553	709	722	768	836
Company securities:										
Debentures	2 585	2 617	1 753	2 154	1 927	1 753	1 894	1 912	2 632	3 382
Preference shares	186	166	115	147	159	166	167	138	196	315
Ordinary shares	4 258	5 062	6 925	10 040	11 185	11 958	16 596	19 815	27 022	35 311
Authorised unit trust units	446	454	515	957	1 013	1 097	1 380	1 709	2 328	3 829
Loans and mortgages	2 984	3 016	2 920	2 961	3 008	3 162	3 472	3 678	3 691	3 968
Land, property and ground rents[5]	3 558	4 350	5 254	6 637	8 446	10 330	12 362	14 490	15 993	17 169
Other financial assets[6]	112	108	262	289	307	275	311	491	1 139	1 643
Borrowing	..	..	..	..	..	−313	−272	−358	−552	−778
General funds										
Total	3 639	4 548	5 462	7 375	8 458	9 585	11 516	13 132	16 156	18 641
Current assets (gross):										
Cash and balances with UK										
monetary sector institutions[2]	361	469	643	686	735	855	901	1 096	1 056	1 342
UK local authority temporary debt	217	124	136	103	106	124	90	66	51	46
Other short-term assets[3]	239	224	213	200	348	460	430	532	620	808
Agents' balances[4]	711	746	970	1 158	1 388	1 733	1 936	2 134	2 575	2 978
British government securities	412	892	1 058	1 724	1 806	2 177	2 777	3 221	4 257	4 897
UK local authority long-term debt	72	119	123	185	209	185	180	113	119	76
Company securities:										
Debentures	136	167	204	293	360	356	442	559	736	750
Preference shares	125	149	151	208	227	241	278	293	348	382
Ordinary shares	793	963	1 266	1 886	1 931	2 078	2 637	2 995	3 651	4 467
Authorised unit trust units	1	1	1	1	4	11	13	16	35	53
Loans and mortgages	178	182	237	251	224	254	297	327	379	462
Land, property and ground rents[5]	346	437	330	516	797	952	1 280	1 450	1 568	1 640
Other financial assets[6]	49	73	129	165	323	368	427	514	963	1 091
Borrowing	..	..	..	..	..	−211	−172	−184	−202	−351

1. Book values.
2. Before 1982 the figures are for cash and balances with UK banks.
3. Including amounts receivable and other debtors.
4. Including reinsurance balances and outstanding interest, dividends and rents.
5. Including overseas land and property for years 1974 and 1975.
6. Including overseas government securities and (from 1976) overseas land and property.

Source Department of Trade and Industry

17.19 Industrial and provident societies[1,2]
Great Britain

	1972	1973	1974	1975	1976	1977	1978	1979	1980	1981	1982
Number of societies	9 429	9 633	9 676	9 583	9 445	9 279	9 321	9 390	9 664	9 736	9 601
Number of members (thousands)	14 014	13 825	13 753	13 993	14 030	14 092	13 995	13 798	13 558	13 547	12 961
Assets (£ thousand)	2 007 502	2 144 172	2 337 105	2 856 075	3 579 086	4 439 155	5 342 578	6 311 910	7 456 987	8 837 347	10 400 488

1. The annual returns from which these figures are derived are mainly made up to dates varying between September of the year shown and January of the following year.
2. 1983 data available early 1985 from: Registry of Friendly Societies, 15/17 Great Marlborough Street, London W1V 2AX Telephone 01 – 437 9992 ext. 225.

Source Registry of Friendly Societies

17.20 Co-operative trading societies[1,2]
Great Britain

	1972	1973	1974	1975	1976	1977	1978	1979	1980	1981	1982
Number of societies											
General trading societies:											
Retail societies	356	335	321	313	312	296	294	280	270	251	243
Principal wholesale societies[3]	3	2	2	2	2	2	2	2	2	2	2
Other wholesale and productive societies	83	76	72	71	78	97	111	118	148	163	187
Agricultural and fishing trading societies	533	536	524	516	521	524	536	539	541	550	584
Number of members (thousands)											
General trading societies:											
Retail societies	10 828.2	10 647.2	10 588.4	10 402.0	10 419.2	10 422.6	10 325.3	10 117.3	9 752.9	9 426.4	8 849.4
Principal wholesale societies[3]	0.4	0.4	0.4	0.4	0.4	0.4	0.3	0.3	0.3	0.3	0.3
Other wholesale and productive societies	41.4	41.3	41.7	39.3	39.8	40.3	41.3	42.6	153.1	43.9	44.3
Agricultural and fishing trading societies	325.8	318.3	315.3	317.4	323.0	315.8	318.8	316.0	312.2	309.4	304.3
Sales (£ million)											
General trading societies:											
Retail societies[4]	1 262.7	1 364.3	1 581.2	1 935.9	2 290.4	2 548.0	2 798.3	3 078.5	3 446.9	3 644.3	3 771.2
Principal wholesale societies[3]	684.1	771.8	877.8	1 070.5	1 230.5	1 391.0	1 500.5	1 613.0	1 755.6	1 833.9	1 933.6
Other wholesale and productive societies	83.8	88.6	101.0	126.6	182.1	213.5	266.7	284.1	407.0	432.6	512.8
Agricultural and fishing trading societies	365.9	470.1	564.1	636.0	774.9	913.0	1 005.4	1 118.6	1 228.7	1 365.3	1 541.9
Share and loan capital[5] (£ thousand)											
General trading societies:											
Retail societies	270 212	290 982	311 206	332 840	371 271	417 327	471 215	524 073	630 210	658 657	679 818
Principal wholesale societies[3]	163 545	143 614	143 768	154 936	164 911	184 621	189 705	231 658	250 084	269 645	301 194
Other wholesale and productive societies	14 963	16 549	18 768	21 179	25 558	30 782	38 442	44 555	53 784	56 186	57 924
Agricultural and fishing trading societies	45 726	52 621	59 874	69 403	79 783	92 454	104 481	117 109	130 938	154 999	161 590
Salaries and wages (£ thousand)											
General trading societies:											
Retail societies	167 744	187 122	223 082	276 025	309 838	332 987	353 925	..	..	..	..
Principal wholesale societies[3]	42 031	47 535	55 550	70 249	80 513	87 139	94 671	..	..	..	..
Other wholesale and productive societies	10 731	10 666	12 083	15 298	18 637	20 790	23 043	..	..	..	..
Agricultural and fishing trading societies	16 172	18 064	21 285	26 663	30 596	35 111	40 223	..	..	..	..

1. These societies are registered under the Industrial and Provident Societies Acts and are included in Table 17.19. See also footnote 1 to that table.
2. 1983 data available early 1985 from: Registry of Friendly Societies, 15/17 Great Marlborough Street, London W1V 2AX. Telephone 01 – 437 9992 ext. 225.
3. Co-operative Wholesale Society Ltd., Scottish Co-operative Society Ltd., and Co-operative Tea Society Ltd. During 1973 the businesses of the last two mentioned societies were transferred to the Co-operative Wholesale Society Ltd. Only in respect of the Scottish Co-operative Society Ltd. has the registry been cancelled.

4. These figures include the sale of goods purchased from the wholesale societies which are also included in the sales of those societies in this table.
5. Including net balance disposable and reserves but excluding loans from non-members.

Source Registry of Friendly Societies

17.21 Collecting societies[1]
Great Britain

£ thousand

	1972	1973	1974	1975	1976	1977	1978	1979	1980	1981	1982
Income: total	93 608	100 473	107 740	119 450	129 092	143 220	159 392	189 667	218 639	251 204	266 778
Premiums	58 852	62 197	66 462	71 679	77 632	84 231	92 766	112 398	129 242	138 529	151 193
Interest	34 083	36 813	40 088	45 460	50 631	57 690	65 721	76 157	88 188	99 263	113 971
Miscellaneous[2]	673	1 463	1 190	2 312	828	1 299	905	1 112	1 209	13 412	1 614
Expenditure: total	72 494	74 458	83 647	97 267	100 600	100 379	108 831	117 211	135 051	147 430	172 724
Claims	37 762	38 206	40 185	41 882	43 923	46 418	49 047	52 822	57 111	55 343	57 956
Cash bonuses	659	678	748	822	798	894	885	964	1 045	1 052	1 383
Surrenders	8 988	8 189	9 166	9 627	10 318	11 789	10 984	12 145	15 848	23 828	29 602
Expenses of management	23 319	24 694	28 378	34 601	39 855	39 996	45 757	49 919	57 784	64 676	72 496
Miscellaneous	1 766	2 691	5 171	10 336	5 707	1 283	2 158	1 362	3 263	2 532	11 287
Funds at end of year	532 135	558 134	582 225	604 408	628 329	671 062	721 514	793 492	877 246	980 971	1 075 063

1. 1983 data available early 1985 from: Registry of Friendly Societies, 15/17
Great Marlborough Street, London W1V 2AX. Telephone 01 – 437 9992 ext. 225.
2. Including accrued interest.

Source Office of the Industrial Assurance Commissioner

17.22 Friendly societies[1,2]
Great Britain

	1972	1973	1974	1975	1976	1977	1978	1979	1980	1981	1982
Number of societies, orders and branches[3]	6 115	5 847	5 490	5 240	4 951	4 793	4 587	4 455	4 242	4 069	3 927
Number of members[3] (Thousands) total	4 543	4 414	4 323	4 259	4 059	3 957	3 744	3 651	3 596	3 431	3 345
Societies without branches	3 717	3 611	3 550	3 505	3 331	3 262	3 073	3 021	2 987	2 830	2 762
Orders and branches	826	803	773	755	727	695	671	630	608	601	583
Benefits paid (£ thousand) Sickness pay: total	5 566	5 630	5 578	5 349	5 702	6 254	6 852	6 841	6 578	7 109	7 982
Societies without branches	4 493	4 547	4 546	4 307	4 739	5 344	5 908	5 929	5 747	6 290	7 193
Orders and branches	1 073	1 083	1 031	1 043	963	910	944	912	831	819	789
Sums at death: total	2 536	2 675	2 694	2 759	3 022	3 183	3 542	3 663	4 039	4 364	4 982
Societies without branches	2 147	2 316	2 339	2 385	2 662	2 812	3 165	3 313	3 700	4 034	4 610
Orders and branches	390	359	356	273	360	371	377	350	339	330	372
Other benefits: total	21 147	22 646	27 050	30 161	41 698	28 201	27 750	31 920	37 384	48 320	48 364
Societies without branches	19 631	21 126	25 326	28 220	39 649	25 629	25 793	29 726	35 205	45 532	44 971
Orders and branches	1 516	1 520	1 724	1 941	2 049	2 572	1 956	2 194	2 179	2 788	3 393
Total funds[2] (£ thousand)	372 434	385 536	400 200	427 690	392 491	407 640	444 635	488 986	545 915	613 817	718 882

1. Excluding collecting societies.
2. 1983 data available early 1985 from: Registry of Friendly Societies, 15/17
Great Marlborough Street, London W1V 2AX. Telephone 01 – 437 9992 ext. 225.
3. At end of year.

Source Registry of Friendly Societies

17.23   Life assurance[1]
Industrial business
Great Britain

£ thousand

	1972	1973	1974	1975	1976	1977	1978	1979	1980	1981	1982
Companies established in Great Britain											
Income: total	472 815	506 978	535 952	700 580	656 959	790 715	854 562	1 080 735	1 296 551	1 430 365	1 685 658
Premiums	283 694	307 041	329 583	361 478	401 261	447 251	501 687	657 172	781 168	841 217	902 175
Interest, etc. (gross)	159 392	174 014	189 602	207 824	235 774	267 548	306 000	375 872	439 128	484 959	564 385
Miscellaneous[2]	29 729	25 923	16 767	131 277	19 924	75 916	46 875	47 692	76 254	104 189	219 098
Expenditure: total	376 300	386 188	648 089	456 969	510 239	557 806	608 959	699 425	829 058	961 773	1 119 894
Claims paid and outstanding	175 531	182 773	192 749	199 489	221 088	235 075	249 587	273 719	317 357	364 321	424 544
Surrenders	63 248	58 634	66 724	68 439	75 320	84 389	85 276	98 217	135 862	189 519	243 322
Expenses of management	104 060	112 301	127 977	158 087	175 365	195 830	225 014	267 812	312 322	339 157	357 047
Shareholders' surplus	7 146	7 062	6 643	7 477	7 942	9 363	10 745	13 060	15 954	20 829	25 140
Miscellaneous (including income tax)	26 315	25 418	253 997	23 476	30 523	33 149	38 337	46 617	47 564	47 946	69 842
Industrial assurance funds at end of year	2 179 075	2 299 508	2 187 262	2 430 873	2 581 942	2 814 851	3 081 954	3 463 264	3 930 757	4 400 480	4 966 243

1. The 'year' is, for each company included, its accounting year which ended between 1 September of the year shown and 31 August of the following year.
2. In 1975 includes £99 million transferred from investment and other reserves by five companies and £10 million written up by two companies on their investments. In 1977 includes £53 million transferred from investment reserves by two companies.

Source   Office of the Industrial Assurance Commissioner

17.24   Returns of industrial assurances taken up and discontinued
Great Britain

Thousands

	1972	1973	1974	1975	1976	1977	1978	1979	1980	1981	1982
Industrial assurance companies[1]											
Paying:											
Assurances taken up during year	3 579	3 355	3 317	3 318	3 398	3 288	3 269	3 354	3 445	3 314	3 330
Assurances discontinued during year:											
Claims on death	880	864	825	799	803	768	757	776	724	696	688
Claims on maturity	922	907	917	901	970	999	985	975	967	1 017	1 054
Surrender for cash	2 143	1 780	1 789	1 733	1 740	1 750	1 628	1 609	1 807	2 051	2 217
Conversion to free policies:											
For full sums assured	438	438	448	372	397	412	429	420	418	462	421
For reduced sums assured	414	353	323	334	320	286	240	284	284	293	296
Forfeiture without grant of free policy or cash surrender value	618	608	603	574	581	580	546	472	484	536	536
Assurances in force at end of year	54 740	53 107	51 516	50 134	48 823	47 282	45 935	44 753	43 514	41 772	39 888
Free:											
Assurances converted to free policies during year	852	791	772	706	717	697	669	704	702	755	717
Assurances discontinued during year:											
Claims on death	513	522	518	504	510	483	473	568	522	521	519
Claims on maturity	38	32	32	33	35	35	36	111	76	84	86
Surrender for cash	332	262	240	209	199	180	158	155	176	192	193
Assurances in force at end of year	15 507	15 479	15 460	15 415	15 418	15 416	15 384	15 254	15 177	15 135	15 055
Collecting societies[2]											
Paying:											
Assurances taken up during year	816	776	746	707	623	594	563	521	516	463	440
Assurances discontinued during year:											
Claims on death	297	278	268	257	253	237	227	225	218	206	211
Claims on maturity	118	115	116	117	118	122	117	117	118	117	127
Surrender for cash	421	344	340	322	320	335	271	290	336	491	500
Conversion to free policies:											
For full sums assured	200	198	200	197	222	213	202	192	178	171	165
For reduced sums assured	285	234	228	214	193	203	185	178	162	93	80
Forfeiture without grant of free policy or cash surrender value	161	136	133	123	107	96	82	69	73	69	65
Assurances in force at end of year	17 095	16 562	16 021	15 499	14 806	14 192	13 667	13 117	12 541	11 847	11 137
Free:											
Assurances converted to free policies during year	485	432	428	411	415	416	388	370	340	264	245
Assurances discontinued during year:											
Claims on death	213	203	201	200	208	198	198	223	222	216	423
Claims on maturity	2	1	1	1	2	2	2	2	3	3	52
Surrender for cash	277	222	212	207	191	183	158	140	118	61	53
Assurances in force at end of year	7 867	7 873	7 892	7 893	7 878	7 910	7 941	7 943	7 945	7 935	7 653

1. Industrial assurance companies incorporated in Great Britain.
2. Collecting societies registered in Great Britain.

Source   Office of the Industrial Assurance Commissioner

17.25 Acquisitions and mergers of companies
Analysis of expenditure by industry group of acquiring company

	Expenditure (£ million) [1]								Number of companies acquired							
	1976	1977	1978	1979	1980	1981	1982	1983	1976	1977	1978	1979	1980	1981	1982	1983
Industrial and commercial companies[2]																
Manufacturing industries:																
Food	75	16	27	7	15	99	48	92	12	19	18	9	15	17	14	19
Drink	20	14	87	8	110	13	34	8	4	12	12	6	6	7	8	3
Tobacco	–	1	38	145	–	39	–	–	1	1	1	4	–	2	–	–
Chemicals and man-made fibres	17	73	72	19	62	17	49	25	17	10	18	12	16	19	20	13
Mineral and ore extraction								–								–
Metals	25	22	14	32	7	13	61	31	13	12	12	19	11	16	19	22
Mechanical and instruments engineering	20	80	54	52	87	49	25	108	34	55	56	35	42	36	31	45
Electrical and electronic engineering																
Office machinery, etc.	20	138	51	327	114	84	31	91	25	31	22	22	13	36	22	29
Shipbuilding and vehicles	2	18	23	15	9	1	–	45	7	17	15	14	9	5	3	6
Metal goods nes	9	19	22	89	12	59	7	5	17	28	16	13	10	10	7	11
Textiles	6	19	52	15	11	21	9	8	18	19	16	23	17	22	15	9
Leather footwear and clothing	3	6	21	32	15	48	5	43	10	13	22	22	19	26	8	12
Non-metallic mineral products	2	18	14	15	44	16	180	31	6	14	11	12	11	10	7	7
Timber and furniture	1	20	10	20	12	5	33	24	7	8	17	13	13	7	8	7
Paper, printing and publishing	15	21	49	31	55	40	60	66	11	19	25	16	30	20	32	29
Other manufacturing	5	18	9	7	6	25	7	20	10	12	14	9	3	2	8	9
Mixed activity (mainly manufacturing)								972								14
Total manufacturing	220	483	543	813	559	529	549	1 568	192	270	275	229	215	235	202	235
Agriculture; forestry and fishing	1	15	23	127	534	107	270	3	6	19	22	12	15	17	20	2
Energy industries								172								18
Construction	37	21	48	69	57	90	140	193	28	29	39	45	42	31	39	31
Wholesaling (excluding petroleum)	25	42	89	116	29	41	210	43	17	26	45	31	27	19	34	39
Retailing	27	44	113	174	70	54	581	69	27	27	41	53	23	17	17	20
Hotels and catering								24								6
Transport and communication	8	10	8	17	37	24	9	55	7	8	9	20	18	9	13	7
Real estate	13	30	30	34	83	108	185	37	9	22	27	36	30	29	51	24
Services	60	47	112	169	47	76	243	141	42	44	72	84	75	59	61	53
Mixed activities (mainly non-manufacturing)								38								12
Mixed activities	57	132	174	137	59	114	20	–[3]	25	36	37	24	24	36	26	–[3]
Total all industrial and commercial companies	448	824	1 140	1 656	1 475	1 143	2 206	2 343	353	481	567	534	469	452	463	447

1. A merger (which takes place when two companies combine to form a new company) is reckoned as the acquisition of the smaller company by the larger and is valued at the market value of the smaller company's share in the newly formed company.
2. The headings relate to the 1983 figures which are based on the 1980 Standard Industrial Classification. There are changes in coverage in nearly all headings. The major ones being the transfer of:
   (a) man-made fibres from textiles to chemicals
   (b) office machinery from mechanical to electrical engineering
   (c) marine engineering from shipbuilding to mechanical engineering
   (d) mineral and ore extraction from energy to form a new heading
   (e) coal and petroleum products, nuclear fuel from chemicals to energy
   (f) distribution of motor vehicles and parts, retail distribution of petroleum products and repair of motor vehicles from services to wholesaling and retailing (repairs with retailing)
   (g) estate agents from real estate to services
   (h) hotels and catering from services to form a new heading
   (i) mixed activities have been split between manufacturing and non-manufacturing
   (j) the definition of total manufacturing in 1983 is not comparable with earlier years
3. Not applicable for 1983.

Sources Department of Trade and Industry

17.26 Income and finance of large companies[1,2]

Balance sheet summary

£ million

Balance sheet at end of accounting 'year'[3]	1977	1978	1979	1980	1981[4]	1982[4]
Estimated number of companies	*1 524*	*1 729*	*1 766*	*1 921*	..	..
Fixed assets:						
Net tangible assets	52 017	64 000	71 301	85 105	102 872	119 641
Intangible assets	3 236	3 218	3 368	6 110	3 533	3 693
Investments in unconsolidated subsidiaries	302	369	572	537	715	723
Total net fixed assets	55 555	67 588	75 242	91 752	107 119	124 058
Current assets and investments:						
Stocks and work-in-progress	37 463	41 801	49 322	53 455	56 512	56 272
Debtors, prepayments and Government grants receivable	32 963	37 549	43 352	46 390	56 006	59 816
Investments	11 172	11 714	13 484	11 855	12 801	12 594
Cash, short-term deposits and tax instruments	9 062	10 256	10 274	11 697	14 911	19 624
Total current assets and investments	90 661	101 321	116 432	123 397	140 235	148 305
Current liabilities:						
Bank loans, overdrafts and short-term loans[5]	19 763	22 251	25 188	30 065	35 006	43 322
Creditors and accruals	36 012	41 072	48 339	52 712	62 499	68 164
Dividends and interest due	1 441	1 634	2 167	2 327	2 514	2 570
Current taxation[6]	3 420	4 643	5 594	6 844	7 114	6 681
Total current liabilities	60 636	69 599	81 288	91 949	107 129	120 740
Net current assets	30 025	31 722	35 144	31 448	33 106	27 564
Total net assets	85 580	99 309	110 386	123 200	140 224	151 618
Financed by:						
Shareholders' interest	59 393	71 873	84 038	94 718	106 854	116 966
Minority shareholders' interest	3 419	4 405	4 984	6 537	7 715	6 278
Deferred taxation[7]	8 623	6 020	5 113	5 455	6 266	11 614
Debentures, mortgages and long-term loans[8]	14 145	17 011	16 251	16 490	19 389	16 764

Income and appropriation account

Accounts for 'year'[3]	1977	1978	1979	1980	1981[4]	1982[4]
Estimated number of companies	*1 524*	*1 729*	*1 766*	*1 921*	..	..
Income from trading and other activities:						
Gross trading profit[4,9]	21 709	23 926	30 391	29 340	36 172	35 494
Total income	23 651	25 987	32 984	32 010	39 467	40 028
Less:						
Interest on bank and short-term loans	2 070	2 395	3 247	4 428	5 488	5 421
Hire of plant and machinery	1 257	1 613	1 758	1 870	2 179	2 503
Gross income	20 324	21 978	27 979	25 712	31 801	32 103
Appropriation of gross income:						
Depreciation and amounts written-off	4 474	5 400	6 325	7 408	9 206	9 687
Taxation	7 178	6 595	6 724	7 168	10 934	10 843
Dividends	2 173	2 610	4 011	3 709	4 331	4 359
Interest on long-term loans	1 135	1 399	1 510	1 545	1 621	1 628
Minority shareholders' interest	313	620	1 025	1 055	1 171	565
Retained income	5 051	5 353	8 384	4 827	4 536	5 028
Total appropriation of gross income	20 324	21 978	27 979	25 712	31 801	32 103

Sources and uses of funds

Accounts for 'year'[3]	1977	1978	1979	1980	1981[4]	1982[4]
Estimated number of companies	*1 524*	*1 729*	*1 766*	*1 921*	..	..
Receipts from issues of share and loan capital	1 573	2 943	1 314	1 334	5 319	249
Increase in amount owing to banks, short-term lenders and creditors	4 282	4 748	10 074	5 480	13 881	17 018
Gross income	20 324	21 978	27 979	25 712	31 801	32 103
Other sources (including exchange differences)	− 959	− 656	− 1 263	− 744	3 115	3 529
Total sources of funds	25 221	29 013	38 104	31 781	54 114	52 900
Payments out of income	8 214	8 519	10 153	11 569	15 714	12 959
Expenditure on fixed assets, etc.	8 143	10 608	12 956	15 900	22 726	27 844
Increase in current assets and investments	8 864	9 885	14 995	4 310	15 674	12 097
Total uses of funds	25 221	29 013	38 104	31 781	54 114	52 900

Note and footnotes on page 307

Source Business Statistics Office

17.26
(continued)

Income and finance of large companies[1,2]

Supplementary information

Accounts for 'year'[3]	1977	1978	1979	1980	1981[4]	1982[4]
Estimated number of companies	*1 524*	*1 729*	*1 766*	*1 921*	..	..
Capital employed[10]	106 402	122 948	137 247	154 777	176 763	193 963
Turnover (where reported)[11]	220 940	245 939	280 676	308 051	331 110	371 237
Exports from UK (where reported)	21 178	23 220	25 381	27 149	23 859	24 277
Contracts placed for capital expenditure but not provided for	5 034	5 948	6 369	5 971	5 973	9 537
Capital expenditure authorised but not contracted for	7 073	9 681	10 502	12 334	14 981	11 729
UK employees' remunerations (where reported)	22 581	25 417	29 758	33 860	35 171	37 723
Average number of UK employees (where reported) (thous)	*(6 871)*	*(6 831)*	*(6 833)*	*(6 912)*	*(6 526)*	*(6 580)*
Number of overseas-owned companies	*486*	*442*	*437*	*508*	..	..

Note: The figures are based on an analysis of company accounts and full details are given in Business Monitor *MA3 Company finance* (HMSO).

1. Listed and unlisted limited companies registered in Great Britain with a capital employed in the current year of more than £4.16 million, excluding companies whose main activity is insurance, banking or finance.
2. There may be a slight discrepancy between a total and the sum of its constituent items due to rounding.
3. The figures for a particular year relate to companies' accounting years ending between 1 April of the year shown and 31 March of the following year. 75% of the larger companies have accounting periods ending in the fourth quarter of the calendar year or in the first quarter of the following year.
4. Provisional.
5. Loans, other than bank loans, which are wholly repayable within five years.
6. Includes all corporation tax, irrespective of the date on which it is payable, but is net of advance corporation tax recoverable.
7. Includes tax equalisation reserve and amounts charged to deferred tax for such things as capital gains tax and betterment levy.

8. Loans, other than bank loans, which are not wholly repayable within five years.
9. Relates to the position after charging directors' fees and emoluments, pensions to past directors, superannuation payments, compensation for loss of office, auditors' fees and any exceptional expenditure (e.g. on reorganisation or closure) but excluding any profit or loss on disposal of assets and before allowing for depreciation provisions, all interest on loans, and hire charges for plant and machinery.
10. Defined for the purpose of this analysis, as shareholders' interest (issued share capital and reserves), minority shareholders' interest, deferred taxation, long-term loans (including debentures and mortgages)—i.e. all the items which finance net assets—*plus* bank loans and overdrafts, short-term loans and indebtedness to directors and group members, *less* amounts due from group members.
11. Excludes VAT but includes excise duties.

Source Business Statistics Office

17.27 Bankruptcies, etc.
England and Wales

	1972	1973	1974	1975	1976	1977	1978	1979	1980	1981	1982	1983
Number of bankruptcies, etc.												
Debtors adjudicated bankrupt [1]	3 860	3 363	5 191	6 676	6 681	4 078	3 526	3 158	3 634	4 730	5 303	6 555
Compositions and schemes of arrangement	5	5	4	2	–	2	–	1	7	3	2	4
Administration orders of deceased debtors' estates	19	12	13	20	19	15	14	11	11	11	14	17
Liabilities (£ thousand)												
Debtors adjudicated bankrupt	20 237	19 102	41 581	81 553	76 692	104 674	205 809	65 805	68 580	169 608	210 615	226 277
Compositions and schemes of arrangement	46	15	43	13	–	11	–	18	116	46	39	81
Administration orders of deceased debtors' estates	164	568	168	2 718	1 517	774	427	532	421	573	380	709
Assets (£ thousand)												
Debtors adjudicated bankrupt	8 231	8 640	14 562	21 215	22 300	15 834	20 093	21 768	39 327	39 433	34 464	54 117
Compositions and schemes of arrangement	15	2	26	6	–	3	–	8	75	63	43	47
Administration orders of deceased debtors' estates	111	245	109	543	212	319	145	124	155	166	135	225

1. Actual net cases administered.

Source Department of Trade and Industry

17.28 Deeds of arrangement
England and Wales

	1972	1973	1974	1975	1976	1977	1978	1979	1980	1981	1982	1983
Number registered												
Assignments of property to trustees for benefit of creditors	85	92	98	120	86	77	67	39	50	72	43	46
Other deeds of arrangement	7	3	8	3	10	5	3	5	2	4	3	5
Liabilities (£ thousand)												
Assignments of property to trustees for benefit of creditors	1 126	1 190	6 261	62 851	36 238	8 165	10 799	7 014	2 700	18 620	4 537	4 736
Other deeds of arrangement	61	148	1 573	51	295	1 125	30	568	456	54	92	402
Assets (£ thousand)												
Assignments of property to trustees for benefit of creditors	654	664	3 152	1 820	1 678	2 491	1 484	813	1 637	3 121	2 867	1 503
Other deeds of arrangement	19	24	413	56	91	120	11	45	67	17	10	244

Source Department of Trade and Industry

17.29 Sequestrations (bankruptcies)
Scotland

	1973	1974	1975	1976	1977	1978	1979	1980	1981	1982	1983
Number of sequestrations [1,2]	47	63	89	80	76	80	66	111	117	144	174
Liabilities (£ thousand)	968	1 619	3 461	3 171	3 213	4 338	2 470	4 843	12 266	9 757	18 434
Assets (£ thousand)	535	559	1 513	1 305	1 025	648	994	2 060	4 228	3 975	5 601

1. In Scotland private trust deeds are not registered with the Accountant and particulars of them are not available. The only deeds of arrangement with creditors registered are those terminating sequestrations.
2. Sequestrations awarded but not brought into operation are excluded from these figures.

Source The Accountant of Court, Edinburgh

17.30 Bankruptcies, etc.
Northern Ireland

	1973	1974	1975	1976	1977	1978	1979	1980	1981	1982	1983
Number of bankruptcies, etc.											
Bankruptcies	19	25	37	49	39	36	23	28	52	56	76
Deeds of arrangement	–	–	1	–	–	–	–	–	–	–	–
Arrangement under the control of the court	4	5	4	1	10	8	8	9	16	17	12
Insolvent estates	2	2	1	1	–	2	2	1	–	–	2
Liabilities[1] (£ thousand)											
Bankruptcies	196	466	1 008	970	588	1 147	551	1 276	2 259	2 171	4 650
Deeds of arrangement	–	–	147	–	–	–	–	–	–	–	–
Arrangement under the control of the court	90	159	277	10	153	323	513	576	1 251	892	533
Insolvent estates	15	63	16	15	–	103	414	587	–	–	342
Assets[1] (£ thousand)											
Bankruptcies	19	98	175	554	299	267	154	252	479	497	1 376
Deeds of arrangement	–	–	53	–	–	–	–	–	–	–	–
Arrangement under the control of the court	49	55	52	5	74	258	235	184	692	352	127
Insolvent estates	11	50	12	11	–	76	242	129	–	–	244

1. Disclosed by debtor or personal representative.

Source Department of Economic Development (Northern Ireland)
Official Assignee Office

17.31 Company liquidations

Number

	1973	1974	1975	1976	1977	1978	1979	1980	1981	1982	1983
England and Wales											
Compulsory liquidations	1 080	1 395	2 287	2 511	2 425	2 265	2 064	2 935	2 771	3 745	4 807
Voluntary liquidations:											
Creditors'	1 495	2 325	3 111	3 428	3 406	2 821	2 473	3 955	5 825	8 322	8 599
Members'	4 297	3 746	3 917	4 173	3 650	3 615	4 030	3 970	3 638	3 908	3 808
Total liquidations notified (all types)	6 872	7 466	9 315	10 112	9 481	8 701	8 567	10 860	12 234	15 975	17 214
Scotland											
Compulsory liquidations	25	42	53	84	67	78	56	135	158	177	263
Voluntary liquidations:											
Creditors'	73	113	151	145	204	196	182	244	280	326	258
Members'	270	264	276	299	222	230	214	242	248	253	243
Total liquidations notified (all types)	368	419	480	528	493	504	452	621	686	756	764
Northern Ireland											
Compulsory liquidations	3	1	3	7	1	8	7	8	16	10	15
Voluntary liquidations:											
Creditors'	12	12	15	42	31	45	27	66	83	111	96
Members'	31	29	36	38	42	36	37	39	39	41	52
Total liquidations notified (all types)	46	42	54	87	74	89	71	113	138	162	163

Sources Department of Trade and Industry; The Registrar of Companies, Edinburgh; Department of Economic Development (Northern Ireland)

18 Prices

Producer price index number (*Table 18.1 – 18.4*)

Introduction of the producer price index

The producer price index is the result of three main changes made to the former wholesale price index.

Firstly the change of name has been made to describe more precisely the purpose of the index in measuring manufacturers' prices and to conform with the established international nomenclature.

Secondly, the index has been rebased to ensure that its weights reflect the changing pattern on industry's sales and purchases; this incorporates a switch from 1975 = 100 to 1980 = 100.

Finally, the index has been reclassified from the 1968 to the 1980 version of the standard industrial classification which has been adopted as the standard basis for classifying economic statistics (see below).

Full details of these changes were given in an article published in *British business,* 15 April 1983.

Revised definition of manufacturing industry

As a result of the adoption of the 1980 standard industrial classification (SIC) the definition of manufacturing industry has been revised. On the 1968 SIC, used by the wholesale price index, manufacturing industry covered orders III to XIX. On the 1980 SIC, used by the producer price index, manufacturing industry covers divisions 2 to 4. The most significant result, in relation to the indices, is that mineral oil refining no longer forms part of manufacturing. Hence petroleum products replace crude oil as a component of the input index for the new definition of manufacturing and no longer feature in the output index.

The indices relate to the average prices for a year. All the index numbers are compiled exclusive of value added tax, therefore changes in V.A.T. are not reflected in the indices.

Purchasing power of the pound (*Table 18.5*)

Changes in the internal purchasing power of a currency may be defined as the 'inverse' of changes in the levels of prices; when prices go up, the amount which can be purchased with a given sum of money goes down. Movements in the internal purchasing power of the pound are based on the consumers' expenditure deflator (CED) prior to 1962 and on the General index of retail prices (RPI) from January 1962 onwards. The CED shows the movement in prices implied by the national accounts estimates of consumers' expenditure valued at current and at constant prices, whilst the RPI is constructed directly by weighting together monthly movements in prices according to a given pattern of household expenditure derived from the Family Expenditure Survey. If the purchasing power of the pound is taken to be 100p in a particular month (quarter, year), the comparable purchasing power in a subsequent month (quarter, year) is

$100 \times \dfrac{\text{earlier period price index}}{\text{later period price index}}$, where the price index used is the CED

for years 1946–1961 and the RPI for periods after 1961.

A long series on the purchasing power of the pound back to 1914, the latest information and a detailed explanation of the estimation of changes in the purchasing power of the pound are given in 'The Internal Purchasing Power of the Pound', a leaflet obtainable from the Press and Information Section, Central Statistical Office, Great George Street, London SW1P 3AQ.

Index of retail prices (*Table 18.6*)

The retail prices index measures the change from month to month in the average level of prices of goods and services purchased by most households in the United Kingdom. The expenditure pattern on which the index is based is revised each year using information from the Family Expenditure Survey. The expenditure of certain higher income households and households of retired people dependent mainly on social security benefits is excluded.

The index covers a large and representative selection of more than 350 separate goods and services, for which price movements are regularly measured in more than 200 towns throughout the country. Approximately 150 000 separate price quotations are used in compiling the index.

Tax and price index (TPI) (*Table 18.7*)

The purpose and methodology of the TPI were described in an article in the August 1979 issue (No. 310) of *Economic Trends* (HMSO). The TPI measures the increase in *gross* taxable income needed to compensate taxpayers for any increase in retail prices. The RPI measures changes in retail prices; the TPI also takes account of the changes to direct taxes (and employees' National Insurance contributions) facing a representative cross-section of taxpayers. It is thus an additional, more comprehensive, index.

Between Budgets the monthly increase in the TPI is normally slightly larger than that in the RPI, since all the extra income needed to offset any rise in retail prices is fully taxed. When direct taxation or employees' National Insurance contributions change the TPI will rise by less than or more than the RPI according to the type of changes made. However, the focus of attention should be the changes over twelve months.

Index numbers of agricultural prices (*Tables 18.8 and 18.9*)

The indices of agricultural prices for the United Kingdom based on the calendar year 1980 are designed to provide short-term indications of movements in the purchase prices of the means of agricultural production and of prices received by producers for their agricultural products. The construction of the indices enables them to be combined with similar indices for other member countries of the European Community, to provide an overall indication of price trends within the Ten, which appear in the Community's Eurostat Series of publications.

18.1 Producer price index numbers of output (home sales)
Annual averages

1980 = 100

	1980 SIC	1979	1980	1981	1982	1983
Output of manufactured products (revised definition)	2 to 4	87.7	100.0	109.5	118.0	124.4
Products of manufacturing industries (revised definition) other than food, drink and tobacco	2 to 4 excluding 41/42	86.7	100.0	107.5	114.9	121.1
Products of the food, drink and tobacco manufacturing industries	41/42	89.4	100.0	112.7	122.8	129.5
Output of selected broad sectors of industry						
Metal manufacturing	22	93.8	100.0	100.4	108.0	111.0
Extraction of minerals not elsewhere specified	23	81.7	100.0	112.3	125.5	133.6[1]
Non-metallic mineral products	24	82.7	100.0	110.4	120.3	126.7[1]
Chemical industry	25	86.5	100.0	106.4	113.5	119.1
Man-made fibres	26	94.3	100.0	99.7	110.2	116.5
Metal goods, engineering and vehicles industries	3	87.9	100.0	107.2	113.8	119.5[1]
Metal goods, not elsewhere specified	31	86.9	100.0	105.3	112.6	117.8[1]
Mechanical engineering	32	87.1	100.0	108.2	117.2	124.6
Electrical and electronic engineering	34	86.9	100.0	106.4	111.2[1]	116.6
Motor vehicles and parts	35	89.0	100.0	108.2	114.5	119.5
Instrument engineering	37	88.5	100.0	110.2	120.2	125.5
Food manufacturing industries	411 to 423	90.5	100.0	108.6	116.4	121.5
Textile industry	43	90.8	100.0	104.5	110.4	116.4
Footwear and clothing industries	45	89.3	100.0	103.8	107.9	112.5
Timber and wooden furniture industries	46	87.0	100.0	107.0	113.2	120.1
Paper and paper products; printing and publishing	47	85.1	100.0	110.0	121.7	129.5[1]
Processing of rubber and plastics	48	86.0	100.0	104.0	109.1	114.1
Other manufacturing industries	49	80.5	100.0	101.2	103.8	113.7

1. Revised.

Sources Business Statistics Office

18.2 Producer price index numbers of materials and fuel purchased
Annual averages

1980 = 100

	1980 SIC Division, class or activity heading	1979	1980	1981	1982	1983
Materials and fuel purchased by manufacturing industry (revised definition)	2 to 4	92.2	100.0	109.2	117.2	125.3
Materials		96.1	100.0	106.1	113.4	121.2
Fuel		78.8	100.0	119.8	130.3	139.3
Materials and fuel purchased by manufacturing industry (revised definition) other than the food, drink and tobacco manufacturing industries	2 to 4 excluding 41/42	89.8	100.0	108.8	116.3	125.3
Materials		95.2	100.0	103.4	109.5	118.8[1]
Fuel		78.9	100.0	119.7	130.0	138.8
Materials and fuel purchased by the food, drink and tobacco manufacturing industries	41/42	94.0	100.0	108.6	116.9	122.8
Materials and fuel purchased by selected broad sectors of industry						
Metal manufacturing	22	91.0	100.0	105.2	112.1	122.3
Extraction of minerals not elsewhere specified	23	82.2	100.0	113.0	123.2	131.1
Non-metallic mineral products	24	82.2	100.0	112.9	123.3	131.8
Chemical Industry	25	88.6	100.0	108.8	115.9[2]	123.4
Man-made fibres	26	88.7	100.0	107.0	115.1[2]	120.9
Metal goods, engineering and vehicles industries	3	90.2	100.0	104.2	111.3	116.6
Metal goods not elsewhere specified	31	91.3	100.0	103.0	109.7	116.1
Mechanical engineering	32	89.4	100.0	105.4	113.4	117.4[1]
Electrical and electronic engineering	34	89.1	100.0	103.3	109.9	117.2[1]
Motor vehicles and parts	35	87.8	100.0	105.7	113.1	117.6[1]
Other transport equipment	36	87.1	100.0	107.0	114.4	120.3[1]
Instrument engineering	37	88.5	100.0	104.3	110.8	116.6[1]
Food manufacturing industries	411 to 423	94.6	100.0	109.1	116.6	122.1
Materials		95.3	100.0	108.6	115.9	121.2
Fuel		78.5	100.0	120.7	132.4	142.3
Textile industry	43	94.7	100.0	105.8	114.8	123.7
Footwear and clothing industries	45	93.6	100.0	102.4	109.9	117.4
Timber and wooden furniture industries	46	88.4	100.0	104.0	110.0	119.3
Paper and paper products; printing and publishing	47	88.4	100.0	108.8	115.6	118.2
Processing of rubber and plastics	48	90.7	100.0	101.5	108.0	117.2
Other manufacturing industries	49	72.8	100.0	86.6	87.7	105.8
Construction materials	5	84.8	100.0	108.2	117.2	125.1[1]
House building materials	Part of 5	84.6	100.0	108.3	117.2	124.9[1]

1. Provisional
2. Revised

Source Business Statistics Office

18.3 Producer price index numbers of commodities produced in the United Kingdom (home sales)
Annual averages

1980 = 100

	1980 SIC[1]	1979	1980	1981	1982	1983
Energy and water supply industries	**1**					
Coal	1113	80.6	100.0	116.1	126.4	136.8
Foundry Coke		89.7	100.0	105.2	100.0	104.8
Mineral oil refining (including duty)	1401	75.1	100.0	122.6	141.1	158.0
Motor spirit (including duty)		76.0	100.0	125.1	143.1	156.9
Kerosene (including duty)		68.6	100.0	118.7	136.8	152.2
Gas oil/derv (including duty)		75.7	100.0	120.0	140.2	158.8
Fuel oil (including duty)		77.8	100.0	124.9	142.9	163.9
Gas oil fuel (including duty)		74.1	100.0	119.4	141.2	160.7
Derv (including duty)		79.2	100.0	121.3	138.0	154.8
Light fuel oil (including duty)		73.8	100.0	121.7	139.2	156.8
Medium fuel oil (including duty)		76.2	100.0	123.0	140.4	159.9
Heavy fuel oil (including duty)		78.2	100.0	125.3	143.4	164.8
Petroleum bitumen		71.1	100.0	122.1	132.3	146.6
Other treatment of petroleum products (excluding petrochemical manufacture)	1402					
Lubricating oils and greases		74.6	100.0	111.1	117.4	123.4
Water supply industry	1700					
Water for Industrial use[2]		85.0	100.0	114.0	125.7	131.7
Metal manufacturing	**22**					
Iron and steel	2210	94.5	100.0	100.8	110.1	110.6
Ordinary steel		94.8	100.0	101.0	110.6	110.9
Ingots for tubes		94.2	100.0	102.9	116.0	117.6
Rounds and squares for tubes		94.0	100.0	101.3	113.9	115.1
Railway material		90.3	100.0	106.1	106.1	111.0
Heavy permanent railway material		90.9	100.0	106.0	106.1	112.7
Light permanent railway material		87.2	100.0	106.4	106.4	103.1
Sheet piling		98.7	100.0	106.2	116.6	121.5
Beams and sections		95.0	100.0	100.6	109.0	104.0
Reinforcing steel in coils		93.6	100.0	100.2	105.9	110.9
Hot rolled narrow strip (less than 600 mm)		96.3	100.0	101.5	108.5	113.2
Hot rolled coil plate and sheet		96.1	100.0	100.1	112.5	115.4
4.76 mm and over		95.8	100.0	100.1	112.4	114.8
3 mm to 4.75 mm		97.9	100.0	100.0	113.5	119.9
Less than 3 mm		97.7	100.0	100.0	110.9	116.7
Cold rolled sheets and plates (including cold rolled wide strip) less than 3 mm thick		97.7	100.0	100.0	109.2	116.4
End products		94.3	100.0	101.2	109.3	115.9
Tinplate and other tinned sheet		87.4	100.0	102.1	112.9	119.4
Black plate		86.3	100.0	101.6	109.6	117.7
Zinc coated, lead coated and other coated sheet		97.6	100.0	100.0	109.7	118.5
Electrical sheet (including Hot rolled elect strip)		92.6	100.0	103.6	103.7	104.7
Electrical sheet grain non-orientated		92.6	100.0	103.6	103.6	104.9
Electrical sheet grain orientated		92.5	100.0	103.8	103.8	103.8
Special steels		93.2	100.0	99.7	107.9	109.5
Semis other than for tubes, non-alloyed		94.4	100.0	101.2	113.9	115.1
Ingots for tubes, alloy steel (other than stainless and heat-resisting)		93.8	100.0	101.9	114.2	115.7
Semis, alloy steel (other than stainless and heat-resisting)		93.0	100.0	100.2	111.0	111.9
Semis for tubes		92.9	100.0	101.3	112.7	113.6
Semis other than for tubes		93.1	100.0	99.6	110.3	111.1
Plate 3 mm and over		95.0	100.0	95.1	99.2	100.2
Stainless and heat-resisting steels		93.2	100.0	99.8	100.3	104.3
Semis		92.6	100.0	99.5	93.7	94.4
Semis for tubes		92.2	100.0	99.3	94.4	95.3
Semis other than for tubes		93.0	100.0	99.7	92.9	93.3
Sheet and strip		92.1	100.0	99.2	100.2	103.2
Steel for reinforcement, cut, bent and delivered		92.6	100.0	102.2	112.0	117.3
Light re-rolled bars and sections		94.0	100.0	100.1	104.8	102.7
Steel tubes	2220	95.2	100.0	103.8	118.9	108.5
Non-alloy steel tubes		95.6	100.0	103.5	117.2	103.5
Drawing and manufacture of steel wire and steel wire products	2234					
Single drawn wire, of high carbon steel, whether covered or not (excluding insulated electric wire)		93.0	100.0	96.3	105.5	107.6
Single drawn wire of other than high carbon and alloy steel, whether covered or not (excluding insulated electric wire)		92.2	100.0	99.6	111.7	106.6
Iron and steel wire ropes (excluding insulated electric wire and cables)		89.6	100.0	108.4	120.7	127.3
Woven wire cloth, gauze, fabric, etc of iron and steel (excluding netting fencing and similar iron and steel manufactures and fabric reinforcements for concrete) in squares or rectangular mesh		87.2	100.0	101.0	115.8	121.1
Stainless steel		87.1	100.0	101.3	113.0	116.2
Other than stainless steel		87.2	100.0	100.6	119.1	126.8
Grille, netting, fencing and similar iron and steel wire manufactures		89.5	100.0	106.6	113.6	115.9
Other drawing, cold rolling and cold forming of steel	2235	94.9	100.0	101.7	116.0	116.3

1. Division, class or activity heading.
2. This index is based on volumetric charges and does not reflect fixed or standing charges.

Source Business Statistics Office

18.3 Producer price index numbers of commodities produced in the United Kingdom (home sales)
Annual averages

(continued)

1980 = 100

	1980 SIC[1]	1979	1980	1981	1982	1983
Aluminium and aluminium alloys	2245					
Primary aluminium and aluminium alloys unwrought (e.g. ingots, slabs, etc.)		90.2	100.0	100.5	100.5	117.2
Plate, sheet, strip circles and blanks		87.2	100.0	92.5	95.0	100.5
Extrusions and tubes (bars, rods, sections, etc.)		86.4	100.0	98.2	98.9	106.0
Copper, brass and other copper alloys	2246					
Copper tubes		89.7	100.0	99.1	106.1	119.7
Copper sheet and copper strip		92.6	100.0	98.3	102.2	116.7
Woven wire cloth, gauze, fabric screening, sieving lawn or meshing (excluding paper machine (fourdrinier) wire)		86.3	100.0	99.9	109.6	115.7
Other non-ferrous metals and their alloys	2247					
Semi-manufactures of lead and lead alloys (e.g. sheet, pipe, shot, etc. but excluding oxides)		124.0	100.0	97.3	89.4	85.6
Unwrought titanium and semi-manufactures		64.7	100.0	108.2	113.1	108.5
Extraction of minerals not elsewhere specified	**23**					
Extraction of stone, clay, sand and gravel	2310					
Extraction and dredging of uncoated sand and gravel (excluding sand for foundry purposes, glassmaking or other industrial uses)		81.9	100.0	114.2	126.6	139.1
Extraction of ball and china clays		83.1	100.0	107.5	120.8	120.8
Non-metallic mineral products	**24**					
Structural clay products	2410	78.1	100.0	113.4	125.3	134.8
Common, facing and engineering bricks		77.5	100.0	113.5	125.7	135.6
Common bricks		76.5	100.0	114.3	126.6	135.4
Non-fletton (ex-works)		74.4	100.0	113.0	122.9	129.2
Fletton (delivered)		79.9	100.0	116.3	132.8	145.7
Facing bricks		78.3	100.0	113.6	125.9	136.0
Non-fletton (ex-works)		79.9	100.0	111.8	124.5	134.8
Fletton (delivered)		76.0	100.0	116.2	128.0	137.7
Clay roofing tiles (plain and single lap)		79.8	100.0	120.1	134.8	149.7
Cement, lime and plaster	2420					
Calcareous cement (other than clinker), delivered – 25 miles		76.5	100.0	113.4	124.1	124.1
Calcareous cement (delivered in bulk – 25 miles)		76.3	100.0	113.4	124.1	124.1
Calcareous cement (delivered in bags – 25 miles)		76.9	100.0	113.5	124.1	124.1
Ready-mixed concrete	2436	81.3	100.0	110.9	121.3	129.1
Other building products of concrete, cement or plaster	2437	85.8	100.0	108.8	119.1	123.7
Plasterboard		83.1	100.0	112.2	123.3	126.3
Flagstones		81.3	100.0	108.9	116.5	125.2
Kerbs and edgings		81.4	100.0	109.0	118.5	123.3
Concrete pipes to BS 556		96.7	100.0	98.6	100.1	94.9
Asbestos goods	2440	84.5	100.0	109.0	120.6	129.3
Working of stone and other non-metallic minerals not elsewhere specified	2450	80.7	100.0	113.3	126.6	138.7
Limestone and dolomite		80.7	100.0	110.7	125.1	137.6
Uncoated limestone roadstone and aggregates		85.8	100.0	106.7	120.1	133.2
Granite		79.2	100.0	114.3	127.0	140.4
Granite and other chippings, aggregates and roadstone		81.7	100.0	110.6	123.8	138.0
Coated granite, and whinstone, roadstone		77.3	100.0	117.1	129.5	142.2
Bituminous and flax felts (incl sarking and sheathing felts)		79.6	100.0	115.2	129.3	141.1
Insulating materials for thermal or acoustic purposes		84.7	100.0	114.6	125.5	136.7
Mineral wool (rock and slag)		86.6	100.0	112.4	123.8	132.7
Abrasive products	2460	85.9	100.0	110.1	121.6	134.7
Abrasive wheels, disc wheels, segments, sharpening stones, and other shapes or forms of bonded abrasives, including diamond		85.3	100.0	111.1	122.8	134.9
Coated abrasives – abrasive paper and cloth		86.9	100.0	108.4	119.6	134.2
Glass containers		85.4	100.0	107.7	112.7	112.3
Glass products (other than flat glass or glass containers)	2479					
Domestic and ornamental glassware		81.6	100.0	107.7	120.9	123.7
Refractory goods	2481					
Refractory bricks and shapes		84.2	100.0	112.2	118.9	123.1
Firebricks and shapes		79.6	100.0	118.0	126.7	131.7
Ceramic goods	2489	82.8	100.0	110.5	119.8	129.0
Vitreous china sanitary ware		79.5	100.0	111.7	123.9	131.7
Wash basins, all types		76.5	100.0	112.1	124.4	128.8
WC pans, all types		79.1	100.0	111.9	124.4	135.9
Chemical industry	**25**					
Inorganic chemicals except industrial gases	2511	83.5	100.0	109.0	118.7	125.4
Chemical elements excl elemental gases		83.7	100.0	110.4	112.6	112.6
Inorganic acids and oxygen compounds of non-metals		82.0	100.0	109.1	122.5	130.2
Sulphuric acid and oleum		75.3	100.0	116.7	130.6	138.2
Metallic oxides and inorganic bases		88.0	100.0	111.7	120.8	124.5
Metallic salts and peroxy salts of inorganic acids		83.9	100.0	105.9	116.1	124.2
Soda ash		82.5	100.0	105.6	117.4	122.6
Metallic salts and peroxy salts of inorganic acids other than soda ash		84.4	100.0	106.0	115.7	124.7
Basic organic chemicals except specialised pharmaceutical chemicals	2512	88.4	100.0	102.6	109.4	113.6
Halogenated sulphonated, nitrated or nitrosated derivatives of hydrocarbons		87.4	100.0	92.9	92.9	100.6
Alcohols, phenols and phenol-alcohols		90.2	100.0	100.1	106.2	109.4
Carboxylic acids and specified derivatives		90.8	100.0	99.9	103.5	103.8
Fertilisers	2513	85.2	100.0	110.5	115.3	116.1

1. Division, class or activity heading.

Source Business Statistics Office

313

18.3

Producer price index numbers of commodities produced in the United Kingdom (home sales)
Annual averages

(continued)

1980 = 100

	1980 SIC[1]	1979	1980	1981	1982	1983
Synthetic resins and plastics materials	2514	91.2	100.0	97.0	100.7	107.4
Products of polymerisation and copolymerisation		92.6	100.0	95.3	97.5	106.6
Acrylic lattices, dispersions and solutions, and moulding and extrusion compounds, cast sheet rod and tube		84.5	100.0	103.4	109.9	120.2
Styrene polymers and copolymers		91.0	100.0	94.5	90.0	95.8
Dyestuffs and pigments	2516	89.2	100.0	100.9	107.8	108.1
Paints, varnishes and painters' fillings	2551					
Building, structural, preservative and decorative products – non-aqueous, oil and/or synthetic based		85.3	100.0	105.0	110.2	114.0
Filling and sealing compounds of all types		85.7	100.0	110.2	115.4	122.8
Chemical treatment of oil and fats	2563					
Fatty acids (excluding acid oils)		109.4	100.0	102.0	110.3	121.6
Miscellaneous chemical products for industrial use	2567					
Wax, refined, blended, bleached, etc. and foundry facings		82.5	100.0	104.6	112.3	116.8
Formulated pesticides	2558	86.4	100.0	107.3	111.5	112.3
Pesticides		80.3	100.0	110.5	117.4	117.9
Insecticides (other than seed dressings) containing organo-phosphorus compounds		94.3	100.0	101.8	109.7	115.9
Preparations for plant control		86.9	100.0	105.8	108.7	109.6
Herbicides containing phenoxy derivatives of acetic, propionic or butyric acids		77.4	100.0	106.1	104.3	98.4
Adhesive film, cloth and foil	2569					
Adhesive film, tape, etc. of plastics or cellulose, adhesive cloth and foil		85.0	100.0	109.6	115.6	123.5
Pharmaceutical products	2570	87.1	100.0	111.7	120.6	126.3
Antipyretics (analgesics)		80.9	100.0	117.9	134.0	143.2
Plain hypotensives (cardiovascular system)		91.8	100.0	101.2	109.4	117.4
Cough and cold preparations		81.0	100.0	121.8	134.5	142.3
Preparations for the alimentary tract and nutrition		86.7	100.0	111.3	122.8	129.3
Antacids and anti-ulcerants		95.3	100.0	104.8	117.7	123.6
Vitamins and mineral supplements		76.8	100.0	112.6	121.1	125.6
Muscular and skeletal systems (systemic)		86.4	100.0	105.1	109.4	111.3
Dermatologicals		83.8	100.0	110.4	117.4	118.8
Antibiotics		87.8	100.0	109.9	114.0	115.1
Disinfectants		82.5	100.0	112.0	122.1	127.8
Surgical and medicated dressings		86.0	100.0	110.9	119.8	129.8
Soap and synthetic detergents	2581	84.6	100.0	104.0	111.0	118.4
Soap (excluding scouring preps)		88.5	100.0	104.3	110.7	116.9
Toilet, in tablet form, (78/80% fatty acid) in packs		91.9	100.0	102.5	106.7	111.8
Finished synthetic detergents (excluding scouring preps) – Liquid		85.0	100.0	97.8	101.7	106.1
Perfumes, cosmetics and toilet preparations	2582					
Men's after shave, cologne and pre-shave lotions in alcoholic lotion form		83.0	100.0	113.3	122.6	128.2
Perfumes, cosmetics and toilet preparations, other than specifically for men		85.2	100.0	110.6	118.3	124.4
Talc and dusting powders and bath preparations		84.1	100.0	110.5	124.1	131.1
Talc and dusting powders		84.0	100.0	108.3	113.7	121.4
Lipsticks and lipglosses, including lipsalve		89.5	100.0	106.2	112.8	115.3
Face powders		81.7	100.0	112.7	128.3	139.2
Liquid and cream		84.6	100.0	109.0	118.9	124.6
Deodorants, anti-perspirants and dipilatories		83.6	100.0	113.9	119.6	120.0
Toothpaste and dental powders		87.1	100.0	105.8	107.4	111.9
Soapless shampoos		83.0	100.0	112.7	119.1	121.5
Photographic materials and chemicals	2591	76.5	100.0	102.5	110.1	116.1
Man-made fibres	**26**					
Man-made fibres	2600	94.2	100.0	99.8	110.3	116.5
Manufacture of metal goods not elsewhere specified	**31**					
Ferrous foundry products	3111	86.4	100.0	106.1	113.2	116.1
Iron castings in the rough or machined		86.8	100.0	105.4	112.2	114.9
Engineers castings		86.8	100.0	105.7	110.7	111.8
Vehicle iron castings		87.8	100.0	105.6	109.4	110.4
Industrial and marine machinery and plant		85.5	100.0	106.0	112.5	113.6
Heavy engineering		84.2	100.0	107.1	115.5	118.8
Light engineering		87.2	100.0	104.8	112.2	115.0
Castings other than engineers		86.9	100.0	104.8	114.6	119.8
Non-alloy steel castings, excluding engineers		81.7	100.0	110.6	118.2	129.5
Stainless and heat resisting alloy steel castings, excluding engineers		82.6	100.0	115.6	127.4	130.4
Other alloy steel castings, excluding engineers		81.6	100.0	115.2	126.4	129.4
Malleable iron castings		90.4	100.0	105.4	112.5	118.5
Forging, pressing and stamping steel forging	3120	88.0	100.0	104.9	111.3	116.8
Bolts, nuts, washers, springs and non-precision chains	3137	87.7	100.0	105.0	121.3	126.3
Bolts, nuts, washers, rivets, etc. of iron or steel		87.8	100.0	104.4	122.5	127.4
All bolt products including machine screws, studs and socket screws		88.2	100.0	107.4	130.8	136.3
Of high tensile steel		88.6	100.0	109.8	136.6	138.9
Of mild steel		87.6	100.0	103.8	122.7	132.3
Metal doors, windows, etc.	3142					
Metal windows and doors (excl strongroom doors and doors for motor vehicles) door frames, window frames, casements and curtain walling		85.3	100.0	107.3	113.9	124.6

1. Division, class or activity heading.

Source Business Statistics Office

18.3

Producer price index numbers of commodities produced in the United Kingdom (home sales)
Annual averages

(*continued*)

1980 = 100

	1980 SIC[1]	1979	1980	1981	1982	1983
Hand tools and implements	3161	83.2	100.0	113.4	121.7	128.2
Agricultural hand tools		84.3	100.0	111.1	119.9	129.1
Other hand tools		82.7	100.0	114.4	122.5	127.8
Handsaws and blades		82.3	100.0	115.0	127.4	136.1
Hacksaw blades		82.2	100.0	115.4	125.9	134.2
Spanners and wrenches		83.8	100.0	111.5	119.8	125.6
Hammers, screwdrivers, chisels and planes		83.5	100.0	112.7	121.1	128.5
Hammers		83.0	100.0	104.7	103.1	105.9
Cutlery, spoons, forks and similar tableware: razors	3162					
Cutlery, spoons, forks and similar tableware		77.6	100.0	106.8	115.3	122.8
Silver plated finished spoons and forks of all kinds		66.4	100.0	107.6	113.5	121.9
Scissors and tailors shears including pinking shears		86.1	100.0	108.8	116.6	120.7
Packaging products of metal	3164	87.5	100.0	103.2	109.5	116.3
Metal cans and boxes		85.8	100.0	104.0	108.2	114.9
Metal kegs, drums and barrels		93.0	100.0	102.9	117.9	124.3
New, of wrought iron and steel		93.5	100.0	103.2	119.9	127.0
Reconditioned		88.5	100.0	99.6	99.9	99.9
Domestic heating and cooking appliances (non-electric)	3165	86.1	100.0	113.7	122.8	129.9
Gas cookers		85.2	100.0	115.1	126.8	134.4
Gas fires and space heaters (excluding gas central heating equipment)		88.0	100.0	112.2	119.6	125.6
Metal furniture and safes	3166					
Office seating, wholly or mainly of metal – other than adjustable		87.1	100.0	110.0	117.0	121.2
Domestic and similar utensils of metal	3167					
Pressure cookers, percolators and other domestic holloware		89.4	100.0	111.5	116.4	103.7
Finished metal products nes	3169	87.1	100.0	105.7	110.2	115.3
Locks, padlocks, latches, keys and blanks including bicycle locks (excluding for motor vehicles and time locks)		82.3	100.0	110.4	120.0	126.3
Knitting machinery elements and needles		86.1	100.0	111.0	117.8	126.3
Base metal fittings and mountings for furniture, builders joinery, leather and travel goods nes		86.9	100.0	105.8	114.6	122.9
Door and door frames		83.1	100.0	109.3	118.8	128.4
Sanitary ware and plumbing fixtures and fittings		88.4	100.0	103.0	100.1	100.8
Bath, basin, sink taps		90.2	100.0	106.1	114.3	119.9
Aluminium ladders and steps		91.9	100.0	104.1	105.8	113.7
Fire extinguishers (hand operated chemical type)		83.4	100.0	111.0	122.2	134.7
Mechanical engineering	**32**					
Agricultural machinery	3211	88.3	100.0	104.9	112.1	114.1
Soil preparations and cultivation machinery		88.5	100.0	101.8	106.3	110.3
Parts for soil preparation and cultivation machinery		90.5	100.0	93.5	100.1	104.7
Harvesting and threshing machinery		88.1	100.0	106.6	113.0	118.4
Pick-up balers		85.5	100.0	108.3	113.9	117.7
Bale handling machinery tractor/trailer mounted		90.0	100.0	106.0	111.3	121.6
Grain and grass dryers		87.9	100.0	110.5	126.8	127.2
Dairy, feed processing and other agricultural machines		88.3	100.0	106.4	115.1	114.1
Milking machinery		90.5	100.0	104.6	116.0	123.9
Agricultural elevators and conveyors (inc. grain augers)		87.3	100.0	106.4	119.5	127.5
Wheeled tractors	3212					
Wheeled tractors, complete (including KD tractors of a minimum value of 50% of a corresponding complete tractor)		89.4	100.0	108.5	114.8	124.9
Metal working machine tools	3221	85.0	100.0	107.4	115.9	123.1
Metal cutting machine tools		84.2	100.0	106.4	114.9	119.9
Non numerically controlled metal cutting machine tools complete		83.0	100.0	107.3	116.2	122.3
Non numerically controlled grinding machines		82.2	100.0	107.8	112.0	115.8
Non numerically controlled milling machines		83.6	100.0	103.9	111.1	118.2
Non numerically controlled turning machines		82.0	100.0	111.0	121.3	125.8
Non numerically controlled metal forming machine tools		88.1	100.0	111.2	120.0	136.6
Presses: mechanical		85.7	100.0	108.4	104.5	101.2
Engineers small tools	3222					
Hard tipped and other metal cutting tools		86.1	100.0	108.7	117.0	125.2
Diamond tipped tools and diamond dies		88.5	100.0	109.9	116.2	122.0
Bandsaws and blades for metal		86.9	100.0	108.6	117.2	120.8
Twist drills and bit stock drills		82.9	100.0	108.7	116.7	122.9
Milling cutters		84.3	100.0	108.7	119.5	127.8
Lathe and planer tools		83.2	100.0	107.3	114.5	122.7
Food, drink and tobacco processing machinery; packaging and bottling machinery	3244	86.4	100.0	111.0	125.7	136.2
Food and drink processing machinery		87.2	100.0	108.6	119.0	125.4
Bakery and confectionary machinery (including parts)		91.2	100.0	104.7	111.8	117.1
Grain milling machinery and plant (including parts)		87.2	100.0	113.6	122.4	123.6
Machines for filling, closing, sealing, capsuling or labelling containers		84.1	100.0	113.2	129.4	136.0

1. Division, class or activity heading.

Source Business Statistics Office

18.3
Producer price index numbers of commodities produced in the United Kingdom (home sales)
Annual averages

(*continued*)

1980 = 100

	1980 SIC[1]	1979	1980	1981	1982	1983
Mining machinery	3251	85.9	100.0	109.8	116.8	133.2
Mineral transport machinery		85.7	100.0	110.2	119.4	124.7
Construction and earth moving equipment	3254	90.4	100.0	108.9	116.4	119.7
Excavators, trenchers, ditchers and similar digging machinery including parts		87.7	100.0	105.8	115.1	120.3
Wheeled tractor shovels		92.5	100.0	108.5	119.6	124.8
Dumpers and dump trucks		88.6	100.0	108.1	117.7	123.5
Equipment for concrete, crushing and screening and road works		87.5	100.0	109.6	116.8	120.2
Concrete mixing and placing machinery and parts		87.6	100.0	107.8	117.8	121.4
Road making and maintenance plant		86.6	100.0	110.9	117.8	124.3
Road rollers and parts		87.6	100.0	103.6	113.9	123.1
Crushing, pulverising and screening plants including parts		88.5	100.0	109.3	114.9	114.7
Mechanical lifting and handling equipment	3255	88.2	100.0	108.2	115.9	120.9
Cranes and transporters		91.5	100.0	106.5	115.5	121.3
Lifting and winding devices		86.4	100.0	110.4	119.8	121.9
Lifting jacks, vehicle jacks and lifts		82.9	100.0	108.3	116.1	120.1
Capstans, winches, windlasses		88.4	100.0	112.2	128.7	124.5
Powered industrial trucks		88.2	100.0	108.6	115.0	121.9
Fork lift trucks		88.4	100.0	108.5	114.6	121.4
Precision chains and other mechanical power transmission equipment	3261					
Transmission chains		84.6	100.0	105.2	115.9	120.1
Ball, needle and roller bearings	3262					
Machinery for working wood, rubber, plastics, leather and making paper, glass, bricks and similar materials; laundry and dry cleaning machinery	3275	83.3	100.0	110.2	118.2	123.7
Woodworking machinery		82.7	100.0	110.6	117.4	124.0
Sawing		87.4	100.0	108.1	116.0	121.6
Brick, tile, cement and concrete block, pottery and other ceramic making machinery		85.1	100.0	109.6	116.4	112.2
Laundry and dry cleaning machinery						
Internal combustion engines (except for road vehicles, wheeled agricultural tractors and aircraft) and other prime movers	3281	90.0	100.0	106.1	112.2	121.4
Compression ignition IC engines. Industrial		85.3	100.0	111.4	119.8	125.5
IC marine engines, propelling, up to 50 kW		89.3	100.0	110.8	120.4	126.1
Compressors and fluid power equipment	3283	85.4	100.0	109.2	119.4	127.8
Compressors		84.4	100.0	110.1	115.7	122.1
Oil hydraulic pumps		84.4	100.0	106.9	115.6	125.0
Oil hydraulic control valves		84.8	100.0	110.1	116.6	124.3
Pneumatic control equipment		86.3	100.0	113.4	125.3	134.3
Directional control, flow control, check and non-return valves and moving and non-moving fluidic devices		86.0	100.0	114.0	125.4	133.9
Other pneumatic control equipment (including pressure control valves)		86.5	100.0	113.0	125.2	134.6
Refrigerating machinery, space heating, ventilating and air conditioning equipment	3284					
Space heating equipment		86.1	100.0	110.5	123.5	134.9
Boilers for central heating		84.3	100.0	109.6	117.3	125.0
Heat emitters		88.3	100.0	111.5	130.9	146.8
Scales, weighing machinery and portable power tools	3285	87.1	100.0	108.8	116.0	120.2
Scales and weighing machinery complete and parts		84.7	100.0	112.0	118.2	121.5
Portable power tools		88.3	100.0	107.1	114.8	119.4
Portable power tools non-electric		86.4	100.0	110.5	120.5	128.0
Pneumatic, petrol, hydraulic and other tools for civil engineering, mining and quarrying		88.7	100.0	110.6	118.1	126.5
Pneumatic, petrol, hydraulic and other tools for general engineering etc		84.1	100.0	110.4	122.8	129.4
Portable power tools (electric)		90.0	100.0	105.2	110.4	112.4
Portable power driven saws, complete and parts		89.6	100.0	100.4	109.3	113.4
Other industrial and commercial machinery	3286					
Garage equipment and plant nes		87.5	100.0	109.9	116.8	123.1
Pumps	3287	85.1	100.0	106.4	113.5	121.6
Centrifugal pumps		87.5	100.0	110.0	113.4	123.4
Positive displacement hand pumps		78.5	100.0	110.4	118.8	125.7
Industrial valves	3288					
Valves of metal		86.0	100.0	111.0	127.4	136.1
Manufacture of office machinery and data processing equipment	**33**					
Office machinery	3301	86.9	100.0	114.8	110.2	112.1
Electrical and electronic engineering	**34**					
Insulated wires and cables	3410	80.8	100.0	102.8	111.5	124.8
Mains (power distribution) cables 600/1000 volts and over		79.3	100.0	103.2	110.4	115.9
Winding wires and strips		87.2	100.0	95.1	103.4	111.2
Batteries and accumulators	3432	90.5	100.0	99.5	103.3	109.1
Electrical equipment for motor vehicles, cycles and aircraft	3434	85.3	100.0	111.7	117.1	122.7

1. Division, class or activity heading.

Source   Business Statistics Office

18.3
Producer price index numbers of commodities produced in the United Kingdom (home sales)
Annual averages

(continued)

1980 = 100

	1980 SIC[1]	1979	1980	1981	1982	1983
Electrical instruments and control systems	3442	86.8	100.0	106.2	112.9	120.6
Electricity supply meters		86.4	100.0	116.2	129.6	137.8
Electrical measuring, testing and controlling instruments and apparatus		89.9	100.0	108.9	121.1	133.9
Ammeters, voltmeters, wattmeters		88.8	100.0	107.4	117.5	130.0
Frequency meters electronic counters and timers, frequency converters and accessories for use with counters		93.4	100.0	106.0	121.8	152.9
Gramophone records and tape recordings	3452	89.5	100.0	103.7	109.5	114.3
Gramophone records		88.0	100.0	105.0	111.6	116.6
33⅓ rpm		89.2	100.0	103.0	106.5	111.0
45 rpm		85.9	100.0	108.4	120.4	126.2
Cassettes		95.2	100.0	96.8	98.3	102.3
Electronic consumer goods and other electronic equipment nes	3454					
Electronic consumer goods		99.1	100.0	100.0	98.1	98.1
Television receivers		99.1	100.0	99.5	97.6	98.5
Colour		99.4	100.0	99.4	97.3	98.4
Domestic-type electric appliances	3460	88.1	100.0	105.2	103.2	106.3
Electric cooking apparatus		83.9	100.0	108.2	112.6	114.6
Electric kettles		83.6	100.0	106.5	105.5	104.2
Electric heating apparatus		85.4	100.0	111.0	120.1	128.1
Space heating apparatus		85.6	100.0	107.1	111.2	115.5
Refrigerators and freezers		87.6	100.0	103.3	106.3	114.7
Electric lamps and other electric lighting equipment	3470					
Electric lamps bulbs and tubes		81.5	100.0	113.7	126.7	137.8
Electric lamps bulbs, filament type		78.9	100.0	114.1	127.6	139.1
Lamp and lighting fittings and parts thereof		82.5	100.0	109.8	119.3	126.4
For tubular fluorescent lamps, of base metal		81.4	100.0	110.7	120.2	124.6
Other, of base metal (excluding for street or domestic lighting)		84.4	100.0	109.9	118.3	128.0
Motor vehicles and parts thereof	**35**					
Motor vehicles and their engines	3510	88.8	100.0	108.8	115.4	119.9
Passenger cars		90.5	100.0	108.7	115.8	119.8
Passenger cars (inclusive of VAT and car tax)		88.0	100.0	108.7	115.9	119.7
Goods vehicles		87.3	100.0	108.0	114.1	120.4
Not exceeding 3.5 tons gvw		87.5	100.0	109.1	115.4	121.9
Exceeding 3.5 tons but not exceeding 16 tons gvw		86.8	100.0	108.3	116.0	124.9
Exceeding 16 tons gvw		87.7	100.0	105.4	109.5	112.5
Other transport equipment	**36**					
Railway and tramway vehicles	3620					
Railway and tramway rolling stock and parts (excluding Diesel and Electric locomotives and parts)		87.1	100.0	106.5	110.1	112.4
Railway and tramway goods vans, goods wagons and trucks, combination road/rail freight vehicles (complete)		88.1	100.0	109.3	113.6	136.9
Instrument engineering	**37**					
Measuring, checking and precision instruments and apparatus	3710	88.1	100.0	111.2	122.1	132.0
Level measuring and control instruments		88.7	100.0	115.0	127.8	138.2
Pressure measuring and control instruments		86.9	100.0	112.5	122.8	133.8
Pressure gauges		82.8	100.0	110.9	120.5	130.0
Surveying, hydrographic, navigational meteorological and geophysical instruments		86.3	100.0	113.6	130.2	144.9
Counting and velocity measuring instruments		86.1	100.0	117.1	131.7	141.8
Speedometers and tachometers		86.1	100.0	117.4	132.4	142.5
Inspection and measuring instruments and tools for measuring and marking out		83.9	100.0	112.3	122.4	128.1
Engineers gauges and measuring instruments		84.7	100.0	110.4	114.1	115.7
Mechanical measuring instruments		84.9	100.0	109.3	115.2	116.5
Medical and surgical equipment and orthopaedic appliances	3720					
Medical surgical veterinary and dissecting instruments, other than hyperdemic syringes and catheters		87.4	100.0	112.4	118.1	122.8
Surgical hosiery		89.6	100.0	112.6	130.9	140.2
Photographic and cinematographic equipment	3733	92.2	100.0	106.3	113.9	104.6
Lenses, prisms, gratings and other optically worked elements, mounted		85.4	100.0	110.4	130.8	151.4
Clocks, watches and other timing devices	3740					
Clocks		91.1	100.0	102.0	101.3	99.2
Complete battery operated electric clocks		95.3	100.0	102.4	106.1	100.6
Food, drink and tobacco manufacturing industries	**41/42**					
Margarine and compound cooking fats	4115	98.2	100.0	101.2	103.5	107.6
Processing organic oils and fats (other than crude animal fat production)	4116	114.4	100.0	103.1	125.3	
Slaughterhouses	4121	97.9	100.0	114.1	123.2	122.2
Bacon curing and meat processing	4122	87.1	100.0	107.7	117.8	120.3
Poultry slaughter and processing	4123	97.1	100.0	99.9	109.2	109.5
Animal by-product processing	4126	119.4	100.0	113.2	119.8	122.6

1. Division, class or activity.

Source Business Statistics Office

18.3

Producer price index numbers of commodities produced in the United Kingdom (home sales)
Annual averages

(continued)

1980 = 100

	1980 SIC[1]	1979	1980	1981	1982	1983
Preparation of milk and milk products	4130	87.1	100.0	111.3	121.0	126.0
Processing of fruit and vegetables	4147	88.6	100.0	106.3	117.9	122.9
Fish processing	4150	90.6	100.0	105.8	109.8	116.6
Grain milling	4160	89.3	100.0	107.4	113.8	119.1
Starch	4180	88.1	100.0	114.3	121.0	121.5
Bread and flour confectionery	4196	86.9	100.0	108.6	115.6	121.3
Biscuits and crispbread	4197	88.1	100.0	103.6	109.1	113.7
Sugar and sugar by-products	4200	87.5	100.0	109.4	121.2	128.6
Ice cream	4213	84.0	100.0	111.9	118.0	123.2
Cocoa, chocolate and sugar confectionery	4214	89.3	100.0	107.4	110.8	115.1
Compound animal feeds	4221	93.5	100.0	107.9	114.8	122.8
Pet foods and non-compound animal feeds	4222	87.7	100.0	106.2	111.4	116.9
Miscellaneous foods	4239	91.4	100.0	106.3	112.5	124.4
Wines, cider and perry	4261	86.9	100.0	115.6	132.1	144.0
Brewing and malting	4270					
Beer		84.6	100.0	123.2	138.7	148.6
Soft drinks	4283	87.6	100.0	110.8	120.2	130.2
Tobacco industries	4290	88.7	100.0	127.3	145.6	156.1
Cigarettes (tipped), duty paid		88.3	100.0	127.8	146.4	157.2
Hand rolling and pipe tobacco, duty paid		92.0	100.0	123.7	140.9	149.4
Textile industry	**43**					
Woollen and Worsted industry	4310					
All wool worsted yarns, spun on the worsted and semi-worsted systems		93.1	100.0	105.9	112.6	119.4
Worsted yarns of man-made fibres, spun on the worsted and semi-worsted systems		90.1	100.0	107.0	114.5	120.5
Wholly of man-made fibres		89.3	100.0	107.4	115.0	121.0
Weaving		91.6	100.0	105.6	112.7	119.3
Apparel cloths containing 50% or more by weight of wool or fine animal hair, woven woollen fabric		91.2	100.0	106.2	113.1	117.1
Apparel cloths containing 50% or more by weight of wool or fine animal hair, woven worsted fabric		92.5	100.0	104.8	112.0	119.2
Spinning and doubling on the cotton system	4321	92.2	100.0	101.8	104.0	112.9
Spinning		93.4	100.0	99.8	100.9	111.5
Finished thread for sewing, embroidery, etc, doubling and winding		86.9	100.0	106.2	111.9	116.6
For industrial uses of man-made fibre		89.7	100.0	105.9	111.9	114.6
Weaving of cotton and silk and man-made fibres	4322					
Woven fabric of glass fibre		82.5	100.0	106.3	117.9	125.5
Jute and polypropylene yarns and fabrics	4350					
Woven cloth of polypropylene		107.5	100.0	90.8	90.9	90.8
Hosiery and other weft knitted goods and fabrics	4363					
Hosiery incl tights and pantie-hose		88.7	100.0	104.9	109.2	113.9
Tights and pantie-hose		85.9	100.0	105.2	107.6	111.2
Children's and infants socks and stockings		86.0	100.0	105.6	106.6	111.8
Men's knitted underwear		84.9	100.0	102.4	109.8	116.4
Men's fully fashioned outerwear of wool		86.7	100.0	109.5	113.5	118.3
Pile carpets, carpeting and rugs	4384	89.2	100.0	104.4	110.2	116.0
Woven carpets, carpeting and carpet type rugs		87.9	100.0	105.6	111.8	117.3
Containing 50% or more of wool yarn		88.2	100.0	106.1	112.5	117.9
Figured and plain Brussels and Wilton		88.1	100.0	106.4	112.5	118.1
Spool and Gripper Axminster		88.2	100.0	105.8	112.6	117.8
Tufted carpets, carpeting and carpet type rugs containing 50% or more by weight of acryllic and polyamide fibres		91.6	100.0	103.2	108.6	115.5
Carpets, carpeting, rugs and matting nes	4385					
Needlefelt for carpet underlay		87.6	100.0	108.0	110.9	112.5
Rope, twine and net	4396	87.1	100.0	103.9	107.7	113.4
Twines, cords, ropes, cables and lines of textile materials other than agricultural twine		86.9	100.0	102.1	104.4	107.6
Narrow fabrics	4398					
Non elastic and non-elastomeric goods not exceeding 30 cms in width – Petersham, galloons and ribbons		84.7	100.0	107.3	114.5	119.4
Miscellaneous textiles nes	4399					
Felt (and bonded fibres fabrics)		85.1	100.0	109.5	120.7	131.1
Leather and leather goods	**44**					
Leather goods	4420	89.9	100.0	104.7	109.3	113.1
Travel goods and similar articles		90.5	100.0	108.8	112.8	117.0
Travel goods of all materials other than metal or wicker; trunks, etc		89.7	100.0	105.9	107.2	109.3
Folio and document cases, satchels, shopping bags, etc.		91.8	100.0	113.3	121.7	129.1

1. Division, class or activity heading.

Source Business Statistics Office

18.3

Producer price index numbers of commodities produced in the United Kingdom (home sales)
Annual averages

(*continued*)

1980 = 100

	1980 SIC[1]	1979	1980	1981	1982	1983
Footwear and clothing industries	**45**					
Footwear	4510	85.2	100.0	107.7	112.3	116.6
Outdoor footwear		85.0	100.0	107.4	112.3	115.9
With uppers wholly or mainly of leather		84.9	100.0	106.8	110.9	114.2
Women's		85.0	100.0	108.1	113.6	117.8
Women's, with uppers wholly or mainly of plastics including poromeric – other than sandals or sandalised shoes		86.1	100.0	111.2	120.2	123.7
Men's and boys' tailored outerwear	4532					
Men's trousers, sold separately		89.8	100.0	102.0	104.3	
Work clothing and men's and boys' jeans	4534					
Cotton boilersuits, men's and boys'		96.6	100.0	104.2	113.7	116.3
Men's and boys' shirts, underwear and nightwear	4535	92.6	100.0	103.2	105.2	108.6
Shirts (other than industrial shirts)		93.4	100.0	102.6	102.4	105.3
Woven		93.4	100.0	102.6	102.4	105.3
Pyjamas and other nightwear		95.2	100.0	101.9	109.9	113.9
Gloves	4538					
Leather/fur gloves, mittens and mitts (Leather/fur contents exceeding 50% value)		84.0	100.0	98.6	95.2	98.4
Men's dresswear		84.8	100.0	103.4	100.2	106.5
Women's dresswear		83.8	100.0	100.0	99.6	103.2
Fabric gloves, mittens and mitts (fabric content exceeding 50% value) for dresswear, other than children's		90.2	100.0	107.9	117.7	121.5
Dress industries nes	4539					
Corsetry		88.4	100.0	105.4	112.8	116.7
Canvas goods, sacks and other made up textiles	4556					
Sacks and bags of vegetable fibre or woven polypropylene		91.6	100.0	95.9	98.9	107.2
Household textiles	4557					
Tea towels		85.1	100.0	102.0	107.8	111.4
Hand and bath towels of terry cotton		87.7	100.0	101.9	103.1	107.0
Nursery squares		87.9	100.0	102.3	105.0	107.6
Timber and wooden furniture industries	**46**					
Sawmilling, planing, etc. of wood	4610					
Homegrown hardwood, sawn		88.4	100.0	99.6	99.4	103.2
Builders carpentry and joinery	4630	87.3	100.0	107.7	116.4	124.7
Builders woodwork and prefabricated building structures		87.2	100.0	107.9	116.9	125.1
Doorsets, leaves and frames and window frames		85.9	100.0	107.0	114.8	124.1
Doorsets, leaves and frames		87.4	100.0	104.7	113.1	121.8
Door leaves flush		90.0	100.0	105.7	114.2	121.5
Door leaves other than flush including louvred doors		84.6	100.0	101.1	109.4	120.7
Window frames		83.9	100.0	110.2	117.1	127.3
Other wooden articles (except furniture)	4650					
Domestic woodware		86.8	100.0	105.8	111.2	115.2
Wooden and upholstered furniture	4671					
Kitchen furniture, wooden		87.1	100.0	108.1	113.3	123.4
Desks and desking		84.5	100.0	111.2	117.5	123.6
Paper and paper products: printing and publishing	**47**					
Pulp, paper and board	4710	89.2	100.0	106.8	115.2	116.8
Printing and writing papers other than newsprint		89.4	100.0	109.9	119.9	122.2
Wrapping and packaging papers		86.6	100.0	105.1	113.1	113.8
Flutings and liners for corrugated board		87.0	100.0	102.8	108.7	108.3
Household toilet papers and tissues		88.8	100.0	105.8	114.2	115.0
Industrial and special purpose papers		91.7	100.0	104.1	111.6	116.1
Packaging boards including corrugated		88.6	100.0	102.9	108.4	109.1
Household and personal hygiene products of paper	4722	83.0	100.0	112.0	127.4	130.6
Toilet paper		81.4	100.0	111.4	129.2	130.8
Kitchen rolls and towels		83.4	100.0	111.8	126.9	128.1
Sanitary towels and tampons		85.1	100.0	119.1	131.7	142.8
Stationery	4723					
Commercial envelopes		82.8	100.0	108.6	118.9	127.5
Filing supplies		89.1	100.0	113.2	122.5	129.9
Packaging products of paper and pulp	4724					
Paper sacks		88.0	100.0	103.9	114.2	118.8
Packaging products of board	4725	85.4	100.0	106.1	114.5	119.3
Fibre-board packing cases		84.5	100.0	107.7	118.9	124.2
Printing and publishing other than of newspapers, periodicals and books	4754					
Atlases, maps, charts and globes		88.7	100.0	115.4	127.2	140.8

1. Division, class or activity heading.

Source Business Statistics Office

18.3 Producer price index numbers of commodities produced in the United Kingdom (home sales)
Annual averages

(*continued*)

1980 = 100

	1980 SIC[1]	1979	1980	1981	1982	1983
Processing of rubber and plastics	**48**					
Rubber tyres and inner tubes	4811					
New tyre covers		86.9	100.0	101.6	108.5	113.2
Radial ply, car and van		87.8	100.0	99.5	105.9	110.8
Commercial vehicles		86.6	100.0	102.3	109.8	115.3
Other rubber products	4812					
Rubber or plastics belting		87.5	100.0	101.6	107.7	110.9
Footwear components		83.7	100.0	106.2	113.7	119.3
Plastics – semi manufactures	4832	88.3	100.0	101.6	108.9	117.6
Plastics floorcoverings	4833	85.6	100.0	108.5	118.0	126.6
Plastics building products	4834					
Pipes and fittings		82.7	100.0	101.3	107.2	114.9
Soil waste pipes and fittings		80.6	100.0	105.8	117.5	124.9
Rainwater pipes and fittings		82.7	100.0	104.0	113.8	120.9
Plastics packaging products	4835					
Bottles up to and including 1 litre capacity – PVC		99.1	100.0	91.2	100.5	103.0
Pots and jars		88.6	100.0	108.1	115.2	112.7
Up to and including 0.25 litre capacity		87.1	100.0	106.2	115.3	116.3
Polystyrene		88.0	100.0	106.3	115.2	115.6
Closed transit containers		82.2	100.0	97.4	107.1	109.5
Plastics products nes	4836					
Haberdashery (including slide and zip fasteners)		88.9	100.0	110.0	111.9	113.6
Other manufacturing industries	**49**					
Muscial instruments	4920					
New keyboard instruments (pianos and organs only)		84.5	100.0	105.7	114.2	119.4
Photographic and cinematographic processing leboratories	4930					
Development and printing of cinematographic film		83.7	100.0	104.1	113.7	123.1
Colour		84.4	100.0	103.4	112.7	121.8
16mm		85.1	100.0	102.8	111.3	119.5
35mm		84.0	100.0	103.9	113.6	123.3
Monochrome		72.1	100.0	115.3	130.0	145.6
Toys and games	4941	87.4	100.0	102.8	109.0	115.1
Dolls and soft toys excluding rubber		86.5	100.0	94.0	99.2	102.9
Dolls		85.2	100.0	90.8	95.4	100.3
Toys, wholly or mainly of metal excluding wheeled toys and construction						
models		84.6	100.0	105.7	109.7	114.9
Sports goods		94.1	100.0	107.0	112.6	122.7
Miscellaneous stationers goods	4954					
Ballpoint pens		94.4	100.0	105.8	111.0	113.8
Propelling and other mechanical pencils		95.3	100.0	105.5	108.6	109.9

1. Division, class or activity heading.

Source Business Statistics Office

18.4 Producer price index numbers of commodities wholly or mainly imported into the United Kingdom
Annual averages

1980 = 100

	1979	1980	1981	1982	1983
Hides, skins and fur skins, raw					
Hides and skins (except fur skins)	181.9	100.0	94.1	111.0	125.6
Hides	175.8	100.0	112.4	122.6	153.2
Wet	176.2	100.0	113.2	122.9	154.1
Dry	169.7	100.0	102.0	117.6	141.2
Oilseeds and oleaginous fruit	116.0	100.0	115.8	107.1	138.6
Groundnuts, cif. Rotterdam[1]	126.7	100.0	143.8	100.9	108.9
Soya beans, US No. 2 grade cif. United Kingdom[1]	109.8	100.0	111.2	109.4	144.3
Copra, Philippine, cif. Europe[1]	164.1	100.0	95.9	92.1	166.2
Palm nuts and kernels, Nigerian, cif. Europe[1]	159.1	100.0	106.5	102.3	163.5
Linseed, Canadian No. 1, cif. Rotterdam[1]	103.8	100.0	108.5	105.0	113.4
Crude rubber					
Natural rubber, smoked sheet[1]	94.6	100.0	87.9	78.0	115.4
Cork and wood	88.8	100.0	99.7	101.1	114.6
Sawn logs and veneer logs in the rough (non-coniferous)	84.1	100.0	93.7	96.8	103.4
Wood sawn lengthwise	89.0	100.0	100.0	101.2	115.1
Softwood (delivered to consumers)	88.1	100.0	98.6	98.3	112.6
Hardwood (ex yard or wharf)	93.3	100.0	106.7	116.2	127.6
Utile	84.9	100.0	109.8	107.2	107.7
Keruing	90.9	100.0	102.8	116.6	126.3
Mahogany	92.8	100.0	118.0	128.8	151.5
Ramin	112.9	100.0	99.1	126.2	143.0
Meranti	89.6	100.0	107.0	112.1	122.6
Sapele	84.8	100.0	108.7	108.3	112.9
Iroko	84.1	100.0	95.6	98.8	102.9
Oak	107.0	100.0	101.3	109.0	138.1
Beech	98.1	100.0	102.8	110.8	112.2
Pulp and waste paper					
Woodpulp	89.9	100.0	119.9	125.7	124.6
Sulphate woodpulp	89.4	100.0	119.0	122.1	118.2
Textile fibres and their wastes	97.3	100.0	105.6	106.0	118.5
Raw cotton[1]	90.5	100.0	103.5	103.4	137.7
Raw jute[1]	117.5	100.0	112.5	123.4	135.3
Vegetable textile fibres	102.0	100.0	94.6	111.1	141.8
Wool and other animal hair	103.4	100.0	112.1	114.5	129.4
Sheep or lamb's wool greasy or fleece washed	103.4	100.0	112.1	114.5	126.4
Merino	95.1	100.0	121.7	129.5	142.2
Crossbred	106.5	100.0	108.4	108.8	120.3
Crude fertilisers and crude minerals					
Natural phosphates	79.3	100.0	111.6	104.6	102.0
Clay	97.1	100.0	95.3	97.5	113.2
Asbestos, Canadian, fob. Quebec[1]	99.1	100.0	132.9	155.0	196.3
Quartz, mica, felspar, etc	94.8	100.0	111.3	119.8	120.7
Metalliferous ores					
Alluminium ores and concentrates (including alumina)	90.0	100.0	107.0	110.0	113.5
Manganese ore, 48–50% Mn grade max. 0.1% P, cif. Europe[1]	90.7	100.0	121.1	133.3	128.3
Chromium ores and concentrates[1]	102.3	100.0	116.6	101.8	105.0
Tungsten ore, min. 65%, cif. Europe[1]	105.4	100.0	114.6	97.6	85.6
Titanium ore[1]	99.9	100.0	141.6	166.3	194.1
Petroleum, petroleum products and related materials					
Crude oil[2]	64.7	100.0	129.0	136.7	142.1
Fixed vegetable oils and fats	123.3	100.0	105.0	97.0	138.8
Soyabean oil, Dutch, ex-mill, fob[1]	120.2	100.0	90.5	92.1	124.9
Palm oil, crude, London, spot price[1]	123.5	100.0	108.1	97.4	125.7
Coconut oil, Philippine, cif. Europe[1]	157.3	100.0	96.5	90.7	166.0
Palm kernel oil, Malaysian, cif. Rotterdam[1]	120.1	100.0	104.2	92.9	166.6

1. Source of information: trade publications.
2. Includes imported oil and North Sea oil; the imported oil component is based on unit value of imports at their time of entry.

Source Business Statistics Office

18.4 Producer price index numbers of commodities wholly or mainly imported into the United Kingdom
Annual averages

(*continued*)

1980 = 100

	1979	1980	1981	1982	1983
Organic chemicals	101.8	100.0	97.9	106.2	115.1
Carboxylic acids and their halogenated, sulphonated, nitrated or nitrosated derivatives	101.3	100.0	90.6	100.6	113.7
Nitrogen function compounds	101.5	100.0	101.9	123.8	138.2
Organo-inorganic and heterocyclic compounds	103.2	100.0	92.1	97.9	103.4
Inorganic chemicals					
Fluorine, bromine and iodine	89.6	100.0	105.7	106.4	110.3
Mercury, min. 99.99%, cif Europe[1]	82.7	100.0	124.8	128.5	123.9
Metallic salts and peroxysalts of inorganic acids	95.0	100.0	93.3	96.0	103.5
Essential oils and perfume materials; toilet, polishing and cleansing preparations					
Essential oils, terpenic by-products	116.3	100.0	105.6	117.1	148.8
Artificial resins and plastic materials, and cellulose esters and ethers					
Polymerisation and copolymerisation products	99.7	100.0	96.4	102.7	117.1
Cork and wood manufactures (excluding furniture)					
Plywood and blockboard (delivered to consumers)	92.0	100.0	102.7	110.1	124.8
Paper, paperboard, and articles of paper pulp, of paper or of paperboard					
Paper and paperboard	93.0	100.0	104.4	110.2	109.4
Newsprint paper	98.5	100.0	105.3	113.3	112.6
Uncoated printing or writing paper, in rolls or sheets	93.1	100.0	102.6	107.3	107.3
Non-ferrous metals					
Silver, refined and partly refined[1]	57.8	100.0	57.2	50.5	83.6
Gold, refined and partly refined[1]	54.8	100.0	86.4	81.8	106.2
Copper, LME settlement price[1]	99.5	100.0	91.9	89.9	111.5
Nickel[1]	93.6	100.0	105.9	100.0	110.3
Lead, LME settlement price[1]	145.2	100.0	92.7	79.4	71.7
Zinc, producers' price[1]	108.5	100.0	132.6	140.9	157.8
Zinc, LME settlement price[1]	107.2	100.0	129.5	129.8	154.3
Tin ingot, min. 99.75%, LME settlement price[1]	100.9	100.0	98.0	101.2	118.5
Magnesium[1]	98.7	100.0	101.3	105.7	129.3
Cobalt	105.1	100.0	85.6	58.0	36.6

1. Source of information: trade publications.

Source Business Statistics Office

18.5 Internal purchasing power of the pound[1] (based on RPI)

pence

	Year in which purchasing power was 100p															
	1968	1969	1970	1971	1972	1973	1974	1975	1976	1977	1978	1979	1980	1981	1982	1983
1968	100	105	112	123	131	143	166	207	241	279	302	343	404	452	491	514
1969	95	100	106	116	125	136	158	196	229	265	287	325	384	429	466	488
1970	89	94	100	109	117	128	148	184	215	249	270	306	361	404	438	458
1971	82	86	91	100	107	117	136	168	196	228	246	279	330	369	400	419
1972	76	80	85	93	100	109	127	157	183	212	230	261	308	344	374	391
1973	70	73	78	86	92	100	116	144	168	195	211	239	282	316	343	358
1974	60	63	67	74	79	86	100	124	145	168	182	206	243	272	295	309
1975	48	51	54	59	64	69	80	100	117	135	146	166	196	219	238	249
1976	42	44	47	51	55	60	69	86	100	116	126	142	168	188	204	213
1977	36	38	40	44	47	51	60	74	86	100	108	123	145	162	176	184
1978	33	35	37	41	44	47	55	68	80	92	100	113	134	150	163	170
1979	29	31	33	36	38	42	49	60	70	81	88	100	118	132	143	150
1980	25	26	28	30	32	35	41	51	60	69	75	85	100	112	122	127
1981	22	23	25	27	29	32	37	46	53	62	67	76	89	100	109	114
1982	20	21	23	25	27	29	34	42	49	57	62	70	82	92	100	105
1983	19	20	22	24	26	28	32	40	47	54	59	67	79	88	96	100

Note To find the purchasing power of the pound in 1980, given that it was 100 pence in 1970, select the column headed 1970 and look at the 1980 row. The result is 28 pence.

Source Central Statistical Office

1. These figures are calculated by taking the inverse ratio of the respective annual averages of the General Index of Retail Prices. See table 18.6

18.6 Index of retail prices
Indices for main groups[1]

	All items	Food	Alcoholic drink	Tobacco	Housing	Fuel and light	Durable household goods	Clothing and footwear	Transport and vehicles	Miscellaneous goods	Services	Meals bought and consumed outside the home
17 January 1956 = 100												
Weights 1956 to 1961	*1 000*	*350*	*71*	*80*	*87*	*55*	*66*	*106*	*68*	*59*	*58*	
1962 January 16	117.5	110.7	108.2	123.6	140.6	130.6	102.1	106.6	126.7	128.2	130.1	
16 January 1962 = 100												
Weights												
1966	*1 000*	*298*	*67*	*77*	*113*	*64*	*57*	*91*	*116*	*61*	*56*	
1967	*1 000*	*293*	*67*	*72*	*118*	*62*	*59*	*92*	*118*	*61*	*58*	
1968	*1 000*	*263*	*63*	*66*	*121*	*62*	*59*	*89*	*120*	*60*	*56*	*41*
1969	*1 000*	*254*	*64*	*68*	*118*	*61*	*60*	*86*	*124*	*66*	*57*	*42*
1970	*1 000*	*255*	*66*	*64*	*119*	*61*	*60*	*86*	*126*	*65*	*55*	*43*
1971	*1 000*	*250*	*65*	*59*	*119*	*60*	*61*	*87*	*136*	*65*	*54*	*44*
1972	*1 000*	*251*	*66*	*53*	*121*	*60*	*58*	*89*	*139*	*65*	*52*	*46*
1973	*1 000*	*248*	*73*	*49*	*126*	*58*	*58*	*89*	*135*	*65*	*53*	*46*
1974	*1 000*	*253*	*70*	*43*	*124*	*52*	*64*	*91*	*135*	*63*	*54*	*51*
Annual averages												
1966	116.5	115.6	121.7	120.8	128.5	120.9	107.2	109.9	109.9	112.5	120.5	
1967	119.4	118.5	125.3	120.8	134.5	124.3	109.0	111.7	112.2	113.7	126.4	
1968	125.0	123.2	127.1	125.5	141.3	133.8	113.2	113.4	119.1	124.5	132.4	126.9
1969	131.8	131.0	136.2	135.5	147.0	137.8	118.3	117.7	123.9	132.3	142.5	135.0
1970	140.2	140.1	143.9	136.3	158.1	145.7	126.0	123.8	132.1	142.8	153.8	145.5
1971	153.4	155.6	152.7	138.5	172.6	160.9	135.4	132.2	147.2	159.1	169.6	165.0
1972	164.3	169.4	159.0	139.5	190.7	173.4	140.5	141.8	155.9	168.0	180.5	180.3
1973	179.4	194.9	164.2	141.2	213.1	178.3	148.7	155.1	165.0	172.6	202.4	211.0
1974	208.2	230.0	182.1	164.8	238.2	208.8	170.8	182.3	194.3	202.7	227.2	248.3
1974 January 15	191.8	216.7	166.0	142.2	225.1	188.6	158.3	166.6	175.0	182.2	212.8	229.5
15 January 1974 = 100												
Weights												
1974	*1 000*	*253*	*70*	*43*	*124*	*52*	*64*	*91*	*135*	*63*	*54*	*51*
1975	*1 000*	*232*	*82*	*46*	*108*	*53*	*70*	*89*	*149*	*71*	*52*	*48*
1976	*1 000*	*228*	*81*	*46*	*112*	*56*	*75*	*84*	*140*	*74*	*57*	*47*
1977	*1 000*	*247*	*83*	*46*	*112*	*58*	*63*	*82*	*139*	*71*	*54*	*45*
1978	*1 000*	*233*	*85*	*48*	*113*	*60*	*64*	*80*	*140*	*70*	*56*	*51*
1979	*1 000*	*232*	*77*	*44*	*120*	*59*	*64*	*82*	*143*	*69*	*59*	*51*
1980	*1 000*	*214*	*82*	*40*	*124*	*59*	*69*	*84*	*151*	*74*	*62*	*41*
1981	*1 000*	*207*	*79*	*36*	*135*	*62*	*65*	*81*	*152*	*75*	*66*	*42*
1982	*1 000*	*206*	*77*	*41*	*144*	*62*	*64*	*77*	*154*	*72*	*65*	*38*
1983	*1 000*	*203*	*78*	*39*	*137*	*69*	*64*	*74*	*159*	*75*	*63*	*39*
Annual averages												
1974	108.5	106.1	109.7	115.9	105.8	110.7	107.9	109.4	111.0	111.2	106.8	108.2
1975	134.8	133.3	135.2	147.7	125.5	147.4	131.2	125.7	143.9	138.6	135.5	132.4
1976	157.1	159.9	159.3	171.3	143.2	182.4	144.2	139.4	166.0	161.3	159.5	157.3
1977	182.0	190.3	183.4	209.7	161.8	211.3	166.8	157.4	190.3	188.3	173.3	185.7
1978	197.1	203.8	196.0	226.2	173.4	227.5	182.1	171.0	207.2	206.7	192.0	207.8
1979	223.5	228.3	217.1	247.6	208.9	250.5	201.9	187.2	243.1	236.4	213.9	239.9
1980	263.7	255.9	261.8	290.1	269.5	313.2	226.3	205.4	288.7	276.9	262.7	290.0
1981	295.0	277.5	306.1	358.2	318.2	380.0	237.2	208.3	322.6	300.7	300.8	318.0
1982	320.4	299.3	341.0	413.3	358.3	433.3	243.8	210.5	343.5	325.8	331.6	341.7
1983	335.1	308.8	366.5	440.9	367.1	465.4	250.4	214.8	366.3	345.6	342.9	364.0
1983 March 15	327.9	302.4	357.0	432.9	349.7	465.6	249.2	213.8	356.5	339.5	337.8	356.5
June 14	334.7	308.8	368.2	444.0	364.0	461.8	251.2	213.7	366.3	345.7	342.7	363.5
September 13	339.5	313.0	371.8	443.5	376.7	466.0	251.6	215.8	373.1	348.6	344.7	368.9
December 13	342.8	318.5	373.2	450.0	381.6	469.0	253.0	217.1	371.7	353.4	350.0	375.7

1. The index of retail prices replaced the interim index from January 1956 (indices of the interim index of retail prices for the period 1952 to January 1956 were last published in *Annual Abstract of Statistics* No. 103, 1965). A new set of weights was introduced, based on ascertained expenditure in 1953–54, valued at January 1956 prices. Between January 1962 and 1974 the weights have been revised each January on the basis of ascertained expenditure in the three years ended in the previous June, valued at prices obtaining at the date of revision. From 1975 the weights have been revised on expenditure for the latest available year.

Source Department of Employment

18.7 Tax and price index
January 1978 = 100

	1974	1975	1976	1977	1978	1979	1980	1981	1982	1983	1984
January	50.2	63.0	80.4	95.3	100.0	106.1	123.2	140.4	162.3	170.7	177.9
February	51.2	64.3	81.6	96.4	100.7	107.2	125.3	141.9	162.4	171.6	178.8
March	51.7	65.8	82.2	97.5	101.5	108.2	127.2	144.3	164.0	171.9	179.4
April	54.3	68.5	82.9	96.4	98.4	110.5	130.8	151.3	166.0	171.8	178.8
May	55.2	71.9	84.0	97.3	99.1	111.6	132.2	152.4	167.4	172.6	179.6
June	55.9	73.5	84.5	98.5	100.0	113.8	133.6	153.5	168.0	173.1	180.1
July	56.5	74.4	84.7	98.6	100.5	113.8	134.9	154.2	169.0	174.2	179.9
August	56.8	74.9	86.1	99.2	101.3	114.9	135.3	155.5	169.0	175.1	181.8
September	57.6	75.7	87.5	99.9	101.8	116.2	136.3	156.6	168.9	176.0	182.2
October	58.9	77.0	89.4	100.4	102.4	117.6	137.3	158.2	169.9	176.7	
November	60.1	78.0	90.9	98.7	103:2	118.8	138.5	160.1	170.9	177.5	
December	61.2	79.2	92.4	99.3	104.3	119.8	139.4	161.2	170.5	178.0	

Percentage changes on one year earlier

Tax and price index											
January		+ 25.5	+ 27.6	+ 18.5	+ 4.9	+ 6.1	+ 16.1	+ 14.0	+ 15.6	+ 5.2	+ 4.2
February		+ 25.6	+ 26.9	+ 18.1	+ 4.5	+ 6.5	+ 16.9	+ 13.2	+ 14.4	+ 5.7	+ 4.2
March		+ 27.3	+ 24.9	+ 18.6	+ 4.1	+ 6.6	+ 17.6	+ 13.4	+ 13.7	+ 4.8	+ 4.4
April		+ 26.2	+ 21.0	+ 16.3	+ 2.1	+ 12.3[1]	+ 18.4[1]	+ 15.7	+ 9.7	+ 3.5	+ 4.1
May		+ 30.3	+ 16.8	+ 15.8	+ 1.8	+ 12.6[1]	+ 18.5[1]	+ 15.3	+ 9.8	+ 3.1	+ 4.1
June		+ 31.5	+ 15.0	+ 16.6	+ 1.5	+ 13.8[1]	+ 17.4[1]	+ 14.9	+ 9.4	+ 3.0	+ 4.0
July		+ 31.7	+ 13.8	+ 16.4	+ 1.9	+ 13.2	+ 18.5	+ 14.3	+ 9.6	+ 3.1	+ 3.3
August		+ 31.9	+ 15.0	+ 15.2	+ 2.1	+ 13.4	+ 17.8	+ 14.9	+ 8.7	+ 3.6	+ 3.8
September		+ 31.4	+ 15.6	+ 14.2	+ 1.9	+ 14.1	+ 17.3	+ 14.9	+ 7.9	+ 4.2	+ 3.5
October		+ 30.7	+ 16.1	+ 12.3	+ 2.0	+ 14.8	+ 16.8	+ 15.2	+ 7.4	+ 4.0	
November		+ 29.8	+ 16.5	+ 8.6	+ 4.6	+ 15.1	+ 16.6	+ 15.6	+ 6.7	+ 3.9	
December		+ 29.4	+ 16.7	+ 7.5	+ 5.0	+ 14.9	+ 16.4	+ 15.6	+ 5.8	+ 4.4	

Retail prices index											
January		+ 19.9	+ 23.4	+ 16.6	+ 9.9	+ 9.3	+ 18.4	+ 13.0	+ 12.0	+ 4.9	+ 5.1
February		+ 19.9	+ 22.9	+ 16.2	+ 9.5	+ 9.6	+ 19.1	+ 12.5	+ 11.0	+ 5.3	+ 5.1
March		+ 21.2	+ 21.2	+ 16.7	+ 9.1	+ 9.8	+ 19.8	+ 12.6	+ 10.4	+ 4.6	+ 5.2
April		+ 21.7	+ 18.9	+ 17.5	+ 7.9	+ 10.1	+ 21.8	+ 12.0	+ 9.4	+ 4.0	+ 5.2
May		+ 25.0	+ 15.4	+ 17.1	+ 7.7	+ 10.3	+ 21.9	+ 11.7	+ 9.5	+ 3.7	+ 5.1
June		+ 26.1	+ 13.8	+ 17.7	+ 7.4	+ 11.4	+ 21.0	+ 11.3	+ 9.2	+ 3.7	+ 5.1
July		+ 26.3	+ 12.9	+ 17.6	+ 7.8	+ 15.6	+ 16.9	+ 10.9	+ 8.7	+ 4.2	+ 4.5
August		+ 26.9	+ 13.8	+ 16.5	+ 8.0	+ 15.8	+ 16.3	+ 11.5	+ 8.0	+ 4.6	+ 5.0
September		+ 26.6	+ 14.3	+ 15.6	+ 7.8	+ 16.5	+ 15.9	+ 11.4	+ 7.3	+ 5.1	+ 4.7
October		+ 25.9	+ 14.7	+ 14.1	+ 7.8	+ 17.2	+ 15.4	+ 11.7	+ 6.8	+ 5.0	
November		+ 25.2	+ 15.0	+ 13.0	+ 8.1	+ 17.4	+ 15.3	+ 12.0	+ 6.3	+ 4.8	
December		+ 24.9	+ 15.1	+ 12.1	+ 8.4	+ 17.2	+ 15.1	+ 12.0	+ 5.4	+ 5.3	

1. These figures are affected by the late timing of the 1979 Budget; the changes introduced by that Budget are included in the Tax and price index from July 1979.

Source Central Statistical Office

18.8 Index of purchase prices of the means of agricultural production
Annual averages

1980 = 100

	Weights	1975	1976	1977	1978	1979	1980	1981	1982	1983
Goods and services currently consumed	100.0	54.7	67.8	78.3	80.1	89.3	100.0	110.0	117.8	126.0
Seeds	4.5	62.4	108.2	109.9	89.4	96.1	100.0	101.0	108.6	116.5
Animals for rearing and production	1.1	58.0	70.6	83.6	100.8	113.1	100.0	130.9	145.5	170.7
Energy	8.5	42.0	51.8	62.0	64.3	76.5	100.0	120.7	137.4	151.3
Fuels for heating	0.8	36.9	46.2	60.9	62.4	75.5	100.0	121.9	140.6	160.2
Motor fuel	5.1	40.1	49.5	60.2	60.7	75.1	100.0	121.6	141.6	158.8
Electricity	2.3	48.1	59.1	66.7	73.6	80.4	100.0	119.9	130.1	135.2
Lubricants	0.3	43.9	51.3	60.0	61.6	74.6	100.0	111.1	117.4	123.2
Fertilisers and soil improvers	13.6	55.5	59.4	68.4	79.2	85.5	100.0	110.2	115.5	116.8
Straight fertilisers	4.7	53.3	56.5	65.5	81.2	88.1	100.0	110.8	122.3	126.5
Compound fertilisers	8.0	57.7	61.6	70.3	78.5	83.7	100.0	110.3	112.0	111.1
Lime	0.9	48.5	55.6	66.2	75.2	87.2	100.0	106.2	111.0	116.2
Plant protection products	3.7	54.5	65.7	76.0	82.3	86.4	100.0	107.4	111.5	112.3
Animal feedingstuffs	45.5	57.7	72.9	86.1	83.5	93.7	100.0	108.0	113.9	123.7
Straight feedingstuffs	11.8	56.7	75.7	88.5	85.4	94.8	100.0	108.3	113.0	122.8
Whole wheat	3.4	54.0	69.7	80.7	84.7	95.2	100.0	109.6	114.0	125.1
Barley meal	2.2	57.2	72.0	82.2	82.2	97.4	100.0	106.3	114.4	123.5
Maize meal	1.5	48.4	57.6	68.9	79.6	89.4	100.0	106.6	115.2	120.0
Wheat offals	0.4	54.7	71.3	88.4	73.7	93.7	100.0	110.0	117.7	127.4
Oilcake	2.5	61.9	95.0	111.0	95.1	98.1	100.0	111.3	112.5	123.2
White fish meal	0.7	53.2	89.1	117.4	103.2	92.5	100.0	109.5	107.5	121.4
Meat and bone meal	0.1	61.2	96.5	115.3	106.5	103.6	100.0	120.2	129.9	129.7
Other	1.0	66.8	73.8	79.2	70.5	89.4	100.0	101.2	105.9	115.3
Compound feedingstuffs	33.7	58.1	71.9	85.3	82.8	93.3	100.0	107.9	114.2	124.0
for calves	1.5	61.2	72.1	84.3	81.0	92.0	100.0	105.6	115.0	122.6
cattle	13.0	58.3	71.1	84.0	80.8	92.5	100.0	105.6	111.8	121.6
pigs	7.1	56.5	71.4	84.7	81.5	91.7	100.0	109.8	115.6	124.7
poultry	11.1	57.9	72.8	87.3	86.4	95.6	100.0	109.9	116.6	127.1
others	1.0	63.3	75.0	84.7	82.0	92.6	100.0	103.8	108.9	116.8
Material and small tools	3.5	52.0	59.3	70.1	76.4	85.8	100.0	106.8	113.0	118.1
Maintenance and repair of plant	6.4	54.5	62.1	70.1	77.2	86.2	100.0	108.7	118.5	128.3
Maintenance and repair of buildings	3.7	49.2	58.1	68.0	73.9	84.5	100.0	109.6	119.1	127.5
Veterinary services	1.8	57.1	63.0	68.5	76.1	84.9	100.0	116.1	125.3	131.5
General expenses	7.7	48.5	61.3	67.6	77.5	85.9	100.0	115.2	127.0	134.2
Goods and services contributing to investment in agriculture	100.0	46.6	56.1	67.3	75.8	85.6	100.0	108.1	116.7	123.5
Machinery and other equipment	63.8	45.5	55.7	68.4	77.7	87.1	100.0	107.7	115.9	121.7
Machinery and plant for cultivation	6.5	47.0	54.6	66.6	76.6	85.5	100.0	104.6	108.0	110.8
Machinery and plant for harvesting	12.4	44.1	53.3	66.5	73.9	81.7	100.0	108.8	119.1	129.9
Farm machinery and installations	18.7	46.8	56.0	66.6	76.7	88.0	100.0	108.3	119.0	118.7
Tractors	22.7	44.6	57.1	71.3	80.8	89.4	100.0	107.3	113.8	123.0
Other vehicles	3.5	46.9	55.3	68.8	79.2	89.1	100.0	108.9	115.6	120.7
Buildings	36.2	48.5	56.9	65.5	72.3	83.1	100.0	108.8	118.3	126.7
Farm buildings	21.7	49.2	58.1	68.0	73.9	84.5	100.0	109.6	119.1	127.5
Engineering and soil improvement operations	14.5	47.5	55.1	61.6	69.9	81.0	100.0	107.5	117.0	125.6

Source Ministry of Agriculture, Fisheries and Food

18.9 Index of producer prices of agricultural products
Annual averages

1980 = 100

	Weights	1975	1976	1977	1978	1979	1980	1981	1982	1983
All products	100.0	62.3	81.7	84.6	86.0	94.5	100.0	110.2	119.5	124.7
All crop products	33.9	68.4	102.6	95.3	86.6	99.2	100.0	110.7	121.0	133.9
Cereals	16.1	60.6	79.8	82.5	88.2	97.8	100.0	110.2	118.7	131.5
Wheat— for milling	3.5	58.6	76.5	85.7	89.7	97.1	100.0	109.8	115.1	127.7
for feeding	5.2	57.9	76.2	81.7	86.8	97.2	100.0	110.0	115.6	128.3
Barley— for feeding	3.1	60.8	78.4	82.2	83.8	98.0	100.0	107.7	116.5	127.8
for malting	4.0	65.8	88.9	81.5	92.7	99.4	100.0	113.3	128.5	142.8
Oats— for milling	0.2	58.0	73.8	75.1	78.5	93.5	100.0	101.0	104.7	118.0
for feeding	0.1	56.0	71.3	74.6	72.7	90.8	100.0	100.1	104.0	117.0
Root crops	5.4	96.4	208.7	129.5	81.1	109.1	100.0	114.3	141.6	153.0
Potatoes—early	0.3	202.8	173.4	131.3	90.9	133.3	100.0	175.9	147.4	158.4
main crop	2.9	105.1	317.4	166.2	75.6	114.0	100.0	114.9	161.1	181.1
Sugar beet	2.2	70.5	75.0	82.3	86.8	99.5	100.0	104.9	115.9	116.4
Fresh vegetables	5.6	70.1	85.6	95.0	80.0	100.8	100.0	109.7	111.9	131.9
Cauliflowers	0.7	50.5	51.2	64.8	58.2	94.7	100.0	118.0	113.9	128.0
Lettuce	0.6	87.9	102.5	88.0	98.2	116.1	100.0	110.8	107.7	141.3
Tomatoes	0.7	66.7	76.0	82.5	91.3	81.0	100.0	92.4	85.6	102.9
Carrots	0.4	85.1	104.4	118.6	62.2	88.6	100.0	133.0	112.3	145.0
Other fresh vegetables	3.2	70.2	90.0	102.5	81.6	105.8	100.0	108.5	118.1	136.0
Fresh fruit	1.8	74.5	83.6	123.2	108.9	96.8	100.0	123.2	130.8	140.2
Dessert apples	0.5	69.3	72.1	125.5	93.9	75.8	100.0	133.7	134.2	139.9
Dessert pears	0.1	87.6	106.9	133.8	123.7	99.7	100.0	118.6	143.5	141.8
Cherries	0.1	69.6	66.9	99.4	115.4	91.3	100.0	121.3	105.9	129.6
Plums	0.1	53.8	37.3	109.4	93.5	91.9	100.0	162.8	108.6	130.1
Strawberries	0.4	87.9	101.4	128.1	126.1	118.0	100.0	113.6	135.3	157.9
Other fresh fruit	0.6	70.1	84.4	119.6	107.6	100.3	100.0	115.8	127.6	130.5
Seeds	1.2	66.9	142.1	126.9	87.7	94.6	100.0	100.9	109.1	109.3
Flowers and plants	1.9	56.7	74.1	82.7	94.7	94.2	100.0	102.8	110.6	117.6
Other crop products	1.9	57.4	67.0	73.8	78.3	89.1	100.0	110.1	117.6	133.2
Pulses	0.5	63.6	79.3	83.9	80.0	99.3	100.0	100.5	108.0	130.6
Hops	0.4	48.7	62.4	63.7	65.4	72.4	100.0	120.9	125.6	141.7
Oilseed rape	1.0	57.5	62.9	72.6	81.9	90.1	100.0	110.9	119.2	131.5
Animals and animal products	66.1	59.1	71.0	79.1	85.6	92.1	100.0	110.0	118.7	119.9
Animals for slaughter	37.6	57.2	69.8	78.2	88.4	94.8	100.0	110.7	119.8	121.8
Large animals	31.6	56.2	69.8	76.7	87.5	94.2	100.0	112.2	121.3	122.9
Cattle (clean)	13.3	51.4	66.0	74.0	84.8	95.0	100.0	110.7	122.2	129.4
Cows	4.3	47.6	66.0	71.5	85.7	92.3	100.0	117.0	127.2	120.9
Pigs (excluding sows)	8.9	70.0	77.9	81.0	91.8	93.7	100.0	108.0	111.5	106.2
Sows	0.3	65.1	78.6	78.9	89.7	85.4	100.0	109.7	126.2	104.8
Sheep over 1 year old	0.1	45.3	62.9	75.1	82.9	89.6	100.0	119.1	134.4	143.3
Lambs	3.4	50.4	68.0	76.7	87.5	91.9	100.0	117.6	128.4	136.4
Sheep under 1 year old	1.0	52.0	63.3	88.9	86.1	104.0	100.0	124.0	135.3	146.8
Ewes	0.3	55.2	89.5	106.2	109.4	107.8	100.0	138.7	152.3	140.3
Poultry	6.0	62.5	69.7	85.8	93.2	97.9	100.0	102.6	112.1	115.7
Chickens	4.5	52.3	56.4	78.7	88.2	95.8	100.0	103.1	111.0	114.6
Turkeys	1.5	92.8	109.4	107.0	108.1	104.2	100.0	101.2	115.3	119.1
Milk	22.5	61.7	73.0	79.8	82.4	88.2	100.0	109.9	120.0	123.2
Eggs	5.6	61.0	70.9	80.9	78.7	87.9	100.0	106.1	107.9	95.9
Other animals products: Wool	0.4	63.2	77.0	103.2	103.9	108.2	100.0	99.1	98.8	99.4

Source Ministry of Agriculture, Fisheries and Food

18.10 Commodity price trends[1]
Calendar years

		1973	1974	1975	1976	1977	1978	1979	1980	1981	1982	1983
Wheat £ per tonne	Average ex-farm price[2]	45.77	59.82	55.75	72.24	83.34	85.69	95.92	99.30	108.92	114.04	125.46
Barley £ per tonne	Average ex-farm price[2]	41.64	57.62	57.44	72.45	77.95	78.35	89.60	92.84	100.45	108.35	118.32
Oats £ per tonne	Average ex-farm price[2]	37.34	56.08	55.79	67.68	74.84	73.92	88.90	97.52	97.42	101.04	111.97
Rye £ per tonne	Average ex-farm price[2]	41.4	56.0	61.1	75.0	70.4	76.2	89.0	101.78	100.97	108.61	120.65
Hops £ per tonne	Average farm-gate price[3]	828	876	1 063	1 360	1 390	1 431	1 578	2 184	2 636	2 740	3 107
Potatoes £ per tonne	Average farm-gate price[4]	20.7	23.6	56.8	143.4	69.9	40.0	58.9	51.2	63.0	78.5	85.5
Sugar beet £ per tonne	Producer price[5]	10.06	13.52	18.48	16.42	21.93	23.72	28.28	27.93	27.74	27.15	31.06
Oilseed rape	Average market price[6]	78.74	172	128	136	162	182	215	230	255	270	310
Apples £ per tonne	Average market price[7]											
Dessert		121	150	175	189	304	224	193	259	335	301	363
Culinary		151	112	172	176	242	195	171	207	270	279	280
Pears £ per tonne	Average market price[7]	144	152	185	188	275	260	200	232	281	331	315
Tomatoes £ per tonne	Average market price[7]	212	237	291	346	411	440	389	504	475	466	632
Cauliflowers £ per tonne	Average market price[7]	73.3	92	122	119	143	133	163	186	207	214	243
Cattle (store) £ per head	1st quality Hereford/Friesian bull calves[8]	64	41	40	56	65	88	103	100	108	125	124
	1st quality yearling steers beef/dairy cross[8]	123	97	110	157	174	213	236	243	275	313	326
Cattle (fat) p per kg liveweight	clean cattle[9]	37.35	33.12	38.51	52.43	56.94	66.26	75.21	76.65[5]	88.72	98.30	95.81
Sheep (store) £ per head	1st quality lambs, hoggets and tegs[8]	13.6	12.0	14.0	19.0	24.0	25.9	26.0	25.9	30.2	33.0	33.4
Sheep (fat)[10] p per kg estimated dressed carcase weight		70.5	64.6	75.5	103.9	124.5	137.4	139.2	125.7	153.3	152.5[14]	146.5
											170.0[15]	180.5
Pigs £ per kg deadweight	Average market price clean pigs	43.79	45.98	61.90	67.32	72.64	80.08	81.35	86.64[2]	93.70	97.09	92.58
Broilers p per kg	Average wholesale price	42.9	45.8	55.0	63.6	76.0	81.1	82.1	91.1	91.6[13]	91.8	99.5
Milk p per litre	Average net return to producers[11]	5.09	6.28	7.98	9.36	10.18	10.61	11.55	12.77	13.79	14.81	15.02[13]
Eggs p per dozen	Average producer price[12]	23.7	24.6	22.8	27.8	31.2	27.0	32.8	37.4	40.5	39.0	35.5
Wool p per kg	Average producer price for clip paid to producers by the British Wool Marketing Board	46.7	48.2	57.1	69.5	93.2	93.8	97.7	91.3	89.5	89.2	90.0

Note Data for 1984 will be published in the *Annual Review of Agriculture* in February 1985

1. This table gives indications of the movement in commodity prices at the first point of sale. The series do not always show total receipts by farmers; for some commodities additional premiums or deficiency payments are made to achieve support price levels.
2. Weighted average ex-farm prices of United Kingdom cereals.
3. Average farm-gate prices paid by Hops Marketing Board to growers in England. Hops are not grown elsewhere in the United Kingdom.
4. Weighted average price paid to growers by registered merchants for early and main crop potatoes in the United Kingdom.
5. Average price paid to growers in the United Kingdom by British Sugar plc for sugar beet of average sugar content.
6. Typical contract price adjusted to delivered basis and 42 per cent oil content. From 1974 the average market price is given.
7. Weighted average wholesale prices for England and Wales. From 1982, for England only.

8. Average prices at representative markets in England and Wales.
9. Based on Meat and Livestock Commission all clean cattle prices.
10. UK weighted average market price for animals certfied under the Fat Sheep Guarantee Scheme/Sheep Variable Premium Scheme.
11. Derived by dividing total value of output by the total quantity of output available for human consumption.
12. Average price of all Class A eggs weighted according to quantity in each grade.
13. Figures forecasted.
14. Great Britain weighted average market price for animals certified under the Sheep Variable Premium Scheme from 1982.
15. Northern Ireland weighted average market price for clean sheep from 1982.

Source Ministry of Agriculture, Fisheries and Food

Index of sources

This index of sources gives the titles of official publications or other sources containing statistics allied to those in the tables of this *Annual Abstract*. These publications provide more detailed analyses than are shown in the *Abstract*. This index includes publications to which reference should be made for short-term (monthly or quarterly) series. No entry is made in this index for items where the data have been obtained from departmental records.

Subject	Table number in *Abstract*	Government department or other organisation	Official publication or other source
1. Area and climate			
Area	1.1	Ordnance Survey	Central Statistical Office: Regional Trends
Climate	1.2 – 1.4	Meteorological Office	Monthly Weather Report Central Statistical Office: Monthly Digest of Statistics
2. Population and vital statistics			
Population census	2.1 – 2.3, 2.5, 2.8	Office of Population Censuses and Surveys	*England and Wales:* Census reports, 1911, 1921, 1931, 1951, 1961, 1971 and 1981 Sample census 1966; Registrar General's statistical review of England and Wales, Part II, Tables Census 1971, Great Britain, Summary tables Census 1981, National Report, Great Britain Part 1 Census 1981 Key statistics for urban areas: Great Britain Welsh Office: Digest of Welsh Statistics (annual)
		General Register Office for Scotland	*Scotland:* Census reports 1951, 1961, 1971 and 1981 Sample census 1966 Census 1971 Census 1981 Key statistics for urban areas: Scotland
		General Register Office (Northern Ireland)	*Northern Ireland:* Census of population 1951, 1961, 1966 and 1971 The Northern Ireland Census 1981. Summary Report
Mid-year estimates	2.1, 2.4, 2.6, 2.9	Office of Population Censuses and Surveys	*England and Wales:* Series FM (Family statistics), DH (Deaths), MB (Morbidity), PP (Population estimates and projections), MN (Migration) and VS (Local authority vital statistics) Population Trends (quarterly) Series PP1, Population estimates: The Registrar General's estimates of the population of regions and local government areas of England and Wales
		General Register Office for Scotland	*Scotland:* Registrar General Scotland Annual Report Quarterly return of births, deaths and marriages Annual estimate of the population of Scotland
		General Register Office (Northern Ireland)	*Northern Ireland:* Annual report of the Registrar General Quarterly return of births, deaths and marriages
Projections	2.7	Government Actuary's Department	Series PP2, Population projections—national figures
Migration	2.10, 2.11	Office of Population Censuses and Surveys	Series MN (Migration) Population Trends (quarterly)
	2.12	Home Office	Control of immigration statistics United Kingdom 1983 Cmnd. 9246
Vital statistics	2.13, 2.14, 2.16 – 2.22	Office of Population Censuses and Surveys	*England and Wales:* Series FM (Family statistics), DH (Deaths), MB (Morbidity), PP (Population estimates and projections), MN (Migration) and VS (Local authority vital statistics) Population Trends (quarterly)
		General Register Office for Scotland	*Scotland:* Registrar General Scotland, Annual Report Quarterly return of births, deaths and marriages
		General Register Office (Northern Ireland)	*Northern Ireland:* Annual report of the Registrar General Quarterly return of births, deaths and marriages

Subject	Table number in *Abstract*	Government department or other organisation	Official publication or other source
Vital statistics (*contd*)	2.15	Lord Chancellor's Department	Judicial statistics, England and Wales (annual)
		Scottish Courts Administration	Judicial statistics, Scotland; Civil judicial statistics (annual)
	2.23	Office of Population Censuses and Surveys; General Register Office for Scotland; General Register Office (Northern Ireland) and Government Actuary's Department	*England and Wales:* Registrar General's Decennial Supplement, England and Wales, 1981 – 83, Life Table *Scotland:* Life Table: 1981 – 83, Registrar General Scotland, Annual Report, Supplement *Northern Ireland:* Life Table 1981 – 83

3. Social conditions

Subject	Table number in *Abstract*	Government department or other organisation	Official publication or other source
Social services	3.1 – 3.6	Central Statistical Office	Civil Appropriation Accounts (annual) Northern Ireland annual abstract of statistics
	3.7, 3.8, 3.9	Department of the Environment	Housing and Construction Statistics (quarterly) Housing return for Scotland (quarterly)
	3.10	Department of the Environment	Housing and Construction Statistics (quarterly) Welsh Office: Welsh housing statistics (annual)
		Scottish Development Department	Housing return for Scotland (quarterly)
		Department of the Environment for Northern Ireland	Digest of Housing Statistics for Northern Ireland (annual)
Social security pensions, benefits and allowances	3.11, 3.12, 3.15	Department of Health and Social Security	National Insurance Fund Account (annual)
		Department of Health and Social Services, Northern Ireland	Northern Ireland National Insurance Fund Account (annual)
	3.13 3.16 – 3.28	Department of Health and Social Security	Social Security Statistics (annual) Health and Personal Social Services Statistics for England (annual) Welsh Office: Health and Personal Social Services Statistics for Wales (annual)
National health service	3.29	Department of Health and Social Security; Welsh Office	Civil Appropriation Accounts (annual) Health and Personal Social Services Statistics for England (annual) Health and Personal Social Services Statistics for Wales (annual)
	3.30	Scottish Health Service, Common Services Agency	Scottish Health Statistics (annual)
	3.31	Department of Health and Social Services, Northern Ireland	Parliament of Northern Ireland Estimates (annual) Summary of Health and Personal Social Services Accounts (annual)
	3.32, 3.33	Department of Health and Social Security	Health and Personal Social Services Statistics for England (annual)
Public health	3.34	Office of Population Censuses and Surveys	Communicable Disease Statistics Series MB2 (annual) Population Trends (quarterly)
		Scottish Health Service, Common Services Agency	Scottish Health Statistics (annual)
		General Register Office (Northern Ireland)	Annual report of the Registrar General Quarterly return of births, deaths and marriages
	3.35, 3.36	Health and Safety Executive	Health and Safety statistics Manufacturing and service industries (annual) Agriculture Mines (annual) Quarries (annual) Department of Energy: Digest of United Kingdom Energy Statistics (annual)
		Department of Trade and Industry	Casualties to vessels and accidents to men. Vessels registered in the United Kingdom (annual)
		Department of Transport	Railway accidents (annual)
		Civil Aviation Authority	Accidents to aircraft on the British Register

Subject	Table number in *Abstract*	Government department or other organisation	Official publication or other source
Public health (*contd*)	3.37	Office of Population Censuses and Surveys; General Register Office for Scotland	Census 1981 National Report Great Britain Part II
Elections	3.38	Home Office; Scottish Home and Health Department	Office of Population Censuses and Surveys Electoral statistics (series EL) Return of election expenses Vachers Parliamentary Companion
	3.39	Home Office	Central Statistical Office: Social Trends
4. Justice and crime	4.2	Home Departments	*England and Wales:* Report of Her Majesty's Chief Inspector of Constabulary (annual) *Scotland:* Report of Her Majesty's Chief Inspector of Constabulary for Scotland (annual)
		Northern Ireland Office	*Northern Ireland:* Chief Constable's Report (Royal Ulster Constabulary)
	4.1, 4.3 – 4.11	Home Office	Central Statistical Office: Monthly Digest of Statistics Criminal statistics, England and Wales (annual) Prison statistics, England and Wales (annual) Welsh Office: Digest of Welsh Statistics (annual)
	4.12 – 4.16	Scottish Home and Health Department	Criminal statistics, Scotland (annual)
	4.17, 4.18	Scottish Home and Health Department	Prisons in Scotland (annual)
	4.19 – 4.22	Northern Ireland Office	Chief Constable's Report (Royal Ulster Constabulary)
5. Education	5.1 – 5.12	Education Departments	Scottish Educational Statistics (annual) Education in Northern Ireland (half-yearly) Education statistics for the United Kingdom (annual) Northern Ireland Annual Abstract of Statistics Welsh Office: Statistics of Education in Wales (annual)
	5.13 – 5.19	University Grants Committee	University statistics (volumes 1 and 3) (annual) Open University Digest of Statistics, Vol. 1, Students and courses (annual)
6. Labour	6.1, 6.2, 6.4, 6.6, 6.8, 6.10, 6.12, 6.14, 6.17, 6.19, 6.20	Department of Employment	Employment Gazette (monthly) Central Statistical Office: Monthly Digest of Statistics Welsh Office: Digest of Welsh Statistics (annual)
	6.3	Engineering Industries Training Board	Employment Gazette (monthly) Annual Report of the Engineering Industries Training Board
	6.9, 6.11, 6.13	Department of Manpower Services (Northern Ireland)	Northern Ireland Annual Abstract of Statistics
	6.5	Ministry of Agriculture, Fisheries and Food	Agricultural Statistics, United Kingdom (annual)
	6.7	HM Treasury	Civil Service Statistics (annual) Central Statistical Office: Monthly Digest of Statistics
	6.15	Office of Population Censuses and Surveys	Census 1981, Definitions Great Britain
	6.16	Business Statistics Office	Analyses of United Kingdom manufacturing (local) units by employment size (Business Monitor PA 1003)
	6.18 – 6.20, 6.22	Department of Employment	Employment Gazette (monthly) New Earnings Survey (annual) Central Statistical Office: Monthly Digest of Statistics
	6.21	Department of Manpower Services (Northern Ireland)	New Earnings Survey Northern Ireland (annual)
	6.23	Department of Employment	Employment Gazette (monthly)

Subject	Table number in *Abstract*	Government department or other organisation	Official publication or other source
7. Defence	7.1 – 7.13	Ministry of Defence	Volume II (Defence Statistics) of the Statement on the Defence Estimates 1984 (Cmnd 9227 – 11)
8. Production Census of production	8.1	Business Statistics Office	Report on the Census of Production (Business Monitor PA 1002.1) (annual)
Index of industrial production	8.2	Central Statistical Office	Monthly Digest of Statistics Economic Trends Annual Supplement Welsh Office: Digest of Welsh Statistics (annual)
Fuel and power	8.3 – 8.14	Department of Energy	Digest of United Kingdom Energy Statistics (annual) Energy Trends (monthly)
Iron and steel	8.15 – 8.17	Department of Trade and Industry; Iron and Steel Statistics Bureau	Iron and steel industry: Annual Statistics published by the British Steel Corporation on behalf of the Iron and Steel Statistics Bureau Regional Trends (annual)
Industrial materials	8.18	World Bureau of Metal Statistics	World Metal Statistics (monthly)
	8.19 – 8.28	Department of Trade and Industry	British business (weekly) Business Monitor (monthly and quarterly) Central Statistical Office: Monthly Digest of Statistics
	8.29	Business Statistics Office	Minerals (Business Monitor PA 1007) Natural Environment Research Council: United Kingdom Mineral Statistics (annual)
		Department of Economic Development (Northern Ireland)	Northern Ireland Annual Abstract of Statistics
Building and construction	8.30	Department of Trade and Industry; Department of the Environment; World Bureau of Metal Statistics	Business Monitor (quarterly) Housing and Construction Statistics (quarterly) Central Statistical Office: Monthly Digest of Statistics
	8.31, 8.32	Department of the Environment	Housing and Construction Statistics (quarterly)
Manufactured goods	8.33 – 8.36	Department of Trade and Industry	Business Monitor (monthly and quarterly) British business (weekly) Central Statistical Office: Monthly Digest of Statistics
	8.37, 8.38	HM Customs and Excise	Annual report of the Commissioners of HM Customs and Excise
9. Agriculture, Fisheries and Food	9.1, 9.2	Agricultural Departments	Agricultural Statistics: England and Wales (annual) Output and utilization of farm produce in the United Kingdom (annual) Scotland: Agricultural statistics (annual)
	9.3 – 9.5		Agricultural Statistics, United Kingdom (annual) Scottish Agricultural Economics (annual) Welsh Office: Welsh Agricultural Statistics (annual)
Forestry	9.6	Forestry Commission	*Great Britain:* Annual report and Accounts of the Forestry Commission
		Department of Agriculture for Northern Ireland	Northern Ireland Annual Abstract of Statistics
Agriculture	9.7	Agricultural Departments	Employment Gazette (monthly)
Food	9.8 – 9.11	Ministry of Agriculture, Fisheries and Food	Central Statistical Office: Monthly Digest of Statistics
Fisheries	9.12 – 9.14	Ministry of Agriculture, Fisheries and Food; Department of Agriculture and Fisheries for Scotland	*England and Wales:* Sea fisheries statistical tables (annual) *Scotland:* Fisheries of Scotland report (annual) Scottish sea fisheries statistical tables (annual)

Subject	Table number in *Abstract*	Government department or other organisation	Official publication or other source
Food supplies	9.15	Ministry of Agriculture, Fisheries and Food	MAFF Food Facts British business (weekly)
	9.16	Ministry of Agriculture, Fisheries and Food	MAFF Food Facts
	9.17	National Food Survey Committee	Annual Report of the National Food Survey Committee: Household Food Consumption and Expenditure

10. Transport and communications

Subject	Table number in *Abstract*	Government department or other organisation	Official publication or other source
Road transport	10.1 – 10.7, 10.11	Department of Transport	Transport Statistics Great Britain (annual) Central Statistical Office: Monthly Digest of Statistics
	10.12 – 10.14	Department of Transport	Road accidents in Great Britain Business Monitor (monthly) Central Statistical Office: Monthly Digest of Statistics Welsh Office: Road accidents: Wales (annual)
	10.8, 10.9	Department of the Environment for Northern Ireland	Northern Ireland annual abstract of statistics
Rail transport	10.15 – 10.18	Department of Transport	Transport Statistics Great Britain (annual)
	10.19 10.20, 10.21	Department of Transport Department of the Environment for Northern Ireland	Health and Safety Executive: Industry and Services (annual) Northern Ireland annual abstract of statistics
Air transport	10.22 – 10.27	Civil Aviation Authority	Central Statistical Office: Monthly Digest of Statistics Civil Aviation Authority: Annual and Monthly Statistics, Accidents to aircraft on the British Register (annual)
Shipping	10.29 – 10.31	Department of Transport	Central Statistical Office: Monthly Digest of Statistics
	10.32 – 10.35	Department of Transport HM Customs and Excise	British business (weekly) Port Statistics (annual) Transport Statistics Great Britain (annual) Nationality of vessels in seaborne trade (Business Monitor M8)
Passenger movement	10.36, 10.37	Department of Transport; Civil Aviation Authority	Central Statistical Office: Monthly Digest of Statistics
Communications	10.38	British Telecom plc; Post Office	British Telecommunications report and accounts (annual) Post Office report and accounts (annual)
Cinemas	10.39, 10.40	Department of Trade and Industry	British business (weekly) Business Monitor MA 2 cinemas Central Statistical Office: Monthly Digest of Statistics

11. Distributive trades and services nes

Subject	Table number in *Abstract*	Government department or other organisation	Official publication or other source
	11.1	Business Statistics Office	Retailing 1982 Business Monitor SDO 25 (biennially) Business Monitor SDA 25
	11.2	Business Statistics Office	British business (weekly) Business Monitor SDO 24
	11.3	Department of Trade and Industry	British business (weekly) Business Monitor SDM 28 (monthly) Central Statistical Office: Monthly Digest of Statistics
	11.4	Business Statistics Office	British business (weekly) Business Monitor SDO 29
Scientific research and development	11.5 – 11.9	Department of Trade and Industry	British business (weekly) Industrial Research and Development Expenditure and Employment Business Monitor MO14 Central Statistical Office: Economic Trends, August 1981, August 1982, September 1983 and August 1984

12. External trade

Subject	Table number in *Abstract*	Government department or other organisation	Official publication or other source
12. External trade	12.1 – 12.6	Department of Trade and Industry	Monthly review of external trade statistics Overseas Trade Statistics of the United Kingdom, (Annual Supplement) Central Statistical Office: Monthly Digest of Statistics

Subject	Table number in *Abstract*	Government department or other organisation	Official publication or other source
13. Balance of payments			
	13.1 – 13.3	Central Statistical Office	United Kingdom Balance of Payments 1984 Edition
	13.3	Bank of England; HM Treasury	United Kingdom Balance of Payments 1984 Edition Quarterly figures: Financial Statistics
	13.1 – 13.3		Quarterly figures: Economic Trends
Overseas aid	13.4, 13.5	Overseas Development Administration	British Aid Statistics 1978 – 1982, Statistics of UK Economic Aid to Developing Countries
14. National income and expenditure			
	14.1 – 14.16	Central Statistical Office	United Kingdom National Accounts 1984 Edition Monthly Digest of Statistics Economic Trends (monthly)
15. Personal income, expenditure and wealth			
	15.1	Central Statistical Office; Department of Employment	Economic Trends, December 1982
	15.2	Board of Inland Revenue	Inland Revenue Statistics (annual) Central Statistical Office: Economic Trends, February 1981
	15.3 – 15.5	Department of Employment	Family Expenditure Survey (annual)
16. Home finance			
Central government	16.1, 16.2	Central Statistical Office	Financial Statistics (monthly)
	16.3 – 16.7, 16.11	HM Treasury; Central Statistical Office; Bank of England	Consolidated Fund and National Loans Fund Accounts Financial Statistics (monthly)
Saving	16.9	Department for National Savings; National Investment and Loans Office	Annual report of the Inspection Committee of Trustee savings banks Accounts of National Savings Bank: Investment Deposit Accounts (annual) Ordinary Deposit Accounts (annual) Accounts of savings banks funds (annual) Accounts of trustee savings banks (annual)
Central government	16.10, 16.11	Board of Inland Revenue	Inland Revenue Statistics (annual)
Rateable values	16.12	Board of Inland Revenue	Rates and Rateable values in England and Wales (annual)
Local authorities	16.13, 16.14	Department of the Environment	Local government financial statistics (England and Wales) (annual) Welsh Office: Welsh local government financial statistics (annual)
		Public Works Loan Board	Annual report of the Public Works Loan Board
		Scottish Office, Central Statistics Unit	Local financial returns (Scotland) (annual)
		Department of the Environment for Northern Ireland	District Council—Summary of Statements of Accounts (annual)
	16.15, 16.16	Department of the Environment	Local government financial statistics (England and Wales) (annual)
	16.17	Water Authorities Association	Digest of Environmental Pollution and Water Statistics, No 6.
	16.18, 16.19	Department of the Environment	Local government financial statistics (England and Wales) (annual)
	16.20 – 16.22	Scottish Office, Central Statistics Unit	Local financial returns (Scotland) (annual)
	16.23 – 16.25	Department of the Environment for Northern Ireland	Local authority financial returns (Northern Ireland) (annual) District Council—Summary of Statement of Accounts (annual)

Subject	Table number in *Abstract*	Government department or other organisation	Official publication or other source
17. Banking, insurance, etc.			
Banking	17.1 17.3 – 17.6	Bank of England	Bank of England Annual Report and Accounts Bank of England Quarterly Bulletin
	17.2	Bankers' Clearing House	Annual report of the Bankers' Clearing House
	17.7	Bank of England; Central Statistical Office	Financial Statistics (monthly)
	17.8	Bank of England	Bank of England Quarterly Bulletin
	17.9	Bank of England	Bank of England Quarterly Bulletin Central Statistical Office: Monthly Digest of Statistics Central Statistical Office: Financial Statistics (monthly)
Capital markets	17.10		Central Statistical Office: Financial Statistics (monthly)
	17.11	Council of The Stock Exchange	Stock Exchange Fact Book (quarterly)
	17.12	Bank of England	Central Statistical Office: Financial Statistics (monthly)
Other financial institutions	17.13	Registry of Friendly Societies	Report of the Chief Registrar of Friendly Societies, incorporating the Report of the Industrial Assurance Commissioner (annual)
	17.14, 17.15	Department of Trade and Industry	British business (weekly) Business Monitor (monthly)
	17.16	Bank of England	Central Statistical Office: Financial Statistics (monthly)
	17.17 17.18	Central Statistical Office; Department of Trade and Industry	Financial Statistics (monthly) Business Monitor M25 (quarterly)
	17.19, 17.20	Registry of Friendly Societies	Report of the Chief Registrar of Friendly Societies, incorporating the Report of the Industrial Assurance Commissioner (annual)
	17.21	Office of the Industrial Assurance Commissioner	Report of the Chief Registrar of Friendly Societies, incorporating the Report of the Industrial Assurance Commissioner (annual)
	17.22	Registry of Friendly Societies	Report of the Chief Registrar of Friendly Societies, incorporating the Report of the Industrial Assurance Commissioner (annual)
Insurance	17.23, 17.24	Office of the Industrial Assurance Commissioner	Report of the Chief Registrar of Friendly Societies, incorporating the Report of the Industrial Assurance Commissioner (annual)
Companies	17.25	Department of Trade and Industry	British business (weekly) Central Statistical Office: Financial Statistics (monthly)
	17.26	Department of Trade and Industry	Business Monitor MA3 (annual)
Insolvency	17.27, 17.28	Department of Trade and Industry	Bankruptcy. General annual report
	17.29	The Account of Court, Edinburgh	Civil judicial statistics, Scotland (annual)
	17.30	Supreme Court	Ulster Yearbook
	17.31	Department of Trade and Industry; The Registrar of Companies, Edinburgh; Department of Economic Development, Northern Ireland	Central Statistical Office: Financial Statistics (monthly) British business (weekly) Companies in (year)
18. Prices	18.1 – 18.4	Business Statistics Office	British business (weekly) Central Statistical Office: Monthly Digest of Statistics
	18.5, 18.7	Central Statistical Office	Monthly Digest of Statistics
	18.6	Department of Employment	Employment Gazette (monthly)
	18.8, 18.9	Ministry of Agriculture, Fisheries and Food	Agricultural Statistics, United Kingdom (annual) Central Statistical Office: Monthly Digest of Statistics
	18.10	Ministry of Agriculture, Fisheries and Food	Annual Review of Agriculture, 1984 (Cmnd 9137)

Index

Figures indicate Table numbers

Printed in the UK for HMSO
Dd737092 12/84 10170 (1466)

SOCIAL TRENDS

For fifteen years Social Trends has provided a valuable insight into life in Britain and its changes

This new edition of Social Trends updates its broad description of British society. The material in it is arranged in chapters corresponding closely to the administrative functions of Government. The focus in each chapter is on current policy concerns. Latest available data are included wherever possible.

Social Trends not only is necessary for people involved in social policy and social work both in government and outside government but is also an invaluable guide for market researchers, journalists, teachers, advertisers, businessmen — anyone, in fact, who has a concern for British society.

Social Trends 15

For the fourth year running price held at £19.95

ISBN 0 11 620102 9*

Central Statistical Office publications are published by Her Majesty's Stationery Office.
They are obtainable from Government bookshops and through booksellers.